CHEAT CODE OVERLOAD

W9-CBQ-962

 Look for faces like this throughout Cheat Code Overload to find the latest and greatest games and the cheats to make playing them even more fun!

XBOX 360™

GAMES

AMPED 3

ALL SLEDS

Select Cheat Codes from the Options menu and press Right Trigger, X, Left Trigger, Down, Right, Left Bumper, Left Trigger, Right Trigger, Y, X.

ALL GEAR

Select Cheat Codes from the Options menu and press Y, Down, Up, Left, Right, Left Bumper, Right, Right Trigger, Right Trigger, Right Bumper.

ALL TRICKS

Select Cheat Codes from the Options menu and press Left Bumper, Right Trigger, Y, Up, Down, X, Left Trigger, Left, Right Bumper, Right Trigger.

ALL LEVELS

Select Cheat Codes from the Options menu and press X, Y, Up, Left, Left Bumper, Left Bumper, Right Trigger, X, Y, Left Trigger.

ALL CONFIGS

Select Cheat Codes from the Options menu and press Down, X, Right, Left Bumper, Right, Right Bumper, X, Right Trigger, Left Trigger, Y.

SUPER SPINS

Select Cheat Codes from the Options menu and press X X (x4), Y (x3), X.

AWESOME METER ALWAYS FULL

Select Cheat Codes from the Options menu and press Up, Right Trigger, X, Y, Left Bumper, X, Down, Left Bumper, Right Trigger, Right Bumper.

ALL AWESOMENESS

Select Cheat Codes from the Options menu and press Right Bumper, Right Bumper, Down, Left, Up, Right Trigger, X, Right Bumper, X, X.

OVERLOAD

ALL BUILD LICENSES

Select Cheat Codes from the Options menu and press Left, Right Trigger, Left Bumper, Right Trigger, X, X, Y, Down, Up, X.

ALL BUILD OBJECTS

Select Cheat Codes from the Options menu and press Left Trigger, Right Trigger, Up, Up, Right Bumper, Left, Right, X, Y, Left Bumper.

ALL CHALLENGES

Select Cheat Codes from the Options menu and press Right, Left Bumper, Left Trigger, X, Left, Right Bumper, Right Trigger, Y, Left Trigger, X.

LOUD SPEAKERS

Select Cheat Codes from the Options menu and press Y, Right Trigger, Right Trigger, Left Bumper, Down, Down, Left, Left, Right, Left Bumper.

LOW GRAVITY BOARDERS

Select Cheat Codes from the Options menu and press Right Trigger, Down, Down, Up, X, Left Bumper, Y, Right Trigger, Y, Down.

NO AI

Select Cheat Codes from the Options menu and press X, X, Left Bumper, Down, Right, Right, Up, Y, Y, Left Trigger.

ALL MUSIC

Select Cheat Codes from the Options menu and press Up, Left, Right Trigger, Right Bumper, Right Trigger, Up, Down, Left, Y, Left Trigger.

AVATAR: THE LAST AIRBENDER — THE BURNING EARTH

UNLIMITED HEALTH

Select Code Entry from the Extras menu and enter 65049.

DOUBLE DAMAGE

Select Code Entry from the Extras menu and enter 90210.

MAXIMUM LEVEL

Select Code Entry from the Extras menu and enter 89121.

UNLIMITED SPECIALS

Select Code Entry from the Extras menu and enter 66206.

ONE-HIT DISHONOR

Select Code Entry from the Extras menu and enter 28260.

ALL BONUS GAMES

Select Code Entry from the Extras menu and enter 99801.

UNLOCKS GALLERY

Select Code Entry from the Extras menu and enter 85061.

BAJA: EDGE OF CONTROL

ALL VEHICLES AND TRACKS

Select Cheat Codes from the Options menu and enter SHOWTIME.

ALL PARTS

Select Cheat Codes from the Options menu and enter SUPERMAX.

BATTLEFIELD 2: MODERN COMBAT

ALL WEAPONS

During a game, hold Right Bumper + Left Bumper and quickly press Right, Right, Down, Up, Left, Left.

BATTLEFIELD: BAD COMPANY

M60

Select Unlocks from the Multiplayer menu, press Start, and enter try4ndrunf0rcov3r.

QBU88
Select Unlocks from the Multiplayer menu, press Start, and enter your3mynextt4rget.

UZI
Select Unlocks from the Multiplayer menu, press Start, and enter cov3r1ngthecorn3r.

FIND ALL FIVE WEAPONS

SNIPER RIFLE
You received a weapon unlock code for this gun if you pre-ordered the game.

MACHINE GUN
Receive a weapon unlock code for this gun after signing up for the newsletter at www.findallfive.com.

SUB-MACHINE GUN
Download the demo and reach rank 4 to receive an unlock code for this weapon.

ASSAULT RIFLE
Go to veteran.battlefield.com and register your previous Battlefield games to receive an unlock code for this weapon.

SEMI-AUTOMATIC SHOTGUN
Check your online stats at www.findallfive.com to get an unlock code for this weapon.

BATTLESTATIONS: MIDWAY

ALL CAMPAIGN AND CHALLENGE MISSIONS
At the mission select, hold Right Bumper + Left Bumper + Right Trigger + Left Trigger and press X.

BEAT'N GROOVY

ALTERNATE CONTROLS
At the Title screen, press Up, Up, Down, Down, Left, Right, Left, Right, B, A.

BIONIC COMMANDO REARMED

The following challenge rooms can be found in the Challenge Room list. Only one code can be active at a time.

AARON SEDILLO'S CHALLENGE ROOM (CONTEST WINNER)
At the Title screen, press Right, Down, Left, Up, Left Bumper, Right Bumper, Y, Y, X, X, Start.

EUROGAMER CHALLENGE ROOM:
At the Title screen, press Down, Up, Down, Up, Left, Left Bumper, X, Left Bumper, X, Y, Start.

GAMESRADAR CHALLENGE ROOM:
At the Title screen, press Right Bumper, Y, X, X, Up, Down, Left Bumper, Left Bumper, Up, Down, Start.

IGN CHALLENGE ROOM:
At the Title screen, press Up, Down, Y, X, X, Y, Down, Up, Left Bumper, Left Bumper, Start.

MAJOR NELSON CHALLENGE ROOM
At the Title screen, press Left Bumper, X, X, X, Right, Down, Left Bumper, Left, Y, Down, Start.

BLAZING ANGELS: SQUADRONS OF WWII

ALL MISSIONS, MEDALS, & PLANES
At the Main menu hold Left Trigger + Right Trigger and press X, Left Bumper, Right Bumper, Y, Y, Right Bumper, Left Bumper, X.

GOD MODE
Pause the game, hold Left Trigger and press X, Y, Y, X. Release Left Trigger, hold Right Trigger and press Y, X, X, Y. Re-enter the code to disable it.

INCREASED DAMAGE
Pause the game, hold Left Trigger and press Left Bumper, Left Bumper, Right Bumper. Release Left Trigger, hold Right Trigger and press Right Bumper, Right Bumper, Left Bumper. Re-enter the code to disable it.

BLAZING ANGELS 2: SECRET MISSIONS OF WWII

Achievements are disabled when using these codes.

ALL MISSIONS AND PLANES UNLOCKED
At the Main menu, hold Left Trigger + Right Trigger, and press X, Left Bumper, Right Bumper, Y, Y, Right Bumper, Left Bumper, X.

GOD MODE
Pause the game, hold Left Trigger, and press X, Y, Y, X. Release Left Trigger, hold Right Trigger and press Y, X, X, Y. Re-enter the code to disable it.

INCREASED DAMAGE WITH ALL WEAPONS
Pause the game, hold Left Trigger, and press Left Bumper, Left Bumper, Right Bumper. Release Left Trigger, hold Right Trigger, and press Right Bumper, Right Bumper, Left Bumper. Re-enter the code to disable it.

BLITZ: THE LEAGUE

The following codes work for Quick Play mode:

UNLIMITED UNLEASH
Select Codes from Extras and enter BIGDOGS.

STAMINA OFF
Select Codes from Extras and enter NOTTIRED.

DOUBLE UNLEASH ICONS
Select Codes from Extras and enter PIPPED.

UNLIMITED CLASH ICONS
Select Codes from Extras and enter CLASHY.

TWO PLAYER CO-OP
Select Codes from Extras and enter CHUWAY.

BALL TRAIL ALWAYS ON
Select Codes from Extras and enter ONFIRE.

BEACH BALL
Select Codes from Extras and enter BOUNCY.

BLITZ: THE LEAGUE II

TOUCHDOWN CELEBRATIONS
Press these button combinations when given the chance after scoring a touchdown

CELEBRATION	CODE
Ball Spike	A, A, A, B
Beer Chug	A, A, B, B

CELEBRATION	CODE
Dance Fever	Y, Y, Y, A
Get Down	B, A, B, Y
Golf Putt	A, X, Y, B
Helmet Fling	A, X, A, X
Knockout	X, X, Y, Y
Man Crush	X, X, X, Y
Nut Shot	Y, Y, B, A
Pylon Darts	A, B, A, B
The Pooper	Y, X, A, B

BROTHERS IN ARMS: HELL'S HIGHWAY

ALL CHAPTERS
Select Enter Codes from the Options and enter GIMMECHAPTERS.

ALL RECON POINTS
Select Enter Codes from the Options and enter 0ZNDRBICRA.

KILROY DETECTOR
Select Enter Codes from the Options and enter SH2VYIVNZF.

TWO MULTIPLAYER SKINS
Select Enter Codes from the Options and enter HI9WTPXSUK.

BULLY: SCHOLARSHIP EDITION

FULL HEALTH
During a game and with a second controller, hold Left Bumper and press Right Trigger, Right Trigger, Right Trigger.

MONEY
During a game and with a second controller, hold Left Bumper and press Y, X, B, A.

INFINITE AMMO
During a game and with a second controller, hold Left Bumper and press Up, Down, Up, Down. Re-enter code to disable.

ALL WEAPONS
During a game and with a second controller, hold Left Bumper and press Up, Up, Up, Up.

ALL GYM GRAPPLE MOVES
During a game and with a second controller, hold Left Bumper and press Up, Left, Down, Down, Y, X, A, A.

ALL HOBO MOVES
During a game and with a second controller, hold Left Bumper and press Up, Left, Down, Right, Y, X, A, B

BURNOUT PARADISE

BEST BUY CAR
Pause the game and select Sponsor Product Code from the Under the Hood menu. Enter Bestbuy. Need A License to use this car offline.

CIRCUIT CITY CAR
Pause the game and select Sponsor Product Code from the Under the Hood menu. Enter Circuitcity. Need Burnout Paradise License to use this car offline.

XBOX 360™

GAMESTOP CAR
Pause the game and select Sponsor Product Code from the Under the Hood menu. Enter Gamestop. Need A License to use this car offline.

WALMART CAR
Pause the game and select Sponsor Product Code from the Under the Hood menu. Enter Walmart. Need Burnout Paradise License to use this car offline.

"STEEL WHEELS" GT
Pause the game and select Sponsor Product Code from the Under the Hood menu. Enter G23X 5K8Q GX2V 04B1 or E60J 8Z7T MS8L 51U6.

LICENSES

LICENSE	NUMBER OF WINS NEEDED
D	2
C	7
B	16
A	26
Burnout Paradise	45
Elite License	All events

CALL OF DUTY 3

ALL CHAPTERS AND BONUS CONTENT
At the Chapter Select screen, hold Back and press Right, Right, Left, Left, X, X.

CALL OF DUTY 4 MODERN WARFARE

ARCADE MODE
After a complete playthrough of the game, Arcade Mode becomes available from the Main menu.

UNLOCKABLE CHEATS
After completing the game, cheats are unlocked based on how many intelligence pieces were gathered. These cheats cannot be used during Arcade Mode. They may also disable the ability to earn Achievements.

CHEAT	INTEL ITEMS	DESCRIPTION
CoD Noir	2	Black and white
Photo-Negative	4	Inverses colors
Super Contrast	6	Increases contrast
Ragtime Warfare	8	Black and white, scratches fill screen, double speed, piano music
Cluster Bombs	10	Four extra grenade explosions after frag grenade explodes
A Bad Year	15	Enemies explode into a bunch of old tires when killed
Slow-Mo Ability	20	Melee button enables/disables slow-motion mode
Infinite Ammo	30	Unlimited ammo and no need to reload. Doesn't work for single-shot weapons such as RPG.

CARS

UNLOCK EVERYTHING
Select Cheat Codes from the Options and enter IF900HP.

ALL CHARACTERS
Select Cheat Codes from the Options and enter YAYCARS.

ALL CHARACTER SKINS
Select Cheat Codes from the Options and enter R4MONE.

ALL MINI-GAMES AND COURSES
Select Cheat Codes from the Options and enter MATTL66.

FAST START
Select Cheat Codes from the Options and enter IMSPEED.

INFINITE BOOST
Select Cheat Codes from the Options and enter VROOOOM.

ART
Select Cheat Codes from the Options and enter CONC3PT.

VIDEOS
Select Cheat Codes from the Options and enter WATCHIT.

CARS MATER-NATIONAL

ALL ARCADE RACES, MINI-GAMES, AND WORLDS
Select Codes/Cheats from the options and enter PLAYALL.

ALL CARS
Select Codes/Cheats from the options and enter MATTEL07.

ALTERNATE LIGHTNING MCQUEEN COLORS
Select Codes/Cheats from the options and enter NCEDUDZ.

ALL COLORS FOR OTHERS
Select Codes/Cheats from the options and enter PAINTIT.

UNLIMITED TURBO
Select Codes/Cheats from the options and enter ZZOOOOM.

EXTREME ACCELERATION
Select Codes/Cheats from the options and enter 0TO200X.

EXPERT MODE
Select Codes/Cheats from the options and enter VRYFAST.

ALL BONUS ART
Select Codes/Cheats from the options and enter BUYTALL.

CASTLEVANIA: SYMPHONY OF THE NIGHT

Before using the following codes, complete the game with 170%.

PLAY AS RICHTER BELMONT
Enter RICHTER as your name.

ALUCARD WITH AXELORD ARMOR
Enter AXEARMOR as your name.

ALUCARD WITH 99 LUCK AND OTHER STATS ARE LOW
Enter X-X!V"Q as your name.

CONDEMNED: CRIMINAL ORIGINS

ALL LEVELS
Enter ShovelFighter as a profile name.

CONDEMNED 2: BLOODSHOT

ALL BONUS ART
Create a profile with the name ShovelFighter. Use this profile to start a game and all of the bonus art is unlocked.

CRASH OF THE TITANS

BIG HEAD CRASH
Pause the game, hold the Right Trigger, and press X, X, Y, A.

SHADOW CRASH
Pause the game, hold the Right Trigger, and press Y, X, Y, A.

DARK MESSIAH OF MIGHT AND MAGIC: ELEMENTS

EXCLUSIVE MAP
Select Exclusive content from the Main menu. Select Exclusivity code and enter 5684219998871395. You can access it through Aranthir's office, in chapter 8.

XBOX 360™

THE DARKNESS

DARKLING OUTFITS

Even Darklings can make a fashion statement. Support your mini minions with an ensemble fit for murderous monsters by collecting these fun and colorful outfits.

OUTFIT	MENTIONED IN	AREA	LOCATION
Potato Sack	Chapter 1	Chinatown	Sitting against alley wall near metro exit
Jungle	Chapter 1	Hunters Point Alley	Inside hidden room
Roadworker	Chapter 3	City Hall station	Inside train car
Lumberjack	Side Objectives	Cutrone objective	Inside Cutrone's apartment
Fireman	Side Objectives	Pajamas objective	Inside room 261
Construction	Side Objectives	Mortarello objective	Inside room of last mission
Baseball	N/A	Dial: 555-4263	N/A
Golfshirt	N/A	Dial: 555-5664	N/A

PHONE NUMBERS

Dialing 'D' for Darkness isn't the only number to punch on a telephone. Sure, you called every number you found on those hard-to-get Collectibles, but you certainly haven't found *all* of the phone numbers. Pay close to attention to the environment as you hunt down Uncle Paulie. Chances are, you overlooked a phone number or two without even knowing it as you ripped out a goon's heart. All 25 'secret' phone numbers are scattered throughout New York and can be seen on anywhere from flyers and storefronts to garbage cans and posters. Dial 18 of the 25 numbers on a phone—in no specific order—to unlock the final secret of the game.

PHONE NUMBERS

555-6118	555-1847	555-6667	555-4569
555-9985	555-1037	555-1206	555-9528
555-3285	555-5723	555-8024	555-6322
555-9132	555-6893	555-2402	555-6557
555-2309	555-4372	555-9723	555-5289
555-6205	555-7658	555-1233	555-3947
555-9562	555-7934	555-7892	555-8930
555-3243	555-3840	555-2349	555-6325
555-4565	555-9898	555-7613	555-6969

DEAD SPACE

REFILL STASIS AND KINESIS ENERGY

Pause the game and press X, Y, Y, X, Y.

REFILL OXYGEN

Pause the game and press X, X, Y (x3).

ADD 2 POWER NODES

Pause the game and press Y, X (x3), Y. This code can only be used once.

ADD 5 POWER NODES

Pause the game and press Y, X, Y, X, X, Y, X, X, Y, X, X, Y. This code can only be used once.

1,000 CREDITS

Pause the game and press X (x3), Y, X. This code can only be used once.

2,000 CREDITS

Pause the game and press X (x3), Y, Y. This code can only be used once.

5,000 CREDITS

Pause the game and press X (x3), Y, X, Y. This code can only be used once.

10,000 CREDITS

Pause the game and press X, Y (x3), X, X, Y. This code can only be used once.

DEF JAM: ICON

IT'S GOING DOWN BY YUNG JOC

At the Title Screen, after "Press Start Button" appears, press Down, B, A, Right.

MAKE IT RAIN BY FAT JOE AND FIGHT AS FAT JOE

At the Title Screen, after "Press Start Button" appears, press B, Up, Right, Left, Y.

DON KING PRESENTS: PRIZEFIGHTER

UNLOCK RICARDO MAYORGA

Select Enter Unlock Code from the Extras menu and enter potsemag.

EXCLUSIVE BEST BUY FIGHT FOOTAGE

Select Enter Unlock Code from the Extras menu and enter 1bestbuybest. Select Watch Videos from the Extras menu to find video.

ERAGON

FURY MODE

Pause the game, hold Left Bumper + Right Bumper + Left Trigger + Right Trigger and press X, X, B, B.

EVERY EXTEND EXTRA EXTREME

FINE ADJUSTMENT MENU

At the Start screen, press Left Bumper, Right Bumper, Left Bumper, Right Bumper, Left Bumper, Right Bumper, Left Bumper, Right Bumper.

FAR CRY INSTINCTS PREDATOR

EVOLUTION GAME

Select the Cheat Menu option from the Main menu or the pause menu and enter GiveMeItAll.

HEAL

Select the Cheat Menu option from the Main menu or the pause menu and enter ImJackCarver.

INFINITE ADRENALINE

Select the Cheat Menu option from the Main menu or the pause menu and enter Bloodlust.

INFINITE AMMO

Select the Cheat Menu option from the Main menu or the pause menu and enter UnleashHell.

OVERLORD

XBOX 360™

ENABLE EVOLUTIONS

Select the Cheat Menu option from the Main menu or the pause menu and enter FeralAttack.

ALL MAPS

Select the Cheat Menu option from the Main menu or the pause menu and enter GiveMeTheMaps.

FAR CRY 2

BONUS MISSIONS

Select Promotional Content from the Additional Content menu and enter the following codes. Each code gives four or six extra missions.

6aPHuswe
Cr34ufrE
2Eprunef
JeM8SpaW
tr99pUkA

FATAL FURY SPECIAL

CHEAT MENU

During a game, hold Start and push A + X + Y.

F.E.A.R.

ALL MISSIONS

Sign in with F3ARDAY1 as your Profile Name. Using this cheat will disable Achievements.

FIGHT NIGHT ROUND 3

ALL VENUES

Create a champ with a first name of NEWVIEW.

FLATOUT: ULTIMATE CARNAGE

MOB CAR IN SINGLE EVENTS

Select Enter Code from Extras and enter BIGTRUCK.

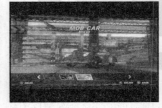

PIMPSTER IN SINGLE EVENTS
Select Enter Code from Extras and enter RUTTO.

ROCKET IN SINGLE EVENTS
Select Enter Code from Extras and enter KALJAKOPPA.

 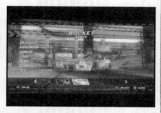

FRACTURE

EXCLUSIVE PRE-ORDER SKIN
Pause the game and press Up, Right, Left, Down, Up, Left, Right, Down.

FROGGER

BIG FROGGER
At the One/Two-Player screen, press Up, Up, Down, Down, Left, Right, Left, Right, B, A.

FULL AUTO

ALL TRACKS, VEHICLES, & WEAPONS
Create a new profile with the name magicman.

THE GODFATHER: THE GAME

FULL AMMO
Pause the game and press Y, Left, Y, Right, X, Right Thumbstick.

FULL HEALTH
Pause the game and press Left, X, Right, Y, Right, Left Thumbstick.

UNLOCK ENTIRE FILM ARCHIVE
After loading a game and before joining the family, press Y, X, Y, X, X, Left Thumbstick. Select Film Archive to view the films.

GRAND THEFT AUTO IV

CHEATS
Call the following phone numbers with Niko's phone to activate the cheats. Some cheats may affect the missions and achievements.

VEHICLE	PHONE NUMBER
Change weather	468-555-0100
Get weapons	486-555-0100
Get different weapons	486-555-0150
Raise wanted level	267-555-0150
Remove wanted level	267-555-0100
Restore armor	362-555-0100
Restore health	482-555-0100
Restore armor, health, and ammo	482-555-0100

SPAWN VEHICLES

Call the following phone numbers with Niko's phone to spawn the corresponding vehicle.

VEHICLE	PHONE NUMBER
Annihilator	359-555-0100
Cognoscenti	227-555-0142
Comet	227-555-0175
FIB Buffalo	227-555-0100
Jetmax	938-555-0100
NRG-900	625-555-0100
Sanchez	625-555-0150
SuperGT	227-555-0168
Turismo	227-555-0147

MAP LOCATIONS

Access a computer in game and enter the following URL:
www.whattheydonotwantyoutoknow.com.

GRID

ALL DRIFT CARS

Select Bonus Codes from the Options. Then choose Enter Code and enter TUN58396.

ALL MUSCLE CARS

Select Bonus Codes from the Options. Then choose Enter Code and enter MUS59279.

BUCHBINDER EMOTIONAL ENGINEERING BMW 320SI

Select Bonus Codes from the Options. Then choose Enter Code and enter F93857372. You can use this in Race Day or in GRID World once you've started your own team.

EBAY

Select Bonus Codes from the Options. Then choose Enter Code and enter DAFJ55E01473M0. You can use this in Race Day or in GRID World once you've started your own team.

GAMESTATION BMW 320SI

Select Bonus Codes from the Options. Then choose Enter Code and enter G29782655. You can use this in Race Day or in GRID World once you've started your own team.

MICROMANIA PAGANI ZONDA R

Select Bonus Codes from the Options. Then choose Enter Code and enter M38572343. You can use this in Race Day or in GRID World once you've started your own team.

PLAY.COM ASTON MARTIN DBR9

Select Bonus Codes from the Options. Then choose Enter Code and enter P47203845. You can use this in Race Day or in GRID World once you've started your own team.

GUITAR HERO II

ALL SONGS

At the Main menu, press Blue, Yellow, Orange, Red, Yellow, Orange, Blue, Yellow, Blue, Yellow, Blue, Yellow, Blue, Yellow, Blue, Yellow.

HYPER SPEED

At the Main menu, press Blue, Orange, Yellow, Orange, Blue, Orange, Yellow, Yellow.

PERFORMANCE MODE

At the Main menu, press Blue, Blue, Yellow, Blue, Blue, Orange, Blue, Blue.

AIR GUITAR

At the Main menu, press Yellow, Blue, Yellow, Orange, Yellow, Blue.

EYEBALL HEAD CROWD

At the Main menu, press Yellow, Orange, Blue, Blue, Blue, Orange, Yellow.

MONKEY HEAD CROWD

At the Main menu, press Orange, Yellow, Blue, Blue, Yellow, Orange, Blue, Blue.

FLAME HEAD

At the Main menu, press Orange, Yellow, Yellow, Orange, Yellow, Yellow, Orange, Yellow, Yellow, Blue, Yellow, Yellow, Blue, Yellow, Yellow.

GUITAR HERO III: LEGENDS OF ROCK

To enter the following cheats, strum the guitar with the given buttons held. For example, if it says Yellow + Orange, hold Yellow and Orange as you strum. Air Guitar, Precision Mode, and Performance Mode can be toggled on and off from the Cheats menu. You can also change between five different levels of Hyperspeed at this menu.

UNLOCK EVERYTHING

Select Cheats from the Options. Choose Enter Cheat and enter Green + Red + Blue + Orange, Green + Red + Yellow + Blue, Green + Red + Yellow + Orange, Green + Yellow + Blue + Orange, Green + Red + Yellow + Blue, Red + Yellow + Blue + Orange, Green + Red + Yellow + Blue, Green + Yellow + Blue + Orange, Green + Red + Yellow + Blue, Green + Red + Yellow + Orange, Green + Red + Yellow + Orange, Green + Red + Yellow + Blue, Green + Red + Yellow + Orange. No sounds play while this code is entered.

An easier way to show this code is by representing Green as 1 down to Orange as 5. For example, if you have 1345, you would hold down Green + Yellow + Blue + Orange while strumming. 1245 + 1234 + 1235 + 1345 + 1234 + 2345 + 1234 + 1345 + 1234 + 1235 + 1235 + 1234 + 1235.

ALL SONGS

Select Cheats from the Options. Choose Enter Cheat and enter Yellow + Orange, Red + Blue, Red + Orange, Green + Blue, Red + Yellow, Yellow + Orange, Red + Yellow, Red + Blue, Green + Yellow, Green + Yellow, Yellow + Blue, Yellow + Blue, Yellow + Orange, Yellow + Orange, Yellow + Blue, Yellow, Red, Red + Yellow, Red, Yellow, Orange.

NO FAIL

Select Cheats from the Options. Choose Enter Cheat and enter Green + Red, Blue, Green + Red, Green + Yellow, Blue, Green + Yellow, Red + Yellow, Orange, Red + Yellow, Green + Yellow, Yellow, Green + Yellow, Green + Red.

AIR GUITAR

Select Cheats from the Options. Choose Enter Cheat and enter Blue + Yellow, Green + Yellow, Green + Yellow, Red + Blue, Red + Blue, Red + Yellow, Red + Yellow, Blue + Yellow, Green + Yellow, Green + Yellow, Red + Blue, Red + Blue, Red + Yellow, Red + Yellow, Green + Yellow, Green + Yellow, Red + Yellow, Red + Yellow.

HYPERSPEED

Select Cheats from the Options. Choose Enter Cheat and enter Orange, Blue, Orange, Yellow, Orange, Blue, Orange, Yellow.

PERFORMANCE MODE

Select Cheats from the Options. Choose Enter Cheat and enter Red + Yellow, Red + Blue, Red + Orange, Red + Blue, Red + Yellow, Green + Blue, Red + Yellow, Red + Blue.

EASY EXPERT

Select Cheats from the Options. Choose Enter Cheat and enter Green + Red, Green + Yellow, Yellow + Blue, Red + Blue, Blue + Orange, Yellow + Orange, Red + Yellow, Red + Blue.

PRECISION MODE

Select Cheats from the Options. Choose Enter Cheat and enter Green + Red, Green + Red, Green + Red, Red + Yellow, Red + Yellow, Red + Blue, Red + Blue, Yellow + Blue, Yellow + Orange, Yellow + Orange, Green + Red, Green + Red, Green + Red, Red + Yellow, Red + Yellow, Red + Blue, Red + Blue, Yellow + Blue, Yellow + Orange, Yellow + Orange.

BRET MICHAELS SINGER

Select Cheats from the Options. Choose Enter Cheat and enter Green + Red, Green + Red, Green + Red, Green + Blue, Green + Blue, Green + Blue, Red + Blue, Red, Red, Red, Red + Blue, Red, Red, Red, Red + Blue, Red, Red, Red.

GUITAR HERO: AEROSMITH

To enter the following cheats, strum the guitar with the given buttons held. For example, if it says Yellow + Orange, hold Yellow and Orange as you strum. Air Guitar, Precision Mode, and Performance Mode can be toggled on and off from the Cheats menu. You can also change between five different levels of Hyperspeed at this menu.

ALL SONGS

Red + Yellow, Green + Red, Green + Red, Red + Yellow, Red + Yellow, Green + Red, Red + Yellow, Red + Yellow, Green + Red, Green + Red, Red + Yellow, Red + Yellow, Green + Red, Red + Yellow, Red + Blue.

AIR GUITAR

Red + Yellow, Green + Red, Red + Yellow, Red + Yellow, Red + Blue, Red + Blue, Red + Blue, Red + Blue, Red + Blue, Yellow + Blue, Yellow + Blue, Yellow + Orange

HYPERSPEED

Yellow + Orange, Yellow + Orange, Yellow + Orange, Yellow + Orange, Yellow + Orange, Red + Yellow, Red + Yellow, Red + Yellow, Red + Yellow, Red + Blue, Red + Blue, Red + Blue, Red + Blue, Red + Blue, Yellow + Blue, Yellow + Orange, Yellow + Orange.

NO FAIL

Select Cheats from the Options. Choose Enter Cheat and enter Green + Red, Blue, Green + Red, Green + Yellow, Blue, Green + Yellow, Red + Yellow, Orange, Red + Yellow, Green + Yellow, Yellow, Green + Yellow, Green + Red.

PERFORMANCE MODE

Green + Red, Green + Red, Red + Orange, Red + Blue, Green + Red, Green + Red, Red + Orange, Red + Blue

PRECISION MODE
Red + Yellow, Red + Blue, Red + Blue, Red + Yellow, Red + Yellow, Yellow + Blue, Yellow + Blue, Yellow + Blue, Red + Blue, Red + Yellow, Red + Blue, Red + Yellow, Red + Yellow, Yellow + Blue, Yellow + Blue, Yellow + Blue, Red + Blue.

GUITAR HERO WORLD TOUR

The following cheats can be toggled on and off at the Cheats menu.

QUICKPLAY SONGS
Select Cheats from the Options menu, choose Enter New Cheat and press Blue, Blue, Red, Green, Green, Blue, Blue, Yellow.

ALWAYS SLIDE
Select Cheats from the Options menu, choose Enter New Cheat and press Green, Green, Red, Red, Yellow, Red, Yellow, Blue.

AT&T BALLPARK
Select Cheats from the Options menu, choose Enter New Cheat and press Yellow, Green, Red, Red, Green, Blue, Red, Yellow.

AUTO KICK
Select Cheats from the Options menu, choose Enter New Cheat and press Yellow, Green, Red, Blue (x4), Red.

EXTRA LINE 6 TONES
Select Cheats from the Options menu, choose Enter New Cheat and press Green, Red, Yellow, Blue, Red, Yellow, Blue, Green.

FLAME COLOR
Select Cheats from the Options menu, choose Enter New Cheat and press Green, Red, Green, Blue, Red, Red, Yellow, Blue.

GEM COLOR
Select Cheats from the Options menu, choose Enter New Cheat and press Blue, Red, Red, Green, Red, Green, Red, Yellow.

STAR COLOR
Select Cheats from the Options menu, choose Enter New Cheat and press Red, Red, Yellow, Red, Blue, Red, Red, Blue.

AIR INSTRUMENTS
Select Cheats from the Options menu, choose Enter New Cheat and press Red, Red, Blue, Yellow, Green (x3), Yellow.

HYPERSPEED
Select Cheats from the Options menu, choose Enter New Cheat and press Green, Blue, Red, Yellow, Yellow, Red, Green, Green. These show up in the menu as HyperGuitar, HyperBass, and HyperDrums.

PERFORMANCE MODE
Select Cheats from the Options menu, choose Enter New Cheat and press Yellow, Yellow, Blue, Red, Blue, Green, Red, Red.

INVISIBLE ROCKER
Select Cheats from the Options menu, choose Enter New Cheat and press Green, Red, Yellow (x3), Blue, Blue, Green.

VOCAL FIREBALL
Select Cheats from the Options menu, choose Enter New Cheat and press Red, Green, Green, Yellow, Blue, Green, Yellow, Green.

AARON STEELE!
Select Cheats from the Options menu, choose Enter New Cheat and press Blue, Red, Yellow (x5), Green.

JONNY VIPER
Select Cheats from the Options menu, choose Enter New Cheat and press Blue, Red, Blue, Blue, Yellow (x3), Green.

NICK
Select Cheats from the Options menu, choose Enter New Cheat and press Green, Red, Blue, Green, Red, Blue, Blue, Green.

RINA
Select Cheats from the Options menu, choose Enter New Cheat and press Blue, Red, Green, Green, Yellow (x3), Green.

HALO 3

TOGGLE HIDE WEAPON
During a local game, hold Left Bumper + Right Bumper + Left Stick + A + Down.

TOGGLE SHOW COORDINATES
During a local game, hold Left Bumper + Right Bumper + Left Stick + A + Up.

TOGGLE BETWEEN PAN-CAM AND NORMAL
During a local game, hold Left Stick + Right Stick and press Left when Show Coordinates is active.

IDOLMASTER: LIVE FOR YOU!

MAMI
At the character select, press R3 while on Ami.

SHORT-HAIRED MIKI
At the character select, press R3 while on Miki.

IRON MAN

CLASSIC ARMOR
Clear One Man Army vs. Mercs.

EXTREMIS ARMOR
Clear One Man Army vs. Maggia.

MARK II ARMOR
Clear One Man Army vs. Ten Rings.

HULKBUSTER ARMOR
Clear One Man Army vs. AIM-X. Can also be unlocked when clear game save data from Incredible Hulk is stored on the same console.

SILVER CENTURION ARMOR
Clear Mission 13: Showdown.

CLASSIC MARK I ARMOR
Clear One Man Army vs. AIM.

JUICED 2: HOT IMPORT NIGHTS

HIDDEN CHALLENGE AND A AUDI TT 1.8 QUATTRO
Select Cheats and Codes from the DNA Lab menu and enter YTHZ. Defeat the challenge to earn the Audi TT 1.8 Quattro.

HIDDEN CHALLENGE AND A BMW Z4
Select Cheats and Codes from the DNA Lab menu and enter GVDL. Defeat the challenge to earn the BMW Z4.

HIDDEN CHALLENGE AND A HOLDEN MONARO
Select Cheats and Codes from the DNA Lab menu and enter RBSG. Defeat the challenge to earn the Holden Monaro.

HIDDEN CHALLENGE AND A HYUNDAI COUPE 2.7 V6
Select Cheats and Codes from the DNA Lab menu and enter BSLU. Defeat the challenge to earn the Hyundai Coupe 2.7 V6.

HIDDEN CHALLENGE AND A INFINITY G35
Select Cheats and Codes from the DNA Lab menu and enter MRHC. Defeat the challenge to earn the Infinity G35.

HIDDEN CHALLENGE AND A KOENIGSEGG CCX
Select Cheats and Codes from the DNA Lab menu and enter KDTR. Defeat the challenge to earn the Koenigsegg CCX.

HIDDEN CHALLENGE AND A MITSUBISHI PROTOTYPE X
Select Cheats and Codes from the DNA Lab menu and enter DOPX. Defeat the challenge to earn the Mitsubishi Prototype X.

HIDDEN CHALLENGE AND A NISSAN 350Z
Select Cheats and Codes from the DNA Lab menu and enter PRGN. Defeat the challenge to earn the Nissan 350Z.

HIDDEN CHALLENGE AND A NISSAN SKYLINE R34 GT-R
Select Cheats and Codes from the DNA Lab menu and enter JWRS. Defeat the challenge to earn the Nissan Skyline R34 GT-R.

HIDDEN CHALLENGE AND A SALEEN S7
Select Cheats and Codes from the DNA Lab menu and enter WIKF. Defeat the challenge to earn the Saleen S7.

HIDDEN CHALLENGE AND A SEAT LEON CUPRA R
Select Cheats and Codes from the DNA Lab menu and enter FAMQ. Defeat the challenge to earn the Seat Leon Cupra R.

KUNG FU PANDA

INFINITE CHI
Select Cheats from the Extra menu and press Down, Right, Left, Up, Down.

INVINCIBILITY
Select Cheats from the Extra menu and press Down, Down, Right, Up, Left.

FULL UPGRADES
Select Cheats from the Extra menu and press Left, Right, Down, Left, Up.

4X DAMAGE MULTIPLAYER
Select Cheats from the Extra menu and press Up, Down, Up, Right, Left.

ALL MULTIPLAYER CHARACTERS
Select Cheats from the Extra menu and press Left, Down, Left, Right, Down.

DRAGON WARRIOR OUTFIT IN MULTIPLAYER
Select Cheats from the Extra menu and press Left, Down, Right, Left, Up.

ALL OUTFITS
Select Cheats from the Extra menu and press Right, Left, Down, Up, Right.

THE LEGEND OF SPYRO: DAWN OF THE DRAGON

UNLIMITED LIFE
Pause the game, hold Left Bumper and press Right, Right, Down, Down, Left with the Left Control Stick.

UNLIMITED MANA
Pause the game, hold Right Bumper and press Up, Right, Up, Left, Down with the Left Control Stick.

MAXIMUM XP
Pause the game, hold Right Bumper and press Up, Left, Left, Down, Up with the Left Control Stick.

ALL ELEMENTAL UPGRADES
Pause the game, hold Left Bumper and press Left, Up, Down, Up, Right with the Left Control Stick.

LEGO BATMAN

BATCAVE CODES
Using the computer in the Batcave, select Enter Code and enter the following codes.

CHARACTERS

CHARACTER	CODE
Alfred	ZAQ637
Batgirl	JKR331
Bruce Wayne	BDJ327
Catwoman (Classic)	M1AAWW
Clown Goon	HJK327
Commissioner Gordon	DDP967
Fishmonger	HGY748
Freeze Girl	XVK541
Joker Goon	UTF782
Joker Henchman	YUN924
Mad Hatter	JCA283
Man-Bat	NYU942
Military Policeman	MKL382
Nightwing	MVY759
Penguin Goon	NKA238
Penguin Henchman	BJH782
Penguin Minion	KJP748
Poison Ivy Goon	GTB899
Police Marksman	HKG984
Police Officer	JRY983
Riddler Goon	CRY928
Riddler Henchman	XEU824
S.W.A.T.	HTF114
Sailor	NAV592
Scientist	JFL786
Security Guard	PLB946
The Joker (Tropical)	CCB199
Yeti	NJL412
Zoo Sweeper	DWR243

VEHICLES

VEHICLE	CODE
Bat-Tank	KNTT4B
Bruce Wayne's Private Jet	LEA664
Catwoman's Motorcycle	HPL826
Garbage Truck	DUS483
Goon Helicopter	GCH328
Harbor Helicopter	CHP735
Harley Quinn's Hammer Truck	RDT637

VEHICLE	CODE
Mad Hatter's Glider	HS000W
Mad Hatter's Steamboat	M4DM4N
Mr. Freeze's Iceberg	ICYICE
The Joker's Van	JUK657
Mr. Freeze's Kart	BCT229
Penguin Goon Submarine	BTN248
Police Bike	LJP234
Police Boat	PLC999
Police Car	KJL832
Police Helicopter	CWR732
Police Van	MAC788
Police Watercraft	VJD328
Riddler's Jet	HAHAHA
Robin's Submarine	TTF453
Two-Face's Armored Truck	EFE933

CHEATS

CHEAT	CODE
Always Score Multiply	9LRGNB
Fast Batarangs	JRBDCB
Fast Walk	ZOLM6N
Flame Batarang	D8NYWH
Freeze Batarang	XPN4NG
Extra Hearts	ML3KHP
Fast Build	EVG26J
Immune to Freeze	JXUDY6
Invincibility	WYD5CP
Minikit Detector	ZXGH9J
More Batarang Targets	XWP645
Piece Detector	KHJ554
Power Brick Detector	MMN786
Regenerate Hearts	HJH7HJ
Score x2	N4NR3E
Score x4	CX9MAT
Score x6	MLVNF2
Score x8	WCCDB9
Score x10	18HW07

LEGO INDIANA JONES: THE ORIGINAL ADVENTURES

CHARACTERS

Approach the blackboard in the Classroom and enter the following codes.

CHARACTER	CODE
Bandit	12N68W
Bandit Swordsman	1MK4RT
Barranca	04EM94
Bazooka Trooper (Crusade)	MK83R7
Bazooka Trooper (Raiders)	S93Y5R
Belloq	CHN3YU
Belloq (Jungle)	TDR197
Belloq (Robes)	VEO29L
British Commander	B73EUA
British Officer	VJ5TI9
British Soldier	DJ5I2W
Captain Katanga	VJ3TT3
Chatter Lal	ENW936
Chatter Lal (Thuggee)	CNH4RY
Chen	3NK48T
Colonel Dietrich	2K9RKS
Colonel Vogel	8EAL4H

CHARACTER	CODE
Dancing Girl	C7EJ21
Donovan	3NFTU8
Elsa (Desert)	JSNRT9
Elsa (Officer)	VMJ5US
Enemy Boxer	8246RB
Enemy Butler	VJ48W3
Enemy Guard	VJ7R51
Enemy Guard (Mountains)	YR47WM
Enemy Officer	572E61
Enemy Officer (Desert	2MK45O
Enemy Pilot	B84ELP
Enemy Radio Operator	1MF94R
Enemy Soldier (Desert)	4NSU7Q
Fedora	V75YSP
First Mate	0GIN24
Grail Knight	NE6THI
Hovitos Tribesman	H0V1SS
Indiana Jones (Desert Disguise)	4J8S4M
Indiana Jones (Officer)	VJ85OS
Jungle Guide	24PF34
Kao Kan	WMO46L
Kazim	NRH23J
Kazim (Desert)	3M29TJ
Lao Che	2NK479
Maharajah	NFK5N2
Major Toht	13NS01
Masked Bandit	N48SF0
Mola Ram	FJUR31
Monkey Man	3RF6YJ
Pankot Assassin	2NKT72
Pankot Guard	VN28RH
Sherpa Brawler	VJ37WJ
Sherpa Gunner	ND762W
Slave Child	0E3ENW
Thuggee	VM683E
Thuggee Acolyte	T2R3F9
Thuggee Slave Driver	VBS7GW
Village Dignitary	KD48TN
Village Elder	4682E1
Willie (Dinner Suit)	VK93R7
Willie (Pajamas)	MEN4IP
Wu Han	3NSLT8

EXTRAS

Approach the blackboard in the Classroom and enter the following codes. Some cheats need to be enabled by selecting Extras from the pause menu.

CHEAT	CODE
Artifact Detector	VIKED7
Beep Beep	VNF59Q
Character Treasure	VIES2R
Disarm Enemies	VKRNS9
Disguises	4ID1N6
Fast Build	V83SLO
Fast Dig	378RS6
Fast Fix	FJ59WS
Fertilizer	B1GW1F
Ice Rink	33GM7J
Parcel Detector	VUT673
Poo Treasure	WWQ1SA
Regenerate Hearts	MDLP69
Secret Characters	3X44AA
Silhouettes	3HE85H

CHEAT	CODE
Super Scream	VN3R7S
Super Slap	0P1TA5
Treasure Magnet	H86LA2
Treasure x10	VI3PS8
Treasure x2	VM4TS9
Treasure x4	VLWEN3
Treasure x6	V84RYS
Treasure x8	A72E1M

LEGO STAR WARS: THE COMPLETE SAGA

The following still need to be purchased after entering the codes.

CHARACTERS

ADMIRAL ACKBAR
At the bar in Mos Eisley Cantina, select Enter Code and enter ACK646.

BATTLE DROID (COMMANDER)
At the bar in Mos Eisley Cantina, select Enter Code and enter KPF958.

BOBA FETT (BOY)
At the bar in Mos Eisley Cantina, select Enter Code and enter GGF539.

BOSS NASS
At the bar in Mos Eisley Cantina, select Enter Code and enter HHY697.

CAPTAIN TARPALS
At the bar in Mos Eisley Cantina, select Enter Code and enter QRN714.

COUNT DOOKU
At the bar in Mos Eisley Cantina, select Enter Code and enter DDD748.

DARTH MAUL
At the bar in Mos Eisley Cantina, select Enter Code and enter EUK421.

EWOK
At the bar in Mos Eisley Cantina, select Enter Code and enter EWK785.

GENERAL GRIEVOUS
At the bar in Mos Eisley Cantina, select Enter Code and enter PMN576.

GREEDO
At the bar in Mos Eisley Cantina, select Enter Code and enter ZZR636.

IG-88
At the bar in Mos Eisley Cantina, select Enter Code and enter GIJ989.

IMPERIAL GUARD
At the bar in Mos Eisley Cantina, select Enter Code and enter GUA850.

JANGO FETT
At the bar in Mos Eisley Cantina, select Enter Code and enter KLJ897.

KI-ADI MUNDI
At the bar in Mos Eisley Cantina, select Enter Code and enter MUN486.

LUMINARA
At the bar in Mos Eisley Cantina, select Enter Code and enter LUM521.

PADMÉ
At the bar in Mos Eisley Cantina, select Enter Code and enter VBJ322.

R2-Q5
At the bar in Mos Eisley Cantina, select Enter Code and enter EVILR2.

STORMTROOPER
At the bar in Mos Eisley Cantina, select Enter Code and enter NBN431.

TAUN WE
At the bar in Mos Eisley Cantina, select Enter Code and enter PRX482.

VULTURE DROID
At the bar in Mos Eisley Cantina, select Enter Code and enter BDC866.

WATTO
At the bar in Mos Eisley Cantina, select Enter Code and enter PLL967.

ZAM WESELL
At the bar in Mos Eisley Cantina, select Enter Code and enter 584HJF.

SKILLS

DISGUISE
At the bar in Mos Eisley Cantina, select Enter Code and enter BRJ437.

FORCE GRAPPLE LEAP
At the bar in Mos Eisley Cantina, select Enter Code and enter CLZ738.

XBOX 360™

VEHICLES

DROID TRIFIGHTER
At the bar in Mos Eisley Cantina, select Enter Code and enter AAB123.

IMPERIAL SHUTTLE
At the bar in Mos Eisley Cantina, select Enter Code and enter HUT845.

TIE INTERCEPTOR
At the bar in Mos Eisley Cantina, select Enter Code and enter INT729.

TIE FIGHTER
At the bar in Mos Eisley Cantina, select Enter Code and enter DBH897.

ZAM'S AIRSPEEDER
At the bar in Mos Eisley Cantina, select Enter Code and enter UUU875.

LEGO STAR WARS II: THE ORIGINAL TRILOGY

BEACH TROOPER
At Mos Eisley Canteena, select Enter Code and enter UCK868. You must still select Characters and purchase this character for 20,000 studs.

BEN KENOBI (GHOST)
At Mos Eisley Canteena, select Enter Code and enter BEN917. You must still select Characters and purchase this character for 1,100,000 studs.

BESPIN GUARD
At Mos Eisley Canteena, select Enter Code and enter VHY832. You must still select Characters and purchase this character for 15,000 studs.

BIB FORTUNA
At Mos Eisley Canteena, select Enter Code and enter WTY721. You must still select Characters and purchase this character for 16,000 studs.

BOBA FETT
At Mos Eisley Canteena, select Enter Code and enter HLP221. You must still select Characters and purchase this character for 175,000 studs.

DEATH STAR TROOPER
At Mos Eisley Canteena, select Enter Code and enter BNC332. You must still select Characters and purchase this character for 19,000 studs.

EWOK
At Mos Eisley Canteena, select Enter Code and enter TTT289. You must still select Characters and purchase this character for 34,000 studs.

GAMORREAN GUARD
At Mos Eisley Canteena, select Enter Code and enter YZF999. You must still select Characters and purchase this character for 40,000 studs.

GONK DROID
At Mos Eisley Canteena, select Enter Code and enter NFX582. You must still select Characters and purchase this character for 1,550 studs.

GRAND MOFF TARKIN
At Mos Eisley Canteena, select Enter Code and enter SMG219. You must still select Characters and purchase this character for 38,000 studs.

GREEDO
At Mos Eisley Canteena, select Enter Code and enter NAH118. You must still select Characters and purchase this character for 60,000 studs.

HAN SOLO (HOOD)
At Mos Eisley Canteena, select Enter Code and enter YWM840. You must still select Characters and purchase this character for 20,000 studs.

IG-88
At Mos Eisley Canteena, select Enter Code and enter NXL973. You must still select Characters and purchase this character for 30,000 studs.

IMPERIAL GUARD
At Mos Eisley Canteena, select Enter Code and enter MMM111. You must still select Characters and purchase this character for 45,000 studs.

IMPERIAL OFFICER
At Mos Eisley Canteena, select Enter Code and enter BBV889. You must still select Characters and purchase this character for 28,000 studs.

IMPERIAL SHUTTLE PILOT
At Mos Eisley Canteena, select Enter Code and enter VAP664. You must still select Characters and purchase this character for 29,000 studs.

IMPERIAL SPY
At Mos Eisley Canteena, select Enter Code and enter CVT125. You must still select Characters and purchase this character for 13,500 studs.

JAWA
At Mos Eisley Canteena, select Enter Code and enter JAW499. You must still select Characters and purchase this character for 24,000 studs.

LOBOT
At Mos Eisley Canteena, select Enter Code and enter UUB319. You must still select Characters and purchase this character for 11,000 studs.

PALACE GUARD
At Mos Eisley Canteena, select Enter Code and enter SGE549. You must still select Characters and purchase this character for 14,000 studs.

REBEL PILOT
At Mos Eisley Canteena, select Enter Code and enter CYG336. You must still select Characters and purchase this character for 15,000 studs.

REBEL TROOPER (HOTH)
At Mos Eisley Canteena, select Enter Code and enter EKU849. You must still select Characters and purchase this character for 16,000 studs.

SANDTROOPER
At Mos Eisley Canteena, select Enter Code and enter YDV451. You must still select Characters and purchase this character for 14,000 studs.

SKIFF GUARD
At Mos Eisley Canteena, select Enter Code and enter GBU888. You must still select Characters and purchase this character for 12,000 studs.

SNOWTROOPER
At Mos Eisley Canteena, select Enter Code and enter NYU989. You must still select Characters and purchase this character for 16,000 studs.

STORMTROOPER
At Mos Eisley Canteena, select Enter Code and enter PTR345. You must still select Characters and purchase this character for 10,000 studs.

THE EMPEROR
At Mos Eisley Canteena, select Enter Code and enter HHY382. You must still select Characters and purchase this character for 275,000 studs.

TIE FIGHTER
At Mos Eisley Canteena, select Enter Code and enter HDY739. You must still select Characters and purchase this item for 60,000 studs.

TIE FIGHTER PILOT
At Mos Eisley Canteena, select Enter Code and enter NNZ316. You must still select Characters and purchase this character for 21,000 studs.

TIE INTERCEPTOR
At Mos Eisley Canteena, select Enter Code and enter QYA828. You must still select Characters and purchase this item for 40,000 studs.

TUSKEN RAIDER
At Mos Eisley Canteena, select Enter Code and enter PEJ821. You must still select Characters and purchase this character for 23,000 studs.

UGNAUGHT
At Mos Eisley Canteena, select Enter Code and enter UGN694. You must still select Characters and purchase this character for 36,000 studs.

LOONEY TUNES: ACME ARSENAL

UNLIMITED AMMO
At the Cheat menu, press Down, Left, Up, Right, Down, Left, Up, Right, Down.

LOST PLANET: EXTREME CONDITION

The following codes are for Single Player Mode on Easy Difficulty only.

500 THERMAL ENERGY
Pause the game and press Up, Up, Down, Down, Left, Right, Left, Right, X, Y, Right Bumper + Left Bumper.

INFINITE AMMUNITION
Pause the game and press Right Trigger, Right Bumper, Y, X, Right, Down, Left, Left Bumper, Left Trigger, Right Trigger, Right Bumper, Y, X, Right, Down, Left, Left Bumper, Left Trigger, Right Trigger, Right Bumper, Y, Left, Down, X, Right Bumper + Left Bumper.

INFINITE HEALTH
Pause the game and press Down (x3), Up, Y, Up, Y, Up, Y, Up(x3), Down, X, Down, X, Down, X, Left, Y, Right, X, Left, Y, Right, X, Right Bumper + Left Bumper.

CHANGE CAMERA ANGLE IN CUT SCENES
During a cut scene, press B, A, X, Y, B, A, X, Y, B, A, X, Y.

MAJOR LEAGUE BASEBALL 2K6

UNLOCK EVERYTHING
Select Enter Cheat Code from the My 2K6 menu and enter Derek Jeter.

TOPPS 2K STARS
Select Enter Cheat Code from the My 2K6 menu and enter Dream Team.

SUPER WALL CLIMB
Select Enter Cheat Code from the My 2K6 menu and enter Last Chance. Enable the cheats by selecting My Cheats or selecting Cheat Codes from the in-game Options screen.

SUPER PITCHES
Select Enter Cheat Code from the My 2K6 menu and enter Unhittable. Enable the cheats by selecting My Cheats or selecting Cheat Codes from the in-game Options screen.

ROCKET ARMS
Select Enter Cheat Code from the My 2K6 menu and enter Gotcha. Enable the cheats by selecting My Cheats or selecting Cheat Codes from the in-game Options screen.

BOUNCY BALL
Select Enter Cheat Code from the My 2K6 menu and enter Crazy Hops. Enable the cheats by selecting My Cheats or selecting Cheat Codes from the in-game Options.

MAJOR LEAGUE BASEBALL 2K7

MICKEY MANTLE ON THE FREE AGENTS LIST
Select Enter Cheat Code from the My 2K7 menu and enter themick.

ALL CHEATS
Select Enter Cheat Code from the My 2K7 menu and enter Black Sox.

ALL EXTRAS
Select Enter Cheat Code from the My 2K7 menu and enter Game On.

UNLOCK EVERYTHING
Select Enter Cheat Code from the My 2K7 menu and enter Derek Jeter. This does not unlock the Topps cheats.

MIGHTY MICK CHEAT
Select Enter Cheat Code from the My 2K7 menu and enter mightymick.

TRIPLE CROWN CHEAT
Select Enter Cheat Code from the My 2K7 menu and enter triplecrown.

PINCH HIT MICK CHEAT
Select Enter Cheat Code from the My 2K7 menu and enter phmantle.

BIG BLAST CHEAT
Select Enter Cheat Code from the My 2K7 menu Rand enter m4murder.

UNLOCK ALL SKINS
At the Team menu, press Up, Down, Left, Right, Left, Right, Start.

UNLOCKS ALL HERO POWERS
At the Team menu, press Left, Right, Up, Down, Up, Down, Start.

ALL HEROES TO LEVEL 99
At the Team menu, press Up, Left, Up, Left, Down, Right, Down, Right, Start.

UNLOCK ALL HEROES
At the Team menu, press Up, Up, Down, Down, Left, Left, Left, Start.

UNLOCK DAREDEVIL
At the Team menu, press Left, Left, Right, Right, Up, Down, Up, Down, Start.

UNLOCK SILVER SURFER
At the Team menu, press Down, Left, Left, Up, Right, Up, Down, Left, Start.

GOD MODE
During gameplay, press Up, Down, Up, Down, Up, Left, Down, Right, Start.

TOUCH OF DEATH
During gameplay, press Left, Right, Down, Down, Right, Left, Start.

SUPER SPEED
During gameplay, press Up, Left, Up, Right, Down, Right, Start.

FILL MOMENTUM
During gameplay, press Left, Right, Right, Left, Up, Down, Down, Up, Start.

UNLOCK ALL COMICS
At the Review menu, press Left, Right, Right, Left, Up, Up, Right, Start.

UNLOCK ALL CONCEPT ART
At the Review menu, press Down, Down, Down, Right, Right, Left, Down, Start.

UNLOCK ALL CINEMATICS
At the Review menu, press Up, Left, Left, Up, Right, Right, Up, Start.

UNLOCK ALL LOAD SCREENS
At the Review menu, press Up, Down, Right, Left, Up, Up Down, Start.

UNLOCK ALL COURSES
At the Comic Missions menu, press Up, Right, Left, Down, Up, Right, Left, Down, Start.

MEDAL OF HONOR: AIRBORNE

Using the following cheats disables saves and achievements. During a game, hold Left Bumper + Right Bumper, and press X, B, Y, A, A. This brings up an Enter Cheat screen. Now you can enter the following:

FULL AMMO
Hold Left Bumper + Right Bumper and press B, B, Y, X, A, Y.

FULL HEALTH
Hold Left Bumper + Right Bumper and press Y, X, X, Y, A, B.

MERCENARIES 2: WORLD IN FLAMES

These codes work with the updated version of Mercenaries 2 only. The cheats will keep you from earning achievements, but anything earned up to that point remains. You can still save with the cheats, but be careful if you want to earn trophies. Quit the game without saving to return to normal.

CHEAT MODE
Access your PDA by pressing Back. Press Left Bumper, Right Bumper, Right Bumper, Left Bumper, Right Bumper, Left Bumper, Left Bumper, Right Bumper, Right Bumper, Right Bumper, Left Bumper and close the PDA. You then need to accept the agreement that says achievements are disabled. Now you can enter the following cheats.

INVINCIBILITY
Access your PDA and press Up, Down, Left, Down, Right, Right. This activates invincibility for you and anyone that joins your game.

INFINITE AMMO
Access your PDA and press Up, Down, Left, Right, Left, Left.

GIVE ALL VEHICLES
Access your PDA and press Up, Down, Left, Right, Right, Left.

GIVE ALL SUPPLIES
Access your PDA and press Left, Right, Right, Left, Up, Up, Left, Up.

XBOX 360™

GIVE ALL AIRSTRIKES (EXCEPT NUKE)
Access your PDA and press Right, Left, Down, Up, Right, Left, Down, Up.

GIVE NUKE
Access your PDA and press Up, Up, Down, Down, Left, Right, Left, Right.

FILL FUEL
Access your PDA and press Up, Up, Up, Down, Down, Down.

ALL COSTUMES
Access your PDA and press Up, Right, Down, Left, Up.

GRAPPLING HOOK
Access your PDA and press Up, Left, Down, Right, Up.

MONSTER MADNESS: BATTLE FOR SUBURBIA

Pause the game and press Up, Up, Down, Down, Left, Right, Left, Right, B, A. This brings up a screen where you can enter the following cheats. With the use of some cheats profile saving, level progression, and Xbox Live Achievements are disabled until you return to the Main menu.

EFFECT	CHEAT
Animal Sounds	patrickdugan
Disable Tracking Cameras	ihatefunkycameras
Faster Music	upthejoltcola
First Person	morgythemole
Infinite Secondary Items	stevebrooks
Objects Move Away from Player	southpeak
Remove Film Grain	reverb

MOTOGP 06

USA EXTREME BIKE
At the Game Mode screen, press Right, Up, B, B, A, B, Up, B, B, A.

MOTOGP 07

ALL CHALLENGES
At the Main menu, press Right, Up, B, A, B, A, Left, Down, Y.

ALL RIDERS
At the Main menu, press Right, Up, B, B, A, Down, Up, B, Down, Up, B.

ALL CHAMPIONSHIPS
At the Main menu, press Right, Up, B, Y, Right, Up, B, Y, Right, Up, B, Y.

ALL TRACKS
At the Main menu, press Left, A, Right, Down, Y, B, A, B, Y.

ALL LIVERIES
At the Main menu, press Right, A, Left, Left, Y, Left, A, Down, Y.

MX VS. ATV UNTAMED

ALL RIDING GEAR
Select Cheat Codes from the Options and enter crazylikea.

ALL HANDLEBARS
Select Cheat Codes from the Options and enter nohands.

27 GRAPHICS
Select Cheat Codes from the Options and enter STICKERS.

NASCAR 08

ALL CHASE MODE CARS
Select cheat codes from the options menu and enter checkered flag.

EA SPORTS CAR
Select cheat codes from the options menu and enter ea sports car.

FANTASY DRIVERS
Select cheat codes from the options menu and enter race the pack.

WALMART CAR AND TRACK
Select cheat codes from the options menu and enter walmart everyday.

NASCAR 09

ALL FANTASY DRIVERS
Select EA Extras from My NASCAR, choose Cheat Codes and enter CHECKERED FLAG.

WAL-MART TRACK AND THE WAL-MART CAR
Select EA Extras from My Nascar, choose Cheat Codes and enter Walmart Everyday.

NBA 2K6

CELEBRITY STREET OPTION
Select Codes from the Features menu and enter ballers.

 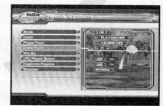

2KSPORTS TEAM
Select Codes from the Features menu and enter 2ksports.

2K6 TEAM
Select Codes from the Features menu and enter nba2k6.

VC TEAM
Select Codes from the Features menu and enter vcteam.

NIKE SHOX MTX SHOES
Select Codes from the Features menu and enter crazylift.

NIKE ZOOM 20-5-5 SHOES
Select Codes from the Features menu and enter lebronsummerkicks.

NIKE ZOOM KOBE 1 SHOES
Select Codes from the Features menu and enter kobe.

NIKE ZOOM LEBRON III ALL-STAR COLORWAY SHOES
Select Codes from the Features menu and enter lb allstar.

NIKE ZOOM LEBRON III BLACK/CRIMSON SHOES
Select Codes from the Features menu and enter lb crimsonblack.

NIKE ZOOM LEBRON III SPECIAL BIRTHDAY EDITION SHOES
Select Codes from the Features menu and enter lb bday.

NIKE ZOOM LEBRON III WHITE/GOLD SHOES
Select Codes from the Features menu and enter lb whitegold.

NIKE UP TEMPO PRO SHOES
Select Codes from the Features menu and enter anklebreakers.

2006 ALL-STAR UNIFORMS
Select Codes from the Features menu and enter fanfavorites.

ST. PATRICK'S DAY UNIFORMS
Select Codes from the Features menu and enter gogreen.

BULLS RETRO UNIFORM
Select Codes from the Features menu and enter chi retro.

CAVALIERS ALTERNATE UNIFORM
Select Codes from the Features menu and enter cle 2nd.

CELTICS ALTERNATE UNIFORM
Select Codes from the Features menu and enter bos 2nd.

CLIPPERS RETRO UNIFORM
Select Codes from the Features menu and enter lac retro.

GRIZZLIES RETRO UNIFORM
Select Codes from the Features menu and enter mem retro.

HEAT RETRO UNIFORM
Select Codes from the Features menu and enter mia retro.

HORNETS RETRO UNIFORM
Select Codes from the Features menu and enter no retro.

KINGS ALTERNATE UNIFORM
Select Codes from the Features menu and enter sac 2nd.

KNICKS RETRO UNIFORM
Select Codes from the Features menu and enter ny retro.

MAGIC RETRO UNIFORM
Select Codes from the Features menu and enter orl retro.

NETS RETRO UNIFORM
Select Codes from the Features menu and enter nj retro.

NUGGETS ALTERNATE UNIFORM
Select Codes from the Features menu and enter den 2nd.

2005-06 PACERS UNIFORM
Select Codes from the Features menu and enter 31andonly.

PISTONS ALTERNATE UNIFORM
Select Codes from the Features menu and enter det 2nd.

ROCKETS RETRO UNIFORM
Select Codes from the Features menu and enter hou retro.

SONICS RETRO UNIFORM
Select Codes from the Features menu and enter sea retro.

SUNS RETRO UNIFORM
Select Codes from the Features menu and enter phx retro.

WIZARDS RETRO UNIFORM
Select Codes from the Features menu and enter was retro.

+10 BONUS FOR DEFENSIVE AWARENESS
Find the PowerBar vending machine in The Crib. Select Enter Code and enter lockdown.

+10 BONUS FOR OFFENSIVE AWARENESS
Find the PowerBar vending machine in The Crib. Select Enter Code and enter getaclue.

MAX DURABILITY
Find the PowerBar vending machine in The Crib. Select Enter Code and enter noinjury.

UNLIMITED STAMINA
Find the PowerBar vending machine in The Crib. Select Enter Code and enter nrgmax.

POWERBAR TATTOO
Find the PowerBar vending machine in The Crib. Select Enter Code and enter pbink. You can now use it in the game's Create Player feature.

NBA 2K7

MAX DURABILITY
Select Codes from the Features menu and enter ironman.

UNLIMITED STAMINA
Select Codes from the Features menu and enter norest.

+10 DEFFENSIVE AWARENESS
Select Codes from the Features menu and enter getstops.

+10 OFFENSIVE AWARENESS
Select Codes from the Features menu and enter inthezone.

TOPPS 2K SPORTS ALL-STARS
Select Codes from the Features menu and enter topps2ksports.

ABA BALL
Select Codes from the Features menu and enter payrespect.

NBA 2K8

ABA BALL
Select Codes from the Features menu and enter Payrespect.

2KSPORTS TEAM
Select Codes from the Features menu and enter 2ksports.

NBA DEVELOPMENT TEAM
Select Codes from the Features menu and enter nba2k.

SUPERSTARS TEAM
Select Codes from the Features menu and enter llmohffaae.

VISUAL CONCEPTS TEAM
Select Codes from the Features menu and enter Vcteam.

2008 ALL STAR NBA JERSEYS
Select Codes from the Features menu and enter haeitgyebs.

BOBCATS RACING JERSEY
Select Codes from the Features menu and enter agtaccsinr.

PACERS SECOND ROAD JERSEY
Select Codes from the Features menu and enter cpares.

ST. PATRICK'S DAY JERSEYS
Select Codes from the Features menu and enter uclerehanp.

VALENTINE'S DAY JERSEYS
Select Codes from the Features menu and enter amcnreo.

NBA 2K9

2K SPORTS TEAM
Select Codes from the Features menu and enter 2ksports.

NBA 2K TEAM
Select Codes from the Features menu and enter nba2k.

SUPERSTARS
Select Codes from the Features menu and enter llmohffaae.

VC TEAM
Select Codes from the Features menu and enter vcteam.

ABA BALL
Select Codes from the Features menu and enter payrespect.

NBA LIVE 07

ADIDAS ARTILLERY II BLACK AND THE RBK ANSWER 9 VIDEO
Select NBA Codes from My NBA Live and enter 99B6356HAN.

ADIDAS ARTILLERY II
Select NBA Codes and enter NTGNFUE87H.

ADIDAS BTB LOW AND THE MESSAGE FROM ALLEN IVERSON VIDEO
Select NBA Codes and enter 7FB3KS9JQ0.

ADIDAS C-BILLUPS
Select NBA Codes and enter BV6877HB9N.

ADIDAS C-BILLUPS BLACK
Select NBA Codes and enter 85NVLDMWS5.

ADIDAS CAMPUS LT
Select NBA Codes and enter CLT2983NC8.

ADIDAS CRAZY 8
Select NBA Codes and enter CC98KKL814.

ADIDAS EQUIPMENT B-BALL
Select NBA Codes and enter 22OIUJKMDR.

ADIDAS GARNETT BOUNCE
Select NBA Codes and enter HYIOUHCAAN.

ADIDAS GARNETT BOUNCE BLACK
Select NBA Codes and enter KDZ2MQL17W.

ADIDAS GIL-ZERO
Select NBA Codes and enter 23DN1PPOG4.

OVERLORD

XBOX 360™

ADIDAS GIL-ZERO BLACK
Select NBA Codes and enter QQQ3JCUYQ7.

ADIDAS GIL-ZERO MID
Select NBA Codes and enter 1GSJC8JWRL.

ADIDAS GIL-ZERO MID BLACK
Select NBA Codes and enter 369V6RVU3G.

ADIDAS STEALTH
Select NBA Codes and enter FE454DFJCC.

ADIDAS T-MAC 6
Select NBA Codes and enter MCJK843NNC.

ADIDAS T-MAC 6 WHITE
Select NBA Codes and enter 84GF7EJG8V.

CHARLOTTE BOBCATS 2006-07 ALTERNATE JERSEY
Select NBA Codes and enter WEDX671H7S.

UTAH JAZZ 2006-07 ALTERNATE JERSEY
Select NBA Codes and enter VCBI89FK83.

NEW JERSEY NETS 2006-07 ALTERNATE JERSEY
Select NBA Codes and enter D4SAA98U5H.

WASHINGTON WIZARDS 2006-07 ALTERNATE JERSEY
Select NBA Codes and enter QV93NLKXQC.

EASTERN ALL-STARS 2006-07 AWAY JERSEY
Select NBA Codes and enter WOCNW4KL7L.

EASTERN ALL-STARS 2006-07 HOME JERSEY
Select NBA Codes and enter 5654ND43N6.

WESTERN ALL-STARS 2006-07 AWAY JERSEY
Select NBA Codes and enter XX93BVL20U.

WESTERN ALL-STARS 2006-07 HOME JERSEY
Select NBA Codes and enter 993NSKL199.

NBA LIVE 08

ADIDAS GIL-ZERO - ALL-STAR EDITION
Select NBA Codes from My NBA and enter 23DN1PPOG4.

ADIDAS TIM DUNCAN STEALTH - ALL-STAR EDITION
Select NBA Codes from My NBA and enter FE454DFJCC.

NBA STREET HOMECOURT

ALL TEAMS
At the Main menu, hold Right Bumper + Left Bumper and press Left, Right, Left, Right.

ALL COURTS
At the Main menu, hold Right Bumper + Left Bumper and press Up, Right, Down, Left.

BLACK/RED BALL
At the Main menu, hold Right Bumper + Left Bumper and press Up, Down, Left, Right.

NCAA FOOTBALL 07

#16 BAYLOR
Select Pennant Collection from My NCAA, then press SELECT and enter Sic Em.

#16 NIKE SPEED TD
Select Pennant Collection from My NCAA, then press SELECT and enter Light Speed.

#63 ILLINOIS
Select Pennant Collection from My NCAA, then press SELECT and enter Oskee Wow.

#160 TEXAS TECH
Select Pennant Collection from My NCAA, then press SELECT and enter Fight.

#200 FIRST AND FIFTEEN
Select Pennant Collection from My NCAA, then press SELECT and enter Thanks.

#201 BLINK
Select Pennant Collection from My NCAA, then press SELECT and enter For.

#202 BOING
Select Pennant Collection from My NCAA, then press SELECT and enter Registering.

#204 BUTTER FINGERS
Select Pennant Collection from My NCAA, then press SELECT and enter With EA.

#205 CROSSED THE LINE
Select Pennant Collection from My NCAA, then press SELECT and enter Tiburon.

#206 CUFFED
Select Pennant Collection from My NCAA, then press SELECT and enter EA Sports.

#207 EXTRA CREDIT
Select Pennant Collection from My NCAA, then press SELECT and enter Touchdown.

#208 HELIUM
Select Pennant Collection from My NCAA, then press SELECT and enter In The Zone.

#209 HURRICANE
Select Pennant Collection from My NCAA, then press SELECT and enter Turnover.

#210 INSTANT FREEPLAY
Select Pennant Collection from My NCAA, then press SELECT and enter Impact.

#211 JUMBALAYA
Select Pennant Collection from My NCAA, then press SELECT and enter Heisman.

#212 MOLASSES
Select Pennant Collection from My NCAA, then press SELECT and enter Game Time.

#213 NIKE FREE
Select Pennant Collection from My NCAA, then press SELECT and enter Break Free.

#214 NIKE MAGNIGRIP
Select Pennant Collection from My NCAA, then press SELECT and enter Hand Picked.

#215 NIKE PRO
Select Pennant Collection from My NCAA, then press SELECT and enter No Sweat.

#219 QB DUD
Select Pennant Collection from My NCAA, then press SELECT and enter Elite 11.

#221 STEEL TOE
Select Pennant Collection from My NCAA, then press SELECT and enter Gridiron.

#222 STIFFED
Select Pennant Collection from My NCAA, then press SELECT and enter NCAA.

#223 SUPER DIVE
Select Pennant Collection from My NCAA, then press SELECT and enter Upset.

#224 TAKE YOUR TIME
Select Pennant Collection from My NCAA, then press SELECT and enter Football.

#225 THREAD & NEEDLE
Select Pennant Collection from My NCAA, then press SELECT and enter 06.

#226 TOUGH AS NAILS
Select Pennant Collection from My NCAA, then press SELECT and enter Offense.

#227 TRIP
Select Pennant Collection from My NCAA, then press SELECT and enter Defense.

#228 WHAT A HIT
Select Pennant Collection from My NCAA, then press SELECT and enter Blitz.

#229 KICKER HEX
Select Pennant Collection from My NCAA, then press SELECT and enter Sideline.

#273 2004 ALL-AMERICANS
Select Pennant Collection from My NCAA, then press SELECT and enter Fumble.

#274 ALL-ALABAMA
Select Pennant Collection from My NCAA, then press SELECT and enter Roll Tide.

#276 ALL-ARKANSAS
Select Pennant Collection from My NCAA, then press SELECT and enter Woopigsooie.

#277 ALL-AUBURN
Select Pennant Collection from My NCAA, then press SELECT and enter War Eagle.

#278 ALL-CLEMSON
Select Pennant Collection from My NCAA, then press SELECT and enter Death Valley.

#279 ALL-COLORADO
Select Pennant Collection from My NCAA, then press SELECT and enter Glory.

#280 ALL-FLORIDA
Select Pennant Collection from My NCAA, then press SELECT and enter Great To Be.

#281 ALL-FSU
Select Pennant Collection from My NCAA, then press SELECT and enter Uprising.

#282 ALL-GEORGIA
Select Pennant Collection from My NCAA, then press SELECT and enter Hunker Down.

#283 ALL-IOWA
Select Pennant Collection from My NCAA, then press SELECT and enter On Iowa.

#284 ALL-KANSAS STATE
Select Pennant Collection from My NCAA, then press SELECT and enter Victory.

#285 ALL-LSU
Select Pennant Collection from My NCAA, then press SELECT and enter Geaux Tigers.

#286 ALL-MIAMI
Select Pennant Collection from My NCAA, then press SELECT and enter Raising Cane.

#287 ALL-MICHIGAN
Select Pennant Collection from My NCAA, then press SELECT and enter Go Blue.

#288 ALL-MISSISSIPPI STATE
Select Pennant Collection from My NCAA, then press SELECT and enter Hail State.

#289 ALL-NEBRASKA
Select Pennant Collection from My NCAA, then press SELECT and enter Go Big Red.

#290 ALL-NORTH CAROLINA
Select Pennant Collection from My NCAA, then press SELECT and enter Rah Rah.

#291 ALL-NOTRE DAME
Select Pennant Collection from My NCAA, then press SELECT and enter Golden Domer.

#292 ALL-OHIO STATE
Select Pennant Collection from My NCAA, then press SELECT and enter Killer Nuts.

#293 ALL-OKLAHOMA
Select Pennant Collection from My NCAA, then press SELECT and enter Boomer.

#294 ALL-OKLAHOMA STATE
Select Pennant Collection from My NCAA, then press SELECT and enter Go Pokes.

#295 ALL-OREGON
Select Pennant Collection from My NCAA, then press SELECT and enter Quack Attack.

#296 ALL-PENN STATE
Select Pennant Collection from My NCAA, then press SELECT and enter We Are.

#297 ALL-PITTSBURGH
Select Pennant Collection from My NCAA, then press SELECT and enter Lets Go Pitt.

#298 ALL-PURDUE
Select Pennant Collection from My NCAA, then press SELECT and enter Boiler Up.

#299 ALL-SYRACUSE
Select Pennant Collection from My NCAA, then press SELECT and enter Orange Crush.

#300 ALL-TENNESSEE
Select Pennant Collection from My NCAA, then press SELECT and enter Big Orange.

#301 ALL-TEXAS
Select Pennant Collection from My NCAA, then press SELECT and enter Hook Em.

#302 ALL-TEXAS A&M
Select Pennant Collection from My NCAA, then press SELECT and enter Gig Em.

#303 ALL-UCLA
Select Pennant Collection from My NCAA, then press SELECT and enter MIGHTY.

#304 ALL-USC
Select Pennant Collection from My NCAA, then press SELECT and enter Fight On.

#305 ALL-VIRGINIA
Select Pennant Collection from My NCAA, then press SELECT and enter Wahoos.

#306 ALL-VIRGINIA TECH
Select Pennant Collection from My NCAA, then press SELECT and enter Tech Triumph.

#307 ALL-WASHINGTON
Select Pennant Collection from My NCAA, then press SELECT and enter Bow Down.

#308 ALL-WISCONSIN
Select Pennant Collection from My NCAA, then press SELECT and enter U Rah Rah.

#311 ARK MASCOT
Select Pennant Collection from My NCAA, then press SELECT and enter Bear Down.

#329 GT MASCOT
Select Pennant Collection from My NCAA, then press SELECT and enter RamblinWreck.

#333 ISU MASCOT
Select Pennant Collection from My NCAA, then press SELECT and enter Red And Gold.

#335 KU MASCOT
Select Pennant Collection from My NCAA, then press SELECT and enter Rock Chalk.

#341 MINN MASCOT
Select Pennant Collection from My NCAA, then press SELECT and enter Rah Rah Rah.

#344 MIZZOU MASCOT
Select Pennant Collection from My NCAA, then press SELECT and enter Mizzou Rah.

#346 MSU MASCOT
Select Pennant Collection from My NCAA, then press SELECT and enter Go Green.

#349 NCSU MASCOT
Select Pennant Collection from My NCAA, then press SELECT and enter Go Pack.

#352 NU MASCOT
Select Pennant Collection from My NCAA, then press SELECT and enter Go Cats.

#360 S CAR MASCOT
Select Pennant Collection from My NCAA, then press SELECT and enter Go Carolina.

#371 UK MASCOT
Select Pennant Collection from My NCAA, then press SELECT and enter On On UK.

#382 WAKE FOREST
Select Pennant Collection from My NCAA, then press SELECT and enter Go Deacs Go.

#385 WSU MASCOT
Select Pennant Collection from My NCAA, then press SELECT and enter All Hail.

#386 WVU MASCOT
Select Pennant Collection from My NCAA, then press SELECT and enter Hail WV.

NEED FOR SPEED CARBON

CASTROL CASH
At the main menu, press Down, Up, Left, Down, Right, Up, X, B. This will give you 10,000 extra cash.

INFINITE CREW CHARGE
At the main menu, press Down, Up, Up, Right, Left, Left, Right, X.

INFINITE NITROUS
At the main menu, press Left, Up, Left, Down, Left, Down, Right, X.

INFINITE SPEEDBREAKER
At the main menu, press Down, Right, Right, Left, Right, Up, Down, X.

NEED FOR SPEED CARBON LOGO VINYLS
At the main menu, press Right, Up, Down, Up, Down, Left, Right, X.

NEED FOR SPEED CARBON SPECIAL LOGO VINYLS
At the main menu, press Up, Up, Down, Down, Down, Down, Up, X.

NEED FOR SPEED PROSTREET

$2,000
Select Career and then choose Code Entry. Enter 1MA9X99.

$4,000
Select Career and then choose Code Entry. Enter W2IOLL01.

$8,000
Select Career and then choose Code Entry. Enter L1IS97A1.

$10,000
Select Career and then choose Code Entry. Enter 1MI9K7E1.

$10,000
Select Career and then choose Code Entry. Enter CASHMONEY.

$10,000
Select Career and then choose Code Entry. Enter REGGAME.

AUDI TT
Select Career and then choose Code Entry. Enter ITSABOUTYOU.

CHEVELLE SS
Select Career and then choose Code Entry. Enter HORSEPOWER.

COKE ZERO GOLF GTI
Select Career and then choose Code Entry. Enter COKEZERO.

DODGE VIPER
Select Career and then choose Code Entry. Enter WORLDSLONGESTLASTING.

MITSUBISHI LANCER EVOLUTION
Select Career and then choose Code Entry. Enter MITSUBISHIGOFAR.

UNLOCK ALL BONUSES
Select Career and then choose Code Entry. Enter UNLOCKALLTHINGS.

5 REPAIR MARKERS
Select Career and then choose Code Entry. Enter SAFETYNET.

ENERGIZER VINYL
Select Career and then choose Code Entry. Enter ENERGIZERLITHIUM.

CASTROL SYNTEC VINYL
Select Career and then choose Code Entry. Enter CASTROLSYNTEC. This also gives you $10,000.

XBOX 360™

NEED FOR SPEED MOST WANTED

BURGER KING CHALLENGE
At the Title screen, press Up, Down, Up, Down, Left, Right, Left, Right.

CASTROL SYNTEC VERSION OF THE FORD GT
At the Title screen, press Left, Right, Left, Right, Up, Down, Up, Down.

MARKER FOR BACKROOM OF THE ONE-STOP SHOP
At the Title screen, press Up, Up, Down, Down, Left, Right, Up, Down.

JUNKMAN ENGINE
At the Title screen, press Up, Up, Down, Down, Left, Right, Up, Down.

PORSCHE CAYMAN
At the Title screen, press L, R, R, R, Right, Left, Right, Down.

NHL 08

ALL RBK EDGE JERSEYS
At the RBK Edge Code option, enter h3oyxpwksf8ibcgt.

NHL 2K6

CHEAT MODE
Select Manage Profiles from the Options menu. Create a new profile with the name Turco813.

NHL 2K8

2007-2008 NHL REEBOK EDGE JERSEYS
From the Features menu, select Unlock 2007-2008/Enter Password. Enter S6j83RMk01.

THE ORANGE BOX

HALF-LIFE 2

The following codes work for Half-Life 2, Half-Life 2: Episode One, and Half-Life 2: Episode Two.

CHAPTER SELECT
While playing, press Left, Left, Left, Left, Left Bumper, Right, Right, Right, Right, Right Bumper. Pause the game and select New Game to skip to another chapter.

RESTORE HEALTH (25 POINTS)
While playing, press Up, Up, Down, Down, Left, Right, Left, Right, B, A.

RESTORE AMMO FOR CURRENT WEAPON
While playing, press Y, B, A, X, Right Bumper, Y, X, A, B, Right Bumper.

INVINCIBILITY
While playing, press Left Shoulder, Up, Right Shoulder, Up, Left Shoulder, Left Shoulder, Up, Right Shoulder, Right Shoulder, Up.

PORTAL

CHAPTER SELECT
While playing, press Left, Left, Left, Left, Left Bumper, Right, Right, Right, Right, Right Bumper. Pause the game and select New Game to skip to another chapter.

GET A BOX
While playing, press Down, B, A, B, Y, Down, B, A, B, Y.

ENERGY BALL
While playing, press Up, Y, Y, X, X, A, A, B, B, Up.

PORTAL PLACEMENT ANYWHERE
While playing, press Y, A, B, A, B, Y, Y, A, Left, Right.

PORTALGUN ID 0
While playing, press Up, Left, Down, Right, Up, Left, Down, Right, Y, Y.

PORTALGUN ID 1
While playing, press Up, Left, Down, Right, Up, Left, Down, Right, X, X.

PORTALGUN ID 2
While playing, press Up, Left, Down, Right, Up, Left, Down, Right, A, A.

PORTALGUN ID 3
While playing, press Up, Left, Down, Right, Up, Left, Down, Right, B, B.

UPGRADE PORTALGUN
While playing, press X, B, Left Bumper, Right Bumper, Left, Right, Left Bumper, Right Bumper, Left Trigger, Right Trigger.

PETER JACKSON'S KING KONG: THE OFFICIAL GAME OF THE MOVIE

At the Main menu hold Left Bumper + Right Bumper + Left Trigger + Right Trigger and press Down, Up, Y, X, Down, Down, Y, Y. Release the buttons to access the Cheat option. The Cheat option is also available on the pause menu. Note that you cannot record your scores using cheat codes.

GOD MODE
Select Cheat and enter 8wonder.

ALL CHAPTERS
Select Cheat and enter KKst0ry.

AMMO 999
Select Cheat and enter KK 999 mun.

MACHINE GUN
Select Cheat and enter KKcapone.

REVOLVER
Select Cheat and enter KKtigun.

SNIPER RIFLE
Select Cheat and enter KKsn1per.

INFINITE SPEARS
Select Cheat and enter lance 1nf.

1-HIT KILLS
Select Cheat and enter GrosBras.

XBOX 360™

EXTRAS
Select Cheat and enter KKmuseum.

QUAKE 4

ALL WEAPONS, FULL ARMOR, HEALTH & AMMO
Press the Back button to access the Objectives, then press Up, Up, Down, Down, Left, Right, Left, Right, B, A.

FULL AMMO
Press the Back button to access the Objectives, then press B, A, X, Y, Left, Right, Left.

FULL HEALTH
Press the Back button to access the Objectives, then press B, A, B, A, Up, Up, Down, X.

RATATOUILLE

UNLIMITED RUNNING
At the cheat code screen, enter SPEEDY.

ALL MULTIPLAYER AND SINGLE PLAYER MINI GAMES
At the cheat code screen, enter MATTELME.

ROBERT LUDLUM'S THE BOURNE CONSPIRACY

LIGHT MACHINE GUNS HAVE SILENCERS
Select Enter Code from the Cheats screen and enter whattheymakeyougive.

EXTRAS UNLOCKED – CONCEPT ART
Select Enter Code from the Cheats screen and enter lastchancemarie. Select Concept Art from the Extras menu.

EXTRAS UNLOCKED – MUSIC TRACKS
Select Enter Code from the Cheats screen and enter jasonbourneisdead. This unlocks Treadstone Appointment and Manheim Suite in the Music Selector found in the Extras menu.

ROCK BAND

ALL SONGS
At the title screen, press Red, Yellow, Blue, Red, Red, Blue, Blue, Red, Yellow, Blue. Saving and all network features are disabled with this code.

TRANSPARENT INSTRUMENTS
Complete the hall of fame concert with that instrument.

GOLD INSTRUMENT
Complete the solo tour with that instrument.

SILVER INSTRUMENT
Complete the bonus tour with that instrument.

Most of these codes disable saving, achievements, and Xbox LIVE play.

UNLOCK ALL SONGS

Select Modify Game from the Extras menu, choose Enter Unlock Code and press Red, Yellow, Blue, Red, Red, Blue, Blue, Red, Yellow, Blue or Y, B, X, Y, Y, X, X, Y, B, X. Toggle this cheat on or off from the Modify Game menu.

SELECT VENUE SCREEN

Select Modify Game from the Extras menu, choose Enter Unlock Code and press Blue, Orange, Orange, Blue, Yellow, Blue, Orange, Orange, Blue, Yellow or X, Left Bumper, Left Bumper, X, B, X, Left Bumper, Left Bumper, X, B. Toggle this cheat on or off from the Modify Game menu.

NEW VENUES ONLY

Select Modify Game from the Extras menu, choose Enter Unlock Code and press Red, Red, Red, Red, Yellow, Yellow, Yellow, Yellow or Y (x4), B (x4). Toggle this cheat on or off from the Modify Game menu.

PLAY THE GAME WITHOUT A TRACK

Select Modify Game from the Extras menu, choose Enter Unlock Code and press Blue, Blue, Red, Red, Yellow, Yellow, Blue, Blue or X, X, Y, Y, B, B, X, X. Toggle this cheat on or off from the Modify Game menu.

AWESOMENESS DETECTION

Select Modify Game from the Extras menu, choose Enter Unlock Code and press Yellow, Blue, Orange, Yellow, Blue, Orange, Yellow, Blue, Orange or B, X, Left Bumper, B, X, Left Bumper, B, X, Left Bumper. Toggle this cheat on or off from the Modify Game menu.

STAGE MODE

Select Modify Game from the Extras menu, choose Enter Unlock Code and press Blue, Yellow, Red, Blue, Yellow, Red, Blue, Yellow, Red or X, B, Y, X, B, Y, X, B, Y. Toggle this cheat on or off from the Modify Game menu.

ROCKSTAR GAMES PRESENTS TABLE TENNIS

Use of the following codes will disable achievements.

SWEATY CHARACTER VIEWER

After loading the map and before accepting the match, press Right Trigger, Up, Down, Left Trigger, Left, Right, Y, X, X, Y.

SMALL CROWD AUDIO

After loading the map and before accepting the match, press Down, Down, Down, Left Bumper, Left Trigger, Left Bumper, Left Trigger.

BIG BALL

After loading the map and before accepting the match, press Left, Right, Left, Right, Up, Up, Up, X.

COLORBLIND SPINDICATOR (ONLY IN NEWER PATCH)

After loading the map and before accepting the match, press Up, Down, X, X, Y, Y.

SILHOUETTE MODE

After loading the map and before accepting the match, press Up, Down, Y, Y, Left Bumper, Left Trigger, Right Trigger, Right Bumper.

XBOX 360™

BIG PADDLES CHEAT (ONLY IN NEWER PATCH)
After loading the map and before accepting the match, press Up, Left, Up, Right, Up, Down, Up, Up, X, X.

UNLOCK ALL
After loading the map and before accepting the match, press Up, Right, Down, Left, Left Bumper, Right, Up, Left, Down, Right Bumper.

VINTAGE AUDIO
After loading the map and before accepting the match, press Up, Up, Down, Down, Left, Right, Left, Right, Left Bumper, Right Bumper.

BIG CROWD AUDIO
After loading the map and before accepting the match, press Up, Up, Up, Right Bumper, Right Trigger, Right Bumper, Right Trigger.

OFFLINE GAMERTAGS
After loading the map and before accepting the match, press X, Y, X, Y, X, Y, Left Trigger, Right Trigger, Down, Down, Down.

SAINTS ROW

Pause the game and select Dial from your phone. Enter the following codes and then press Call. Select Cheats to enable the first set of codes, the ones that start with "#." You cannot earn achievements if using these cheats. Note that vehicles are delivered to your garage.

CODE NAME	DIAL	CODE NAME	DIAL
Give Cash	#MONEY	Hannibal	#42664225
Full Health	#FULLHEALTH	Hollywood	#HOLLYWOOD
Repair Car	#778	Jackrabbit	#JACKRABBIT
Infinite Ammo	#AMMO	The Job	#THEJOB
Infinite Sprint	#SPRINT	K6	#K6KRUKOV
No Cop Notoriety	#NOCOPS	Keystone	#KEYSTONE
No Gang Notoriety	#NOGANGS	Knife	#KNIFE
Evil Cars	#EVILCARS	Komodo	#KOMODO
Clear Skies	#SUNNY	La Fuerza	#LAFUER9A
Wrath of God	#10	Mag	#MAG
44	#SHEPHERD	McManus	#MACMANUS
12 Gauge	#12GAUGE	Mockingbird	#MOCKINGBIRD
Ambulance	#AMBULANCE	Molotov	#MOLOTOV
Anchor	#ANCHOR	Nelson	#635766
Ant	#ANT	Newman	#NEWMAN
Aqua	#A7UA	Nightstick	#NIGHTSTICK
AR40	#AR40XTND	Nordberg	#NORDBERG
AS12	#AS12RIOT	NR4	#NR4
Baron	#BARON	Pimp Cane	#PIMPCANE
Baseball Bat	#BASEBALL	Pipebomb	#PIPEBOMB
Betsy	#BETSY	Quasar	#7UASAR
Bulldog	#BULLDOG	Quota	#7UOTA
Cavallaro	#CAVALLARO	Rattler	#RATTLER
Compton	#COMPTON	Reaper	#REAPER
Cosmos	#COSMOS	RPG	#ROCKET
Destiny	#DESTINY	Shogun	#SHOGUN
Justice	#JUSTICE	SKR7	#SKRSPREE
FBI	#FBI	T3K	#T3KURBAN
Ferdelance	#FERDELANCE	Taxi	#TAXI
Gdhc	#GDHC50	Titan	#TITAN
Grenade	#GRENADE	Tombstone	#TOMBSTONE
Gunslinger	#GUNSLINGER	Traxxmaster	#TRAXXMASTER
Halberd	#HALBERD	VICE9	#Vice9
Hammerhead	#HAMMERHEAD	Vortex	#VORTEX
Hannibal	#42664225	Voxel	#VOXEL

CODE NAME	DIAL	CODE NAME	DIAL
Zenith	#9ENITH	GameStop	#42637867
Zimos	#9IMOS	Chicken Ned	5552445 (select Homies from your Phone to access Chicken Ned)
Zircon	#9IRCON		

For the following codes, select the Phone Book to call.

CODE NAME	DIAL
EagleLine Yellow	5550180174
Big Willy's Cab	5558198415
Brown Baggers	5553765
Crash Landing	5556278
The Dead Cow	5556238
Emergency	911
Eye for an Eye	5555966
Freckle Bitch's	5556328
Grounds for Divorce	5559473
Impression	5553248
Legal Lee's	5559467
Lik-a-Chick	5553863
On the Fence	5557296
On the Rag	5555926
On Thin Ice	5552564
Rim Jobs	5553493
$tock$	5552626
Suicide Hotline	5554876837
TNA Taxis	5554558008

SAINTS ROW 2

CHEAT CODES

Select Dial from the Phone menu and enter these numbers followed by the Call button. Activate the cheats by selecting Cheats from the Phone menu. Enabling a cheat prevents the acquisition of Achievements

PLAYER ABILITY

CHEAT	NUMBER
Give Cash	#2274666399
No Cop Notoriety	#50
No Gang Notoriety	#51
Infinite Sprint	#6
Full Health	#1
Player Pratfalls	#5
Milk Bones	#3
Car Mass Hole	#2
Infinite Ammo	#11
Heaven Bound	#12
Add Police Notoriety	#4
Add Gang Notoriety	#35
Never Die	#36
Unlimited Clip	#9

XBOX 360™

VEHICLES

XBOX 360™

CHEAT	NUMBER
Repair Car	#1056
Venom Classic	#1079
Five-0	#1055
Stilwater Municipal	#1072
Baron	#1047
Attrazione	#1043
Zenith	#1081
Vortex	#1080
Phoenix	#1064
Bootlegger	#1049
Raycaster	#1068
Hollywood	#1057
Justice	#1058
Compton	#1052
Eiswolf	#1053
Taxi	#1074
Ambulance	#1040
Backhoe	#1045
Bagboy	#1046
Rampage	#1067
Reaper	#1069
The Job	#1075
Quota	#1066
FBI	#1054
Mag	#1060
Bulldog	#1050
Quasar	#1065
Titan	#1076
Varsity	#1078
Anchor	#1041
Blaze	#1044
Sabretooth	#804
Sandstorm	#805
Kaneda	#801
Widowmaker	#806
Kenshin	#802
Melbourne	#803
Miami	#826
Python	#827
Hurricane	#825
Shark	#828
Skipper	#829
Mongoose	#1062
Superiore	#1073
Tornado	#713
Horizon	#711
Wolverine	#714
Snipes 57	#712
Bear	#1048
Toad	#1077
Kent	#1059
Oring	#1063
Longhauler	#1061
Atlasbreaker	#1042
Septic Avenger	#1070
Shaft	#1071
Bulldozer	#1051

WEAPONS

CHEAT	NUMBER
AR-50	#923
K6	#935
GDHC	#932
NR4	#942
44	#921
Tombstone	#956
T3K	#954
VICE9	#957
AS14 Hammer	#925
12 Gauge	#920
SKR-9	#951
McManus 2010	#938
Baseball Bat	#926
Knife	#936
Molotov	#940
Grenade	#933
Nightstick	#941
Pipebomb	#945
RPG	#946
Crowbar	#955
Pimp Cane	#944
AR200	#922
AR-50/Grenade Launcher	#924
Chainsaw	#927
Fire Extinguisher	#928
Flamethrower	#929
Flashbang	#930
GAL43	#931
Kobra	#934
Machete	#937
Mini-gun	#939
Pepperspray	#943
Annihilator RPG	#947
Samurai Sword	#948
Satchel Charge	#949
Shock Paddles	#950
Sledgehammer	#952
Stungun	#953
XS-2 Ultimax	#958
Pimp Slap	#969

WEATHER

CHEAT	NUMBER
Clear Skies	#78669
Heavy Rain	#78666
Light Rain	#78668
Overcast	#78665
Time Set Midnight	#2400
Time Set Noon	#1200
Wrath Of God	#666

WORLD

CHEAT	NUMBER
Super Saints	#8
Super Explosions	#7
Evil Cars	#16
Pedestrian War	#19
Drunk Pedestrians	#15
Raining Pedestrians	#20
Low Gravity	#18

XBOX 360™

SAMURAI SHODOWN 2

PLAY AS KUROKO IN 2-PLAYER
At the character select, press Up, Down, Left, Up, Down, Right + X.

SEGA SUPERSTARS TENNIS

UNLOCK CHARACTERS
Complete the following missions to unlock the corresponding character.

CHARACTER	COMPLETE THIS MISSION
Alex Kidd	Mission 1 of Alex Kidd's World
Amy Rose	Mission 2 of Sonic the Hedgehog's World
Gilius	Mission 1 of Golden Axe's World
Gum	Mission 12 of Jet Grind Radio's World
Meemee	Mission 8 of Super Monkey Ball's World
Pudding	Mission 1 of Space Channel 5's World
Reala	Mission 2 of NiGHTs' World
Shadow The Hedgehog	Mission 14 of Sonic the Hedgehog's World

SHREK THE THIRD

10,000 GOLD COINS
At the gift shop, press Up, Up, Down, Up, Right, Left.

SILENT HILL: HOMECOMING

YOUNG ALEX COSTUME
At the Title screen, press Up, Up, Down, Down, Left, Right, Left, Right, B.

THE SIMPSONS GAME

After unlocking the following, the outfits can be changed at the downstairs closet in the Simpson's house. The Trophies can be viewed at different locations in the house: Bart's room, Lisa's room, Marge's room, and the garage.

BART'S OUTFITS AND TROPHIES (POSTER COLLECTION)
At the Main menu, press Right, Left, X, X, Y, Right Thumb Stick.

HOMER'S OUTFITS AND TROPHIES (BEER BOTTLE COLLECTION)
At the Main menu, press Left, Right, Y, Y, X, Left Thumb Stick.

LISA'S OUTFITS AND TROPHIES (DOLLS)
At the Main menu, press X, Y, Y, X, X, Y, Left Thumb Stick.

MARGE'S OUTFITS AND TROPHIES (HAIR PRODUCTS)
At the Main menu, press Y, X, Y, Y, X, Right Thumb Stick.

SKATE

EXCLUSIVE BEST BUY CLOTHES
At the Main menu, press Up, Down, Left, Right, X, Right Bumper, Y, Left Bumper. You can get the clothes at Reg's or Slappy's Skate Shop. Find it under Skate.

DEM BONES CHARACTER
Break each bone in your body at least three times.

NEW GREEN GOBLIN AS A SIDEKICK

While standing in the Helicarrier between levels, press Left, Down, Right, Right, Down, Left.

VENOM AS A SIDEKICK

While standing in the Helicarrier between levels, press Left, Left, Right, Up, Down, Down.

SANDMAN AS A SIDEKICK

While standing in the Helicarrier between levels, press Right, Right, Right, Up, Down, Left.

5000 TECH TOKENS

While standing in the Helicarrier between levels, press Up, Up, Down, Down, Left, Right.

STAR WARS: THE FORCE UNLEASHED

CHEAT CODES

Pause the game and select Input Code. Here you can enter the following codes. Activating any of the following cheat codes will disable some unlockables, and you will be unable to save your progress.

CHEAT	CODE
All Force Powers at Max Power	KATARN
All Force Push Ranks	EXARKUN
All Saber Throw Ranks	ADEGAN
All Repulse Ranks	DATHOMIR
All Saber Crystals	HURRIKANE
All Talents	JOCASTA
Deadly Saber	LIGHTSABER

COMBOS

Pause the game and select Input Code. Here you can enter the following codes. Activating any of the following cheat codes will disable some unlockables, and you will be unable to save your progress.

COMBO	CODE
All Combos	MOLDYCROW
Aerial Ambush	VENTRESS
Aerial Assault	EETHKOTH
Aerial Blast	YADDLE
Impale	BRUTALSTAB
Lightning Bomb	MASSASSI
Lightning Grenade	RAGNOS
Saber Slam	PLOKOON
Saber Sling	KITFISTO
Sith Saber Flurry	LUMIYA
Sith Slash	DARAGON
Sith Throw	SAZEN
New Combo	FREEDON
New Combo	MARAJADE

ALL DATABANK ENTRIES

Pause the game and select Input Code. Enter OSSUS.

MIRRORED LEVEL

Pause the game and select Input Code. Enter MINDTRICK. Re-enter the code to return level to normal.

SITH MASTER DIFFICULTY

Pause the game and select Input Code. Enter SITHSPAWN.

COSTUMES

Pause the game and select Input Code. Here you can enter the following codes.

COSTUME	CODE
All Costumes	SOHNDANN
Bail Organa	VICEROY
Ceremonial Jedi Robes	DANTOOINE
Drunken Kota	HARDBOILED
Emperor	MASTERMIND

OVERLORD

XBOX 360™

COSTUME	CODE
Incinerator Trooper	PHOENIX
Jedi Adventure Robe	HOLOCRON
Kashyyyk Trooper	TK421GREEN
Kota	MANDALORE
Master Kento	WOOKIEE
Proxy	PROTOTYPE
Scout Trooper	FERRAL
Shadow Trooper	BLACKHOLE
Sith Stalker Armor	KORRIBAN
Snowtrooper	SNOWMAN
Stormtrooper	TK421WHITE
Stormtrooper Commander	TK421BLUE

STUNTMAN IGNITION

3 PROPS IN STUNT CREATOR MODE
Select Cheats from Extras and enter COOLPROP.

ALL ITEMS UNLOCKED FOR CONSTRUCTION MODE
Select Cheats from Extras and enter NOBLEMAN.

MVX SPARTAN
Select Cheats from Extras and enter fastride.

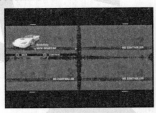

ALL CHEATS
Select Cheats from Extras and enter Wearefrozen. This unlocks the following cheats: Slo-mo Cool, Thrill Cam, Vision Switcher, Nitro Addiction, Freaky Fast, and Ice Wheels.

ALL CHEATS
Select Cheats from Extras and enter Kungfoopete.

ICE WHEELS CHEAT
Select Cheats from Extras and enter IceAge.

NITRO ADDICTION CHEAT
Select Cheats from Extras and enter TheDuke.

VISION SWITCHER CHEAT
Select Cheats from Extras and enter GFXMODES.

SUPERMAN RETURNS: THE VIDEOGAME

GOD MODE
Pause the game, select Options and press Up, Up, Down, Down, Left, Right, Left, Right, Y, X.

INFINITE CITY HEALTH
Pause the game, select Options and press Y, Right, Y, Right, Up, Left, Right, Y.

ALL POWER-UPS
Pause the game, select Options and press Left, Y, Right, X, Down, Y, Up, Down, X, Y, X.

ALL UNLOCKABLES
Pause the game, select Options and press Left, Up, Right, Down, Y, X, Y, Up, Right, X.

FREE ROAM AS BIZARRO
Pause the game, select Options and press Up, Right, Down, Right, Up, Left, Down, Right, Up.

PLAY AS AKUMA

At the character select, highlight Hsien-Ko and press Down.

PLAY AS DAN

At the character select, highlight Donovan and press Down.

PLAY AS DEVILOT

At the character select, highlight Morrigan and press Down.

PLAY AS ANITA

At the character select, hold Left Bumper + Right Bumper and choose Donovan.

PLAY AS HSIEN-KO'S TALISMAN

At the character select, hold Left Bumper + Right Bumper and choose Hsien-Ko.

PLAY AS MORRIGAN AS A BAT

At the character select, hold Left Bumper + Right Bumper and choose Morrigan.

PLAY AS ANITA

At the character select, hold Left Bumper + Right Bumper and choose Donovan.

PLAY AS HSIEN-KO'S TALISMAN

At the character select, hold Left Bumper + Right Bumper and choose Hsien-Ko.

PLAY AS MORRIGAN AS A BAT

At the character select, hold Left Bumper + Right Bumper and choose Morrigan.

SURF'S UP

ALL CHAMPIONSHIP LOCATIONS

Select Cheat Codes from the Extras menu and enter FREEVISIT.

ALL LEAF SLIDE STAGES

Select Cheat Codes from the Extras menu and enter GOINGDOWN.

ALL MULTIPLAYER LEVELS

Select Cheat Codes from the Extras menu and enter MULTIPASS.

ALL BOARDS

Select Cheat Codes from the Extras menu and enter MYPRECIOUS.

ASTRAL BOARD

Select Cheat Codes from the Extras menu and enter ASTRAL.

MONSOON BOARD

Select Cheat Codes from the Extras menu and enter MONSOON.

TINE SHOCKWAVE BOARD

Select Cheat Codes from the Extras menu and enter TINYSHOCKWAVE.

ALL CHARACTER CUSTOMIZATIONS

Select Cheat Codes from the Extras menu and enter TOPFASHION.

PLAY AS ARNOLD

Select Cheat Codes from the Extras menu and enter TINYBUTSTRONG.

PLAY AS ELLIOT

Select Cheat Codes from the Extras menu and enter SURPRISEGUEST.

PLAY AS GEEK

Select Cheat Codes from the Extras menu and enter SLOWANDSTEADY.

PLAY AS TANK EVANS

Select Cheat Codes from the Extras menu and enter IMTHEBEST.

PLAY AS TATSUHI KOBAYASHI

Select Cheat Codes from the Extras menu and enter KOBAYASHI.

PLAY AS ZEKE TOPANGA

Select Cheat Codes from the Extras menu and enter THELEGEND.

ALL VIDEOS AND SPEN GALLERY

Select Cheat Codes from the Extras menu and enter WATCHAMOVIE.

ART GALLERY

Select Cheat Codes from the Extras menu and enter NICEPLACE.

OVERLOAD

XBOX 360™

THRILLVILLE: OFF THE RAILS

$50,000
While in a park, press X, B, Y, X, B, Y, A.

500 THRILL POINTS
While in a park, press B, X, Y, B, X, Y, X.

ALL PARKS
While in a park, press X, B, Y, X, B, Y, X.

ALL RIDES IN CURRENT PARK
While in a park, press X, B, Y, X, B, Y, Y.

MISSION UNLOCK
While in a park, press X, B, Y, X, B, Y, B.

ALL MINI-GAMES IN PARTY PLAY
While in a park, press X, B, Y, X, B, Y, Right.

TIGER WOODS PGA TOUR 06

ALL GOLFERS
Select Password from the Options menu and enter itsinthegame.

ALL CLUBS
Select Password from the Options menu and enter clubs11.

GOLD COLLECTION EA SPORTS BALL
Select Password from the Options menu and enter golfisfun.

NICKLAUS ITEMS
Select Password from the Options menu and enter goldenbear.

ALL COURSES
Select Password from the Options menu and enter eyecandy.

VIJAY SINGH
Select Password from the Options menu and enter victory.

TIGER WOODS PGA TOUR 07

BIG HEAD MODE FOR CROWDS
Select Password and enter tengallonhat.

TIGER WOODS PGA TOUR 08

ALL COURSES
Select Password from EA Sports Extras and enter greensfees.

ALL GOLFERS
Select Password from EA Sports Extras and enter allstars.

WAYNE ROONEY
Select Password from EA Sports Extras and enter playfifa08.

INFINITE MONEY
Select Password from EA Sports Extras and enter cream.

TIGER WOODS PGA TOUR 09

SPECTATORS BIG HEAD MODE
Select EA SPORTS Extras from My Tiger '09, choose Password and enter cephalus.

TIMESHIFT

KRONE IN MULTIPLAYER
Select Multiplayer from the Options menu. Highlight Model and press Left to get to Krone. Press Y and enter RXYMCPENCJ.

TMNT

CHALLENGE MAP 2
At the Main menu, hold the Left Bumper and press A, A, B, A.

DON'S BIG HEAD GOODIE
At the Main menu, hold the Left Bumper and press B, Y, A, X.

TOMB RAIDER: LEGEND

You must unlock the following codes in the game before using them.

BULLETPROOF
During a game, hold Left Trigger and press A, Right Trigger, Y, Right Trigger, X, Left Bumper.

DRAIN ENEMY HEALTH
During a game, hold Left Trigger and press X, B, A, Left Bumper, Right Trigger, Y.

INFINITE ASSAULT RIFLE AMMO
During a game, hold Left Bumper and press A, B, A, Left Trigger, X, Y.

INFINITE GRENADE LAUNCHER AMMO
During a game, hold Left Bumper and press Left Trigger, Y, Right Trigger, B, Left Trigger, X.

INFINITE SHOTGUN AMMO
During a game, hold Left Bumper and press Right Trigger, B, X, Left Trigger, X, A.

INFINITE SMG AMMO
During a game, hold Left Bumper and press B, Y, Left Trigger, Right Trigger, A, B.

EXCALIBUR
During a game, hold Left Bumper and press Y, A, B, Right Trigger, Y, Left Trigger.

SOUL REAVER
During a game, hold Left Bumper and press A, Right Trigger, B, Right Trigger, Left Trigger, X.

1-SHOT KILL
During a game, hold Left Trigger and press Y, A, Y, X, Left Bumper, B.

TEXTURELESS MODE
During a game, hold Left Trigger and press Left Bumper, A, B, A, Y, Right Trigger.

TOM CLANCY'S GHOST RECON ADVANCED WARFIGHTER

ALL MISSIONS
At the Mission Select screen, hold Back + Left Trigger + Right Trigger and press Y, Right Bumper, Y, Right Bumper, X.

FULL HEALTH
Pause the game, hold Back + Left Trigger + Right Trigger and press Left Bumper, Left Bumper, Right Bumper, X, Right Bumper, Y.

INVINCIBLE
Pause the game, hold Back + Left Trigger + Right Trigger and press Y, Y, X, Right Bumper, X, Left Bumper.

TEAM INVINCIBLE
Pause the game, hold Back + Left Trigger + Right Trigger and press X, X, Y, Right Bumper, Y, Left Bumper.

UNLIMITED AMMO
Pause the game, hold Back + Left Trigger + Right Trigger and press Right Bumper, Right Bumper, Left Bumper, X, Left Bumper, Y.

TOM CLANCY'S GHOST RECON ADVANCED WARFIGHTER 2

FAMAS IN QUICK MISSION MODE
Create a new campaign with the name: GRAW2QUICKFAMAS.

TOM CLANCY'S RAINBOW SIX VEGAS

The following codes work in single player only.

BIG HEADS
Pause the game, hold Left Trigger and press B, X, A, Y, Left Thumbstick, Y, A, X, B, Right Thumbstick.

CHANGE BULLET TRACER COLOR
Pause the game, hold Left Trigger and press Left Thumbstick, Left Thumbstick, A, Right Thumbstick, Right Thumbstick, B, Left Thumbstick, Left Thumbstick, X, Right Thumbstick, Right Thumbstick, Y.

ONE SHOT KILLS
Pause the game, hold the Left Bumper and press Left Thumbstick, Right Thumbstick, Left Thumbstick, Right Thumbstick, A, B, Left Thumbstick, Right Thumbstick, Left Thumbstick, Right Thumbstick, X, Y.

THIRD PERSON VIEW
Pause the game, hold Left Trigger and press X, B, X, B, Left Thumbstick, Left Thumbstick, Y, A, Y, A, Right Thumbstick, Right Thumbstick.

GI JOHN DOE MODE
Pause the game, hold the Right Bumper and press Left Thumbstick, Left Thumbstick, A, Right Thumbstick, Right Thumbstick, B, Left Thumbstick, Left Thumbstick, X, Right Thumbstick, Right Thumbstick, Y.

SUPER RAGDOLL
Pause the game, hold the Right Bumper and press A, A, B, B, X, X, Y, Y, A, B, X, Y.

THIRD PERSON MODE
Pause the game, hold the Right Bumper and press X, B, X, B, Left Thumbstick, Left Thumbstick, Y, A, Y, A, Right Thumbstick, Right Thumbstick.

TAR-21 ASSAULT RIFLE
At the Character Customization screen, hold Right Bumper and press Down, Down, Up, Up, X, B, X, B, Y, Up, Up, Y.

MULTIPLAYER MAP: COMCAST EVENT
Select Extras from the Main menu. Choose Comcast Gift and enter Comcast Faster.

M468 ASSAULT RIFLE
While customizing your character, hold down RB and press Up, Y, Down, A, Left, X, Right, B, Left, Left, Right, X

TONY HAWK'S AMERICAN WASTELAND

ALWAYS SPECIAL
Select Cheat Codes from the Options menu and enter uronfire. Pause the game and select Cheats from the Game Options to enable the code.

PERFECT RAIL
Select Cheat Codes from the Options menu and enter grindxpert. Pause the game and select Cheats from the Game Options to enable the code.

PERFECT SKITCH
Select Cheat Codes from the Options menu and enter h!tchar!de. Pause the game and select Cheats from the Game Options to enable the code.

PERFECT MANUAL
Select Cheat Codes from the Options menu and enter 2wheels!. Pause the game and select Cheats from the Game Options to enable the code.

MOON GRAVITY
Select Cheat Codes from the Options menu and enter 2them00n. Pause the game and select Cheats from the Game Options to enable the code.

MAT HOFFMAN
Select Cheat Codes from the Options menu and enter the_condor.

TONY HAWK'S PROJECT 8

SPONSOR ITEMS

As you progress through Career mode and move up the rankings, you gain sponsors. Each sponsor comes with its own Create-a-Skater item.

RANK	CAS ITEM UNLOCKED
Rank 040	Adio Kenny V2 Shoes
Rank 050	Quiksilver Hoody 3
Rank 060	Birdhouse Tony Hawk Deck
Rank 080	Vans No Skool Gothic Shoes
Rank 100	Volcom Scallero Jacket
Rank 110	eS Square One Shoes
Rank 120	Almost Watch What You Say Deck
Rank 140	DVS Adage Shoe
Rank 150	Element Illuminate Deck
Rank 160	Etnies Sheckler White Lavender Shoes
Complete Skateshop Goal	Stereo Soundwave Deck

SKATERS

You must unlock all of the skaters, except for Tony Hawk, by completing challenges in the Career Mode. They are playable in Free Skate and 2-Player modes.

SKATER	HOW TO UNLOCK
Tony Hawk	Always unlocked
Lyn-z Adams Hawkins	Complete Pro Challenge
Bob Burquist	Complete Pro Challenge
Dustin Dollin	Complete Pro Challenge
Nyjah Huston	Complete Pro Challenge
Bam Margera	Complete Pro Challenge
Rodney Mullen	Complete Pro Challenge
Paul Rodriguez	Complete Pro Challenge
Ryan Sheckler	Complete Pro Challenge
Daewon Song	Complete Pro Challenge
Mike Vallely	Complete Pro Challenge
Stevie Willams	Complete Pro Challenge
Travis Barker	Complete Pro Challenge
Kevin Staab	Complete Pro Challenge
Zombie	Complete Pro Challenge
Christaian Hosoi	Rank #1
Jason Lee	Complete Final Tony Hawk Goal
Photographer	Unlock Shops
Security Guard	Unlock School
Bum	Unlock Car Factory
Beaver Mascot	Unlock High School
Real Estate Agent	Unlock Downtown
Filmer	Unlock High School
Skate Jam Kid	Rank #4
Dad	Rank #1
Colonel	All Gaps
Nerd	Complete School Spirit Goal

CHEAT CODES

Select Cheat Codes from the Options menu to enter the following codes. You can access some of these codes from the Options menu.

CODE	WHAT IT UNLOCKS
plus44	Travis Barker
hohohosoi	Christian Hosoi
notmono	Jason Lee
mixitup	Kevin Staab
strangefellows	Dad & Skater Jam Kid
themedia	Photog Girl & Filmer
militarymen	Colonel & Security Guard
jammypack	Always Special

CODE	WHAT IT UNLOCKS
balancegalore	Perfect Rail
frontandback	Perect Manual
shellshock	Unlimited Focus
shescaresme	Big Realtor
birdhouse	Inkblot Deck
allthebest	Full Stats
needaride	All Decks unlocked and free, except for Inkblot Deck and Gamestop Deck
yougotitall	All specials unlocked and in player's special list and set as owned in Skate Shop
wearelosers	Nerd and a Bum
manineedadate	Beaver Mascot
suckstobedead	Officer Dick
HATEDANDPROUD	The Vans unlockable item

TONY HAWK'S PROVING GROUND

Select Cheat Codes from the Options and enter the following cheats. Some codes need to be enabled by selecting Cheats from the Options during a game.

UNLOCK	CHEAT
Unlocks Boneman	CRAZYBONEMAN
Unlocks Bosco	MOREMILK
Unlocks Cam	NOTACAMERA
Unlocks Cooper	THECOOP
Unlocks Eddie X	SKETCHY
Unlocks El Patinador	PILEDRIVER
Unlocks Eric	FLYAWAY
Unlocks Mad Dog	RABBIES
Unlocks MCA	INTERGALACTIC
Unlocks Mel	NOTADUDE
Unlocks Rube	LOOKSSMELLY
Unlocks Spence	DAPPER
Unlocks Shayne	MOVERS
Unlocks TV Producer	SHAKER
Unlock FDR	THEPREZPARK
Unlock Lansdowne	THELOCALPARK
Unlock Air & Space Museum	THEINDOORPARK
Unlocks all Fun Items	OVERTHETOP
Unlocks all CAS items	GIVEMESTUFF
Unlocks all Decks	LETSGOSKATE
Unlock all Game Movies	WATCHTHIS
Unlock all Lounge Bling Items	SWEETSTUFF
Unlock all Lounge Themes	LAIDBACKLOUNGE
Unlock all Rigger Pieces	IMGONNABUILD
Unlock all Video Editor Effects	TRIPPY
Unlock all Video Editor Overlays	PUTEMONTOP
All specials unlocked and in player's special list	LOTSOFTRICKS
Full Stats	BEEFEDUP
Give player +50 skill points	NEEDSHELP
THE FOLLOWING CHEATS LOCK YOU OUT OF THE LEADERBOARDS:	
Unlocks Perfect Manual	STILLAINTFALLIN
Unlocks Perfect Rail	AINTFALLIN
Unlock Super Check	BOOYAH
Unlocks Unlimited Focus	MYOPIC
Unlock Unlimited Slash Grind	SUPERSLASHIN
Unlocks 100% branch completion in NTT	FOREVERNAILED
No Bails	ANDAINTFALLIN
YOU CAN NOT USE THE VIDEO EDITOR WITH THE FOLLOWING CHEATS:	
Invisible Man	THEMISSING
Mini Skater	TINYTATER
No Board	MAGICMAN

TRANSFORMERS: THE GAME

The following cheats disable saving and achievements:

INFINITE HEALTH
At the Main menu, press Left, Left, Up, Left, Right, Down, Right.

INFINITE AMMO
At the Main menu, press Up, Down, Left, Right, Up, Up, Down.

NO MILITARY OR POLICE
At the Main menu, press Right, Left, Right, Left, Right, Left, Right.

ALL MISSIONS
At the Main menu, press Down, Up, Left, Right, Right, Right, Up, Down.

BONUS CYBERTRON MISSIONS
At the Main menu, press Right, Up, Up, Down, Right, Left, Left.

GENERATION 1 SKIN: JAZZ
At the Main menu, press Left, Up, Down, Down, Left, Up, Right.

GENERATION 1 SKIN: MEGATRON
At the Main menu, press Down, Left, Left, Down, Right, Right, Up.

GENERATION 1 SKIN: OPTIMUS PRIME
At the Main menu, press Down, Right, Left, Up, Down, Down, Left.

GENERATION 1 SKIN: ROBOVISION OPTIMUS PRIME
At the Main menu, press Down, Down, Up, Up, Right, Right, Right.

GENERATION 1 SKIN: STARSCREAM
At the Main menu, press Right, Down, Left, Left, Down, Up, Up.

UNDERTOW

GAMER PIC 1 - SCUBA DIVER
Total 100 kills.

GAMER PIC 2 - ATLANTIS MAN
Total 10,000 kills.

VIRTUA TENNIS 3

KING & DUKE
At the Main menu, press Up, Up, Down, Down, Left, Right, LB, RB.

ALL GEAR
At the Main menu, press Left, Right, B, Left, Right, B, Up, Down.

ALL COURTS
At the Main menu, press Up, Up, Down, Down, Left, Right, Left, Right.

WIN ONE MATCH TO WIN TOURNAMENT
At the Main menu, press B, Left, B, Right, B, Up, B, Down.

VIVA PINATA

NEW ITEMS IN PET STORE
Select New Garden and enter chewnicorn as the name.

NEW ITEMS IN PET STORE
Select New Garden and enter bullseye as the name.

NEW ITEMS IN PET STORE
Select New Garden and enter goobaa as the name.

NEW ITEMS IN PET STORE
Select New Garden and enter kittyfloss as the name.

CLASSIC GAMER AWARD ACHIEVEMENT

At the START screen, press Up, Up, Down, Down, Left, Right, Left, Right, B, A. This earns you 10 points toward your Gamerscore.

VIVA PINATA: TROUBLE IN PARADISE

CREDITS

Select Play Garden and name your garden Piñata People. This unlocks the ability to view the credits on the Main menu.

WALL-E

The following cheats will disable saving. The five possible characters starting with Wall-E and going down are: Wall-E, Auto, EVE, M-O, GEL-A Steward.

ALL BONUS FEATURES UNLOCKED

Select Cheats from the Bonus Features menu and enter Wall-E, Auto, EVE, GEL-A Steward.

ALL GAME CONTENT UNLOCKED

Select Cheats from the Bonus Features menu and enter M-O, Auto, GEL-A Steward, EVE.

ALL SINGLE PLAYER LEVELS UNLOCKED

Select Cheats from the Bonus Features menu and enter Auto, GEL-A Steward, M-O, Wall-E.

ALL MULTIPLAYER MAPS UNLOCKED

Select Cheats from the Bonus Features menu and enter EVE, M-O, Wall-E, Auto.

ALL HOLIDAY COSTUMES UNLOCKED

Select Cheats from the Bonus Features menu and enter Auto, Auto, GEL-A Steward, GEL-A Steward.

ALL MULTIPLAYER COSTUMES UNLOCKED

Select Cheats from the Bonus Features menu and enter GEL-A Steward, Wall-E, M-O, Auto.

UNLIMITED HEALTH UNLOCKED

Select Cheats from the Bonus Features menu and enter Wall-E, M-O, Auto, M-O.

WALL-E: MAKE ANY CUBE AT ANY TIME

Select Cheats from the Bonus Features menu and enter Auto, M-O, Auto, M-O.

WALL-EVE: MAKE ANY CUBE AT ANY TIME

Select Cheats from the Bonus Features menu and enter M-O, GEL-A Steward, EVE, EVE.

WALL-E WITH A LASER GUN AT ANY TIME

Select Cheats from the Bonus Features menu and enter Wall-E, EVE, EVE, Wall-E.

WALL-EVE WITH A LASER GUN AT ANY TIME

Select Cheats from the Bonus Features menu and enter GEL-A Steward, EVE, M-O, Wall-E.

WALL-E: PERMANENT SUPER LASER UPGRADE

Select Cheats from the Bonus Features menu and enter Wall-E, Auto, EVE, M-O.

EVE: PERMANENT SUPER LASER UPGRADE

Select Cheats from the Bonus Features menu and enter EVE, Wall-E, Wall-E, Auto.

CREDITS

Select Cheats from the Bonus Features menu and enter Auto, Wall-E, GEL-A Steward, M-O.

XBOX 360

HBK AND HHH'S DX OUTFIT

Select Cheat Codes from the Options and enter DXCostume69K2.

KELLY KELLY'S ALTERNATE OUTFIT

Select Cheat Codes from the Options and enter KellyKG12R.

BRET HART

Complete the March 31, 1996 Hall of Fame challenge by defeating Bret Hart with Shawn Michaels in a One-On-One 30-Minute Iron Man Match on Legend difficulty. Purchase from WWE Shop for $210,000.

MICK FOLEY

Complete the June 28, 1998 Hall of Fame challenge by defeating Mick Foley with The Undertaker in a Hell In a Cell Match on Legend difficulty. Purchase from WWE Shop for $210,000.

MR. MCMAHON

Win or successfully defend a championship (WWE or World Heavyweight) at WrestleMania in WWE 24/7 GM Mode. Purchase from WWE Shop for $110,000.

THE ROCK

Complete the April 1, 2001 Hall of Fame challenge by defeating The Rock with Steve Austin in a Single Match on Legend Difficulty. Purchase from WWE Shop for $210,000.

STEVE AUSTIN

Complete the March 23, 1997 Hall of Fame challenge by defeating Steve Austin with Bret Hart in a Submission Match on Legend Difficulty. Purchase from WWE Shop for $210,000.

TERRY FUNK

Complete the April 13, 1997 Hall of Fame challenge by defeating Tommy Dreamer, Sabu and Sandman with any Superstar in an ECW Extreme Rules 4-Way Match on Legend difficulty. Purchase from WWE Shop for $210,000.

MR. MCMAHON BALD

Must unlock Mr. McMahon as a playable character first. Purchase from WWE Shop for $60,000.

XBOX 360™ ACHIEVEMENTS

GAMES

007 QUANTUM OF SOLACE

ACHIEVEMENTS

NAME	GOAL/REQUIREMENT	POINT VALUE
Live and Let Die	Takedown 50 enemies.	20
Diamonds Are Forever	Hack all locks.	20
For Your Eyes Only	Disable 10 cameras.	20
The Man with the Golden Gun	Defeat 50 enemies with one shot each.	20
Time to face gravity	In White's Estate, open the cellar door with one shot.	15
We have people everywhere	In Siena, shoot all seven satellite dishes on the rooftops.	15
Opera isn't for everyone	In Opera House, move through backstage without alerting the guards.	15
He's coming fast!	In Sink Hole, kill the helicopter pilot while the gunners are still alive.	15
I miss the Cold War	Outside Science Center, defeat each sniper guard with one shot.	15
Half-monk, half-hitman	Inside the Science Center, shoot down all the lights in the main hall.	15

NAME	GOAL/REQUIREMENT	POINT VALUE
ELLIPSIS	In Airport, save the Skyfleet servers without breaking stealth.	15
I'm the money	In Train, only use the P99 while on the freight train.	15
Any thug can kill	In Casino Royale, reach the spa room without alerting or attacking the guards.	15
I've got a little itch	In Barge, save Vesper in under two minutes.	15
Allow me	In Venice, defeat Gettler with one shot.	15
You just need one shot	In Eco Hotel, kill the driver of the car.	15
The World is Not Enough	Collect all cell phones.	40
Thunderball	Collect all power weapons.	40
License to Kill	Defeat an enemy with one shot.	10
Octopussy	Complete game on New Recruit.	20
Tomorrow Never Dies	Complete game on Field Operative.	25
You Only Live Twice	Complete game on Agent.	30
The name is Bond, James Bond.	Complete game on 007.	70
A View to a Kill	Complete White's Estate.	15
From Russia With Love	Complete Siena, Opera House, and Sink Hole.	15
The Living Daylights	Complete Shanty Town and Construction Site.	15
On Her Majesty's Secret Service	Complete Science Center Exterior, Interior, and Airport.	15
Casino Royale	Complete Montenegro Train, Casino Royale, and Casino Poison.	15
The Spy Who Loved Me	Complete Barge and Venice.	15
Quantum of Solace	Complete Eco Hotel.	15
I know where you keep your gun	Unlock and purchase all weapons.	20
Quite the body count	Unlock and purchase all weapon attachments.	15
Ejector seat, you're joking?	Unlock and purchase all gadgets.	20
Goldfinger	Unlock and purchase all golden weapons.	25
Chemin de Fer	Unlock and purchase all weapons, grenades, attachments, gadgets, and golden weapons.	50
You've defused hundreds of these	Defuse a bomb in Bond Versus once.	15
I admire your courage	Earn over 1,000 in credits.	15
Life is full of small challenges	Earn over 10,000 in credits.	20
For England, James?	Earn over 100,000 in credits.	25
The best player in the service.	Be a top player in an online match.	15
Yes. Considerably.	Play 100 online matches.	20
Shaken, not stirred	Win 5 Territory Control online matches.	15
A licensed troubleshooter	Eliminate 100 players with the Golden Gun in Golden Gun mode.	20
A measure of comfort	Eliminate 1,000 players across all games played.	20
The nature of evil	Eliminate 10 players while blind firing from cover across all games.	20
3030 was a double	Eliminate 100 players while in cover across all games.	20
He's playing his golden harp	Melee the player with the Golden Gun.	15
Die Another Day	Escape as Bond in Bond Evasion mode.	15
Dr. No	Win a round as Bond in Bond Versus mode.	15
Moonraker	Collect 30 cell phones.	20

ARMY OF TWO

ACHIEVEMENTS

NAME	GOAL/REQUIREMENT	POINTS
Elite PMC	Complete all missions as a Professional.	50
My Virtual Friend	Complete all missions with the Partner AI.	35
Say Hello to my Little Friends	Purchase the MP7, M134, DAO-X Protecta, MGL MK-X, and the M107 Light Fifty.	45

NAME	GOAL/REQUIREMENT	POINTS
Man of Many Masks	Purchase every mask variant.	50
If I Were a Rich Man	Earn one million dollars in total over the course of campaign mode.	40
Fear is The Mind Killer	Spend 1 minute straight at full Aggro.	45
Starting a Riot	Kill 50 enemies total in Co-op Riot Shield.	30
Two Eyes are Better Than One	Kill 5 enemies total using Co-op Snipe.	35
Seven-six-two Millimeter	Kill 250 enemies total using Assault Rifles.	20
This is my Boom Stick!	Kill 250 enemies total using Shotguns.	20
Spray and Pray	Kill 250 enemies total using Machine Guns.	20
Dead Man's Hand	Kill 150 enemies total using Handguns.	20
Alright, Who Wants Some?	Kill 250 enemies total using SMGs.	20
One Shot. One Kill.	Kill 100 enemies total using Sniper Rifles.	20
Big Boom! Big Bada Boom!	Kill 25 enemies total using RPGs.	20
Flip You. Flip You For Real	Kill 50 enemies total using the Melee Attack.	20
Fission Mailed	Kill 25 Martyrs by shooting the Bomb Packs on their chests.	20
If It Bleeds, We Can Kill It	Kill 25 Heavy Armor enemies.	30
Field Medic	Drag and heal your partner 25 times.	30
Boots on the Ground	Finish playing a versus ranked match.	10
The Devil's in the Details	Complete 20 minor objectives in a ranked match.	20
Surviving The Game	Complete a ranked match without ever needing to be revived.	25
Retirement Savings Plan	Earn one billion dollars in total in ranked matches.	40
Out of Debt	Heal your partner for the first time. Training does not count.	15
One Gun is Enough	Win a ranked match without purchasing any additional weapons.	35
Beast with Two Fronts	Kill 50 enemies total in Back-to-Back.	20
Running Man	Kill 75 enemies while in the stealth mode of Overkill.	30
L'Abattoir	Kill 100 enemies while in the power mode of Overkill.	30
Weapon Specialist	Purchase 3 weapons.	15
Stonewall	Kill 30 enemies using the Riot Shield melee attack	30
My Kind of Case!	Collect all of the information cases in the entire game.	40
True SSC Challenger	Win every stage of a ranked three round SSC Challenge match	25
Barrel SSC Challenger	Destroy 500 barrels in ranked SSC Challenge matches	25
SSC Challenge Win	Win a ranked SSC Challenge match	25
SSC Challenge Marksman	Achieve 75% accuracy at the conclusion of a ranked three round SSC Challenge match	25

SECRET ACHIEVEMENTS

NAME	GOAL/REQUIREMENT	POINTS
Mission 1 Complete	Complete Mission 1 as Contractor or higher.	30
Mission 2 Complete	Complete Mission 2 as Contractor or higher.	30
Mission 3 Complete	Complete Mission 3 as Contractor or higher.	15
Mission 4 Complete	Complete Mission 4 as Contractor or higher.	15
Mission 5 Complete	Complete Mission 5 as Contractor or higher.	15
Mission 6 Complete	Complete Mission 6 as Contractor or higher.	15

ASSASSIN'S CREED

ACHIEVEMENTS

NAME	GOAL/REQUIREMENT	POINTS
The Eagle and The Apple - 1191	Complete Assassin's Creed.	100
Personal Vendetta	Kill every Templar.	40

XBOX 360™ ACHIEVEMENTS

OVERLOAD

NAME	GOAL/REQUIREMENT	POINTS
Keeper of the Lions Passant	Find All of Richard's Flags in the Kingdom.	25
Keeper of the Creed	Find All Flags in Masyaf.	10
Keeper of the Four Gospels	Find All Flags in Jerusalem.	20
Keeper of the Crescent	Find All Flags in Damascus.	20
Absolute Symbiosis	Have a complete Synchronization bar.	45
Fearless	Complete all Reach High Points.	25
Hungerer of Knowledge	See 85% of all the memory glitches.	20
Defender of the People: Acre	Complete every free mission in Acre.	20
Defender of the People: Jerusalem	Complete every free mission in Jerusalem.	20
Defender of the People: Damascus	Complete every free mission in Damascus.	20
Conversationalist	Go through every dialog with Lucy.	20
Disciple of the Creed	Assassinate all your targets with a full DNA bar.	30
Eagle's Will	Defeat 100 opponents without dying.	20
Eagle's Flight	Last 10 minutes in open conflict.	20
Eagle's Prey	Assassinate 100 guards.	20
Blade in the Crowd	Kill one of your main targets like a true assassin.	30
Eagle's Challenge	Defeat 25 guards in a single fight.	20
Eagle's Swiftness	Perform 100 Counter Kill in Fights.	20
Eagle's Dive	Perform 50 Combo Kills in Fights.	20
Eagle's Talon	Perform 50 stealth assassinations.	15
Eagle's Dance	Perform 50 leap of faith.	10
The hands of a Thief	Pickpocket 200 throwing knives.	15
March of the Pious	Use Scholar blending 20 times.	5
Eagle's Eye	Kill 75 guards by throwing knives.	15
Enemy of the Poor	Grab and Throw 25 Harassers.	5
Gifted Escapist	Jump through 20 merchant stands.	5
Keeper of the Black Cross	Find All Teutonic Flags in Acre.	10
Keeper of the Order	Find all Templar Flags in Acre.	10
Keeper of the 8 Virtues	Find All Hospitalier Flags in Acre.	10

SECRET ACHIEVEMENTS

NAME	GOAL/REQUIREMENT	POINTS
Visions of the Future	A strange vision has appeared to you. What could it mean?	50
The Blood of a Corrupt Merchant	You've slain Tamir, Black Market Merchant in Damascus.	25
The Blood of a Slave Trader	You've slain Talal, Slave Trader of Jerusalem.	25
The Blood Of A Doctor	You've slain Garnier de Naplouse, Hospitlier Leader in Acre.	25
The Blood of a Regent	You've slain Majd Addin, Regent of Jerusalem.	25
The Blood of the Merchant King	You've slain Abul Nuqoud, Merchant King of Damascus.	25
The Blood of a Liege-Lord	You've slain William of Montferrat, Liege-Lord of Acre.	25
The Blood of a Scribe	You've slain Jubair, the Scribe of Damascus.	25
The Blood of a Teutonic Leader	You've slain Sibrand, the Teutonic Leader of Acre.	25
The Blood of a Nemesis	You've slain Robert de Sable, but there is one more...	25
Welcome to the Animus	You've successfully completed the Animus tutorial.	20
Hero of Masyaf	You've protected Masyaf from the Templar invasion.	20
The Punishment for Treason	You have found the traitor and have brought him before Al Mualim.	20

ACHIEVEMENTS

NAME	GOAL/REQUIREMENT	POINTS
High Roller	Earn $150,000 in one Campaign Mode game.	15
Whale	Earn $250,000 in one Campaign Mode game.	25
Bombs Away	Win a game by only passing the ball.	13
Ground Attack	Win a game by only running the ball.	17
Underdog	Defeat the Nightmare in Hard Difficulty in Quickplay when using the Grizzlies or Hammerheads.	15
Butterfingaz	Defeat the computer in bonus Quick Play game of Butterfingaz.	10
Domination	Defeat the computer in a bonus Quick Play game of Domination.	10
Special Teamer	Return a punt or a kickoff for a touchdown game in a Campaign Mode.	25
Shutout	Complete one shutout game in Campaign Mode.	10
Juiced	Train both Rookie and Veteran up to an A+ rating during Campaign Mode.	15
Top Dog	Defeat an online opponent with your Campaign Mode custom team.	6
Custom Pain	Defeat 10 online opponents with your Campaign Mode custom team.	14
Air Supremacy	Gain 400 passing yards in any Campaign Mode game.	20
Groundhog	Gain 200 rushing yards in any Campaign Mode game.	35
Sticky Fingers	Gain 200 receiving yards in any Campaign Mode game.	20
Ownage	Win 10 games online.	20
Pwnage	Win 25 games online.	50
Mexico'd	Knock Mexico out of the game with a game-ending injury (Quickplay or Campaign Mode).	11
Headhunter	Knock Julius Williams out of the game (Quickplay or Campaign).	10
Shutdown	Hold an opposing team to under 100 combined (pass/rush) in a Campaign Mode game.	10
Buffet Victory	Win a Quick Play game with every team.	30
Fast Learner	Complete every Training Camp task.	10
Playmaker	Score a 90+ yard touchdown in Campaign mode.	5
Romo	Cause 3 or more injuries to your opponent in a single Campaign Mode game.	25
Gunslinger	Throw at least 6 TD passes in a single game in Campaign Mode.	6
Scrubs Champ	Defeat Division 3 in Campaign Mode.	25
Division 2 Champ	Defeat Division 2 in Campaign Mode.	70
The End	Defeat Campaign Mode.	150
Rushing Champ	Win the rushing title with your rookie (any division in Campaign Mode).	15
Passing Champ	Win the passing title with your rookie (any division in Campaign Mode).	15
Receiving Champ	Win the receiving title with your rookie (any division in Campaign Mode).	15
LT's Pride	Get 20 sacks with a veteran in one Division Season.	25
Thief	Force 7 turnovers with your veteran in a Division Season in Campaign Mode.	15
L33T	Win every game in Campaign Mode.	50
Arsenal	Score 19 points in a quarter in Campaign Mode.	9
Greatest Show	Score 24 points in a quarter in Campaign Mode.	15
Manvalanche	Get 12 sacks in one Campaign Mode game.	15
Bling Bling	Buy every piece of bonus equipment that's unlocked after you Defeat Campaign Mode.	25
Deep Pockets	Earn $500,000 dollars online.	10
Mad Bank	Earn $1,000,000 dollars online.	20
Weak Sauce	Lost to Arizona in game 1 of Campaign Mode .	0
O RLY?	Lost by more than 24 pts in Campaign Mode .	0
Blind	Threw 5+ interceptions in one game .	0
ROFL Waffle	Lost 5 games in a row online.	0
Lollercoaster	Fumble the ball 5 times in a game.	0

XBOX 360™ ACHIEVEMENTS

NAME	GOAL/REQUIREMENT	POINTS
Tables Turn	Injured Quentin Sands in Division 1.	30
Burning Sensation	You feel itchy down below. Did you pick something up from your last opponent?	69

CALL OF DUTY 4: MODERN WARFARE

ACHIEVEMENTS

NAME	GOAL/REQUIREMENT	POINTS
Make the Jump	Infiltrate a cargo ship.	20
Earn a Winged Dagger	Complete 'F.N.G.'	20
Win the War	Complete the game on any difficulty.	40
Dancing in the Dark	Kill the power.	20
Save the Bacon	Protect 'War Pig', the Abrams tank.	20
Death From Above	Operate an AC-130 gun ship.	20
Wrong Number	Find Al-Asad's safehouse.	20
Piggyback Ride	Carry Cpt. MacMillian to safety.	20
Desperate Measures	Corner Zakhaev's Son.	20
Look Sharp	Find 15 enemy intel items.	20
Eyes and Ears	Find 30 enemy intel items.	20
Down Boy Down	Survive a dog attack.	20
New Squadron Record	Complete the cargo ship mockup in less than 20 seconds.	20
Rescue Roycewicz	Save Pvt. Roycewicz on the stairs.	20
Your Show Sucks	Destroy all the TVs showing Al-Asad's speech.	20
Man of the People	Save the farmer.	10
Straight Flush	Kill 5 enemies with one shot while in the AC-130 gunship.	20
Ghillies In The Mist	Complete 'All Ghillied Up' without alerting any enemies.	20
Mile High Club	Sky dive to safety on Veteran difficulty.	20
No Rest for the Weary	Stab an injured crawling enemy.	10
Deep and Hard	Complete the game on Hardened or Veteran difficulty.	90
The Package	Complete 'Crew Expendable' on Veteran difficulty.	40
The Rescue	Complete 'Blackout' on Veteran difficulty.	40
The Search	Complete 'Charlie Don't Surf' on Veteran difficulty.	40
The Bog	Complete 'The Bog' and 'War Pig' on Veteran difficulty.	40
The Escape	Complete 'Hunted' and 'Death From Above' on Veteran difficulty.	40
The First Horseman	Complete 'Shock and Awe' on Veteran difficulty.	40
The Second Horseman	Complete 'Safehouse' on Veteran difficulty.	40
The Shot	Complete 'All Ghillied Up' and 'One Shot, One Kill' on Veteran difficulty.	40
The Third Horseman	Complete 'Heat' and 'The Sins of the Father' on Veteran difficulty.	40
The Ultimatum	Complete 'Ultimatum', 'All In', and 'No Fighting in the War Room' on Veteran difficulty.	40
The Fourth Horseman	Complete 'Game Over' on Veteran difficulty.	40
Daredevil	Kill an enemy while blinded by a flashbang in the single player campaign.	10
Roadkill	Kill 2 enemies by blowing up a car in the single player campaign.	10
Bird on the Ground	Shoot down an enemy helicopter with an RPG in the single player campaign.	20
Four of a Kind	Kill 4 enemies in a row with headshots in the single player campaign.	20
Three of a Kind	Kill 3 enemies in a row with your knife in the single player campaign.	10

ACHIEVEMENTS

NAME	GOAL/REQUIREMENT	POINTS
Hands-On	5 Grapple Kills	10
Man Handle	50 Grapple Kills	15
Death Grip	250 grapple kills	20
Fatal Touch	500 grapple kills	30
Shish Kabob	Impale an enemy	10
Enemy Appetizers	Impale 100 enemies	30
Now You See It, Now You Don't	Disarm an enemy	10
Master Looter	Disarm 100 enemies	30
Rock of Ages	Kill 100 enemies by boulder throw	30
Free Fall	Kill an enemy by death fall	10
Death Rain	Kill 100 enemies by death fall	30
Slice 'n Dice	100 dismemberments	10
Chop Shop	500 dismemberments	20
Meat Market	1000 dismemberments	30
Parry Farm	Perform every parry kill move	10
Parry Assassin	100 parry kills	15
Parry King	200 parry kills	20
Chained Attacker	Combo Counter reaches 100	10
Chain of Fools	Combo Counter reaches 325	20
Mob Massacre	Kill 5 or more enemies simultaneously	15
Treasure Seeker	Find 5 treasure chests	10
Treasure Hunter	Find 50 treasure chests	20
Filthy Rich	Find all treasure chests	30
Noble Conan	Save a Maiden	10
Triumvirate Seeker	Activate 5 rune triumvirates	10
Triumvirates United	Activate all rune triumvirates	20
The Legendary Set	Collect all armor pieces	10
Mighty Conan	Complete the game on Hard mode	30
Master Conan	Complete the game on King mode	50
Bill of Health	Find all Health Meter powerups	20
Armored Up	Find all Power Meter powerups	20
Adrenaline Rush	Find all Song of Death meter powerups	20
Master Swordsman	All one-handed blade attacks mastered	10
Master Dual Wielder	All dual wield attacks mastered	10
Master Two-Handed Swordsman	All two-handed blade attacks mastered	10
Bring out the Gimp	Kill at least 25 enemies during the Giant Squid boss battle	15
Losing His Mind	Decapitate a captain with a shield	20
Untouchable	Complete a mission without taking any damage	40
High and Mighty	Score 20000 points in a level	10
The Bloody Crown	Score 100000 total points	40

SECRET ACHIEVEMENTS

NAME	GOAL/REQUIREMENT	POINTS
Rest In Peace	Send Graven into the Netherworld in the Ocean Ruins and complete the game	40
My Hero	Save all maidens	20
Defeat Cleaver's Army	Defeat the Bone Cleaver and his army in Barachan Isles and obtain The Ward of Fire	10
Dragon Slayer	Defeat the Sand Dragon in the lost city of Shem and obtain The Ward of the Earth	10
Demon Slayer	Defeat the Elephant Demon in the Kush caves and obtain The Ward of the Abyss	20
Snake Charmer	Defeat the Sorceress Queen in Stygia and obtain The Ward of Souls	20
Sink the Squid	Defend the ship and defeat the Giant Squid	30
Who's your Daddy?	Defeat the Bone Cleaver in Argos and obtain The Ward of the Departed	30
Strength of 10 Men	Kill 10 or more enemies simultaneously	40

CRACKDOWN

ACHIEVEMENTS

NAME	GOAL/REQUIREMENT	POINTS
Agency Explosives Expert	Bomb your way to a 4-star Explosives rating.	20
Agency Athlete	Run & jump your way to a 4-star Agility rating.	20
Agency Wheelman	Accelerate and slide your way to a 4-star Driving rating.	20
Agency Brawler	Punch, jab, kick, and throw your way to a 4-star Strength rating.	20
Agency Marksman	Hit your target every time to achieve a 4-star Firearms rating.	20
Master Agent	Earn 4-star ratings in all five skill areas and then max out your Skills Status meters.	40
Roadkill King	Mow down and massacre 175 gang members while driving.	15
High Flyer	Make your way to the top of the Agency Tower.	10
Firing Squad	Fire away - shoot and kill 500 gang members using firearms.	15
Bare-Knuckle Brawler	Kill 150 gang members with your bare hands (or thrown objects).	15
Mad Bomber	Show your explosive personality - kill 500 gang members using explosives.	15
Untouchable Agent	Kill 200 gang members without dying yourself.	15
Body Juggler	Use explosives to keep a body up in the air for 10 seconds.	20
Car Juggler	Use explosives to keep a car up in the air for seven seconds.	20
Hazardous Hangtime	Execute a 6-second jump in a vehicle.	10
Driving High	Achieve a height of 115 feet or more in a vehicle.	10
Front Flipper	Execute two forward flips in a single jump in a moving vehicle.	20
Timed Stunt Driver	Execute six car stunts in 60 seconds.	20
Base Jumper	Jump from the top of the Agency Tower and land in the water below.	10
Stunt Driver	Successfully execute five car stunts - front & back flips, barrel rolls, a long jump.	20
Orb Hunter	Collect 300 Hidden Orbs.	50
Free Runner	Collect 500 Agility Orbs.	50
Repo Man	Commandeer 100 gang-controlled vehicles.	10
Los Muertos Intel Master	Locate all Los Muertos dossier targets.	10
Volk Intel Master	Locate all Volk dossier targets.	10
Shai-Gen Intel Master	Locate all Shai-Gen dossier targets.	10
First Blood	Eliminate the first of 21 gang bosses.	10
Los Muertos Cleanser	Murder Los Muertos - kill all Los Muertos gang members.	20
Volk Cleanser	Eviscerate the Volk - take out all Volk gang members.	40
Shai-Gen Cleanser	Assassinate Shai-Gen - kill all Shai-Gen gang members.	50
The Trifecta	Wipe the city clean by taking out all members of all three gangs.	50
Rampage	Wreak havoc in 60-second increments.	20
Take Me To Your Supply Point	Unlock your first Supply Point.	10
It's Good To Be Connected	Unlock all Supply Points.	30
Airtime Assassin	Shoot and kill 5 gang members in a single jump (while airborne).	10
Shot-putter	Throw any object (other than a grenade) 205 feet or more.	10
Global Impact	Kill 15 gang members using the Observatory Globe.	15
Ring Leader	Drive through all of the unique Stunt Markers.	20
Chain Banger	Blow up 100 explosive objects in 60 seconds.	10
Double Trouble	Double your fun - complete your first mission in Co-op mode.	10
Tag Teamer	Partner up and complete every mission in Co-op mode.	40
Road Warrior	Successfully complete all 14 Road Races.	30
Over Our Heads	Successfully complete all 12 Rooftop Races.	30

DARK SECTOR

ACHIEVEMENTS

NAME	GOAL/REQUIREMENT	POINTS
Prologue	Complete Chapter 1.	10
Exposure	Complete Chapter 2.	10
Baggage Claim	Complete Chapter 3.	10
Moths To The Flame	Complete Chapter 4.	10
The Shipment	Complete Chapter 5.	10
The Bait	Complete Chapter 6.	10
Industrial Evolution	Complete Chapter 7.	10
Unnatural History	Complete Chapter 8.	10
Threshold Guardian	Complete Chapter 9.	10
The Dark Sector	Complete the Game.	100
Dark Sector - Brutal Difficulty	Complete the Game on Brutal Difficulty.	110
Headhunter	Decapitate 30 Enemies.	10
Incinerator	Incinerate 30 Enemies.	10
Electrician	Electrocute 30 Enemies.	10
Jack Frost	Kill 30 Frozen Enemies.	10
Finesse	Kill 30 enemies with Aftertouch.	40
Hardball	Kill 30 enemies with Power-throw.	35
Sharpshooter	Get 30 Headshots.	10
Glaive Master	Complete a Level by Only Using the Glaive.	10
The Finisher	Perform 30 Finishers.	10
Double Decap Latte	Get Two Decapitations In One Shot.	15
Skeet Shooter	Shoot 10 Projectiles in Mid-flight.	10
Weaponsmith	Apply 5 Upgrades in the Black Market.	10
Greed	Collect over 50,000 rubles.	10
Researcher	Collect 10 Weapon Upgrades.	10
Master Researcher	Collect All the Weapon Upgrades.	15
Rebound	Kill an Enemy With a Reflected Projectile.	15
Glory	Finish Best Overall in a Ranked Infection Match (Multiplayer).	30
Veteran	Score 500 Points in Ranked Infection Games (Multiplayer).	30
Hero	Score 2000 Points in Ranked Infection Games (Multiplayer).	40
Champion	Finish Best Overall in a Ranked Epidemic Match (Multiplayer).	30
Comrade	Score 500 Points in Ranked Epidemic Games (Multiplayer).	30
Hero of the People	Score 2000 Points in Ranked Epidemic Games (Multiplayer).	40

SECRET ACHIEVEMENTS

NAME	GOAL/REQUIREMENT	POINTS
Colossus	Defeated the Colossus.	50
Stalker	Defeated the Stalker.	65
Nemesis	Defeated the Nemesis.	85
Ghost	Used Shifting to Get a Finisher.	35
Jack the Jackal	Take the Jackal for a Rid	35

THE DARKNESS

ACHIEVEMENTS
GENERAL AWARDS

NAME	GOAL/REQUIREMENT	POINTS
Beginnings	Complete the first part of the game.	25
Into the Dark	Complete the second part of the game.	50
Happy Birthday	Acquire Creeping Dark.	25
No Man's Land	Acquire Demon Arm.	25
Hills	Acquire Darkness Guns.	25
Crazy for You	Acquire Black Hole.	25
Darkling Master	Collect all Darkling types.	15
One with the Dark	Achieve maximum Darkness level.	25

OVERLORD

NAME	GOAL/REQUIREMENT	POINTS
Anti Hero	Complete the game on Normal difficulty.	25
Legendary Dark	Complete the game on Hard difficulty.	55
Roadkill	Kill the workers in the tunnel.	10
Ghandi	Explore Dutch Oven Harry's club without resorting to violence.	10
Romantic	Spend quality time with Jenny in her Chinatown apartment.	10
Heart of Gold	Complete all sub-missions.	50
Gunslinger	Kill seven enemies in 15 seconds.	25
Anti Air	Take out the Turkish Baths helicopter.	25
Take a Look at the Sky	Take down six airplanes.	10
Keeper of Secrets	Call 18 secret numbers.	10
Knuckle, Meet Face	Perform a melee kill for the first time.	5
Up Close and Personal	Perform an execution kill for the first time.	5
Executioner	Perform 25 execution kills.	10
Legendary Executioner	Perform 50 execution kills.	25
Picking Up Stuff	Unlock a collectible for the first time.	5
Gatherer	Unlock 25 collectibles.	5
The Collector	Unlock 50 collectibles.	10
The Obesessive Collector	Unlock 75 collectibles.	15
Completionist	Unlock 100 collectibles.	25

DARKNESS AWARDS

NAME	GOAL/REQUIREMENT	POINTS
Cannibal	Devour 300 enemies.	25
Rogue Killer	Kill 15 enemies using Creeping Dark.	15
Void Bringer	Kill 20 enemies using Black Hole.	15
Gunner	Kill 30 enemies using Darkness Guns.	15
Ripper	Kill 30 enemies using Demon Arm.	15
Fashionable	Collect all the Darkling outfits.	25
Summoner	Spawn five Darklings.	5
Legendary Summoner	Spawn 50 Darklings.	25
Bringing People Together	Trap five enemies within the Black Hole at the same time.	5
Darkness Master	Master all Darkness powers: Kill 30 enemies using Creeping Dark. Kill 40 enemies using Black Hole. Kill 60 enemies using Darkness Guns. Kill 60 enemies using Demon Arm. Spawn 50 Darklings.	100

MULTIPLAYER AWARDS

NAME	GOAL/REQUIREMENT	POINTS
Patriot	Capture the flag in a Capture the Flag game.	5
Flag Runner	Capture 20 flags in a Capture the Flag game.	5
Flag Owner	Capture 50 flags in a Capture the Flag game.	10
Hard to Kill	Get over 600 damage in multiplayer without dying.	5
Murderer	Kill enough players to achieve a Killing Streak within a multiplayer match.	5
Butcher	Claim 20 Killing Streaks in multiplayer.	25
Hoodlum	Be on the winning side in a multiplayer match in any of the multiplayer modes.	5
Mook	Be on the winning side in five multiplayer matches.	5
Henchman	Be on the winning side in 20 multiplayer matches.	15
Contract Killer	Be on the winning side in 50 multiplayer matches.	25
Made Man	Be on the winning side in 100 multiplayer matches.	35
The Don	Be on the winning side in 250 multiplayer matches.	45
Bullet Dodger	Finish a multiplayer match with less than five deaths (minimum of four players).	20

ACHIEVEMENTS

NAME	GOAL/REQUIREMENT	POINT VALUE
Dead On Arrival	Complete Chapter 1 on any difficulty setting	20
Lab Rat	Complete Chapter 2 on any difficulty setting	20
All Systems Go	Complete Chapter 3 on any difficulty setting	20
Cannon Fodder	Complete Chapter 4 on any difficulty setting	20
True Believer	Complete Chapter 5 on any difficulty setting	20
Greenhouse Effect	Complete Chapter 6 on any difficulty setting	20
S.O.S.	Complete Chapter 7 on any difficulty setting	20
Strange Transmissions	Complete Chapter 8 on any difficulty setting	20
Wreckage	Complete Chapter 9 on any difficulty setting	20
Keeper of the Faith	Complete Chapter 10 on any difficulty setting	20
Betrayed	Complete Chapter 11 on any difficulty setting	20
Exodus	Complete Chapter 12 on any difficulty setting	20
Epic Tier 3 Engineer	Complete the game on the hardest difficulty setting	150
Survivor	Complete the game on any difficulty setting	50
Pack Rat	Store 25 Items in the Safe	10
Story Teller	Collect 75 Logs	20
Legend Teller	Collect 150 Logs	40
Full Arsenal	Own every Weapon in the game	30
Z-Baller	Complete Level 6 in Zero-G Basketball	5
Merchant	Collect 8 schematics	10
Armstrong	Shoot 50 objects using Kinesis	10
Marksman	Dismember 20 Limbs	5
Surgeon	Dismember 500 Limbs	20
Butcher	Dismember 1000 Limbs	40
Freeze	Use Stasis on 50 enemies	15
Crackshot	Achieve a perfect score in the Shooting Gallery	5
Air Alert	Zero-G Jump over 100 times	10
One Gun	Beat the game using only the Plasma Cutter	40
Brawler	Kill at least 30 enemies with a melee attack	10
Maxed Out	Upgrade all weapons and equipment	75
Ragdoll Check	Force an enemy into a Gravity Panel 5 times	5
Big Spender	Spend 300,000 credits at the store	10
Full Contact	Kill 30 enemies with the Contact Beam	10
A Cut Above	Kill 30 enemies with the Ripper	10
Tool Time	Kill 30 enemies with the Plasma Cutter	10
Pusher	Kill 30 enemies with the Force Gun	10
Live With The Hot Ones	Kill 30 enemies with the Flamethrower	10
Autofire	Kill 30 enemies with the Pulse Rifle	10
Eviscerator	Kill 30 enemies with the Line Gun	10
There's Always Peng!	Find the Peng Treasure	15

SECRET ACHIEVEMENTS

NAME	GOAL/REQUIREMENT	POINT VALUE
Exterminator	Kill the Leviathan	15
Brute Force	Kill a Brute	15
Mindless Prey	Kill the Hive Mind	30
Playing Catch	Catch a Brute or Leviathan Pod using Kinesis	10
Don't get cocky, kid	Survive the ADS Cannon with over 50% shield strength remaining	10
Kickin it	Escape from a Lurker's grab attack 10 times	10
Slugger	Kill the Slug Boss with more than 50% shield strength remaining	10
Get off my ship!	Kill the Slug Boss	15

DEVIL MAY CRY 4

ACHIEVEMENTS

NAME	GOAL/REQUIREMENT	POINTS
A Comfortable Pace	Clear mission 11 in Human Mode.	10
Easy Does It	Clear all missions in Human Mode.	10
Half Way There	Clear mission 11 in Devil Hunter Mode.	10
Done and Done	Clear all missions in Devil Hunter Mode.	20
Rock and a Hard Place	Clear Mission 11 in Son of Sparda Mode	10
Hardly A Simple Task	Clear All Missions in Son of Sparda Mode	30
Easier Said Than Done	Clear Mission 11 in Dante Must Die Mode	10
All Bow Before You	Clear All Missions in Dante Must Die Mode	40
Step into the Light	Clear All Missions in Heaven or Hell Mode	10
Tonight, We Dine in Hell	Clear All Missions in Hell or Hell Mode	10
The Best of the Rest	Clear all missions in Human Mode with an S ranking.	20
A Cut Above	Clear all missions in Devil Hunter Mode with an S ranking.	30
A Stunning Feat	Clear all Missions in Son of Sparda Mode with an S Ranking	40
Never Say Die	Clear all Missions in Dante Must Die Mode with an S Ranking	50
A Throne of Glory	Clear all Game Modes	50
Nothing Left Unsaid	Clear all Secret Missions	10
The First Circle	Complete Stage 10 of the Bloody Palace	10
The Second Circle	Clear stage 20 of Bloody Palace Mode	10
The Third Circle	Clear stage 30 of Bloody Palace Mode	10
The Fourth Circle	Clear stage 40 of Bloody Palace Mode	10
The Fifth Circle	Clear stage 50 of Bloody Palace Mode	10
The Sixth Circle	Clear stage 60 of Bloody Palace Mode	10
The Seventh Circle	Clear stage 70 of Bloody Palace Mode	10
The Eight Circle	Clear stage 80 of Bloody Palace Mode	10
The Ninth Circle	Clear stage 90 of Bloody Palace Mode	10
Covered in Blood	Clear All Bloody Palace Mode stages	40
King of the Palace	Clear All Bloody Palace stages with an S Ranking	50
Speak of the Devil	Clear the game with Super Nero (Dante)	20
Smokin'!	Complete a Stylish Rank S (Smokin'!) combo.	10
Smokin' Style!!	Complete a Stylish Rank SS (Smokin' Style!!) combo.	10
Smokin' Sick Style!!!	Complete a Stylish Rank SSS (Smokin' Sick Style!!!) combo.	10
Simply Spectacular	Complete a mission with an S ranking.	10
Modus Vivendi	Extend the Vitality Gauge to maximum capacity	10
Bat Out of Hell	Extend the Devil Trigger Gauge to maximum capacity	10
River of Red	Acquire 10,000 Red Orbs.	10
Your Cup Runeth Over	Acquire 100,000 Red Orbs.	20
Red Orb Millionaire	Acquire 1,000,000 Red Orbs.	40
Filled with Pride	Acquire 10,000 Proud Souls.	10
Brimming with Pride	Acquire 100,000 Proud Souls.	20
Proud Millionaire	Acquire 1,000,000 Proud Souls.	40
Rookie Devil Hunter	Defeat a total of 100 enemies.	10
Skilled Devil Hunter	Defeat a total of 1,000 enemies.	30
Legendary Devil Hunter	Defeat a total of 10,000 enemies.	50
Item Collector	Acquire a maximum number of all items	50
Skill Collector - Nero	Acquire all of Nero's skills	50
Skill Collector - Dante	Acquire all of Dante's skill	50

ETERNAL SONATA

ACHIEVEMENTS

NAME	GOAL/REQUIREMENT	POINTS
Raindrops	Chapter 1 Raindrops has been completed.	10
Revolution	Chapter 2 Revolution has been completed.	10
Fantaisie-Impromptu	Chapter 3 Fantaisie-Impromptu has been completed.	10

NAME	GOAL/REQUIREMENT	POINTS
Grande Valse Brilliante	Chapter 4 Grande Valse Brilliante has been completed.	10
Nocturne	Chapter 5 Nocturne has been completed.	10
Tristesse	Chapter 6 Tristesse has been completed.	10
Heroic	Chapter 7 Heroic has been completed.	10
Heaven's Mirror	Final Chapter Heaven's Mirror has been completed.	10
Grand Finale	Final Chapter Heaven's Mirror has been completed with all characters remaining.	70
Unlocked Party Level 2	Party Level 2 can now be selected.	10
Unlocked Party Level 3	Party Level 3 can now be selected.	10
Unlocked Party Level 4	Party Level 4 can now be selected.	10
Unlocked Party Level 5	Party Level 5 can now be selected.	10
Unlocked Party Level 6	Party Level 6 can now be selected.	20
Hero's Gate	The Hero's Gate has been opened.	30
Rondo's Return	Rondo has been defeated in Unison.	50
Claves's Resurrection	Unison has been completed and Claves has been resurrected.	50
Soul Released	The soul of Chord, the first mineral powder test subject, has been released.	79
Xylophone's Treasure	The hidden treasure in the secret room on the top floor of Xylophone Tower has been acquired.	80
Pirates' Treasure	The mystery behind the the pirates' treasure has been solved and the treasure has been acquired.	80
Score Piece Collector	All the score pieces scattered throughout the world have been collected.	100
EZI Worshipper	All the items related to EZI have been collected.	321

FALLOUT 3

ACHIEVEMENTS

NAME	GOAL/REQUIREMENT	POINT VALUE
Vault 101 Citizenship Award	Got the Pip-Boy 3000	10
The G.O.A.T. Whisperer	Took the G.O.A.T.	10
Escape!	Completed "Escape!"	20
Following in His Footsteps	Completed "Following in His Footsteps"	20
Galaxy News Radio	Completed "Galaxy News Radio"	20
Scientific Pursuits	Completed "Scientific Pursuits"	20
Tranquility Lane	Completed "Tranquility Lane"	20
The Waters of Life	Completed "The Waters of Life"	20
Picking up the Trail	Completed "Picking up the Trail"	20
Rescue from Paradise	Completed "Rescue from Paradise"	20
Finding the Garden of Eden	Completed "Finding the Garden of Eden"	20
The American Dream	Completed "The American Dream"	20
Take it Back!	Completed "Take it Back!"	40
Big Trouble in Big Town	Completed "Big Trouble in Big Town"	20
The Superhuman Gambit	Completed "The Superhuman Gambit"	20
The Wasteland Survival Guide	Completed "The Wasteland Survival Guide"	20
Those!	Completed "Those!"	20
The Nuka-Cola Challenge	Completed "The Nuka-Cola Challenge"	20
Head of State	Completed "Head of State"	20
The Replicated Man	Completed "The Replicated Man"	20
Blood Ties	Completed "Blood Ties"	20
Oasis	Completed "Oasis"	20
The Power of the Atom	Completed "The Power of the Atom"	20
Tenpenny Tower	Completed "Tenpenny Tower"	20
Strictly Business	Completed "Strictly Business"	20
You Gotta Shoot 'Em in the Head	Completed "You Gotta Shoot 'Em in the Head"	20

OVERLORD

NAME	GOAL/REQUIREMENT	POINT VALUE
Stealing Independence	Completed "Stealing Independence"	20
Trouble on the Homefront	Completed "Trouble on the Homefront"	20
Agatha's Song	Completed "Agatha's Song"	20
Reilly's Rangers	Completed "Reilly's Rangers"	20
Reaver	Reached Level 8 with Bad Karma	10
Mercenary	Reached Level 8 with Neutral Karma	10
Protector	Reached Level 8 with Good Karma	10
Harbinger of War	Reached Level 14 with Bad Karma	20
Pinnacle of Survival	Reached Level 14 with Neutral Karma	20
Ambassador of Peace	Reached Level 14 with Good Karma	20
Scourge of Humanity	Reached Level 20 with Bad Karma	30
Paradigm of Humanity	Reached Level 20 with Neutral Karma	30
Last, Best Hope of Humanity	Reached Level 20 with Good Karma	30
Weaponsmith	Made one of every custom weapon	30
Doesn't Play Well with Others	Killed 300 people	20
Slayer of Beasts	Killed 300 creatures	20
Silver-Tongued Devil	Won 50 Speech Challenges	20
Data Miner	Hacked 50 terminals	20
Keys are for Cowards	Picked 50 locks	20
One-Man Scouting Party	Discovered 100 locations	20
Psychotic Prankster	Placed a grenade or mine while pickpocketing	10
The Bigger They Are…	Kill all the Super Mutant Behemoths	20
Yes, I Play with Dolls	Collected 10 Vault-Tec Bobbleheads	10
Vault-Tec C.E.O.	Collected 20 Vault-Tec Bobbleheads	30

GEARS OF WAR

CAMPAIGN ACHIEVEMENTS

GAME COMPLETION ON CASUAL CAMPAIGN ACHIEVEMENTS	TYPE	DIFFICULTY	POINTS	DESCRIPTION
Prison Breakout	Campaign	Easy	10	Complete the Tutorial (on any difficulty).
Completed Act 1 on Casual	Campaign	Easy	10	Complete Act 1 on Casual Difficulty.
Completed Act 2 on Casual	Campaign	Easy	10	Complete Act 2 on Casual Difficulty.
Completed Act 3 on Casual	Campaign	Easy	10	Complete Act 3 on Casual Difficulty.
Completed Act 4 on Casual	Campaign	Easy	10	Complete Act 4 on Casual Difficulty.
Completed Act 5 on Casual	Campaign	Easy	10	Complete Act 5 on Casual Difficulty.
Mercenary (unlocks Gamer Pic)	Campaign	Easy	10	Complete all Acts on Casual Difficulty.

GEARS OF WAR 2

ACHIEVEMENTS

NAME	GOAL/REQUIREMENT	POINT VALUE
Green as Grass	Train the rook (any difficulty)	10
It's a Trap!	Story progression in Act 1, Chapter 2	10
Escort Service	Story progression in Act 1, Chapter 4	10
Girl About Town	Story progression in Act 1, Chapter 6	10
That Sinking Feeling	Story progression in Act 2, Chapter 1	10
Freebaird!	Story progression in Act 2, Chapter 5	10
Heartbroken	Story progression in Act 2, Chapter 6	10

NAME	GOAL/REQUIREMENT	POINT VALUE
Longitude and Attitude	Story progression in Act 3, Chapter 3	10
Tanks for the Memories	Story progression in Act 3, Chapter 4	10
Water Sports	Story progression in Act 3, Chapter 6	10
There's a Time for Us	Story progression in Act 4, Chapter 2	10
Better Wrapped in Beacon	Story progression in Act 4, Chapter 3	10
Have Fun Storming the Castle	Story progression in Act 4, Chapter 6	10
And the Horse You Rode in On	Story progression in Act 5, Chapter 1	10
You Are the Support, Son	Story progression in Act 5, Chapter 2	10
Brumak Rodeo	Story progression in Act 5, Chapter 4	10
Does This Look Infected to You?	Story progression in Act 5, Chapter 5	10
Tourist of Duty	Complete all campaign acts on Casual Difficulty	25
Guerilla Tactician	Complete all campaign acts on Normal Difficulty	50
Artist of War	Complete all campaign acts on Hardcore Difficulty	75
Suicide Missionary	Complete all campaign acts on Insane Difficulty	150
Collector	Recover 5 collectibles (any difficulty)	5
Pack Rat	Recover 20 collectibles (any difficulty)	15
Completionist	Recover all 41 collectibles (any difficulty)	30
One-Night Stand	Complete 1 chapter in co-op on any difficulty (Marcus or Dom)	10
Open Relationship	Complete 10 chapters in co-op on any difficulty (Marcus or Dom)	30
Friends with Benefits	Complete all acts in co-op on any difficulty (Marcus or Dom)	50
Once More, With Feeling	Perform 30 perfect active reloads (any mode)	10
Takes a Licking	Melee 30 Tickers (any mode)	30
Organ Grinder	Kill 30 enemies with a cover mounted Mulcher (any mode)	10
Shock and Awe	Kill 30 enemies with the heavy Mortar (any mode)	10
Said the Spider to the Fly	Kill 10 enemies with a planted grenade (any mode)	10
Crowd Control	Melee 10 enemies down with the Boomshield equipped (any mode)	10
Smells Like Victory	Kill 30 enemies with the Scorcher Flamethrower (any mode)	10
Variety is the Spice of Death	Kill an enemy with every weapon in the game (any mode)	30
Seriously 2.0	Kill 100,000 enemies (any mode)	50
Standing Here, Beside Myself	Win 3 matches of Wingman (public)	10
Beat the Meatflag	Capture 10 meatflags in Submission (public)	10
It's Good to be the King	Win 10 rounds of Guardian as the leader (public)	10
You Go Ahead, I'll Be Fine	Win three matches of King of the Hill (public)	10
Back to Basic	Successfully complete the 5 lessons of multiplayer Training Grounds	10
Party Like It's 1999	Play 1999 rounds of multiplayer (any mode)	30
Around the World, Again	Win a multiplayer match on each map (any mode)	30
Dirty, Dirty Horde	Survive the first 10 waves of Horde (any difficulty, any map)	20
Hoard the Horde	Survive all 50 waves of Horde (any difficulty, any map)	30
Crossed Swords	Win 10 chainsaw duels (any mode)	10
A Parting Gift	Kill 10 enemies with a grenade while down but not out (any mode)	20
Pound of Flesh	Use a meatshield to save your life 10 times (any mode)	10
Photojournalist	Submit a spectator photo	10
Kick 'Em When They're Down	Perform all 11 unique executions on a downed enemy	10

XBOX 360™ ACHIEVEMENTS

GAME COMPLETION ON HARDCORE

CAMPAIGN ACHIEVEMENTS	TYPE	DIFFICULTY	POINTS	DESCRIPTION
Completed Act 1 on Hardcore	Campaign	Medium	20	Complete Act 1 on Hardcore Difficulty.
Completed Act 2 on Hardcore	Campaign	Medium	20	Complete Act 2 on Hardcore Difficulty.
Completed Act 3 on Hardcore	Campaign	Medium	20	Complete Act 3 on Hardcore Difficulty.
Completed Act 4 on Hardcore	Campaign	Medium	20	Complete Act 4 on Hardcore Difficulty.
Completed Act 5 on Hardcore	Campaign	Medium	20	Complete Act 5 on Hardcore Difficulty.
Soldier (unlocks Gamer Pic)	Campaign	Medium	20	Complete all Acts on Hardcore Difficulty.

GAME COMPLETION ON INSANE

CAMPAIGN ACHIEVEMENTS	TYPE	DIFFICULTY	POINTS	DESCRIPTION
Completed Act 1 on Insane	Campaign	Hard	30	Complete Act 1 on Insane Difficulty.
Completed Act 2 on Insane	Campaign	Hard	30	Complete Act 2 on Insane Difficulty.
Completed Act 3 on Insane	Campaign	Hard	30	Complete Act 3 on Insane Difficulty.
CAMPAIGN ACHIEVEMENTS	TYPE	DIFFICULTY	POINTS	DESCRIPTION
Completed Act 4 on Insane	Campaign	Hard	30	Complete Act 4 on Insane Difficulty.
Completed Act 5 on Insane	Campaign	Hard	30	Complete Act 5 on Insane Difficulty.
Commando (unlocks Gamer Pic)	Campaign	Hard	30	Complete all Acts on Insane Difficulty.

COG TAGS

CAMPAIGN ACHIEVEMENTS	TYPE	DIFFICULTY	POINTS	DESCRIPTION
Time to Remember	Campaign	Easy	10	Recover 10 COG Tags (on any difficulty).
Honor Bound	Campaign	Medium	20	Recover 20 COG Tags (on any difficulty).
For the Fallen	Campaign	Hard	30	Recover 30 COG Tags (on any difficulty).

KILLING BOSSES

CAMPAIGN ACHIEVEMENTS	TYPE	DIFFICULTY	POINTS	DESCRIPTION
My Love for You is Like a Truck	Campaign	Hard	30	Defeat a Berserker on Hardcore Difficulty.
Broken Fingers	Campaign	Hard	30	Defeat a Corpser on Hardcore Difficulty.
A Dish Best Served Cold	Campaign	Hard	30	Defeat General RAAM on Hardcore Difficulty.

GAME SKILLS

CAMPAIGN ACHIEVEMENTS	TYPE	DIFFICULTY	POINTS	DESCRIPTION
Zen and the Art of Reloading	Campaign	Easy	10	Perform 25 Perfect Active Reloads (on any difficulty).
Zen and the Art Part 2	Campaign	Medium	20	Perform 5 Perfect Active Reloads in a row (on any difficulty).
Clusterluck	Campaign	Medium	20	Kill 3 enemies at once 10 different times (on any difficulty).

CO-OP ACHIEVEMENTS

CO-OP SPECIFIC ACHIEVEMENTS	TYPE	DIFFICULTY	POINTS	DESCRIPTION
Dom-curious	Co-op	Easy	10	Complete 1 chapter as Dominic Santiago on any difficulty.
Domination	Co-op	Medium	20	Complete 10 chapters as Dominic Santiago on any difficulty.

CO-OP SPECIFIC ACHIEVEMENTS	TYPE	DIFFICULTY	POINTS	DESCRIPTION
I Can't Quit You Dom	Co-op	Hard	30	Complete all Acts in Co-Op on any difficulty.

VERSUS ACHIEVEMENTS

VERSUS ACHIEVEMENTS	TYPE	DIFFICULTY	POINTS	DESCRIPTION
Don't You Die on Me	Versus	Easy	10	Revive 100 teammates in Ranked Matches.
A Series of Tubes	Versus	Medium	20	Host 50 complete Ranked Matches.

WEAPON MASTERY

CAMPAIGN ACHIEVEMENTS	TYPE	DIFFICULTY	POINTS	DESCRIPTION
Fall Down Go Boom	Versus	Easy	10	Kill 100 enemies in Ranked Matches with the Boomshot.
Pistolero	Versus	Medium	20	Kill 100 enemies in Ranked Matches with a Pistol.
The Nuge	Versus	Medium	20	Kill 100 enemies in Ranked Matches with the Torquebow.
I Spy With My Little Eye	Versus	Medium	20	Kill 100 enemies in Ranked Matches with the Longshot.
Don't Hurt 'Em	Versus	Medium	20	Kill 100 enemies in Ranked Matches with the Hammer of Dawn.

HUMILIATION MASTERY

CAMPAIGN ACHIEVEMENTS	TYPE	DIFFICULTY	POINTS	DESCRIPTION
It's a Massacre	Versus	Easy	10	Kill 100 enemies in Ranked Matches with the Chainsaw.
Curb Appeal	Versus	Medium	20	Kill 100 enemies in Ranked Matches with the Curb Stomp.
Capital Punishment	Versus	Medium	20	Kill 100 enemies in Ranked Matches with an Execution.
Crackdown	Versus	Medium	20	Kill 100 enemies in Ranked Matches with Melee.
Is it a Spider?	Versus	Medium	20	Kill 100 enemies in Ranked Matches with Grenade Tag.
The Money Shot	Versus	Medium	20	Kill 100 enemies in Ranked Matches with a Head Shot.

VERSUS SUCCESS

CAMPAIGN ACHIEVEMENTS	TYPE	DIFFICULTY	POINTS	DESCRIPTION
Always Remember Your First	Versus	Easy	10	Finish playing a Versus Ranked Match.
Don't Hate the Player	Versus	Easy	10	Finish with the highest points in a Ranked Match.
Mix it Up	Versus	Medium	20	Win a Ranked Match in every Versus game type.
Can't Touch Us	Versus	Medium	20	Win 10 Ranked Matches without losing a Round.
Around the World	Versus	Hard	30	Win a Ranked Match on every Versus map.
Seriously... (unlocks Gamer Pic)	Versus	Hard	50	Kill 10,000 people in Versus Ranked Match total.

ACHIEVEMENTS

NAME	GOAL/REQUIREMENT	POINTS
Off The Boat	Complete the first mission.	5
One Hundred And Eighty	In a darts game score 180 with 3 darts.	10
Pool Shark	Beat a friend at pool.	10
King of QUB3D	Beat the High Score in QUB3D.	15
Finish Him	Complete 10 melee counters in 4 minutes.	15
Genetically Superior	Come first in 20 singleplayer street races.	25
Wheelie Rider	Do a wheelie lasting at least 500 feet on a motorbike.	30
Gobble Gobble	Score 3 strikes in a row, a turkey, in 10-pin bowling.	10
Driving Mr. Bellic	Unlock the special ability of taxi.	10
Rolled Over	Do 5 car rolls in a row from one crash.	30
Walk Free	Lose a 4 star wanted rating by outrunning the cops.	50
Courier Service	Complete all 10 package delivery jobs.	10
Retail Therapy	Unlock the special ability of buying guns from a friend.	10
Chain Reaction	You must blow up 10 vehicles in 10 seconds.	20
One Man Army	Survive 5 minutes on 6 star wanted level.	40
Lowest Point	Complete mission "Roman's Sorrow."	5
Order Fulfilled	Complete all 10 Exotic Export orders.	10
Manhunt	Complete the most wanted side missions from the police computer.	15
Cleaned The Mean Streets	Capture 20 criminals through the police computer.	20
Fed The Fish	Complete the mission "Uncle Vlad."	5
It'll Cost Ya	Complete a taxi ride without skipping from one island to another.	5
Sightseer	Fly on all helicopter tours of Liberty City.	5
Warm Coffee	Successfully date a girl to be invited into her house.	5
That's How We Roll!	Unlock the special ability of helicopter.	10
Half Million	Reach a balance of $500,000.	55
Impossible Trinity	Complete mission "Museum Piece."	10
Full Exploration	Unlock all the islands.	20
You Got The Message	Deliver all 30 cars ordered through text message.	20
Dare Devil	Complete 100% of the unique stunt jumps.	30
Assassin's Greed	Complete all 9 assassin missions.	20
Endangered Species	Collect every hidden package in the game.	50
Under The Radar	Fly underneath the main bridges in the game that cross water with a helicopter.	40
Dial B For Bomb	Unlock the special ability of phoning for a bomb to be placed.	10
Gracefully Taken	Complete mission "I'll Take Her."	10
Liberty City (5)	After meeting all possible friends, the ones left alive all like you above 90%.	20
No More Strangers	Meet all random characters.	5
That Special Someone	Complete mission "That Special Someone".	10
You Won!	Complete the final mission.	60
Liberty City Minute	Complete the story missions in less than 30 hours.	30
Key To The City	Achieve 100% in "Game progress" statistic.	100
Teamplayer	Kill 5 players who are not in your team, in any ranked multiplayer team game.	10
Cut Your Teeth	Earn a personal rank promotion in multiplayer.	5
Join The Midnight Club	Win a ranked multiplayer race without damaging your vehicle too much and with damage enabled.	10
Fly The Co-op	Beat our time in ranked versions of "Deal Breaker", "Hangman's NOOSE" and "Bomb da Base II."	15
Taking It For The Team	Be on the winning team in all ranked multiplayer team games.	10
Top Of The Food Chain	Kill 20 players with a pistol in a ranked multiplayer deathmatch.	10
Top The Midnight Club	Come first in 20 different ranked standard multiplayer races.	20
Wanted	Achieve the highest personal rank in multiplayer.	20

NAME	GOAL/REQUIREMENT	POINTS
Auf Wiedersehen Petrovic	Win all ranked multiplayer variations, all races and "Cops 'n Crooks," as both sides.	30
Let Sleeping Rockstars Lie	Kill a Rockstar developer in a ranked multiplayer match.	10

GUITAR HERO II

ACHIEVEMENTS

NAME	GOAL/REQUIREMENT	POINTS
100K Club	Get 100,000 points in a song.	10
200K Club	Get 200,000 points in a song.	10
300K Club	Get 300,000 points in a song.	30
400K Club	Get 400,000 points in a song.	30
Champagne Room V.I.P.	Get 500,000 points in a song.	30
Roadie	Unlock Rat Cellar.	10
New Kid	Unlock Blackout Bar.	10
Young Gun	Unlock RedOctane Club.	10
Axe Grinder	Unlock Rock City Theater.	10
Shredder	Unlock Vans Warped Tour.	10
Rock Star	Unlock Harmonix Arena.	10
Guitar Hero	Unlock Stonehenge.	10
Dimebag Darrell Award	Get a 100 note streak.	10
Eddie Van Halen Award	Get a 500 note streak.	30
Yngwie Malmsteen Award	Get a 1000 note streak.	30
Easy Tour Champ	Beat the Easy tour.	10
Medium Tour Champ	Beat the Medium tour.	30
Hard Tour Champ	Beat the Hard tour.	30
Expert Tour Champ	Beat the Expert tour.	30
Sandbox Hero Award	Earn five stars on all songs in the Easy tour.	30
Most Likely to Succeed Award	Earn five stars on all songs in the Medium tour.	30
Guitarmaggedon Award	Earn five stars on all songs in the Hard tour.	30
Start a Real Band Already Award	Earn five stars on all songs in the Expert tour.	30
Rock School Grad	Complete all tutorials.	10
Scoremonger Award	Get an 8x multiplier.	10
Perfectionist Award	Get 100% notes hit on a song.	30
Rock Snob Award	Refuse to play an encore.	10
Long Road Ahead Award	Fail a song on Easy.	10
Hendrix Award	Beat a song with lefty flip on.	10
Teacher's Pet Award	Practice three different songs.	10
Saturday Morning Award	Beat Trogdor and Thunder Horse.	10
Kick the Bucket Award	Beat Jordan on Expert.	30
Gear Head Award	Buy all guitars.	30
Fanatical Completionist Award	Buy all guitar finishes.	30
Record Collector Award	Buy all songs.	10
Life of the Party Award	Buy all characters.	10
Fashion Plate Award	Buy all outfits.	10
Extra Credit Award	View the credits.	10
Big Spender Award	Spend $10,000 at the store.	10
Scenester Award	Beat all the unlock songs.	10
Joan & Lita Award	Get a 100 note streak in Cooperative.	30
Joe & Steven Award	Get a 500 note streak in Cooperative.	30
Keef & Mick Award	Get a 1000 note streak in Cooperative.	30
Lennon & McCartney Award	Get an 8x streak in Cooperative.	10
Page & Plant Award	Get 100% notes hit on a song in Cooperative.	30
200K Pair	Get 200,000 points on a song in Cooperative.	30
400K Pair	Get 400,000 points on a song in Cooperative.	30
600K Pair	Get 600,000 points on a song in Cooperative.	30
800K Pair	Get 800,000 points on a song in Cooperative.	30
Millionaire Pair	Get 1,000,000 points on a song in Cooperative.	30

OVERLOAD

GUITAR HERO III

ACHIEVEMENTS

NAME	GOAL/REQUIREMENT	POINTS
Enlightened Guitarist	Gold Star 20 songs on Expert	30
Hendrix Reborn	Complete Career Lefty and Righty	10
Who Needs the Power	200k on Cult of Personality without Star Power	15
Whammy Mania	Use the Whammy Bar on every held note on Number of the Beast	15
Star Mania	Activate Star Power 3 times on Through the Fire and Flames on Expert	15
Life of the Party	Host Ranked Online matches and win 15 consecutive songs	10
Search and Destroy	Join Ranked Online matches and win 15 consecutive songs	10
Too Many to Count	Hit 250,000 notes in Career	25
Never Gonna Spend It All	Earn $350,000 in career lifetime earnings	10
That's What Friends Are For	Complete Co-op Career	25
Back Up Hero	Complete all songs as the back-up guitar player	10
Guitar Wizard	Complete all Co-op as the lead guitarist	10
100 Million!?! Gulp!?!	Earn 100,000,000 points total in Career	30
Streaker	Earn a 150 note streak in a Ranked Online Battle mode match	10
Tone Deaf	Beat any song on the expert difficulty with the games sound options turned down to zero	5
Easy Rider	Complete a Career on the Easy Difficulty	5
Medium Rare	Complete Career Mode on the Medium difficulty	10
Always Hard	Complete Career on the Hard difficulty	15
Solo Career	Complete all Career difficulties	25
Button Masher	Win 15 consecutive Ranked songs online using a standard controller	5
Buy a Guitar Already	Play through a career on the Hard or Expert difficulty using a standard controller	15
Big Ol' Pile of Wins	Win 500 Online Ranked matches	20
The Long Road Ahead	Complete all difficulties in Career, buy everything from the shop and complete 100 online matches	100
Meet Your Maker	Beat one of the creators of Guitar Hero 3 at their own game	20
Right Hand of God	Complete Career Mode on the Expert difficulty	20
Bronze Streaker	Earn a 100 note Streak in Career or Quick Play	5
Silver Streaker	Earn a 250 note streak in Career or Quick Play	10
Gold Streaker	Earn a 500 note streak in Career or Quick Play	15
Streak Master	Earn a 1000 note streak in Career or Quick Play	20
First Big Score	Score 250,000 on a song	5
Half a Mill'	Score 500,000 on a song	10
Now That's Impressive	Score 750,000 on a song	20
Axe Grinder	Earn 5 stars on all songs on the Easy difficulty	10
Rock Guru	Earn 5 stars on all songs on the Medium difficulty	20
Shredder	Earn 5 stars on all songs on the Hard difficulty	30
Guitar Hero	Earn 5 stars on all songs on the Expert difficulty	75
Perfectionist	100% a song	10
Ready to Rock	Complete the tutorial	5
Axe Collector	Buy all the Guitars from the shop	5
Track Master	Buy all songs from the shop	5
Got 'em All	Buy all characters from the shop	5
A Couple of Streakers	Earn a 200 note streak in a Co-op match	5
Two Timer	Earn a 500 note streak in a Co-op match	10
Dynamic Duo	Earn a 1000 note streak in a Co-op match	15
Streak Masters	Earn a 2000 note streak in a Co-op match	20
Millionaire Club	Score 1,000,000 on any song in a Co-op match	20
Higher Than Most	Score 700,000 on any song in a Co-op match	20
Easy Duo	Earn 5 stars on all Co-op songs for the Easy difficulty	10
Medium Duo	Earn 5 stars on all Co-op songs for the Medium difficulty	20

NAME	GOAL/REQUIREMENT	POINTS
Hard Duo	Earn 5 stars on all Co-op songs on the Hard difficulty	30
Living Legends	5 Star all Co-op songs on Expert	75
Leaders of the Pack	100% a song in a Co-op match	10
Two by Four	Get an 8X multiplier in a Co-op game	5
Half Mill' Club	Score 500,000 on any song in a Co-op match	10
Burnin' a Hole in Your Pocket	Buy everything from the store	10
The Inhuman Achievement	Complete Through the Fire and Flames on Expert	15

SECRET ACHIEVEMENTS

NAME	GOAL/REQUIREMENT	POINTS
Tail Between Your Legs	Refuse a boss battle	0
Blowin' It	Fail any song 10 times	5
Almost Got It	Fail a song past 90% completion	5

GUITAR HERO: AEROSMITH

ACHIEVEMENTS

NAME	GOAL/REQUIREMENT	POINT VALUE
Get Your Wings	Complete the Tutorial	10
Make It	Complete the Career on Easy	20
Movin' Out	Complete the Career on Medium	30
Rock in a Hard Place	Complete the Career on Hard	50
Dream On	Complete the Career on Expert	75
Aerosmith	Unlock Aerosmith as the playable band	15
Jailbait	Play a song at the Nipmuc venue	5
Cheesecake	Earn a 100 note streak in Career or Quick Play (Local only)	10
Crazy	Earn a 500 note streak in Career or Quick Play (Local Only)	20
No More, No More	Perform all the Encores	10
Kings and Queens	Purchase all the playable characters from The Vault	20
Big Ten Inch Record	Purchase all the bonus songs	20
Toys in the Attic	Purchase all guitars from The Vault (Bass/Lead/Rhythm)	20
Same Old Song and Dance	Complete every song in the setlist and the Vault (Local only)	50
Score Hero	Score "325,000" or more on the song "Train Kept a Rollin'"	30
Get it Up	Score 2,000,000 in the Career	30
Eat the Rich	Earn $50,000 in career earnings	30
I Don't Want to Miss a Thing	Earn a gold star rating on a song on Medium or harder difficulty (Local only)	30
Gems	Hit every star power phrase on a song (Local or Xbox LIVE)	25
Sick as a Dog	Earn a 5 star rating for a song on Medium or harder (Local or Xbox LIVE)	25
Ain't That a B***h	Earn a gold star rating on a song (Local only)	20
Big Ones	Earn a 300 note streak in Co-op (Local or Xbox LIVE)	15
Cryin'	Earn a 600 note streak in Co-op (Local or Xbox LIVE)	25
Combination	Earn an 8x multiplier in Co-op (Local or Xbox LIVE)	5
Let the Music Do the Talking	Earn a gold star rating on a Co-op song (Local or Xbox LIVE)	40
When I Needed You	Activate Star Power 3 times in a song in a Co-op match (Local or Xbox LIVE)	15
What it Takes	Play 20 online ranked matches of any game type	35
Deuces Are Wild	Complete all songs on the setlist as the lead guitarist (Local or Xbox LIVE)	40
My Fist Your Face	Win an online ranked Pro Face-Off match	20
Don't Get Mad, Get Even	Win an online ranked Face-Off match	20
Walkin' the Dog	Win an online ranked Pro-Face Off match by 10,000 or more points	20

NAME	GOAL/REQUIREMENT	POINT VALUE
Soul Saver	Win a ranked online Battle Mode match with a Death Drain attack	20
Love Me Two Times	Complete all songs on the setlist as the Bass/Rhythm guitarist (Local or Xbox LIVE - primary user)	40

SECRET ACHIEVEMENTS

NAME	GOAL/REQUIREMENT	POINT VALUE
Subway	Played a song at the Max's Kansas City venue	10
On The Road Again	You unlocked the Orpheum Theater of Boston venue	10
Nine Lives	You unlocked the Moscow venue	10
Critical Mass	You unlocked the Half-Time Show venue	15
March 19th, 2001	You unlocked the Hall of Fame venue	20
Woman Of The World	You played a song with a female guitarist	10
Draw The Line	You turned down an encore	5
Spaced	You completed a song earning Star Power, but never used it	10
Dude Looks Like a Lady	Played a song as Izzy Sparks	10
Walk This Way	You purchased DMC from The Vault	10
Night in the Ruts	Bummer, you failed a song 10 times	10
Fallen Angels	Keep trying, you failed a Co-op song beyond 95% completion	15
Nobody's Fault	You failed 5 Co-op songs. Don't give up!	5
You See Me Crying	You lost an online ranked Pro Face-Off match	5
Falling Off	You lost an online ranked Face-Off match	5
Back in the Saddle	You rocked out as Tom Hamilton and Brad Whitford in a Co-op match	10

GUITAR HERO WORLD TOUR

ACHIEVEMENTS

NAME	GOAL/REQUIREMENT	POINT VALUE
Learning the Ropes	Complete a tutorial	5
One Time Solo Artist	Completed a song (Solo)	5
Stix	Perform as a Drummer (Band or Solo)	5
Yodeler	Perform as a Vocalist (Band or Solo)	5
Pick and Axe	Perform as a Guitarist (Band or Solo)	5
Feeding the Beast	Upload a song to GHTunes	5
Download Junkie	Download a few songs from GHTunes	5
A Pair Beats A Pair	Complete an Xbox LIVE 2 v 2 Pro Face-Off match (win or lose)	5
Survival of the Fittest	Complete an Xbox LIVE Battle Mode match win or lose	5
Mine is Bigger Than Yours	Complete an Xbox LIVE Band v Band match (win or lose)	5
First of Many	Complete a gig (Band or Solo)	10
One Man Band	Perform as every instrument at least once (Vocals, Lead, Bass & Drums)	10
Should We Stick Together?	Complete a song in a band (4 player band)	10
50 Note Posse	All band members get a 50 note streak at the same time (4 player band)	15
Easy There	Complete a Career on easy (Band or Solo)	25
Solo Artist	Complete a solo career (any difficulty)	25
Band on a Mission	Complete the majority of the gigs (Band or Solo)	25
Bling, Bling	Earn $1,000,000 in lifetime earnings	30
Top of the Charts	Complete a band career (any difficulty)	30
Medium Musician	Complete a Career on medium (Band or Solo)	30
Solid Gold Rockstars	100% a song as a band (4 player band)	30
Platinum Rockstars	100% a song as a band, hard or expert only (4 player band)	50

NAME	GOAL/REQUIREMENT	POINT VALUE
Hardcore	Complete a Career on hard (Band or Solo)	60
Hall of Famer	Complete a Career on expert (Band or Solo)	100
Jack of All Trades	Complete all instrument careers - any difficulty (Band or Solo)	150

SECRET ACHIEVEMENTS

NAME	GOAL/REQUIREMENT	POINT VALUE
Stamp Of Approval	You created your own band logo	5
One Of A Kind Axe	You created your own custom guitar	5
Warrior Of Rock	You created a male band member	5
Custom Beats	You created your own custom drums	5
Rock Maiden	You created a female band member	5
Inked	You created a custom tattoo	5
Leading Lady	You rocked out as Hayley Williams	10
The Experience	You rocked out as Jimi Hendrix	10
The Dark Prince	You rocked out as Ozzy Osbourne	10
Pumpkin Smasher	You rocked out as Billy Corgan	10
Bad to the Bone	You rocked out as the Skeleton	10
Wylde Man	You rocked out as Zack Wylde	10
Motorcity Madman	You rocked out as Ted Nugent	10
Don't Blink	You rocked out as Travis Barker	10
Shiny Metal Thingy	You rocked out as the Rockubot	10
Guitarist's Coattails	Get the highest score in the band as the lead or bass guitar (4 player band)	10
Vocalist's Coattails	You got the highest score in a band as the vocalist	10
1.21 Jigowatts?!?!	All band members activated star power at the same time	15
Super Group Unite	You earned an 8x multiplier with the rest of the band at the same time	15
Axe Museum	You unlocked all of the guitars	20
Get Your Boogie On	You scored 222,222 or higher on the song Satch Boogie as the Lead guitarist	30
Muse to My Ears	You scored 222,222 or higher on the song Assassin as a Drummer	30
Mike Checka'	You scored 123,450 or higher on the song Beat It as a Vocalist	30
Heavy Metall…	You scored 444,444 or more on the song Trapped Under Ice	35
TOOL of Destruction	You scored 444,444 or more on the song Schism	35

INFINITE UNDISCOVERY

ACHIEVEMENTS

NAME	GOAL/REQUIREMENT	POINT VALUE
Surprise!	Attack the enemy without being detected.	5
Blitzkrieg	Keep on surprising the enemy.	10
Infinitely Unobservant	Keep on getting surprised by the enemy.	10
Groundbreaking	Work on your ground combos.	20
Aerial Acrobat	Work on your aerial combos.	20
Down to Earth	Work on your down strikes.	20
Stalwart	Learn every battle skill.	30
Sagacious	Learn every spell.	30
Artistic	Learn every tune.	30
Compulsive	Obtain every item.	50
Mister Chef	Improve your cooking skills!	5
Claridian Chef	Keep improving your cooking skills!	10
Aspiring Chemist	Improve your alchemy skills!	5
Claridian Mind	Keep improving your alchemy skills!	10
Goldsmith	Improve your forging skills!	5
Claridian Hammer	Keep improving your forging skills!	10
Bestselling Author	Improve your writing skills!	5
Claridian Scribe	Keep improving your writing skills!	10
High Enchanter	Improve your enchanting skills!	5

NAME	GOAL/REQUIREMENT	POINT VALUE
Claridian Hand	Keep improving your enchanting skills!	10
Social Butterfly	Take advantage of your party's skills.	10
Filthy Rich	Gather as much Fol as you can.	20
Hero of the Millennium	Defeat as many enemies as you can.	20
Time for Glasses?	Keep on clocking hours.	30
Barrel of Lulz	Detonate all the barrels in prison.	15
On the Run	Deliver Aya to the village without getting hurt.	30
Rock, Stock, and Barrel	Use machines of war to destroy your foes.	30
Capell to the Rescue	Rescue the imprisoned.	30
Guardian	Deliver the villagers without letting any of them perish.	30
For the Children	Rescue the child before he gets hurt.	30
Reckless Driver	Use the carts in the mine.	30
The Tide of Battle	Watch out for the tsunami.	20
Imperial Guard	Hurry to the empress.	20
Marathon Man	Hurry to the village under attack.	20

SECRET ACHIEVEMENTS

NAME	GOAL/REQUIREMENT	POINT VALUE
Hephaestus's Hammer	Forged an azureal blade.	30
Creme de la Creme	Cooked a Heaven and Earth Dish.	30
Mad Scientist	Alchemized a Holy Grail.	30
Summa Cum Laude	Wrote "Will of the Universe"	30
Bad Influence	Allowed nine characters to vermify.	30
Cherubic Gatekeeper	Defeated Ethereal Queen in Hard mode.	30
Azure Avenger	Destroyed the Azure Chain.	10
Crimson Crusader	Destroyed the Crimson Chain.	10
Orange Officer	Destroyed the Orange Chain.	10
Cerulean Savior	Destroyed the Cerulean Chain.	10
Amber Ace	Destroyed the Amber Chain.	10
Ashen Assailant	Destroyed the Ashen Chain.	10
Vengeance at Last	Defeated the Dreadknight.	30
Decide	Defeated Veros.	45
Big Daddy's Back	Sigmund joined your party in the Seraphic Gate.	49
Seraphic Gatekeeper	Defeated Ethereal Queen in Infinity mode.	1

IRON MAN

ACHIEVEMENTS

NAME	GOAL/REQUIREMENT	POINTS
Sidekick	Complete all missions on Easy difficulty (or harder)	75
Hero	Complete all missions on Normal difficulty (or harder)	75
Super Hero	Complete all missions on Formidable difficulty	75
Disarmed	Destroy stockpiled Stark weapons in the Escape mission	25
City Protector	Destroy drones without civilian damage in the First Flight mission	25
Decommissioner	Destroy all Prometheus missiles in the Maggia Compound mission	25
In the Drink	Avoid civilian casualties in the Flying Fortress mission	25
Tatyana, Interrupted	Protect the nuclear facility in the Arctic Battle mission	25
Not a Scratch	Avoid harming the destroyer and its crew in the Lost Destroyer mission	25
Power Saver	Avoid disrupting the city's power supply in the On Defense mission	25
Shocking!	Protect outlying occupied buildings in the Save Pepper mission	25
Proton Shut Out	Prevent cannon attacks on civilian targets in the Island Meltdown mission	25
Escape Velocity	Sever the tether before the satellite overloads in the Space Tether mission	25

NAME	GOAL/REQUIREMENT	POINTS
You're Fired!	Destroy power regulators in the Iron Monger mission	25
Excelsior!	Complete Hero Objectives for all missions	70
Ten Rings Obsoleted	Complete the One Man Army vs. Ten Rings challenge without an armor breach	25
Maggia Obsoleted	Complete the One Man Army vs. Maggia challenge without an armor breach	25
Mercs Obsoleted	Complete the One Man Army vs. Mercs challenge without an armor breach	25
AIM Obsoleted	Complete the One Man Army vs. AIM challenge without an armor breach	25
AIM-X Obsoleted	Complete the One Man Army vs. AIM-X challenge without an armor breach	25
Air Superiority	Destroy all dropships before the Stark Gunship is stolen in the First Flight mission	15
Road King	Destroy all convoy vehicles in less than 2 minutes in the Stark Weapons mission	15
Launch Aborted	Destroy all Prometheus missiles within 10 minutes in the Maggia Compound mission	15
Collateral Damage	Destroy a Prometheus missile by destroying a fuel truck in the Maggia Compound mission	15
Personnel Vendetta	Defeat 20 soldiers in the Arctic Battle mission	15
Overkill	Defeat a soldier using the Unibeam	15
Smack down	Defeat Titanium Man before his second recharge in the On Defense mission	15
Impenetrable	Complete a mission (other than Escape or First Flight) without an armor breach	15
An Object in Motion	Destroy any target using a ramming attack	15
Grounded	Successfully grapple and throw a plane	15
Your Own Medicine	Damage or destroy another enemy while grappling a SAM launcher.	15
Long Shot	Damage or destroy another enemy while grappling a howitzer.	15
Hulk Smash!	Successfully grapple an opponent in the Hulkbuster armor	15
Ground Pound	Defeat an opponent using the ground pound in the Extremis armor	15
Classic Confrontation	Defeat Titanium Man using the Classic armor	15
Old School	Defeat Iron Monger using the Silver Centurion armor	15
Pugilist	Complete any mission (other than Escape) without using weapons systems	15
Eject!	Spare the US fighter pilots in the Stark Weapons mission	25
Guardian	Protect warehouse workers in the Maggia Factories mission	25

LEGO BATMAN

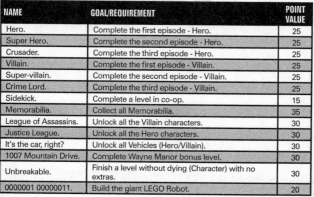

ACHIEVEMENTS

NAME	GOAL/REQUIREMENT	POINT VALUE
Hero.	Complete the first episode - Hero.	25
Super Hero.	Complete the second episode - Hero.	25
Crusader.	Complete the third episode - Hero.	25
Villain.	Complete the first episode - Villain.	25
Super-villain.	Complete the second episode - Villain.	25
Crime Lord.	Complete the third episode - Villain.	25
Sidekick.	Complete a level in co-op.	15
Memorabilia.	Collect all Memorabilia.	35
League of Assassins.	Unlock all the Villain characters.	30
Justice League.	Unlock all the Hero characters.	30
It's the car, right?	Unlock all Vehicles (Hero/Villain).	30
1007 Mountain Drive.	Complete Wayne Manor bonus level.	30
Unbreakable.	Finish a level without dying (Character) with no extras.	30
0000001 00000011.	Build the giant LEGO Robot.	20

NAME	GOAL/REQUIREMENT	POINT VALUE
The city is safe... for now.	100% game completion.	50
Cobblepot School of Driving.	Smash all the cars in the robot level.	20
Vigilante.	Rescue 25 civilians.	25
Be a Hero.	Super Hero on every level.	40
Super Builder.	Build 50 LEGO build-its.	20
Nice Outfit!	Collect all suits.	20
Dressed to Impress.	Get all suit upgrades.	20
The Richest Man in Gotham.	Max out the stud counter.	40
The Most Dangerous Man on Earth.	Defeat Joker, Two-Face, Riddler and Catwoman as Batman.	20
Heads I win, tails you lose.	Defeat 10 goons and 10 police officers with Two-Face in a level.	20
Who needs curiosity?	Defeat Catwoman 9 times.	20
Shot to the goon.	Defeat 8 goons in 8 seconds.	20
Throwing up.	Throw 50 policemen with superstrength.	20
Atomic Backbreaker.	As Bane do the Backbreaker on Batman.	20
Oh, I got a live one here!	Shock 30 people with Joker's hand buzzer.	10
Kill-a moth.	Defeat Killer Moth.	20
Smash Gordon.	Defeat Commissioner Gordon with Harley Quinn's Hammer.	20
Start of something wonderful.	Shock the Joker with the Joker.	15
Boy Wonder.	Perform 20 backflips in a row with Robin.	10
Thanks a million.	Complete Arkham Bonus level.	30
Is it a bird? Is it a plane?	Glide for 9 seconds.	10
Gentlemen, start your screaming.	Knock 5 people into the ground with a vehicle at once.	15
Natural Habitat.	Smash all street lights in Episode 1 Chapter 1.	10
Make it snappy.	Build the Croc ride on.	20
The Destroyer of Worlds.	Destroy 12 objects at once with Bat Bombs.	15
There and back.	Destroy 10 objects in one Batarang throw.	10
Kiss from a Rose.	Eat 15 enemies with the Venus ride on .	15
Ice to see you.	Freeze 50 enemies as Mr. Freeze.	15
Say hello to my little friends.	Destroy 20 policemen with penguin bombers.	15
Scare Tactics.	Scare 5 enemies with Scarecrow.	10
Down the rabbit hole.	Use Mad Hatter's mind control to walk 5 enemies to their deaths.	20
Eat floor... High fiber.	Slam 20 goons into the floor with Batman.	15

LEGO STAR WARS: THE COMPLETE SAGA

ACHIEVEMENTS

NAME	GOAL/REQUIREMENT	POINTS
The Phantom Menace	Finish Episode I in story mode.	20
Attack of the Clones	Finish Episode II in story mode.	20
Revenge of the Sith	Finish Episode III in story mode.	20
A New Hope	Finish Episode IV in story mode.	20
The Empire Strikes Back	Finish Episode V in story mode.	20
Return of the Jedi	Finish Episode VI in story mode.	20
Collector	Unlock all characters.	60
Secret Master	Collect all available red bricks.	60
Going for gold	Collect all available Gold Bricks.	60
Mini Mayhem	Collect all mini-kits.	60
100%	Complete the game to 100%	100
Lightsaber master	Perform 20 unblockable combo attacks.	20
Lightsaber defender	Perform 200 perfect lightsaber deflections.	20
Dodger	Perform 200 blaster character dodges.	20
Stormtrooper Slayer	Destroy 300 stormtroopers.	20

NAME	GOAL/REQUIREMENT	POINTS
Droid Slayer	Destory 300 droids.	20
Fighter Ace	Destroy 50 TIE fighters.	20
Yee Haw	Ride all mounts types & ride-ons.	20
Cash In	Sell your landspeeder to the Jawas.	20
Crowd Pleaser	Break Jar Jar 20 times.	20
Slam Dunk	Destroy 5 people with one attack (Jedi super slam).	20
Harmless?	Disable 5 Droidikas with R2D2.	20
Fire in the hole!	Destroy 10 characters with one thermal detonator.	20
Let the Wookiee win	Pull 25 arms off other characters.	20
Disco King	Set off all three Discos.	20
Use the Force Luke	Death Star Trench Run without Firing.	20
Bar Room Brawl	Start a Cantina Fight with 50 casualties.	20
LEGO build-master	Make 100 Build-its throughout the game.	20
Gopher	Max out the stud counter.	20
Cloud Cover	Finish Cloud City still wearing a Helmet.	20
Follower of Fashion	Wear Every Hat.	20
Undecided.	Crossover: Destroy Anakin with Vader.	10
Love is...	Crossover: Destroy Jango Fett with Boba Fett.	10
Unfaithful	Crossover: Destroy The Emperor with Darth Maul.	10
Did I Break your Concentration?	Revenge: Destroy The Emperor with Mace Windu.	10
Nobody Expects...	Revenge: Destroy The Emperor with Kit Fisto.	10
Hands Off!	Revenge: Destroy Anakin with Dooku.	10
Who needs Obi-Wan?	Revenge: Destroy Darth Maul with Qui-Gon.	10
Strike me down	Revenge: Destroy Darth Vader with Obi-Wan.	10
Arcade Master	Get 100 points in Arcade Mode.	20
Online Player	Play through an entire level online.	20
Shoot First	Shoot first.	20

LEGO STAR WARS II: THE ORIGINAL TRILOGY

ACHIEVEMENTS

NAME	GOAL/REQUIREMENT	POINTS
Secret Plans Level Complete	Complete the first level of the game—Secret Plans.	20
Episode IV Complete	Complete all six levels in this Episode in Story Mode.	50
Episode V Complete	Complete all six levels in this Episode in Story Mode.	50
Episode VI Complete	Complete all six levels in this Episode in Story Mode.	50
LEGO City Complete	Complete the LEGO City level.	50
Bounty Hunter Missions Complete	Complete all of the 10 Bounty Hunter Missions.	40
Game 20% Complete	Complete 20% of the game.	20
Game 40% Complete	Complete 40% of the game.	40
Game 60% Complete	Complete 60% of the game.	60
Game 80% Complete	Complete 80% of the game.	80
Game 100% Complete	Complete everything in the game!	180
Secret Plans— Undefeated	Complete this level without dying. No Extras should be turned on.	20
Jundland Wastes— Undefeated.	Complete this level without dying. No Extras should be turned on.	20
Mos Eisley— Undefeated.	Complete this level without dying. No Extras should be turned on.	20
Rescue the Princess— Undefeated	Complete this level without dying. No Extras should be turned on.	20
Death Star Escape— Undefeated	Complete this level without dying. No Extras should be turned on.	20
Rebel Attack— Undefeated	Complete this level without dying. No Extras should be turned on.	20
Hoth Battle— Undefeated	Complete this level without dying. No Extras should be turned on.	20

Echo Base—Undefeated	Complete this level without dying. No Extras should be turned on.	20
Facon Flight—Undefeated	Complete this level without dying. No Extras should be turned on.	20
Dagobah—Undefeated	Complete this level without dying. No Extras should be turned on.	20
Cloud City Trap—Undefeated	Complete this level without dying. No Extras should be turned on.	20
Bespin—Undefeated	Complete this level without dying. No Extras should be turned on.	20
Jabba's Palace—Undefeated	Complete this level without dying. No Extras should be turned on.	20
Carkoon—Undefeated.	Complete this level without dying. No Extras should be turned on.	20
Speeder Showdown—Undefeated	Complete this level without dying. No Extras should be turned on.	20
Endor—Undefeated.	Complete this level without dying. No Extras should be turned on.	20
Jedi Destiny—Undefeated.	Complete this level without dying. No Extras should be turned on.	20
Death Star II—Undefeated	Complete this level without dying. No Extras should be turned on	20

MADDEN NFL 09

ACHIEVEMENTS

NAME	GOAL/REQUIREMENT	POINT VALUE
2 TD Kickoff Returns in a game	Return 2 Kickoffs for a TD in a game (non co-op)	75
Shut out Rival in a Franchise	Shut out Rival in a Franchise game (non co-op)	50
Kick a FG for over 50 yards	Kick a FG for over 50 yards in a Franchise game (non co-op)	15
Complete a game without an INT	Complete a game without an interception, 5 min+ quarter length (non co-op)	30
6 Rush TDs with the Dolphins	6 Rush TDs in a game with the Dolphins (non co-op)	50
Catch 10 passes in a game	Catch 10 passes in a game with one receiver (non co-op)	50
Complete game without fumbling	Complete a game without fumbling, 5 min+ quarter length (non co-op)	25
2 TD Punt Returns in a game	2 TD Punt Returns in a game (non co-op)	65
Intercept 6 passes in a game	Intercept 6 passes in a game (non co-op)	50
Hold a Rival to under 300 yards	Hold a Rival to under 300 yards total offense in a game (non co-op)	50
Score 60 points in a Rival game	Score 60 points in a Rival game (non co-op)	30
Score 40 points in a Rival game	Score 40 points in a Rival game (non co-op)	20
Record 12 sacks in a game	Record 12 sacks in a game (non co-op)	50
6 sacks with 1 player in a game	6 sacks with 1 player in a game (non co-op)	50
80% completion for a game	80% pass completion in a Franchise game, 5 min+ quarter length (non co-op)	50
7 Pass TDs with the Falcons	Throw 7 pass TDs in a game with the Falcons (non co-op)	50
550 Pass Yds with the Titans	550 Pass Yds in a game with the Titans (non co-op)	50
300 Rush Yds with the Jets	300 Rush Yds in a game with the Jets (non co-op)	10
Hold a Rival to under 20 points	Hold a Rival team to under 20 points in a game (non co-op)	10
Midway Monster	Create a legendary player from the past.	50
Can You Believe These Seats?!	Celebrate a touchdown in a wall hotspot	30
Steal Their Thunder	Steal an opposing player's touchdown celebration	30

NAME	GOAL/REQUIREMENT	POINT VALUE
Slam Dunk All-Star	Dunk the ball over the goalpost (or at least attempt to) after a touchdown	30
Shine In The Spotlight	Celebrate a touchdown in an endzone hotspot	30

SECRET ACHIEVEMENTS

NAME	GOAL/REQUIREMENT	POINT VALUE
Now Here's a Guy...	Thank you for purchasing Madden NFL 09. Here's to another 20 years!	50

MAJOR LEAGUE BASEBALL 2K7

ACHIEVEMENTS

NAME	GOAL/REQUIREMENT	POINTS
Moonshot!	Hit a mammoth 450+ foot home run.	20
Super Slugger	Hit 3 home runs in one game with the same player on "Pro" or higher difficulty setting.	30
Offensive Explosion	Score 20 runs in one game on "Pro" or higher difficulty setting.	40
5 Hit Game	Have a player get 5 base hits in one game.	50
Closing Time	Have a pitcher record a "save" by coming into a close ballgame to finish off a win.	10
Payoff	Make 10 successful "Payoff Pitches" in one game.	30
Strikeout the Side	Strike out all 3 batters you face in an inning.	20
Unhittable	Strikeout 15 batters with one pitcher on "Pro" or higher difficulty setting.	50
Thief	Successfully steal 2 bases in a game with one player.	10
Double Steal	Make a successful double steal (2 players steal a base on the same play)	20
Organized Crime	Have your team successfully steal 6 bases in one game.	40
Robbery!	Make a wall climb catch (rob a home run.)	20
Triple Double	Turned 3 double plays in one game. "Triple Double" done baseball style.	30
Strikeout Leader	During a season, franchise, or GM Career, have a pitcher lead his league in strikeouts.	30
Home Run Leader	During a season, franchise, or GM Career, have a player lead the league in HRs.	30
Cy Young Winner	During a season, franchise, or GM Career, have a player win the Cy Young award.	30
World Series Winner	Play through a season (offline) and win the World Series.	75
Trivia Time	Successfully answer a trivia question between innings of a ball game.	5
League Participation	Play at least one game in an online league or tournament.	20
Get Connected	Play a full 9 inning game versus an online opponent	20
Win 10 Online	Win ten 9 inning games online.	10
3-Game Streak	Go on a 3-game winning streak online.	20
5-Game Streak	Go on a 5-game winning streak online.	30
Win 20 Online	Win twenty 9 inning games online.	20
Join Up	Join an online league or tournament.	10

SECRET ACHIEVEMENTS

NAME	GOAL/REQUIREMENT	POINTS
No-Hitter	Pitched a complete game no-hitter.	100
Online Champion	Won an online tourney/league. Most impressive.	50
MVP Winner	Won the league MVP award.	30
Rail Lean Catch	Made an acrobatic catch leaning over foul territory railing.	10
Burglar	Stole home plate. You the man.	30
Ejected!	Ejected from a ballgame? Double Check!	10
Win 50 Online	Your dedication and skill are an inspiration to us all.	50
The Cycle	Hit a single, double, triple, and Home Run in one game with the same player. Astounding.	50

MAJOR LEAGUE BASEBALL 2K8

ACHIEVEMENTS

NAME	GOAL/REQUIREMENT	POINTS
Control Artist	Throw a Total Control Pitch with superb execution.	5
Frozen Rope	Get a line drive base hit using Right Stick Hitting (Pro difficulty or higher).	5
Advanced Mind, Advanced Pleasure	Complete 10 games using advanced controls.	50
Fantasy Cards	Create a complete card team.	10
Buy a Pack	Use your duplicate cards to buy a new pack of cards.	20
Earn a Team	Unlock all the cards for a team in card series 1.	30
Earn 100 Cards	Unlock 100 different types of cards.	50
Quality Start	Have your starting pitcher give up 3 or fewer runs in 6+ innings of work (Pro difficulty or higher).	5
Hold!	Get credit for a hold (Pro difficulty or higher).	5
Save!	Get credit for a save (min 3 batters faced, Pro difficulty or higher).	5
Keep it Down	Complete a 9-inning game without giving up a home run (Pro difficulty or higher).	5
1-2-3	Retire all 3 batters faced in an inning (Pro difficulty or higher).	10
Strikeout the Side	Strikeout all 3 batters faced in an inning (Pro difficulty or higher).	50
A Day To Remember	Throw a no-hitter using any number of pitchers (minimum 9 innings, Pro difficulty or higher).	100
Skillz	Make a spectacular defensive play (Pro difficulty or higher).	5
Catch 'em Nappin	Successfully bunt for a hit (Pro difficulty or higher).	10
Red-Handed	Throw out a runner attempting to steal a base (Pro difficulty or higher).	10
He's Got a Gun!	Throw out a runner at homeplate from the outfield using Right Stick Throwing.	20
The Train's Comin' Through	Score a run after plowing over the catcher at homeplate (Pro difficulty or higher).	20
De-Railed	Successfully prevent a runner from plowing over your catcher and scoring (Pro difficulty or higher).	20
Triple Double	Turn 3 double plays in one game (Pro difficulty or higher).	20
Eagle Eye	Get a Base on Balls (Pro difficulty or higher).	10
Double Triple	Hit two triples in one game (Pro difficulty or higher).	30
Goliath	Hit 5 home runs in one game (Pro difficulty or higher).	20
Legendary	Win a 9-inning game on Legend difficulty.	50
What's Your Fantasy?	Complete at least 25 rounds of a fantasy draft in franchise mode.	5
Glove of Gold	In franchise, have a player win the Player's Choice Best Fielder award (min 20 games played).	10
Platinum Bat	In franchise, have a player win the Player's Choice Best Hitting award (min. 20 games played).	10
Star-Studded	In franchise, have 3 or more players make the All-Star Team (min 15 games played).	20
Makin' a Splash	In franchise, have a rookie earn the Rookie of the Year award (min 20 games played).	20
Contender	In franchise, have your team make the playoffs (min 20 games played).	20
Domination	Win at least 105 games in one season (min 20 games played)	30
Layer Cake	In franchise, win a game at each minor league level (A, AA, and AAA).	10
The Brink of Stardom	In franchise, have a player win the Minor League Player of the Year award.	10
I'm a Winner!	Win a ranked match on Xbox LIVE.	10
Win 20 Online	Win 20 ranked matches on Xbox LIVE.	30
Card Master	Win a Card Battle match on Xbox LIVE.	50
Slugger	Win a Strikes Only match on Xbox LIVE.	20
League Participation	Play a game in a league or tournament on Xbox LIVE.	10
Cards Shmards	Top 'em: In a ranked match on Xbox LIVE, beat an opponent who has unlocked 'Earn 100 Cards'.	20
David vs. Goliath	Top 'em: In a ranked match on Xbox LIVE, beat an opponent who has unlocked 'Goliath'.	20

NAME	GOAL/REQUIREMENT	POINTS
Another Level	Top 'em: In a ranked match on Xbox LIVE, beat an opponent who has unlocked 'Legendary'.	20
Live Wire	Top 'em: In a ranked match on Xbox LIVE, beat an opponent who has unlocked 'Win 20 Online'.	20
You're Not So Tough	Top 'em: In a ranked match on Xbox LIVE, beat an opponent who has unlocked 'A Day to Remember'.	50
What Makes YOU So Special?	Top 'em: In a ranked match on Xbox LIVE, beat an opponent who has unlocked a Top 'em achievement.	50

MARVEL ULTIMATE ALLIANCE

ACHIEVEMENTS

NAME	GOAL/REQUIREMENT	POINTS
Mandarin's Downfall	The evil Mandarin was crushed by the forces of good.	45
Mephisto's Defeat	Mephisto was struck down.	45
The Trickster	Loki was defeated.	45
The Power Cosmic	The mighty Galactus was toppled.	45
Doomed Ending	Dr. Doom was utterly defeated.	45
Scarlet Swashbuckler	Daredevil was unlocked as a playable hero.	30
Wakandan Royalty	Black Panther was unlocked as a playable hero.	30
Agent of S.H.I.E.L.D.	Nick Fury was unlocked as a playable hero.	30
Surfs Up	Silver Surfer was unlocked as a playable hero.	30
Dragon Slayer	Fin Fang Foom was defeated.	15
Blue Screen of Death	M.O.D.O.K was defeated.	15
Underwater Battle	Tigershark and Attuma were defeated.	15
Swimming with the Fish	The mighty Kraken was defeated.	15
Defeated Grey Gargoyle	Grey Gargoyle was defeated.	15
Game Over	Arcade was defeated.	15
Son of a Devil	Blackheart was defeated.	15
The Executioner's Blade	Executioner and Enchantress were defeated.	15
Giant Relief	Ymir fell to the forces of good.	15
Warrior's Path	Gladiator was defeated.	15
Deathbird's Defeat	Deathbird was crushed.	15
Titanic Victory	Titannus was defeated.	15
Golden Age of Comics	Attained gold on all comic missions.	30
The Ultimate Super Hero	Defeated 4000 enemies.	50
Marvel Geek	Answered 15 trivia questions correctly.	5
Comic God	Answered 20 trivia questions correctly in a row.	15
Marvel Master	Answered 150 trivia questions correctly.	10
I have a friend	Completed a level with at least 1 other player.	5
Super Hero Team	Completed 25 levels with at least 1 other player.	15
Excelsior!	Beat Marvel: Ultimate Alliance in Hard Mode.	50
Fall to Death	Threw 5 enemies off a ledge.	10
Scared of Heights	Threw 50 enemies off a ledge	20
Widowmaker	Threw 500 enemies off a ledge.	30
Battle Tested	Won 1 Arcade mode level.	5
Battle Hardened	Won 20 Arcade mode levels.	15
Mad Skillz	Won 3 Arcade mode levels consecutively.	10
Teh Mast3r	Won 15 Arcade mode levels consecutively.	25
The Destroyer	Won 100 Arcade mode (Competitive) games.	25
Teamwork	Completed 1 level with 3 other players.	5
Ultimate Team Alliance	Completed 25 levels with 3 other players.	15
Fledging superhero	Defeated 10 enemies.	5
Legendary Superhero	Defeated 100 enemies.	15
Pugilist	Performed 5 finishing moves.	5
Melee Master	Performed 50 finishing moves.	15
Touch of Death	Performed 200 finishing moves.	30
Good Samaritan	Completed Skrull Cityscape level without defeating a single enemy.	20
Dressed for Success	Unlocked ALL outfits for EVERY hero.	45

XBOX 360™ ACHIEVEMENTS

ACHIEVEMENTS

NAME	GOAL/REQUIREMENT	POINTS
Medal of Honor	Complete 1 Mass Effect Playthrough on any setting	100
Medal of Heroism	Complete Feros	25
Distinguished Service Medal	Complete Eden Prime	25
Council Legion of Merit	Complete Virmire	25
Honorarium of Corporate Service	Complete Noveria	25
Long Service Medal	Complete 2 Mass Effect Playthroughs on any setting	25
Distinguished Combat Medal	Complete 1 Mass Effect playthrough on the Hardcore difficulty setting. Do not change the setting.	25
Medal of Valor	Complete 1 Mass Effect playthrough on the Insanity difficulty setting. Do not change the setting.	50
Pistol Expert	Register 150 Pistol Kills	10
Shotgun Expert	Register 150 Shotgun Kills	15
Assault Rifle Expert	Register 150 Assault Rifle Kills	15
Sniper Expert	Register 150 Sniper Rifle Kills	15
Lift Mastery	Use biotic Lift 75 times	15
Throw Mastery	Use biotic Throw 75 times	15
Warp Mastery	Use biotic Warp 75 times	15
Singularity Mastery	Use biotic Singularity 75 times	15
Barrier Mastery	Use biotic Barrier 75 times	15
Stasis Mastery	Use biotic Stasis 75 times	15
Damping Specialist	Use Damping Field 75 times	15
AI Hacking Specialist	Use AI Hacking 75 times	15
Overload Specialist	Use Shield Overload 75 times	15
Sabotage Specialist	Use Sabotage 75 times	15
First Aid Specialist	Use medi-gel 150 times	15
Neural Shock Specialist	Use Neural Shock 75 times	15
Scholar	Find all primary Alien: Council Races, Extinct Races and Non-Council Races codex entries	25
Completionist	Complete the majority of the game	25
Tactician	Complete playthrough with shield damage greater than health damage	25
Medal of Exploration	Land on an uncharted world	50
Rich	Exceed 1,000,000 Credits	25
Dog of War	Register 150 organic enemy kills	25
Geth Hunter	Register 250 synthetic enemy kills	25
Soldier Ally	Complete the majority of the game with the Alliance soldier squad member	20
Sentinel Ally	Complete the majority of the game with the Alliance sentinel squad member	20
Krogan Ally	Complete the majority of the game with the krogan squad member	20
Turian Ally	Complete the majority of the game with the turian squad member	20
Quarian Ally	Complete the majority of the game with the quarian squad member	20
Asari Ally	Complete the majority of the game with the asari squad member	20
Power Gamer	Reach 50th level with one character	20
Extreme Power Gamer	Reach 60th level with one character	50
Renegade	Accumulate 75% of total Renegade points	15
Paragon	Accumulate 75% of total Paragon points	15
Paramour	Complete any romance subplot	10
Spectre Inductee	Become a Spectre	15
Charismatic	Use Charm or Intimidate to resolve an impossible situation	10
Search and Rescue	Locate Dr. T'soni in the Artemis Tau cluster	10
Colonial Savior	Complete the Bring Down the Sky mission.	50

ACHIEVEMENTS

NAME	GOAL/REQUIREMENT	POINTS
Utilized Time Machine	Escape from Egypt in the time machine.	10
Obtained Scanning Technology	Complete the mission to create the scanner gadget.	10
Obtain the Charge Ball Gadget	Obtain the Charge Ball Glove.	10
Obtain Disassembler Gadget	Obtain the Disassembler Gadget.	10
Overwhelmed Menacing Automaton	Defeat Robot guarding the time machine.	40
Restored Space/Time Continuum	Complete Science Fair Level.	20
Obtained Havoc Gadget	Obtain Havoc Gloves.	10
Obtain LEV Gadget	Obtain the LEV Gun.	10
Undermined Prometheus Project	Defeat Prometheus.	60
Defeat Mega Doris	Defeat Mega Doris.	100
Scan 130 Items	Scan 130 items throughout the game.	100
Earn Uncle Art VR Disk	Earn Uncle Art's VR Disk.	10
Earn Billie VR Disk	Earn Billie's VR Disk.	10
Earn Franny's VR Disk	Earn Franny's VR Disk.	10
Earn Grandpa's VR Disk	Earn Grandpa's VR Disk.	10
Earn Laszlo's VR Disk	Earn Laszlo's VR Disk.	10
Earn Tallulah's VR Disk	Earn Tallulah's VR Disk.	10
Find Magma Charge Ball Court	Find Magma Charge Ball VR Disk.	10
Find Hive Charge Ball Court	Find Hive Charge Ball VR Disk.	10
Find Garden Charge Ball Court	Find Robinson Garden Charge Ball VR Disk.	10
Find Egypt Charge Ball Court	Find Egypt Charge Ball VR Disk.	10
Find Train Room Court	Find Train Room Charge Ball VR Disk.	10
Find Frog Room Charge Ball Court	Find Frog Room Charge Ball VR Disk.	10
Found All Charge Ball Courts	All Charge Ball VR Disks Collected.	50
Ambush Art in Charge Ball	Defeat Art in Charge Ball Mini-Game.	10
Best Billie in Charge Ball	Defeat Billie in Charge Ball Mini-Game.	10
Finish off Franny in Charge Ball	Defeat Franny in Charge Ball Mini-Game.	10
Bear Down on Bud in Charge Ball	Defeat Grandpa in Charge Ball Mini-Game.	10
Lambaste Laszlo in Charge Ball	Defeat Laszlo in Charge Ball Mini-Game.	10
Trounce Tallulah in Charge Ball	Defeat Tallulah in Charge Ball Mini-Game.	10
Clobber the Champ in Charge Ball	Defeat the Champ in Charge Ball Mini-Game.	10
Completed First Havoc Puzzle	Complete First Havoc Glove Puzzle.	10
Complete All Havoc Puzzles	Complete Every Havoc Glove Puzzle.	50
Acolyte of Protectospheres	Complete First Protectosphere Course.	10
Grand Master of Protectospheres	Complete all Protectosphere Courses.	50
Vanquish Army of Giant Ants	Defeat Lizzy.	60
Master of Security	Score 100,000 in the Security System.	100
Security Specialist	Score 25,000 in the Security System.	100

THE OUTFIT

MEDAL OPPORTUNITIES—SINGLE-PLAYER

NAME	GOAL/REQUIREMENT	POINTS
Air Defense	Shoot down at least 5 Nazi Stukas (Mission 1: Beyond the Beachhead).	15
Combat Aid	Protect at least five of the Allied paratroopers (Mission 1: Beyond the Beachhead).	10
Troop Car Destroyed	Destroy the Axis troop car (Mission 2: Into the Fray).	15
Searchlights Destroyed	Destroy all Nazi spotlights in the mission (Mission 2: Into the Fray).	10
Destroy the Nazi convoy	Convoy Ambush (Mission 3: Yo Adrienne).	20
Propaganda Destroyed	Destroy the Nazi propaganda statues (Mission 3: Yo Adrienne).	15
Tank Crew Rescue	Protect the Allied tank crew (Mission 4: Mortain).	15
Reinforcement Rescue	Protect the Allied paratroops from Nazi Stukas (Mission 4: Mortain).	20
Allied Rescue	Protect the Allied soldiers at the armory (Mission 5: Assault on Rochereau).	15
Panther Tank Capture	Secure the Nazi Panther (Mission 5: Assault on Rochereau; must locate Allied engineers to activate this medal).	20
Transport Ship Destruction	Destroy the offshore transports (Mission 6: See the Light).	20
Submarine Destruction	Destroy the Nazi submarines (Mission 6: See the Light).	20
Train Destroyed	Destroy the Armored train (Mission 7: Sole Survivors).	25
POW Savior	Protect the Wehrmacht POWs (Mission 7: Sole Survivors).	25
Fuel Depot Destroyed	Destroy the Nazi fuel barrels (Mission 8: Vengeance).	20
Allied Savior	Protect the Allied emplacements from Nazi Panzers/ Panther (Mission 8: Vengeance).	20
Howitzer Defense	Protect the Allied emplacements from Nazi Stukas (Mission 9: Crossing Over).	20
Tank Column Destroyed	Destroy Nazi tank column (Mission 9: Crossing Over).	20
Prototype Jet Destroyed	Destroy Nazi prototype jet (Mission 10: Iron Zeppelin).	25
V1 Rockets Destroyed	Destroy the Nazi V1 rockets (Mission 10: Iron Zeppelin).	20
AA Guns Destroyed	Destroy all the Nazi Flak guns (Mission 11: The Gates of Hell).	20
Bunker Defense	Protect the Wehrmacht bunker from Nazi SS (Mission 11: The Gates of Hell).	25
Radar Tower Destroyed	Destroy the Nazi radar tower (Mission 12: The Fortress).	20
Airfield Saved	Defeat the Nazi counterattack at the airfield (Mission 12: The Fortress).	25
Game Completion Award	Complete the Single-Player Campaign.	30

MEDAL OPPORTUNITIES—MULTIPLAYER

NAME	GOAL/REQUIREMENT	POINTS
Wounded in Action	Awarded for an average lifetime shorter than 30 seconds in Ranked Quick Match games.	20
Master of Capturing	Must capture more than 10 objectives in a single Ranked Quick Match game.	20
Great Score	Must achieve a score greater than 350 in a single Ranked Quick Match game.	30
Lightning Victory	Must achieve victory in less than two minutes in any Ranked Quick Match game.	30
Prisoner of War	Awarded when your total number of losses exceeds 200 in Ranked Quick Match games.	20
Victories Keep Piling Up	Awarded for winning 500 Ranked Quick Match games.	75
Persistence Counts	Must die 1000 times in Ranked Quick Match games.	20
Infantry Killer	Achieve 1000 infantry kills in Ranked Quick Match games.	25

NAME	GOAL/REQUIREMENT	POINTS
Vehicle Killer	Get 200 vehicle kills in Ranked Quick Match games.	25
Emplacement Killer	Attain 250 emplacement kills in Ranked Quick Match games.	25
Great Shooting	Achieve accuracy greater than 40% in a single Ranked Quick Match game.	25
Marksman	Attain accuracy greater than 25% over your Ranked Quick Match game career.	50
Feared	Achieve more than 15 enemy player kills in a single Ranked Quick Match game.	25
Clear Winner	Awarded for victories totaling 1000 Command Points in Ranked Quick Match games.	35
Guns Blazing	Complete an average score of over 18 per minute of play in Ranked Quick Match games.	45
Focused Fire	Must kill enemy players at a rate of 1.7 or greater per minute of play in Ranked Quick Match games.	40

PHANTASY STAR UNIVERSE

ACHIEVEMENTS

NAME	GOAL/REQUIREMENT	POINTS
De Ragan Slayer	Defeat the Chapter 3 boss.	100
Onmagoug Slayer	Defeat the Chapter 5 boss.	100
Adahna Degahna Slayer	Defeat the Chapter 7 boss.	100
De Ragnus Slayer	Defeat the Chapter 8 boss.	100
Magas Maggahna Slayer	Defeat the Chapter 9 boss.	100
Dimmagolus Slayer	Defeat the Chapter 11 boss.	100
Dulk Fakis Slayer	Defeat the Chapter 12 boss.	200
Dulk Fakis 2 Slayer	Defeat the last boss.	200

ROCK BAND

ACHIEVEMENTS

NAME	GOAL/REQUIREMENT	POINTS
Breakthrough Act	Unlock a Big Club in Solo Tour on Easy, Medium, Hard or Expert	10
Hot Artist	Unlock a Theater in Solo Tour on Easy, Medium, Hard or Expert	10
Top Artist	Unlock an Arena in Solo Tour on Medium, Hard or Expert	10
String Shredder	Finish Guitar Solo Tour on Easy	20
Fret Ripper	Finish Guitar Solo Tour on Medium	30
Axe Assassin	Finish Guitar Solo Tour on Hard	40
Lord of the Strings	Finish Guitar Solo Tour on Expert	50
Rhythm Rocker	Finish Drum Solo Tour on Easy	20
Groove Technician	Finish Drum Solo Tour on Medium	30
Heavy Hitter	Finish Drum Solo Tour on Hard	40
AN-I-MAL!!!	Finish Drum Solo Tour on Expert	50
Howler	Finish Vocal Solo Tour on Easy	20
Screamer	Finish Vocal Solo Tour on Medium	30
Crooner	Finish Vocal Solo Tour on Hard	40
Virtuoso	Finish Vocal Solo Tour on Expert	50
Got Wheels	Unlock the Van in Band World Tour	20
Open Road	Unlock the Bus in Band World Tour	20
Jet Setter	Unlock the Jet in Band World Tour	20
One Million Fans	Reach 1 million fans in Band World Tour	10
Hall of Fame Inductee	Finish the Hall of Fame Induction in Band World Tour	100
Vinyl Artist	Finish the Endless Setlist in Band World Tour on Medium	10
Gold Artist	Finish the Endless Setlist in Band World Tour on Hard	20
Platinum Artist	Finish the Endless Setlist in Band World Tour on Expert	25
Big In London	Finish the last remaining gig in London (Band World Tour)	10
Big In Paris	Finish the last remaining gig in Paris (Band World Tour)	10

NAME	GOAL/REQUIREMENT	POINTS
Big In Amsterdam	Finish the last remaining gig in Amsterdam (Band World Tour)	10
Big In Berlin	Finish the last remaining gig in Berlin (Band World Tour)	10
Big In Stockholm	Finish the last remaining gig in Stockholm (Band World Tour)	10
Big In Rome	Finish the last remaining gig in Rome (Band World Tour)	10
Big In Boston	Finish the last remaining gig in Boston (Band World Tour)	10
Big In NYC	Finish the last remaining gig in New York (Band World Tour)	10
Big In Chicago	Finish the last remaining gig in Chicago (Band World Tour)	10
Big In LA	Finish the last remaining gig in Los Angeles (Band World Tour)	10
Big In Seattle	Finish the last remaining gig in Seattle (Band World Tour)	10
Big In San Francisco	Finish the last remaining gig in San Francisco (Band World Tour)	10
Big In Japan	Finish the last remaining gig in Tokyo (Band World Tour)	10
Big In Sydney	Finish the last remaining gig in Sydney (Band World Tour)	10
Big In Reykjavik	Finish the last remaining gig in Reykjavik (Band World Tour)	10
Big In Rio de Janeiro	Finish the last remaining gig in Rio de Janeiro (Band World Tour)	10
Big In Moscow	Finish the last remaining gig in Moscow (Band World Tour)	10
Tug of War Champ	Win 20 Tug of War ranked matches	30
Tug of War Streak	Win 5 Tug of War ranked matches in a row	20
Score Duel Champ	Win 20 Score Duel ranked matches	30
Score Duel Streak	Win 5 Score Duel ranked matches in a row	20
Killer Performance	Five Star a song on Easy, Medium, Hard or Expert	10
Flawless Groove	Score 100% notes hit as bassist, up-strums only, on Expert	10
Flawless Drumming	Score 100% notes hit as a drummer on Expert	10
Flawless Fretwork	Score 100% notes hit as a guitarist on Expert	10
Flawless Singing	Score a 100% rating as a vocalist on Expert	10
Riding on Coattails	Play with a "Platinum Artist"	5

ROCK BAND 2

ACHIEVEMENTS

NAME	GOAL/REQUIREMENT	POINT VALUE
Solid Gold, Baby!	Gold Star a song	25
The Bachman-Turner Award	Maintain deployed Overdrive for 90 seconds	25
Flawless Fretwork	Score 100% notes hit as a guitarist on Expert	25
Flawless Guitar Solo	100% a guitar solo on Expert, using only the solo buttons	20
Flawless Drumming	Score 100% notes hit as a drummer on Expert	25
Flawless Singing	Score a 100% rating as a vocalist on Expert	25
Flawless Groove	Score 100% notes hit as bassist, up-strums only, on Expert	25
Comeback Kid	Defeat the last player that defeated you over Xbox LIVE in either Score Duel or Tug of War.	15
Victory!	Defeat a player in either Score Duel or Tug of War.	15
Band Savior	Be a savior three times during a single song	20
Overdrive Overdose	Achieve an 8x Band Multiplier	25
Hello Cleveland!	Deploy Vocal Overdrive 4 times in a single song	20
Million Point Club	Earn more than 1,000,000 points in a single song.	25
You're Hired!	Hire a staff member	10
Needs more Umlauts!	Make a band logo	10
The San Dimas 4th Annual Award	Compete in a Battle of the Bands event	15
You Killed the Radio Star	Make a music video in World Tour	15
Clothes to the Edge	Buy over $100,000 worth of items from the Rock Shop	20
Along for the Ride	Beat an instrument-specific challenge while playing another instrument	10
Challenge Novice	Complete either 25 challenges on Medium, 10 challenges on Hard, or 5 challenges on Expert	10

OVERLOAD

NAME	GOAL/REQUIREMENT	POINT VALUE
Challenge Master	Complete 25 Challenges on Hard Difficulty or 10 Challenges on Expert Difficulty	15
Challenge Savant	Complete 25 Challenges on Expert Difficulty	25
The Final Countdown	Unlock an Impossible Challenge	15
Groove Assassin	Beat the Impossible Bass Challenge	20
Lord of the Strings	Beat the Impossible Guitar Challenge	25
Stage Igniters	Beat the Impossible Band Challenge	25
AN-I-MAL!!!	Beat the Impossible Drum Challenge	25
Virtuoso	Beat the Impossible Vocal Challenge	25
West Coast Performer	Play a set on the West Coast of North America	10
Heartland Performer	Play a set in Middle America	10
East Coast Performer	Play a set on the East Coast of North America	10
God Save the Band	Play a set in the United Kingdom	10
Western Europe Performer	Play a set in Western Europe.	10
Eastern European Performer	Play a set in Eastern Europe	10
Worldwide Sensation	Gain access to every venue in the world	25
Road Dog	Play in every venue in the world	30
One Million Fans	Reach 1 million fans in World Tour	30
Open Road	Win a Bus in World Tour	20
Got Wheels	Win a Van in World Tour	20
Jet Setter	Win a Jet in World Tour	20
Beat It!	Complete all beats at 60 BPM or higher or half of the beats at 140 BPM or higher	10
The Beat Goes On	Complete all beats at 100 BPM or higher or half of the beats at 180 BPM or higher	20
Fill Me In	Complete all fills at 60 BPM or higher or half of the fills at 140 BPM or higher	10
Fill Legend	Complete all fills at 100 BPM or higher or half of the fills at 180 BPM or higher	20

SECRET ACHIEVEMENTS

NAME	GOAL/REQUIREMENT	POINT VALUE
Buy a Real Instrument Already!	Beat an "Impossible" Challenge with all players on Expert Difficulty	35
Rock Immortal Inductee	Joined the Rolling Stone Rock Immortals list	20
Vinyl Artist	Finished the Endless Setlist 2 in World Tour on Medium	20
Gold Artist	Finished the Endless Setlist 2 in World Tour on Hard	30
Platinum Artist	Finished the Endless Setlist 2 in World Tour on Expert	50
The Bladder of Steel Award	Completed the Endless Setlist 2 without pausing or failing.	25

SAINTS ROW 2

ACHIEVEMENTS

NAME	GOAL/REQUIREMENT	POINT VALUE
Welcome Back	Complete the Saints Revival prologue	5
Seppuku	Defeat the Ronin	40
Brother's Keeper	Defeat the Brotherhood	40
Remind Me of the Babe	Defeat the Sons of Samedi	40
Crime Lord	Complete all levels of all activities	50
Velvet Rope	Complete all levels of Crowd Control	15
Demolition Man	Complete all levels of Demolition Derby	15
Purple Haze	Complete all levels of Drug Trafficking	15
Trickster	Complete all levels of Escort	15
Do Not Talk About It	Complete all levels of Fight Club	15
Reality Star	Complete all levels of FUZZ	15
HeliGood	Complete all levels of Heli Assault	15

NAME	GOAL/REQUIREMENT	POINT VALUE
Stuntman	Complete all levels of Trail Blazing	15
Ambulance Chaser	Complete all levels of Insurance Fraud	15
Wrecking Crew	Complete all levels of Mayhem	15
Splatster Chief	Complete all levels of Septic Avenger	15
...But It Sure Is Fun	Complete all levels of Snatch	15
Blue Collar	Complete all levels of Tow Truck, Fire Truck, Ambulance, and Taxi diversions	10
Duke of Stilwater	Find all stunt jumps in Stilwater	10
Maverick Goose	Find all flying stunt locations in Stilwater	10
Hi Fidelity	Find all CDs in Stilwater	15
All-City	Find and spray all 50 tags in Stilwater	10
Where's My Car?	Deliver all the cars to the chop shops	10
Hello 47	Kill all Hitman targets	10
2 Quick 2 Pissed	Complete all races in Stilwater	15
Romero's Hero	Complete the Zombie Uprising video game	5
Surf's Up	Get 3 gold stars in Vehicle Surfing	5
Duelist	Complete all Ronin missions in co-op	25
Pot Luck	Complete all Samedi missions in co-op	25
Separated at Birth	Complete all Brotherhood missions in co-op	25
Partners in Crime	Complete all campaign missions in co-op	100
Confidence Men	Complete all levels of all activities in co-op	25
True Pal	Defeat your partner in a co-op diversion	10
Strong Armed	Complete the Strong Arm tutorial	10
Saint's Seven	Win all seven Ranked Strong Arm Activities, and win on all seven Strong Arm maps	30
Spread the Love	Host and win an Xbox LIVE Party Game	30
Tested	Win 10 Xbox LIVE Strong Arm matches	10
Hoodlum	Earn 7 Multiplayer Badges	30
Made	Earn 15 Multiplayer Badges	30
Kingpin	Earn 30 Multiplayer Badges	40

SECRET ACHIEVEMENTS

NAME	GOAL/REQUIREMENT	POINT VALUE
A Brighter Future	Defeated the Ultor Corporation epilogue	80
Vengeance	Exacted revenge on Julius	15
Going the Distance	Threw someone a long, long way	5
Love Thy Neighbor	Grabbed 50 human shields	5
Aww Nuts!	Hit 100 lifetime nut shots	5
Stilwater Welcoming Committee	Mugged 50 citizens of Stilwater	5
I'm Not Addicted!	Gambled $500,000 total lifetime	5
Trash Talker	Taunted 50 gang members	5
Soprano	Sung Along to the Radio	10
Still Addicted to tha Row	Played Saints Row 2 in single player or co-op for a combined 50 hours	20

SHREK THE THIRD

ACHIEVEMENTS

NAME	GOAL/REQUIREMENT	POINTS
Spoon Fed Ogre	Complete the game in Charming Difficulty.	30
Glorious Liege	Complete the game in Grimm Difficulty.	80
Hail to the King!	Complete all 20 missions of the game for the first time in any difficulty.	60
Questing Rookie	Complete 33% of the Challenge Quests in the game.	40
Questing Fiend	Complete 66% of the Challenge Quests in the game.	50
Questing Ogre	Complete all the Challenge Quests in the game.	80
For the Fridge	Collect 33% of Coloring Book Pages in the game. (Any Difficulty).	30
Upstart Artist	Collect 66% of Coloring Book Pages in the game. (Any Difficulty).	40

NAME	GOAL/REQUIREMENT	POINTS
Art Collector	Collect 100% of Coloring Book Pages in the game. (Any Difficulty).	50
The Finisher	Perform 100 finishing moves.	50
The Juggler	Launch 50 Enemies into the air then catch them with Shrek.	40
Survivor Shrek	Achieve a Perfect on every level. (Normal difficulty or higher).	60
Super Ogre	Use Super Ogre Power 5 times with Shrek or Fiona.	30
Novice Collector	Collect 33% of all Souvenir Mugs in the game. (Any Difficulty).	30
Amateur Collector	Collect 66% Souvenir Mugs in the game. (Any Difficulty).	40
Master Collector	Collect all Souvenir Mugs in the game. (Any Difficulty)	50
Ice Dragon Tamer	Defeat the Ice Dragon. (Normal Difficulty or higher).	30
Music Critic	Defeat Captain Hook. (Normal Difficulty or higher).	30
Upstaged Charming	Defeat Prince Charming. (Normal Difficulty or higher).	30
The Collector	Complete all of The Collector series of quests.	60
Super Ogre Power Extreme	Use Super Ogre Power 10 times with any character.	60
Ogre Smash!	Use Fairy Dust Attack 50 times with any character.	30

SID MEIER'S CIVILIZATION REVOLUTION

ACHIEVEMENTS

NAME	GOAL/REQUIREMENT	POINT VALUE
One Mistress and No Master	Win as an English civilization.	15
I Will Not Be Triumphed Over	Win as an Egyptian civilization.	15
Flower and Song	Win as an Aztec civilization.	15
A Short Life of Glory	Win as a Greek civilization.	15
Fair and Softly Goes Far	Win as a Spanish civilization.	15
Blood and Iron	Win as a German civilization.	15
Veni Vidi Vici	Win as a Roman civilization.	15
A Great Wind is Blowing	Win as a Russian civilization.	15
Let a Hundred Flowers Bloom	Win as a Chinese civilization.	15
We the People	Win as an American civilization.	15
Imagination Rules the World	Win as a French civilization.	15
An Indomitable Will	Win as an Indian civilization.	15
A Knight Without Fear or Blame	Win as an Arab civilization.	15
This World is a Harsh Place	Win as an African civilization.	15
All Others Must Fail	Win as a Mongolian civilization.	15
Victory Over Lesser Men	Win as a Japanese civilization.	15
Difficulties Mastered	Win a victory with each civilization.	30
A Revelation of Man	Win a Cultural Victory.	20
Embiggens the Smallest Man	Win a Cultural Victory on at least King difficulty.	30
Citizen of the World	Win a Cultural victory on Deity difficulty.	45
Have Fun Storming the Castle	Win a Domination Victory.	20
Vi Victa Vis	Win a Domination Victory on at least King difficulty.	30
Such Joy Ambition Finds	Win a Domination victory on Deity difficulty.	45
A Penny Saved is a Penny Earned	Win an Economic Victory.	20
The Guy Who Signs the Checks	Win an Economic Victory on at least King difficulty.	30
Playing the Game	Win an Economic victory on Deity difficulty.	45
Ideas Control the World	Win a Technology Victory.	20

NAME	GOAL/REQUIREMENT	POINT VALUE
640K Ought to be Enough	Win a Technology Victory on at least King difficulty.	30
Indistinguishable From Magic	Win a Technology victory on Deity difficulty.	45
Destroyer of Worlds	Win all types of victories (Domination, Technology, Cultural, and Economic).	30
The Universal Brotherhood of Man	Develop a city to produce 200 culture per turn.	25
Organized Knowledge	Develop a city to produce 200 science per turn.	25
The Root of All Evil	Develop a city to produce 200 gold per turn.	25
Curse of the Drinking Class	Develop a city to produce 200 resources per turn.	25
Buy the Ticket, Take the Ride	Make contact with another civilization.	3
Culture is Worth a Little Risk	Build a Wonder of the World.	9
Once More Unto the Breach	Combine three identical units into an army.	5
80% of Success is Showing Up	Accumulate culture to unlock a famous person.	5
Home is Where One Starts From	Construct a special building.	3
Good Afternoon, Doctor Jones.	Discover an ancient artifact.	9
Before all Else, Be Armed	Earn a special unit ability in combat.	5
Scientia Potentia Est	Complete development of any technology.	3
Napalm in the Morning	Defeat an enemy unit.	3
The Fruit of Labor	Build a second city in a game.	5
What is the City But the People?	Grow a city to size 20.	25
The Will to Win is Everything	Win 20 battles with one unit.	25
Here's Looking at You, Kid	Unlock all famous persons.	45
That We May Live in Peace	Win the game by year 1000 AD on King difficulty or higher.	25
Absolute Power is Kind of Neat	Win without changing governments on King difficulty or higher.	25
Power Never Takes a Back Step	Win with only one city on at least King difficulty.	25

SOUL CALIBUR IV

ACHIEVEMENTS

NAME	GOAL/REQUIREMENT	POINT VALUE
Encounter with the Unknown	Fight against Yoda.	10
Pursuer of the Secret	Clear STORY MODE on difficulty: NORMAL.	10
Mystery of the Swords	Clear STORY MODE on difficulty: HARD.	20
May the Force be with You	Clear STORY MODE with Yoda.	20
War Veteran	Clear ARCADE MODE.	10
Hero on the Battlefield	Clear ARCADE MODE with over 450,000 points.	20
Legendary Hidden Treasures	Acquire over 30 treasures in TOWER OF LOST SOULS.	20
Never Ending Advance	Descend 20 floors in TOWER OF LOST SOULS.	20
Tower's New Guardian	Clear all upper floors of TOWER OF LOST SOULS.	30
Scorpion's Sting	Win a battle with Critical Finish.	10
Smasher	Destroy all of the opponent's equipment.	10
Iron Hammer	Land an attack on a taunting opponent.	10

NAME	GOAL/REQUIREMENT	POINT VALUE
Death on the Battlefield	Perform 100 Critical Finishes.	30
Like a Flowing Stream	Perform 200 Impacts.	20
Lost in the Moment	Perform 20 Just Impacts.	30
Quick Strike	Perform 5 First Attacks in a row in Arcade.	10
Swift Strike	Perform 100 First Attacks.	20
Mad Destroyer	Perform 100 Soul Crushes.	20
Violent Storm	Perform 50 Wall Hits.	20
10,000 Strikes of Proof	Land 10,000 attacks.	30
Endure 1,000	Guard 1,000 times against attacks.	30
Water Moon	Perform 30 grapple breaks.	20
Distance will not Betray	Reach over 10,000 meters in total movement distance in battle.	20
First Step as an Artist	Customize a regular character.	5
Chosen by History	Create a custom character.	5
Sharpened Teeth	Maximize a style's level.	20
Equal Skill and Power	Use all skill points and set up 4 skills.	20
Engraved into History	Fight 100 times (Online).	30
World Class Fighter	Fight against 20 different fighting styles (Online).	30
World Traveler	Fight on all stages (Online).	30
Gladiator	Win consecutive Ranked Matches (Online).	20
Unknown Swordsman	Win 10 times (Online).	20
Hero King	Level up to 20 (Online).	30
Divine Punishment	K.O. with an Unblockable Attack.	20
Reversal Wizard	Win 20 times with low HP.	20
Phoenix	Win with all equipment destroyed.	10
Wandering Assassin	K.O. opponent with over 20 types of weapons.	10
Repel All Blades	Win perfect 30 times.	30
Numeric God	Measure the two passages of time and win.	20
Two Cannot Exist Together	Exhaust each other's power.	20
Gathering of the Best	Complete CHAIN OF SOULS.	20
Observer of Souls	Collect all illustrations in Art Gallery.	30
Sword Hunter	Collect all weapons for 5 characters.	15
The Controller	Get Soul Calibur (Final Form).	20
Wild Run to Tragedy	Get Soul Edge (Final Form).	20
Looter of the Battlefield	Collect all accessories.	20
Wandering Weapon Merchant	Collect 350 pieces of equipment.	20
Transcend History and the World	Acquire all weapons and equipment.	50

SECRET ACHIEVEMENTS

NAME	GOAL/REQUIREMENT	POINT VALUE
tart of a New Era	Welcome to the new world of SOULCALIBUR!	5
Tower of Gold	Acquire 1,000,000 gold.	20

SPIDER-MAN 3

ACHIEVEMENTS

NAME	GOAL/REQUIREMENT	POINTS
Police Sergeant	Complete all Bank Robbery missions.	30
Police Officer	Complete all Crime Spree missions.	30
Police Corporal	Complete all Petty Theft missions.	30
Cold Blooded Super Master	Complete all Connors missions.	30
Deputy	Complete all DeWolfe missions.	30
Frequent Flyer	Collect all Skyscraper tokens.	10
Splat Master 2007	Splat into the ground 25 times.	20
Police Detective	Complete 25 random city missions.	30
Police Chief	Complete all combat tours.	30
Punk Rocker	Collect all Apocalypse Gang tokens.	10
Sweet Tooth	Collect all Arsenic Candy tokens.	10

NAME	GOAL/REQUIREMENT	POINTS
Fire Breather	Collect all Order of the Dragon Tail tokens.	10
Arachnophile	Collect all Secret tokens.	10
Pied Piper	Collect all Subway tokens.	10
Hitch Hiker	Ride a car or truck for 5 miles.	20
Eddie Brock	Defeat this nemesis.	40
Flint Marko	Defeat this nemesis.	30
Harry Osborn	Defeat this nemesis.	30
Wilson Fisk	Defeat this nemesis.	30
Aleksei Sytsevich	Defeat this nemesis.	30
Macdonald Gargan	Rescue this adversary.	40
Sergei Kravinoff	Defeat this nemesis.	30
Curtis Connors	Defeat this nemesis.	30
Luke Carlyle	Defeat this nemesis.	30
Gold Medal Winner	Get Gold on all trick races.	30
Silver Finalist	Get at least Silver on all trick races.	20
Bronze Finalist	Get at least Bronze on all trick races.	20
Trick Novice	Get at least Bronze on all easy trick races.	20
Mary Jane Thriller	Complete all Mary Jane thrill rides.	20
Bomb Squad	Get at least Bronze on all bomb tours.	20
Mega Tourist	Take a photograph from a great height.	10
Master Tourist	Take a 500-point photograph.	20
Shutterbug	Complete all Daily Bugle photo missions.	20
Web Slinger	Web up 25 enemies.	20
Fast Swinger	Swing at 200 miles per hour.	20
Pole Swinger	Swing on 50 poles.	10
Spider-Man	Complete all missions.	50
Collateral Damage	Destroy 25 objects.	10
A Dark Reward	Secret Achievement	20
Web Swinger	Swing a total of 10 miles.	20
Master Web Swinger	Swing a total of 50 miles.	20
Mega Web Swinger	Swing a total of 200 miles.	30
Intermediate Racer	Get at least Bronze on all easy and medium trick races.	20

SPIDER-MAN FRIEND OR FOE

ACHIEVEMENTS

NAME	GOAL/REQUIREMENT	POINTS
Tokyo Complete	Find all collectibles, find all secrets, and defeat all bosses in this location.	125
Tangaroa Island Complete	Find all collectibles, find all secrets, and defeat all bosses in this location.	125
Egypt Complete	Find all collectibles, find all secrets, and defeat all bosses in this location.	125
Transylvania Complete	Find all collectibles, find all secrets, and defeat all bosses in this location.	125
Nepal Complete	Find all collectibles, find all secrets, and defeat all bosses in this location.	125
Lightning Strikes	Obtain a Hit Chain higher than 15.	25
Combo Meter Master	Fill the Combo Meter all the way to Level 4.	25
Our Powers Combined	Initiate a Hero Strike Power-Up.	25
Web Slinger	Fully upgrade Web Line with all available Modifications.	75
Arachnid Artillery	Fully upgrade Web Shoot with all available Abilities and Mods.	75
All Tied Up	Fully upgrade Web Stun with all available Abilities and Mods.	75
Fury's Fourteen	All characters are fully upgraded with all Attacks and Attributes.	75

ACHIEVEMENTS

NAME	GOAL/REQUIREMENT	POINT VALUE
Complete Story, Act One	Complete Act One	50
Complete Story, Act Two	Complete Act Two	50
Complete Web of Shadows	Complete Game	75
Ultimate Spider-Man	Purchase all Upgrades	50
Obsessive Spider-Man	Complete 60 Bonus Goals	25
Excessive Spider-Man	Complete Half of All Optional Goals	15
Max Out Spider-Man	Max Out Spider-Man	75
Heroic Accumulation	Find Half of all Collectibles	25
First One Hundred	Find 100 Collectibles	15
50 Hit Combo - Spider Silk	Execute 50 Hit Combo "Spider Silk"	10
100 Hit Combo - Ownership	Execute 100 Hit Combo "Ownership"	25
250 Hit Combo - Neighborly	Execute 250 Hit Combo "Neighborly"	50
Great Power	Thwart 25 City Crimes	10
Great Responsibility	Thwart 100 City Crimes	25
Defeat 100 Enemies	Defeat 100 Enemies	20
Defeat 500 Enemies	Defeat 500 Enemies	35
No Sweat	Defeat 1000 Enemies	50
The Bigger They Come...	Defeat First Tech Mech	5
Eviction	Pull Tech Mech Pilot from his seat	5
Encountered	Parry then Counter Attack one enemy	5
Over the Counter	Parry then Counter Attack 100 enemies	10
Bowling Ball	Web Swing-Kick 5 Enemies in a single pass	5
Trampoline	Web-Strike Bounce 20 Enemies in succession	25
Overkill	Perform all three types of attacks (Ground, Air, Wall) on a single enemy 10 times	20
Ground Combo Skill	Defeat 50 Enemies using only Ground Combos	15
Air Combo Skill	Defeat 50 Enemies using only Air Combos	15
Wall Combo Skill	Defeat 50 Enemies using only Wall Combos	15

SECRET ACHIEVEMENTS

NAME	GOAL/REQUIREMENT	POINT VALUE
Hero	Red Suit Conclusion earned	20
Mary Jane and Spider-Man	Mary Jane Conclusion achieved	20
Black Cat and Spider-Man	Black Cat Conclusion achieved	20
Antihero	Black Suit Conclusion earned	20
Bad Kitty	Black Cat defeated	15
Defeat Venom, Round One	Defeated Venom once	15
Grounded	Electro defeated	15
Declawed	Wolverine defeated	15
Defeat Symbiote Vulture	Symbiote Vulture Defeated	20
Defeat Symbiote Black Cat	Symbiote Black Cat defeated	20
Defeat Symbiote Wolverine	Symbiote Wolverine Defeated	20
Defeat Symbiote Electro	Symbiote Electro defeated	20
Winged	Vulture defeated	15
Defeat Venom, Round Two	Defeated Venom twice	20
Id	Spent time with Black Cat	5
Vice	First Black Suit Choice	5
Super-ego	Black Cat Spurned	5
Virtue	First Red Suit Choice	5

OVERLORD

XBOX 360™ ACHIEVEMENTS

STAR WARS: THE FORCE UNLEASHED

ACHIEVEMENTS

NAME	GOAL/REQUIREMENT	POINT VALUE
Apprentice	Complete Game - Apprentice difficulty. Do not change the difficulty after the game has started.	75
Sith Warrior	Complete Game - Sith Warrior difficulty. Do not change the difficulty after the game has started.	100
Sith Lord	Complete Game - Sith Lord difficulty. Do not change the difficulty after the game has started.	100
Sith Master	Complete Game - Sith Master difficulty. Do not change the difficulty after the game has started.	100
Pushed	Defeat 100 enemies with Force Push	5
Gripped	Defeat 100 enemies with Force Grip	5
Shocked	Defeat 100 enemies with Force Lightning	5
Repulsed	Defeat 100 enemies with Force Repulse	5
Impaled	Defeat 100 enemies with Saber Throw	5
Stormed	Defeat 100 enemies with Lightning Shield	5
Grappled	Defeat 100 enemies with a grapple move	15
Launched	Defeat 100 enemies with Aerial Ambush juggle combos	20
PROXY Won't Be Happy	Destroy 35 droids	15
Rebel Leader	Defeat 500 Imperials	15
Bossk	Defeat 200 Wookiees on Kashyyyk Prologue	15
Bully	Defeat 25 Ugnaughts or Jawas	15
Skilled	Earn 250,000 Force Points on a single level	5
Expert	Earn 500,000 Force Points on a single level	10
Legend	Earn 600,000 Force Points on a single level	25
Frenzy	Get a Frenzy x4 bonus	5
Sith Frenzy	Get a Frenzy x8 bonus	10
Sith Lord Frenzy	Get a Frenzy x12 bonus	15
Holocron Collector	Collect all Jedi holocrons in the game	75
Corellian Star	Complete all bonus objectives on one level	10
Force Push Mastery	Defeat 500 enemies with Force Push	20
Force Grip Mastery	Defeat 500 enemies with Force Grip	20
Force Lightning Mastery	Defeat 500 enemies with Force Lightning	20
Force Repulse Mastery	Defeat 500 enemies with Repulse	20
Lightsaber Throw Mastery	Defeat 500 enemies with Saber Throw	20
Lightning Shield Mastery	Defeat 500 enemies with Lightning Shield	20
The Bigger They Are	Defeat 6 Rancors	15
The Harder They Fall	Defeat 10 AT-STs or AT-KTs	15
Cannon Fodder	Defeat 150 Stormtroopers	15
Sith Trials	Complete all Training Room challenges and Combat Modules	20
Sith Training	Complete all Training Room lessons	20

SECRET ACHIEVEMENTS

NAME	GOAL/REQUIREMENT	POINT VALUE
Invasion	Complete Level - Prologue	10
Insurrection	Complete Level - TIE Factory, act 1	10
Junkyard	Complete Level - Raxus Prime, act 1	10
Jedi Hunt	Complete Level - Felucia, act 1	10
Empirical	Complete Level - Empirical, act 2	10
Vapor Room	Complete Level - Cloud City, act 2	10
Skyhook	Complete Level - Kashyyyk, act 2	10
Infestation	Complete Level - Felucia, act 2	10
Destroyer	Complete Level - Raxus Prime, act 2	10
Redemption	Complete Game - Light Side	20
Revenge	Complete Game - Dark Side	20
Worst Day-Shift Manager Ever	Kill 12 Stormtroopers as Vader during the Prologue	10

ACHIEVEMENTS

NAME	GOAL/REQUIREMENT	POINTS
Aftershocker	Earn a 1 star ranking in all Aftershock scenes.	30
Aftershocker Legend	Earn a 5 star ranking in all Aftershock scenes.	30
Architect	Earn a 4 star ranking in all Constructor Challenges.	15
Big Pipe	Host 50 ranked matches.	10
Commando	Earn a 1 star ranking in all Strike Force Omega scenes.	30
Commando Legend	Earn a 5 star ranking in all Strike Force Omega scenes.	30
Cranker	Perform 30 180-degree turn stunts.	10
Crazy Horse	Earn 400 or more wheelie points in one movie scene.	10
Death Wish	Drive or jump into a hazard zone 30 times.	5
Drifter	Earn 500 or more drift points in one movie scene.	10
Duster	Perform 20 over-take stunts.	10
Entertainer	Custom Arena selected for boards the first time.	10
Flammable	Ignite your vehicle for the first time.	5
Hillbilly	Earn a 1 star ranking in all Whoopin' and a Hollerin II scenes.	30
Hillbilly Legend	Earn a 5 star ranking in all Whoopin' and a Hollerin II scenes.	30
Hollywood	Unlock all of the Taurus Awards.	30
Legend	Earn a 4 star ranking in all movie scenes.	20
Lord Challenger	Earn a 5 star ranking in all Quick Fixes.	30
Master Challenger	Earn a 4 star ranking in all Quick Fixes.	20
MasterMC	Custom Arena selected for boards 10 times.	10
Millionaire	Earn over a million points in any scene.	10
Most Wanted!	Earn a 5 star ranking for all Odd Jobs.	30
Nitro Head	Earn 10 Nitrous in any ranked MP match.	10
Outlaw	Earn a 4 star ranking in all Odd Jobs.	20
Plugged In	Steal a 100,000+ point string in any ranked Backlot Battle.	10
Race Ruler	Earn over 20 first places in a ranked Movie Challenge.	20
Racer	Finish 1st in 10 ranked Backlot Races.	20
Rammer	Earn 20,000 ramming points in any ranked Backlot Battle.	10
Screwdriver	Earn 300 or more airborne rotation points in one movie scene.	10
Secret Agent	Earn a 1 star ranking in all Never Kill Me Again scenes.	30
Secret Agent Legend	Earn a 5 star ranking in all Never Kill Me Again scenes.	30
Shaver	Earn 500 or more close points in one movie scene.	10
Soldier	Finish 1st in 10 consecutive ranked Backlot Battles.	20
Spinner	Perform 10 reverse-180 stunts..	10
Stealer	Steal 6 or more strings in 1 ranked Backlot Battle.	20
String'n King	Get your multiplier to a x100 in any movie scene.	10
Stunt Constructor	Earn a 5 star ranking in all Constructor Challenges.	30
Super Hero	Earn a 1 star ranking in all Night Avenger scenes.	30
Super Hero Legend	Earn a 5 star ranking in all Night Avenger scenes.	30
Threader	String an entire movie scene.	10
Thrill Seeker	Earn a 1 star ranking for all Odd Jobs.	30
Tornado	Earn a 200x Multiplier in any ranked Backlot Battle.	10
Trooper	Finish in 1st place with each of the vehicles in Backlot Battle.	20
Turtle	Flip your car on its back for the first time.	5
Unbreakable!	Earn a 5 star ranking in all movie scenes.	100
Untouchable	Place 1st in 12 ranked Backlot Battles without getting your string stolen.	10
Wheel'n	Earn 100 or more 2-wheel points in one movie scene.	10
Wheelman	Earn a 1 star ranking in all Overdrive scenes.	30
Wheelman Legend	Earn a 5 star ranking in all Overdrive scenes.	30
Wings	Earn 300 or more airborne points in one movie scene.	10

OVERLOAD

XBOX 360™ ACHIEVEMENTS

SUPERMAN RETURNS

ACHIEVEMENTS

NAME	GOAL/REQUIREMENT	POINTS
Hero of Metropolis	Complete All Metro Events and Mini-Games .	200
Armageddon Averted	Complete Level 01: Meteor Storm .	30
Mr. What's-his-name	Complete All Mini-Games .	50
You Am Bizarro!	Complete The Bizarro Mini-Game .	20
Super Sonic	Finished All Fast Flyer Mini-Games .	20
Mr. Whiskers	Find All Kittens .	50
Souped-Up Superman	Obtain All 15 Power-Ups .	30
Frequent Flyer	Travel For 10,000 Miles .	30
Roadside Assistance	Pick Up 100 Cars Throughout The Game .	30
The Greatest Day	Play A Total Of 12 Hours .	30
Heavy Lifting	Lift 10,000 Tons Throughout The Game .	30
Warworld	Visited and Dominated Warworld .	50
Twisted	Saved Metropolis from the rampaging tornado.	100
The Mongul Hordes	Vanquished Mongul once again.	100
Me aM savE yOU!	By you is Bizarro not undefeated!	100
Metallo Mastered	Stopped Metallo in the name of justice.	100
Versatile Fighter	Perform 99 fighting combos.	30
Not that Super	Entered a cheat code in a desperate plea for help .	0

TALES OF VESPERIA

ACHIEVEMENTS

NAME	GOAL/REQUIREMENT	POINT VALUE
Too Much Free Time	Patience. Hours and hours of patience.	20
To Points Unknown	The journey of 100,000 km begins with a single step.	10
Grand Battles	Monsters! Bring on the monsters!	10
Jackpot	Win more chips!	10
Piggybank	Save more Gald. More. No, seriously. A lot more.	10
They Call Me...	Clear sub events to acquire titles.	30
Character Study	Careful! Some skits are only available for a limited time.	10
No More Grinding	Just fight and fight until you don't really need to fight anymore.	10
Map Nerd	The camera reveals what the World Map holds...	50
Monster Nerd	Don't forget to use a Magic Lens or two. Or more.	30
Item Nerd	Careful! Some items are only available through synthesis.	30
Little Mad Scientist	Synthesize! Mash stuff up! Make lots of things!	10
Back Up Plan	Save points are located all over the world.	10
Vesperia master	Aim for total completion.	0
The Hit that Keeps On Hitting	Keep that combo going and going and going!	20

SECRET ACHIEVEMENTS

NAME	GOAL/REQUIREMENT	POINT VALUE
Eureka!	You used Synthesis to create new equipment and items. Keep it up!	10
First Strike	Took out your enemy in a single shot! Master this technique to gain advantage in battles.	20
Big Game Greenhorn	Giganto Monsters are...special. Big. Strong. Nasty. Have fun!	20
Big Game Hunter	You slew all Giganto Monsters! Nothing can stand before you! Careful, though. It's a big world...	50
Smarty-pants	Hey! You answered every quiz question right! You are a true Tales fan. Thank you.	10
Speedster	Whoa! Easy! Could you be any faster?! Relax. Take your time. There's much more to discover...	15
Ahhh, Memories	You have cleared the Labyrinth of Memories. Did you enjoy the surprise?	30

NAME	GOAL/REQUIREMENT	POINT VALUE
Recovered the Aque Blastia	You took back the aque blastia core from Barbos. This should fix the lower quarter's fountain.	100
Ended Alexei's Ambitions	You put an end to Alexei's ambitions. However, the Adephagos remains. The battle continues...	150
Defeated the Adephagos	You defeated the Adephagos with Duke! A new world begins. A world without blastia.	200
Bunny Guild Member	Somehow, somewhere, you became an official member of the Bunny Guild. Who needs Brave Vesperia?	10
Low Level Challenger	You defeated Barbos at Lv. 15 or under! Amazing! You sure know how to take this guy down.	10
Secret Mission 1	Defeated Zagi while protecting Estellise from Zagi's attacks.	5
Secret Mission 2	Downed Goliath by attacking its Achilles' heel while it charged X Buster.	5
Secret Mission 3	Learning from Karol's experience, you used the billybally plants to stun Gattuso.	5
Secret Mission 4	Lured Zagi to the side of the ship and knocked him overboard to cool him off!	5
Secret Mission 5	Downed the Dreaded Giant when it reared back and left itself wide open.	5
Secret Mission 6	Raven used Serpent to set a trap for the Gigalarva and prevented it from healing itself.	5
Secret Mission 7	VS Barbos. You took out the bridge supports, keeping him from calling out more of his thugs.	5
Secret Mission 8	Third battle VS. Zagi. Let him absorb too much magic, destroying his bohdi blastia.	5
Secret Mission 9	You defeated the Leader Bat and prevented Pteropus from recombining.	5
Secret Mission 10	VS. Outbreaker. You destroyed the core and prevented magic from inverting day and night.	5
Secret Mission 11	VS. Belius. You lit up all candlesticks and eliminated the illusions.	5
Secret Mission 12	VS. Nan and Tison. Timed your strikes between their attacks and knocked them down.	5
Secret Mission 13	VS. Schwann. Downed him by attacking when he was clutching his heart after his mystic arte.	5
Secret Mission 14	Fourth battle VS. Zagi. Used Karol's Nice Recovery Smash arte to force him to recover from poison.	5
Secret Mission 15	VS. Baitojoh. Hit it 3 times during it's Ice Edge attack and fished it out of the water.	5
Secret Mission 16	VS. Estellise. Used the item, Mother's Memento.	5
Secret Mission 17	VS. Yeager. Made his heart explode using Raven's Rain arte.	5
Secret Mission 18	VS. Alexei. Downed him by attacking when he was tired after his mystic arte.	5
Secret Mission 19	VS. Gusios. Attacked his tail, then downed him with a close attack while his feet were raised.	5
Secret Mission 20	VS. Khroma. Downed her by timing your strikes between certain of her attacks.	5
Secret Mission 21	VS. Flynn. He used every arte he could, including a mystic arte.	5
Secret Mission 22	Fifth battle VS. Zagi. Downed him by attacking after he becomes exhausted from Blastia Bane.	5
Secret Mission 23	Defeated Duke using a mystic arte.	5

TONY HAWK'S PROJECT 8

ACHIEVEMENTS

NAME	GOAL/REQUIREMENT	POINTS
Training Complete	You completed the training, go put what you learned into practice.	10
Outta the Houses	You escaped the suburban life, explore the world.	10
School Unlocked	Unlocked the School.	10
Slums Unlocked	Unlocked the Slums.	10
Skate Park Unlocked	You made your way to the skate park. Enjoy yourself.	10
Funpark Unlocked	Unlocked the Funpark.	10
Factory Unlocked	Go shred the factory, you deserve it.	10

NAME	GOAL/REQUIREMENT	POINTS
First Sick Goal	Congratulations, you completed a goal at Sick difficulty.	5
All Pro Challenges Completed	You stepped up to the challenge. You did everything the pro's challenged you to do.	20
Sick Chalk Challenges	Incredible, you beat all the goals at Sick difficulty.	30
Sick Classic Goals	All classic goals at Sick? That's amazing.	30
Hit 50% of the Gaps	Wow! 50 percent of the gaps found… Keep going you're halfway there.	20
Hit All of the Gaps	You've skated the world and found every gap. Congratulations!	35
Scored Over 1,000,000 Points!	That's a nice highs core run, but you can do better right?	10
Nice Combo!	Well done, you landed over a 500,000 point combo.	20
Played Xbox Live	Play an online game.	10
50 games Online	Finish 50 games online.	15
100 games Online	Finish 100 games online.	20
You Made It into Project 8	Congratulations you cracked the top 8, can you get higher?	50
You Made It to Spot 4!	Congratulations you cracked the top 4, can you get to number 1?	75
Ranked Number 1!	You did it. You are the number one skater on Project 8.	100
Secret Area Found	You found your first secret area. Don't tell anyone.	5
Manual Master	You've manualed for 140,000 feet!	20
Hang Time	14,000 seconds of air time.	20
The Daily Grind	You've managed to grind for 140,000 total feet.	20
Beat a Developer	Win a skate session against a member of the Project 8 development team, or someone who already has.	50
Suburbia Classic Beaten at Sick	Amazing. You got Sick on the Suburbia classic goal.	15
Main St Classic Beaten at Sick	Amazing. You got Sick on the Main St classic goal.	15
Capitol Classic Beaten at Sick	Capitol Classic beaten at Sick.	15
School Classic Beaten at Sick	Amazing. You got Sick on the School classic goal.	15
Slums Classic Beaten at Sick	Amazing. You got Sick on the Slums classic goal.	15
Skate Classic Beaten at Sick	Amazing. You got Sick on the Skate Park classic goal.	15
Fun Park Classic Beaten at Sick	Amazing. You got Sick on the Fun Park classic goal.	15
Factory Classic Beaten at Sick	Amazing. You got Sick on the Factory classic goal.	15
Full Stats	You got every stat maxed. How long did that take you?	50
Mullen Pro Challenge	Find Rodney and beat his challenge.	10
Vallely Pro Challenge	Find Mike V and beat his challenge.	10
Song Pro Challenge	Find Daewon and beat his challenge.	10
Burnquist Pro Challenge	Find Bob and beat his challenge.	10
Sheckler Pro Challenge	Find Ryan and beat his challenge.	10
Margera Pro Challenge	Find Bam and beat his challenge.	10
Nyjah & Lyn-Z Pro Challenge	Find Nyjah and Lyn-Z and beat their challenge.	10
Williams & Dollin Pro Challenge	Find Stevie and Dustin and beat their challenge.	10
P-Rod Pro Challenge	Find P-Rod and beat his challenge.	10
Shhhh it's a secret	You found all the secret areas, nice going Sherlock.	25
That combo was sick!	Wow you landed a combo over 5,000,000 points .	35
Sick Highscore Run	That's a huge high score.	20
Impressing the locals	Congratulations, you got 1000 Stokens.	25
Break 15 bones in one bail	Man that hurt.	10

ACHIEVEMENTS

NAME	GOAL/REQUIREMENT	POINTS
All Gaps	Find all the Gaps on the View Gaps list.	50
Cashtastic	Find all cash spots.	40
AM all goals	Complete all goals at AM ranking or better.	40
All Pro	Complete all goals at PRO ranking or better.	70
All Classic	Complete all Classic goals at AM ranking or better.	10
Pro all Classic	Complete all Classic goals at PRO ranking or better.	15
Sick all Classic	Complete all Classic goals at SICK.	40
All Hawk-man	Complete all Hawk-man Goals at AM ranking or better.	10
Complete All Hawk Man Goals Pro	Complete all Hawk-man Goals at PRO ranking or better.	15
Sick all Hawk-man	Complete all Hawk-man Goals at SICK.	40
High Score Video	Make a Video worth 20,000 points	10
All Skill Goals	Complete all Skill Challenges at AM ranking or better.	10
Pro all Skill Goals	Complete all Skill Challenges at PRO ranking or better.	15
Sick all Skill Goals	Completed all Skill Challenges at SICK.	40
Thug Check Distance	Knock Thug 150 feet.	5
All Skill Upgrades	Upgrade all skater skills.	10
All Skater Items	Purchase all Skater Gear including unlocked items.	20
All Photo Goals	Complete all Photo goals at AM ranking or better.	10
Pro all Photo Goals	Complete all Photo goals at PRO ranking or better.	15
Sick all Photo Goals	Complete all Photo goals at SICK	40
All Film Goals	Complete all Film goals at AM ranking or better.	10
Pro all Film Goals	Complete all Film goals at PRO ranking or better.	15
Sick all Film Goals	Completed all Film Goals at SICK	40
All Line Goals	Complete all Line goals at AM ranking or better.	10
Pro all Line Goals	Complete all Line goals at PRO ranking or better.	15
Sick all Line Goals	Complete all Line goals at SICK	40
All Uber Goals	Complete all Lifestyle Uber Goals.	20
1000 online games played.	Accumulate 1000 games played.	20
5 out of 5! Online Domination.	Win all 5 rounds in a match with at least 4 gamertags in the room.	20

SECRET ACHIEVEMENTS

NAME	GOAL/REQUIREMENT	POINTS
Deck Milestone	Achieved 'Get Your Own Skate Deck' Game Milestone.	10
Sponsored Milestone	Achieved the 'Sponsored' Game Milestone progress.	15
Win $100,000 in wagers online.	Win enough wagers to accumulate $100,000 in winnings. Ranked Match only.	25
Shoe Milestone	Achieved 'Get Your Own Skate Shoe' Game Milestone.	10
Skate Check Episode	Dustin's Skate Checking episode completed.	15
Mod the World Episode	Daewon and Rodney's Modify the World episode completed	25
Aggro Episode	Mike V's Go Epic episode completed.	10
Climbing Episode	Bam's Climbing episode completed.	15
Bowl Skating Episode	Lance's Bowl Skating episode completed.	25
NTG Episode	Bob's Nail the Grab episode completed.	15
Join Team Milestone	Achieved the 'Join Team' Game Milestone.	30
NTT Episode	Arto's episode completed.	10
Build Your Team	Achieved 'Build Your Team' Game Milestone.	10
Rigging Episode	Jeff's Rigging episode completed.	10
Team Built	Achieved 'Team Built' Game Milestone.	20
Mod all Spots	Modified all environment areas.	35
NTM Episode	Stevie's Nail the Manual episode completed.	25

OVERLORD

XBOX 360™ ACHIEVEMENTS

TRANSFORMERS THE GAME

ACHIEVEMENTS

ACHIEVEMENT	OBTAIN	POINTS
Suburban Hero	Complete "The Suburbs".	25
Suburban Hero Challenger	Complete all "The Suburbs" sub-missions.	20
Neighboorhood Watch	Complete "More Than Meets the Eye".	25
Neighboorhood Watch Challenger	Complete all "More Than Meets the Eye" sub-missions.	20
Could You Describe the Ruckus?	Complete "Inside Hoover Dam".	25
Could You Describe the Ruckus? Challenger	Complete all "Inside Hoover Dam" sub-missions.	20
Downtown Defender	Complete "The Last Stand".	25
Downtown Defender Challenger	Complete all "The Last Stand" sub-missions.	20
Look to the Stars	Complete "The Ultimate Doom".	50
Sand Blaster	Complete "Soccent Military Base".	25
Sand Blaster Challenger	Complete all "Soccent Military Base" sub-missions.	20
Suburban Scourge	Complete "The Hunt For Sam Witwicky".	25
Suburban Scourge Challenger	Complete all "The Hunt For Sam Witwicky" sub-missions.	20
Air Traffic Destroyer	Complete "A Gathering Force".	25
Air Traffic Destroyer Challenger	Complete all "A Gathering Force" sub-missions.	20
Downtown Demolisher	Complete "City of the Machines".	25
Downtown Demolisher Challenger	Complete all "City of the Machines" sub-missions.	20
Finish this Planet	Complete "Day of the Machines".	50
Pride of Bumblebee	Collect all faction sigil shields.	60
Pride of Megatron	Defeat 200 Autobot drones.	20
Pride of Optimus Prime	Defeat 200 Decepticon drones.	20
Transform and Roll Out	Transform for the first time.	10
Robots in Disguise	Transform 500 times.	25
Keeper of the AllSpark	Get a 100% save file.	75
Batter Up	Hit an enemy with a baseball bat swing.	10
Weapons Systems Inactive	Complete "Uninvited Guests" using only melee.	20
Land Shark	Stay underground for 2:00 (Scorponok).	10
Sharp Shooter	Complete "Fireworks" with over 2:30 remaining.	40
I Know Kung Fu	Perform 1000 melee attacks.	30
Sideways Motion	Obtain your first Slide skill mark.	15
Turbo?! We Don't Need No Turbo!	Complete "Tunnel Vision" without using turbo.	30
Ring-A-Ding-Ding	Use the giant phone to hit an enemy.	10
Pit Crew	Use a large tire to hit an enemy.	10
Wrong Way!!	Ram 250 cars.	15
Shot Putter	Obtain your first Throw skill mark.	15
Speed Demon	Obtain your first Speed skill mark.	15
What Challenge?	Complete your first sub-mission.	10
Pride of Ironhide	Obtain your first Heroic skill mark.	15
Pride of Brawl	Obtain your first Destruction skill mark.	15
Mad Skillz	Obtain all skill marks in all areas.	40
We Don't Need Roads	Obtain your first Jump skill mark.	15
Root Of All Evil	Obtain your first Evil skill mark.	15

TUROK

ACHIEVEMENTS

NAME	GOAL/REQUIREMENT	POINTS
Triple Kill	Kill 3 opponents within 4 seconds of each other in a ranked match	20
Thorn in Side	Kill the Flag carrier 5 times in a ranked match	20
Co-Op 1	Finish Co-op Map 1	30
Co-Op 2	Finish Co-op Map 2	30
Co-Op 3	Finish Co-op Map 3	30

NAME	GOAL/REQUIREMENT	POINTS
Hometown Hero	Return 5 Flags to your base in one public game	25
Arch-Nemesis	Kill the same player 5 times in a row without killing anyone else in between during a public match	15
Crack Shot	Kill 5 opponents in a public game with headshots	15
Accuracy Award	Achieve an accuracy of 75% or greater with at least 20 shots fired in one ranked match	20
Great Round	Finish a public DM match with a Battle Rating of greater than 100	15
Grab Bag	Kill at least 1 creature, 1 enemy, 1 teammate, and yourself in the same round of a public match	10
Unbreakable	Play through a ranked match without dying	30
Pacifist	Play a public match with no shots fired or kills awarded, capturing the flag at least twice	15
Dino Hunter	Kill 20 Dinos in one public game	15
Exterminator	Kill 20 Bugs in one public game	15
Resurrection	Finish a player match free-for-all game with at least 10 deaths and 10 kills	15
Gamesman	Play a full round of each gametype in public or private matches	15
Retribution	Knife kill your Rival in a public match	15
Primitive Weapons	Play a public match using only the bow or knife, earning at least 10 kills	15
All-Purpose Warrior	Win 10 public games of each team game option (Small Team, Large Team, Co-Op)	30
Medal of Citation	Achieve 100 player kills in ranked matches	25
Medal of Commendation	Achieve 500 player kills in ranked matches	50
Boomstick	Destroy a dilo with the stickygun during a public match	10
Arsenal	Kill at least one enemy with every weapon in the game during public play	20
Massive Battle	Participate in a public 6 on 6 team game	10
Buddy Blowout	Play a full 8 on 8 private team game	20
Multiplayer First-Class	Finish a ranked match with 100% accuracy and at least 5 kills	35
Multiplayer Master-Class	Finish a ranked match with all headshots and at least 5 kills	40
Practically Canadian	How aboot defending your flag, eh? And that's in ranked matches, sorry.	20
Big Game Ribbon	Whoa momma!	20
Angler Ribbon	Fishing anyone?	20
Sell Your Shotguns	Complete "Mother Superior" without using the ORO Shotgun	35
Dino Dominance	Knife kill 50 creatures in the Story Mode campaign	25
Turok Service Ribbon	Complete the Story Mode campaign and unlock Inhuman difficulty	40
Turok Campaign Ribbon	Complete the Story Mode campaign on Inhuman	60
Sniper!	Head shot 10 enemies in a row during the Story Mode campaign	40
Impaler Ribbon	Pin an enemy to the wall with an arrow in the Story Mode campaign	10
Turok Defense Force	Successfully fight off 20 Raptor mauls during the Story Mode campaign	25
It's A Trap!	Get dinos to kill 5 soldiers by sticking them with the flare in the Story Mode campaign	15
Loud Love	Kill 3 soldiers with one ORO Copperhead Rocket Launcher shot in the Story Mode campaign	15
5, 4, 3, 2, 1... BOOM!	Kill 3 Soldiers with one Frag Grenade in the Story Mode campaign	15
Pincushion	Pin 50 enemies with the Bow in the Story Mode campaign	25
Man or Animal	Record 100 stealth kills of soldiers with the ORO P23 Combat Knife	30

XBOX 360™ ACHIEVEMENTS

OVERLOAD

ACHIEVEMENTS

NAME	GOAL/REQUIREMENT	POINTS
Viking Conqueror Normal	Reach the end of the game on normal difficulty	30
Viking Conqueror Hard	Reach the end of the game on hard difficulty	60
Niflberg Supplies Freed	Liberate the farm and the quarry in Niflberg	20
Dragon Summoner	Find and charge the dragon gem Hugin and dragon amulet, and summon a dragon	15
Skullbagger 1	Collect the 6 skulls in Darkwater	15
Savior of Niflberg Normal	Liberate Niflberg completely on the normal difficulty level	25
Savior of Niflberg Hard	Liberate Niflberg completely on the hard difficulty level	35
Galcliff Supplies Freed	Liberate the farm, still, lumber mill, and the quarry in Galcliff	20
Dragon Master	Complete the second dragon gem, and summon a dragon	15
Skullbagger 2	Collect the 6 skulls in Holdenfort and the 6 skulls in Caldberg	15
Demon's Nemesis	Kill Hel's Harbinger Drakan	40
Redeemer Of Galcliff Normal	Liberate Galcliff completely on the normal difficulty level	30
Redeemer of Galcliff Hard	Liberate Galcliff completely on the hard difficulty level	40
Isaholm Supplies Freed	Liberate the farm, still, lumber mill, and the quarry in Isaholm	20
Dragon Overlord	Recover the final dragon gem, and summon a dragon	15
Skullbagger 3	Collect all the 4 skulls in Thornvik	15
Death King	Finish off 150 Legion with fatality moves	25
Demon Eviscerator	Finish off 100 Legion with fatality moves	20
They Never Saw Me Coming	Execute 100 sneaky kills	20
Giant Killer	Find and slaughter a Legion Giant	25
The Flames of Freya	Buy flamepots and incinerate 10 Legion soldiers with them	20
Thor's Mortal Lightning Rod	Send a Legion back to the underworld in the most lightning-tastic way imaginable	5
Odin's Doomsinger	Use the ultimate fire attack to kill a Legion	5
Heimdall's Enforcer	Glacially wipe out a Legion using the ultimate ice attack	5
Deadly Axe Juggler	Kill 5 Legion just using Throwing axes	15
Euthanasia Euphoria	Use your defensive bash to knock your Legion foes to their doom!	5
Friend Of The People	Power-up over 500 Vikings in your armies with runic magic	10
Assassin of Assassins	Locate and kill a Legion Assassin	15
Blinded To Fear	Kill 50 Legion without using a health potion	45
Viking Slaughterer	Learn a total of 4 new moves	12
Viking Butcher	Master the first new move at the Battle Arena	10
Viking Slayer	Master a total of 8 new moves	14
Viking Warrior	Master a total of 12 new moves	16
Viking Blademaster	Learn all the moves in the game	18
Demon Hacker	Finish off 25 Legion with fatality moves	5
Secretive Rogue	Complete the quest to sneak into Darkwater	20
The Perfect Killer	Kill a Legion Champion without being hit	20
Killer of Champions	Kill 10 Champions	5
Killer of Giants	Kill 5 Giants	5
Hero Of Darkwater	Lead your army to victory at the battle for Darkwater	10
Hero Of Holdenfort	Lead your army to victory at the battle for Holdenfort	10
Hero Of Caldberg	Lead your army to victory at the battle for Caldberg	10
Hero Of Thornvik	Lead your army to victory at the battle for Thornvik	10
Hero Of Midgard	Lead your army to victory at the final battle for all Midgard	20
No Need For Immortality	Lead your army to victory at Hel's Fortress without need for immortality	50
Thirst For Blood	Kill 50 Legion soldiers	10

NAME	GOAL/REQUIREMENT	POINTS
Lust For Blood	Kill 100 Legion soldiers	20
Champion of Champions	Find and defeat a Legion Champion	25
Berzerker	Kill 200 Legion soldiers	35
Slaughter Master	Kill 500 Legion soldier	50

VIVA PIÑATA

ACHIEVEMENTS

NAME	GOAL/REQUIREMENT	POINTS
Challenger	Successfully completed 5 Factory requests.	20
Master Challenger	Successfully completed 20 Factory requests.	20
Romancer	Become Master Romancer for 5 species.	20
Master Romancer	Become Master Romancer for 20 species.	20
Collector	Made 5 species resident.	20
Master Collector	Made 50 species resident.	20
Longevity	Played the game for 10 hours (real time).	20
Garden Value	Garden worth 25,000 chocolate coins.	20
Garden Value Master	Garden worth 100,000 chocolate coins.	20
Piñata Value	One Piñata worth 5,000 chocolate coins.	20
Piñata Value Master	One Piñata worth 10,000 chocolate coins.	20
Green Fingers	Grown 5 plants to maturity.	20
Master Green Fingers	Grown 25 plants to maturity.	20
Wealthy	Player has 25,000 chocolate coins.	20
Label Designer	Made a Custom Label.	20
Piñata Name Caller	Named a Piñata.	20
Helper Name Caller	Named a Helper.	20
Talent	Player has reached Level 10.	20
Master Talent	Player has reached Level 50.	20
Wealth Master	Player has 100,000 chocolate coins.	20
Land Owner	Garden Size increased Once.	20
Sprinkling	Employed a sprinkling.	20
Gatherling	Employed a Gatherling.	20
Super Shovel	All the Shovel Head upgrades.	20
Weedling	Employed a Weedling.	20
Harvester	Collected produce from a Buzzlegum, Moozipan, or Goobaa.	20
Watchling	Employed a Watchling.	20
Generosity	Player turned the Beggar into a Trader.	20
Sour Tower	Tower of Sour has 2 pieces.	20
Taffly Fertilizer	Player has made fertilizer with the Taffly.	20
Evolver	Evolved 2 species.	20
Master Land Owner	Garden size at maximum.	20
Variants	Made 5 variant Piñatas.	20
Pigxie Prize	Cross romancing a Swanana and a Rashberry.	20
Shovel Strength	All the Shovel Handle upgrades.	20
Watering Can Do	All the Watering Can upgrades.	20
Diggerling	Employed a Diggerling.	20
Master Sour Tower	Tower of Sour has 6 pieces.	20
Cluckles Hatches Egg	Player has hatched an egg using the Cluckles.	20
Horticulturist	Full bonus growth for 5 plants.	20
Macaracoon Gift	Player has been brought a Romance Sweet by a Macaracoon.	20
Variants Master	Made 20 variant Pinatas.	20
Crowla Delay	Player has distracted Dastardos with the Crowla.	20
Longevity Master	Played the game for 50 hours (real time).	20
Sherbat Dance	Player has distracted Dastardos with the Sherbat.	20
Master Evolver	Evolved 8 species.	20
Cocoadile Tears	Player has attained full bonus growth for a plant using the Cocodile Tears.	20
Master Horticulturist	Full bonus growth for 25 plants.	20
Mallowolf Howl	Player has used the Mallowolf to scare off Ruffians.	20
Chewnicorn Healing	Player has healed a Piñata with the Chewnicorn's power.	20

VIVA PIÑATA: TROUBLE IN PARADISE

ACHIEVEMENTS

NAME	GOAL/REQUIREMENT	POINT VALUE
Card Sharp	Use a Piñata Card	10
Famous Piñata	Obtain a special Piñata from the website (or trade one with someone who has)	20
Records Keeper	Restore 10 of Piñata Central's Computer Records	30
Master Exhibitor	Win 10 Piñata shows	20
Desert Collector	Make 3 Desert species resident	10
Couch Socialite	Play One Box Co-op for 1 hour	10
Master Couch Socialite	Play One Box Co-op for 3 Hours	20
Region 7 Challenger	Complete all Challenges in Region 7	20
Desert Green Fingers	Grow all Desert plants to maturity	20
Arctic Green Fingers	Grow all Arctic plants to maturity	20
Come And Have A Go	Earn a Gold Combat Medal	20
Master Arctic Collector	Make all Arctic species resident	20
Region 2 Challenger	Complete all Challenges in Region 2	20
Packet Bulger	Packet contains all surface types	20
Region 1 Challenger	Complete all of Langston's Destination Challenges in Region 1	20
Full House	Play 4 Player Online Co-op for 1 hour	10
Master Card Sharp	Use 10 different Piñata Cards	20
SpeedFreak	Win a Piñata race	10
Expert Records Keeper	Restore all of Piñata Central's Computer Records	50
Master Records Keeper	Restore 30 of Piñata Central's Computer Records	40
Exhibitor	Win a Piñata show	10
Region 3 Challenger	Complete all Challenges in Region 3	20
Region 4 Challenger	Complete all Challenges in Region 4	20
Region 5 Challenger	Complete all Challenges in Region 5	20
Master Speedfreak	Win 10 Piñata races	20
Region 6 Challenger	Complete all Challenges in Region 6	20
Master Desert Collector	Make all Desert species resident	20
Arctic Collector	Make 3 Arctic species resident	10
Master Challenger	Complete all Challenges in all Regions	50

SECRET ACHIEVEMENTS

NAME	GOAL/REQUIREMENT	POINT VALUE
Moojoo Evolution	Evolve a Moojoo from a Doenut	20
Twin Birth	Create One Set of Twin Pinata's	10
Hoghurt Evolution	Evolve a Hoghurt from a Rashberry	20
Yakity Yak	Collect milk from a Flapyak	20
Dinokeeper	Obtain a Choclodocus	50
Polollybear Evolution	Evolve a Polollybear from a Fizzlybear	20
Fancy Dress	Wear a complete Piñata "costume" of accessories	30
Wildcard Variant	Create a Wildcard Pinata	10
Chocstrich Evolution	Evolve a Chocstrich from a Cluckles	20
Candied Camera	Take 10 Photographs (Normal)	10
Master Candied Camera	Take a Special Photograph	20
Choo-Choo	Have a Woo Woo Train in the Garden	10
Pieena Evolution	Evolve a Pieena from a Pretztail	20
Parmadillo Evolution	Evolve a Parmadillo from a Fudgehog	20
Wildcard Variant Master	Create 10 Wildcard Piñatas	20
Twin Birth Master	Create 10 sets of twin Piñatas	20
Master Instructor	Teach 10 Piñatas both of its tricks	20
Long Shot	Knock 1 Sweet into a seed hole from a long distance	20
Instructor	Teach a Piñata both of its tricks	10

NAME	GOAL/REQUIREMENT	POINT VALUE
Choo-Choo Master	Have a Spectral Locomotive in the Garden	20
Gone Clubbing	Knock 5 Sweets into seed holes using the Shovel	10

WWE SMACKDOWN VS. RAW 2009

ACHIEVEMENTS

Name	Goal/Requirement	Point Value
Congrats are in order	Win an Exhibition match.	10
Smokin'	Defeat Kane in an Inferno Match.	20
Create A Finisher	Defeat an opponent using a Created Finisher in a match.	10
A brawl to end them all	Win in both a Locker Room Brawl and Backstage Brawl.	30
Cena Story	Complete Cena's story in Road to WrestleMania mode.	20
Triple H Story	Complete Triple H's DX and Evolution route in Road to WrestleMania mode.	40
Undertaker Story	Complete Undertaker's story in Road to WrestleMania mode.	20
Chris Jericho Story	Complete Chris Jericho's story in Road to WrestleMania mode.	20
Mysterio & Batista Story	Complete Mysterio & Batista's story in Road to WrestleMania mode using both Superstars.	40
Bonus Collector	Obtain all bonuses in Road to WrestleMania mode.	150
Gold Rush	In Career mode, win every WWE Championship at least once.	60
A year in the life	Complete 1 year of Career Mode playing each match.	100
Unstoppable	Use a created Superstar and obtain 6 abilities in Career Mode.	60
5 Hall of Famers	In Career mode, induct 5 Superstars to the Hall of Fame.	100

SECRET ACHIEVEMENTS

NAME	GOAL/REQUIREMENT	POINT VALUE
Lights, Camera, Action!	Create at least 1 original WWE highlight reel.	30
Hot Tag	Perform a hot tag in a tag team match and win.	30
The end of the road	Complete Road to WrestleMania mode using each selectable Superstar.	200
5 Stars	In Career mode, Obtain a 5-Star match rating	60

XBOX 360™ ACHIEVEMENTS

OVERLORD

NINTENDO Wii™

GAMES

WII VIRTUAL CONSOLE

AVATAR: THE LAST AIRBENDER

UNLIMITED HEALTH
Select Code Entry from Extras and enter 94677.

UNLIMITED CHI
Select Code Entry from Extras and enter 24463.

UNLIMITED COPPER
Select Code Entry from Extras and enter 23637.

NEVERENDING STEALTH
Select Code Entry from Extras and enter 53467.

1 HIT DISHONOR
Select Code Entry from Extras and enter 54641.

DOUBLE DAMAGE
Select Code Entry from Extras and enter 34743.

ALL TREASURE MAPS
Select Code Entry from Extras and enter 37437.

THE CHARACTER CONCEPT ART GALLERY
Select Code Entry from Extras and enter 97831.

AVATAR: THE LAST AIRBENDER— THE BURNING EARTH

DOUBLE DAMAGE
Go to the code entry section and enter 90210.

INFINITE LIFE
Go to the code entry section and enter 65049.

INFINITE SPECIAL ATTACKS
Go to the code entry section and enter 66206.

MAX LEVEL
Go to the code entry section and enter 89121.

ONE-HIT DISHONOR
Go to the code entry section and enter 28260.

ALL BONUS GAMES
Go to the code entry section and enter 99801.

ALL GALLERY ITEMS
Go to the code entry section and enter 85061.

BEN 10: PROTECTOR OF EARTH

INVINCIBILITY
Select a game from the Continue option. Go to the Map Selection screen, press Plus and choose Extras. Select Enter Secret Code and enter XLR8, Heatblast, Wildvine, Fourarms.

ALL COMBOS
Select a game from the Continue option. Go to the Map Selection screen, press Plus and choose Extras. Select Enter Secret Code and enter Cannonblot, Heatblast, Fourarms, Heatblast.

ALL LOCATIONS
Select a game from the Continue option. Go to the Map Selection screen, press Plus and choose Extras. Select Enter Secret Code and enter Heatblast, XLR8, XLR8, Cannonblot.

DNA FORCE SKINS
Select a game from the Continue option. Go to the Map Selection screen, press Plus and choose Extras. Select Enter Secret Code and enter Wildvine, Fourarms, Heatblast, Cannonbolt.

DARK HEROES SKINS
Select a game from the Continue option. Go to the Map Selection screen, press Plus and choose Extras. Select Enter Secret Code and enter Cannonbolt, Cannonbolt, Fourarms, Heatblast.

ALL ALIEN FORMS
Select a game from the Continue option. Go to the Map Selection screen, press Plus and choose Extras. Select Enter Secret Code and enter Wildvine, Fourarms, Heatblast, Wildvine.

MASTER CONTROL
Select a game from the Continue option. Go to the Map Selection screen, press Plus and choose Extras. Select Enter Secret Code and enter Cannonbolt, Heatblast, Wildvine, Fourarms.

OVERLORD

NINTENDO Wii™

BLAZING ANGELS: SQUADRONS OF WWII

ALL AIRCRAFT AND CAMPAIGNS
After you have chosen a pilot, hold Minus + Plus and press Left, Right, 1, 2, 2, 1.

GOD MODE
Pause the game, hold Minus and press 1, 2, 1, 2.

WEAPON DAMAGE INCREASED
Pause the game, hold Minus and press 2, 1, 1, 2.

BOOM BLOX

ALL TOYS IN CREATE MODE
At the Title screen, press Up, Right, Down, Left to bring up a cheats menu. Enter Tool Pool.

SLOW-MO IN SINGLE PLAYER
At the Title screen, press Up, Right, Down, Left to bring up a cheats menu. Enter Blox Time.

CHEERLEADERS BECOME PROFILE CHARACTER
At the Title screen, press Up, Right, Down, Left to bring up a cheats menu. Enter My Team.

FLOWER EXPLOSIONS
At the Title screen, press Up, Right, Down, Left to bring up a cheats menu. Enter Flower Power.

JINGLE BLOCKS
At the Title screen, press Up, Right, Down, Left to bring up a cheats menu. Enter Maestro.

CALL OF DUTY 3

ALL CHAPTERS AND BONUS CONTENT
At the Chapter Select screen, hold Plus and press Right, Right, Left, Left, 2 Button, 2 Button.

CARS MATER-NATIONAL

ALL ARCADE RACES, MINI-GAMES, AND WORLDS
Select Codes/Cheats from the options and enter PLAYALL.

ALL CARS
Select Codes/Cheats from the options and enter MATTEL07.

ALTERNATE LIGHTNING MCQUEEN COLORS
Select Codes/Cheats from the options and enter NCEDUDZ.

ALL COLORS FOR OTHERS
Select Codes/Cheats from the options and enter PAINTIT.

UNLIMITED TURBO
Select Codes/Cheats from the options and enter ZZOOOOM.

EXTREME ACCELERATION
Select Codes/Cheats from the options and enter 0TO200X.

EXPERT MODE
Select Codes/Cheats from the options and enter VRYFAST.

ALL BONUS ART
Select Codes/Cheats from the options and enter BUYTALL.

UNLOCK EVERYTHING
Pause the game and press 2, 1, C, Z, 2, 1.

UNLIMITED HEALTH AND POWER
Pause the game and press 2, 2, Z, Z, 1, 1.

INCREASE SPEED
Pause the game and press Z, 1, 2, 1(x3).

INCREASE DAMAGE
Pause the game and press 1, Z, Z, C x3).

CONFIGURATION A
Pause the game and press 2, Z, 1, Z, C, Z.

CONFIGURATION B
Pause the game and press C, C, 1, C, Z, C.

ALL ABILITIES
Pause the game and press Z, C, Z, C(x3).

ALL BONUSES
Pause the game and press 1, 2, C, 2(x3).

ALL GOODIES
Pause the game and press C, 2, 2, Z, C, Z.

DE BLOB

INVULNERABILITY
During a game, hold C and press 1, 1, 1, 1. Re-enter the code to disable.

LIFE UP
During a game, hold C and press 1, 1, 2, 2.

TIME BONUS
During a game, hold C and press 1, 2, 1, 2. This adds 10 minutes to your time.

ALL MOODS
At the Main menu, hold C and press B, B, 1, 2, 1, 2, B, B.

ALL MULTIPLAYER LEVELS
At the Main menu, hold C and press 2, 2, B, B, 1, 1, B, B.

DEFEND YOUR CASTLE

CATAPULTS ONLY
Show the credits and click on IM IN UR CONSOLZ DFENDIN UR CASLEZ when it shows up.

GIANT STICK FIGURE
Show the credits and click on SMB3W4 when it shows up.

TINY UNITS
Show the credits and click on Chuck Norris when it shows up.

DESTROY ALL HUMANS! BIG WILLY UNLEASHED

Pause the game and go to the Unlockables screen. Hold the analog stick Up until a Enter Unlock Code window appears. You can now enter the following cheats with the directional-pad. Press A after entering a code.

NINTENDO Wii™

OVERLORD

Use this menu to toggle cheats on and off.

UNLOCK ALL GAME WORLDS
Up, Right, Down, Right, Up

CAN'T BE KILLED
Left, Down, Up, Right, Up

LOTS OF GUNS
Right, Left, Down, Left, Up

INFINITE AMMO
Right, Up, Up, Left, Right

UNLIMITED BIG WILLY BATTERY
Left, Left, Up, Right, Down

UNLIMITED JETPACK FUEL
Right, Right, Up, Left, Left

PK PICK UP HEAVY THINGS
Down, Up, Left, Up, Right

STEALTH SPACE NINJA
Up, Right, Down, Down, Left

CRYPTO DANCE FEVER SKIN
Right, Left, Right, Left, Up

KLUCKIN'S CHICKEN BLIMP SKIN
Left, Up, Down, Up, Down

LEISURE SUIT SKIN
Left, Down, Right, Left, Right

PIMP MY BLIMP SKIN
Down, Up, Right, Down, Right

DISNEY'S CHICKEN LITTLE: ACE IN ACTION

ALL LEVELS
Select the Cheats option and enter Right, Up, Left, Right, Up.

ALL WEAPONS
Select the Cheats option and enter Right, Down, Right, Left.

UNLIMITED SHIELD
Select the Cheats option and enter Right, Down, Right, Down, Right.

DISNEY PRINCESS: ENCHANTED JOURNEY

BELLE'S KINGDOM
Select Secrets and enter GASTON.

GOLDEN SET
Select Secrets and enter BLUEBIRD.

FLOWER WAND
Select Secrets and enter SLEEPY.

HEART WAND
Select Secrets and enter BASHFUL.

SHELL WAND
Select Secrets and enter RAJAH.

SHIELD WAND
Select Secrets and enter CHIP.

STAR WAND
Select Secrets and enter SNEEZY.

SURVIVAL MODE
Clear 30 missions in Mission 100 mode.

DRAGON BLADE: WRATH OF FIRE

ALL LEVELS
At the Title screen, hold Plus +
Minus and select New Game or Load
game. Hold the buttons until the
stage select appears.

EASY DIFFICULTY
At the Title screen, hold Z + 2 when
selecting "New Game."

HARD DIFFICULTY
At the Title screen, hold C + 2 when
selecting "New Game."

To clear the following codes, hold Z at the stage select.

DRAGON HEAD
At the stage select, hold Z and press Plus. Immediately Swing Wii-mote
Right, swing Wii-mote Down, swing Nunchuck Left, swing Nunchuck Right.

DRAGON WINGS
At the stage select, hold Z and press Plus. Immediately Swing Nunchuck
Up + Wii-mote Up, swing Nunchuck Down + Wii-mote Down, swing
Nunchuck Right + Wii-mote Left, swing Nunchuck Left + Wii-mote Right.

TAIL POWER
At the stage select, hold Z and press Plus. Immediately Swing your Wii-
mote Down, Up, Left, and Right

DOUBLE FIST POWER
At the stage select, hold Z and press Plus. Immediately swing your
Nunchuck Right, swing your Wii-mote left, swing your Nunchuck right
while swinging your Wii-mote left, then swing both Wii-mote and
Nunchuck down

DRIVER: PARALLEL LINES

ALL VEHICLES
Pause the game, select cheats and
enter carshow.

ALL WEAPONS
Pause the game, select cheats and
enter gunrange.

INVINCIBILITY
Pause the game, select cheats and
enter steelman.

INFINITE AMMUNITION
Pause the game, select cheats and
enter gunbelt.

INFINITE NITROUS
Pause the game, select cheats and
enter zoomzoom.

INDESTRUCTIBLE CARS
Pause the game, select cheats and
enter rollbar.

WEAKER COPS
Pause the game, select cheats and
enter keystone.

ZERO COST
Pause the game, select cheats and
enter tooledup. This gives you free
upgrades.

FAR CRY VENGEANCE

ALL MAPS
Select Cheats Menu from the Options menu and enter GiveMeTheMaps.

GHOST SQUAD

COSTUMES
Reach the following levels in single player to unlock the corresponding costume.

LEVEL	COSTUME
07	Desert Camouflage
10	Policeman
15	Tough Guy
18	Sky Camouflage
20	World War II
23	Cowboy
30	Urban Camouflage
34	Virtua Cop
38	Future Warrior
50	Ninja
60	Panda Suit
99	Gold Uniform

NINJA MODE
Play through Arcade Mode.

PARADISE MODE
Play through Ninja Mode.

THE GODFATHER: BLACKHAND EDITION

The following pause screen codes can be used only once every five minutes.

$5000
Pause the game and press Minus, 2, Minus, Minus, 2, Up.

FULL AMMO
Pause the game and press 2, Left, 2, Right, Minus, Down.

FULL HEALTH
Pause the game and press Left, Minus, Right, 2, Right, Up.

FILM CLIPS
After loading your game, before selecting Play Game, press 2, Minus, 2, Minus, Minus, Up.

GODZILLA UNLEASHED

UNLOCK ALL
At the Main menu, press A + Up to bring up the cheat entry screen. Enter 204935.

90000 STORE POINTS
At the Main menu, press A + Up to bring up the cheat entry screen. Enter 031406.

SET DAY
At the Main menu, press A + Up to bring up the cheat entry screen. Enter 0829XX, where XX represents the day. Use 00 for day one.

SHOW MONSTER MOVES
At the Main menu, press A + Up to bring up the cheat entry screen. Enter 411411.

VERSION NUMBER
At the Main menu, press A + Up to bring up the cheat entry screen. Enter 787321.

MOTHERSHIP LEVEL
Playing as the Aliens, destroy the mothership in the Invasion level.

THE GRIM ADVENTURES OF BILLY & MANDY

CONCEPT ART
At the Main menu, hold 1 and press Up, Up, Down, Down, Left, Right, Left, Right.

GUITAR HERO III: LEGENDS OF ROCK

To enter the following cheats, strum the guitar with the given buttons held. For example, if it says Yellow + Orange, hold Yellow and Orange as you strum. Air Guitar, Precision Mode and Performance Mode can be toggled on and off from the Cheats menu. You can also change between five different levels of Hyperspeed at this menu.

UNLOCK EVERYTHING

Select Cheats from the Options. Choose Enter Cheat and enter Green + Red + Blue + Orange, Green + Red + Yellow + Blue, Green + Red + Yellow + Orange, Green + Yellow + Blue + Orange, Green + Red + Yellow + Blue, Red + Yellow + Blue + Orange, Green + Red + Yellow + Blue, Green + Yellow + Blue + Orange, Green + Red + Yellow + Blue, Green + Red + Yellow + Orange, Green + Red + Yellow + Orange, Green + Red + Yellow + Blue, Green + Red + Yellow + Orange. No sounds play while this code is entered.

An easier way to show this code is by representing Green as 1 down to Orange as 5. For example, if you have 1345, you would hold down Green + Yellow + Blue + Orange while strumming. 1245 + 1234 + 1235 + 1345 + 1234 + 2345 + 1234 + 1345 + 1234 + 1235 + 1234 + 1235.

ALL SONGS

Select Cheats from the Options. Choose Enter Cheat and enter Yellow + Orange, Red + Blue, Red + Orange, Green + Blue, Red + Yellow, Yellow + Orange, Red + Yellow, Red + Blue, Green + Yellow, Green + Yellow, Yellow + Blue, Yellow + Blue, Yellow + Orange, Yellow + Blue, Yellow, Red, Red + Yellow, Red, Yellow, Orange.

NO FAIL

Select Cheats from the Options. Choose Enter Cheat and enter Green + Red, Blue, Green + Red, Green + Yellow, Blue, Green + Yellow, Red + Yellow, Orange, Red + Yellow, Green + Yellow, Yellow, Green + Yellow, Green + Red.

AIR GUITAR

Select Cheats from the Options. Choose Enter Cheat and enter Blue + Yellow, Green + Yellow, Green + Yellow, Red + Blue, Red + Blue, Red + Yellow, Red + Yellow, Blue + Yellow, Green + Yellow, Green + Yellow, Red + Blue, Red + Blue, Red + Yellow, Red + Yellow, Green + Yellow, Green + Yellow, Red + Yellow, Red + Yellow.

HYPERSPEED

Select Cheats from the Options. Choose Enter Cheat and enter Orange, Blue, Orange, Yellow, Orange, Blue, Orange, Yellow.

PERFORMANCE MODE

Select Cheats from the Options. Choose Enter Cheat and enter Red + Yellow, Red + Blue, Red + Orange, Red + Blue, Red + Yellow, Green + Blue, Red + Yellow, Red + Blue.

EASY EXPERT

Select Cheats from the Options. Choose Enter Cheat and enter Green + Red, Green + Yellow, Yellow + Blue, Red + Blue, Blue + Orange, Yellow + Orange, Red + Yellow, Red + Blue.

PRECISION MODE

Select Cheats from the Options. Choose Enter Cheat and enter Green + Red, Green + Red, Green + Red, Red + Yellow, Red + Yellow, Red + Blue, Red + Blue, Yellow + Blue, Yellow + Orange, Yellow + Orange, Green + Red, Green + Red, Green + Red, Red + Yellow, Red + Yellow, Red + Blue, Red + Blue, Yellow + Blue, Yellow + Orange, Yellow + Orange.

LARGE GEMS

Select Cheats from the Options. Choose Enter Cheat and enter Green, Red, Green, Yellow, Green, Blue, Green, Orange, Green, Blue, Green, Yellow, Green, Red, Green, Green + Red, Red + Yellow, Green + Red, Yellow + Blue, Green + Red, Blue + Orange, Green + Red, Yellow + Blue, Green + Red, Red + Yellow, Green + Red, Green + Yellow.

GUITAR HERO: AEROSMITH

Select Cheats from the Options menu and enter the following.
To do this, strum the guitar while holding the indicated buttons.
For example, if it says Yellow + Orange, hold Yellow and Orange as you strum. Air Guitar, Precision Mode, and Performance Mode can be toggled on and off from the Cheats menu. You can also change between five different levels of Hyperspeed at this menu.

ALL SONGS

Red + Yellow, Green + Red, Green + Red, Red + Yellow, Red + Yellow, Green + Red, Red + Yellow, Red + Yellow, Green + Red, Green + Red, Red + Yellow, Red + Yellow, Green + Red, Red + Yellow, Red + Blue. This code does not unlock Pandora's Box.

AIR GUITAR

Red + Yellow, Green + Red, Red + Yellow, Red + Yellow, Red + Blue, Red + Blue, Red + Blue, Red + Blue, Red + Blue, Yellow + Blue, Yellow + Blue, Yellow + Orange

HYPERSPEED

Yellow + Orange, Yellow + Orange, Yellow + Orange, Yellow + Orange, Yellow + Orange, Red + Yellow, Red + Yellow, Red + Yellow, Red + Yellow, Red + Blue, Red + Blue, Red + Blue, Red + Blue, Red + Blue, Yellow + Blue, Yellow + Orange, Yellow + Orange.

NO FAIL

Select Cheats from the Options. Choose Enter Cheat and enter Green + Red, Blue, Green + Red, Green + Yellow, Blue, Green + Yellow, Red + Yellow, Orange, Red + Yellow, Green + Yellow, Yellow, Green + Yellow, Green + Red.

PERFORMANCE MODE

Green + Red, Green + Red, Red + Orange, Red + Blue, Green + Red, Green + Red, Red + Orange, Red + Blue.

PRECISION MODE

Red + Yellow, Red + Blue, Red + Blue, Red + Yellow, Red + Yellow, Yellow + Blue, Yellow + Blue, Yellow + Blue, Red + Blue, Red + Yellow, Red + Blue, Red + Blue, Red + Yellow, Red + Yellow, Yellow + Blue, Yellow + Blue, Yellow + Blue, Red + Blue.

GUITAR HERO WORLD TOUR

The following cheats can be toggled on and off at the Cheats menu.

QUICKPLAY SONGS

Select Cheats from the Options menu, choose Enter New Cheat and press Blue, Blue, Red, Green, Green, Blue, Blue, Yellow.

ALWAYS SLIDE

Select Cheats from the Options menu, choose Enter New Cheat and press Green, Green, Red, Red, Yellow, Red, Yellow, Blue.

AT&T BALLPARK

Select Cheats from the Options menu, choose Enter New Cheat and press Yellow, Green, Red, Red, Green, Blue, Red, Yellow.

AUTO KICK

Select Cheats from the Options menu, choose Enter New Cheat and press Yellow, Green, Red, Blue (x4), Red.

EXTRA LINE 6 TONES

Select Cheats from the Options menu, choose Enter New Cheat and press Green, Red, Yellow, Blue, Red, Yellow, Blue, Green.

FLAME COLOR

Select Cheats from the Options menu, choose Enter New Cheat and press Green, Red, Green, Blue, Red, Red, Yellow, Blue.

GEM COLOR

Select Cheats from the Options menu, choose Enter New Cheat and press Blue, Red, Red, Green, Red, Green, Red, Yellow.

STAR COLOR

Select Cheats from the Options menu, choose Enter New Cheat and press Red, Red, Yellow, Red, Blue, Red, Red, Blue.

AIR INSTRUMENTS

Select Cheats from the Options menu, choose Enter New Cheat and press Red, Red, Blue, Yellow, Green (x3), Yellow.

HYPERSPEED

Select Cheats from the Options menu, choose Enter New Cheat and press Green, Blue, Red, Yellow, Yellow, Red, Green, Green. These show up in the menu as HyperGuitar, HyperBass, and HyperDrums.

PERFORMANCE MODE

Select Cheats from the Options menu, choose Enter New Cheat and press Yellow, Yellow, Blue, Red, Blue, Green, Red, Red.

INVISIBLE ROCKER

Select Cheats from the Options menu, choose Enter New Cheat and press Green, Red, Yellow (x3), Blue, Blue, Green.

VOCAL FIREBALL

Select Cheats from the Options menu, choose Enter New Cheat and press Red, Green, Green, Yellow, Blue, Green, Yellow, Green.

AARON STEELE!

Select Cheats from the Options menu, choose Enter New Cheat and press Blue, Red, Yellow (x5), Green.

JONNY VIPER

Select Cheats from the Options menu, choose Enter New Cheat and press Blue, Red, Blue, Blue, Yellow (x3), Green.

NICK

Select Cheats from the Options menu, choose Enter New Cheat and press Green, Red, Blue, Green, Red, Blue, Blue, Green.

RINA

Select Cheats from the Options menu, choose Enter New Cheat and press Blue, Red, Green, Green, Yellow (x3), Green.

ICE AGE 2: THE MELTDOWN

INFINITE PEBBLES

Pause the game and press Down, Down, Left, Up, Up, Right, Up, Down.

INFINITE ENERGY

Pause the game and press Down, Left, Right, Down, Down, Right, Left, Down.

INFINITE HEALTH

Pause the game and press Up, Right, Down, Up, Left, Down, Right, Left.

IRON MAN

ARMOR SELECTION

Iron Man's different armor suits are unlocked by completing certain missions. Refer to the following tables for when each is unlocked. After selecting a mission to play, you get the opportunity to pick the armor you wish to use.

COMPLETE MISSION	SUIT UNLOCKED
1: Escape	Mark I
2: First Flight	Mark II
3: Fight Back	Mark III
6: Flying Fortress	Comic Tin Can
9: Home Front	Classic
13: Showdown	Silver Centurion

CONCEPT ART

Concept Art is unlocked after finding certain numbers of Weapon Crates.

CONCEPT ART UNLOCKED	NUMBER OF WEAPON CRATES FOUND
Environments Set 1	6
Environments Set 2	12
Iron Man	18
Environments Set 3	24
Enemies	30
Environments Set 4	36
Villains	42
Vehicles	48
Covers	50

NINTENDO Wii™

KUNG FU PANDA

INFINITE CHI
Select Cheats from the Extra menu and press Down, Right, Left, Up, Down.

INVINCIBILITY
Select Cheats from the Extra menu and press Down, Down, Right, Up, Left.

4X DAMAGE MULTIPLIER
Select Cheats from the Extra menu and press Up, Down, Up, Right, Left.

ALL MULTIPLAYER CHARACTERS
Select Cheats from the Extra menu and press Left, Down, Left, Right, Down.

DRAGON WARRIOR OUTFIT IN MULTIPLAYER
Select Cheats from the Extra menu and press Left, Down, Right, Left, Up.

LEGO BATMAN

BATCAVE CODES
Using the computer in the Batcave, select Enter Code and enter the following codes.

CHARACTERS

CHARACTER	CODE
Alfred	ZAQ637
Batgirl	JKR331
Bruce Wayne	BDJ327
Catwoman (Classic)	M1AAWW
Clown Goon	HJK327
Commissioner Gordon	DDP967
Fishmonger	HGY748
Freeze Girl	XVK541
Joker Goon	UTF782
Joker Henchman	YUN924
Mad Hatter	JCA283
Man-Bat	NYU942
Military Policeman	MKL382
Nightwing	MVY759
Penguin Goon	NKA238
Penguin Henchman	BJH782
Penguin Minion	KJP748
Poison Ivy Goon	GTB899
Police Marksman	HKG984
Police Officer	JRY983
Riddler Goon	CRY928
Riddler Henchman	XEU824
S.W.A.T.	HTF114
Sailor	NAV592
Scientist	JFL786
Security Guard	PLB946
The Joker (Tropical)	CCB199
Yeti	NJL412
Zoo Sweeper	DWR243

VEHICLES

VEHICLE	CODE
Bat-Tank	KNTT4B
Bruce Wayne's Private Jet	LEA664
Catwoman's Motorcycle	HPL826
Garbage Truck	DUS483
Goon Helicopter	GCH328
Harbor Helicopter	CHP735
Harley Quinn's Hammer Truck	RDT637
Mad Hatter's Glider	HS000W

VEHICLE	CODE
Mad Hatter's Steamboat	M4DM4N
Mr. Freeze's Iceberg	ICYICE
The Joker's Van	JUK657
Mr. Freeze's Kart	BCT229
Penguin Goon Submarine	BTN248
Police Bike	LJP234
Police Boat	PLC999
Police Car	KJL832
Police Helicopter	CWR732
Police Van	MAC788
Police Watercraft	VJD328
Riddler's Jet	HAHAHA
Robin's Submarine	TTF453
Two-Face's Armored Truck	EFE933

CHEATS

CHEAT	CODE
Always Score Multiply	9LRGNB
Fast Batarangs	JRBDCB
Fast Walk	ZOLM6N
Flame Batarang	D8NYWH
Freeze Batarang	XPN4NG
Extra Hearts	ML3KHP
Fast Build	EVG26J
Immune to Freeze	JXUDY6
Invincibility	WYD5CP
Minikit Detector	ZXGH9J
More Batarang Targets	XWP645
Piece Detector	KHJ554
Power Brick Detector	MMN786
Regenerate Hearts	HJH7HJ
Score x2	N4NR3E
Score x4	CX9MAT
Score x6	MLVNF2
Score x8	WCCDB9
Score x10	18HW07

LEGO INDIANA JONES: THE ORIGINAL ADVENTURES

EXTRAS

Approach the blackboard in the Classroom and enter the following codes. Pause the game and select Extras. Here you can enable the cheat.

EXTRA	CODE
Artifact Detector	VIKED7
Beep Beep	VNF59Q
Character Treasure	VIES2R
Disarm Enemies	VKRNS9
Disguises	4ID1N6
Fast Build	V83SLO
Fast Dig	378RS6
Fast Fix	FJ59WS
Fertilizer	B1GW1F
Ice Rink	33GM7J
Parcel Detector	VUT673
Poo Treasure	WWQ1SA
Regenerate Hearts	MDLP69
Secret Characters	3X44AA
Silhouettes	3HE85H
Super Scream	VN3R7S
Super Slap	0P1TA5

Treasure Magnet	H86LA2
Treasure x2	VM4TS9
Treasure x4	VLWEN3
Treasure x6	V84RYS
Treasure x8	A72E1M
Treasure x10	VI3PS8

CHARACTERS

Approach the blackboard in the Classroom and enter the following codes.

CHARACTER	CODE
Bandit	12N68W
Bandit Swordsman	1MK4RT
Barranca	04EM94
Bazooka Trooper (Crusade)	MK83R7
Bazooka Trooper (Raiders)	S93Y5R
Belloq	CHN3YU
Belloq (Jungle)	TDR197
Belloq (Robes)	VEO29L
British Commander	B73EUA
British Officer	VJ5TI9
British Soldier	DJ5I2W
Captain Katanga	VJ3TT3
Chatter Lal	ENW936
Chatter Lal (Thuggee)	CNH4RY
Chen	3NK48T
Colonel Dietrich	2K9RKS
Colonel Vogel	8EAL4H
Dancing Girl	C7EJ21
Donovan	3NFTU8
Elsa (Desert)	JSNRT9
Elsa (Officer)	VMJ5US
Enemy Boxer	8246RB
Enemy Butler	VJ48W3
Enemy Guard	VJ7R51
Enemy Guard (Mountains)	YR47WM
Enemy Officer	572E61
Enemy Officer (Desert	2MK45O
Enemy Pilot	B84ELP
Enemy Radio Operator	1MF94R
Enemy Soldier (Desert)	4NSU7Q
Fedora	V75YSP
First Mate	0GIN24
Grail Knight	NE6THI
Hovitos Tribesman	H0V1SS
Indiana Jones (Desert Disguise)	4J8S4M
Indiana Jones (Officer)	VJ85OS
Jungle Guide	24PF34
Kao Kan	WMO46L
Kazim	NRH23J
Kazim (Desert)	3M29TJ
Lao Che	2NK479
Maharajah	NFK5N2
Major Toht	13NS01
Masked Bandit	N48SF0
Mola Ram	FJUR31
Monkey Man	3RF6YJ
Pankot Assassin	2NKT72
Pankot Guard	VN28RH
Sherpa Brawler	VJ37WJ
Sherpa Gunner	ND762W
Slave Child	0E3ENW
Thuggee	VM683E
Thuggee Acolyte	T2R3F9

CHARACTER	CODE
Thuggee Slave Driver	VBS7GW
Village Dignitary	KD48TN
Village Elder	4682E1
Willie (Dinner Suit)	VK93R7
Willie (Pajamas)	MEN4IP
Wu Han	3NSLT8
Extras	

Approach the blackboard in the Classroom and enter the following codes. Some cheats must be enabled by selecting Extras from the Pause menu.

CHEAT	CODE
Artifact Detector	VIKED7
Beep Beep	VNF59Q
Character Treasure	VIES2R
Disarm Enemies	VKRNS9
Disguises	4ID1N6
Fast Build	V83SLO
Fast Dig	378RS6
Fast Fix	FJ59WS
Fertilizer	B1GW1F
Ice Rink	33GM7J
Parcel Detector	VUT673
Poo Treasure	WWQ1SA
Regenerate Hearts	MDLP69
Secret Characters	3X44AA
Silhouettes	3HE85H
Super Scream	VN3R7S
Super Slap	0P1TA5
Treasure Magnet	H86LA2
Treasure x10	VI3PS8
Treasure x2	VM4TS9
Treasure x4	VLWEN3
Treasure x6	V84RYS
Treasure x8	A72E1M

LEGO STAR WARS: THE COMPLETE SAGA

The following must still be purchased after entering the codes.

CHARACTERS

ADMIRAL ACKBAR
At the bar in Mos Eisley Cantina, select Enter Code and enter ACK646.

BATTLE DROID (COMMANDER)
At the bar in Mos Eisley Cantina, select Enter Code and enter KPF958.

BOBA FETT (BOY)
At the bar in Mos Eisley Cantina, select Enter Code and enter GGF539.

BOSS NASS
At the bar in Mos Eisley Cantina, select Enter Code and enter HHY697.

CAPTAIN TARPALS
At the bar in Mos Eisley Cantina, select Enter Code and enter QRN714.

COUNT DOOKU
At the bar in Mos Eisley Cantina, select Enter Code and enter DDD748.

DARTH MAUL
At the bar in Mos Eisley Cantina, select Enter Code and enter EUK421.

EWOK
At the bar in Mos Eisley Cantina, select Enter Code and enter EWK785.

GENERAL GRIEVOUS
At the bar in Mos Eisley Cantina, select Enter Code and enter PMN576.

GREEDO
At the bar in Mos Eisley Cantina, select Enter Code and enter ZZR636.

IG-88
At the bar in Mos Eisley Cantina, select Enter Code and enter GIJ989.

IMPERIAL GUARD
At the bar in Mos Eisley Cantina, select Enter Code and enter GUA850.

JANGO FETT
At the bar in Mos Eisley Cantina, select Enter Code and enter KLJ897.

KI-ADI MUNDI
At the bar in Mos Eisley Cantina, select Enter Code and enter MUN486.

LUMINARA
At the bar in Mos Eisley Cantina, select Enter Code and enter LUM521.

PADMÉ
At the bar in Mos Eisley Cantina, select Enter Code and enter VBJ322.

R2-Q5
At the bar in Mos Eisley Cantina, select Enter Code and enter EVILR2.

STORMTROOPER
At the bar in Mos Eisley Cantina, select Enter Code and enter NBN431.

TAUN WE
At the bar in Mos Eisley Cantina, select Enter Code and enter PRX482.

VULTURE DROID
At the bar in Mos Eisley Cantina, select Enter Code and enter BDC866.

WATTO
At the bar in Mos Eisley Cantina, select Enter Code and enter PLL967.

ZAM WESELL
At the bar in Mos Eisley Cantina, select Enter Code and enter 584HJF.

SKILLS

DISGUISE
At the bar in Mos Eisley Cantina, select Enter Code and enter BRJ437.

FORCE GRAPPLE LEAP
At the bar in Mos Eisley Cantina, select Enter Code and enter CLZ738.

VEHICLES

DROID TRIFIGHTER
At the bar in Mos Eisley Cantina, select Enter Code and enter AAB123.

IMPERIAL SHUTTLE
At the bar in Mos Eisley Cantina, select Enter Code and enter HUT845.

TIE INTERCEPTOR
At the bar in Mos Eisley Cantina, select Enter Code and enter INT729.

TIE FIGHTER
At the bar in Mos Eisley Cantina, select Enter Code and enter DBH897.

ZAM'S AIRSPEEDER
At the bar in Mos Eisley Cantina, select Enter Code and enter UUU875.

MADDEN NFL 07

MADDEN CARDS
Select Madden Cards from My Madden. Then select Madden Codes and enter the following:

CARD	PASSWORD
#199 Gold Lame Duck Cheat	5LAWO0
#200 Gold Mistake Free Cheat	XL7SP1
#210 Gold QB on Target Cheat	WROA0R
#220 Super Bowl XLI Gold	RLA9R7
#221 Super Bowl XLII Gold	WRLUF8
#222 Super Bowl XLIII Gold	NIEV4A
#223 Super Bowl XLIV Gold	M5AB7L
#224 Aloha Stadium Gold	YI8P8U
#225 1958 Colts Gold	B57QLU
#226 1966 Packers Gold	1PL1FL
#227 1968 Jets Gold	MIE6WO
#228 1970 Browns Gold	CL2TOE
#229 1972 Dolphins Gold	NOEB7U
#230 1974 Steelers Gold	YO0FLA
#231 1976 Raiders Gold	MOA11I
#232 1977 Broncos Gold	C8UM7U
#233 1978 Dolphins Gold	VIU0O7
#234 1980 Raiders Gold	NLAPH3
#235 1981 Chargers Gold	COAGI4
#236 1982 Redskins Gold	WL8BRI
#237 1983 Raiders Gold	H0EW71
#238 1984 Dolphins Gold	M1AM1E
#239 1985 Bears Gold	QOETO8
#240 1986 Giants Gold	ZI8S2L
#241 1988 49ers Gold	SP2A8H
#242 1990 Eagles Gold	2L4TRO
#243 1991 Lions Gold	J1ETRI
#244 1992 Cowboys Gold	W9UVI9

CARD	PASSWORD
#245 1993 Bills Gold	DLA3I7
#246 1994 49ers Gold	DR7EST
#247 1996 Packers Gold	F8LUST
#248 1998 Broncos Gold	FIES95
#249 1999 Rams Gold	S9OUSW
#250 Bears Pump Up the Crowd	B1OUPH
#251 Bengals Cheerleader	DRL2SW
#252 Bills Cheerleader	1PLUYO
#253 Broncos Cheerleader	3ROUJO
#254 Browns Pump Up the Crowd	T1UTOA
#255 Buccaneers Cheerleader	S9EWRI
#256 Cardinals Cheerleader	57IEPI
#257 Chargers Cheerleader	F7UHL8
#258 Chiefs Cheerleader	PRI5SL
#259 Colts Cheerleader	1R5AMI
#260 Cowboys Cheerleader	Z2ACHL
#261 Dolphins Cheerleader	C5AHLE
#262 Eagles Cheerleader	PO7DRO
#263 Falcons Cheerleader	37USPO
#264 49ers Cheerleader	KL0CRL
#265 Giants Pump Up the Crowd	C4USPI
#266 Jaguars Cheerleader	MIEH7E
#267 Jets Pump Up the Crowd	C0LUXI
#268 Lions Pump Up the Crowd	3LABLU
#269 Packers Pump Up the Crowd	4HO7VO
#270 Panthers Cheerleader	F2IASP
#282 All AFC Team Gold	PRO9PH
#283 All NFC Team Gold	RLATH7

MANHUNT 2

INFINITE AMMO
At the Main menu, press Up, Up, Down, Down, Left, Right, Left, Right.

LEVEL SELECT
At the Main menu, press Up, Down, Left, Right, Up, Down, Left, Right.

MARIO & SONIC AT THE OLYMPIC GAMES

UNLOCK 4X100M RELAY EVENT
Medal in Mercury, Venus, Jupiter, and Saturn.

UNLOCK SINGLE SCULLS EVENT
Medal in Mercury, Venus, Jupiter, and Saturn.

UNLOCK DREAM RACE EVENT
Medal in Mercury, Venus, Jupiter, and Saturn.

UNLOCK ARCHERY EVENT
Medal in Moonlight Circuit.

UNLOCK HIGH JUMP EVENT
Medal in Stardust Circuit.

UNLOCK 400M EVENT
Medal in Planet Circuit.

UNLOCK DREAM FENCING EVENT
Medal in Comet Circuit.

UNLOCK DREAM TABLE TENNIS EVENT
Medal in Satellite Circuit.

UNLOCK 400M HURDLES EVENT
Medal in Sunlight Circuit.

UNLOCK POLE VAULT EVENT
Medal in Meteorite Circuit.

UNLOCK VAULT EVENT
Medal in Meteorite Circuit.

UNLOCK DREAM PLATFORM EVENT
Medal in Cosmos Circuit.

CROWNS
Get all gold medals in all events with a character to unlock their crown.

MARIO KART WII

CHARACTERS

CHARACTER	UNLOCK BY...
Baby Daisy	Earn 1 Star in 50cc for Mushroom, Flower, Star, and Special Cups.
Baby Luigi	Unlock 8 Expert Staff Ghost Data in Time Trials.
Birdo	Race 16 different courses in Time Trials or win 250 versus races.
Bowser Jr.	Earn 1 Star in 100cc for Shell, Banana, Leaf, and Lightning Cups.
Daisy	Win 150cc Special Cup.
Diddy Kong	Win 50cc Lightning Cup.
Dry Bones	Win 100cc Leaf Cup.
Dry Bowser	Earn 1 Star in 150cc for Mushroom, Flower, Star, and Special Cups.
Funky Kong	Unlock 4 Expert Staff Ghost Data in Time Trials.
King Boo	Win 50cc Star Cup.
Mii Outfit A	Win 100cc Special Cup.
Mii Outfit B	Unlock all 32 Expert Staff Ghost Data in Time Trials.
Mii Outfit C	Get 15,000 points in Versus Mode.
Rosalina	Have a Super Mario Galaxy save file and she is unlocked after 50 races or earn 1 Star in all Mirror Cups.
Toadette	Race 32 different courses in Time Trials.

KARTS

KART	UNLOCK BY...
Blue Falcon	Win Mirror Lightning Cup.
Cheep Charger	Earn 1 Star in 50cc for Mushroom, Flower, Star, and Special Cups.
Rally Romper	Unlock an Expert Staff Ghost Data in Time Trials.
B Dasher Mk. 2	Unlock 24 Expert Staff Ghost Data in Time Trials.
Royal Racer	Win 150cc Leaf Cup.
Turbo Blooper	Win 50cc Leaf Cup.
Aero Glider	Earn 1 Star in 150cc for Mushroom, Flower, Star, and Special Cups.
Dragonetti	Win 150cc Lightning Cup.
Piranha Prowler	Win 50cc Special Cup.

BIKES

KART	UNLOCK BY...
Bubble Bike	Win Mirror Leaf Cup.
Magikruiser	Race 8 different courses in Time Trials.
Quacker	Win 150cc Star Cup.
Dolphin Dasher	Win Mirror Star Cup.
Nitrocycle	Earn 1 Star in 100cc for all cups.
Rapide	Win 100cc Lightning Cup.
Phantom	Win Mirror Special Cup.
Torpedo	Unlock 12 Expert Staff Ghost Data in Time Trials.
Twinkle Star	Win 100cc Star Cup.

MARVEL ULTIMATE ALLIANCE

UNLOCK ALL SKINS
At the Team menu, press Up, Down, Left, Right, Left, Right, Plus.

UNLOCKS ALL HERO POWERS
At the Team menu, press Left, Right, Up, Down, Up, Down, Plus.

ALL HEROES TO LEVEL 99
At the Team menu, press Up, Left, Up, Left, Down, Right, Down, Right, Plus.

UNLOCK ALL HEROES
At the Team menu, press Up, Up, Down, Down, Left, Left, Left, Plus.

UNLOCK DAREDEVIL
At the Team menu, press Left, Left, Right, Right, Up, Down, Up, Down, Plus.

UNLOCK SILVER SURFER
At the Team menu, press Down, Left, Left, Up, Right, Up, Down, Left, Plus.

GOD MODE
During gameplay, press Up, Down, Up, Down, Up, Left, Down, Right, Plus.

TOUCH OF DEATH
During gameplay, press Left, Right, Down, Down, Right, Left, Plus.

SUPER SPEED
During gameplay, press Up, Left, Up, Right, Down, Right, Plus.

FILL MOMENTUM
During gameplay, press Left, Right, Right, Left, Up, Down, Down, Up, Plus.

UNLOCK ALL COMICS
At the Review menu, press Left, Right, Right, Left, Up, Up, Right, Plus.

UNLOCK ALL CONCEPT ART
At the Review menu, press Down, Down, Down, Right, Right, Left, Down, Plus.

UNLOCK ALL CINEMATICS
At the Review menu, press Up, Left, Left, Up, Right, Right, Up, Plus.

UNLOCK ALL LOAD SCREENS
At the Review menu, press Up, Down, Right, Left, Up, Up Down, Plus.

UNLOCK ALL COURSES
At the Comic Missions menu, press Up, Right, Left, Down, Up, Right, Left, Down, Plus.

MEDAL OF HONOR: VANGUARD

EXTRA ARMOR
Pause the game and press Up, Down, Up, Down to display the words Enter Cheat Code. Then press Right, Left, Right, Down, Up, Right.

DECREASE ENEMY ACCURACY
Pause the game and press Up, Down, Up, Down to display the words Enter Cheat Code. Then press Right, Left, Right, Down, Up, Right.

INVISIBLE
Pause the game and press Up, Down, Up, Down to display the words Enter Cheat Code. Then press Up, Right, Left, Down, Down, Up.

MLB POWER PROS

EXTRA FORMS
At the Main menu, press Right, Left, Up, Down, Down, Right, Right, Up, Up, Left, Down, Left.

VIEW MLB PLAYERS AT CUSTOM PLAYER MENU
Select View or Delete Custom Players/Password Display from My Data and press Up, Up, Down, Down, Left, Right, Left, Right, 1, 2.

MONSTER JAM

TRUCKS
As you collect monster points, they are tallied toward your Championship Score. Trucks are unlocked when you reach certain point totals.

TRUCK	POINTS
Destroyer	10,000
Blacksmith	50,000
El Toro Loco	70,000
Suzuki	110,000
Maximum Destruction	235,000

MORTAL KOMBAT: ARMAGEDDON

The following codes are for the Wii Remote and Nunchuck. Directions are input with the Nunchuck stick, except where noted to use the Wii Remote's D-pad. You need to use a Classic Controller to input ZL and ZR where called for.

You can also use the Classic Controller alone to input the codes with the following chart:

REMOTE/NUNCHUCK	CLASSIC CONTROLLER
Nunchuck Directions	D-pad
Down on Wii Remote D-pad	B
Up on Wii Remote D-pad	X
Left on Wii Remote D-pad	Y
Right on Wii Remote D-pad	A
A	R
C	L
ZL on Classic Controller	Same
ZR on Classic Controller	Same

BLAZE CHARACTER

While in The Krypt, select the "?" and press Up on D-pad, Left on D-pad, Left, C, Left, Right on D-pad.

DAEGON CHARACTER

While in The Krypt, select the "?" and press A, C, Up on D-pad, Down, Down, Left on D-pad.

MEAT CHARACTER

While in The Krypt, select the "?" and press Up, Left on D-pad, Left on D-pad, Right on D-pad, Right on D-pad, Up.

TAVEN CHARACTER

While in The Krypt, select the "?" and press C, Left, ZR, Up, Right on D-pad, Down.

DRAHMIN'S ALTERNATE COSTUME

While in The Krypt, select the "?" and press C, Right, Down on D-pad, A, Up, Up.

FROST'S ALTERNATE COSTUME

While in The Krypt, select the "?" and press Down, A, A, C, Right on D-pad, C.

NITARA'S ALTERNATE COSTUME

While in The Krypt, select the "?" and press Down, C, Up, C, C, Right.

SHANG TSUNG'S ALTERNATE COSTUME

While in The Krypt, select the "?" and press C, Left, Up, Right on D-pad, Up, L (or ZL).

FALLING CLIFFS ARENA

While in The Krypt, select the "?" and press ZR, Right on D-pad, Left on D-pad, Down on D-pad, Right on D-pad, Up on D-pad.

KRIMSON FOREST ARENA

While in The Krypt, select the "?" and press Right on D-pad, C, Up, Left on D-pad, Right on D-pad, Down.

NETHERSHIP INTERIOR ARENA

While in The Krypt, select the "?" and press A, Left, Left, Down, C, Left on D-pad.

THE PYRAMID OF ARGUS ARENA

While in The Krypt, select the "?" and press A, C, Left on D-pad, Down on D-pad, A, Up.

REIKO'S WAR ROOM ARENA

While in The Krypt, select the "?" and press A, Up on D-pad, A, Up, Down on D-pad, Down on D-pad.

SHINNOK'S SPIRE ARENA

While in The Krypt, select the "?" and press Left, Left, Right on D-pad, Up, Up on D-pad, C.

ARMAGEDDON PROMO MOVIE

While in The Krypt, select the "?" and press Up, Up, Down, Up, ZL, Right on D-pad.

CYRAX FATALITY BLOOPER MOVIE

While in The Krypt, select the "?" and press Right, C, ZR, Down, Up, C.

MOTOR GAMEPLAY MOVIE

While in The Krypt, select the "?" and press Up on D-pad, Up, ZR, L (or ZL), A, ZR.

BLAZE BOSS SKETCH KONCEPT ART

While in The Krypt, select the "?" and press C, Up on D-pad, C, C, A, Left on D-pad.

COLOR STUDY FOR OPENING MOVIE 3 KONCEPT ART

While in The Krypt, select the "?" and press Up on D-pad, Left, Left, Down on D-pad, Down, Right on D-pad.

FIREWELL SKETCH 3 KONCEPT ART

While in The Krypt, select the "?" and press Up, Left on D-pad, R (or ZR), L (or ZL), Right on D-pad, C.

GAUNTLET TRAP SKETCH KONCEPT ART

While in The Krypt, select the "?" and press Right on D-pad, RZ, Up on D-pad, Down, Right on D-pad, Left.

HERO SKETCHES 1 KONCEPT ART

While in The Krypt, select the "?" and press Up, Down on D-pad, RZ, Down, L (or LZ), Down on D-pad.

MILEENA'S CAR SKETCH KONCEPT ART

While in The Krypt, select the "?" and press R (or ZR), Right, Up, R (or ZR), Up on D-pad, Up.

SCORPION THROW SKETCH KONCEPT ART

While in The Krypt, select the "?" and press L (or ZL), Left, Up, Right on D-pad, R (or ZR), C.

SEKTOR'S 2-HAND PULSE BLADE SKETCH KONCEPT ART

While in The Krypt, select the "?" and press A, C, Left, Down on D-pad, Up, A.

ARMORY FIGHT TUNE

While in The Krypt, select the "?" and press Down on D-pad, Left on D-pad, Left, Up on D-pad, Left on D-pad, Down on D-pad.

LIN KUEI PALACE TUNE

While in The Krypt, select the "?" and press L (or ZL), Left, Right on D-pad, Down on D-pad, RZ, Right.

PYRAMID OF ARGUS TUNE

While in The Krypt, select the "?" and press Down, Left, A, C, Up, C.

TEKUNIN WARSHIP TUNE

While in The Krypt, select the "?" and press Up, Right on D-pad, C, A, A, Down on D-pad.

MYSIMS

PASSWORD SCREEN

Press the – Button to bring up the pause screen. Then enter the following with the Wii Remote: 2, 1, Down, Up, Down, Up, Left, Left, Right, Right. Now you can enter the following passwords:

OUTFITS	
Camouflage pants	N10ng5g
Diamond vest	Tglg0ca
Genie outfit	Gvsb3k1
Kimono dress	I3hkdvs
White jacket	R705aan

FURNITURE	
Bunk bed	F3nevr0
Hourglass couch	Ghtymba
Modern couch	T7srhca
Racecar bed	Ahvmrva
Rickshaw bed	Itha7da

MYSIMS KINGDOM

DETECTIVE OUTFIT

Pause the game and press Left, Right, Left, Right, Left, Right.

TATTOO VEST OUTFIT

Pause the game and press C, Z, C, Z, B, A, B, A.

NBA LIVE 08

AGENT ZERO SHOES

At the Extras menu, enter ADGILLIT6BE as a code.

CUBA SHOES

At the Extras menu, enter ADGILLIT4BC as a code.

CUSTOMIZE SHOES

At the Extras menu, enter ADGILLIT5BD as a code.

DUNCAN ALL STAR SHOES

At the Extras menu, enter FE454DFJCC as a code.

GIL WOOD SHOES

At the Extras menu, enter ADGILLIT1B9 as a code.

GIL ZERO ALL STAR SHOES

At the Extras menu, enter 23DN1PPOG4 as a code.

TS LIGHTSWITCH AWAY SHOES

At the Extras menu, enter ADGILLIT0B8 as a code.

TS LIGHTSWITCH HOME SHOES

At the Extras menu, enter ADGILLIT2BA as a code.

NEED FOR SPEED CARBON

CASTROL CASH
At the Main menu, press Down, Up, Left, Down, Right, Up, Button 1, B. This gives you 10,000 extra cash.

INFINITE CREW CHARGE
At the Main menu, press Down, Up, Up, Right, Left, Left, Right, Button 1.

INFINITE NITROUS
At the Main menu, press Left, Up, Left, Down, Left, Down, Right, Button 1.

INFINITE SPEEDBREAKER
At the Main menu, press Down, Right, Right, Left, Right, Up, Down, Button 1.

NEED FOR SPEED CARBON LOGO VINYLS
At the Main menu, press Right, Up, Down, Up, Down, Left, Right, Button 1.

NEED FOR SPEED CARBON SPECIAL LOGO VINYLS
At the Main menu, press Up, Up, Down, Down, Down, Down, Up, Button 1.

NEED FOR SPEED PROSTREET

$2,000
Select Career and then choose Code Entry. Enter 1MA9X99.

$4,000
Select Career and then choose Code Entry. Enter W2IOLL01.

$8,000
Select Career and then choose Code Entry. Enter L1IS97A1.

$10,000
Select Career and then choose Code Entry. Enter 1MI9K7E1.

$10,000
Select Career and then choose Code Entry. Enter CASHMONEY.

$10,000
Select Career and then choose Code Entry. Enter REGGAME.

AUDI TT
Select Career and then choose Code Entry. Enter ITSABOUTYOU.

CHEVELLE SS
Select Career and then choose Code Entry. Enter HORSEPOWER.

COKE ZERO GOLF GTI
Select Career and then choose Code Entry. Enter COKEZERO.

DODGE VIPER
Select Career and then choose Code Entry. Enter WORLDSLONGESTLASTING.

MITSUBISHI LANCER EVOLUTION
Select Career and then choose Code Entry. Enter MITSUBISHIGOFAR.

UNLOCK ALL BONUSES
Select Career and then choose Code Entry. Enter UNLOCKALLTHINGS.

5 REPAIR MARKERS
Select Career and then choose Code Entry. Enter SAFETYNET.

ENERGIZER VINYL
Select Career and then choose Code Entry. Enter ENERGIZERLITHIUM.

CASTROL SYNTEC VINYL
Select Career and then choose Code Entry. Enter CASTROLSYNTEC. This also gives you $10,000.

NICKTOONS: ATTACK OF THE TOYBOTS

DAMAGE BOOST
Select Cheats from the Extras menu. Choose Enter Cheat Code and enter 456645.

INVULNERABILITY
Select Cheats from the Extras menu. Choose Enter Cheat Code and enter 313456.

UNLOCK EXO-HUGGLES 9000
Select Cheats from the Extras menu. Choose Enter Cheat Code and enter 691427.

132

UNLOCK MR. HUGGLES
Select Cheats from the Extras menu. Choose Enter Cheat Code and enter 654168.

UNLIMITED LOBBER GOO
Select Cheats from the Extras menu. Choose Enter Cheat Code and enter 118147.

UNLIMITED SCATTER GOO
Select Cheats from the Extras menu. Choose Enter Cheat Code and enter 971238.

UNLIMITED SPLITTER GOO
Select Cheats from the Extras menu. Choose Enter Cheat Code and enter 854511.

PRINCE OF PERSIA RIVAL SWORDS

BABY TOY WEAPON
Pause the game and enter the following code. Use the D-pad for the directions.
Left, Left, Right, Right, Z, Nunchuck down, Nunchuck down, Z, Up, Down

CHAINSAW
Pause the game and enter the following code. Use the D-pad for the directions.
Up, Up, Down, Down, Left, Right, Left, Right, Z, Nunchuck down, Z, Nunchuck down

SWORDFISH
Pause the game and enter the following code. Use the D-pad for the directions.
Up, Down, Up, Down, Left, Right, Left, Right, Z, Nunchuck down, Z, Nunchuck down

TELEPHONE SWORD
Pause the game and enter the following code. Use the D-pad for the directions.
Right, Left, Right, Left, Down, Down, Up, Up, Z, Nunchuck Down, Z, Z, Nunchuck Down, Nunchuck Down

RAMPAGE: TOTAL DESTRUCTION

ALL MONSTERS
At the Main menu, press Minus + Plus to access the Cheat menu and enter 141421.

INVULNERABLE TO ATTACKS
At the Main menu, press Minus + Plus to access the Cheat menu and enter 986960.

ALL SPECIAL ABILITIES
At the Main menu, press Minus + Plus to access the Cheat menu and enter 011235.

ALL LEVELS
At the Main menu, press Minus + Plus to access the Cheat menu and enter 271828.

CPU VS CPU DEMO
At the Main menu, press Minus + Plus to access the cheat menu and enter 082864.

FAST CPU VS CPU DEMO
At the Main menu, press Minus + Plus to access the Cheat menu and enter 874098.

ONE-HIT DESTROYS BUILDINGS
At the Main menu, press Minus + Plus to access the Cheat menu and enter 071767.

OPENING MOVIE
At the Main menu, press Minus + Plus to access the Cheat menu and enter 667300.

ENDING MOVIE
At the Main menu, press Minus + Plus to access the Cheat menu and enter 667301.

CREDITS
At the Main menu, press Minus + Plus to access the Cheat menu and enter 667302.

NINTENDO Wii™

VERSION INFORMATION
At the Main menu, press Minus + Plus to access the Cheat menu and enter 314159.

CLEAR CHEATS
At the Main menu, press Minus + Plus to access the Cheat menu and enter 000000.

RATATOUILLE

Select Gusteau's Shop from the Extras menu. Choose Secrets, select the appropriate code number, and then enter the code. Once the code is entered, select the cheat you want to activate it.

CODE NUMBER	CODE	EFFECT
1	Pieceocake	Very Easy difficulty mode
2	Myhero	No impact and no damage from enemies
3	Shielded	No damage from enemies
4	Spyagent	Move undetected by any enemy
5	Ilikeonions	Fart every time Remy jumps
6	Hardfeelings	Head butt when attacking instead of tailswipe
7	Slumberparty	Multiplayer mode
8	Gusteauart	All Concept Art
9	Gusteauship	All four championship modes
10	Mattelme	All single player and multiplayer minigames
11	Gusteauvid	All Videos
12	Gusteaures	All Bonus Artworks
13	Gusteaudream	All Dream Worlds in Gusteau's Shop
14	Gusteauslide	All Slides in Gusteau's Shop
15	Gusteaulevel	All single player minigames
16	Gusteaucombo	All items in Gusteau's Shop
17	Gusteaupot	5,000 Gusteau points
18	Gusteaujack	10,000 Gusteau points
19	Gusteauomni	50,000 Gusteau points

RAYMAN RAVING RABBIDS 2

FUNKYTOWN
Play each game at least once.

RABBID COSTUMES
Costumes are unlocked as you score 12,000 points in certain games, as well as when you shoot the correct rabbid in the shooting games.

COSTUME	MINIGAME	HOW TO UNLOCK
Cossack	Chess	Earn 12,000 points
Crash Test Dummy	Shopping Cart Downhill	Earn 12,000 points
Cupid	Burgerinnii	Earn 12,000 points
Doctor	Anesthetics	Earn 12,000 points
Fireman	Paris, Pour Troujours	Shoot fireman rabbid
French Maid	Little Chemist	Earn 12,000 points
Fruit-Hat Dancer	Year of the Rabbids	Shoot rabbid wearing fruit hat
Gingerbread	Hot Cake	Earn 12,000 points
HAZE Armor	Big City Fights	Shoot rabbid with armor
Indiana Jones	Rolling Stone	Earn 12,000 points
Jet Trooper	Greatest Hits	Earn 12,000 points
Ken	RRR Xtreme Beach Volleyball	Earn 12,000 points
Martian	Bumper Cars	Earn 12,000 points
Party Girl	Paris, Mon Amour	Once inside boat, shoot girl rabbid
Raider's	American Football	Earn 12,000 points
Sam Fisher	Rabbid School	Earn 12,000 points
Samurai	The Office	Earn 12,000 points
Space	Year of the Rabbids	Earn 12,000 points
Spider-	Spider Rabbid	Play the "Spider Rabbid" Game
TMNT, Leonardo	Usual Rabbids	Earn 12,000 points
Transformer	Plumber Rabbids	Earn 12,000 points

COSTUME	MINIGAME	HOW TO UNLOCK
Vegas Showgirl	Burp	Earn 12,000 points
Voodoo	Voodoo Rabbids	Earn 12,000 points
Wrestler	Greatest Hits	Shoot rabbid in green outfit

RESIDENT EVIL: THE UMBRELLA CHRONICLES

UNLIMITED AMMO

Earn S rank in all scenarios on hard difficulty.

ARCHIVE ITEMS

Defeat the following scenarios with the indicated rank to earn that item. Get an S rank to get both A and S items.

SCENARIO	A RANK	S RANK
Train Derailment 1	Mixing Set	Briefcase
Train Derailment 2	Statue of Evil/Good	Relief of Discipline/Obedience/Unity
Train Derailment 3	Blue/Green Leech Charm	Sterilizing Agent
Beginnings 1	Motherboard	Valve Handle
Beginnings 2	Fire/Water Key	Microfilm A/B
Mansion Incident 1	Lighter/Lockpick	Great Eagle/Wolf Medal
Mansion Incident 2	Sun/Star/Moon Crest	V-Jolt
Mansion Incident 3	MO Disc	Fuel Canteen
Nightmare 1	Cylinder Shaft	Hex Crank
Nightmare 2	Last Book, Vol. 1/2	Emblem/Gold Emblem
Rebirth 1	Clark/Gail X-Ray	Slide Cartridge
Rebirth 2	Blue/Red/Yellow Gemstone	Death Mask
Raccoon's Destruction 1	S.T.A.R.S. Card (Jill's)	Book of Wisdom/Future Compass
Raccoon's Destruction 2	Joint N/S Plug	Lighter Fluid
Raccoon's Destruction 3	Crystal/Obsidian/Amber Ball	Chronos Key
Death's Door	Picture (Ada and Jon)	S.T.A.R.S. Card (Brad's)
Fourth Survivor	G-virus	Eagle/Serpent/Jaguar Stone
Umbrella's End 1	Plastic Bomb/Detonator	Square Crank
Umbrella's End 2	Blue/Red/Green Chemical	Ink Ribbon
Umbrella's End 3	Vaccine	Medium Base
Dark Legacy 1	King/Knight/Bishop/Rook Plug	Battery
Dark Legacy 2	Film A/B/D/C	Spade/Diamond/Club/Heart Key

ROCK BAND

UNLOCK ALL SONGS

At the Title screen, press Red, Yellow, Blue, Red, Red, Blue, Blue, Red, Yellow, Blue. This code disables saving.

SCARFACE: THE WORLD IS YOURS

MAX AMMO

Pause the game, select Cheats and enter AMMO.

REFILL HEALTH

Pause the game, select Cheats and enter MEDIK.

BULLDOZER

Pause the game, select Cheats and enter DOZER.

INCREASE GANG HEAT

Pause the game, select Cheats and enter GOBALLS.

DECREASE GANG HEAT

Pause the game, select Cheats and enter NOBALLS.

INCREASE COP HEAT

Pause the game, select Cheats and enter DONUT.

NINTENDO Wii™

DECREASES COP HEAT
Pause the game, select Cheats and enter FLYSTRT.

FILL BALLS METER
Pause the game, select Cheats and enter FPATCH.

GRAY SUIT TONY WITH SUNGLASSES
Pause the game, select Cheats and enter GRAYSH.

TOGGLE RAIN
Pause the game, select Cheats and enter RAINY.

SHREK THE THIRD

10,000 GOLD COINS
At the gift shop, press Up, Up, Down, Up, Right, Left.

THE SIMPSONS GAME

UNLIMITED POWER FOR ALL CHARACTERS
At the Extras menu, press Plus, Left, Right, Plus, Minus, Z.

ALL MOVIES
At the Extras menu, press Minus, Left, Minus, Right, Plus, C.

ALL CLICHÉS
At the Extras menu, press Left, Minus, Right, Plus, Right, Z.

SIMCITY CREATOR

EGYPTIAN BUILDING SET
Name your city Mummy's desert.

GREEK BUILDING SET
Name your city Ancient culture.

JUNGLE BUILDING SET
Name your city Become wild.

SCI-FI BUILDING SET
Name your city Future picture.

THE SIMS 2: CASTAWAY

CHEAT GNOME
During a game, press B, Z, Up, Down, B. You can now use this Gnome to get the following:

MAX ALL MOTIVES
During a game, press Minus, Plus, Z, Z, A.

MAX CURRENT INVENTORY
During a game, press Left, Right, Left, Right, A.

MAX RELATIONSHIPS
During a game, press Z, Plus, A, B, 2.

ALL RESOURCES
During a game, press A, A, Down, Down, A.

ALL CRAFTING PLANS
During a game, press Plus, Plus, Minus, Minus, Z.

ADD 1 TO SKILL
During a game, press 2, Up, Right, Z, Right.

SPACE HARRIER

CONTINUE AFTER GAME OVER
At the Game Over screen, press Up, Up, Down, Down, Left, Right, Left, Right, Down, Up, Down, Up.

SPEED RACER

INVULNERABILITY
Select Enter Code from the Options menu and enter A, B, A, Up, Left, Down, Right.

UNLIMITED BOOST
Select Enter Code from the Options menu and enter B, A, Down, Up, B, A, Down.

LAST 3 CARS
Select Enter Code from the Options menu and enter 1, 2, 1, 2, B, A, Plus.

GRANITE CAR
Select Enter Code from the Options menu and enter B, Up, Minus, Plus, 1, Up, Plus.

MONSTER TRUCK
Select Enter Code from the Options menu and enter B, Up, Minus, 2, B, Up, Minus.

AGGRESSIVE OPPONENTS
Select Enter Code from the Options menu and enter Up, Left, Down, Right, Up, Left, Down.

PACIFIST OPPONENTS
Select Enter Code from the Options menu and enter Up, Right, Down, Left, Up, Right, Down.

TINY OPPONENTS
Select Enter Code from the Options menu and enter B, A, Left, Down, Minus, Up, Minus.

HELIUM
Select Enter Code from the Options menu and enter Minus, Up, Minus, 2, Minus, Up, Minus.

MOON GRAVITY
Select Enter Code from the Options menu and enter Up, Plus, Up, Right, Minus, Up, Minus.

OVERKILL
Select Enter Code from the Options menu and enter A, Minus, Plus, Down, Up, Plus, 1.

PSYCHEDELIC
Select Enter Code from the Options menu and enter Left, A, Right, Down, B, Up, Minus.

SPIDER-MAN: FRIEND OR FOE

NEW GREEN GOBLIN AS A SIDEKICK
While standing in the Helicarrier between levels, press Left, Down, Right, Right, Down, Left.

SANDMAN AS A SIDEKICK
While standing in the Helicarrier between levels, press Right, Right, Right, Up, Down, Left.

VENOM AS A SIDEKICK
While standing in the Helicarrier between levels, press Left, Left, Right, Up, Down, Down.

5000 TECH TOKENS
While standing in the Helicarrier between levels, press Up, Up, Down, Down, Left, Right.

SPONGEBOB SQUAREPANTS: CREATURE FROM THE KRUSTY KRAB

30,000 EXTRA Z'S
Select Cheat Codes from the Extras menu and enter ROCFISH.

PUNK SPONGEBOB IN DIESEL DREAMING
Select Cheat Codes from the Extras menu and enter SPONGE. Select Activate Bonus Items to enable this bonus item.

HOT ROD SKIN IN DIESEL DREAMING
Select Cheat Codes from the Extras menu and enter HOTROD. Select Activate Bonus Items to enable this bonus item.

PATRICK TUX IN STARFISHMAN TO THE RESCUE
Select Cheat Codes from the Extras menu and enter PATRICK. Select Activate Bonus Items to enable this bonus item.

SPONGEBOB PLANKTON IN SUPER-SIZED PATTY

Select Cheat Codes from the Extras menu and enter PANTS. Select Activate Bonus Items to enable this bonus item.

PATRICK LASER COLOR IN ROCKET RODEO

Select Cheat Codes from the Extras menu and enter ROCKET. Select Activate Bonus Items to enable this bonus item.

PATRICK ROCKET SKIN COLOR IN ROCKET RODEO

Select Cheat Codes from the Extras menu and enter SPACE. Select Activate Bonus Items to enable this bonus item.

PLANKTON ASTRONAUT SUIT IN REVENGE OF THE GIANT PLANKTON MONSTER

Select Cheat Codes from the Extras menu and enter ROBOT. Select Activate Bonus Items to enable this bonus item.

PLANKTON EYE LASER COLOR IN REVENGE OF THE GIANT PLANKTON MONSTER

Select Cheat Codes from the Extras menu and enter LASER. Select Activate Bonus Items to enable this bonus item.

PIRATE PATRICK IN ROOFTOP RUMBLE

Select Cheat Codes from the Extras menu and enter PIRATE. Select Activate Bonus Items to enable this bonus item.

HOVERCRAFT VEHICLE SKIN IN HYPNOTIC HIGHWAY - PLANKTON

Select Cheat Codes from the Extras menu and enter HOVER. Select Activate Bonus Items to enable this bonus item.

SPONGEBOB SQUAREPANTS FEATURING NICKTOONS: GLOBS OF DOOM

When entering the following codes, the order of the characters going down is: SpongeBob SquarePants, Nicolai Technus, Danny Phantom, Dib, Zim, Tlaloc, Tak, Beautiful Gorgeous, Jimmy Neutron, Plankton. These names are shortened to the first name in the following.

ATTRACT COINS

Using the Upgrade Machine on the bottom level of the lair, select "Input cheat codes here". Enter Tlaloc, Plankton, Danny, Plankton, Tak. Coins are attracted to you making them much easier to collect.

DON'T LOSE COINS

Using the Upgrade Machine on the bottom level of the lair, select "Input cheat codes here." Enter Plankton, Jimmy, Beautiful, Jimmy, Plankton. You don't lose coins when you get knocked out.

GOO HAS NO EFFECT

Using the Upgrade Machine on the bottom level of the lair, select "Input cheat codes here". Enter Danny, Danny, Danny, Nicolai, Nicolai. Goo does not slow you down.

MORE GADGET COMBO TIME

Using the Upgrade Machine on the bottom level of the lair, select "Input cheat codes here". Enter SpongeBob, Beautiful, Danny, Plankton, Nicolai. You have more time to perform gadget combos.

SSX BLUR

ALL CHARACTERS

Select Cheats from the Options menu and enter NoHolds.

ENTIRE MOUNTAIN UNLOCKED

Select Cheats from the Options menu and enter MasterKey.

ALL OUTFITS

Select Cheats from the Options menu and enter ClothShop.

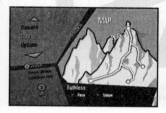 

YETI OUTFIT

Select Cheats from the Options
menu and enter WildFur.

STAR WARS: THE FORCE UNLEASHED

CHEATS

Once you have accessed the Rogue Shadow, select Enter Code from
the Extras menu. Now you can enter the following codes:

CHEAT	CODE
Invincibility	CORTOSIS
Unlimited Force	VERGENCE
1,000,000 Force Points	SPEEDER
All Force Powers	TYRANUS
Max Force Power Level	KATARN
Max Combo Level	COUNTDOOKU
Stronger Lightsaber	LIGHTSABER

COSTUMES

Once you have accessed the Rogue Shadow, select Enter Code from the
Extras menu. Now you can enter the following codes:

COSTUME	CODE
All Costumes	GRANDMOFF
501st Legion	LEGION
Aayla Secura	AAYLA
Admiral Ackbar	ITSATWAP
Anakin Skywalker	CHOSENONE
Asajj Ventress	ACOLYTE

COSTUME	CODE
Ceremonial Jedi Robes	DANTOOINE
Chop'aa Notimo	NOTIMO
Classic stormtrooper	TK421
Count Dooku	SERENNO
Darth Desolous	PAUAN
Darth Maul	ZABRAK
Darth Phobos	HIDDENFEAR
Darth Vader	SITHLORD
Drexl Roosh	DREXLROOSH
Emperor Palpatine	PALPATINE
General Rahm Kota	MANDALORE
Han Solo	NERFHERDER
Heavy trooper	SHOCKTROOP
Juno Eclipse	ECLIPSE
Kento's Robe	WOOKIEE
Kleef	KLEEF
Lando Calrissian	SCOUNDREL
Luke Skywalker	T16WOMPRAT
Luke Skywalker (Yavin)	YELLOWJCKT
Mace Windu	JEDIMASTER
Mara Jade	MARAJADE
Maris Brook	MARISBROOD
Navy commando	STORMTROOP
Obi Wan Kenobi	BENKENOBI
Proxy	HOLOGRAM
Qui Gon Jinn	MAVERICK
Shaak Ti	TOGRUTA
Shadow trooper	INTHEDARK
Sith Robes	HOLOCRON
Sith Stalker Armor	KORRIBAN
Twi'lek	SECURA

STRONG BAD'S COOL GAME FOR ATTRACTIVE PEOPLE EPISODE 1: HOMESTAR RUINER

COBRA MODE IN SNAKE BOXER 5
At the Snake Boxer 5 title screen, press Up, Up, Down, Up, Plus.

SUPER MARIO GALAXY

PLAY AS LUIGI
Collect all 120 stars and fight Bowser. After the credits you will get a message that Luigi is playable.

GRAND FINALE GALAXY
Collect all 120 stars with Luigi and beat Bowser.

STAR 121
Collect 100 purple coins.

SURF'S UP

ALL CHAMPIONSHIP LOCATIONS
Select Cheat Codes from the Extras menu and enter FREEVISIT.

ALL LEAF SLIDE STAGES
Select Cheat Codes from the Extras menu and enter GOINGDOWN.

ALL MULTIPLAYER LEVELS
Select Cheat Codes from the Extras menu and enter MULTIPASS.

ALL BOARDS
Select Cheat Codes from the Extras menu and enter MYPRECIOUS.

ASTRAL BOARD
Select Cheat Codes from the Extras menu and enter ASTRAL.

MONSOON BOARD
Select Cheat Codes from the Extras menu and enter MONSOON.

TINE SHOCKWAVE BOARD
Select Cheat Codes from the Extras menu and enter TINYSHOCKWAVE.

ALL CHARACTER CUSTOMIZATIONS
Select Cheat Codes from the Extras menu and enter TOPFASHION.

PLAY AS ARNOLD
Select Cheat Codes from the Extras menu and enter TINYBUTSTRONG.

PLAY AS ELLIOT
Select Cheat Codes from the Extras menu and enter SURPRISEGUEST.

PLAY AS GEEK
Select Cheat Codes from the Extras menu and enter SLOWANDSTEADY.

PLAY AS TANK EVANS
Select Cheat Codes from the Extras menu and enter IMTHEBEST.

PLAY AS TATSUHI KOBAYASHI
Select Cheat Codes from the Extras menu and enter KOBAYASHI.

PLAY AS ZEKE TOPANGA
Select Cheat Codes from the Extras menu and enter THELEGEND.

ALL VIDEOS AND SPEN GALLERY
Select Cheat Codes from the Extras menu and enter WATCHAMOVIE.

ART GALLERY
Select Cheat Codes from the Extras menu and enter NICEPLACE.

THRILLVILLE: OFF THE RAILS

$50,000
During a game, press C, Z, B, C, Z, B, A.

500 THRILL POINTS
During a game, press Z, C, B, Z, C, B, C.

ALL MISSIONS
During a game, press C, Z, B, C, Z, B, Z.

ALL PARKS
During a game, press C, Z, B, C, Z, B, C.

ALL RIDES
During a game, press C, Z, B, C, Z, B, B.

ALL MINIGAMES
During a game, press C, Z, B, C, Z, B, Right.

TIGER WOODS PGA TOUR 07

ALL CHARACTERS
Select Password from the Options menu and enter gameface.

UNLOCK ADIDAS ITEMS
Select Password from the Options menu and enter three stripes.

UNLOCK BRIDGESTONE ITEMS
Select Password from the Options menu and enter shojiro.

UNLOCK COBRA ITEMS
Select Password from the Options menu and enter snakeking.

UNLOCK EA SPORTS ITEMS
Select Password from the Options menu and enter inthegame.

UNLOCK GRAFALLOY ITEMS
Select Password from the Options menu and enter just shafts.

UNLOCK MACGREGOR ITEMS
Select Password from the Options menu and enter mactec.

UNLOCK MIZUNO ITEMS
Select Password from the Options menu and enter rihachinrzo.

UNLOCK NIKE ITEMS
Select Password from the Options menu and enter justdoit.

UNLOCK OAKLEY ITEMS
Select Password from the Options menu and enter jannard.

UNLOCK PGA TOUR ITEMS
Select Password from the Options menu and enter lightning.

UNLOCK PING ITEMS
Select Password from the Options menu and enter solheim.

UNLOCK PRECEPT ITEMS
Select Password from the Options menu and enter guys are good.

UNLOCK TAYLORMADE ITEMS
Select Password from the Options menu and enter mradams.

TIGER WOODS PGA TOUR 08

ALL CLUBS
Select Passwords from the Options and enter PROSHOP.

ALL GOLFERS
Select Passwords from the Options and enter GAMEFACE.

BRIDGESTONE ITEMS
Select Passwords from the Options and enter NOTJUSTTIRES.

BUICK ITEMS
Select Passwords from the Options and enter THREESTRIPES.

CLEVELAND GOLF ITEMS
Select Passwords from the Options and enter CLEVELAND.

COBRA ITEMS
Select Passwords from the Options and enter SNAKEKING.

EA ITEMS
Select Passwords from the Options and enter INTHEGAME.

GRAFALLOY ITEMS
Select Passwords from the Options and enter JUSTSHAFTS.

MIZUNO ITEMS
Select Passwords from the Options and enter RIHACHINRIZO.

NIKE ITEMS
Select Passwords from the Options and enter JUSTDOIT.

PRECEPT ITEMS
Select Passwords from the Options and enter GUYSAREGOOD.

TIGER WOODS PGA TOUR 09 ALL-PLAY

SPECTATORS BIG HEAD MODE
Select EA SPORTS Extras from My Tiger '09, choose Password and enter cephalus.

TMNT

CHALLENGE MAP 2
At the Main menu, hold Z and press A, A, A, 1, A.

DON'S BIG HEAD GOODIE
At the Main menu, hold Z and press 1, A, C, 2.

BOARDS

BOARD	COMPLETE EVENT
Street Issue	Street Issue Slalom (Tier 1)
Solar	Tourist Trap (Tier 1)
Chaos	Vista Point Race (Random)
Kuni	Hong Kong Race (Tier 2)
Red Rascal	San Francisco Elimination (Tier 3)
Cruiser	Grind Time (Tier 4)
Illuminate	Machu Pichu Top to Bottom Tricks (Tier 4)
Dark Sign	He-Man Club/Girl Power (Tier 5)
Spooky	Clearance Sale (Tier 6)
Black Icer	Precision Shopping Slalom (Tier 7)
Ripper	Del Centro Slalom (Tier 7)
Dispersion	Machu Picchu Top to Bottom Race (Tier 7)
Makonga	Mall Rats (Tier 8)
Goddess of Speed	The Hills Are Alive Tricks (Tier 9)
Dragon	Swiss Elimination (Tier 9)

OUTFITS

CHARACTER	OUTFIT	COMPLETE EVENT
Gunnar	High-G Armor	Gunnar's Threads (Tier 1)
Kyla	Shooting Star	Cuzco Challenge Race (Tier 2)
Tony	Business Camouflage	Mountain High Race (Random)
Budd	The Bohemian	Catacombs Slalom (Tier 2)
Tiffany	Baby Blue	Tourist Spot Slalom (Tier 2)
Ammon	Money Suit	Edinburgh Full Tricks (Tier 3)
Jynx	Black Tuesday	Road to Cuzco Race (Tier 3)
Jynx	Graveyard Casual	Cable Car Tricks (Random)
Crash	Bombs Away	Fallen Empire Race (Tier 4)
MacKenzie	Spitfire Squadron	Edinburgh Full Race (Tier 4)
Gunnar	Street Creds	Favela Rush (Tier 4)
Crash	Brace for Impact	Out of the Woods Race (Tier 5)
Kyla	Touchdown	Clear the Streets (Tier 5)
Tony	Mariachi Loco	Out of the Woods Tricks (Random)
MacKenzie	Killer Bee	High Street Slalom (Tier 6)
Ammon	Tommy T	Seaside Village Race (Tier 6)
Budd	Power of Chi	Rome Elimination (Tier 6)
Crash	Space Monkey	Lift Off (Tier 7)
Jynx	Funeral Fun	Del Centro Race (Tier 7)
Budd	Toys for Bob	Waterfront Race (Random)
MacKenzie	Street Combat	Parking Lot Shuffle (Tier 7)
Gunnar	Black Knight	Park It Anywhere (Tier 7)
Tiffany	Nero Style	Rome Burning (Tier 7)
Tiffany	Military Chic	Shopping Spree (Tier 8)
Ammon	Tan Suit	Saturday Matinee (Tier 9)
Tony	Downhill Jam	Hills Are Alive Race (Tier 9)
Kyla	Alpine Red	San Francisco Full Slalom (Tier 9)

SKATERS

SKATER	COMPLETE EVENT
Kevin Staab	Kevin's Challenge (Random)
MacKenzie	MacKenzie's Challenge (Tier 2)
Crash	Crash Test (Tier 3)
Armando Gnutbagh	Unknown Skater (Tier 10)

CHEAT CODES

Select Cheat Codes from the Options menu and enter the following cheats. Select Toggle Cheats to enable/disable them.

FREE BOOST
Enter OOTBAGHFOREVER.

ALWAYS SPECIAL
Enter POINTHOGGER.

UNLOCK MANUALS
Enter IMISSMANUALS.

PERFECT RAIL
Enter LIKETILTINGAPLATE.

PERFECT MANUAL
Enter TIGHTROPEWALKER.

PERFECT STATS
Enter IAMBOB.

EXTREME CAR CRASHES
Enter WATCHFORDOORS.

FIRST-PERSON SKATER
Enter FIRSTPERSONJAM.

SHADOW SKATER
Enter CHIMNEYSWEEP.

DEMON SKATER
Enter EVILCHIMNEYSWEEP.

MINI SKATER
Enter DOWNTHERABBITHOLE.

GIGANTO-SKATER
Enter IWANNABETALLTALL.

INVISIBLE BOARD
Enter LOOKMANOBOARD.

INVISIBLE SKATER
Enter NOWYOUSEEME.

PICASSO SKATER
Enter FOURLIGHTS.

CHIPMUNK VOICES
Enter HELLOHELIUM.
Enter DISPLAYCOORDINATES.

LARGE BIRDS
Enter BIRDBIRDBIRDBIRD.

REALLY LARGE BIRDS
Enter BIRDBIRDBIRDBIRDBIRD.

TINY PEOPLE
Enter SHRINKTHEPEOPLE.
*There is no need to toggle on the following cheats. They take effect after entering them.

ALL EVENTS
Enter ADVENTURESOFKWANG.

ALL SKATERS
Enter IMINTERFACING.

144

ALL BOARDS/OUTFITS
Enter RAIDTHEWOODSHED.

ALL MOVIES
Enter FREEBOZZLER.

TONY HAWK'S PROVING GROUND

Select Cheat Codes from the Options and enter the following cheats. Some codes need to be enabled by selecting Cheats from the Options during a game.

UNLOCK	CHEAT
Unlocks Bosco	MOREMILK
Unlocks Cam	NOTACAMERA
Unlocks Cooper	THECOOP
Unlocks Eddie X	SKETCHY
Unlocks El Patinador	PILEDRIVER
Unlocks Eric	FLYAWAY
Unlocks Judy Nails	LOVEROCKNROLL
Unlocks Mad Dog	RABBIES
Unlocks MCA	INTERGALACTIC
Unlocks Mel	NOTADUDE
Unlocks Rube	LOOKSSMELLY
Unlocks Spence	DAPPER
Unlocks Shayne	MOVERS
Unlocks TV Producer	SHAKER
Unlock FDR	THEPREZPARK
Unlock Lansdowne	THELOCALPARK
Unlock Air & Space Museum	THEINDOORPARK
Unlocks all Fun Items	OVERTHETOP
Unlock all Game Movies	WATCHTHIS
Unlock all Rigger Pieces	IMGONNABUILD
All specials unlocked and in player's special list	LOTSOFTRICKS
Full Stats	BEEFEDUP
Give player +50 skill points	NEEDSHELP

The following cheats lock you out of the Leaderboards:

UNLOCK	CHEAT
Unlocks Perfect Manual	STILLAINTFALLIN
Unlocks Perfect Rail	AINTFALLIN
Unlocks Unlimited Focus	MYOPIC

You can not use the Video Editor with the following cheats:

UNLOCK	CHEAT
Invisible Man	THEMISSING
Mini Skater	TINYTATER

TRANSFORMERS: THE GAME

INFINITE HEALTH
At the Main menu, press Left, Left, Up, Left, Right, Down, Right.

INFINITE AMMO
At the Main menu, press Up, Down, Left, Right, Up, Up, Down.

NO MILITARY OR POLICE
At the Main menu, press Right, Left, Right, Left, Right, Left, Right.

ALL MISSIONS
At the Main menu, press Down, Up, Left, Right, Right, Right, Up, Down.

BONUS CYBERTRON MISSIONS
At the Main menu, press Right, Up, Up, Down, Right, Left, Left.

GENERATION 1 SKIN: JAZZ
At the Main menu, press Left, Up, Down, Down, Left, Up, Right.

GENERATION 1 SKIN: MEGATRON
At the Main menu, press Down, Left, Left, Down, Right, Right, Up.

GENERATION 1 SKIN: OPTIMUS PRIME
At the Main menu, press Down, Right, Left, Up, Down, Down, Left.

GENERATION 1 SKIN: ROBOVISION OPTIMUS PRIME
At the Main menu, press Down, Down, Up, Up, Right, Right, Right.

GENERATION 1 SKIN: STARSCREAM
At the Main menu, press Right, Down, Left, Left, Down, Up, Up.

GENERATION 1 SKIN: MEGATRON
At the Main menu, press Down, Left, Left, Down, Right, Right, Up.

GENERATION 1 SKIN: OPTIMUS PRIME
At the Main menu, press Down, Right, Left, Up, Down, Down, Left.

GENERATION 1 SKIN: ROBOVISION OPTIMUS PRIME
At the Main menu, press Down, Down, Up, Up, Right, Right, Right.

GENERATION 1 SKIN: STARSCREAM
At the Main menu, press Right, Down, Left, Left, Down, Up, Up.

WALL-E

The following cheats will disable saving. The five possible characters starting with Wall-E and going down are: Wall-E, Auto, EVE, M-O, GEL-A Steward.

ALL BONUS FEATURES UNLOCKED
Select Cheats from the Bonus Features menu and enter Wall-E, Auto, EVE, GEL-A Steward.

ALL GAME CONTENT UNLOCKED
Select Cheats from the Bonus Features menu and enter M-O, Auto, GEL-A Steward, EVE.

ALL SINGLE PLAYER LEVELS UNLOCKED
Select Cheats from the Bonus Features menu and enter Auto, GEL-A Steward, M-O, Wall-E.

ALL MULTIPLAYER MAPS UNLOCKED
Select Cheats from the Bonus Features menu and enter EVE, M-O, Wall-E, Auto.

ALL HOLIDAY COSTUMES UNLOCKED
Select Cheats from the Bonus Features menu and enter Auto, Auto, GEL-A Steward, GEL-A Steward.

ALL MULTIPLAYER COSTUMES UNLOCKED
Select Cheats from the Bonus Features menu and enter GEL-A Steward, Wall-E, M-O, Auto.

UNLIMITED HEALTH UNLOCKED
Select Cheats from the Bonus Features menu and enter Wall-E, M-O, Auto, M-O.

WALL-E: MAKE ANY CUBE AT ANY TIME
Select Cheats from the Bonus Features menu and enter Auto, M-O, Auto, M-O.

WALL-EVE: MAKE ANY CUBE AT ANY TIME
Select Cheats from the Bonus Features menu and enter M-O, GEL-A Steward, EVE, EVE.

WALL-E WITH A LASER GUN AT ANY TIME
Select Cheats from the Bonus Features menu and enter Wall-E, EVE, EVE, Wall-E.

WALL-EVE WITH A LASER GUN AT ANY TIME
Select Cheats from the Bonus Features menu and enter GEL-A Steward, EVE, M-O, Wall-E.

WALL-E: PERMANENT SUPER LASER UPGRADE
Select Cheats from the Bonus Features menu and enter Wall-E, Auto, EVE, M-O.

EVE: PERMANENT SUPER LASER UPGRADE
Select Cheats from the Bonus Features menu and enter EVE, Wall-E, Wall-E, Auto.

CREDITS

Select Cheats from the Bonus Features menu and enter Auto, Wall-E, GEL-A Steward, M-O.

WII SPORTS

BOWLING BALL COLOR

After selecting your Mii, hold the following direction on the D-pad and press A at the warning screen:

DIRECTION	COLOR
Up	Blue
Right	Gold
Down	Green
Left	Red

NO HUD IN GOLF

Hold 2 as you select a course to disable the power meter, map, and wind speed meter.

BLUE TENNIS COURT

After selecting your Mii, hold 2 and press A at the warning screen.

WWE SMACKDOWN! VS RAW 2008

HBK AND HHH'S DX OUTFIT

Select Cheat Codes from the Options and enter DXCostume69K2.

KELLY KELLY'S ALTERNATE OUTFIT

Select Cheat Codes from the Options and enter KellyKG12R.

NINTENDO Wii: VIRTUAL CONSOLE

For the Virtual Console games, a Classic Controller may be needed to enter some codes.

ADVENTURES OF LOLO

PASSWORDS

LEVEL	PASSWORD	LEVEL	PASSWORD
1-2	BCBT	6-2	CQZG
1-3	BDBR	6-3	CRZD
1-4	BGBQ	6-4	CTZC
1-5	BHBP	6-5	CVZB
2-1	BJBM	7-1	CYYZ
2-2	BKBL	7-2	CZYY
2-3	BLBK	7-3	DBYV
2-4	BMBJ	7-4	DCYT
2-5	BPBH	7-5	DDYR
3-1	BQBG	8-1	DGYQ
3-2	BRBD	8-2	DHYP
3-3	BTBC	8-3	DJYM
3-4	BVBB	8-4	DKYL
3-5	BYZZ	8-5	DLYK
4-1	BZZY	9-1	DMYJ
4-2	CBZV	9-2	DPYH
4-3	CCZT	9-3	DQYG
4-4	CDZR	9-4	DRYD
4-5	CGZQ	9-5	DTYC
5-1	CHZP	10-1	DVYB
5-2	CJZM	10-2	DYVZ
5-3	CKZL	10-3	DZVY
5-4	CLZK	10-4	GBVV
5-5	CMZJ	10-5	GCVT
6-1	CPZH		

ADVENTURES OF LOLO 2

MORE DIFFICULTIES
Enter PROA, PROB, PROC, or PROD as a password.

PASSWORDS

LEVEL	PASSWORD	LEVEL	PASSWORD
1-1	PPHP	4-2	HPPP
1-2	PHPK	4-3	HHKK
1-3	PQPD	4-4	HQKD
1-4	PVPT	4-5	HVKT
1-5	PRPJ	5-1	HRKJ
2-5	PCPZ	5-2	HBKM
2-5	PLPY	5-3	HLKY
2-5	PBPM	5-4	HCKZ
2-5	PGPG	5-5	HGKG
2-5	PZPC	6-1	HZKC
3-1	PYPL	6-2	HYKL
3-2	PMPB	6-3	HMKB
3-3	PJPR	6-4	HJKR
3-4	PTPV	6-5	HTKV
3-5	PDPQ	7-1	HDKQ
4-1	PKPH	7-2	HKKH

LEVEL	PASSWORD
7-3	QPKP
7-4	QHDK
7-5	QQDD
8-1	QVDT
8-2	QRDJ
8-3	QBDM
8-4	QLDY
8-5	QCDZ
9-1	QGDG

LEVEL	PASSWORD
9-2	QZDC
9-3	QYDL
9-4	QMDB
9-5	QJDR
10-1	QTDV
10-2	QDDQ
10-3	QKDH
10-4	VPDP
10-5	VHTK

ALTERED BEAST

LEVEL SELECT
At the Title screen, press B + Start.

BEAST SELECT
At the Title screen, hold A + B + C + Down/Left and press Start.

SOUND TEST
At the Title screen, hold A + C + Up/Right and press Start.

BOMBERMAN '93

PASSWORDS

LEVEL	PASSWORD
A-1	CBCCBBDB
A-2	DDCDBBGB
A-3	FFDDBBJB
A-4	GHFDBCLB
A-5	GJFDBCMB
A-6	HKFDBCNB
A-7	HLFDBCPB
A-8	JNFDBCQB
B-1	GCDDCCKB
B-2	HFFFCCMB
B-3	JGFFCCNB
B-4	JHFFCCPB
B-5	KKGFCCRB
B-6	LLGFCCSB
B-7	LMGFCCTB
B-8	CKFFCHBC
C-1	LFGFFCQB
C-2	LGGFFCRB
C-3	MHGFFCSB
C-4	DFGFFHBC
C-5	DGGFFHCC
C-6	FHGFFJFC
C-7	GKGFFJGC
C-8	GLGFFJHC
D-1	GBGFKJFC
D-2	HDGFKJGC
D-3	HFGFKJHC
D-4	JGGFKJJC

LEVEL	PASSWORD
D-5	JHGFKJKC
D-6	KKHFKJLC
D-7	KLHFKJMC
D-8	LMHFKJNC
E-1	NFHFTJQC
E-2	PGJFTJSC
E-3	PHJFTJTC
E-4	GFHFTDBD
E-5	GGHFTDCD
E-6	HHHFTDDD
E-7	JKHGTDGD
E-8	KLJGTDJD
F-1	KCJGTJGD
F-2	LDKGTJJD
F-3	LFKGTJKD
F-4	MHLGTJLD
F-5	MJLGTHLD
F-6	MKLGTJND
F-7	NLLGTJPD
F-8	QNMHTJSD
G-1	JBLHTXBF
G-2	KCMHTXDF
G-3	KDMHTXFF
G-4	LGNHTXHF
G-5	MHNHTXJF
G-6	MJNHTXKF
G-7	NLPHTXLF
G-8	NMPHTXMF

CHEW MAN FU

GAME COMPLETE PASSWORDS
Select Password and enter 573300 or 441300.

COMIX ZONE

STAGE SELECT

At the Jukebox menu, press C on the following numbers:

14, 15, 18, 5, 13, 1, 3, 18, 15, 6

A voice says "Oh Yeah" when entered correctly. Then, press C on 1 through 6 to warp to that stage.

INVINCIBLE

At the Jukebox menu, press C on the following numbers:

3, 12, 17, 2, 2, 10, 2, 7, 7, 11

A voice says "Oh Yeah" when entered correctly.

CREDITS

At the Options menu press A + B + C.

DONKEY KONG COUNTRY 2: DIDDY'S KONG QUEST

SOUND TEST

Highlight Two Player and press Down (x5).

CHEAT MODE

Press Down (x5) again after getting Sound Test to access the cheat mode. Now you can enter the following:

50 LIVES

Press Y, A, Select, A, Down, Left, A, Down.

HARD MODE

Press B, A, Right, Right, A, Left, A, X. This gets rid of the barrels.

DR. ROBOTNIK'S MEAN BEAN MACHINE

EASY PASSWORDS

STAGE	PASSWORD
02: Frankly	Red Bean, Red Bean, Red Bean, Has Bean
03: Humpty	Clear Bean, Purple Bean, Clear Bean, Green Bean
04: Coconuts	Red Bean, Clear Bean, Has Bean, Yellow Bean
05: Davy Sprocket	Clear Bean, Blue Bean, Blue Bean, Purple Bean
06: Skweel	Clear Bean, Red Bean, Clear Bean, Purple Bean
07: Dynamight	Purple Bean, Yellow Bean, Red Bean, Blue Bean
08: Grounder	Yellow Bean, Purple Bean, Has Bean, Blue Bean
09: Spike	Yellow Bean, Purple Bean, Has Bean, Blue Bean
10: Sir Ffuzy-Logik	Red Bean, Yellow Bean, Clear Bean, Has Bean
11: Dragon Breath	Green Bean, Purple Bean, Blue Bean, Clear Bean
12: Scratch	Red Bean, Has Bean, Has Bean, Yellow Bean
13: Dr. Robotnik	Yellow Bean, Has Bean, Blue Bean, Blue Bean

NORMAL PASSWORDS

STAGE	PASSWORD
02: Frankly	Has Bean, Clear Bean, Yellow Bean, Yellow Bean
03: Humpty	Blue Bean, Clear Bean, Red Bean, Yellow Bean
04: Coconuts	Yellow Bean, Blue Bean, Clear Bean, Purple Bean
05: Davy Sprocket	Has Bean, Green Bean, Blue Bean, Yellow Bean
06: Skweel	Green Bean, Purple Bean, Purple Bean, Yellow Bean
07: Dynamight	Purple Bean, Blue Bean, Green Bean, Has Bean
08: Grounder	Green Bean, Has Bean, Clear Bean, Yellow Bean
09: Spike	Blue Bean, Purple Bean, Has Bean, Has Bean
10: Sir Ffuzy-Logik	Has Bean, Red Bean, Yellow Bean, Clear Bean
11: Dragon Breath	Clear Bean, Red Bean, Red Bean, Blue Bean
12: Scratch	Green Bean, Green Bean, Clear Bean, Yellow Bean
13: Dr. Robotnik	Purple Bean, Yellow Bean, Has Bean, Clear Bean

HARD PASSWORDS

STAGE	PASSWORD
02: Frankly	Clear Bean, Green Bean, Yellow Bean, Yellow Bean
03: Humpty	Yellow Bean, Purple Bean, Clear Bean, Purple Bean
04: Coconuts	Blue Bean, Green Bean, Clear Bean, Blue Bean
05: Davy Sprocket	Red Bean, Purple Bean, Green Bean, Green Bean
06: Skweel	Yellow Bean, Yellow Bean, Clear Bean, Green Bean
07: Dynamight	Purple Bean, Clear Bean, Blue Bean, Blue Bean
08: Grounder	Clear Bean, Yellow Bean, Has Bean, Yellow Bean
09: Spike	Purple Bean, Blue Bean, Blue Bean, Green Bean
10: Sir Ffuzy-Logik	Clear Bean, Green Bean, Red Bean, Yellow Bean
11: Dragon Breath	Blue Bean, Yellow Bean, Yellow Bean, Has Bean
12: Scratch	Green Bean, Clear Bean, Clear Bean, Blue Bean
13: Dr. Robotnik	Has Bean, Clear Bean, Purple Bean, Has Bean

HARDEST PASSWORDS

STAGE	PASSWORD
02: Frankly	Blue Bean, Blue Bean, Green Bean, Yellow Bean
03: Humpty	Green Bean, Yellow Bean, Green Bean, Clear Bean
04: Coconuts	Purple Bean, Purple Bean, RedBean, Has Bean
05: Davy Sprocket	Green Bean, Red Bean, Purple Bean, Blue Bean
06: Skweel	Purple Bean, Clear Bean, Green Bean, Yellow Bean
07: Dynamight	Blue Bean, Purple Bean, Green Bean, Has Bean
08: Grounder	Clear Bean, Purple Bean, Yellow Bean, Has Bean
09: Spike	Purple Bean, Green Bean, Has Bean, Clear Bean
10: Sir Ffuzy-Logik	Green Bean, Blue Bean, Yellow Bean, Has Bean
11: Dragon Breath	Green Bean, Purple Bean, Has Bean, Red Bean
12: Scratch	Red Bean, Green Bean, Has Bean, Blue Bean
13: Dr. Robotnik	Red Bean, Red Bean, Clear Bean, Yellow Bean

DUNGEON EXPLORER

PLAY AS PRINCESS AKI
Enter JBBNJ HDCOG as a password.

PLAY AS THE HERMIT
Enter IMGAJ MDPAI as a password.

HOMING WEAPON
Enter HOMIN GAAAA as a password.

CHANGE NAMES
Enter CHECK NAMEA as a password.

INVINCIBILITY
Enter DEBDE DEBDA as a password, then press Plus + 2.

JUMP TO ANY LOCATION
After enabling the Invincibility code, enter one of the 15 bushes in front of Axis castle to jump to the following locations:

LOCATION	BUSH (STARTING FROM LEFT)
Natas	1
Balamous Tower	2
Rotterroad	3
Mistose Dungeon	4
Ratonix Dungeon	5
Reraport Maze	6
Rally Maze	7
Bullbeast	8
Melba Village	9
After Gutworm	10
Nostalgia Dungeon	11
Water Castle	12
Road to Cherry Tower	13
Stonefield	14
Karma Castle	15

OVERLOAD

NINTENDO Wii™

ECCO THE DOLPHIN

DEBUG MENU
Pause the game with Ecco facing the screen and press Right, B, C, B, C, Down, C, Up.

INFINITE AIR
Enter LIFEFISH as a password.

PASSWORDS

LEVEL	PASSWORD	LEVEL	PASSWORD
The Undercaves	WEFIDNMP	Deep City	DDXPQQLJ
The Vents	BQDPXJDS	City of Forever	MSDBRQLA
The Lagoon	JNSBRIKY	Jurassic Beach	IYCBUNLB
Ridge Water	NTSBZTKB	Pteranodon Pond	DMXEUNLI
Open Ocean	YWGTTJNI	Origin Beach	EGRIUNLB
Ice Zone	HZIFZBMF	Trilobite Circle	IELMUNLB
Hard Water	LRFJRQLI	Dark Water	RKEQUNLN
Cold Water	UYNFRQLC	City of Forever 2	HPQIGPLA
Island Zone	LYTIOQLZ	The Tube	JUMFKMLB
Deep Water	MNOPOQLR	The Machine	GXUBKMLF
The Marble	RJNTQQLZ	The Last Fight	TSONLMLU
The Library	RTGXQQLE		

F-ZERO X

ALL TRACKS, VEHICLES, AND DIFFICULTIES
At the mode select, press Up on the D-pad, L, R, Up on the Right control stick, X, Y, ZR, Plus.

GOLDEN AXE

LEVEL SELECT
At the character select in Arcade mode, hold Down/Left and press B+Start.

START WITH 9 CONTINUES
At the character select in Arcade mode, hold Down/Left and then hold A+C. Release the buttons and select a character.

GRADIUS

MAX OUT WEAPONS
Pause the game and press Up, Up, Down, Down, Left, Right, Left, Right, B, A.

GRADIUS III

FULL POWER-UP
Pause the game and press Up, Up, Down, Down, L, R, L, R, B, A.

SUICIDE
Pause the game and press Up, Up, Down, Down, Left, Right, Left, Right, B, A.

ICE HOCKEY

NO GOALIES
At the title screen, hold A + B on controllers 1 and 2. Then, press start on controller 1.

MILITARY MADNESS

PASSWORDS

LEVEL	PASSWORD	LEVEL	PASSWORD
01	REVOLT	17	MILTON
02	ICARUS	18	IRAGAN
03	CYRANO	19	LIPTUS
04	RAMSEY	20	INAKKA
05	NEWTON	21	TETROS
06	SENECA	22	ARBINE
07	SABINE	23	RECTOS
08	ARATUS	24	YEANTA
09	GALIOS	25	MONOGA
10	DARWIN	26	ATTAYA
11	PASCAL	27	DESHTA
12	HALLEY	28	NEKOSE
13	BORMAN	29	ERATIN
14	APOLLO	30	SOLCIS
15	KAISER	31	SAGINE
16	NECTOR	32	WINNER

SOUND TEST
Enter ONGAKU as a password.

RISTAR

Select Passwords from the Options menu and enter the following:

LEVEL SELECT
ILOVEU

BOSS RUSH MODE
MUSEUM

TIME ATTACK MODE
DOFEEL

TOUGHER DIFFICULTY
SUPER

ONCHI MUSIC
MAGURO. Activate this from the Sound Test.

CLEARS PASSWORD
XXXXXX

GAME COPYRIGHT INFO
AGES

SOLOMON'S KEY

CONTINUE GAME
At the Game Deviation Value screen, hold Up + A + B.

SONIC THE HEDGEHOG

LEVEL SELECT
At the Title screen, press Up, Down, Left, Right. A sound of a ring being collected plays if the code is entered correctly. Hold A and press Start to access the Level Select.

CONTROL MODE
At the Title screen, press Up, C, Down, C, Left, C, Right, C. Then, hold A and press Start.

DEBUG MODE
After entering the Control Mode, hold A and press Start. Press A to change Sonic into another sprite. Press B to change back to Sonic. Press C to place that sprite. Pause the game and press A to restart. Hold B for slow motion and press C to advance a frame.

CHANGE DEMO
During the demo, hold C. Sonic will start making mistakes.

WARIO'S WOODS

HARD BATTLES
Highlight VS. Computer Mode, hold Left and press Start.

GAMES

CAREER COMPLETE 100%
Select Cheat Codes from the Options menu and enter SHOWTIME.

INSTALL ALL PARTS
Select Cheat Codes from the Options menu and enter SUPERMAX.

BATTLEFIELD: BAD COMPANY

M60
Select Unlocks from the Multiplayer menu, press Start and enter
try4ndrunf0rcov3r.

QBU88
Select Unlocks from the Multiplayer menu, press Start and enter
your3mynextt4rget.

UZI
Select Unlocks from the Multiplayer menu, press Start and enter
cov3r1ngthecorn3r.

THE BIGS

START A ROOKIE WITH HIGHER STATS
When you create a rookie, name him HOT DOG. His stats will be higher
than when you normally start.

BIONIC COMMANDO REARMED

The following challenge rooms can be found in the Challenge Room list.
Only one code can be active at a time.

AARON SEDILLO'S CHALLENGE ROOM (CONTEST WINNER)
At the Title screen, Right, Down, Left, Up, L1, R1, ⬤, ⬤, ⊗, ⊗, Start.

EUROGAMER CHALLENGE ROOM
At the Title screen, press Down, Up, Down, Up, Left, L1, ⬤, L1, ⬤, ⬤, Start.

GAMESRADAR CHALLENGE ROOM
At the Title screen, R1, ⬤, ⬤, ⬤, Up, Down, L1, L1, Up, Down, Start.

IGN CHALLENGE ROOM
At the Title screen, Up, Down, ⬤, ⬤, ⬤, ⬤, Down, Up, L1, L1, Start.

BLAZING ANGELS: SQUADRONS OF WWII

ALL MISSIONS AND PLANES UNLOCKED
At the Main menu, hold L2 + R2, and press ⬤, L1, R1, ⬤, ⬤, R1, L1, ⬤.

GOD MODE
Pause the game, hold L2, and press ⬤, ⬤, ⬤, ⬤. Release L2, hold R2 and
press ⬤, ⬤, ⬤, ⬤. Re-enter the code to disable it.

INCREASED DAMAGE WITH ALL WEAPONS
Pause the game, hold L2, and press L1, L1, R1. Release L2, hold R2, and
press R1, R1, L1. Re-enter the code to disable it.

BROTHERS IN ARMS: HELL'S HIGHWAY

ALL CHAPTERS
Select Enter Code from the Options and enter gimmechapters.

ALL RECON POINTS
Select Enter Code from the Options and enter 0zndrbicra.

KILROY DETECTOR
Select Enter Code from the Options and enter sh2vyivnzf.

TWO MULTIPLAYER SKINS
Select Enter Code from the Options and enter hi9wtpxsuk.

BURNOUT PARADISE

BEST BUY CAR
Pause the game and select Sponsor Product Code from the Under the Hood menu. Enter Bestbuy. Need A License to use this car offline.

CIRCUIT CITY CAR
Pause the game and select Sponsor Product Code from the Under the Hood menu. Enter Circuitcity. Need Burnout Paradise License to use this car offline.

GAMESTOP CAR
Pause the game and select Sponsor Product Code from the Under the Hood menu. Enter Gamestop. Need A License to use this car offline.

WALMART CAR
Pause the game and select Sponsor Product Code from the Under the Hood menu. Enter Walmart. Need Burnout Paradise License to use this car offline.

"STEEL WHEELS" GT
Pause the game and select Sponsor Product Code from the Under the Hood menu. Enter G23X 5K8Q GX2V 04B1 or E60J 8Z7T MS8L 51U6.

LICENSES

LICENSE	NUMBER OF WINS NEEDED
D	2
C	7
B	16
A	26
Burnout Paradise	45
Elite License	All events

CALL OF DUTY 3

ALL CHAPTERS & BONUS CONTENT
At the Chapter Select screen, hold Select and press Right, Right, Left, Left, ●, ●.

CALL OF DUTY 4: MODERN WARFARE

ARCADE MODE
After a complete playthrough of the game, Arcade Mode becomes available from the Main menu.

UNLOCKABLE CHEATS

After completing the game, cheats are unlocked based on how many intelligence pieces were gathered. These cheats cannot be used during Arcade Mode. These cheats may also disable the ability to earn Achievements.

CHEAT	INTEL ITEMS	DESCRIPTION
CoD Noir	2	Black and white
Photo-Negative	4	Inverses colors
Super Contrast	6	Increases contrast
Ragtime Warfare	8	Black and white, scratches fill screen, double speed, piano music
Cluster Bombs	10	Four extra grenade explosions after frag grenade explodes.
A Bad Year	15	Enemies explode into a bunch of old tires when killed.
Slow-Mo Ability	20	Melee button enables/disables slow-motion mode.
Infinite Ammo	30	Unlimited ammo and no need to reload. Doesn't work for single-shot weapons such as RPG.

CARS MATER-NATIONAL

ALL ARCADE RACES, MINI-GAMES, AND WORLDS
Select Codes/Cheats from the options and enter PLAYALL.

ALL CARS
Select Codes/Cheats from the options and enter MATTEL07.

ALTERNATE LIGHTNING MCQUEEN COLORS
Select Codes/Cheats from the options and enter NCEDUDZ.

ALL COLORS FOR OTHERS
Select Codes/Cheats from the options and enter PAINTIT.

UNLIMITED TURBO
Select Codes/Cheats from the options and enter ZZOOOOM.

EXTREME ACCELERATION
Select Codes/Cheats from the options and enter 0TO200X.

EXPERT MODE
Select Codes/Cheats from the options and enter VRYFAST.

ALL BONUS ART
Select Codes/Cheats from the options and enter BUYTALL.

CONAN

PROMOTIONAL UNLOCKABLE #1 CONCEPT ART
Go to the Concept Art menu in Extras and press Up, Down, Up, Down, Left, Right, Left, Right, ●, ▲.

PROMOTIONAL UNLOCKABLE #2 CONCEPT ART
Go to the Concept Art menu in Extras and press Up, Down, Left, Left, ●, ●, ●.

PROMOTIONAL UNLOCKABLE #3 CONCEPT ART
Go to the Concept Art menu in Extras and press L3, L3, ▲, ▲, ●, R3.

PROMOTIONAL UNLOCKABLE #4 CONCEPT ART
Go to the Concept Art menu in Extras and press Left, ●, Left, ▲, Down, R3, R3.

PROMOTIONAL UNLOCKABLE #5 CONCEPT ART
Go to the Concept Art menu in Extras and press Right, Right, Left, Left, Up, Down, Up, Down, ●, ●.

PROMOTIONAL UNLOCKABLE #6 CONCEPT ART
Go to the Concept Art menu in Extras and press ▲, ▲, L3, ●, ●, R3, Up, Down.

PROMOTIONAL UNLOCKABLE #7 CONCEPT ART
Go to the Concept Art menu in Extras and press Up, L1, Down, R1, ●, ●, ▲, ▲, R3.

PROMOTIONAL UNLOCKABLE #8 CONCEPT ART
Go to the Concept Art menu in Extras and press L3, ●, R3, ▲, L1, L1, Down, Down.

PROMOTIONAL UNLOCKABLE #9 CONCEPT ART
Go to the Concept Art menu in Extras and press Down, L1, Down, R1, ●, L2.

THE DARKNESS

DARKLING OUTFITS
Even Darklings can make a fashion statement. Support your mini minions with an ensemble fit for murderous monsters by collecting these fun and colorful outfits.

OUTFIT	MENTIONED IN	AREA	LOCATION
Potato Sack	Chapter 1	Chinatown	Sitting against alley wall near metro exit
Jungle	Chapter 1	Hunters Point Alley	Inside hidden room
Roadworker	Chapter 3	City Hall station	Inside train car
Lumberjack	Side Objectives	Cutrone objective	Inside Cutrone's apartment
Fireman	Side Objectives	Pajamas objective	Inside room 261
Construction	Side Objectives	Mortarello objective	Inside room of last mission
Baseball	N/A	Dial: 555-4263	N/A
Golfshirt	N/A	Dial: 555-5664	N/A

PHONE NUMBERS
Dialing 'D' for Darkness isn't the only number to punch on a telephone. Sure, you called every number you found on those hard-to-get Collectibles, but you certainly haven't found *all* of the phone numbers. Pay close to attention to the environment as you hunt down Uncle Paulie. Chances are, you overlooked a phone number or two without even knowing it as you ripped out a goon's heart. All 25 'secret' phone numbers are scattered throughout New York and can be seen on anywhere from flyers and storefronts to garbage cans and posters. Dial 18 of the 25 numbers on a phone—in no specific order—to unlock the final secret of the game.

PHONE NUMBERS	PHONE NUMBERS	PHONE NUMBERS	PHONE NUMBERS
555-6118	555-5723	555-9723	555-8930
555-1847	555-8024	555-5289	555-3243
555-6667	555-6322	555-6205	555-3840
555-4569	555-9132	555-7658	555-2349
555-9985	555-6893	555-1233	555-6325
555-1037	555-2402	555-3947	555-4565
555-1206	555-6557	555-9562	555-9898
555-9528	555-2309	555-7934	555-7613
555-3285	555-4372	555-7892	555-6969

DEAD SPACE

REFILL STASIS AND KINESIS ENERGY
Pause the game and press ●, ▲, ▲, ●, ▲.

REFILL OXYGEN
Pause the game and press ●, ●, ▲ (x3).

ADD 2 POWER NODES
Pause the game and press ▲, ● (x3), ▲. This code can only be used once.

ADD 5 POWER NODES
Pause the game and press ⬆, ⬇, ⬆, ⬇, ⬇, ⬆, ⬇, ⬆, ⬇, ⬇, ⬆. This code can only be used once.

1,000 CREDITS
Pause the game and press ⬇ (x3), ⬆, ⬇. This code can only be used once.

2,000 CREDITS
Pause the game and press ⬇ (x3), ⬆, ⬆. This code can only be used once.

5,000 CREDITS
Pause the game and press ⬇ (x3), ⬆, ⬇, ⬆. This code can only be used once.

10,000 CREDITS
Pause the game and press ⬇, ⬆ (x3), ⬇, ⬇, ⬆. This code can only be used once.

DEF JAM: ICON

IT'S GOING DOWN BY YUNG JOC
At the Title Screen, after "Press Start Button" appears, press Down, ⬇, ✖, Right.

MAKE IT RAIN BY FAT JOE AND FIGHT AS FAT JOE
At the Title Screen, after "Press Start Button" appears, press ⬇, Up, Right, Left, ⬇.

FAR CRY 2

BONUS MISSIONS
Select Promotional Content from the Additional Content menu and enter the following codes. Each code gives four or six extra missions.

6aPHuswe
Cr34ufrE
2Eprunef
JeM8SpaW
tr99pUkA

F.E.A.R.

ALL MISSIONS
Enter F3ARDAY1 as your profile name.

FIGHT NIGHT ROUND 3

ALL VENUES
Create a champ with a first name of NEWVIEW.

FRACTURE

EXCLUSIVE PRE-ORDER SKIN
Pause the game and press Up, Right, Left, Down, Up, Left, Right, Down.

FULL AUTO 2: BATTLELINES

ALL CARS
Select Cheat Codes from Extras and enter 47GIV3MECARS.

ALL MISSIONS
Select Cheat Codes from Extras and enter IMFEDUPWITHTHIS.

SCEPTRE AND MINI-ROCKETS
Select Cheat Codes from Extras and enter 10E6CUSTOMER. This vehicle and weapon become available in Arcade Mode and Head to Head.

THE GODFATHER: THE DON'S EDITION

The following codes can be used only once every five minutes.

$5,000
Pause the game and press ●, ▲, ●, ●, ▲, L3.

FULL HEALTH
Pause the game and press Left, ●, Right, ▲, Right, L3.

FULL AMMO
Pause the game and press ▲, Left, ▲, Right, ●, R3.

ALL MOVIES
At the Main menu, press ▲, ●, ▲, ●, ●, L3.

GRAND THEFT AUTO IV

CHEATS
Call the following phone numbers with Niko's phone to activate the cheats. Some cheats may affect the missions and achievements.

VEHICLE	PHONE NUMBER
Change weather	468-555-0100
Get weapons	486-555-0100
Get different weapons	486-555-0150

VEHICLE	PHONE NUMBER
Raise wanted level	267-555-0150
Remove wanted level	267-555-0100
Restore armor	362-555-0100
Restore health	482-555-0100
Restore armor, health, and ammo	482-555-0100

SPAWN VEHICLES
Call the following phone numbers with Niko's phone to spawn the corresponding vehicle.

VEHICLE	PHONE NUMBER
Annihilator	359-555-0100
Cognoscenti	227-555-0142
Comet	227-555-0175
FIB Buffalo	227-555-0100
Jetmax	938-555-0100
NRG-900	625-555-0100
Sanchez	625-555-0150
SuperGT	227-555-0168
Turismo	227-555-0147

MAP LOCATIONS
Access a computer in-game and enter the following URL: www.whattheydonotwantyoutoknow.com.

ALL DRIFT CARS

Select Bonus Codes from the Options. Then choose Enter Code and enter TUN58396.

ALL MUSCLE CARS

Select Bonus Codes from the Options. Then choose Enter Code and enter MUS59279.

BUCHBINDER EMOTIONAL ENGINEERING BMW 320SI

Select Bonus Codes from the Options. Then choose Enter Code and enter F93857372. You can use this in Race Day or in GRID World once you've started your own team.

EBAY MOTORS MUSTANG

Select Bonus Codes from the Options. Then choose Enter Code and enter DAFJ55E01473M0. You can use this in Race Day or in GRID World once you've started your own team.

GAMESTATION BMW 320SI

Select Bonus Codes from the Options. Then choose Enter Code and enter G29782655. You can use this in Race Day or in GRID World once you've started your own team.

MICROMANIA PAGANI ZONDA R

Select Bonus Codes from the Options. Then choose Enter Code and enter M38572343. You can use this in Race Day or in GRID World once you've started your own team.

PLAY.COM ASTON MARTIN DBR9

Select Bonus Codes from the Options. Then choose Enter Code and enter P47203845. You can use this in Race Day or in GRID World once you've started your own team.

GUITAR HERO III: LEGENDS OF ROCK

To enter the following cheats, strum the guitar with the given buttons held. For example, if it says Yellow + Orange, hold Yellow and Orange as you strum. Air Guitar, Precision Mode, and Performance Mode can be toggled on and off from the Cheats menu. You can also change between five different levels of Hyperspeed at this menu.

UNLOCK EVERYTHING

Select Cheats from the Options. Choose Enter Cheat and enter Green + Red + Blue + Orange, Green + Red + Yellow + Blue, Green + Red + Yellow + Orange, Green + Yellow + Blue + Orange, Green + Red + Yellow + Blue, Red + Yellow + Blue + Orange, Green + Red + Yellow + Blue, Green + Yellow + Blue + Orange, Green + Red + Yellow + Blue, Green + Red + Yellow + Orange, Green + Red + Yellow + Orange, Green + Red + Yellow + Blue, Green + Red + Yellow + Orange. No sounds play while this code is entered.

An easier way to show this code is by representing Green as 1 down to Orange as 5. For example, if you have 1345, you would hold down Green + Yellow + Blue + Orange while strumming. 1245 + 1234 + 1235 + 1345 + 1234 + 2345 + 1234 + 1345 + 1234 + 1235 + 1235 + 1234 + 1235.

ALL SONGS

Select Cheats from the Options. Choose Enter Cheat and enter Yellow + Orange, Red + Blue, Red + Orange, Green + Blue, Red + Yellow, Yellow + Orange, Red + Yellow, Red + Blue, Green + Yellow, Green + Yellow, Yellow + Blue, Yellow + Blue, Yellow + Orange, Yellow + Orange, Yellow + Blue, Yellow, Red, Red + Yellow, Red, Yellow, Orange.

NO FAIL

Select Cheats from the Options. Choose Enter Cheat and enter Green + Red, Blue, Green + Red, Green + Yellow, Blue, Green + Yellow, Red + Yellow, Orange, Red + Yellow, Green + Yellow, Yellow, Green + Yellow, Green + Red.

AIR GUITAR

Select Cheats from the Options. Choose Enter Cheat and enter Blue + Yellow, Green + Yellow, Green + Yellow, Red + Blue, Red + Blue, Red + Yellow, Red + Yellow, Blue + Yellow, Green + Yellow, Green + Yellow, Red + Blue, Red + Blue, Red + Yellow, Red + Yellow, Green + Yellow, Green + Yellow, Red + Yellow, Red + Yellow.

HYPERSPEED

Select Cheats from the Options. Choose Enter Cheat and enter Orange, Blue, Orange, Yellow, Orange, Blue, Orange, Yellow.

PERFORMANCE MODE

Select Cheats from the Options. Choose Enter Cheat and enter Red + Yellow, Red + Blue, Red + Orange, Red + Blue, Red + Yellow, Green + Blue, Red + Yellow, Red + Blue.

EASY EXPERT

Select Cheats from the Options. Choose Enter Cheat and enter Green + Red, Green + Yellow, Yellow + Blue, Red + Blue, Blue + Orange, Yellow + Orange, Red + Yellow, Red + Blue.

PRECISION MODE

Select Cheats from the Options. Choose Enter Cheat and enter Green + Red, Green + Red, Green + Red, Red + Yellow, Red + Yellow, Red + Blue, Red + Blue, Yellow + Blue, Yellow + Orange, Yellow + Orange, Green + Red, Green + Red, Green + Red, Red + Yellow, Red + Yellow, Red + Blue, Red + Blue, Yellow + Blue, Yellow + Orange, Yellow + Orange.

BRET MICHAELS SINGER

Select Cheats from the Options. Choose Enter Cheat and enter Green + Red, Green + Red, Green + Red, Green + Blue, Green + Blue, Green + Blue, Red + Blue, Red, Red, Red, Red + Blue, Red, Red, Red, Red + Blue, Red, Red, Red.

GUITAR HERO: AEROSMITH

Select Cheats from the Options menu and enter the following. To do this, strum the guitar with the given buttons held. For example, if it says Yellow + Orange, hold Yellow and Orange as you strum. Air Guitar, Precision Mode, and Performance Mode can be toggled on and off from the Cheats menu. You can also change between five different levels of Hyperspeed at this menu.

ALL SONGS

Red + Yellow, Green + Red, Green + Red, Red + Yellow, Red + Yellow, Green + Red, Red + Yellow, Red + Yellow, Green + Red, Green + Red, Red + Yellow, Red + Yellow, Green + Red, Red + Yellow, Red + Blue. This code does not unlock Pandora's Box.

AIR GUITAR

Red + Yellow, Green + Red, Red + Yellow, Red + Yellow, Red + Blue, Red + Blue, Red + Blue, Red + Blue, Red + Blue, Yellow + Blue, Yellow + Blue, Yellow + Orange

HYPERSPEED

Yellow + Orange, Yellow + Orange, Yellow + Orange, Yellow + Orange, Yellow + Orange, Red + Yellow, Red + Yellow, Red + Yellow, Red + Yellow, Red + Blue, Red + Blue, Red + Blue, Red + Blue, Red + Blue, Yellow + Blue, Yellow + Orange, Yellow + Orange.

NO FAIL

Select Cheats from the Options. Choose Enter Cheat and enter Green + Red, Blue, Green + Red, Green + Yellow, Blue, Green + Yellow, Red + Yellow, Orange, Red + Yellow, Green + Yellow, Yellow, Green + Yellow, Green + Red.

PERFORMANCE MODE

Green + Red, Green + Red, Red + Orange, Red + Blue, Green + Red, Green + Red, Red + Orange, Red + Blue.

PRECISION MODE

Red + Yellow, Red + Blue, Red + Blue, Red + Yellow, Red + Yellow, Yellow + Blue, Yellow + Blue, Yellow + Blue, Red + Blue, Red + Yellow, Red + Blue, Red + Blue, Red + Yellow, Red + Yellow, Yellow + Blue, Yellow + Blue, Yellow + Blue, Red + Blue.

The following cheats can be toggled on and off at the Cheats menu.

QUICKPLAY SONGS

Select Cheats from the Options menu, choose Enter New Cheat and press Blue, Blue, Red, Green, Green, Blue, Blue, Yellow.

ALWAYS SLIDE

Select Cheats from the Options menu, choose Enter New Cheat and press Green, Green, Red, Red, Yellow, Red, Yellow, Blue.

AT&T BALLPARK

Select Cheats from the Options menu, choose Enter New Cheat and press Yellow, Green, Red, Red, Green, Blue, Red, Yellow.

AUTO KICK

Select Cheats from the Options menu, choose Enter New Cheat and press Yellow, Green, Red, Blue (x4), Red.

EXTRA LINE 6 TONES

Select Cheats from the Options menu, choose Enter New Cheat and press Green, Red, Yellow, Blue, Red, Yellow, Blue, Green.

FLAME COLOR

Select Cheats from the Options menu, choose Enter New Cheat and press Green, Red, Green, Blue, Red, Red, Yellow, Blue.

GEM COLOR

Select Cheats from the Options menu, choose Enter New Cheat and press Blue, Red, Red, Green, Red, Green, Red, Yellow.

STAR COLOR

Select Cheats from the Options menu, choose Enter New Cheat and press Red, Red, Yellow, Red, Blue, Red, Red, Blue.

AIR INSTRUMENTS

Select Cheats from the Options menu, choose Enter New Cheat and press Red, Red, Blue, Yellow, Green (x3), Yellow.

HYPERSPEED

Select Cheats from the Options menu, choose Enter New Cheat and press Green, Blue, Red, Yellow, Yellow, Red, Green, Green. These show up in the menu as HyperGuitar, HyperBass, and HyperDrums.

PERFORMANCE MODE

Select Cheats from the Options menu, choose Enter New Cheat and press Yellow, Yellow, Blue, Red, Blue, Green, Red, Red.

INVISIBLE ROCKER

Select Cheats from the Options menu, choose Enter New Cheat and press Green, Red, Yellow (x3), Blue, Blue, Green.

VOCAL FIREBALL

Select Cheats from the Options menu, choose Enter New Cheat and press Red, Green, Green, Yellow, Blue, Green, Yellow, Green.

AARON STEELE!

Select Cheats from the Options menu, choose Enter New Cheat and press Blue, Red, Yellow (x5), Green.

JONNY VIPER

Select Cheats from the Options menu, choose Enter New Cheat and press Blue, Red, Blue, Blue, Yellow (x3), Green.

NICK

Select Cheats from the Options menu, choose Enter New Cheat and press Green, Red, Blue, Green, Red, Blue, Blue, Green.

RINA

Select Cheats from the Options menu, choose Enter New Cheat and press Blue, Red, Green, Green, Yellow (x3), Green.

OVERLORD

PLAYSTATION 3®

IRON MAN

CLASSIC ARMOR
Clear One Man Army vs. Mercs.

EXTREMIS ARMOR
Clear One Man Army vs. Maggia.

MARK II ARMOR
Clear One Man Army vs. Ten Rings.

HULKBUSTER ARMOR
Clear One Man Army vs. AIM-X. Can also be unlocked when clear game save data from Incredible Hulk is stored on the same console.

CLASSIC MARK I ARMOR
Clear One Man Army vs. AIM.

ULTIMATE ARMOR
Clear Mission 13: Showdown.

JUICED 2: HOT IMPORT NIGHTS

ASCARI KZ1
Select Cheats and Codes from the DNA Lab menu and enter KNOX. Defeat the challenge to earn the car.

AUDI TT 1.8L QUATTRO
Select Cheats and Codes from the DNA Lab menu and enter YTHZ. Defeat the challenge to earn the car.

BMW Z4 ROADSTER
Select Cheats and Codes from the DNA Lab menu and enter GVDL. Defeat the challenge to earn the car.

FRITO-LAY INFINITI G35
Select Cheats and Codes from the DNA Lab menu and enter MNCH. Defeat the challenge to earn the car.

HOLDEN MONARO
Select Cheats and Codes from the DNA Lab menu and enter RBSG. Defeat the challenge to earn the car.

HYUNDAI COUPE 2.7L V6
Select Cheats and Codes from the DNA Lab menu and enter BSLU. Defeat the challenge to earn the car.

INFINITI G35
Select Cheats and Codes from the DNA Lab menu and enter MRHC. Defeat the challenge to earn the car.

KOENIGSEGG CCX
Select Cheats and Codes from the DNA Lab menu and enter KDTR. Defeat the challenge to earn the car.

MITSUBISHI PROTOTYPE X
Select Cheats and Codes from the DNA Lab menu and enter DOPX. Defeat the challenge to earn the car.

NISSAN 350Z
Select Cheats and Codes from the DNA Lab menu and enter PRGN. Defeat the challenge to earn the car.

NISSAN SKYLINE R34 GT-R
Select Cheats and Codes from the DNA Lab menu and enter JWRS. Defeat the challenge to earn the car.

SALEEN S7
Select Cheats and Codes from the DNA Lab menu and enter WIKF. Defeat the challenge to earn the car.

SEAT LEON CUPRA R
Select Cheats and Codes from the DNA Lab menu and enter FAMQ. Defeat the challenge to earn the car.

KUNG FU PANDA

UNLIMITED CHI
Select Cheats from the Extra menu and enter Down, Right, Left, Up, Down.

INVULNERABILITY
Select Cheats from the Extra menu and enter Down, Down, Right, Up, Left.

FULL UPGRADES
Select Cheats from the Extra menu and enter Left, Right, Down, Left, Up.

FULL AWESOME METER
Select Cheats from the Extra menu and enter Up, Down, Up, Right, Left. This gives Po 4X damage.

MULTIPLAYER CHARACTERS

Select Cheats from the Extra menu and enter Left, Down, Left, Right, Down.

OUTFITS

Select Cheats from the Extra menu and enter Right, Left, Down, Up, Right.

LAIR

CHICKEN VIDEO

At the Cheat menu, enter chicken.

COFFEE VIDEO

At the Cheat menu, enter 686F7420636F66666565.

UNLOCKS STABLE OPTION FOR ALL LEVELS

At the Cheat menu, enter koelsch. Saving is disabled with this code.

THE LEGEND OF SPYRO: DAWN OF THE DRAGON

UNLIMITED LIFE

Pause the game, hold L1 and press Right, Right, Down, Down, Left with the Left Analog Stick.

UNLIMITED MANA

Pause the game, hold R1 and press Up, Right, Up, Left, Down with the Left Analog Stick.

MAXIMUM XP

Pause the game, hold R1 and press Left, Right, Right, Up, Up with the Left Analog Stick.

ALL ELEMENTAL UPGRADES

Pause the game, hold L1 and press Left, Up, Down, Up, Right with the Left Analog Stick.

LEGO BATMAN

BATCAVE CODES

Using the computer in the Batcave, select Enter Code and enter the following:

CHARACTERS

CHARACTER	CODE
Alfred	ZAQ637
Batgirl	JKR331
Bruce Wayne	BDJ327
Catwoman (Classic)	M1AAWW
Clown Goon	HJK327
Commissioner Gordon	DDP967

PLAYSTATION®3

CHARACTER	CODE
Fishmonger	HGY748
Freeze Girl	XVK541
Joker Goon	UTF782
Joker Henchman	YUN924
Mad Hatter	JCA283
Man-Bat	NYU942
Military Policeman	MKL382
Nightwing	MVY759
Penguin Goon	NKA238
Penguin Henchman	BJH782
Penguin Minion	KJP748
Poison Ivy Goon	GTB899
Police Marksman	HKG984
Police Officer	JRY983
Riddler Goon	CRY928
Riddler Henchman	XEU824
S.W.A.T.	HTF114
Sailor	NAV592
Scientist	JFL786
Security Guard	PLB946
The Joker (Tropical)	CCB199
Yeti	NJL412
Zoo Sweeper	DWR243

VEHICLES

VEHICLE	CODE
Bat-Tank	KNTT4B
Bruce Wayne's Private Jet	LEA664
Catwoman's Motorcycle	HPL826
Garbage Truck	DUS483
Goon Helicopter	GCH328
Harbor Helicopter	CHP735
Harley Quinn's Hammer Truck	RDT637
Mad Hatter's Glider	HS000W
Mad Hatter's Steamboat	M4DM4N
Mr. Freeze's Iceberg	ICYICE
The Joker's Van	JUK657
Mr. Freeze's Kart	BCT229
Penguin Goon Submarine	BTN248
Police Bike	LJP234
Police Boat	PLC999
Police Car	KJL832
Police Helicopter	CWR732
Police Van	MAC788
Police Watercraft	VJD328
Riddler's Jet	HAHAHA
Robin's Submarine	TTF453
Two-Face's Armored Truck	EFE933

CHEATS

CHEAT	CODE
Always Score Multiply	9LRGNB
Fast Batarangs	JRBDCB
Fast Walk	ZOLM6N
Flame Batarang	D8NYWH
Freeze Batarang	XPN4NG
Extra Hearts	ML3KHP
Fast Build	EVG26J
Immune to Freeze	JXUDY6
Invincibility	WYD5CP

CHEAT	CODE
Minikit Detector	ZXGH9J
More Batarang Targets	XWP645
Piece Detector	KHJ554
Power Brick Detector	MMN786
Regenerate Hearts	HJH7HJ
Score x2	N4NR3E
Score x4	CX9MAT
Score x6	MLVNF2
Score x8	WCCDB9
Score x10	18HW07

LEGO INDIANA JONES: THE ORIGINAL ADVENTURES

CHARACTERS

Approach the blackboard in the Classroom and enter the following codes.

CHARACTER	CODE
Bandit	12N68W
Bandit Swordsman	1MK4RT
Barranca	04EM94
Bazooka Trooper (Crusade)	MK83R7
Bazooka Trooper (Raiders)	S93Y5R
Belloq	CHN3YU
Belloq (Jungle)	TDR197
Belloq (Robes)	VEO29L
British Commander	B73EUA
British Officer	VJ5TI9
British Soldier	DJ5I2W
Captain Katanga	VJ3TT3
Chatter Lal	ENW936
Chatter Lal (Thuggee)	CNH4RY
Chen	3NK48T
Colonel Dietrich	2K9RKS
Colonel Vogel	8EAL4H
Dancing Girl	C7EJ21
Donovan	3NFTU8
Elsa (Desert)	JSNRT9
Elsa (Officer)	VMJ5US
Enemy Boxer	8246RB
Enemy Butler	VJ48W3
Enemy Guard	VJ7R51
Enemy Guard (Mountains)	YR47WM
Enemy Officer	572E61
Enemy Officer (Desert	2MK45O
Enemy Pilot	B84ELP
Enemy Radio Operator	1MF94R
Enemy Soldier (Desert)	4NSU7Q
Fedora	V75YSP
First Mate	0GIN24
Grail Knight	NE6THI
Hovitos Tribesman	H0V1SS
Indiana Jones (Desert Disguise)	4J8S4M
Indiana Jones (Officer)	VJ85OS
Jungle Guide	24PF34
Kao Kan	WMO46L
Kazim	NRH23J
Kazim (Desert)	3M29TJ
Lao Che	2NK479
Maharajah	NFK5N2
Major Toht	13NS01
Masked Bandit	N48SF0

PLAYSTATION®3

OVERLOAD

CHARACTER	CODE
Mola Ram	FJUR31
Monkey Man	3RF6YJ
Pankot Assassin	2NKT72
Pankot Guard	VN28RH
Sherpa Brawler	VJ37WJ
Sherpa Gunner	ND762W
Slave Child	0E3ENW
Thuggee	VM683E
Thuggee Acolyte	T2R3F9
Thuggee Slave Driver	VBS7GW
Village Dignitary	KD48TN
Village Elder	4682E1
Willie (Dinner Suit)	VK93R7
Willie (Pajamas)	MEN4IP
Wu Han	3NSLT8

EXTRAS

Approach the blackboard in the Classroom and enter the following codes. Some cheats need to be enabled by selecting Extras from the Pause menu.

CHEAT	CODE
Artifact Detector	VIKED7
Beep Beep	VNF59Q
Character Treasure	VIES2R
Disarm Enemies	VKRNS9
Disguises	4ID1N6
Fast Build	V83SLO
Fast Dig	378RS6
Fast Fix	FJ59WS
Fertilizer	B1GW1F
Ice Rink	33GM7J
Parcel Detector	VUT673
Poo Treasure	WWQ1SA
Regenerate Hearts	MDLP69
Secret Characters	3X44AA
Silhouettes	3HE85H
Super Scream	VN3R7S
Super Slap	0P1TA5
Treasure Magnet	H86LA2
Treasure x10	VI3PS8
Treasure x2	VM4TS9
Treasure x4	VLWEN3
Treasure x6	V84RYS
Treasure x8	A72E1M

LEGO STAR WARS: THE COMPLETE SAGA

The following still need to be purchased after entering the codes.

CHARACTERS

ADMIRAL ACKBAR
At the bar in Mos Eisley Cantina, select Enter Code and enter ACK646.

BATTLE DROID (COMMANDER)
At the bar in Mos Eisley Cantina, select Enter Code and enter KPF958.

BOBA FETT (BOY)
At the bar in Mos Eisley Cantina, select Enter Code and enter GGF539.

BOSS NASS
At the bar in Mos Eisley Cantina, select Enter Code and enter HHY697.

CAPTAIN TARPALS
At the bar in Mos Eisley Cantina, select Enter Code and enter QRN714.

COUNT DOOKU
At the bar in Mos Eisley Cantina, select Enter Code and enter DDD748.

DARTH MAUL
At the bar in Mos Eisley Cantina, select Enter Code and enter EUK421.

EWOK
At the bar in Mos Eisley Cantina, select Enter Code and enter EWK785.

GENERAL GRIEVOUS
At the bar in Mos Eisley Cantina, select Enter Code and enter PMN576.

GREEDO
At the bar in Mos Eisley Cantina, select Enter Code and enter ZZR636.

IG-88
At the bar in Mos Eisley Cantina, select Enter Code and enter GIJ989.

IMPERIAL GUARD
At the bar in Mos Eisley Cantina, select Enter Code and enter GUA850.

JANGO FETT
At the bar in Mos Eisley Cantina, select Enter Code and enter KLJ897.

KI-ADI MUNDI
At the bar in Mos Eisley Cantina, select Enter Code and enter MUN486.

LUMINARA
At the bar in Mos Eisley Cantina, select Enter Code and enter LUM521.

PADMÉ
At the bar in Mos Eisley Cantina, select Enter Code and enter VBJ322.

R2-Q5
At the bar in Mos Eisley Cantina, select Enter Code and enter EVILR2.

STORMTROOPER
At the bar in Mos Eisley Cantina, select Enter Code and enter NBN431.

TAUN WE
At the bar in Mos Eisley Cantina, select Enter Code and enter PRX482.

VULTURE DROID
At the bar in Mos Eisley Cantina, select Enter Code and enter BDC866.

WATTO
At the bar in Mos Eisley Cantina, select Enter Code and enter PLL967.

ZAM WESELL
At the bar in Mos Eisley Cantina, select Enter Code and enter 584HJF.

SKILLS

DISGUISE
At the bar in Mos Eisley Cantina, select Enter Code and enter BRJ437.

FORCE GRAPPLE LEAP
At the bar in Mos Eisley Cantina, select Enter Code and enter CLZ738.

VEHICLES

DROID TRIFIGHTER
At the bar in Mos Eisley Cantina, select Enter Code and enter AAB123.

IMPERIAL SHUTTLE
At the bar in Mos Eisley Cantina, select Enter Code and enter HUT845.

TIE INTERCEPTOR
At the bar in Mos Eisley Cantina, select Enter Code and enter INT729.

TIE FIGHTER
At the bar in Mos Eisley Cantina, select Enter Code and enter DBH897.

ZAM'S AIRSPEEDER
At the bar in Mos Eisley Cantina, select Enter Code and enter UUU875.

LINGER IN SHADOWS

CREDITS AND HIDDEN PART
At the Title screen, press L3 + R3.

MADDEN NFL 07

MADDEN CARDS
Select Madden Cards from My Madden. Then select Madden Codes and enter the following:

CARD	PASSWORD
#199 Gold Lame Duck Cheat	5LAWO0
#200 Gold Mistake Free Cheat	XL7SP1
#210 Gold QB on Target Cheat	WROA0R
#220 Super Bowl XLI Gold	RLA9R7
#221 Super Bowl XLII Gold	WRLUF8
#222 Super Bowl XLIII Gold	NIEV4A
#223 Super Bowl XLIV Gold	M5AB7L
#224 Aloha Stadium Gold	YI8P8U
#225 1958 Colts Gold	B57QLU
#226 1966 Packers Gold	1PL1FL
#227 1968 Jets Gold	MIE6WO
#228 1970 Browns Gold	CL2TOE

CARD	PASSWORD
#229 1972 Dolphins Gold	NOEB7U
#230 1974 Steelers Gold	YO0FLA
#231 1976 Raiders Gold	MOA11I
#232 1977 Broncos Gold	C8UM7U
#233 1978 Dolphins Gold	VIU0O7
#234 1980 Raiders Gold	NLAPH3
#235 1981 Chargers Gold	COAGI4
#236 1982 Redskins Gold	WL8BRI
#237 1983 Raiders Gold	H0EW71
#238 1984 Dolphins Gold	M1AM1E
#239 1985 Bears Gold	QOETO8
#240 1986 Giants Gold	ZI8S2L
#241 1988 49ers Gold	SP2A8H
#242 1990 Eagles Gold	2L4TRO
#243 1991 Lions Gold	J1ETRI
#244 1992 Cowboys Gold	W9UVI9
#245 1993 Bills Gold	DLA3I7
#246 1994 49ers Gold	DR7EST
#247 1996 Packers Gold	F8LUST
#248 1998 Broncos Gold	FIES95
#249 1999 Rams Gold	S9OUSW
#250 Bears Pump Up the Crowd	B1OUPH
#251 Bengals Cheerleader	DRL2SW
#252 Bills Cheerleader	1PLUYO
#253 Broncos Cheerleader	3ROUJO
#254 Browns Pump Up the Crowd	T1UTOA
#255 Buccaneers Cheerleader	S9EWRI
#256 Cardinals Cheerleader	57IEPI
#257 Chargers Cheerleader	F7UHL8
#258 Chiefs Cheerleader	PRI5SL
#259 Colts Cheerleader	1R5AMI
#260 Cowboys Cheerleader	Z2ACHL
#261 Dolphins Cheerleader	C5AHLE
#262 Eagles Cheerleader	PO7DRO
#263 Falcons Cheerleader	37USPO
#264 49ers Cheerleader	KL0CRL
#265 Giants Pump Up the Crowd	C4USPI
#266 Jaguars Cheerleader	MIEH7E
#267 Jets Pump Up the Crowd	C0LUXI
#268 Lions Pump Up the Crowd	3LABLU
#269 Packers Pump Up the Crowd	4HO7VO
#270 Panthers Cheerleader	F2IASP
#282 All AFC Team Gold	PRO9PH
#283 All NFC Team Gold	RLATH7

MAJOR LEAGUE BASEBALL 2K7

MICKEY MANTLE ON THE FREE AGENTS LIST
Select Enter Cheat Code from the My 2K7 menu and enter themick.

ALL CHEATS
Select Enter Cheat Code from the My 2K7 menu and enter Black Sox.

ALL EXTRAS
Select Enter Cheat Code from the My 2K7 menu and enter Game On.

UNLOCK EVERYTHING
Select Enter Cheat Code from the My 2K7 menu and enter Derek Jeter. This does not unlock the Topps cheats.

MIGHTY MICK CHEAT
Select Enter Cheat Code from the My 2K7 menu and enter mightymick.

TRIPLE CROWN CHEAT
Select Enter Cheat Code from the My 2K7 menu and enter triplecrown.

BIG BLAST CHEAT
Select Enter Cheat Code from the My 2K7 menu and enter m4murder.

MARVEL ULTIMATE ALLIANCE

UNLOCK ALL SKINS
At the Team menu, press Up, Down, Left, Right, Left, Right, Start.

UNLOCKS ALL HERO POWERS
At the Team menu, press Left, Right, Up, Down, Up, Down, Start.

ALL HEROES TO LEVEL 99
At the Team menu, press Up, Left, Up, Left, Down, Right, Down, Right, Start.

UNLOCK ALL HEROES
At the Team menu, press Up, Up, Down, Down, Left, Left, Left, Start.

UNLOCK DAREDEVIL
At the Team menu, press Left, Left, Right, Right, Up, Down, Up, Down, Start.

UNLOCK SILVER SURFER
At the Team menu, press Down, Left, Left, Up, Right, Up, Down, Left, Start.

GOD MODE
During gameplay, press Up, Down, Up, Down, Up, Left, Down, Right, Start.

TOUCH OF DEATH
During gameplay, press Left, Right, Down, Down, Right, Left, Start.

SUPER SPEED
During gameplay, press Up, Left, Up, Right, Down, Right, Start.

FILL MOMENTUM
During gameplay, press Left, Right, Right, Left, Up, Down, Down, Up, Start.

UNLOCK ALL COMICS
At the Review menu, press Left, Right, Right, Left, Up, Up, Right, Start.

UNLOCK ALL CONCEPT ART
At the Review menu, press Down, Down, Down, Right, Right, Left, Down, Start.

UNLOCK ALL CINEMATICS
At the Review menu, press Up, Left, Left, Up, Right, Right, Up, Start.

UNLOCK ALL LOAD SCREENS
At the Review menu, press Up, Down, Right, Left, Up, Up Down, Start.

UNLOCK ALL COURSES
At the Comic Missions menu, press Up, Right, Left, Down, Up, Right, Left, Down, Start.

MEDAL OF HONOR: AIRBORNE

Using the following cheats disables saves. During a game, hold L1 + R1, and press ●, ●, ▲, ✕, ✕. This brings up an Enter Cheat screen. Now you can enter the following:

FULL AMMO
Hold L1 + R1 and press ●, ●, ▲, ●, ✕, ▲.

FULL HEALTH
Hold L1 + R1 and press ▲, ●, ●, ▲, ✕, ●.

MERCENARIES 2: WORLD IN FLAMES

To use Cheat Mode, you must update the game by being online when the game is started. The cheats will keep you from earning trophies, but anything earned up to that point remains. You can still save with the cheats, but be careful if you want to earn trophies. Quit the game without saving to return to normal.

PLAYSTATION®3

CHEAT MODE

Access your PDA by pressing Select. Press L2, R2, R2, L2, R2, L2, L2, R2, R2, R2, L2 and close the PDA. You then need to accept the agreement that says trophies are disabled. Now you can enter the following cheats.

INVINCIBILITY

Access your PDA and press Up, Down, Left, Down, Right, Right. This activates invincibility for you and anyone that joins your game.

INFINITE AMMO

Access your PDA and press Up, Down, Left, Right, Left, Left.

GIVE ALL VEHICLES

Access your PDA and press Up, Down, Left, Right, Right, Left.

GIVE ALL SUPPLIES

Access your PDA and press Left, Right, Right, Left, Up, Up, Left, Up.

GIVE ALL AIRSTRIKES (EXCEPT NUKE)

Access your PDA and press Right, Left, Down, Up, Right, Left, Down, Up.

GIVE NUKE

Access your PDA and press Up, Up, Down, Down, Left, Right, Left, Right.

FILL FUEL

Access your PDA and press Up, Up, Up, Down, Down, Down.

ALL COSTUMES

Access your PDA and press Up, Right, Down, Left, Up.

GRAPPLING HOOK

Access your PDA and press Up, Left, Down, Right, Up.

METAL GEAR SOLID 4: GUNS OF THE PATRIOTS

100,000 DREBIN POINTS

At Otacon's computer in Shadow Moses, enter 14893.

OPENING – OLD L.A. 2040 IPOD SONG

At Otacon's computer in Shadow Moses, enter 78925.

POLICENAUTS END TITLE IPOD SONG

At Otacon's computer in Shadow Moses, enter 13462.

You must first defeat the game to use the following passwords.

DESPERATE CHASE IPOD SONG

Select password from the Extras menu and enter thomas.

GEKKO IPOD SONG

Select password from the Extras menu and enter george.

MIDNIGHT SHADOW IPOD SONG

Select password from the Extras menu and enter theodore.

MOBS ALIVE IPOD SONG

Select password from the Extras menu and enter abraham.

DESERT EAGLE - LONG BARREL

Select password from the Extras menu and enter deskyhstyl.

MK. 23 SOCOM PISTOL

Select password from the Extras menu and enter mekakorkkk.

MOSIN NAGANT

Select password from the Extras menu and enter mnsoymsyhn.

TYPE 17 PISTOL

Select password from the Extras menu and enter jmsotsynrn.

ALTAIR COSTUME

Select password from the Extras menu and enter aottrykmyn.

MLB 07: THE SHOW

CLASSIC STADIUMS
At the Main menu, press Down, Up, Right, Down, Up, Left, Down, Up.

GOLDEN/SLIVER ERA PLAYERS
At the Main menu, press Left, Up, Right, Down, Down, Left, Up, Down.

MLB 08: THE SHOW

ALL CLASSIC STADIUMS
At the Main menu, press Down, Right, ●, ●, Left, ●, Up, L1. The controller will vibrate if entered correctly.

MOTOSTORM

UNLOCK EVERYTHING
At the Main menu, hold L1 + L2 + R1 + R2 + R3 (while pressed Up) + L3 (while pressed Down).

BIG HEADS ON ATVS AND BIKES
Pause the game and hold L1 + L2 + R1 + R2 + R3 (while pressed Right), + L3 (while pressed Left).

MX VS. ATV UNTAMED

ALL RIDING GEAR
Select Cheat Codes from the Options and enter crazylikea.

ALL HANDLEBARS
Select Cheat Codes from the Options and enter nohands.

NASCAR 08

ALL CHASE MODE CARS
Select cheat codes from the Options menu and enter checkered flag.

EA SPORTS CAR
Select cheat codes from the Options menu and enter ea sports car.

FANTASY DRIVERS
Select cheat codes from the Options menu and enter race the pack.

WALMART CAR AND TRACK
Select cheat codes from the Options menu and enter walmart everyday.

NASCAR 09

ALL FANTASY DRIVERS
Select EA Extras from My Nascar, choose Cheat Codes and enter CHECKERED FLAG.

WALMART TRACK AND THE WALMART CAR
Select EA Extras from My Nascar, choose Cheat Codes and enter Walmart Everyday.

NBA 07

2006 CHARLOTTE BOBCATS ALTERNATE JERSEY
Select NBA.com from the Trophy Room. Press ● to bring up the Enter Code screen. Enter JKL846ETK5.

2006 NOK HORNETS ALTERNATE JERSEY
Select NBA.com from the Trophy Room. Press ● to bring up the Enter Code screen. Enter EL2E3T8H58.

2006 NEW JERSEY NETS ALTERNATE JERSEY
Select NBA.com from the Trophy Room. Press ● to bring up the Enter Code screen. Enter NB79D965D2.

2006 UTAH JAZZ ALTERNATE JERSEY
Select NBA.com from the Trophy Room. Press ● to bring up the Enter Code screen. Enter 228GG7585G.

2006 WAS WIZARDS ALTERNATE JERSEY
Select NBA.com from the Trophy Room. Press ● to bring up the Enter Code screen. Enter PL5285F37F.

2007 EASTERN ALL STARS
Select NBA.com from the Trophy Room. Press ● to bring up the Enter Code screen. Enter 5F89RE3H8G.

2007 WESTERN ALL STARS
Select NBA.com from the Trophy Room. Press ● to bring up the Enter Code screen. Enter 2H5E89EH8C.

NBA 2K7

ABA BALL
Select Codes from the Features menu and enter payrespect.

ALL-STAR BALL
Select Codes from the Features menu and enter ply8mia.

MAXIMUM DURABILITY
Select Codes from the Features menu and enter ironman.

UNLIMITED STAMINA
Select Codes from the Features menu and enter norest.

+10 DEFENSIVE AWARENESS
Select Codes from the Features menu and enter getstops.

+10 OFFENSIVE AWARENESS
Select Codes from the Features menu and enter inthezone.

2007 ALL-STAR UNIFORMS
Select Codes from the Features menu and enter syt6cii.

BOBCATS SECONDARY
Select Codes from the Features menu and enter bcb8sta.

JAZZ SECONDARY
Select Codes from the Features menu and enter zjb3lau.

NETS SECONDARY
Select Codes from the Features menu and enter nrd4esj.

WIZARDS SECONDARY
Select Codes from the Features menu and enter zw9idla.

ST. PATRICK'S DAY UNIFORMS
Select Codes from the Features menu and enter tpk7sgn.

VALENTINE'S DAY UNIFORMS
Select Codes from the Features menu and enter vdr5lya.

INTERNATIONAL ALL-STARS
Select Codes from the Features menu and enter tns9roi.

NBA 2K TEAM
Select Codes from the Features menu and enter bestsim.

SUPERSTARS
Select Codes from the Features menu and enter rta1spe

TOPPS 2K SPORTS ALL-STARS
Select Codes from the Features menu and enter topps2ksports.

NBA 2K8

ABA BALL
Select Codes from the Features menu and enter Payrespect.

2KSPORTS TEAM
Select Codes from the Features menu and enter 2ksports.

NBA DEVELOPMENT TEAM
Select Codes from the Features menu and enter nba2k.

SUPERSTARS TEAM
Select Codes from the Features menu and enter llmohffaae.

VISUAL CONCEPTS TEAM
Select Codes from the Features menu and enter Vcteam.

2008 ALL STAR NBA JERSEYS
Select Codes from the Features menu and enter haeitgyebs.

BOBCATS RACING JERSEY
Select Codes from the Features menu and enter agtaccsinr.

PACERS SECOND ROAD JERSEY
Select Codes from the Features menu and enter cpares.

ST. PATRICK'S DAY JERSEYS
Select Codes from the Features menu and enter uclerehanp.

VALENTINE'S DAY JERSEYS
Select Codes from the Features menu and enter amcnreo.

NBA 2K9

2K SPORTS TEAM
Select Codes from the Features menu and enter 2ksports.

NBA 2K TEAM
Select Codes from the Features menu and enter nba2k.

SUPERSTARS
Select Codes from the Features menu and enter llmohffaae.

VC TEAM
Select Codes from the Features menu and enter vcteam.

ABA BALL
Select Codes from the Features menu and enter payrespect.

NBA LIVE 07

AIR JORDAN V
Select NBA Codes from My NBA Live 07 and enter PNBBX1EVT5.

AIR JORDAN V
Select NBA Codes from My NBA Live 07 and enter VIR13PC451.

AIR JORDAN V
Select NBA Codes from My NBA Live 07 and enter IB7G8NN91Z.

JORDAN MELO M3
Select NBA Codes from My NBA Live 07 and enter JUL38TC485.

C-BILLUPS ALL-STAR EDITION
Select NBA Codes from My NBA Live 07 and enter BV6877HB9N.

ADIDAS C-BILLUPS VEGAS EDITION
Select NBA Codes from My NBA Live 07 and enter 85NVLDMWS5.

ADIDAS GARNETT BOUNCE ALL-STAR EDITION
Select NBA Codes from My NBA Live 07 and enter HYIOUHCAAN.

ADIDAS GARNETT BOUNCE VEGAS EDITION
Select NBA Codes from My NBA Live 07 and enter KDZ2MQL17W.

ADIDAS GIL-ZERO ALL-STAR EDITION
Select NBA Codes from My NBA Live 07 and enter 23DN1PPOG4.

ADIDAS GIL-ZERO VEGAS EDITION
Select NBA Codes from My NBA Live 07 and enter QQQ3JCUYQ7.

ADIDAS GIL-ZERO MID
Select NBA Codes from My NBA Live 07 and enter 1GSJC8JWRL.

ADIDAS GIL-ZERO MID
Select NBA Codes from My NBA Live 07 and enter 369V6RVU3G.

ADIDAS STEALTH ALL-STAR EDITION
Select NBA Codes from My NBA Live 07 and enter FE454DFJCC.

ADIDAS T-MAC 6 ALL-STAR EDITION
Select NBA Codes from My NBA Live 07 and enter MCJK843NNC.

ADIDAS T-MAC 6 VEGAS EDITION
Select NBA Codes from My NBA Live 07 and enter 84GF7EJG8V.

CHARLOTTE BOBCATS SECOND ROAD JERSEY
Select NBA Codes from My NBA Live 07 and enter WEDX671H7S.

UTAH JAZZ SECOND ROAD JERSEY
Select NBA Codes from My NBA Live 07 and enter VCBI89FK83.

NEW JERSEY NETS SECOND ROAD JERSEY
Select NBA Codes from My NBA Live 07 and enter D4SAA98U5H.

WASHINGTON WIZARDS SECOND ROAD JERSEY

Select NBA Codes from My NBA Live 07 and enter QV93NLKXQC.

EASTERN ALL-STARS 2007 ROAD JERSEY

Select NBA Codes from My NBA Live 07 and enter WOCNW4KL7L.

EASTERN ALL-STARS 2007 HOME JERSEY

Select NBA Codes from My NBA Live 07 and enter 5654ND43N6.

WESTERN ALL-STARS 2007 ROAD JERSEY

Select NBA Codes from My NBA Live 07 and enter XX93BVL20U.

WESTERN ALL-STARS 2007 HOME JERSEY

Select NBA Codes from My NBA Live 07 and enter 993NSKL199.

NBA LIVE 08

ADIDAS GIL-ZERO - ALL-STAR EDITION

Select NBA Codes from My NBA and enter 23DN1PPOG4.

ADIDAS TIM DUNCAN STEALTH - ALL-STAR EDITION

Select NBA Codes from My NBA and enter FE454DFJCC.

NBA STREET HOMECOURT

ALL TEAMS

At the Main menu, hold R1 + L1 and press Left, Right, Left, Right.

ALL COURTS

At the Main menu, hold R1 + L1 and press Up, Right, Down, Left.

BLACK/RED BALL

At the Main menu, hold R1 + L1 and press Up, Down, Left, Right.

NEED FOR SPEED PROSTREET

$2,000

Select Career and then choose Code Entry. Enter 1MA9X99.

$4,000

Select Career and then choose Code Entry. Enter W2IOLL01.

$8,000

Select Career and then choose Code Entry. Enter L1IS97A1.

$10,000

Select Career and then choose Code Entry. Enter 1MI9K7E1.

$10,000

Select Career and then choose Code Entry. Enter CASHMONEY.

$10,000

Select Career and then choose Code Entry. Enter REGGAME.

AUDI TT

Select Career and then choose Code Entry. Enter ITSABOUTYOU.

CHEVELLE SS

Select Career and then choose Code Entry. Enter HORSEPOWER.

COKE ZERO GOLF GTI

Select Career and then choose Code Entry. Enter COKEZERO.

DODGE VIPER

Select Career and then choose Code Entry. Enter WORLDSLONGESTLASTING.

MITSUBISHI LANCER EVOLUTION
Select Career and then choose Code Entry. Enter MITSUBISHIGOFAR.

UNLOCK ALL BONUSES
Select Career and then choose Code Entry. Enter UNLOCKALLTHINGS.

5 REPAIR MARKERS
Select Career and then choose Code Entry. Enter SAFETYNET.

ENERGIZER VINYL
Select Career and then choose Code Entry. Enter ENERGIZERLITHIUM.

CASTROL SYNTEC VINYL
Select Career and then choose Code Entry. Enter CASTROLSYNTEC. This also gives you $10,000.

NHL 08

ALL RBK EDGE JERSEYS
At the RBK Edge Code option, enter h3oyxpwksf8ibcgt.

NINJA GAIDEN SIGMA

5 EXTRA MISSIONS IN MISSION MODE.
At the mission mode screen, press Up, Down, Left, Down, Right, Up, ●.

THE ORANGE BOX

HALF-LIFE 2
The following codes work for Half-Life 2, Half-Life 2: Episode One, and Half-Life 2: Episode Two.

CHAPTER SELECT
While playing, press Left, Left, Left, Left, L1, Right, Right, Right, Right, R1. Pause the game and select New Game to skip to another chapter.

RESTORE HEALTH (25 POINTS)
While playing, press Up, Up, Down, Down, Left, Right, Left, Right, ●, ✕.

RESTORE AMMO FOR CURRENT WEAPON
While playing, press R1, ▲, ●, ✕, ■, R1, ▲, ■, ✕, ●, R1.

PORTAL

CHAPTER SELECT
While playing, press Left, Left, Left, Left, L1, Right, Right, Right, Right, R1. Pause the game and select New Game to skip to another chapter.

GET A BOX
While playing, press Down, ●, ✕, ●, ▲, Down, ●, ✕, ●, ▲.

ENERGY BALL
While playing, press Up, ▲, ▲, ●, ■, ✕, ✕, ●, ●, Up.

PORTAL PLACEMENT ANYWHERE
While playing, press ▲, ✕, ●, ✕, ●, ▲, ●, ✕, Left, Right.

PORTALGUN ID 0
While playing, press Up, Left, Down, Right, Up, Left, Down, Right, ▲, ▲.

PORTALGUN ID 1
While playing, press Up, Left, Down, Right, Up, Left, Down, Right, ●, ●.

PORTALGUN ID 2
While playing, press Up, Left, Down, Right, Up, Left, Down, Right, ✕, ✕.

PORTALGUN ID 3
While playing, press Up, Left, Down, Right, Up, Left, Down, Right, ●, ●.

UPGRADE PORTALGUN
While playing, press ■, ●, L1, R1, Left, Right, L1, R1, L2, R2.

RATATOUILLE

Select Gusteau's Shop from the Extras menu. Choose Secrets, select the appropriate code number, and then enter the code. Once the code is entered, select the cheat you want to activate it.

CODE NUMBER	CODE	EFFECT
1	Pieceocake	Very Easy difficulty mode.
2	Myhero	No impact and no damage from enemies.
3	Shielded	No damage from enemies .
4	Spyagent	Move undetected by any enemy.
5	Ilikeonions	Fart every time Remy jumps.
6	Hardfeelings	Head butt when attacking instead of tailswipe.
7	Slumberparty	Multiplayer mode .
8	Gusteauart	All Concept Art .
9	Gusteauship	All four championship modes .
10	Mattelme	All single player and multiplayer minigames.
11	Gusteauvid	All Videos .
12	Gusteaures	All Bonus Artworks.
13	Gusteaudream	All Dream Worlds in Gusteau's Shop.
14	Gusteauslide	All Slides in Gusteau's Shop.
15	Gusteaulevel	All single player minigames.
16	Gusteaucombo	All items in Gusteau's Shop.
17	Gusteaupot	5,000 Gusteau points.
18	Gusteaujack	10,000 Gusteau points.
19	Gusteauomni	50,000 Gusteau points.

RATCHET & CLANK FUTURE: TOOLS OF DESTRUCTION

CHALLENGE MODE

After defeating the game, you can replay it in Challenge Mode with all of Ratchet's current upgraded weapons and armor.

SKILL POINTS

Complete the following objectives to earn skill points. Each one is worth 10 to 40 points and you can use these points to unlock Cheats in the Cheats menu. The list below lists the skill points with a location and description.

SKILL POINT	LOCATION	DESCRIPTION
Smashing Good Time	Cobalia	Destroy all crates and consumer bots in the trade port and gel factory.
I Should Have Gone Down in a Barrel	Cobalia	Jump into each of the two gel waterfall areas in Cobalia gel factory.
Giant Hunter	Cobalia	Kill several Basilisk Leviathans in the Cobalia wilderness.
Wrench Ninja 3	Stratus City	Use only the Omniwrench to get through the level to the Robo-Wings segment.
We Don't Need No Stinkin' Bridges!	Stratus City	Cross the tri-pad sequence using gel-cube bounces.
Surface-to-Air Plasma Beasts	Stratus City	Take out several flying targets using a specific weapon.
Been Around	Stratus City	Take off from every Robo-wing launch pad in Stratus City.
Collector's Addition	Voron	Be very thorough in your collection of goodies.
Minesweeper	Voron	Clear out a bunch of mines.
What's That, R2?	Voron	Barrel roll multiple times.
I Think I'm Gonna Be Sick	IFF	Ride the ferris wheel for 5 loops without getting off or taking damage.
Fast and the Fire-ious	IFF	Use the Charge Boots to cross the bridge to the arena without being burned.
One Heckuva Peephole	IFF	Return after receiving the Geo-laser and complete the Geo-laser setup.
Alphabet City	Apogee	Teleport to each of the six asteroids in alphabetical order.

SKILL POINT	LOCATION	DESCRIPTION
Knock You Down to Size	Apogee	Wrench Slam 5 centipedes.
Dancin' with the Stars	Apogee	Make 5 enemies dance at once on an asteroid.
Taste o' Yer Own Medicine	Pirate Base	Destroy all of the Shooter Pirates with the Combuster.
Preemptive Strike	Pirate Base	Destroy all of the "sleeping bats" while they are still sleeping.
It's Mutant-E Cap'n!	Pirate Base	Change 5 pirates into penguins in one blast.
You Sunk My Battleship!	Rakar	Shoot down a large percentage of the big destroyers.
Pretty Lights	Rakar	Complete the level without destroying any of the snatchers that fire beams at Ratchet.
I've Got Places To Be	Rakar	Destroy the boss in under 2:30.
The Consumer Is Not (Always) Right	Rykan V	Destroy a bunch of consumer bots in the level.
Live Strong	Rykan V	Complete the Gryo Cycle in 1:45.
Untouchable	Rykan V	Don't take damage in the Gyro-Cycle.
It Sounded Like a Freight Train	Sargasso	Get 10 Swarmers in one tornado.
Head Examiner	Sargasso	Land on all of the dinosaur heads in Sargasso.
Extinction	Sargasso	Kill all of the Sargasso Predators.
Lombaxes Don't Like Cold	Iris	Break all the breakable icicles.
Mow Down Ho-Down	Iris	Use turrets to destroy 10 dancing pirates.
Dancin' on the Ceiling	Zordoom	Successfully use a Groovitron while on a Magboot surface.
Seared Ahi	Zordoom	Use the Pyroblaster on 3 Drophid creatures after freeing them from their robotic suits.
Shocking Ascent	Zordoom	Destroy all enemies on the elevator using just the Shock Ravager.
Expert Marksman	Borag	Kill 75% of all of the enemies.
Can't Touch This	Borag	Don't take damage before fighting the boss.
Pyoo, Pyoo!	Borag	Complete the level without secondary fire.
Dead Aim	Kerchu	Destroy several destructible towers while on the pirate barge.
Fire With Fire	Kerchu	Kill a few Kerchu Flamethrowers with the Pyro Blaster.
Rocket Jump	Kerchu	Successfully jump over a row of three rockets while on the grindrail during the boss fight in Kerchu City.
Your Friendly Neighborhood...	Slag Fleet	Destroy 5 enemies while on the grav ramp before Slag's ship.
Turret Times Two	Slag Fleet	Destroy at least 2 pirates with each turret in the level.
Six Gun Salute	Slag Fleet	Get six pirates in a row to salute Ratchet while in the Pirate Disguise.
Gotta Catch 'Em All	Cragmite Ruins	Hit all Cragmite soldiers with the Mag-Net Launcher.
Ratchet and Goliath	Cragmite Ruins	Destroy multiple walkers using just the Nano-Swarmers.
Ratchet &...Not Clank?!	Cragmite Ruins	Use Mr. Zurkon in Cragmite's Ratchet-only segment.
Stay Still So I Can Shoot You!	Meridian	Use strafe-flip 10 times while fighting the Cragmite soldiers.
Now Boarding...	Meridian	Complete the Gyro-Cycle in 55 seconds.
Low Flying Howls	Meridian	Fly under an electrified barrier in the Robo-wings segment.
Extreme Alien Makeover	Fastoon2	Turn 10 Cragmites into penguins.
Empty Bag o' Tricks	Fastoon2	Complete the level without using any devices.

SKILL POINT	LOCATION	DESCRIPTION
Nowhere to Hide	Fastoon2	Destroy every piece of breakable cover.
No, Up Your Arsenal	Global	Upgrade every weapon to the max.
Roflcopter	Global	Turn enemies into penguins, then use the Visicopter to destroy the penguins.
Stir Fry	Global	Kill 2 different enemy types using the Shock Ravager while they are trapped in a tornado.
Golden Children	Overall	Find all of the Gold Bolts.
Sacagawea	Global	Complete all of the maps 100%, leaving no area undiscovered.
Cheapskate	Global	Purchase a single Combustor round.
Everybody Dance Now	Global	Make every type of enemy in the game dance.
F5 on the Fujita Scale	Global	Pick up more than 10 enemies with one tornado.
Chorus line	Global	Get 10+ enemies to dance together.
Happy Feet	Global	Get several penguins to dance on-screen.
Disco Inferno	Global	Use the Groovitron followed by the Pyro Blaster.
Bolts in the Bank	Global	Sell a bunch of Leviathan Souls to the Smuggler.
It's Like the North Pole Here	Global	Have at least 12-15 enemies and/or citizens turned into penguins at one time.
Say Hello to My Little Friend	Global	Kill 15 enemies with one RYNO shot.
For the Hoard!	Global	Get every item.
Promoted to Inspector	Global	Get every gadget.
Global Thermonuclear War	Global	Get every weapon.
It's Even Better the Second Time!	Global	Complete Challenge Mode.
The Hardest of Core	Global	Get all skill points and everything else in the game.

RESISTANCE: FALL OF MAN

HARD DIFFICULTY
Complete the game on Medium difficulty.

SUPERHUMAN DIFFICULTY
Complete the game on Hard difficulty.

SKILL POINTS
You can access the Skill Points and Rewards menus during gameplay by pressing START to access the Pause Menu, then selecting EXTRAS.

ENEMIES

NAME	LEVEL ACQUIRED	DESCRIPTION
Hybrid	The Gauntlet	After defeating first set of Hybrids.
Leaper	A Lone Survivor	After defeating first few Leapers.
Crawler	A Lone Survivor	After the cinematic and FPNICS.
Menial	Fate Worse Than Death	After the first room.
Cocoon	Conversion	At the third checkpoint.
Carrier	Fate Worse Than Death	At the window when you first see the Carriers.
Howler	Path of Least Resistance	After defeating the Howlers at the end of the level.
Steelhead	Cathedral	After defeating the first two Steelheads in the church.
Titan	Conduits	After defeating the Titan at the beginning of Conduits.
Slipskull	No Way Out	After defeating all three Slipskulls in the burrower room.
Leaper Pod	No Way Out or 61	After finding the Leaper Pods for the first time.
Gray Jack	Angel	After the cryo room.

NAME	LEVEL ACQUIRED	DESCRIPTION
Hardfang	Evacuation	After defeating the first Hardfang in the cafeteria.
Roller	Into the Depths	After defeating the Rollers in the room with the tunnel in the floor.
Widowmaker	Ice and Iron	After defeating the first Widowmaker.
Hybrid 2.0	Angel's Lair	After the first wave of Hybrids in the node.
Angel	Angel's Lair	After defeating the first Angel on the bridge.

VEHICLES

NAME	LEVEL ACQUIRED	DESCRIPTION
Hawk	The Gauntlet	Player automatically starts with this.
Kingfisher	Path of Least Resistance	At the start of the level.
Sabertooth	A Lone Survivor	After getting inside the tank.
Dropship	Hunted Down	After spotting a Dropship in the parking lot area.
Stalker	Outgunned	After spotting the first one in Outgunned.
Burrower	No Way Out	After spotting the first one in No Way Out.
Lynx	Common Ground	After getting inside the Lynx.
Goliath	Giant Slayer	After spotting the first one.

WEAPONS—1ST PLAYTHROUGH

NAME	LEVEL ACQUIRED	DESCRIPTION
M5A2 Carbine	The Gauntlet	Automatically unlocked at start of the game.
Frag Grenade	The Gauntlet	Automatically unlocked at start of the game.
Bullseye	The Gauntlet	In the alleyway after checkpoint 2.
Shotgun	Fate Worse Than Death or 32 or 40	Fate Worse Than Death: Behind the stairs in the outdoor area. Hunted Down: Behind the bar. Hunted Down: In the docks area. Path of Least Resistance: Forced here on the stairs between hill 1 and 2.
Auger	Cathedral	After defeating the first two advanced Hybrids.
Fareye	Conduits	After defeating the large Hybrid and reaching checkpoint 1.
Hailstorm	Search and Rescue	After leaving the first area.
Sapper	A Disturbing Discovery	At the back of the first mech factory.
LAARK	In a Darker Place	On the ground in the first room.
Bullseye Mark 2	Angel's Lair	After leaving the first room and going into the node.

WEAPONS—2ND PLAYTHROUGH

NAME	LEVEL ACQUIRED	DESCRIPTION
Reapers	The Gauntlet	Inside the house at the bottom of the hill.
Backlash Grenade	Cathedral	After crossing alley just past the cathedral; it's the first room on the left.
Arc Charger	No Way Out	At the end of the long hallway prior to the burrower.
L11-Dragon	Evacuation	Before the first elevator leading to the hangar.
Splitter	A Desperate Gambit	At checkpoint 1, near the big windows.

LOCATIONS

NAME	LEVEL ACQUIRED	DESCRIPTION
York	The Gauntlet	Unlocked at the start of the level.
Grimsby	Fate Worse Than Death	Unlocked at the start of the level.
Manchester	Path of Least Resistance	Unlocked at the start of the level.

PLAYSTATION®3

NAME	LEVEL ACQUIRED	DESCRIPTION
Nottingham	Into the Fire	Unlocked at the start of the level.
Cheshire	No Way Out	Unlocked at the start of the level.
Somerset	Search and Rescue	Unlocked at the start of the level.
Bristol	Devil at the Door	Unlocked at the start of the level.
Bracknell	Into the Depths	Unlocked at the start of the level.
London	A Desperate Gambit	Unlocked at the start of the level.
Thames	Burning Bridges	Unlocked at the start of the level.
Tower	Angel's Lair	Unlocked at the start of the level.

REWARDS

NAME	HOW TO UNLOCK
Concept Art Pack 1	10 points
Concept Art Pack 2	20 points
The Mighty Wrench - Gives allies wrench	40 points
Flip Levels	70 points
Clank Backpacks	100 points
MP Mechanic Skin	126 points
MP Soldier Skin	Beat game on Superhuman mode.
MP Soldier head skin	Beat game on Superhuman mode and collect all Skill Points.
Movie player	Beat game once.

ROBERT LUDLUM'S THE BOURNE CONSPIRACY

AUTOMATIC SHOTGUNS REPLACE SIMI-AUTOS

Select Cheats from the Main menu, press ●, and then enter alwaysanobjective.

LIGHT MACHINE GUNS HAVE SILENCERS

Select Enter Code from the Cheats screen and enter whattheymakeyougive.

EXTRAS UNLOCKED – CONCEPT ART

Select Enter Code from the Cheats screen and enter lastchancemarie. Select Concept Art from the Extras menu.

EXTRAS UNLOCKED – MUSIC TRACKS

Select Enter Code from the Cheats screen and enter jasonbourneisdead. This unlocks Treadstone Appointment and Manheim Suite in the Music Selector found in the Extras menu.

ROCK BAND

ALL SONGS

At the Title screen, press Red, Yellow, Blue, Red, Red, Blue, Blue, Red, Yellow, Blue. Saving and all network features are disabled with this code.

TRANSPARENT INSTRUMENTS

Complete the hall of fame concert with that instrument.

GOLD INSTRUMENT

Complete the solo tour with that instrument.

SILVER INSTRUMENT

Complete the bonus tour with that instrument.

ROCK BAND 2

Most of these codes disable saving, achievements, and Xbox LIVE play. The first code listed is with the guitar and the second is an alternative using a controller.

UNLOCK ALL SONGS
Select Modify Game from the Extras menu, choose Enter Unlock Code and press Red, Yellow, Blue, Red, Red, Blue, Blue, Red, Yellow, Blue or ●, ▲, ■, ●, ●, ■, ■, ●, ▲, ■. Toggle this cheat on or off from the Modify Game menu.

SELECT VENUE SCREEN
Select Modify Game from the Extras menu, choose Enter Unlock Code and press Blue, Orange, Orange, Blue, Yellow, Blue, Orange, Orange, Blue, Yellow or ■, L1, L1, ■, ▲, ■, L1, L1, ■, ▲. Toggle this cheat on or off from the Modify Game menu.

NEW VENUES ONLY
Select Modify Game from the Extras menu, choose Enter Unlock Code and press Red, Red, Red, Red, Yellow, Yellow, Yellow, Yellow or ● (x4), ▲ (x4). Toggle this cheat on or off from the Modify Game menu.

PLAY THE GAME WITHOUT A TRACK
Select Modify Game from the Extras menu, choose Enter Unlock Code and press Blue, Blue, Red, Blue, Yellow, Yellow, Blue, Blue or ■, ■, ●, ■, ▲, ▲, ■, ■. Toggle this cheat on or off from the Modify Game menu.

AWESOMENESS DETECTION
Select Modify Game from the Extras menu, choose Enter Unlock Code and press Yellow, Blue, Orange, Yellow, Blue, Orange, Yellow, Blue, Orange or ▲, ■, L1, ▲, ■, L1, ▲, ■, L1. Toggle this cheat on or off from the Modify Game menu.

STAGE MODE
Select Modify Game from the Extras menu, choose Enter Unlock Code and press Blue, Yellow, Red, Blue, Yellow, Red, Blue, Yellow, Red or ▲, ●, ■, ▲, ●, ■, ▲, ●. Toggle this cheat on or off from the Modify Game menu.

SAINTS ROW 2

CHEAT CODES
Select Dial from the Phone menu and enter these numbers followed by the Call button. Activate the cheats by selecting Cheats from the Phone menu. Enabling a cheat prevents the acquisition of Achievements

PLAYER ABILITY

Give Cash	#2274666399
No Cop Notoriety	#50
No Gang Notoriety	#51

Infinite Sprint	#6
Full Health	#1
Player Pratfalls	#5
Milk Bones	#3
Car Mass Hole	#2
Infinite Ammo	#11
Heaven Bound	#12
Add Police Notoriety	#4
Add Gang Notoriety	#35
Never Die	#36
Unlimited Clip	#9

VEHICLES

Repair Car	#1056
Venom Classic	#1079
Five-0	#1055
Stilwater Municipal	#1072
Baron	#1047
Attrazione	#1043
Zenith	#1081
Vortex	#1080
Phoenix	#1064
Bootlegger	#1049
Raycaster	#1068
Hollywood	#1057
Justice	#1058
Compton	#1052
Eiswolf	#1053
Taxi	#1074
Ambulance	#1040
Backhoe	#1045
Bagboy	#1046
Rampage	#1067
Reaper	#1069
The Job	#1075
Quota	#1066
FBI	#1054
Mag	#1060
Bulldog	#1050
Quasar	#1065
Titan	#1076
Varsity	#1078
Anchor	#1041
Blaze	#1044
Sabretooth	#804
Sandstorm	#805
Kaneda	#801
Widowmaker	#806
Kenshin	#802
Melbourne	#803
Miami	#826
Python	#827
Hurricane	#825
Shark	#828
Skipper	#829
Mongoose	#1062
Superiore	#1073
Tornado	#713
Horizon	#711
Wolverine	#714
Snipes 57	#712
Bear	#1048
Toad	#1077

VEHICLES CONT.

Kent	#1059
Oring	#1063
Longhauler	#1061
Atlasbreaker	#1042
Septic Avenger	#1070
Shaft	#1071
Bulldozer	#1051

WEAPONS

AR-50	#923
K6	#935
GDHC	#932
NR4	#942
44	#921
Tombstone	#956
T3K	#954
VICE9	#957
AS14 Hammer	#925
12 Gauge	#920
SKR-9	#951
McManus 2010	#938
Baseball Bat	#926
Knife	#936
Molotov	#940
Grenade	#933
Nightstick	#941
Pipebomb	#945
RPG	#946
Crowbar	#955
Pimp Cane	#944
AR200	#922
AR-50/Grenade Launcher	#924
Chainsaw	#927
Fire Extinguisher	#928
Flamethrower	#929
Flashbang	#930
GAL43	#931
Kobra	#934
Machete	#937
Mini-gun	#939
Pepperspray	#943
Annihilator RPG	#947
Samurai Sword	#948
Satchel Charge	#949
Shock Paddles	#950
Sledgehammer	#952
Stungun	#953
XS-2 Ultimax	#958
Pimp Slap	#969

WEATHER

Clear Skies	#78669
Heavy Rain	#78666
Light Rain	#78668
Overcast	#78665
Time Set Midnight	#2400
Time Set Noon	#1200
Wrath Of God	#666

PLAYSTATION®3

WORLD

Super Saints	#8
Super Explosions	#7
Evil Cars	#16
Pedestrian War	#19
Drunk Pedestrians	#15
Raining Pedestrians	#20
Low Gravity	#18

SEGA SUPERSTARS TENNIS

UNLOCK CHARACTERS
Complete the following missions to unlock the corresponding character.

CHARACTER	COMPLETE THIS MISSION
Alex Kidd	Mission 1 of Alex Kidd's World
Amy Rose	Mission 2 of Sonic the Hedgehog's World
Gilius	Mission 1 of Golden Axe's World
Gum	Mission 12 of Jet Grind Radio's World
Meemee	Mission 8 of Super Monkey Ball's World
Pudding	Mission 1 of Space Channel 5's World
Reala	Mission 2 of NiGHTs' World
Shadow The Hedgehog	Mission 14 of Sonic the Hedgehog's World

SILENT HILL: HOMECOMING

YOUNG ALEX COSTUME
At the Title screen, press Up, Up, Down, Down, Left, Right, Left, Right, ●.

THE SIMPSONS GAME

After unlocking the following, the outfits can be changed at the downstairs closet in the Simpson's house. The Trophies can be viewed at different locations in the house: Bart's room, Lisa's room, Marge's room, and the garage.

BART'S OUTFITS AND TROPHIES (POSTER COLLECTION)
At the Main menu, press Right, Left, ●, ●, ▲, R3.

HOMER'S OUTFITS AND TROPHIES (BEER BOTTLE COLLECTION)
At the Main menu, press Left, Right, ▲, ▲, ●, L3.

LISA'S OUTFITS AND TROPHIES (DOLLS)
At the Main menu, press ●, ▲, ●, ●, ●, ▲, L3.

MARGE'S OUTFITS AND TROPHIES (HAIR PRODUCTS)
At the Main menu, press ▲, ●, ▲, ●, ▲, ●, R3.

SKATE

BEST BUY CLOTHES
At the Main menu, press Up, Down, Left, Right, ●, R1, ▲, L1.

SOLDIER OF FORTUNE: PAYBACK

ACR-2 SNIPER RIFLE
At the difficulty select, press Up, Up, Down, Left, Right, Right, Down.

CHEAT CODES

Pause the game and select Input Code. Here you can enter the following codes. Activating any of the following cheat codes will disable some unlockables, and you will be unable to save your progress.

CHEAT	CODE
All Force Powers at Max Power	KATARN
All Force Push Ranks	EXARKUN
All Saber Throw Ranks	ADEGAN
All Repulse Ranks	DATHOMIR
All Saber Crystals	HURRIKANE
All Talents	JOCASTA
Deadly Saber	LIGHTSABER

COMBOS

Pause the game and select Input Code. Here you can enter the following codes. Activating any of the following cheat codes will disable some unlockables, and you will be unable to save your progress.

COMBO	CODE
All Combos	MOLDYCROW
Aerial Ambush	VENTRESS
Aerial Assault	EETHKOTH
Aerial Blast	YADDLE
Impale	BRUTALSTAB
Lightning Bomb	MASSASSI
Lightning Grenade	RAGNOS
Saber Slam	PLOKOON
Saber Sling	KITFISTO
Sith Saber Flurry	LUMIYA
Sith Slash	DARAGON
Sith Throw	SAZEN
New Combo	FREEDON
New Combo	MARAJADE

ALL DATABANK ENTRIES

Pause the game and select Input Code. Enter OSSUS.

MIRRORED LEVEL

Pause the game and select Input Code. Enter MINDTRICK. Re-enter the code to return level to normal.

SITH MASTER DIFFICULTY

Pause the game and select Input Code. Enter SITHSPAWN.

COSTUMES

Pause the game and select Input Code. Here you can enter the following codes.

COSTUME	CODE
All Costumes	SOHNDANN
Bail Organa	VICEROY
Ceremonial Jedi Robes	DANTOOINE
Drunken Kota	HARDBOILED
Emperor	MASTERMIND
Incinerator Trooper	PHOENIX
Jedi Adventure Robe	HOLOCRON
Kashyyyk Trooper	TK421GREEN
Kota	MANDALORE
Master Kento	WOOKIEE
Proxy	PROTOTYPE
Scout Trooper	FERRAL
Shadow Trooper	BLACKHOLE
Sith Stalker Armor	KORRIBAN
Snowtrooper	SNOWMAN
Stormtrooper	TK421WHITE
Stormtrooper Commander	TK421BLUE

STUNTMAN IGNITION

3 PROPS IN STUNT CREATOR MODE

Select Cheats from Extras and enter COOLPROP.

ALL ITEMS UNLOCKED FOR CONSTRUCTION MODE

Select Cheats from Extras and enter NOBLEMAN.

MVX SPARTAN

Select Cheats from Extras and enter fastride.

ALL CHEATS

Select Cheats from Extras and enter Wearefrozen. This unlocks the following cheats: Slo-mo Cool, Thrill Cam, Vision Switcher, Nitro Addiction, Freaky Fast, and Ice Wheels.

ALL CHEATS

Select Cheats from Extras and enter Kungfoopete.

ICE WHEELS CHEAT

Select Cheats from Extras and enter IceAge.

NITRO ADDICTION CHEAT

Select Cheats from Extras and enter TheDuke.

VISION SWITCHER CHEAT

Select Cheats from Extras and enter GFXMODES.

SUPER PUZZLE FIGHTER II TURBO HD REMIX

PLAY AS AKUMA

At the character select, highlight Hsien-Ko and press Down.

PLAY AS DAN

At the character select, highlight Donovan and press Down.

PLAY AS DEVILOT

At the character select, highlight Morrigan and press Down.

PLAY AS ANITA

At the character select, hold L1 + R1 and choose Donovan.

PLAY AS HSIEN-KO'S TALISMAN

At the character select, hold L1 + R1 and choose Hsien-Ko.

PLAY AS MORRIGAN AS A BAT

At the character select, hold L1 + R1 and choose Morrigan.

SURF'S UP

ALL CHAMPIONSHIP LOCATIONS

Select Cheat Codes from the Extras menu and enter FREEVISIT.

ALL LEAF SLIDE STAGES

Select Cheat Codes from the Extras menu and enter GOINGDOWN.

ALL MULTIPLAYER LEVELS

Select Cheat Codes from the Extras menu and enter MULTIPASS.

ALL BOARDS

Select Cheat Codes from the Extras menu and enter MYPRECIOUS.

ASTRAL BOARD

Select Cheat Codes from the Extras menu and enter ASTRAL.

MONSOON BOARD

Select Cheat Codes from the Extras menu and enter MONSOON.

TINE SHOCKWAVE BOARD

Select Cheat Codes from the Extras menu and enter TINYSHOCKWAVE.

ALL CHARACTER CUSTOMIZATIONS

Select Cheat Codes from the Extras menu and enter TOPFASHION.

PLAY AS ARNOLD

Select Cheat Codes from the Extras menu and enter TINYBUTSTRONG.

PLAY AS ELLIOT

Select Cheat Codes from the Extras menu and enter SURPRISEGUEST.

PLAY AS GEEK

Select Cheat Codes from the Extras menu and enter SLOWANDSTEADY.

PLAY AS TANK EVANS

Select Cheat Codes from the Extras menu and enter IMTHEBEST.

PLAY AS TATSUHI KOBAYASHI

Select Cheat Codes from the Extras menu and enter KOBAYASHI.

PLAY AS ZEKE TOPANGA

Select Cheat Codes from the Extras menu and enter THELEGEND.

ALL VIDEOS AND SPEN GALLERY

Select Cheat Codes from the Extras menu and enter WATCHAMOVIE.

ART GALLERY

Select Cheat Codes from the Extras menu and enter NICEPLACE.

TIGER WOODS PGA TOUR 08

ALL COURSES

Select Password from EA Sports Extras and enter greensfees.

ALL GOLFERS

Select Password from EA Sports Extras and enter allstars.

WAYNE ROONEY

Select Password from EA Sports Extras and enter playfifa08.

INFINITE MONEY

Select Password from EA Sports Extras and enter cream.

TIMESHIFT

KRONE IN MULTIPLAYER

Select Multiplayer from the Options menu. Highlight Model and press ● to get to Krone. Press Y and enter RXYMCPENCJ.

TONY HAWK'S PROJECT 8

SPONSOR ITEMS

As you progress through Career mode and move up the rankings, you gain sponsors and each comes with its own Create-a-skater item.

RANK REQUIRED	CAS ITEM UNLOCKED
Rank 040	Adio Kenny V2 Shoes
Rank 050	Quiksilver_Hoody_3
Rank 060	Birdhouse Tony Hawk Deck
Rank 080	Vans No Skool Gothic Shoes
Rank 100	Volcom Scallero Jacket
Rank 110	eS Square One Shoes
Rank 120	Almost Watch What You Say Deck
Rank 140	DVS Adage Shoe
Rank 150	Element Illuminate Deck
Rank 160	Etnies Sheckler White Lavender Shoes
Complete Skateshop Goal	Stereo Soundwave Deck

SKATERS

All of the skaters, except for Tony Hawk, must be unlocked by completing challenges in the Career Mode. They are useable in Free Skate and 2 Player modes.

SKATER	HOW TO UNLOCK
Tony Hawk	Always Unlocked
Lyn-z Adams Hawkins	Complete Pro Challenge
Bob Burquist	Complete Pro Challenge
Dustin Dollin	Complete Pro Challenge
Nyjah Huston	Complete Pro Challenge
Bam Margera	Complete Pro Challenge
Rodney Mullen	Complete Pro Challenge
Paul Rodriguez	Complete Pro Challenge
Ryan Sheckler	Complete Pro Challenge
Daewon Song	Complete Pro Challenge
Mike Vallely	Complete Pro Challenge
Stevie Willams	Complete Pro Challenge
Travis Barker	Complete Pro Challenge
Kevin Staab	Complete Pro Challenge
Zombie	Complete Pro Challenge
Christaian Hosoi	Rank #1
Jason Lee	Complete Final Tony Hawk Goal
Photographer	Unlock Shops
Security Guard	Unlock School
Bum	Unlock Car Factory
Beaver Mascot	Unlock High School
Real Estate Agent	Unlock Downtown
Filmer	Unlock High School
Skate Jam Kid	Rank #4
Dad	Rank #1
Colonel	All Gaps
Nerd	Complete School Spirit Goal

CHEAT CODES

Select Cheat Codes from the Options and enter the following codes. In game you can access some codes from the Options menu.

CHEAT CODE	RESULTS
plus44	Unlocks Travis Barker
hohohosoi	Unlocks Christian Hosoi
notmono	Unlocks Jason Lee
mixitup	Unlocks Kevin Staab
strangefellows	Unlocks Dad & Skater Jam Kid
themedia	Unlocks Photog Girl & Filmer
militarymen	Unlocks Colonel & Security Guard
Cheat Code	Results
jammypack	Unlocks Always Special
balancegalore	Unlocks Perfect Rail
frontandback	Unlocks Perect Manual
shellshock	Unlocks Unlimited Focus
shescaresme	Unlocks Big Realtor
birdhouse	Unlocks Inkblot deck
allthebest	Full stats
needaride	All decks unlocked and free, except for Inkblot Deck and Gamestop Deck
yougotitall	All specials unlocked and in player's special list and set as owned in skate shop
wearelosers	Unlocks Nerd and a Bum
manineedadate	Unlocks Beaver Mascot
suckstobedead	Unlocks Officer Dick
HATEDANDPROUD	Unlocks the Vans item

TONY HAWK'S PROVING GROUND

Select Cheat Codes from the Options and enter the following cheats. Some codes need to be enabled by selecting Cheats from the Options during a game.

UNLOCK	CHEAT
Unlocks Boneman	CRAZYBONEMAN
Unlocks Bosco	MOREMILK
Unlocks Cam	NOTACAMERA
Unlocks Cooper	THECOOP
Unlocks Eddie X	SKETCHY
Unlocks El Patinador	PILEDRIVER
Unlocks Eric	FLYAWAY
Unlocks Mad Dog	RABBIES
Unlocks MCA	INTERGALACTIC
Unlocks Mel	NOTADUDE
Unlocks Rube	LOOKSSMELLY
Unlocks Spence	DAPPER
Unlocks Shayne	MOVERS
Unlocks TV Producer	SHAKER
Unlock FDR	THEPREZPARK
Unlock Lansdowne	THELOCALPARK
Unlock Air & Space Museum	THEINDOORPARK
Unlocks all Fun Items	OVERTHETOP
Unlocks all CAS items	GIVEMESTUFF
Unlocks all Decks	LETSGOSKATE
Unlock all Game Movies	WATCHTHIS
Unlock all Lounge Bling Items	SWEETSTUFF
Unlock all Lounge Themes	LAIDBACKLOUNGE
Unlock all Rigger Pieces	IMGONNABUILD
Unlock all Video Editor Effects	TRIPPY
Unlock all Video Editor Overlays	PUTEMONTOP
All specials unlocked and in player's special list	LOTSOFTRICKS
Full Stats	BEEFEDUP
Give player +50 skill points	NEEDSHELP

The following cheats lock you out of the Leaderboards:

UNLOCK	CHEAT
Unlocks Perfect Manual	STILLAINTFALLIN
Unlocks Perfect Rail	AINTFALLIN
Unlock Super Check	BOOYAH
Unlocks Unlimited Focus	MYOPIC
Unlock Unlimited Slash Grind	SUPERSLASHIN
Unlocks 100% branch completion in NTT	FOREVERNAILED
No Bails	ANDAINTFALLIN

You can not use the Video Editor with the following cheats:

UNLOCK	CHEAT
Invisible Man	THEMISSING
Mini Skater	TINYTATER
No Board	MAGICMAN

TOM CLANCY'S RAINBOW SIX VEGAS

SUPER RAGDOLL
Pause the game, hold L2 and press ✕, ✕, ◉, ◉, ⬤, ⬤, ▲, ▲, ✕, ◉, ⬤, ▲.

THIRD PERSON MODE
Pause the game, hold L2 and press ⬤, ◉, ⬤, ◉, L3, L3, ▲, ✕, ▲, ✕, R3, R3.

BIG HEAD
Pause the game, hold L2 and press ◉, ⬤, ✕, ▲, L3, ▲, ✕, ⬤, ◉, R3.

ONE HIT KILLS
Pause the game, hold L2 and press L3, R3, L3, R3, ✕, ◉, L3, R3, L3, R3 ⬤, ▲.

TOM CLANCY'S RAINBOW SIX VEGAS 2

GI JOHN DOE MODE
Pause the game, hold the R1 and press L3, L3, ✕, R3, R3, ◉, L3, L3, ⬤, R3, R3, ▲.

SUPER RAGDOLL
Pause the game, hold the R1 and press ✕, ✕, ◉, ◉, ⬤, ⬤, ▲, ▲, ✕, ◉, ⬤, ▲.

THIRD PERSON MODE
Pause the game, hold the R1 and press ⬤, ◉, ⬤, ◉, L3, L3, ▲, ✕, ▲, ✕, R3, R3.

TAR-21 ASSAULT RIFLE
At the Character Customization screen, hold R1 and press Down, Down, Up, Up, ⬤, ◉, ⬤, ◉, ▲, Up, Up, ▲.

MULTIPLAYER MAP: COMCAST EVENT
Select Extras from the Main menu. Choose Comcast Gift and enter Comcast Faster.

INFINITE HEALTH
At the Main menu, press Left, Left, Up, Left, Right, Down, Right.

INFINITE AMMO
At the Main menu, press Up, Down, Left, Right, Up, Up, Down.

NO MILITARY OR POLICE
At the Main menu, press Right, Left, Right, Left, Right, Left, Right.

ALL MISSIONS
At the Main menu, press Down, Up, Left, Right, Right, Right, Up, Down.

BONUS CYBERTRON MISSIONS
At the Main menu, press Right, Up, Up, Down, Right, Left, Left.

GENERATION 1 SKIN: JAZZ
At the Main menu, press Left, Up, Down, Down, Left, Up, Right.

GENERATION 1 SKIN: MEGATRON
At the Main menu, press Down, Left, Left, Down, Right, Right, Up.

GENERATION 1 SKIN: OPTIMUS PRIME
At the Main menu, press Down, Right, Left, Up, Down, Down, Left.

GENERATION 1 SKIN: ROBOVISION OPTIMUS PRIME
At the Main menu, press Down, Down, Up, Up, Right, Right, Right.

GENERATION 1 SKIN: STARSCREAM
At the Main menu, press Right, Down, Left, Left, Down, Up, Up.

UNCHARTED: DRAKE'S FORTUNE

DRAKE'S BASEBALL T-SHIRT
At the costume select, press Left, Right, Down, Up, ▲, R1, L1, ●.

MAKING A CUTSCENE - GRAVE ROBBING
At the rewards screen, highlight Making a Cutscene - Grave Robbing and press Left, R2, Right, Up, L2, ▲, ●, Down.

MAKING A CUTSCENE - TIME'S UP
At the rewards screen, highlight Making a Cutscene - Time's Up and press L1, Right, ●, Down, Left, ▲, R1, Up.

CONCEPT ART - BONUS 1
At the rewards screen, highlight Concept Art - Bonus 1 and press L2, Right, Up, ●, Left, ▲, R1, Down.

CONCEPT ART - BONUS 2
At the rewards screen, highlight Concept Art - Bonus 2 and press ●, L1, Right, Left, Down, R2, ▲, Up.

VIRTUA FIGHTER 5

WATCH MODE
Select Exhibition Mode, then at the character select, hold L1 + R1 and press ✖.

WALL-E

The following cheats will disable saving. The five possible characters starting with Wall-E and going down are: Wall-E, Auto, EVE, M-O, GEL-A Steward.

ALL BONUS FEATURES UNLOCKED
Select Cheats from the Bonus Features menu and enter Wall-E, Auto, EVE, GEL-A Steward.

ALL GAME CONTENT UNLOCKED
Select Cheats from the Bonus Features menu and enter M-O, Auto, GEL-A Steward, EVE.

ALL SINGLE PLAYER LEVELS UNLOCKED
Select Cheats from the Bonus Features menu and enter Auto, GEL-A Steward, M-O, Wall-E.

ALL MULTIPLAYER MAPS UNLOCKED
Select Cheats from the Bonus Features menu and enter EVE, M-O, Wall-E, Auto.

ALL HOLIDAY COSTUMES UNLOCKED
Select Cheats from the Bonus Features menu and enter Auto, Auto, GEL-A Steward, GEL-A Steward.

ALL MULTIPLAYER COSTUMES UNLOCKED
Select Cheats from the Bonus Features menu and enter GEL-A Steward, Wall-E, M-O, Auto.

UNLIMITED HEALTH UNLOCKED
Select Cheats from the Bonus Features menu and enter Wall-E, M-O, Auto, M-O.

WALL-E: MAKE ANY CUBE AT ANY TIME
Select Cheats from the Bonus Features menu and enter Auto, M-O, Auto, M-O.

WALL-EVE: MAKE ANY CUBE AT ANY TIME
Select Cheats from the Bonus Features menu and enter M-O, GEL-A Steward, EVE, EVE.

WALL-E WITH A LASER GUN AT ANY TIME
Select Cheats from the Bonus Features menu and enter Wall-E, EVE, EVE, Wall-E.

WALL-EVE WITH A LASER GUN AT ANY TIME
Select Cheats from the Bonus Features menu and enter GEL-A Steward, EVE, M-O, Wall-E.

WALL-E: PERMANENT SUPER LASER UPGRADE
Select Cheats from the Bonus Features menu and enter Wall-E, Auto, EVE, M-O.

EVE: PERMANENT SUPER LASER UPGRADE
Select Cheats from the Bonus Features menu and enter EVE, Wall-E, Wall-E, Auto.

CREDITS
Select Cheats from the Bonus Features menu and enter Auto, Wall-E, GEL-A Steward, M-O.

WORLD SERIES OF POKER 2008 BATTLE FOR THE BRACELETS

PHILLIP J. HELLMUTH
Enter BEATTHEBRAT as the player name.

WWE SMACKDOWN! VS RAW 2008

HBK AND HHH'S DX OUTFIT
Select Cheat Codes from the Options and enter DXCostume69K2.

KELLY KELLY'S ALTERNATE OUTFIT
Select Cheat Codes from the Options and enter KellyKG12R.

BRET HART
Complete the March 31, 1996 Hall of Fame challenge by defeating Bret Hart with Shawn Michaels in a One-On-One 30-Minute Iron Man Match on Legend difficulty. Purchase from WWE Shop for $210,000.

MICK FOLEY

Complete the June 28, 1998 Hall of Fame challenge by defeating Mick Foley with The Undertaker in a Hell In a Cell Match on Legend difficulty. Purchase from WWE Shop for $210,000.

MR. MCMAHON

Win or successfully defend a championship (WWE or World Heavyweight) at WrestleMania in WWE 24/7 GM Mode. Purchase from WWE Shop for $110,000.

THE ROCK

Complete the April 1, 2001 Hall of Fame challenge by defeating The Rock with Steve Austin in a Single Match on Legend Difficulty. Purchase from WWE Shop for $210,000.

STEVE AUSTIN

Complete the March 23, 1997 Hall of Fame challenge by defeating Steve Austin with Bret Hart in a Submission Match on Legend Difficulty. Purchase from WWE Shop for $210,000.

TERRY FUNK

Complete the April 13, 1997 Hall of Fame challenge by defeating Tommy Dreamer, Sabu and Sandman with any Superstar in an ECW Extreme Rules 4-Way Match on Legend difficulty. Purchase from WWE Shop for $210,000.

MR. MCMAHON BALD

Must unlock Mr. McMahon as a playable character first. Purchase from WWE Shop for $60,000.

GAMES

OVERLOAD

PLAYSTATION 2

AMPLITUDE

BLUR
During a game, press R3 (x4), L3 (x4), then R3.

MONKEY NOTES
During a game, press L3 (x4), R3 (x4), then L3. Quit the game and go back into the song to see the effect. Re-enter the code to disable it.

RANDOM NOTE PLACEMENT
During a game, press ⊗, ✕, ⊗, Left, Left, R3, R3, Right, Right. Quit the game and go back into the song to see the effect. Re-enter the code to disable it.

CHANGE SHAPE OF TRACK LAYOUT
During the game, press L3 (x3), R3 (x3), L3, R3, and L3. Quit the game and go back into the song to see the effect. Enter it once for a tunnel appearance and a second time for a Tempest-style look. Enter the code a third time to disable it.

APE ESCAPE: PUMPED & PRIMED

ALL GADGETS
Complete Story Mode. At the mode select, hold R1 + L1 + R2 + L2 to access the password screen. Enter Go Wild!.

DISABLE ALL GADGETS CHEAT
Complete Story Mode. At the mode select, hold R1 + L1 + R2 + L2 to access the password screen. Enter Limited!.

NORMAL DIFFICULTY
Complete Story Mode. At the mode select, hold R1 + L1 + R2 + L2 to access the password screen. Enter NORMAL!.

HARD DIFFICULTY
Complete Story Mode. At the mode select, hold R1 + L1 + R2 + L2 to access the password screen. Enter HARD!.

AVATAR: THE LAST AIRBENDER—THE BURNING EARTH

1 HIT DISHONOR
At the Main menu, press L1 and select Code Entry. Enter 28260.

ALL BONUS GAME
At the Main menu, press L1 and select Code Entry. Enter 99801.

ALL GALLERY ITEMS
At the Main menu, press L1 and select Code Entry. Enter 85061.

DOUBLE DAMAGE
At the Main menu, press L1 and select Code Entry. Enter 90210.

INFINITE HEALTH
At the Main menu, press L1 and select Code Entry. Enter 65049.

MAX LEVEL
At the Main menu, press L1 and select Code Entry. Enter 89121.

UNLIMITED SPECIAL ATTACKS
At the Main menu, press L1 and select Code Entry. Enter 66206.

OVERLOAD

AVATAR: THE LAST AIRBENDER— INTO THE INFERNO

ALL CHAPTERS
Select Game Secrets at Ember Islands and enter 52993833.

MAX COINS
Select Game Secrets at Ember Islands and enter 66639224.

ALL ITEMS AVAILABLE AT SHOP
Select Game Secrets at Ember Islands and enter 34737253.

ALL CONCEPT ART
Select Game Secrets at Ember Islands and enter 27858343.

BEN 10: ALIEN FORCE THE GAME

LEVEL LORD
Enter Gwen, Kevin, Big Chill, Gwen as a code.

INVINCIBILITY
Enter Kevin, Big Chill, Swampfire, Kevin as a code.

ALL COMBOS
Enter Swampfire, Gwen, Kevin, Ben as a code.

INFINITE ALIENS
Enter Ben, Swampfire, Gwen, Big Chill as a code.

BEN 10: PROTECTOR OF EARTH

INVINCIBILITY
Select a game from the Continue option. Go to the Map Selection screen, press Start and choose Extras. Select Enter Secret Code and enter XLR8, Heatblast, Wildvine, Fourarms.

ALL COMBOS
Select a game from the Continue option. Go to the Map Selection screen, press Start and choose Extras. Select Enter Secret Code and enter Cannonblot, Heatblast, Fourarms, Heatblast.

ALL LOCATIONS
Select a game from the Continue option. Go to the Map Selection screen, press Start and choose Extras. Select Enter Secret Code and enter Heatblast, XLR8, XLR8, Cannonblot.

DNA FORCE SKINS
Select a game from the Continue option. Go to the Map Selection screen, press Start and choose Extras. Select Enter Secret Code and enter Wildvine, Fourarms, Heatblast, Cannonbolt.

DARK HEROES SKINS
Select a game from the Continue option. Go to the Map Selection screen, press Start and choose Extras. Select Enter Secret Code and enter Cannonbolt, Cannonbolt, Fourarms, Heatblast.

ALL ALIEN FORMS
Select a game from the Continue option. Go to the Map Selection screen, press Start and choose Extras. Select Enter Secret Code and enter Wildvine, Fourarms, Heatblast, Wildvine.

MASTER CONTROL
Select a game from the Continue option. Go to the Map Selection screen, press Start and choose Extras. Select Enter Secret Code and enter Cannonbolt, Heatblast, Wildvine, Fourarms.

OVERLORD

PLAYSTATION 2

BRATZ: FOREVER DIAMONDZ

1000 BLINGZ
While in the Bratz Office, use the Cheat computer to enter SIZZLN.

2000 BLINGZ
While in the Bratz Office, use the Cheat computer to enter FLAUNT.

PET TREATS
While in the Bratz Office, use the Cheat computer to enter TREATZ.

GIFT SET A
While in the Bratz Office, use the Cheat computer to enter STYLIN.

GIFT SET B
While in the Bratz Office, use the Cheat computer to enter SKATIN.

GIFT SET C
While in the Bratz Office, use the Cheat computer to enter JEWELZ.

GIFT SET E
While in the Bratz Office, use the Cheat computer to enter DIMNDZ.

BROTHERS IN ARMS: EARNED IN BLOOD

ALL LEVELS AND REWARDS
Create a profile with the name 2ndsquad.

BULLY

The following codes must be entered with a controller plugged into port 2:

FULL HEALTH
During a game, hold L1 and press R2, R2, R2.

ALL WEAPONS
During a game, hold L1 and press Up, Up, Up, Up.

INFINITE AMMO
During a game, hold L1 and press Up, Down, Up, Down.

MAX AMMO
During a game, hold L1 and press Up, Up.

MONEY
During a game, hold L1 and press ▲, ●, ●, ✕.

ALL CLOTHES
During a game, press L1, L1, R1, L1, L1, L1, R1, R1.

ALL GYM GRAPPLE MOVES
During a game, hold L1 and press Up, Left, Down, Down, ▲, ●, ✕, ✕.

ALL HOBO FIGHTING MOVES
During a game, hold L1 and press Up, Left, Down, Right, ▲, ●, ✕, ●.

CAPCOM CLASSICS COLLECTION VOL 2

UNLOCK EVERYTHING
At the title screen, press Left, Right, Up, Down, L1, R1, L1, R1. This code unlocks Cheats, Tips, Art, and Sound Tests.

CARS MATER-NATIONAL

ALL ARCADE RACES, MINI-GAMES, AND WORLDS
Select Codes/Cheats from the options and enter PLAYALL.

ALL CARS
Select Codes/Cheats from the options and enter MATTEL07.

ALTERNATE LIGHTNING MCQUEEN COLORS
Select Codes/Cheats from the options and enter NCEDUDZ.

ALL COLORS FOR OTHERS
Select Codes/Cheats from the options and enter PAINTIT.

UNLIMITED TURBO
Select Codes/Cheats from the options and enter ZZOOOOM.

EXTREME ACCELERATION
Select Codes/Cheats from the options and enter 0TO200X.

EXPERT MODE
Select Codes/Cheats from the options and enter VRYFAST.

ALL BONUS ART
Select Codes/Cheats from the options and enter BUYTALL.

CRASH OF THE TITANS

BIG HEAD CRASH
Pause the game, hold R1, and press ●, ●, ▲, ✕. Re-enter the code to disable.

SHADOW CRASH
Pause the game, hold R1, and press ▲, ●, ▲, ●. Re-enter the code to disable.

THE DA VINCI CODE

GOD MODE
Select Codes from the Options menu and enter VITRUVIAN MAN.

EXTRA HEALTH
Select Codes from the Options menu and enter SACRED FEMININE.

MISSION SELECT
Select Codes from the Options menu and enter CLOS LUCE 1519.

1-HIT FIST KILL
Select Codes from the Options menu and enter PHILLIPS EXETER.

1-HIT WEAPON KILL
Select Codes from the Options menu and enter ROYAL HOLLOWAY.

ALL VISUAL DATABASE
Select Codes from the Options menu and enter APOCRYPHA.

ALL VISUAL DATABASE & CONCEPT ART
Select Codes from the Options menu and enter ET IN ARCADIA EGO.

DESTROY ALL HUMANS! 2

SALAD DAYS WITH POX & CRYPTO
Pause the game and select Archives. Then press and hold L3 and press ✕, ●, ▲, ●, ●, ●, ▲, ✕, ✕.

OVERLOAD

DRAGON BALL Z: SAGAS

PENDULUM ROOMS

Select Options from the Main menu and press Up, Down, Up, Down, Left, Right, Left, Right, Select, Start, Select, Start, ●, ●, ●, ●, ✖, ✖, Start. When entered correctly, the message "Pendulum Rooms Unlocked" will appear on-screen. This unlocks the Pendulum mode, all Extras, all Sagas, and all Upgrades.

INVINCIBILITY

Pause the game, select Controller and press Down, ✖, Select, Start, Right, ●, Left, ●, Up, ▲.

ALL UPGRADES

Pause the game, select Controller and press Up, Left, Down, Right, Select, Start, ●, ✖, ●, ▲.

DUEL MASTERS

ALL LOCATIONS

At the Map screen, hold R3 and press ● (x3).

4 OF EVERY CARD & UNLOCK CHUCK IN ARCADE MODE

At the Deck Building screen, hold R3 and press L1, L1, L1.

PLAYER 1 LOSES SHIELD

During a duel, hold R3 and press ▲, ●, ✖. Release R3.

PLAYER 2 LOSES SHIELD

During a duel, hold R3 and press ▲, ●, ✖. Release R3.

PLAYER 1 GAINS SHIELD

During a duel, hold R3 and press ✖, ●, ▲. Release R3.

PLAYER 2 GAINS SHIELD

During a duel, hold R3 and press ✖, ●, ▲. Release R3.

PLAYER 1 WINS

During a duel, hold R3 and press L1, R1, L1.

PLAYER 2 WINS

During a duel, hold R3 and press R1, L1, R1.

TURN OFF DECK OUTS

During a duel, hold R3 and press ● (x3).

ERAGON

FURY MODE

Pause the game, hold L1 + L2 + R1 + R2 and press ●, ●, ●, ●.

FIGHT NIGHT ROUND 3

ALL VENUES

Select Create Champ and change the first name to NEWVIEW.

ALL CARS & 1,000,000 CREDITS

Select Enter Code from the Extras menu and enter GIEVEPIX.

1,000,000 CREDITS

Select Enter Code from the Extras menu and enter GIVECASH.

PIMPSTER CAR

Select Enter Code from the Extras menu and enter RUTTO.

FLATMOBILE CAR

Select Enter Code from the Extras menu and enter WOTKINS.

MOB CAR

Select Enter Code from the Extras menu and enter BIGTRUCK.

SCHOOL BUS

Select Enter Code from the Extras menu and enter GIEVCARPLZ.

ROCKET CAR

Select Enter Code from the Extras menu and enter KALJAKOPPA.

TRUCK

Select Enter Code from the Extras menu and enter ELPUEBLO.

You can use one of these for each level completed.

DOUBLE SHOT POWER

After the first boss, pause the game and press Up, Up, Down, Down, Left, Right, Left, Right, L2, R2.

LASER POWER

After the first boss, pause the game and press Up, Up, Down, Down, Left, Right, Left, Right, L1, R1.

GRAFFITI KINGDOM

PLAY AS FAKE PASTEL IN VS BOSSES
After completing the game, select VS Mode. Then hold L2 + R1 while selecting VS Bosses.

PLAY AS FAKE PIXEL IN VS BOSSES
After completing the game, select VS Mode. Then hold L1 + L2 while selecting VS Bosses.

PLAY AS PASTEL IN VS BOSSES
After completing the game, select VS Mode. Then hold L1 + R1 while selecting VS Bosses.

PLAY AS PIXEL IN VS BOSSES
After completing the game, select VS Mode. Then hold L1 + R2 while selecting VS Bosses.

FAKE PASTEL VS PASTEL IN 2-PLAYER TOURNAMENT
After completing the game, select VS Mode. Then hold L1 + L2 + R1 while selecting 2 Player Tournament.

FAKE PASTEL VS PIXEL IN 2-PLAYER TOURNAMENT
After completing the game, select VS Mode. Then hold L2 + R1 while selecting 2 Player Tournament.

FAKE PIXEL VS FAKE PASTEL IN 2-PLAYER TOURNAMENT
After completing the game, select VS Mode. Then hold L2 + R2 while selecting 2 Player Tournament.

FAKE PIXEL VS PIXEL IN 2-PLAYER TOURNAMENT
After completing the game, select VS Mode. Then hold L1 + L2 while selecting 2 Player Tournament.

PASTEL VS FAKE PASTEL IN 2-PLAYER TOURNAMENT
After completing the game, select VS Mode. Then hold L1 + R1 while selecting 2 Player Tournament.

PASTEL VS FAKE PIXEL IN 2-PLAYER TOURNAMENT
After completing the game, select VS Mode. Then hold R1 + R2 while selecting 2 Player Tournament.

PIXEL VS FAKE PIXEL IN 2-PLAYER TOURNAMENT
After completing the game, select VS Mode. Then hold L1 + R2 while selecting 2 Player Tournament.

GRAND THEFT AUTO: SAN ANDREAS

During a game, enter the following cheats:

FULL HEALTH, FULL ARMOR & $250,000
Press R1, R2, L1, ✪, Left, Down, Right, Up, Left, Down, Right, Up.

INFINITE LUNG CAPACITY
Press Down, Left, L1, Down, Down, R2, Down, L2, Down.

0 FAT & 0 MUSCLE
Press ▲, Up, Up, Left, Right, ■, ●, Right.

MAXIMUM MUSCLES
Press ▲, Up, Up, Left, Right, ■, ●, Left.

MAXIMUM FAT
Press ▲, Up, Up, Left, Right, ■, ●, Down.

BIG JUMPS
Press Up, Up, ▲, ▲, Up, Up, Left, Right, ●, R2, R2.

BIG BUNNY HOPS ON BMX
Press ▲, ■, ●, ●, ■, ●, ●, L1, L2, L2, R1, R2.

SUICIDE
Press Right, L2, Down, R1, Left, Left, R1, L1, L2, L1.

FASTER GAMEPLAY
Press ▲, Up, Right, Down, L2, L1, ■.

SLOWER GAMEPLAY
Press ▲, Up, Right, Down, ■, R2, R1.

FASTER TIME
Press ●, ●, L1, ■, L1, ■, ■, ■, L1, ▲, ●, ▲.

BLACK CARS
Press ●, L2, Up, R1, Left, ✪, R1, L1, Left, ●.

PINK CARS
Press ●, L1, Down, L2, Left, ✪, R1, L1, Right, ●.

FAST CARS
Press Up, L1, R1, Up, Right, Up, ✪, L2, ✪, L1.

TAXIS HAVE NITROUS & HOP WITH L3
Press Up, ✪, ▲, ✪, ▲, ✪, ■, R2, Right.

INVISIBLE VEHICLES
Press ▲, L1, ▲, R2, ●, L1, L1.

INVINCIBLE VEHICLE
Press L1, L2, L2, Up, Down, Down, Up, R1, R2, R2.

DRIVE-BY WHILE DRIVING
Press Up, Up, ●, L2, Right, ✕, R1, Down, R2, ●.

GREEN STOPLIGHTS
Press Right, R1, Up, L2, L2, Left, R1, L1, R1, R1.

AGGRESSIVE TRAFFIC
Press R2, ●, R1, L2, Left, R1, L1, R2, L2.

LESS TRAFFIC
Press ✕, Down, Up, R2, Down, ▲, L1, ▲, Left.

FASTER CARS
Press Right, R1, Up, L2, L2, Left, R1, L1, R1, R1.

BETTER CAR HANDLING
Press ▲, R1, R1, Left, R1, L1, R2, L1.

CARS FLOAT
Press Right, R2, ●, R1, L2, ●, R1, R2.

GRAND THEFT AUTO: SAN ANDREAS

During a game, enter the following cheats:

FULL HEALTH, FULL ARMOR & $250,000
Press R1, R2, L1, ✕, Left, Down, Right, Up, Left, Down, Right, Up.

INFINITE LUNG CAPACITY
Press Down, Left, L1, Down, Down, R2, Down, L2, Down.

0 FAT & 0 MUSCLE
Press ▲, Up, Up, Left, Right, ●, ●, Right.

MAXIMUM MUSCLES
Press ▲, Up, Up, Left, Right, ●, ●, Left.

MAXIMUM FAT
Press ▲, Up, Up, Left, Right, ●, ●, Down.

BIG JUMPS
Press Up, Up, ▲, ▲, Up, Up, Left, Right, ●, R2, R2.

BIG BUNNY HOPS ON BMX
Press ▲, ●, ●, ●, ●, ●, ●, L1, L2, L2, R1, R2.

SUICIDE
Press Right, L2, Down, R1, Left, Left, R1, L1, L2, L1.

FASTER GAMEPLAY
Press ▲, Up, Right, Down, L2, L1, ●.

SLOWER GAMEPLAY
Press ▲, Up, Right, Down, ●, R2, R1.

FASTER TIME
Press ●, ●, L1, ●, L1, ●, ●, ●, L1, ▲, ●, ▲.

BLACK CARS
Press ●, L2, Up, R1, Left, ✕, R1, L1, Left, ●.

PINK CARS
Press ●, L1, Down, L2, Left, ✕, R1, L1, Right, ●.

FAST CARS
Press Up, L1, R1, Up, Right, Up, ✕, L2, ✕, L1.

TAXIS HAVE NITROUS & HOP WITH L3
Press Up, ✕, ▲, ✕, ▲, ✕, ●, R2, Right.

INVISIBLE VEHICLES
Press ▲, L1, ▲, R2, ●, L1, L1.

INVINCIBLE VEHICLE
Press L1, L2, L2, Up, Down, Down, Up, R1, R2, R2.

DRIVE-BY WHILE DRIVING
Press Up, Up, ●, L2, Right, ✕, R1, Down, R2, ●.

GREEN STOPLIGHTS
Press Right, R1, Up, L2, L2, Left, R1, L1, R1, R1.

AGGRESSIVE TRAFFIC
Press R2, ●, R1, L2, Left, R1, L1, R2, L2.

LESS TRAFFIC
Press ✕, Down, Up, R2, Down, ▲, L1, ▲, Left.

FASTER CARS
Press Right, R1, Up, L2, L2, Left, R1, L1, R1, R1.

BETTER CAR HANDLING
Press ▲, R1, R1, Left, R1, L1, R2, L1.

CARS FLOAT
Press Right, R2, ●, R1, L2, ●, R1, R2.

CARS FLY
Press Up, Down, L1, R1, L1, Right, Left, L1, Left.

ALL CARS EXPLODE
Press R2, L2, R1, L1, L2, R2, ●, ▲, ●, ▲, L2, L1.

FLYING BOATS
Press R2, ●, Up, L1, Right, R1, Right, Up, ●, ▲.

PEDESTRIANS ATTACK YOU
Press Down, Up, Up, Up, ✕, R2, R1, L2, L2.

PEDESTRIANS ATTACK EACH OTHER
Press Down, Left, Up, Left, ✕, R2, R1, L2, L1.

PEDESTRIANS CARRY WEAPONS
Press R2, R1, ✕, ▲, ✕, ▲, Up, Down.

ELVISES EVERYWHERE
Press L1, ●, ▲, L1, L1, ●, L2, Up, Down, Left.

CJ IS A CLOWN, CIVILIANS IN FAST FOOD APPAREL & MORE!
Press ▲, ▲, L1, ●, ●, ●, ●, Down, ●.

PEOPLE IN SWIMSUITS
Press Up, Up, Down, Down, ●, ●, L1, R1, ▲, Down.

GANGS
Press L2, Up, R1, R1, Left, R1, R1, R2, Right, Down.

REDUCE WANTED LEVEL
Press R1, R1, ●, R2, Up, Down, Up, Down, Up, Down.

RAISE WANTED LEVEL
Press R1, R1, ●, R2, Left, Right, Left, Right, Left, Right.

CLEAR WEATHER
Press R2, ✕, L1, L1, L2 (x3), ▲.

SUNNY WEATHER
Press R2, ✕, L1, L1, L2 (x3), Down.

FOGGY WEATHER
Press R2, ✕, L1, L1, L2 (x3), ✕.

CLOUDY WEATHER
Press R2, ✕, L1, L1, L2 (x3), ●.

RAINY WEATHER
Press R2, ✕, L1, L1, L2 (x3), ●.

WEAPON SET 1
Press R1, R2, L1, R2, Left, Down, Right, Up, Left, Down, Right, Up.

WEAPON SET 2
Press R1, R2, L1, R2, Left, Down, Right, Up, Left, Down, Down, Left.

WEAPON SET 3
Press R1, R2, L1, R2, Left, Down, Right, Up, Left, Down, Down, Down.

PARACHUTE
Press Left, Right, L1, L2, R1, R2, R2, Up, Down, Right, L1.

JETPACK
Press L1, L2, R1, R2, Up, Down, Left, Right, L1, L2, R1, R2, Up, Down, Left, Right.

BLOODRING BANGER
Press Down, R1, ●, L2, L2, ✕, R1, L1, Left, Left.

CADDY
Press ●, L1, Up, R1, L2, ✕, R1, L1, ●, ✕.

DOZER
Press R2, L1, L1, Right, Right, Up, Up, ✕, L1, Left.

HOTRING RACER 1
Press R1, ●, R2, Right, L1, L2, ✕, ✕, ●, R1.

HOTRING RACER 2
Press R2, L1, ●, Right, L1, R1, Right, Up, ●, R2.

HYDRA
Press ▲, ▲, ●, ●, ✕, L1, L1, Down, Up.

Enter the following cheats during a game.

$250000
Press Up, Down, Left, Right, ✕, ✕, L1, R1.

ARMOR
Press Up, Down, Left, Right, ○, ○, L1, R1.

HEALTH
Press Up, Down, Left, Right, ○, ○, L1, R1.

NEVER WANTED
Press Up, Right, △, △, Down, Left, ○, ○.

LOWER WANTED LEVEL
Press Up, Right, △, △, Down, Left, ✕, ✕.

RAISE WANTED LEVEL
Press Up, Right, △, ○, Down, Left, ○, ○.

WEAPON SET 1
Press Left, Right, ✕, Up, Down, ○, Left, Right.

WEAPON SET 2
Press Left, Right, ○, Up, Down, △, Left, Right.

WEAPON SET 3
Press Left, Right, △, Up, Down, ○, Left, Right.

SPAWN RHINO
Press Up, L1, Down, R1, Left, L1, Right, R1.

SPAWN TRASHMASTER
Press Down, Up, Right, △, L1, △, L1, △.

BLACK CARS
Press L1, R1, L1, R1, Left, ○, Up, ✕.

CHROME CARS
Press Right, Up, Left, Down, △, △, L1, R1.

CARS AVOID YOU
Press Up, Up, Right, Left, △, ○, ○, ○.

DESTROY ALL CARS
Press L1, R1, R, Left, Right, ○, Down, R1.

GUYS FOLLOW YOU
Press Right, L1, Down, L1, ○, Up, L1, ○.

NO TRACTION
Press Down, Left, Up, L1, R1, △, ○, ✕.

PEDESTRIAN GETS INTO YOUR VEHICLE
Press Down, Up, Right, L1, L1, ○, Up, L1.

PEDESTRIANS ATTACK YOU
Press Down, △, Up, ✕, L1, R1, L1, R1.

PEDESTRIANS HAVE WEAPONS
Press Up, L1, Down, R1, Left, ○, Right, △.

PEDESTRIANS RIOT
Press R1, L1, L1, Down, Left, ○, Down, L1.

SUICIDE
Press Right, Right, ○, ○, L1, R1, Down, ✕.

UPSIDE DOWN 1
Press ○, △, ○, L1, L1, R1, Left, Right.

UPSIDE DOWN 2
Press Left, Left, Left, R1, R1, L1, Right, Left.

FASTER CLOCK
Press R1, L1, L, Down, Up, ✕, Down, L1.

FASTER GAMEPLAY
Press Left, Left, R1, R1, Up, △, Down, ✕.

SLOWER GAMEPLAY
Press Left, Left, ○, ○, Down, Up, △, ✕.

CLEAR WEATHER
Press Left, Down, R1, L1, Right, Up, Left, ✕.

FOGGY WEATHER
Press Left, Down, △, ✕, Right, Up, Left, L1.

OVERCAST WEATHER
Press Left, Down, L1, R1, Right, Up, Left, ○.

RAINY WEATHER
Press Left, Down, L1, R1, Right, Up, Left, △.

SUNNY WEATHER
Press Left, Down, R1, L1, Right, Up, Left, ○.

GRAN TURISMO 4

EXTRA TRACKS FOR ARCADE MODE

Play through the indicated number of days to unlock the corresponding track in Arcade Mode.

DAYS	UNLOCKS
15	Deep Forest Raceway
29	Opera Paris
43	Fuji Speedway 80s
57	Special Stage Route 5
71	Suzuka Circuit
85	Twin Ring Motegi Road Course East Short
99	Grand Valley Speedway
113	Hong Kong
127	Suzuka Circuit West Course
141	Fuji Speedway 2005 GT
155	Ice Arena
169	Apricot Hill Raceway
183	Cote d Azur
197	Tahiti Maze
211	Twin Ring Motegi Road Course
225	George V Paris
239	Cathedral Rocks Trail I
253	Costa di Amalfi
267	Circuit de la Sarthe 1
281	Autumn Ring
309	Chamonix
309	Infineon Raceway Stock Car Course
323	Fuji Speedway 2005 F
337	Tsukuba Circuit Wet
351	Circuit de la Sarthe 2 (not chicaned)

GUITAR HERO

UNLOCK ALL CHEATS

At the Main menu, press Yellow, Orange, Blue, Blue, Orange, Yellow, Yellow.

GUITAR HERO GUITAR CHEAT

At the Main menu, press Blue, Orange, Yellow, Blue, Blue.

CROWD METER CHEAT

At the Main menu, press Yellow, Blue, Orange, Orange, Blue, Blue, Yellow, Orange.

MONKEY HEAD CROWD

At the Main menu, press Blue, Orange, Yellow, Yellow, Yellow, Blue, Orange.

SKULL HEAD CROWD

At the Main menu, press Orange, Yellow, Blue, Blue, Orange, Yellow, Blue, Blue.

AIR GUITAR CHEAT

At the Main menu, press Orange, Orange, Blue, Yellow, Orange.

NO VENUE CHEAT

At the Main menu, press Blue, Yellow, Orange, Blue, Yellow, Orange.

GUITAR HERO II

AIR GUITAR

At the Main menu, press Yellow, Yellow, Blue, Orange, Yellow, Blue.

EYEBALL HEAD CROWD

At the Main menu, press Blue, Orange, Yellow, Orange, Yellow, Orange, Blue.

MONKEY HEAD CROWD

At the Main menu, press Orange, Blue, Yellow, Yellow, Orange, Blue, Yellow, Yellow.

FLAMING HEAD

At the Main menu, press Orange, Yellow, Orange, Orange, Yellow, Orange, Yellow, Yellow.

HORSE HEAD

At the Main menu, press Blue, Orange, Orange, Blue, Orange, Orange, Blue, Orange, Orange, Blue.

HYPER SPEED DEACTIVATE

At the Main menu, press Orange, Blue, Orange, Yellow, Orange, Blue, Orange, Yellow.

PERFORMANCE MODE

At the Main menu, press Yellow, Yellow, Blue, Yellow, Orange, Yellow, Yellow, Yellow.

GUITAR HERO III: LEGENDS OF ROCK

To enter the following cheats, strum the guitar with the given buttons held. For example, if it says Yellow + Orange, hold Yellow and Orange as you strum. Some cheats can be toggled on and off from the Cheats menu. You can also change between five different levels of Hyperspeed at this menu.

UNLOCK EVERYTHING

Select Cheats from the Options. Choose Enter Cheat and enter Green + Red + Blue + Orange, Green + Red + Yellow + Blue, Green + Red + Yellow + Orange, Green + Yellow + Blue + Orange, Green + Red + Yellow + Blue, Red + Yellow + Blue + Orange, Green + Red + Yellow + Blue, Green + Yellow + Blue + Orange, Green + Red + Yellow + Blue, Green + Red + Yellow + Orange, Green + Red + Yellow + Orange, Green + Red + Yellow + Blue, Green + Red + Yellow + Orange. No sounds play while this code is entered.

An easier way to show this code is by representing Green as 1 down to Orange as 5. For example, if you have 1345, you would hold down Green + Yellow + Blue + Orange while strumming. 1245 + 1234 + 1235 + 1345 + 1234 + 2345 + 1234 + 1345 + 1234 + 1235 + 1235 + 1234 + 1235.

ALL SONGS

Select Cheats from the Options. Choose Enter Cheat and enter Yellow + Orange, Red + Blue, Red + Orange, Green + Blue, Red + Yellow, Yellow + Orange, Red + Yellow, Red + Blue, Green + Yellow, Green + Yellow, Yellow + Blue, Yellow + Blue, Yellow + Orange, Yellow + Orange, Yellow + Blue, Yellow, Red, Red + Yellow, Red, Yellow, Orange.

ANO FAIL

Select Cheats from the Options. Choose Enter Cheat and enter Green + Red, Blue, Green + Red, Green + Yellow, Blue, Green + Yellow, Red + Yellow, Orange, Red + Yellow, Green + Yellow, Yellow, Green + Yellow, Green + Red.

AIR GUITAR

Select Cheats from the Options. Choose Enter Cheat and enter Blue + Yellow, Green + Yellow, Green + Yellow, Red + Blue, Red + Blue, Red + Yellow, Red + Yellow, Blue + Yellow, Green + Yellow, Green + Yellow, Red + Blue, Red + Blue, Red + Yellow, Red + Yellow, Green + Yellow, Green + Yellow, Red + Yellow, Red + Yellow.

HYPERSPEED

Select Cheats from the Options. Choose Enter Cheat and enter Orange, Blue, Orange, Yellow, Orange, Blue, Orange, Yellow.

PERFORMANCE MODE

Select Cheats from the Options. Choose Enter Cheat and enter Red + Yellow, Red + Blue, Red + Orange, Red + Blue, Red + Yellow, Green + Blue, Red + Yellow, Red + Blue.

EASY EXPERT

Select Cheats from the Options. Choose Enter Cheat and enter Green + Red, Green + Yellow, Yellow + Blue, Red + Blue, Blue + Orange, Yellow + Orange, Red + Yellow, Red + Blue.

PRECISION MODE

Select Cheats from the Options. Choose Enter Cheat and enter Green + Red, Green + Red, Green + Red, Red + Yellow, Red + Yellow, Red + Blue, Red + Blue, Yellow + Blue, Yellow + Orange, Yellow + Orange, Green + Red, Green + Red, Green + Red, Red + Yellow, Red + Yellow, Red + Blue, Red + Blue, Yellow + Blue, Yellow + Orange, Yellow + Orange.

LARGE GEMS

Select Cheats from the Options. Choose Enter Cheat and enter Green, Red, Green, Yellow, Green, Blue, Green, Orange, Green, Blue, Green, Yellow, Green, Red, Green, Green + Red, Red + Yellow, Green + Red, Yellow + Blue, Green + Red, Blue + Orange, Green + Red, Yellow + Blue, Green + Red, Red + Yellow, Green + Red, Green + Yellow.

GUITAR HERO: AEROSMITH

At the Main menu, select "Options", "Cheats", "Enter New Cheat", then enter one of the following codes to unlock the corresponding cheat option. Note: Each note or chord must be strummed. Press Green at the "Cheats" menu to turn off a particular cheat.

AIR GUITAR

Press Red + Yellow, Green + Red, [Red + Yellow] two times, [Red + Blue] five times, [Yellow + Blue] two times, Yellow + Orange.

HYPERSPEED

YO, YO, YO, YO, YO, RY, RY, RY, RY, RB, RB, RB, RB, RB, YB, YO, YO

NO FAIL

Press Green + Red, Blue, Green + Red, Green + Yellow, Blue, Green + Yellow, Red + Yellow, Orange, Red + Yellow, Green + Yellow, Yellow, Green + Yellow.

ALL SONGS

Press Red + Yellow, [Green + Red] two times, [Red + Yellow] two times, Green + Red, [Red + Yellow] two times, [Green + Red] two times, [Red + Yellow].

GUITAR HERO ENCORE: ROCKS THE 80S

UNLOCK EVERYTHING

At the Main menu, press Blue, Orange, Yellow, Red, Orange, Yellow, Blue, Yellow, Red, Yellow, Blue, Yellow, Red, Yellow, Blue, Yellow.

HYPERSPEED

At the Main menu, press Yellow, Blue, Orange, Orange, Blue, Yellow, Yellow, Orange.

PERFORMANCE MODE

At the Main menu, press Blue, Blue, Orange, Yellow, Yellow, Blue, Orange, Blue.

AIR GUITAR

At the Main menu, press Yellow, Blue, Yellow, Orange, Blue, Blue.

EYEBALL HEAD CROWD

At the Main menu, press Yellow, Blue, Orange, Orange, Blue, Yellow.

MONKEY HEAD CROWD

At the Main menu, press Blue, Blue, Orange, Yellow, Blue, Blue, Orange, Yellow.

FLAME HEAD

At the Main menu, press Yellow, Orange, Yellow, Orange, Yellow, Orange, Blue, Orange.

HORSE HEAD

At the Main menu, press Blue, Orange, Orange, Blue, Yellow, Blue, Orange, Orange, Blue, Yellow.

GUITAR HERO WORLD TOUR

ALL SONGS IN QUICK PLAY

At the Cheats menu, select Enter New Cheat and press Blue, Blue, Red, Green, Green, Blue, Blue, Yellow.

AIR INSTRUMENTS

At the Cheats menu, select Enter New Cheat and press Red, Red, Blue, Yellow, Green, Green, Green, Yellow.

ALWAYS SLIDE

At the Cheats menu, select Enter New Cheat and press Green, Green, Red, Red, Yellow, Red, Yellow, Blue.

AT&T BALL PARK

At the Cheats menu, select Enter New Cheat and press Yellow, Green, Red, Red, Green, Blue, Red, Yellow.

AUTO KICK

At the Cheats menu, select Enter New Cheat and press Yellow, Green, Red, Blue, Blue, Blue, Blue, Red.

EXTRA LINE 6 TONES

At the Cheats menu, select Enter New Cheat and press Green, Red, Yellow, Blue, Red, Yellow, Blue, Green.

FLAME COLORS

At the Cheats menu, select Enter New Cheat and press Green, Red, Green, Blue, Red, Red, Yellow, Blue.

GEM COLORS

At the Cheats menu, select Enter New Cheat and press Blue, Red, Red, Green, Red, Green, Red, Yellow.

HYPER SPEED

At the Cheats menu, select Enter New Cheat and press Green, Blue, Red, Yellow, Yellow, Red, Green, Green.

INVISIBLE ROCKER

At the Cheats menu, select Enter New Cheat and press Green, Red, Yellow, Yellow, Yellow, Blue, Blue, Green.

PERFORMANCE MODE

At the Cheats menu, select Enter New Cheat and press Yellow, Yellow, Blue, Red, Blue, Green, Red, Red.

STAR COLORS

At the Cheats menu, select Enter New Cheat and press Red, Red, Yellow, Red, Blue, Red, Red, Blue.

AARON STEELE

At the Cheats menu, select Enter New Cheat and press Blue, Red, Yellow, Yellow, Yellow, Yellow, Yellow, Green.

JOHNNY VIPER

At the Cheats menu, select Enter New Cheat and press Blue, Red, Blue, Blue, Yellow, Yellow, Yellow, Green.

NICK

At the Cheats menu, select Enter New Cheat and press Green, Red, Blue, Green, Red, Blue, Blue, Green.

RINA

At the Cheats menu, select Enter New Cheat and press Blue, Red, Green, Green, Yellow, Yellow, Yellow, Green.

VOCAL FIREBALL

At the Cheats menu, select Enter New Cheat and press Red, Green, Green, Yellow, Blue, Green, Yellow, Green.

HOT SHOTS GOLF FORE!

Select Password from the Options menu and enter the following codes to enable these cheats.

ALL CHARACTERS IN VS MODE

Enter REZTWS.

PRICE REDUCTION SALE IN SHOP

Enter MKJEFQ.

ALOHA BEACH RESORT COURSE IN SHOP

Enter XSREHD.

BAGPIPE CLASSIC COURSE IN SHOP

Enter CRCNHZ.

BLUE LAGOON C.C. COURSE IN SHOP
Enter WVRJQS.

DAY DREAM G.C. IN SHOP
Enter OQUTNA.

MINI-GOLF 2 G.C. IN SHOP
Enter RVMIRU.

SILKROAD CLASSIC COURSE IN SHOP
Enter ZKOGJM.

UNITED FOREST G.C. IN SHOP
Enter UIWHLZ.

WESTERN VALLEY COUNTRY CLUB COURSE IN SHOP
Enter LIBTFL.

WILD GREEN C.C. COURSE IN SHOP
Enter YZLOXE.

CAPSULE 01 IN SHOP
Enter WXAFSJ.

CAPSULE 2 IN SHOP
Enter OEINLK.

CAPSULE 3 IN SHOP
Enter WFKVTG.

CAPSULE 4 IN SHOP
Enter FCAVDO.

CAPSULE 5 IN SHOP
Enter YYPOKK.

CAPSULE 6 IN SHOP
Enter GDQDOF.

CAPSULE 7 IN SHOP
Enter HHXKPV.

CAPSULE 8 IN SHOP
Enter UOKXPS.

CAPSULE 9 IN SHOP
Enter LMIRYD.

CAPSULE 10 IN SHOP
Enter MJLJEQ.

CAPSULE 11 IN SHOP
Enter MHNCQI

LOWER TOURNEY STAGE
Enter XKWGFZ.

CADDIE CLANK IN SHOP
Enter XCQGWJ.

CADDIE DAXTER IN SHOP
Enter WSIKIN.

CADDIE KAYLA IN SHOP
Enter MZIMEL.

CADDIE KAZ IN SHOP
Enter LNNZJV.

CADDIE MOCHI IN SHOP
Enter MYPWPA.

CADDIE SIMON IN SHOP
Enter WRHZNB.

CADDIE SOPHIE IN SHOP
Enter UTWIVQ.

BEGINNER'S BALL IN SHOP
Enter YFQJJI.

BIR AIR BALL IN SHOP
Enter CRCGKR.

INFINITY BALL IN SHOP
Enter DJXBRG.

PIN HOLE BALL IN SHOP
Enter VZLSGP.

SIDESPIN BALL IN SHOP
Enter JAYQRK.

TURBO SPIN BALL IN SHOP
Enter XNETOK.

100T HAMMER CLUB (B-CLASS) IN SHOP
Enter NFSNHR.

UPGRADE 100T HAMMER CLUB (A-CLASS) IN SHOP
Enter BVLHSI.

UPGRADE 100T HAMMER CLUB (S-CLASS) IN SHOP
Enter MCSRUK.

BIG AIR CLUB (B-CLASS) IN SHOP
Enter DLJMFZ.

UPGRADE BIG AIR CLUB (A-CLASS) IN SHOP
Enter TOSXUJ.

UPGRADE BIG AIR CLUB (S-CLASS) IN SHOP
Enter JIDTQI.

INFINITY CLUB IN SHOP
Enter RZTQGV.

UPGRADE INFINITY CLUB (A-CLASS) IN SHOP
Enter WTGFOR.

UPGRADE INFINITY CLUB (S-CLASS) IN SHOP
Enter EIPCUL.

PIN HOLE CLUB (B-CLASS) IN SHOP
Enter DGHFRP.

UPGRADE PIN HOLE CLUB (A-CLASS) IN SHOP
Enter TTIMHT.

UPGRADE PIN HOLE CLUB (S-CLASS) IN SHOP
Enter RBXVEL.

UPGRADE TURBO SPIN CLUB (A-CLASS) IN SHOP
Enter NIWKWP.

UPGRADE TURBO SPIN CLUB (S-CLASS) IN SHOP
Enter DTIZAB.

EXTRA POSE CAM IN SHOP
Enter UEROOK.

EXTRA SWING CAM IN SHOP
Enter RJIFQS.

EXTRA VIDEO IN SHOP
Enter DPYHIU.

HECKLETS IN SHOP
Enter DIXWFE.

HSG CD/VOICE IN SHOP
Enter UITUGF.

HSG CD/MUSIC IN SHOP
Enter PAJXLI.

HSG RULES IN SHOP
Enter FKDHDS.

LANDING GRID IN SHOP
Enter MQTIMV.

REPLAY CAM A IN SHOP
Enter PVJEMF.

REPLAY CAM B IN SHOP
Enter EKENCR.

REPLAY CAM C IN SHOP
Enter ZUHHAC.

MENU CHARACTER BRAD IN SHOP
Enter ZKJSIO.

MENU CHARACTER PHOEBE IN SHOP
Enter LWVLCB.

MENU CHARACTER RENEE IN SHOP
Enter AVIQXS.

WALLPAPER SET 2 IN SHOP
Enter RODDHQ.

MIKE'S COSTUME IN SHOP
Enter YKCFEZ.

LIN'S COSTUME IN SHOP
Enter BBLSKQ.

MEL'S COSTUME IN SHOP
Enter ARFLCR.

PHOEBE'S COSTUME IN SHOP
Enter GJBCHY.

IRON MAN

ARMOR SELECTION

Iron Man's different armor suits are unlocked by completing certain missions. Refer to the following tables for when each is unlocked. After selecting a mission to play, you get the opportunity to pick the armor you wish to use.

COMPLETE MISSION	SUIT UNLOCKED
1: Escape	Mark I
2: First Flight	Mark II
3: Fight Back	Mark III
6: Flying Fortress	Comic Tin Can
9: Home Front	Classic
13: Showdown	Silver Centurion

CONCEPT ART

Concept Art is unlocked after finding certain numbers of Weapon Crates.

CONCEPT ART UNLOCKED	NUMBER OF WEAPON CRATES FOUND
Environments Set 1	6
Environments Set 2	12
Iron Man	18
Environments Set 3	24
Enemies	30
Environments Set 4	36
Villains	42
Vehicles	48
Covers	50

JUICED 2: HOT IMPORT NIGHTS

ASCARI KZ1
Select Cheats and Codes from the DNA Lab menu and enter KNOX. Defeat the challenge to earn the car.

NISSAN SKYLINE R34 GT-R
Select Cheats and Codes from the DNA Lab menu and enter JWRS. Defeat the challenge to earn the car.

KARAOKE REVOLUTION VOLUME 3

BANANA MICROPHONE
Score gold at each venue in Showtime mode. At the Extras menu, press Down, Up, Left, Right, ●, ●, ●, ● at Cheat Collection 1.

BIG EYED CHARACTER
Score gold at each venue in Showtime mode. At the Extras menu, press ●, ●, ●, Down, Left, Left, Down at Cheat Collection 1.

DWAYNE DOLL MICROPHONE
Score gold at each venue in Showtime mode. At the Extras menu, press ●, ●, R3, ●, Up, Down, Right, Left at Cheat Collection 1.

TOOTHBRUSH MICROPHONE
Score gold at each venue in Showtime mode. At the Extras menu, press L2, L2, ●, ●, Down, Up, Left, L3 at Cheat Collection 1.

BIG HEAD CHARACTER
Score gold at each venue in Showtime mode. At the Extras menu, press ●, ●, ●, ●, Up, Right, Down, Left at Cheat Collection 2.

FISH MICROPHONE
Score gold at each venue in Showtime mode. At the Extras menu, press ●, Down, Up, Left, ●, ●, L2, L1 at Cheat Collection 2.

MERCURY CHARACTER
Score gold at each venue in Showtime mode. At the Extras menu, press Down, Down, Right, Left, Right, Left, ●, ● at Cheat Collection 2.

WRAITH CHARACTER
Score gold at each venue in Showtime mode. At the Extras menu, press L2, L2, Right, Right, ●, ●, R1, R1 at Cheat Collection 2.

GLASS CHARACTER
Score gold at each venue in Showtime mode. At the Extras menu, press Down, L2, R1, R2, L1, ●, ●, ● at Cheat Collection 3.

ICE CREAM MICROPHONE
Score gold at each venue in Showtime mode. At the Extras menu, press ●, ●, ●, R2, L2, R1, L1 at Cheat Collection 3.

OIL SLICK CHARACTER
Score gold at each venue in Showtime mode. At the Extras menu, press L3, L3, R2, R1, L2, L1, Down, Up at Cheat Collection 3.

SMALL HEAD CHARACTER
Score gold at each venue in Showtime mode. At the Extras menu, press ●, R2, L2, R1, L1, Down, Down, Up at Cheat Collection 3.

ALIEN CROWD
Score gold at each venue in Showtime mode. At the Extras menu, press Up, Up, Down, ●, ●, L2, R2, ● at Cheat Collection 4.

PIRATE CROWD
Score gold at each venue in Showtime mode. At the Extras menu, press Down, L2, L2, R2, R2, ●, ●, ● at Cheat Collection 4.

ROBOT CROWD
Score gold at each venue in Showtime mode. At the Extras menu, press L3, Down, Down, R1, ●, ●, ●, ● at Cheat Collection 4.

TOUGH AUDIO CROWD
Score gold at each venue in Showtime mode. At the Extras menu, press ●, L1, L2, R1, R2, Right, Right, Down at Cheat Collection 4.

ZOMBIE CROWD
Score gold at each venue in Showtime mode. At the Extras menu, press ●, ●, ●, ●, Up, Right, Right, Up at Cheat Collection 4.

KATAMARI DAMACY

COMETS
Finish a "Make a Star" level under a certain time to earn a comet.

LEVEL	FINISH WITHIN
Make a Star 1	1 minute
Make a Star 2	3 minutes
Make a Star 3	4 minutes
Make a Star 4	6 minutes
Make a Star 5	8 minutes
Make a Star 6	8 minutes
Make a Star 7	8 minutes
Make a Star 8	12 minutes
Make a Star 9	15 minutes
Make the Moon	20 minutes

KUNG FU PANDA

INVULNERABILITY
Select Cheats from the Extras menu and enter Down, Down, Right, Up, Left.

INFINITE CHI
Select Cheats from the Extras menu and enter Down, Right, Left, Up, Down.

BIG HEAD MODE
Select Cheats from the Extras menu and enter Down, Up, Left, Right, Right.

ALL MULTIPLAYER CHARACTERS
Select Cheats from the Extras menu and enter Left, Down, Left, Right, Down.

DRAGON WARRIOR OUTFIT IN MULTIPLAYER
Select Cheats from the Extras menu and enter Left, Down, Right, Left, Up.

LEGO BATMAN

BATCAVE CODES
Using the computer in the Batcave, select Enter Code and enter the following:

CHARACTERS

CHARACTER	CODE
Alfred	ZAQ637
Batgirl	JKR331
Bruce Wayne	BDJ327
Catwoman (Classic)	M1AAWW
Clown Goon	HJK327
Commissioner Gordon	DDP967
Fishmonger	HGY748
Freeze Girl	XVK541
Joker Goon	UTF782
Joker Henchman	YUN924
Mad Hatter	JCA283
Man-Bat	NYU942
Military Policeman	MKL382
Nightwing	MVY759
Penguin Goon	NKA238
Penguin Henchman	BJH782
Penguin Minion	KJP748
Poison Ivy Goon	GTB899

CHARACTER	CODE
Police Marksman	HKG984
Police Officer	JRY983
Riddler Goon	CRY928
Riddler Henchman	XEU824
S.W.A.T.	HTF114
Sailor	NAV592
Scientist	JFL786
Security Guard	PLB946
The Joker (Tropical)	CCB199
Yeti	NJL412
Zoo Sweeper	DWR243

VEHICLES

VEHICLE	CODE
Bat-Tank	KNTT4B
Bruce Wayne's Private Jet	LEA664
Catwoman's Motorcycle	HPL826
Garbage Truck	DUS483
Goon Helicopter	GCH328
Harbor Helicopter	CHP735
Harley Quinn's Hammer Truck	RDT637
Mad Hatter's Glider	HS000W
Mad Hatter's Steamboat	M4DM4N
Mr. Freeze's Iceberg	ICYICE
The Joker's Van	JUK657
Mr. Freeze's Kart	BCT229
Penguin Goon Submarine	BTN248
Police Bike	LJP234
Police Boat	PLC999
Police Car	KJL832
Police Helicopter	CWR732
Police Van	MAC788
Police Watercraft	VJD328
Riddler's Jet	HAHAHA
Robin's Submarine	TTF453
Two-Face's Armored Truck	EFE933

CHEATS

CHEAT	CODE
Always Score Multiply	9LRGNB
Fast Batarangs	JRBDCB
Fast Walk	ZOLM6N
Flame Batarang	D8NYWH
Freeze Batarang	XPN4NG
Extra Hearts	ML3KHP
Fast Build	EVG26J
Immune to Freeze	JXUDY6
Invincibility	WYD5CP
Minikit Detector	ZXGH9J
More Batarang Targets	XWP645
Piece Detector	KHJ554
Power Brick Detector	MMN786
Regenerate Hearts	HJH7HJ
Score x2	N4NR3E
Score x4	CX9MAT
Score x6	MLVNF2
Score x8	WCCDB9
Score x10	18HW07

PLAYSTATION 2

EACH TROOPER
At Mos Eisley Canteena, select Enter Code and enter UCK868. You must still select Characters and purchase this character for 20,000 studs.

BEN KENOBI (GHOST)
At Mos Eisley Canteena, select Enter Code and enter BEN917. You must still select Characters and purchase this character for 1,100,000 studs.

BESPIN GUARD
At Mos Eisley Canteena, select Enter Code and enter VHY832. You must still select Characters and purchase this character for 15,000 studs.

BIB FORTUNA
At Mos Eisley Canteena, select Enter Code and enter WTY721. You must still select Characters and purchase this character for 16,000 studs.

BOBA FETT
At Mos Eisley Canteena, select Enter Code and enter HLP221. You must still select Characters and purchase this character for 175,000 studs.

DEATH STAR TROOPER
At Mos Eisley Canteena, select Enter Code and enter BNC332. You must still select Characters and purchase this character for 19,000 studs.

EWOK
At Mos Eisley Canteena, select Enter Code and enter TTT289. You must still select Characters and purchase this character for 34,000 studs.

GAMORREAN GUARD
At Mos Eisley Canteena, select Enter Code and enter YZF999. You must still select Characters and purchase this character for 40,000 studs.

GONK DROID
At Mos Eisley Canteena, select Enter Code and enter NFX582. You must still select Characters and purchase this character for 1,550 studs.

GRAND MOFF TARKIN
At Mos Eisley Canteena, select Enter Code and enter SMG219. You must still select Characters and purchase this character for 38,000 studs.

GREEDO
At Mos Eisley Canteena, select Enter Code and enter NAH118. You must still select Characters and purchase this character for 60,000 studs.

HAN SOLO (HOOD)
At Mos Eisley Canteena, select Enter Code and enter YWM840. You must still select Characters and purchase this character for 20,000 studs.

IG-88
At Mos Eisley Canteena, select Enter Code and enter NXL973. You must still select Characters and purchase this character for 30,000 studs.

IMPERIAL GUARD
At Mos Eisley Canteena, select Enter Code and enter MMM111. You must still select Characters and purchase this character for 45,000 studs.

IMPERIAL OFFICER
At Mos Eisley Canteena, select Enter Code and enter BBV889. You must still select Characters and purchase this character for 28,000 studs.

IMPERIAL SHUTTLE PILOT
At Mos Eisley Canteena, select Enter Code and enter VAP664. You must still select Characters and purchase this character for 29,000 studs.

IMPERIAL SPY
At Mos Eisley Canteena, select Enter Code and enter CVT125. You must still select Characters and purchase this character for 13,500 studs.

JAWA
At Mos Eisley Canteena, select Enter Code and enter JAW499. You must still select Characters and purchase this character for 24,000 studs.

LOBOT
At Mos Eisley Canteena, select Enter Code and enter UUB319. You must still select Characters and purchase this character for 11,000 studs.

PALACE GUARD
At Mos Eisley Canteena, select Enter Code and enter SGE549. You must still select Characters and purchase this character for 14,000 studs.

REBEL PILOT
At Mos Eisley Canteena, select Enter Code and enter CYG336. You must still select Characters and purchase this character for 15,000 studs.

REBEL TROOPER (HOTH)
At Mos Eisley Canteena, select Enter Code and enter EKU849. You must still select Characters and purchase this character for 16,000 studs.

SANDTROOPER
At Mos Eisley Canteena, select Enter Code and enter YDV451. You must still select Characters and purchase this character for 14,000 studs.

SKIFF GUARD
At Mos Eisley Canteena, select Enter Code and enter GBU888. You must still select Characters and purchase this character for 12,000 studs.

SNOWTROOPER
At Mos Eisley Canteena, select Enter Code and enter NYU989. You must still select Characters and purchase this character for 16,000 studs.

STORMTROOPER

At Mos Eisley Canteena, select Enter Code and enter PTR345. You must still select Characters and purchase this character for 10,000 studs.

THE EMPEROR

At Mos Eisley Canteena, select Enter Code and enter HHY382. You must still select Characters and purchase this character for 275,000 studs.

TIE FIGHTER

At Mos Eisley Canteena, select Enter Code and enter HDY739. You must still select Characters and purchase this item for 60,000 studs.

TIE FIGHTER PILOT

At Mos Eisley Canteena, select Enter Code and enter NNZ316. You must still select Characters and purchase this character for 21,000 studs.

TIE INTERCEPTOR

At Mos Eisley Canteena, select Enter Code and enter QYA828. You must still select Characters and purchase this item for 40,000 studs.

TUSKEN RAIDER

At Mos Eisley Canteena, select Enter Code and enter PEJ821. You must still select Characters and purchase this character for 23,000 studs.

UGNAUGHT

At Mos Eisley Canteena, select Enter Code and enter UGN694. You must still select Characters and purchase this character for 36,000 studs.

MADDEN NFL 07

MADDEN CARDS

Select Madden Cards from My Madden. Then select Madden Codes and enter the following:

CARD	PASSWORD
#199 Gold Lame Duck Cheat	5LAWO0
#200 Gold Mistake Free Cheat	XL7SP1
#210 Gold QB on Target Cheat	WROA0R
#220 Super Bowl XLI Gold	RLA9R7
#221 Super Bowl XLII Gold	WRLUF8
#222 Super Bowl XLIII Gold	NIEV4A
#223 Super Bowl XLIV Gold	M5AB7L
#224 Aloha Stadium Gold	YI8P8U
#225 1958 Colts Gold	B57QLU
#226 1966 Packers Gold	1PL1FL
#227 1968 Jets Gold	MIE6WO
#228 1970 Browns Gold	CL2TOE
#229 1972 Dolphins Gold	NOEB7U
#230 1974 Steelers Gold	YO0FLA
#231 1976 Raiders Gold	MOA11I
#232 1977 Broncos Gold	C8UM7U
#233 1978 Dolphins Gold	VIU0O7
#234 1980 Raiders Gold	NLAPH3
#235 1981 Chargers Gold	COAGI4
#236 1982 Redskins Gold	WL8BRI
#237 1983 Raiders Gold	H0EW71
#238 1984 Dolphins Gold	M1AM1E
#239 1985 Bears Gold	QOETO8
#240 1986 Giants Gold	ZI8S2L
#241 1988 49ers Gold	SP2A8H
#242 1990 Eagles Gold	2L4TRO
#243 1991 Lions Gold	J1ETRI
#244 1992 Cowboys Gold	W9UVI9
#245 1993 Bills Gold	DLA3I7
#246 1994 49ers Gold	DR7EST
#247 1996 Packers Gold	F8LUST
#248 1998 Broncos Gold	FIES95
#249 1999 Rams Gold	S9OUSW
#250 Bears Pump Up the Crowd	B1OUPH
#251 Bengals Cheerleader	DRL2SW
#252 Bills Cheerleader	1PLUYO
#253 Broncos Cheerleader	3ROUJO
#254 Browns Pump Up the Crowd	T1UTOA
#255 Buccaneers Cheerleader	S9EWRI
#256 Cardinals Cheerleader	57IEPI

CARD	PASSWORD
#257 Chargers Cheerleader	F7UHL8
#258 Chiefs Cheerleader	PRI5SL
#259 Colts Cheerleader	1R5AMI
#260 Cowboys Cheerleader	Z2ACHL
#261 Dolphins Cheerleader	C5AHLE
#262 Eagles Cheerleader	PO7DRO
#263 Falcons Cheerleader	37USPO
#264 49ers Cheerleader	KL0CRL
#265 Giants Pump Up the Crowd	C4USPI
#266 Jaguars Cheerleader	MIEH7E
#267 Jets Pump Up the Crowd	C0LUXI
#268 Lions Pump Up the Crowd	3LABLU
#269 Packers Pump Up the Crowd	4HO7VO
#270 Panthers Cheerleader	F2IASP
#282 All AFC Team Gold	PRO9PH
#283 All NFC Team Gold	RLATH7

MAJOR LEAGUE BASEBALL 2K8

BIG HEAD MODE
Select Enter Cheat Code from the My 2K8 menu and enter Black Sox. This unlocks the Smart Choice cheat. Go to My Cheats to toggle the cheat on and off.

MANHUNT 2

EXTRA LEVEL AS LEO
Defeat the game.

RELIVE SCENE
Defeat the game. This allows you to replay any level.

MARC ECKO'S GETTING UP: CONTENTS UNDER PRESSURE

ALL LEVELS
Select Codes from the Options menu and enter IPULATOR.

INFINITE HEALTH
Select Codes from the Options screen and enter MARCUSECKOS.

MAX HEALTH
Select Codes from the Options screen and enter BABYLONTRUST.

INFINITE SKILLS
Select Codes from the Options screen and enter FLIPTHESCRIPT.

MAX SKILLS
Select Codes from the Options screen and enter VANCEDALLISTER.

ALL COMBAT UPGRADES
Select Codes from the Options menu and enter DOGTAGS.

ALL CHARACTERS IN VERSUS MODE
Select Codes from the Options menu and enter STATEYOURNAME.

ALL VERSUS ARENAS
Select Codes from the Options menu and enter WORKBITCH.

ALL ART
Select Codes from the Options menu and enter SIRULLY.

ALL BLACK BOOK
Select Codes from the Options menu and enter SHARDSOFGLASS.

ALL IPOD
Select Codes from the Options menu and enter GRANDMACELIA.

ALL LEGENDS
Select Codes from the Options menu and enter NINESIX.

ALL MOVIES
Select Codes from the Options menu and enter DEXTERCROWLEY.

MEDAL OF HONOR: VANGUARD

EXTRA ARMOR
Pause the game and press Up, Down, Up, Down to get the Enter Cheat Code message. Then, press Right, Left, Right, Down, Up, Right.

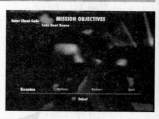

MERCENARIES 2: WORLD IN FLAMES

$1,000,000
At the Faction menu, press Right, Down, Left, Up, Up, Left, Down, Right.

INFINITE AMMO
At the Faction menu, press Right, Left, Right, Right, Left, Right, Left, Left.

INFINITE HEALTH
At the Faction menu, press Press Up, Down, Up, Down, Left, Right, Left, Right.

ALL FACTIONS TO NEUTRAL
At the Faction menu, press Up, Up, Up, Up, Down, Down, Right, Left.

MLB 07: THE SHOW

CLASSIC STADIUMS
At the Main menu, press Down, Up, Right, Down, Up, Left, Down, Up.

GOLDEN/SLIVER ERA PLAYERS
At the Main menu, press Left, Up, Right, Down, Down, Left, Up, Down.

MLB 08: THE SHOW

ALL CLASSIC STADIUMS
At the Main menu, press Down, Right, ⊚, ⊛, Left, ⊗, Up, L1. The controller will vibrate if entered correctly.

ALL GOLDEN & SILVER ERA PLAYERS IN EXHIBITION
At the Main menu, press L1, L2, ⊛, ⊛, ⊗, ⊚, Down. The controller will vibrate if entered correctly.

MLB POWER PROS

VIEW MLB PLAYERS AT CREATED PLAYERS MENU
Select View or Delete Custom Players/Password Display from the My Data menu. Press Up, Up, Down, Down, Left, Right, Left Right, L1, R1.

ALVIN LOCKHART'S BATTING STANCE AND PITCHING FORM
At the Main menu, press Right, Left, Up, Down, Down, Right, Right, Up, Up, Left, Down, Left. These will be available at the shop.

MVP 07 NCAA BASEBALL

ALL CHALLENGE ITEMS
In Dynasty Mode, create a player with the name David Hamel.

MX VS. ATV UNTAMED

EVERYTHING
Select Cheat Codes from the Options menu and enter YOUGOTIT.

1000000 STORE POINTS
Select Cheat Codes from the Options menu and enter MANYZEROS.

50CC BIKE CLASS
Select Cheat Codes from the Options menu and enter LITTLEGUY.

ALL BIKES
Select Cheat Codes from the Options menu and enter ONRAILS.

ALL CHALLENGES
Select Cheat Codes from the Options menu and enter MORESTUFF.

ALL FREESTYLE TRACKS
Select Cheat Codes from the Options menu and enter ALLSTYLE.

ALL GEAR
Select Cheat Codes from the Options menu and enter WELLDRESSED.

ALL MACHINES
Select Cheat Codes from the Options menu and enter MCREWHEELS.

ALL RIDERS
Select Cheat Codes from the Options menu and enter WHOSTHAT.

ALL TRACKS
Select Cheat Codes from the Options menu and enter FREETICKET.

MONSTER TRUCK
Select Cheat Codes from the Options menu and enter PWNAGE.

NARUTO: ULTIMATE NINJA 2

In Naruto's house, select Input Password. Here you are able to enter an element, then three signs. Enter the following here:

1,000 RYO
Water, Hare, Monkey, Monkey
Water, Ram, Horse, Dog
Water, Horse, Horse, Horse
Water, Rat, Rooster, Boar
Water, Rat, Monkey, Rooster
Fire, Rat, Dragon, Dog

5,000 RYO
Water, Tiger, Dragon, Tiger
Water, Snake, Rooster, Horse

10,000 RYO
Fire, Tiger, Tiger, Rooster
Fire, Tiger, Dragon, Hare

NASCAR 08

ALL CHASE MODE CARS
Select cheat codes from the options menu and enter checkered flag.

EA SPORTS CAR
Select cheat codes from the options menu and enter ea sports car.

FANTASY DRIVERS
Select cheat codes from the options menu and enter race the pack.

WALMART CAR AND TRACK
Select cheat codes from the options menu and enter walmart everyday.

NASCAR 09

WALMART TRACK AND THE WALMART CAR
In Chase for the Sprint Cup, enter the driver's name as WalMart EveryDay.

2006 CHARLOTTE BOBCATS ALTERNATE JERSEY
Select NBA.com from the Trophy Room. Press ● to bring up the Enter Code screen. Enter JKL846ETK5.

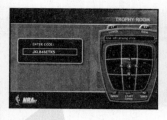 

2006 NOK HORNETS ALTERNATE JERSEY
Select NBA.com from the Trophy Room. Press ● to bring up the Enter Code screen. Enter EL2E3T8H58.

2006 NEW JERSEY NETS ALTERNATE JERSEY
Select NBA.com from the Trophy Room. Press ● to bring up the Enter Code screen. Enter NB79D965D2.

2006 UTAH JAZZ ALTERNATE JERSEY
Select NBA.com from the Trophy Room. Press ● to bring up the Enter Code screen. Enter 228GG7585G.

2006 WAS WIZARDS ALTERNATE JERSEY
Select NBA.com from the Trophy Room. Press ● to bring up the Enter Code screen. Enter PL5285F37F.

2007 EASTERN ALL STARS
Select NBA.com from the Trophy Room. Press ● to bring up the Enter Code screen. Enter 5F89RE3H8G.

2007 WESTERN ALL STARS
Select NBA.com from the Trophy Room. Press ● to bring up the Enter Code screen. Enter 2H5E89EH8C.

NBA 09 THE INSIDE

ALL-STAR 09 EAST
Select Trophy Room from the Options. Press L1, then ●, and enter SHPNV2K699.

ALL-STAR 09 WEST
Select Trophy Room from the Options. Press L1, then ●, and enter K8AV6YMLNF.

ALL TROPHIES
Select Trophy Room from the Options. Press L1, then ●, and enter K@ZZ@@M!.

LA LAKERS LATIN NIGHTS
Select Trophy Room from the Options. Press L1, then ●, and enter NMTWCTC84S.

MIAMI HEAT LATIN NIGHTS
Select Trophy Room from the Options. Press L1, then ●, and enter WCTGSA8SPD.

PHOENIX SUNS LATIN NIGHTS
Select Trophy Room from the Options. Press L1, then ●, and enter LKUTSENFJH.

SAN ANTONIO LATIN NIGHTS
Select Trophy Room from the Options. Press L1, then ●, and enter JFHSY73MYD.

NBA 2K8

2K SPORTS TEAM
Select Codes from the Features menu and enter 2ksports.

NBA DEVELOPMENT TEAM
Select Codes from the Features menu and enter nba2k.

VISUAL CONCEPTS TEAM
Select Codes from the Features menu and enter vcteam.

ABA BALL
Select Codes from the Features menu and enter payrespect.

NBA LIVE 08

ADIDAS GIL II ZERO SHOE CODES
Select NBA Codes from My NBA Live and enter the following:

SHOES	CODE
Agent Zero	ADGILLIT6BE
Black President	ADGILLIT7BF
Cuba	ADGILLIT4BC
Cust0mize Shoe	ADGILLIT5BD
GilWood	ADGILLIT1B9
TS Lightswitch Away	ADGILLIT0B8
TS Lightswitch Home	ADGILLIT2BA

NCAA FOOTBALL 08

PENNANT CODES
Go to My Shrine and select Pennants. Press Select and enter the following:

PENNANT	CODE
#200 1st & 15 Cheat	Thanks
#201 Blink Cheat	For
#202 Boing Cheat	Registering
#204 Butter Fingers Cheat	With EA
#205 Crossed The Line Cheat	Tiburon
#206 Cuffed Cheat	EA Sports
#207 Extra Credit Cheat	Touchdown
#208 Helium Cheat	In The Zone
#209 Hurricane Cheat	Turnover
#210 Instant FrePlay Cheat	Impact
#211 Jumbalaya Cheat	Heisman
#212 Molasses Cheat	Game Time
#213 Nike Free Cheat	Break Free
#214 Nike Magnigrip Cheat	Hand Picked
#215 Nike Pro Cheat	No Sweat
#219 QB Dud Cheat	Elite 11
#221 Steel Toe Cheat	Gridiron
#222 Stiffed Cheat	NCAA
#223 Super Dive Cheat	Upset
#226 Tough As Nail Cheats	Offense
#228 What A Hit Cheat	Blitz
#229 Kicker Hex Cheat	Sideline
#273 2004 All-American Team	Fumble
#274 All-Alabama Team	Roll Tide
#276 All-Arkansas Team	Woopigsooie
#277 All-Auburn Team	War Eagle

PENNANT	CODE
#278 All-Clemson Team	Death Valley
#279 All-Colorado Team	Glory
#281 All-FSU Team	Uprising
#282 All-Georgia Team	Hunker Down
#283 All-Iowa Team	On Iowa
#285 All-LSU Team	Geaux Tigers
#287 All-Michigan Team	Go Blue
#288 All-Mississippi State Team	Hail State
#289 All-Nebraska Team	Go Big Red
#291 All-Notre Dame Team	Golden Domer
#292 All-Ohio State Team	Killer Nuts
#293 All-Oklahoma Team	Boomer
#294 All-Oklahoma State Team	Go Pokes
#296 All-Penn State Team	We Are
#298 All-Purdue Team	Boiler Up
#300 All-Tennessee Team	Big Orange
#301 All-Texas Team	Hook Em
#302 All-Texas A&M Team	Gig Em
#303 All-UCLA Team	Mighty
#304 All-USC Team	Fight On
#305 All-Virginia Team	Wahoos
#307 All-Washington Team	Bow Down
#308 All-Wisconsin Team	U Rah Rah
#344 MSU Mascot Team	Mizzou Rah
#385 Wyo Mascot	All Hail
#386 Zips Mascot	Hail WV

NEED FOR SPEED PROSTREET

$2,000
Select Career and then choose Code Entry. Enter 1MA9X99.

$4,000
Select Career and then choose Code Entry. Enter W2IOLL01.

$8,000
Select Career and then choose Code Entry. Enter L1IS97A1.

$10,000
Select Career and then choose Code Entry. Enter 1MI9K7E1.

$10,000
Select Career and then choose Code Entry. Enter CASHMONEY.

$10,000
Select Career and then choose Code Entry. Enter REGGAME.

AUDI TT
Select Career and then choose Code Entry. Enter ITSABOUTYOU.

CHEVELLE SS
Select Career and then choose Code Entry. Enter HORSEPOWER.

COKE ZERO GOLF GTI
Select Career and then choose Code Entry. Enter COKEZERO.

DODGE VIPER
Select Career and then choose Code Entry. Enter WORLDSLONGESTLASTING.

MITSUBISHI LANCER EVOLUTION
Select Career and then choose Code Entry. Enter MITSUBISHIGOFAR.

UNLOCK ALL BONUSES
Select Career and then choose Code Entry. Enter UNLOCKALLTHINGS.

5 REPAIR MARKERS
Select Career and then choose Code Entry. Enter SAFETYNET.

ENERGIZER VINYL
Select Career and then choose Code Entry. Enter ENERGIZERLITHIUM.

CASTROL SYNTEC VINYL
Select Career and then choose Code Entry. Enter CASTROLSYNTEC. This also gives you $10,000.

NHL 08

ALL RBK EDGE JERSEYS
At the RBK Edge Code option, enter h3oyxpwksf8ibcgt.

NICKTOONS: ATTACK OF THE TOYBOTS

DAMAGE BOOST
Select Cheats from the Extras menu. Choose Enter Cheat Code and enter 456645.

INVULNERABILITY
Select Cheats from the Extras menu. Choose Enter Cheat Code and enter 313456.

UNLOCK EXO-HUGGLES 9000
Select Cheats from the Extras menu. Choose Enter Cheat Code and enter 691427.

UNLOCK MR. HUGGLES
Select Cheats from the Extras menu. Choose Enter Cheat Code and enter 654168.

UNLIMITED LOBBER GOO
Select Cheats from the Extras menu. Choose Enter Cheat Code and enter 118147.

UNLIMITED SCATTER GOO
Select Cheats from the Extras menu. Choose Enter Cheat Code and enter 971238.

UNLIMITED SPLITTER GOO
Select Cheats from the Extras menu. Choose Enter Cheat Code and enter 854511.

OVER THE HEDGE

COMPLETE LEVELS
Pause the game, hold L1 + R1 and press ▲, ●, ▲, ●, ●, ■.

ALL MINI-GAMES
Pause the game, hold L1 + R1 and press ●, ●, ▲, ▲, ●, ■.

MORE HP FROM FOOD
Pause the game, hold L1 + R1 and press ▲, ●, ▲, ●, ■, ▲.

ALWAYS POWER PROJECTILE
Pause the game, hold L1 + R1 and press ▲, ●, ▲, ●, ■, ●.

BONUS COMIC 14
Pause the game, hold L1 + R1 and press ▲, ●, ■, ●, ●, ▲.

BONUS COMIC 15
Pause the game, hold L1 + R1 and press ▲, ▲, ■, ●, ●, ●.

PRINCE OF PERSIA: THE TWO THRONES

BABY TOY HAMMER WEAPON
Pause the game and press Left, Left, Right, Right, ● ■, ●, ●, Up, Down.

CHAINSAW WEAPON
Pause the game and press Up, Up, Down, Down, Left, Right, Left, Right, ●, ■, ●, ■.

SWORDFISH WEAPON
Pause the game and press Up, Down, Up, Down, Left, Right, Left, Right, ●, ■, ●, ■.

TELEPHONE OF SORROW WEAPON
Pause the game and press Left, Right, Left, Right, ●, ■, ●, ●, ■, ●.

RATATOUILLE

Select Gusteau's Shop from the Extras menu. Choose Secrets, select the appropriate code number, and then enter the code. Once the code is entered, select the cheat you want to activate it.

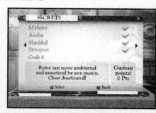

CODE #	CODE	EFFECT
1	Pieceocake	Very Easy difficulty mode
2	Myhero	no impact and no damage from enemies
3	Asobo	Plays the Asobo logo
4	Shielded	No damage from enemies
5	Spyagent	Move undetected by any enemy
6	Ilikeonions	Fart every time Remy jumps
7	Hardfeelings	Head butt when attacking instead of tailswipe
8	Slumberparty	Multiplayer mode
9	Gusteauart	All Concept Art
10	Gusteauship	All four championship modes
11	Mattelme	All single player and multiplayer minigames
12	Gusteauvid	All Videos
13	Gusteaures	All Bonus Artworks
14	Gusteaudream	All Dream Worlds in Gusteau's Shop
15	Gusteauslide	All Slides in Gusteau's Shop
16	Gusteaulevel	All single player minigames
17	Gusteaucombo	All items in Gusteau's Shop
18	Gusteaupot	5,000 Gusteau points
19	Gusteaujack	10,000 Gusteau points
20	Gusteauomni	50,000 Gusteau points

RATCHET AND CLANK: UP YOUR ARSENAL

DUEL BLADE LASER SWORD
Pause the game and press ●, ●, ●, ●, ●, Up, Down, Left, Left.

QWARK'S ALTERNATE COSTUME
Start a game of Qwark Vid-Comic and press Up, Up, Down, Down, Left, Right, ●, ●, ●.

PIRATE VS NINJA MINI-GAME
At the Qwark Comics Issue select, press ● to bring up a password screen. Enter _MEGHAN_ as a password.

4-PLAYER BOMB MINI-GAME
At the Qwark Comics Issue select, press ● to bring up a password screen. Enter YING_TZU as a password. Press Start, Select to return to Starship Phoenix.

SLY 2: BAND OF THIEVES DEMO
At the Title screen, hold L1 + L2 + R1 + R2.

RESERVOIR DOGS

UNLIMITED AMMO
Select Cheats from the Extras menu and press R2, L2, ●, L2, ✖, R2.

ALL LEVELS
Select Cheats from the Extras menu and press L2, R2, L2, R2, L1, R1.

ART GALLERY
Select Cheats from the Extras menu and press ●, ✖, L2, R2, ●, ✖.

MOVIE GALLERY
Select Cheats from the Extras menu and press L1, L1, ●, ✖, L1, R1.

RESIDENT EVIL 4

ALTERNATE TITLE SCREEN
Complete the game.

MATILDA
Complete the game.

MERCENARIES
Complete the game.

PROFESSIONAL DIFFICULTY
Complete the game.

SEPERATE WAYS
Complete the game.

ASHLEY'S ARMOR OUTFIT
Defeat Separate Ways.

LEON'S GANGSTER OUTFIT
Defeat Separate Ways.

ROBOTS

BIG HEAD
Pause the game and press Up, Down, Down, Up, Right, Right, Left, Right.

UNLIMITED HEALTH
Pause the game and press Up, Right, Down, Up, Left, Down, Right, Left.

UNLIMITED SCRAP
Pause the game and press Down, Down, Left, Up, Up, Right, Up, Down.

ROCK BAND

ALL SONGS
At the Title screen, press Red, Yellow, Blue, Red, Red, Blue, Blue, Red, Yellow, Blue. Using this code disables the ability to save your game.

SAMURAI JACK: THE SHADOW OF AKU

MAXIMUM HEALTH
During a game, hold Left on the Left Analog Stick + Right on the Right Analog Stick and press ✖, ●, ▲, ■.

MAXIMUM ZEN
During a game, hold Left on the Left Analog Stick + Right on the Right Analog Stick and press ●, ✖, ■, ▲.

CRYSTAL SWORD
During a game, press Left on the Left Analog Stick Down + Up on the Right Analog Stick and press ✖, ●, ■, ▲.

FIRE SWORD
During a game, press Down on the Left Analog Stick + Up on the Right Analog Stick and press ■, ✖, ●, ▲.

LIGHTNING SWORD
During a game, press Down on the Left Analog Stick + Up on the Right Analog Stick and press ●, ✖, ▲, ■.

After entering the following Cheats, highlight the cheat and press A to "DO IT."

MAX AMMO
Pause the game, select Cheats and enter AMMO.

REFILL HEALTH
Pause the game, select Cheats and enter MEDIK.

FILL BALLS METER
Pause the game, select Cheats and enter FPATCH.

KILL TONY
Pause the game, select Cheats and enter KILTONY.

DECREASE COP HEAT
Pause the game, select Cheats and enter FLYSTRT.

INCREASE COP HEAT
Pause the game, select Cheats and enter DONUT.

DECREASE GANG HEAT
Pause the game, select Cheats and enter NOBALLS.

INCREASE GANG HEAT
Pause the game, select Cheats and enter GOBALLS.

REPAIR TONY'S VEHICLE
Pause the game, select Cheats and enter TBURGLR.

SPAWN ARIEL MK III
Pause the game, select Cheats and enter OLDFAST.

SPAWN BACINARI
Pause the game, select Cheats and enter 666999.

SPAWN BODOG STAMPEDE
Pause the game, select Cheats and enter BUMMER.

SPAWN BULLDOZER
Pause the game, select Cheats and enter DOZER.

SPAWN ODIN VH88
Pause the game, select Cheats and enter DUMPER.

BLACK SUIT TONY
Pause the game, select Cheats and enter BLACK.

BLUE PINSTRIPE SUIT TONY WITH SHADES
Pause the game, select Cheats and enter BLUESH.

GRAY SUIT TONY
Pause the game, select Cheats and enter GRAY.

GRAY SUIT TONY WITH SHADES
Pause the game, select Cheats and enter GRAYSH.

HAWAIIAN SHIRT TONY
Pause the game, select Cheats and enter HAWAII.

HAWAIIAN SHIRT TONY WITH SHADES
Pause the game, select Cheats and enter HAWAIIG.

SANDY SHIRT TONY
Pause the game, select Cheats and enter SANDY.

SANDY SHIRT TONY WITH SHADES
Pause the game, select Cheats and enter SANDYSH.

WHITE SUIT TONY
Pause the game, select Cheats and enter WHITE.

WHITE SUIT TONY WITH SHADES
Pause the game, select Cheats and enter WHITESH.

CHANGE TIME OF DAY
Pause the game, select Cheats and enter MARTHA.

TOGGLE LIGHTNING
Pause the game, select Cheats and enter SHAZAAM.

TOGGLE RAIN
Pause the game, select Cheats and enter RAINY.

BREAL "THE WORLD IS YOURS" MUSIC TRACK
Pause the game, select Cheats and enter TUNEME.

SEGA GENESIS COLLECTION

Before using the following cheats, select the ABC Control option. This sets the controller to the following: ● is A, ✕ is B, ● is C.

ALTERED BEAST

OPTIONS MENU
At the title screen, hold B and press Start.

LEVEL SELECT
After enabling the Options menu, select a level from the menu. At the title screen, hold A and press Start.

BEAST SELECT
At the title screen, hold A + B + C + Down/Left and then press Start

SOUND TEST
At the title screen, hold A + C + Up/Right and press Start.

COMIX ZONE

INVINCIBILITY
At the jukebox screen, press C on the following sounds:
3, 12, 17, 2, 2, 10, 2, 7, 7, 11

LEVEL SELECT
At the jukebox screen, press C on the following sounds:
14, 15, 18, 5, 13, 1, 3, 18, 15, 6
Press C on the desired level.

ECCO THE DOLPHIN

INVINCIBILITY
When the level name appears, hold A + Start until the level begins.

DEBUG MENU
Pause the game with Ecco facing the screen and press Right, B, C, B, C, Down, C, Up.

INFINITE AIR
Enter LIFEFISH as a password.

PASSWORDS

LEVEL	PASSWORD	LEVEL	PASSWORD
The Undercaves	WEFIDNMP	Deep City	DDXPQQLJ
The Vents	BQDPXJDS	City of Forever	MSDBRQLA
The Lagoon	JNSBRIKY	Jurassic Beach	IYCBUNLB
Ridge Water	NTSBZTKB	Pteranodon Pond	DMXEUNLI
Open Ocean	YWGTTJNI	Origin Beach	EGRIUNLB
Ice Zone	HZIFZBMF	Trilobite Circle	IELMUNLB
Hard Water	LRFJRQLI	Dark Water	RKEQUNLN
Cold Water	UYNFRQLC	City of Forever 2	HPQIGPLA
Island Zone	LYTIOQLZ	The Tube	JUMFKMLB
Deep Water	MNOPOQLR	The Machine	GXUBKMLF
The Marble	RJNTQQLZ	The Last Fight	TSONLMLU
The Library	RTGXQQLE		

FLICKY

ROUND SELECT
Begin a new game. Before the first round appears, hold A + C + Up + Start. Press Up or Down to select a Round.

GAIN GROUND

LEVEL SELECT
At the Options screen, press A, C, B, C.

GOLDEN AXE

LEVEL SELECT
Select Arcade Mode. At the character select, hold Down/Left + B and press Start. Press Up or Down to select a level.

RISTAR

Select Passwords from the Options menu and enter the following:

LEVEL SELECT
ILOVEU

BOSS RUSH MODE
MUSEUM

TIME ATTACK MODE
DOFEEL

TOUGHER DIFFICULTY
SUPER

ONCHI MUSIC
MAGURO. Activate this from the Sound Test.

CLEARS PASSWORD
XXXXXX

GAME COPYRIGHT INFO
AGES

SONIC THE HEDGEHOG

LEVEL SELECT
At the title screen, press Up, Down, Left, Right. Hold A and press Start.

SONIC THE HEDGEHOG 2

LEVEL SELECT
Select Sound Test from the options. Press C on the following sounds in order: 19, 65, 09, 17. At the title screen, hold A and press Start.

VECTORMAN

DEBUG MODE
At the options screen, press A, B, B, A, Down, A, B, B, A.

REFILL LIFE
Pause the game and press A, B, Right, A, C, A, Down, A, B, Right, A.

VECTORMAN 2

LEVEL SELECT
Pause the game and press Up, Right, A, B, A, Down, Left, A, Down.

EXTRA LIFE
Pause the game and press Right, Up, B, A, Down, Up, B, Down, Up, B. Repeat for more lives.

FULL ENERGY
Pause the game and press B, A, B, A, Left, Up, Up.

NEW WEAPON
Pause the game and press C, A, Left, Left, Down, A, Down. Repeat for more weapons.

SEGA SUPERSTARS TENNIS

UNLOCK CHARACTERS
Complete the following missions to unlock the corresponding character.

CHARACTER	COMPLETE THIS MISSION
Alex Kidd	Mission 1 of Alex Kidd's World
Amy Rose	Mission 2 of Sonic the Hedgehog's World
Gilius	Mission 1 of Golden Axe's World
Gum	Mission 12 of Jet Grind Radio's World
Meemee	Mission 8 of Super Monkey Ball's World
Pudding	Mission 1 of Space Channel 5's World
Reala	Mission 2 of NiGHTs' World
Shadow The Hedgehog	Mission 14 of Sonic the Hedgehog's World

SHAMAN KING: POWER OF SPIRIT

VERSUS MODE
Complete all 20 episodes in Story Mode.

MASKED MERIL IN VERSUS MODE
Press Select on Meril.

MATILDA IN VERSUS MODE
Press Select on Kanna.

MARION FAUNA IN VERSUS MODE
Press Select on Matilda.

ZEKE ASAKURA IN VERSUS MODE
Press Select on Yoh Asakura.

SHREK THE THIRD

10,000 GOLD COINS
At the gift shop, press Up, Up, Down, Up, Right, Left.

SILENT HILL: ORIGINS

CODEBREAKER SUIT
During a game, press Up, Up, Down, Down, Left, Right, Left, Right, ✕, ●.
You must first finish the game to get this suit.

THE SIMPSONS GAME

UNLIMITED POWER FOR ALL CHARACTERS
At the Extras menu, press ●, Left, Right, ●, ●, L1.

ALL CLICHÉS.
At the Extras menu, press Left, ●, Right, ●, Right, L1.

ALL MOVIES
At the Extras menu, press ●, Left, ●, Right, ●, R1.

THE SIMS 2: CASTAWAY

CHEAT GNOME
During a game, press R1, L1, Down, ●, R2. You can now use this Gnome to get the following:

EXCLUSIVE VEST AND TANKTOP
Pause the game and go to Fashion and Grooming. Press ●, R2, R2, ▲, Down.

MAX ALL MOTIVES
During a game, press R2, Up, X, ●, L1.

MAX CURRENT INVENTORY
During a game, press Left, Right, ●, R2, ●.

MAX RELATIONSHIPS
During a game, press L1, Up, R2, Left, ▲.

ALL RESOURCES
During a game, press ●, ▲, Down, X, Left.

ALL CRAFTING PLANS
During a game, press X, ▲, L2, ●, R1.

ADD 1 TO SKILL
During a game, press ▲, L1, L1, Left, ▲.

CHEAT GNOME

During a game, press L1, L1, R1, ✖, ✖, Up.

GIVE SIM PET POINTS

After activating the Cheat Gnome, press ▲, ●, ✖, ■, L1, R1 during a game.
Select the Gnome to access the cheat.

ADVANCE 6 HOURS

After activating the Cheat Gnome, press Up, Left, Down, Right, R1 during a
game. Select the Gnome to access the cheat.

GIVE SIM SIMOLEONS

After activating the Cheat Gnome,
enter the Advance 6 Hours cheat.
Access the Gnome and exit. Enter
the cheat again. Now, Give Sim
Simoleons should be available from
the Gnome.

CAT AND DOG CODES

When creating a family, press ●
to Enter Unlock Code. Enter the
following for new fur patterns.

FUR PATTERN/CAT OR DOG	UNLOCK CODE
Bandit Mask Cats	EEGJ2YRQZZAIZ9QHA64
Bandit Mask Dogs	EEGJ2YRQZQARQ9QHA64
Black Dot Cats	EEGJ2YRQZQQ1IQ9QHA64
Black Dot Dogs	EEGJ2YRQZZ1IQ9QHA64
Black Smiley Cats	EEGJ2YRQQZ1RQ9QHA64
Black Smiley Dogs	EEGJ2YRZQQARQ9QHA64
Blue Bones Cats	EEGJ2YRQZZARQ9QHA64
Blue Bones Dogs	EEGJ2YRZZZ1IZ9QHA64
Blue Camouflage Cats	EEGJ2YRZZQ1IQ9QHA64
Blue Camouflage Dogs	EEGJ2YRZZZ1RQ9QHA64
Blue Cats	EEGJ2YRQZZAIQ9QHA64
Blue Dogs	EEGJ2YRQQQ1IZ9QHA64
Blue Star Cats	EEGJ2YRQQZ1IZ9QHA64
Blue Star Dogs	EEGJ2YRQQQZ1IQ9QHA64
Deep Red Cats	EEGJ2YRQQQAIQ9QHA64
Deep Red Dogs	EEGJ2YRQZQ1RQ9QHA64
Goofy Cats	EEGJ2YRQZQ1IZ9QHA64
Goofy Dogs	EEGJ2YRZZZARQ9QHA64
Green Cats	EEGJ2YRQQQAIZ9QHA64
Green Dogs	EEGJ2YRZQQAIQ9QHA64
Green Flower Cats	EEGJ2YRQZQAIQ9QHA64
Green Flower Dogs	EEGJ2YRQZZ1RQ9QHA64
Light Green Cats	EEGJ2YRZZQ1RQ9QHA64
Light Green Dogs	EEGJ2YRZQQ1RQ9QHA64
Navy Hearts Cats	EEGJ2YRZQZ1IQ9QHA64
Navy Hearts Dogs	EEGJ2YRQQZ1IQ9QHA64
Neon Green Cats	EEGJ2YRZZQAIQ9QHA64
Neon Green Dogs	EEGJ2YRZQQAIQ9QHA64
Neon Yellow Cats	EEGJ2YRZZQARQ9QHA64
Neon Yellow Dogs	EEGJ2YRQQQAIZ9QHA64
Orange Diagonal Cats	EEGJ2YRQQZAIQ9QHA64
Orange Diagonal Dogs	EEGJ2YRZQZ1IZ9QHA64
Panda Cats	EEGJ2YRQZQAIZ9QHA64
Pink Cats	EEGJ2YRQQZ1IZ9QHA64
Pink Dogs	EEGJ2YRZQZ1IZ9QHA64
Pink Vertical Strip Cats	EEGJ2YRQQQARQ9QHA64
Pink Vertical Strip Dogs	EEGJ2YRZZZAIQ9QHA64
Purple Cats	EEGJ2YRQQZARQ9QHA64
Purple Dogs	EEGJ2YRQQZAIZ9QHA64
Star Cats	EEGJ2YRZQZARQ9QHA64

FUR PATTERN/CAT OR DOG	UNLOCK CODE
Star Dogs	EEGJ2YRZQZAIZ9QHA64
White Paws Cats	EEGJ2YRQQQ1RQ9QHA64
White Paws Dogs	EEGJ2YRZQQ1IZ9QHA64
White Zebra Stripe Cats	EEGJ2YRZZQ1IZ9QHA64
White Zebra Stripe Dogs	EEGJ2YRZZZ1IQ9QHA64
Zebra Stripes Dogs	EEGJ2YRZZQAIZ9QHA64

SLY 3: HONOR AMONG THIEVES

TOONAMI PLANE

While flying the regular plane, pause the game and press R1, R1, Right, Down, Down, Right.

RESTART EPISODES

Pause the game during the Episode and enter the following codes to restart that Episode. You must first complete that part of the Episode to use the code.

EPISODE	CODE
Episode 1, Day 1	Left, R2, Right, L1, R2, L1
Episode 1, Day 2	Down, L2, Up, Left, R2, L2
Episode 2, Day 1	Right, L2, Left, Up, Right, Down
Episode 2, Day 2	Down, Up, R1, Up, R2, L2
Episode 3, Day 1	R2, R1, L1, Left, L1, Down
Episode 3, Day 2	L2, R1, R2, L2, L1, Up
Episode 4, Day 1	Left, Right, L1, R2, Right, R2
Episode 4, Day 2	L1, Left, L2, Left, Up, L1
Episode 5, Day 1	Left, R2, Right, Up, L1, R2
Episode 5, Day 2	R2, R1, L1, R1, R2, R1
Operation Laptop Retrieval	L2, Left, R1, L2, L1, Down
Operation Moon Crash	L2, Up, Left, L1, L2, L1
Operation Reverse Double Cross	Right, Left, Up, Left, R2, Left
Operation Tar Be-Gone	Down, L2, R1, L2, R1, Right
Operation Turbo Dominant Eagle	Down, Right, Left, L2, R1, Right
Operation Wedding Crasher	L2, R2, Right, Down, L1, R2

SOCOM 3: US NAVY SEALS

DISPLAY COORDINATES

Pause the game and press ●, ▲, ●, ●, L1, ▲, ●, ●, ▲, ●.

SOCOM U.S. NAVY SEALS: COMBINED ASSAULT

SHOW COORDINATES

Pause the game and press ●, ▲, ●, ●, L1, ▲, ●, ●, ▲, ●.

THE SOPRANOS: ROAD TO RESPECT

INFINITE AMMO

During a game, hold L2 + R2 and press ●, ●, ✕, ●, ▲, ▲.

INFINITE RESPECT

During a game, hold L2 + R2 and press ✕, ●, ✕, ●, ▲, ▲.

SPIDER-MAN: FRIEND OR FOE

NEW GREEN GOBLIN AS A SIDEKICK

While standing in the Helicarrier between levels, press Left, Down, Right, Right, Down, Left.

SANDMAN AS A SIDEKICK

While standing in the Helicarrier between levels, press Right, Right, Right, Up, Down, Left.

VENOM AS A SIDEKICK
While standing in the Helicarrier between levels, press Left, Left, Right, Up, Down, Down.

5000 TECH TOKENS
While standing in the Helicarrier between levels, press Up, Up, Down, Down, Left, Right.

THE SPIDERWICK CHRONICLES

INVULNERABILITY
During the game, hold L1 + R1 and press ▲, ▲, ▲, ▲, ✕, ✕, ▲, ▲.

HEAL
During the game, hold L1 + R1 and press ▲, ■, ✕, ●, ▲, ■, ✕, ●.

COMBAT LOADOUT
During the game, hold L1 + R1 and press ▲, ▲, ✕, ✕, ■, ●, ■, ●.

INFINITE AMMO
During the game, hold L1 + R1 and press ●, ●, ■, ●, ✕, ✕, ✕, ▲.

FIELD GUIDE UNLOCKED
During the game, hold L1 + R1 and press ●, ●, ●, ■, ▲, ▲, ▲, ✕.

SPRITE A
During the game, hold L2 + R2 and press ▲, ✕, ●, ■, ✕, ✕, ▲, ●.

SPRITE B
During the game, hold L2 + R2 and press ✕, ✕, ▲, ■, ■, ●, ▲, ✕.

SPRITE C
During the game, hold L2 + R2 and press ●, ▲, ■, ✕, ●, ▲, ■, ✕.

SPONGEBOB SQUAREPANTS: CREATURE FROM THE KRUSTY KRAB

30,000 EXTRA Z'S
Select Cheat Codes from the Extras menu and enter ROCFISH.

PUNK SPONGEBOB IN DIESEL DREAMING
Select Cheat Codes from the Extras menu and enter SPONGE. Select Activate Bonus Items to enable this bonus item.

HOT ROD SKIN IN DIESEL DREAMING
Select Cheat Codes from the Extras menu and enter HOTROD. Select Activate Bonus Items to enable this bonus item.

PATRICK TUX IN STARFISHMAN TO THE RESCUE
Select Cheat Codes from the Extras menu and enter PATRICK. Select Activate Bonus Items to enable this bonus item.

SPONGEBOB PLANKTON IN SUPER-SIZED PATTY
Select Cheat Codes from the Extras menu and enter PANTS. Select Activate Bonus Items to enable this bonus item.

PATRICK LASER COLOR IN ROCKET RODEO
Select Cheat Codes from the Extras menu and enter ROCKET. Select Activate Bonus Items to enable this bonus item.

PATRICK ROCKET SKIN COLOR IN ROCKET RODEO
Select Cheat Codes from the Extras menu and enter SPACE. Select Activate Bonus Items to enable this bonus item.

PLANKTON EYE LASER COLOR IN REVENGE OF THE GIANT PLANKTON MONSTER
Select Cheat Codes from the Extras menu and enter LASER. Select Activate Bonus Items to enable this bonus item.

PLAYSTATION®2

PIRATE PATRICK IN ROOFTOP RUMBLE

Select Cheat Codes from the Extras menu and enter PIRATE. Select Activate Bonus Items to enable this bonus item.

HOVERCRAFT VEHICLE SKIN IN HYPNOTIC HIGHWAY—PLANKTON

Select Cheat Codes from the Extras menu and enter HOVER. Select Activate Bonus Items to enable this bonus item.

SPONGEBOB SQUAREPANTS FEATURING NICKTOONS: GLOBS OF DOOM

When entering the following codes, the order of the characters going down is: SpongeBob SquarePants, Nicolai Technus, Danny Phantom, Dib, Zim, Tlaloc, Tak, Beautiful Gorgeous, Jimmy Neutron, Plankton. These names are shortened to the first name in the following.

ATTRACT COINS

Using the Upgrade Machine on the bottom level of the lair, select "Input cheat codes here". Enter Tlaloc, Plankton, Danny, Plankton, Tak. Coins are attracted to you making them much easier to collect.

DON'T LOSE COINS

Using the Upgrade Machine on the bottom level of the lair, select "Input cheat codes here". Enter Plankton, Jimmy, Beautiful, Jimmy, Plankton. You don't lose coins when you get knocked out.

GOO HAS NO EFFECT

Using the Upgrade Machine on the bottom level of the lair, select "Input cheat codes here". Enter Danny, Danny, Danny, Nicolai, Nicolai. Goo does not slow you down.

MORE GADGET COMBO TIME

Using the Upgrade Machine on the bottom level of the lair, select "Input cheat codes here". Enter SpongeBob, Beautiful, Danny, Plankton, Nicolai. You have more time to perform gadget combos.

SPY HUNTER: NOWHERE TO RUN

SPY HUNTER ARCADE

You must activate the machine when you come across it in the safe house on Level 7 (Cleaning Up).

SSX ON TOUR

NEW THREADS

Select Cheats from the Extras menu and enter FLYTHREADS.

THE WORLD IS YOURS

Select Cheats from the Extras menu and enter BACKSTAGEPASS.

SHOW TIME (ALL MOVIES)

Select Cheats from the Extras menu and enter THEBIGPICTURE.

BLING BLING (INFINITE CASH)

Select Cheats from the Extras menu and enter LOOTSNOOT.

FULL BOOST, FULL TIME

Select Cheats from the Extras menu and enter ZOOMJUICE.

MONSTERS ARE LOOSE (MONSTER TRICKS)

Select Cheats from the Extras menu and enter JACKALOPESTYLE.

SNOWBALL FIGHT

Select Cheats from the Extras menu and enter LETSPARTY.

FEEL THE POWER (STAT BOOST)

Select Cheats from the Extras menu and enter POWERPLAY.

CHARACTERS ARE LOOSE

Select Cheats from the Extras menu and enter ROADIEROUNDUp.

UNLOCK CONRAD

Select Cheats from the Extras menu and enter BIGPARTYTIME.

UNLOCK MITCH KOOBSKI

Select Cheats from the Extras menu and enter MOREFUNTHANONE.

UNLOCK NIGEL

Select Cheats from the Extras menu and enter THREEISACROWD.

UNLOCK SKI PATROL

Select Cheats from the Extras menu and enter FOURSOME.

STAR TREK: ENCOUNTERS

ALL LEVELS AND SHIPS
Get a high score in Onslaught Mode and enter your name as 4jstudios.

ALL CREW CARDS
Get a high score in Onslaught Mode and enter your name as Bethesda.

STAR WARS: BATTLEFRONT II

INFINITE AMMO
Pause the game, hold L2 + R2 and press Up, Down, Left, Down, Down, Left, Down, Down, Left, Down, Down, Down, Left, Right.

INVINCIBILITY
Pause the game, hold L2 + R2 and press Up, Up, Up, Left, Down, Down, Down, Left, Up, Up, Up, Left, Right.

NO HUD
Pause the game, hold L2 + R2 and press Up, Up, Up, Up, Left, Up, Up, Down, Left, Down, Up, Up, Left, Right. Re-enter the code to enable the HUD again.

ALTERNATE SOLDIERS
Pause the game, hold L2 + R2 and press Down, Down, Down, Up, Up, Left, Down, Down, Down, Down, Down, Left, Up, Up, Up, Left.

ALTERNATE SOUNDS
Pause the game, hold L2 + R2 and press Up, Up, Up, Left, Up, Down, Up, Up, Left, Down, Down, Down, Left, Up, Down, Down, Left, Right.

FUNNY MESSAGES WHEN REBELS DEFEATED
Pause the game, hold L2 + R2 and press Up, Down, Left, Down, Left, Right.

STAR WARS EPISODE III: REVENGE OF THE SITH

INFINITE FORCE
Select Codes from the Settings menu and enter KAIBURR.

INFINITE HEALTH
Select Codes from the Settings menu and enter XUCPHRA.

QUICK HEALTH & FORCE RESTORATION
Select Codes from the Settings menu and enter BELSAVIS.

ALL STORY, BONUS & CO-OP MISSIONS AND DUELISTS
Select Codes from the Settings menu and enter 021282.

ALL STORY MISSIONS
Select Codes from the Settings menu and enter KORRIBAN.

ALL BONUS MISSIONS
Select Codes from the Settings menu and enter NARSHADDAA.

ALL DUEL ARENAS
Select Codes from the Settings menu and enter TANTIVIEV.

ALL DUELISTS
Select Codes from the Settings menu and enter ZABRAK.

ALL POWERS & MOVES
Select Codes from the Settings menu and enter JAINA.

SUPER LIGHTSABER MODE
Select Codes from the Settings menu and enter SUPERSABERS.

TINY DRIOD MODE
Select Codes from the Settings menu and enter 071779.

ALL REPLAY MOVIES
Select Codes from the Settings menu and enter COMLINK.

ALL CONCEPT ART
Select Codes from the Settings menu and enter AAYLASECURA.

PLAYSTATION 2

CHEATS

Once you have accessed the Rogue Shadow, select Enter Code from the Extras menu. Now you can enter the following:

CHEAT	CODE
Invincibility	CORTOSIS
Unlimited Force	VERGENCE
1,000,000 Force Points	SPEEDER
All Force Powers	TYRANUS
Max Force Power Level	KATARN
Max Combo Level	COUNTDOOKU
Stronger Lightsaber	LIGHTSABER

COSTUMES

Once you have accessed the Rogue Shadow, select Enter Code from the Extras menu. Now you can enter the following codes:

COSTUME	CODE
All Costumes	GRANDMOFF
501st Legion	LEGION
Aayla Secura	AAYLA
Admiral Ackbar	ITSATWAP
Anakin Skywalker	CHOSENONE
Asajj Ventress	ACOLYTE
Ceremonial Jedi Robes	DANTOOINE
Chop'aa Notimo	NOTIMO
Classic stormtrooper	TK421
Count Dooku	SERENNO
Darth Desolous	PAUAN
Darth Maul	ZABRAK
Darth Phobos	HIDDENFEAR
Darth Vader	SITHLORD
Drexl Roosh	DREXLROOSH
Emperor Palpatine	PALPATINE
General Rahm Kota	MANDALORE
Han Solo	NERFHERDER
Heavy trooper	SHOCKTROOP
Juno Eclipse	ECLIPSE
Kento's Robe	WOOKIEE
Kleef	KLEEF
Lando Calrissian	SCOUNDREL
Luke Skywalker	T16WOMPRAT
Luke Skywalker (Yavin)	YELLOWJCKT
Mace Windu	JEDIMASTER
Mara Jade	MARAJADE
Maris Brook	MARISBROOD
Navy commando	STORMTROOP
Obi Wan Kenobi	BENKENOBI
Proxy	HOLOGRAM
Qui Gon Jinn	MAVERICK
Shaak Ti	TOGRUTA
Shadow trooper	INTHEDARK
Sith Robes	HOLOCRON
Sith Stalker Armor	KORRIBAN
Twi'lek	SECURA

OVERLOAD 2

STREET FIGHTER ALPHA

PLAY AS DAN

At the character select screen in Arcade Mode, hold the Start button and place the cursor on the Random Select space then input one of the following commands within 1 second:

LP LK MK HK HP MP

HP HK MK LK LP MP

LK LP MP HP HK MK

HK HP MP LP LK HK

PLAY AS M.BISON

At the character select screen, hold the Start button, place the cursor on the random select box, and input:

1P side: Down, Down, Back, Back, Down, Back, Back + LP + HP

2P side: Down, Down, Forward, Forward, Down, Forward, Forward + LP + HP

PLAY AS AKUMA

At the character select screen, hold the Start button, place the cursor on the random select box, and input:

1P side: Down, Down, Down, Back, Back, Back + LP + HP

2P side: Down, Down, Down, Forward, Forward, Forward + LP + HP

AKUMA MODE

Select your character in Arcade mode, then press and hold Start + MP + MK as the character selection screen ends.

RYU AND KEN VS. M.BISON

On both the 1p and 2p side in Arcade mode, press and hold Start, then:

1P side: place the cursor on Ryu and input Up, Up, release Start, Up, Up + LP

2P side: place the cursor on Ken and input Up, Up, release Start, Up, Up + HP

LAST BOSS MODE

Select Arcade mode while holding ●, ✖, and R1.

DRAMATIC BATTLE MODE

Select Dramatic Battle mode while holding ●, ✖, and R2.

RANDOM BATTLE MODE

Select Versus mode while holding ●, ✖, and R2.

STREET FIGHTER ALPHA 2

PLAY AS ORIGINAL CHUN-LI

Highlight Chun-Li on the character select screen, hold the Start button for 3 seconds, then select Chun-Li normally.

PLAY AS SHIN AKUMA

Highlight Akuma on the character select screen, hold the Start button for 3 seconds, then select Akuma normally.

PLAY AS EVIL RYU

Highlight Ryu on the character select screen, hold the Start button, input Forward, Up, Down, Back, then select Ryu normally.

PLAY AS EX DHALSIM

Highlight Dhalsim on the character select screen, hold the Start button, input Back, Down, Forward, Up, then select Dhalsim normally.

PLAY AS EX ZANGIEF

Highlight Zangief on the character select screen, hold the Start button, input Down, Back, Back, Back, Back, Up, Up, Forward, Forward, Forward, Forward, Down, then select Zangief normally.

LAST BOSS MODE

Select Arcade mode while holding the ●, ●, and R1 buttons.

DRAMATIC BATTLE MODE

Select Dramatic Battle mode while holding the ● + ✖ + R2.

SELECT SPECIAL ROUTE IN SURVIVAL MODE

Select Survival Battle while holding the R1 or R2.

RANDOM BATTLE MODE

Select Versus mode while holding the ● + ✖ + R2.

STREET FIGHTER ALPHA 2 GOLD

PLAY AS EX RYU

Highlight Ryu and press the Start button once before selecting normally.

PLAY AS EVIL RYU

Highlight Ryu and press the Start button twice before selecting normally.

PLAY AS ORIGINAL CHUN-LI

Highlight Chun-Li and press the Start button once before selecting normally.

PLAY AS EX CHUN-LI

Highlight Chun-Li and press the Start button twice before selecting normally.

PLAY AS EX KEN

Highlight Ken and press the Start button once before selecting normally.

PLAY AS EX DHALSIM

Highlight Dhalsim and press the Start button once before selecting normally.

PLAY AS EX ZANGIEF

Highlight Zangief and press the Start button once before selecting normally.

PLAY AS EX SAGAT

Highlight Sagat and press the Start button once before selecting normally.

PLAY AS EX M.BISON

Highlight M.Bison and press the Start button once before selecting normally.

PLAY USING SAKURA'S ALTERNATE COLORS

Highlight Sakura and press the Start button five times before selecting normally.

PLAY AS SHIN AKUMA

Highlight Akuma and press the Start button five times before selecting normally.

PLAY AS CAMMY

Highlight M.Bison and press the Start button twice before selecting normally.

HIDDEN MODES

LAST BOSS MODE

Select Arcade mode while holding ● + ● + R1.

SELECT SPECIAL ROUTE IN SURVIVAL MODE

Select Survival Battle while holding the R1 or R2.

DRAMATIC BATTLE MODE

Select Dramatic Battle mode while holding ● + ✖ + R2.

RANDOM BATTLE MODE

Select Versus mode while holding ● + ✖ + R2.

STREET FIGHTER ALPHA 3

PLAY AS BALROG

Highlight Karin for one second, then move the cursor to the random select box and hold Start before selecting normally.

PLAY AS JULI

Highlight Karin for one second, then move the cursor to the random select box and press Up, or Down, while selecting normally.

PLAY AS JUNI

Highlight Karin for one second, then move the cursor to the random select box and press Back, or Forward, while selecting normally.

CLASSICAL MODE

Press and hold HP + HK while starting game.

SPIRITED MODE

Press and hold MP + MK while starting game.

SAIKYO MODE

Press and hold LP + LK while starting game.

SHADALOO MODE
Press and hold LK + MK + HK while starting game.

SELECT SPECIAL ROUTE IN SURVIVAL MODE
Select Survival mode while holding R1 or R2.

DRAMATIC BATTLE MODE
Select Dramatic Battle mode while holding ● + ✖ + R2.

RANDOM BATTLE MODE
Select Versus mode while holding ● + ✖ + R2.

STUNTMAN IGNITION

3 PROPS IN STUNT CREATOR MODE
Select Cheats from Extras and enter COOLPROP.

ALL ITEMS UNLOCKED FOR CONSTRUCTION MODE
Select Cheats from Extras and enter NOBLEMAN.

MVX SPARTAN
Select Cheats from Extras and enter fastride.

ALL CHEATS
Select Cheats from Extras and enter Wearefrozen. This unlocks the following cheats: Slo-mo Cool, Thrill Cam, Vision Switcher, Nitro Addiction, Freaky Fast, and Ice Wheels.

ALL CHEATS
Select Cheats from Extras and enter Kungfoopete.

ICE WHEELS CHEAT
Select Cheats from Extras and enter IceAge.

NITRO ADDICTION CHEAT
Select Cheats from Extras and enter TheDuke.

VISION SWITCHER CHEAT
Select Cheats from Extras and enter GFXMODES.

THE SUFFERING: TIES THAT BIND

SUICIDE
During gameplay, hold L1 + R1 + ✖ and press Down, Down, Down, Down.

SHOTGUN & AMMO
During gameplay, hold L1 + R1 + ✖ and press Left, Left, Left, Down, Down, Down.

MOLOTOV COCKTAILS
During gameplay, hold L1 + R1 + ✖ and press Down, Down, Down, Up, Up, Up.

FULL FLASHLIGHT
During gameplay, hold L1 + R1 + ✖ and press Up, Left, Down, Right, Up, Right, Down, Left, R2.

FULL AMMO CURRENT WEAPON
During gameplay, hold L1 + R1 + ✖ and press Right, Right, Down, Up, Left, Right, Left, Left, R2.

FULL AMMO CURRENT THROWN
During gameplay, hold L1 + R1 + ✖ and press Left, Left, Up, Down, Right, Left, Right, Right, R2.

FULL INSANITY
During gameplay, hold L1 + R1 + ✖ and press Right, Right, Right, R2, Left, Left, Right, Left, R2.

FULL HEALTH
During gameplay, hold L1 + R1 + ✖ and press Down, Down, Down, R2, Up, Up, Down, Up, R2.

ARSENAL
During gameplay, hold L1 + R1 + ✖ and press Down, Right, Up, Left, Down, R2, Left, Left, Right, Right, R2, Down, Up, Left, Right, R2.

INVINCIBILITY
During gameplay, hold L1 + R1 + ✖ and press Down, Up, Down, Up.

MINUS 50 REP
During gameplay, hold L1 + R1 + ✖ and press Left, Left, Down, Up.

PLUS 50 REP
During gameplay, hold L1 + R1 + ✖ and press Up, Up, Right, Up.

FULL BLOOD
During gameplay, hold L1 + R1 + ✖ and press Up, Down, Left, Right.

ZERO BLOOD
During gameplay, hold L1 + R1 + ✖ and press Down, Up, Right, Left.

SHRAPNEL
During gameplay, hold L1 + R1 + ✖ and press Right, Right, Right, Left, Left, Left.

PLAYSTATION®2

MAX EVIL REP
During gameplay, hold L1 + R1 + ✪ and press Left, Down, Left, Down, Left, Down, R2.

MAX GOOD REP
During gameplay, hold L1 + R1 + ✪ and press Up, Right, Up, Right, Up, Right, R2.

FULL BOTTLES
During gameplay, hold L1 + R1 + ✪ and press Right, Right, Up, Up, R2, Left, Right, R2, Right, Up, Right, R2.

SUPER BAD DUDE
During gameplay, hold L1 + R1 + ✪ and press Down, Up, Down, Left, Right, Left, R2, Up, Left, Down, Right, Up, Right, Down, Left, R2, Down, Down, Down, R2, R2.

PROJECTOR STATE
During gameplay, hold L1 + R1 + ✪ and press Up, R2, Left, R2, Down, R2, Right, R2.

DREAM STATE
During gameplay, hold L1 + R1 + ✪ and press Left, Left, R2, Right, Right, R2, Up, Up, R2, Down, Down, R2.

ALL NOTES
During gameplay, hold L1 + R1 + ✪ and press Right, Left, Up, Left, R2, Right, Down, Right.

ALL MAPS
During gameplay, hold L1 + R1 + ✪ and press Left, Right, Down, Right, R2, Left, Up, Left.

SUPERMAN RETURNS

GOD MODE
Pause the game, select Options and press Up, Up, Down, Down, Left, Right, Left, Right, ◉, ●.

INFINITE CITY HEALTH
Pause the game, select Options and press ◉, Right, ◉, Right, Up, Left, Right, ◉.

ALL POWER-UPS
Pause the game, select Options and press Left, ◉, Right, ◉, Down, ◉, Up, Down, ◉, ◉, ◉.

ALL UNLOCKABLES
Pause the game, select Options and press Left, Up, Right, Down, ◉, ◉, ◉, Up, Right, ◉.

FREE ROAM AS BIZARRO
Pause the game, select Options and press Up, Right, Down, Right, Up, Left, Down, Right, Up.

SUZUKI TT SUPERBIKES

CHEAT SCREEN
At the Main menu, press R1, R2, L1, L2, R1, R2, L1, L2. Now you can enter the following:

ALL EVENTS
Enter BORN FREE.

RED BULL MAD SUNDAY EVENTS
Enter SUNDAYSUNDAY.

ALL HELMETS
Enter SKID LIDS.

ALL LEATHERS
Enter COLORED HIDE.

ALL BIKES
Enter ROCKETS.

ALL WHEELS
Enter TIRE CITY.

ALL COLLECTION BOOK
Enter COUCH POTATO.

TAITO LEGENDS

EXTRA GAMES
At the Title screen, press L1, R1, R2, L2, Select, Start.

INVULNERABILITY
Select Cheat Codes from the Extras menu and enter KRUNKIN.

INFINITE NOVA
Select Cheat Codes from the Extras menu and enter CAKEDAY.

WEAK ENEMIES
Select Cheat Codes from the Extras menu and enter CODMODE.

ALL LEVELS
Select Cheat Codes from the Extras menu and enter GUDGEON.

ALL MINIGAMES
Select Cheat Codes from the Extras menu and enter CURLING.

ALL AWARDS
Select Cheat Codes from the Extras menu and enter SNEAKER.

ALL CONCEPT ART
Select Cheat Codes from the Extras menu and enter FRIVERS.

RAINBOW TRAIL
Select Cheat Codes from the Extras menu and enter UNICORN.

TAK: THE GREAT JUJU CHALLENGE

BONUS SOUND EFFECTS
In Juju's Potions, select Universal Card and enter the following for Bugs, Crystals and Fruits respectively: 20, 17, 5.

BONUS SOUND EFFECTS 2
In Juju's Potions, select Universal Card and enter the following for Bugs, Crystals and Fruits respectively: 50, 84, 92.

BONUS MUSIC TRACK 1
In Juju's Potions, select Universal Card and enter the following for Bugs, Crystals and Fruits respectively: 67, 8, 20.

BONUS MUSIC TRACK 2
In Juju's Potions, select Universal Card and enter the following for Bugs, Crystals and Fruits respectively: 6, 18, 3.

MAGIC PARTICLES
In Juju's Potions, select Universal Card and enter the following for Bugs, Crystals and Fruits respectively: 24, 40, 11.

MORE MAGIC PARTICLES
In Juju's Potions, select Universal Card and enter the following for Bugs, Crystals and Fruits respectively: 48, 57, 57.

VIEW JUJU CONCEPT ART
In Juju's Potions, select Universal Card and enter the following for Bugs, Crystals and Fruits respectively: 33, 22, 28.

VIEW VEHICLE ART
In Juju's Potions, select Universal Card and enter the following for Bugs, Crystals and Fruits respectively: 11, 55, 44.

VIEW WORLD ART
In Juju's Potions, select Universal Card and enter the following for Bugs, Crystals and Fruits respectively: 83, 49, 34.

TEENAGE MUTANT NINJA TURTLES 3: MUTANT NIGHTMARE

INVINCIBILITY
Select Passwords from the Options menu and enter MDLDSSSLR.

HEALTH POWER-UPS BECOME SUSHI
Select Passwords from the Options menu and enter SLLMRSLD.

NO HEALTH POWER-UPS
Select Passwords from the Options menu and enter DMLDMRLD.

ONE HIT DEFEATS TURTLE
Select Passwords from the Options menu and enter LDMSLRDD.

PLAYSTATION®2

MAX OUGI
Select Passwords from the Options menu and enter RRDMLSDL.

UNLIMITED SHURIKEN
Select Passwords from the Options menu and enter LMDRRMSR.

NO SHURIKEN
Select Passwords from the Options menu and enter LLMSRDMS.

DOUBLE ENEMY ATTACK
Select Passwords from the Options menu and enter MSRLSMML.

DOUBLE ENEMY DEFENSE
Select Passwords from the Options menu and enter SLRMLSSM.

TEST DRIVE UNLIMITED

ALL CARS AND MONEY
At the Main menu, press ▲, ●, L1, R1, ▲.

THRILLVILLE: OFF THE RAILS

ALL PARKS
While in a park, press ■, ●, ▲, ■, ●, ▲, ■.

ALL RIDES IN PARK
While in a park, press ■, ●, ▲, ■, ●, ▲, ▲.

$50,000
While in a park, press ■, ●, ▲, ■, ●, ▲, ✕.

MISSION COMPLETE
While in a park, press ■, ●, ▲, ■, ●, ▲, ●.

TIGER WOODS PGA TOUR 07

ALL CHARACTERS
Select Password from the Options menu and enter gameface.

UNLOCK ADIDAS ITEMS
Select Password from the Options menu and enter three stripes.

UNLOCK BRIDGESTONE ITEMS
Select Password from the Options menu and enter shojiro.

UNLOCK COBRA ITEMS
Select Password from the Options menu and enter snakeking.

UNLOCK EA SPORTS ITEMS
Select Password from the Options menu and enter inthegame.

UNLOCK GRAFALLOYE ITEMS
Select Password from the Options menu and enter just shafts.

UNLOCK MACGERGOR ITEMS
Select Password from the Options menu and enter mactec.

UNLOCK MIZUNO ITEMS
Select Password from the Options menu and enter rihachinrzo.

UNLOCK NIKE ITEMS
Select Password from the Options menu and enter justdoit.

UNLOCK OAKLEY ITEMS
Select Password from the Options menu and enter jannard.

UNLOCK PGA TOUR ITEMS
Select Password from the Options menu and enter lightning.

UNLOCK PING ITEMS
Select Password from the Options menu and enter solheim.

UNLOCK PRECEPT ITEMS
Select Password from the Options menu and enter guys are good.

UNLOCK TAYLORMADE ITEMS
Select Password from the Options menu and enter mradams.

TIGER WOODS PGA TOUR 08

ALL GOLFERS
Select Passwords from the Options and enter GAMEFACE.

BRIDGESTONE ITEMS
Select Passwords from the Options and enter SHOJIRO.

COBRA ITEMS
Select Passwords from the Options and enter SNAKEKING.

GRAFALLOY ITEMS
Select Passwords from the Options and enter JUSTSHAFTS.

MACGREGOR ITEMS
Select Passwords from the Options and enter MACTEC.

MIZUNO ITEMS
Select Passwords from the Options and enter RIHACHINRIZO.

NIKE ITEMS
Select Passwords from the Options and enter JUSTDOIT.

OAKLEY ITEMS
Select Passwords from the Options and enter JANNARD.

PING ITEMS
Select Passwords from the Options and enter SOLHEIM.

PRECEPT ITEMS
Select Passwords from the Options and enter GUYSAREGOOD.

TAYLORMADE ITEMS
Select Passwords from the Options and enter MRADAMS.

TIGER WOODS PGA TOUR 08

$1,000,000
Select Passwords from the Extras menu and enter JACKPOT.

MAX SKILL POINTS
Select Passwords from the Extras menu and enter IAMRUBBISH.

ALL CLOTHING & EQUIPMENT
Select Passwords from the Extras menu and enter SHOP2DROP.

ALL PGA TOUR EVENTS
Select Passwords from the Extras menu and enter BEATIT.

ALL COVER STORIES
Select Passwords from the Extras menu and enter HEADLINER.

TIM BURTON'S THE NIGHTMARE BEFORE CHRISTMAS: OOGIE'S REVENGE

ALL LEVELS
At the title screen, press L1, L2, L1, L2, L3, R1, R2, R1, R2, R3.

INVINCIBILITY
During a game, press Right, Left, L3, R3, Left, Right, R3, L3.

PUMPKIN JACK AND SANTA JACK COSTUMES
During gameplay, press Down, Up, Right, Left, L3, R3.

TMNT

DON'S BIG HEAD GOODIE
At the Main menu, hold L1 and press ●, ▲, ✖, ■.

CHALLENGE MAP 2
At the Main menu, hold L1 and press ✖, ✖, ●, ✖.

TOMB RAIDER: LEGEND

You must unlock the following codes in the game before using them.

BULLETPROOF
During gameplay, hold L1 and press ✖, R1, ▲, R1, ●, L2.

DRAIN ENEMY HEALTH
During gameplay, hold L1 and press ●, ●, ✖, L2, R1, ▲.

INFINITE ASSAULT RIFLE AMMO
During gameplay, hold L2 and press ✖, ●, ✖, L1, ●, ▲.

INFINITE GRENADE LAUNCHER AMMO
During gameplay, hold L2 and press L1, ▲, R1, ●, L1, ●.

INFINITE SHOTGUN AMMO
During gameplay, hold L2 and press R1, ●, ●, L1, ●, ✖.

INFINITE SMG AMMO
During gameplay, hold L2 and press ●, ▲, L1, R1, ✖, ●.

EXCALIBUR
During gameplay, hold L2 and press ▲, ✖, ●, R1, ▲, L1.

ONE-SHOT KILL
During gameplay, hold L1 and press ▲, ✖, ▲, ●, L2, ●.

NO TEXTURE MODE
During gameplay, hold L1 and press L2, ✖, ●, ✖, ▲, R1.

OVERLORD

PLAYSTATION®2

TOM CLANCY'S SPLINTER CELL CHAOS THEORY

ALL SOLO LEVELS
At the Solo menu, hold L1 + L2 + R1 + R2 and press ● (x5), ● (x5).

ALL COOP LEVELS
At the Coop menu, hold L1 + L2 + R1 + R2 and press ● (x5), ● (x5).

TEAM PICTURE
At the Main menu, press R2, ● (x5), ●.

TONY HAWK'S DOWNHILL JAM

CHEAT CODES

Select Cheat Codes from the Options menu and enter the following cheats. Select Toggle Cheats to enable/disable them.

FREE BOOST
Enter OOTBAGHFOREVER.

ALWAYS SPECIAL
Enter POINTHOGGER.

UNLOCK MANUALS
Enter IMISSMANUALS.

PERFECT RAIL
Enter LIKETILTINGAPLATE.

PERFECT MANUAL
Enter TIGHTROPEWALKER.

PERFECT STATS
Enter IAMBOB.

FIRST-PERSON SKATER
Enter FIRSTPERSONJAM.

SHADOW SKATER
Enter CHIMNEYSWEEP.

DEMON SKATER
Enter EVILCHIMNEYSWEEP.

MINI SKATER
Enter DOWNTHERABBITHOLE.

GIGANTO-SKATER
Enter IWANNABETALLTALL.

INVISIBLE SKATER
Enter NOWYOUSEEME.

FREE BOOST
Enter OOTBAGHFOREVER.

ALWAYS SPECIAL
Enter POINTHOGGER.

UNLOCK MANUALS
Enter IMISSMANUALS.

PERFECT RAIL
Enter LIKETILTINGAPLATE.

PERFECT MANUAL
Enter TIGHTROPEWALKER.

PERFECT STATS
Enter IAMBOB.

FIRST-PERSON SKATER
Enter FIRSTPERSONJAM.

SHADOW SKATER
Enter CHIMNEYSWEEP.

DEMON SKATER
Enter EVILCHIMNEYSWEEP.

MINI SKATER
Enter DOWNTHERABBITHOLE.

GIGANTO-SKATER
Enter IWANNABETALLTALL.

INVISIBLE SKATER
Enter NOWYOUSEEME.

SKATE AS A WORK OF ART
Enter FOURLIGHTS.

DISPLAY COORDINATES
Enter DISPLAYCOORDINATES.

LARGE BIRDS
Enter BIRDBIRDBIRDBIRD.

ESPECIALLY LARGE BIRDS
Enter BIRDBIRDBIRDBIRDBIRD.

TINY PEOPLE
Enter SHRINKTHEPEOPLE.
*There is no need to toggle on the following cheats. They take effect after entering them.

ALL EVENTS
Enter ADVENTURESOFKWANG.

ALL SKATERS
Enter IMINTERFACING.

ALL BOARDS/OUTFITS
Enter RAIDTHEWOODSHED.

ALL MOVIES
Enter FREEBOZZLER.

CHEAT CODES

Select Cheat Codes from the Options and enter the following cheats. Some codes need to be enabled by selecting Cheats from the Options during a game.

UNLOCK	CHEAT
Unlocks Bosco	MOREMILK
Unlocks Cam	NOTACAMERA
Unlocks Cooper	THECOOP
Unlocks Eddie X	SKETCHY
Unlocks El Patinador	PILEDRIVER
Unlocks Eric	FLYAWAY
Unlocks Judy Nails	LOVEROCKNROLL
Unlocks Mad Dog	RABBIES
Unlocks MCA	INTERGALACTIC
Unlocks Mel	NOTADUDE
Unlocks Rube	LOOKSSMELLY
Unlocks Spence	DAPPER
Unlocks Shayne	MOVERS
Unlocks TV Producer	SHAKER
Unlock FDR	THEPREZPARK
Unlock Lansdowne	THELOCALPARK
Unlock Air & Space Museum	THEINDOORPARK
Unlocks all Fun Items	OVERTHETOP
Unlock all Game Movies	WATCHTHIS
Unlock all Rigger Pieces	IMGONNABUILD
All specials unlocked and in player's special list	LOTSOFTRICKS
Full Stats	BEEFEDUP
Give player +50 skill points	NEEDSHELP
Unlocks Perfect Manual	STILLAINTFALLIN
Unlocks Perfect Rail	AINTFALLIN
Unlocks Unlimited Focus	MYOPIC
Invisible Man	THEMISSING
Mini Skater	TINYTATER

TOTAL OVERDOSE: A GUNSLINGER'S TALE IN MEXICO

CHEAT MODE

Hold L1 + R1 + L2 + R2 + L3 + R3 for a few seconds, then you can enter the following codes.

RESTORE HEALTH

Press ✕, ●, ○, ▲.

ALL LOCO MOVES

During a game, hold L1 + L2 + L3 + R1 + R2 + R3 for three seconds. Then press ●, ●, L2, R2.

MAXIMUM HEALTH

During a game, hold L1 + L2 + L3 + R1 + R2 + R3 for three seconds. Then press ✕, ●, ○, ▲.

MAXIMUM OF REWINDINGS

During a game, hold L1 + L2 + L3 + R1 + R2 + R3 for three seconds. Then press R1, R2, L2, ✕.

FREE ALL WEAPONS

During a game, hold L1 + L2 + L3 + R1 + R2 + R3 for three seconds. Then press ▲, L1, R2, ●.

TRANSFORMERS: THE GAME

INFINITE HEALTH

At the Main menu, press Left, Left, Up, Left, Right, Down, Right.

INFINITE AMMO

At the Main menu, press Up, Down, Left, Right, Up, Up, Down.

NO MILITARY OR POLICE

At the Main menu, press Right, Left, Right, Left, Right, Left, Right.

ALL MISSIONS

At the Main menu, press Down, Up, Left, Right, Right, Right, Up, Down.

BONUS CYBERTRON MISSIONS
At the Main menu, press Right, Up, Up, Down, Right, Left, Left.

GENERATION 1 SKIN: JAZZ
At the Main menu, press Left, Up, Down, Down, Left, Up, Right.

GENERATION 1 SKIN: MEGATRON
At the Main menu, press Down, Left, Left, Down, Right, Right, Up.

GENERATION 1 SKIN: OPTIMUS PRIME
At the Main menu, press Down, Right, Left, Up, Down, Down, Left.

GENERATION 1 SKIN: ROBOVISION OPTIMUS PRIME
At the Main menu, press Down, Down, Up, Up, Right, Right, Right.

GENERATION 1 SKIN: STARSCREAM
At the Main menu, press Right, Down, Left, Left, Down, Up, Up.

TWISTED METAL: HEAD ON – EXTRA TWISTED EDITION

Hold L1 + R1 + L2 + R2 during gameplay, then press the button combination. Do the same thing to turn it off.

INVULNERABILITY
During a game, hold L1 + R1 + L2 + R2 and press Up, Down, Left, Right, Right, Left, Down, Up.

TRADE WEAPONS FOR HEALTH
During a game, hold L1 + R1 + L2 + R2 and press ▲, ✕, ●, ●.

INFINITE WEAPONS
During a game, hold L1 + R1 + L2 + R2 and press ●, ▲, Down, Down.

KILLER WEAPONS
During a game, hold L1 + R1 + L2 + R2 and press ✕, ✕, Up, Up.

MEGA GUNS
During a game, hold L1 + R1 + L2 + R2 and press ✕, ▲, ✕, ▲.

RADIAL BLAST
During a game, hold L1 + R1 + L2 + R2 and press Left, Left, Up, Down, Left, Right.

ULTIMATE SPIDER-MAN

ALL CHARACTERS
Pause the game and select Controller Setup from the Options menu. Press Right, Down, Right, Down, Left, Up, Left, Right.

ALL COVERS
Pause the game and select Controller Setup from the Options menu. Press Left, Left, Right, Left, Up, Left, Left, Down.

ALL CONCEPT ART
Pause the game and select Controller Setup from the Options menu. Press Down, Down, Down, Up, Down, Up, Left, Left.

ALL LANDMARKS
Pause the game and select Controller Setup from the Options menu. Press Up, Right, Down, Left, Down, Up, Right, Left.

URBAN CHAOS: RIOT RESPONSE

At the Main menu, press Up, Up, Down, Down, ●, Down, Up, ●. This opens the Cheat screen. Select Add Cheat and enter the following:

ALL LEVELS & EMERGENCIES
Enter KEYTOTHECITY.

TERROR MODE
Enter BURNERSREVENGE.

ASSUALT RIFLE MK. 3 WITH INFINITE SHELLS
Enter ULTIMATEPOWER.

MINI-GUN
Enter MINIFUN.

PISTOL MK. 4
Enter ZEROTOLERANCE.

ENHANCED STUN GUN
Enter FRYINGTIME.

BURNING BULLETS
Enter BURNINGBULLET.

DISCO CHEAT
Enter DANCINGFEET.

HEADLESS CHEAT
Enter KEEPYOURHEAD.

SQUEAKY VOICES
Enter WHATWASTHAT.

VICTORIOUS BOXERS 2: FIGHTING SPIRIT

EXTRA CHARACTERS IN EXHIBITION
Select Password from the Options menu and enter NEL SAZ UMA.

BROCCOMAN IN EXHIBITION MODE
Select Password from the Options menu and enter BRC MAN EXH.

LUNSAKU PAUDY, JUNICHI HOTTA & HIROSHI YAMANAKA
Select Password from the Options menu and enter ALL *ST ARS.

KAMOGAWA, NEKOTA AND HAMA IN EXHIBITION MODE
Select Password from the Options menu and enter MRS AND MAN.

DATE VS. RAMIREZ MATCH IN STORY MODE
Select Password from the Options menu and enter DAT EVS RMZ.

TAKAMURA VS. YAJIMA MATCH IN STORY MODE
Select Password from the Options menu and enter ASA CT3 CLR.

EXTRA STAGES
Select Password from the Options menu and enter DAM ATA MAQ.

THE WARRIORS

100% COMPLETE
During gameplay, press L1, Select, ●, Down, L2, Right.

99 CREDITS IN ARMIES OF THE NIGHT
During the Armies of the Night mini-game, press Up, Up, Down, Down, Left, Right.

$200, FLASH, & SPRAY PAINT
During gameplay, press R1, R2, L1, ✖, Down, L1.

INFINITE HEALTH
During gameplay, press Up, ▲, L3, Select, ✖, L2.

INFINITE RAGE
During gameplay, press ●, ●, ▲, Select, ✖, Left.

INFINITE SPRINT
During gameplay, press Down, ●, left, ✖, L1, Select.

COMPLETE MISSION
During gameplay, press Down, ●, ✖, Select, R1, Left.

BAT
During gameplay, press ●, R2, Down, Down, L1, L1.

UNBREAKABLE BAT
During gameplay, press L3, L3, ●, Up, ●, Select.

BRASS KNUCKLES
During gameplay, press ●, ●, ●, L1, Select, ▲.

KNIFE
During gameplay, press Down, Down, Select, Up, Up, L3.

MACHETE
During gameplay, press L1, ✖, R1, R1, Select, R2.

PIPE
During gameplay, press R2, ●, Select, Up, L1, Right.

STEEL-TOE BOOTS
During gameplay, press R3, R2, R1,

BUM ADVICE UPGRADE
During gameplay, press ●, ●, Down, R2, L2, ●.

COMBAT STAMINA UPGRADE
During gameplay, press ✖, L1, Down, ●, Up, ✖.

FLASH CAPACITY UPGRADE
During gameplay, press L2, ✖, R2, L1, L1, ●.

FLASH UPGRADE
During gameplay, press Down, Left, Up, Up, ●, Right.

SPRINT STAMINA UPGRADE
During gameplay, press L2, Select, Select, Select, Select, ▲.

CUFF DROPS
During gameplay, press Up, ✖, Up, Select, L3, L1.

CUFF KEY DROPS
During gameplay, press Left, ✖, ✖, R2, L1, Down.

UNCUFF SELF
During gameplay, press ▲, ▲, ▲, Select, ▲, R1.

LOSE THE POLICE
During gameplay, press Up, Select, ✖, ▲, ▲, ●.

HOBO ALLIANCE
During gameplay, press R1, R1, L1, R1, L1, Up.

WEAPONS DEALER
During gameplay, press Right, R1, ●, ✖, Select, ●.

HOBO ALLIANCE
During gameplay, press R1, R1, L1, R1, L1, Up.

WEAPONS DEALER
During gameplay, press Right, R1, ●, ✖, Select, ●.

WAY OF THE SAMURAI 2

MORE CHARACTER MODELS
At the Character Customization screen, highlight Name and press L1, R2, R1, L2, L1, R2, R1, L2, ●. Press Right or Left to change character models.

HBK AND HHH'S DX OUTFIT
Select Cheat Codes from the Options and enter DXCostume69K2.

KELLY KELLY'S ALTERNATE OUTFIT
Select Cheat Codes from the Options and enter KellyKG12R.

X-MEN: THE OFFICIAL GAME

DANGER ROOM ICEMAN
At the Cerebro Files menu, press Right, Right, Left, Left, Down, Up, Down, Up, Start.

DANGER ROOM NIGHTCRAWLER
At the Cerebro Files menu, press Up, Up, Down, Down, Left, Right, Left, Right, Start.

DANGER ROOM WOLVERINE
At the Cerebro Files menu, press Down, Down, Up, Up, Right, Left, Right, Left, Start.

YS: THE ARK OF NAPISHTIM

Enter the cheat codes as follows:

1. **Select New Game.**

2. **Select Cheat to enter the Cheat Room.**

3. **To activate Cheat Mode, strike the colored crystals in this sequence: Red, Blue, Yellow, Red, Blue, Yellow. The sequence appears at the top left as you strike each crystal.**

4. **Perform a Downward Thrust strike on the center pedestal to complete the code and activate Cheat Mode.**

5. **You can now use the same method to enter one of the cheat codes listed below, then exit the Cheat Room.**

6. **The game selection buttons are now red. Games saved with the Cheat Mode enabled will appear in red.**

CLEARFLAG
Hit the crystals in the following order: Red, Red, Red, Red, Blue, Blue, Blue, Blue, Yellow, Yellow, Yellow, Yellow, Blue, Blue, Yellow, Yellow, Red, Red. Turns on all special features normally available only after you've completed the game once—Nightmare Mode, Time Attack, and Red Spirit Monuments. **Note:** When enabled, Red Spirit Monuments appear after you reach Port Rimorge. They allow you to warp between the Rehdan Village and Port Rimorge monuments to save travel time.

OPENING MOVIE WITH ENGLISH VOICE/ENGLISH TEXT
Hit the crystals in the following order: Blue, Blue, Yellow, Red.

OPENING MOVIE WITH ENGLISH VOICE/JAPANESE TEXT
Hit the crystals in the following order: Blue, Blue, Blue, Yellow, Red.

OPENING MOVIE WITH JAPANESE VOICE/ENGLISH TEXT
Hit the crystals in the following order: Blue, Blue, Blue, Blue, Yellow, Red.

OPENING MOVIE WITH JAPANESE VOICE/NO TEXT
Hit the crystals in the following order: Blue, Yellow, Red.

ALTERNATE OPENING MOVIE
Hit the crystals in the following order: Red, Blue, Red.

BEACH MOVIE WITH ENGLISH VOICE/ENGLISH TEXT
Hit the crystals in the following order: Blue, Blue, Red, Yellow

BEACH MOVIE WITH ENGLISH VOICE/JAPANESE TEXT
Hit the crystals in the following order: Blue, Blue, Blue, Red, Yellow.

BEACH MOVIE WITH JAPANESE VOICE/ENGLISH TEXT
Hit the crystals in the following order: Blue, Red, Red, Yellow.

BEACH MOVIE WITH JAPANESE VOICE/JAPANESE TEXT
Hit the crystals in the following order: Blue, Red, Yellow.

ROMUN FLEET ENTRANCE ANIME MOVIE
Hit the crystals in the following order: Blue, Red, Yellow, Red, Red, Yellow, Blue, Blue, Blue.

ROMUN FLEET ENTRANCE CG MOVIE
Hit the crystals in the following order: Blue, Red, Yellow, Red, Red, Yellow, Blue.

ROMUN FLEET DESTROYED ANIME MOVIE
Hit the crystals in the following order: Blue, Red, Yellow, Red, Red, Yellow, Red, Red, Red.

ROMUN FLEET DESTROYED CG MOVIE
Hit the crystals in the following order: Blue, Red, Yellow, Red, Red, Yellow, Red.

NAPISHTIM DESTROYED MOVIE WITH ENGLISH VOICE/ENGLISH TEXT
Hit the crystals in the following order: Blue, Red, Yellow, Red, Red, Blue, Yellow, Yellow.

NAPISHTIM DESTROYED MOVIE WITH ENGLISH VOICE/JAPANESE TEXT
Hit the crystals in the following order: Blue, Red, Yellow, Red, Red, Blue, Yellow, Yellow, Yellow.

NAPISHTIM DESTROYED MOVIE WITH JAPANESE VOICE/ENGLISH TEXT
Hit the crystals in the following order: Blue, Red, Yellow, Red, Red, Blue, Yellow, Yellow, Yellow, Yellow.

NAPISHTIM DESTROYED MOVIE WITH JAPANESE VOICE/JAPANESE TEXT
Hit the crystals in the following order: Blue, Red, Yellow, Red, Red, Blue, Yellow.

OLHA IN BIKINI
Hit the crystals in the following order: Blue, Blue, Blue, Blue, Blue, Yellow, Yellow, Yellow, Red, Blue, Yellow, Yellow, Red, Red, Red.

OLHA DEMO AFTER CLEARING TIME ATTACK ON HARD (JAPANESE)
Hit the crystals in the following order: Red, Red, Red, Red, Red, Blue, Blue, Blue, Yellow, Red, Blue, Blue, Yellow, Yellow, Yellow.

GAME IN JAPANESE
Hit the crystals in the following order: Yellow, Yellow, Red, Blue.

LEVEL 10
Hit the crystals in the following order: Red, Blue, Blue, Red, Red, Blue.

LEVEL 20
Hit the crystals in the following order: Red, Blue, Blue, Red, Red, Blue, Blue.

LEVEL 30
Hit the crystals in the following order: Red, Red, Blue, Blue, Red, Red, Blue, Blue.

LEVEL 40
Hit the crystals in the following order: Red, Red, Blue, Red, Red, Blue, Blue, Yellow.

LEVEL 60
Hit the crystals in the following order: Red, Red, Blue, Blue, Yellow, Yellow, Red, Red, Blue, Blue, Yellow, Yellow.

HALF PRICE ITEMS

Hit the crystals in the following order: Yellow, Yellow, Blue, Blue, Red, Red, Red, Yellow, Yellow, Yellow, Red, Red, Blue, Blue.

20 ITEM TOOL MAX INCREASE

Hit the crystals in the following order: Yellow, Yellow, Red, Red, Blue, Blue, Yellow, Red.

MAXED OUT BLIRANTE SWORD

Hit the crystals in the following order: Blue, Blue, Yellow, Yellow, Yellow, Red, Blue, Red, Red, Red, Yellow, Yellow.

MAXED OUT LIVART SWORD

Hit the crystals in the following order: Blue, Blue, Blue, Yellow, Yellow, Red, Blue, Red, Red, Yellow, Yellow, Yellow.

MAXED OUT ERICCIL SWORD

Hit the crystals in the following order: Blue, Yellow, Yellow, Red, Red, Red, Blue, Blue, Blue, Red, Red, Yellow.

MAXED OUT ALL 3 SWORDS

Hit the crystals in the following order: Blue, Yellow, Red, Blue, Blue, Blue, Red, Red, Red, Yellow, Yellow, Yellow, Blue, Yellow, Red.

ALTERNATE ENDING MOVIES

In the Rehdan Village (Festival at Night): Toksa and Nahrya look toward Adol as he walks by.

At the Entrance of the Village: Isha runs toward the back, then returns.

On the Tres Mares: The cat is on the front of the ship.

ENDING CHANGE CRITERIA

Direction Calman is facing: Faces Adol if he has gotten the Gold Locket.

Number of Pikkards: Found all four pikkards and returned them to Emilio.

XBOX®

GAMES

XBOX

OVERLOAD

ALIEN HOMINID

ALL LEVELS, MINI-GAMES, AND HATS
Select Player 1 Setup or Player 2 Setup and change the name to ROYGBIV.

HATS FOR 2-PLAYER GAME
Go to the Options menu and rename your alien one of the following:

ALIEN	HAT STYLE	HAT NUMBER
ABE	Top Hat	#11
APRIL	Blond Wig	#4
BEHEMOTH	Red Cap	#24
CLETUS	Hunting Hat	#3
DANDY	Flower Petal Hat	#13
GOODMAN	Black Curly Hair	#7
GRRL	Flowers	#10
PRINCESS	Tiara	#12
SUPERFLY	Afro	#6
TOMFULP	Brown Messy Hair	#2

AVATAR: THE LAST AIRBENDER

ALL TREASURE MAPS
Select Code Entry from the Extras menu and enter 37437.

1 HIT DISHONOR
Select Code Entry from the Extras menu and enter 54641.

DOUBLE DAMAGE
Select Code Entry from the Extras menu and enter 34743.

UNLIMITED COPPER
Select Code Entry from the Extras menu and enter 23637.

UNLIMITED CHI
Select Code Entry from the Extras menu and enter 24463.

UNLIMITED HEALTH
Select Code Entry from the Extras menu and enter 94677.

NEVERENDING STEALTH
Select Code Entry from the Extras menu and enter 53467.

CHARACTER CONCEPT ART GALLERY
Select Code Entry from the Extras menu and enter 97831.

THE BARD'S TALE

During a game, hold L + R and enter the following:

EVERYTHING ON (SILVER AND ADDERSTONES)
Up, Up, Down, Down, Left, Right, Left, Right

FULL HEALTH AND MANA
Left, Left, Right, Right, Up, Down, Up, Down

CAN'T BE HURT
Right, Left, Right, Left, Up, Down, Up, Down

CAN'T BE STRUCK
Left, Right, Left, Right, Up, Down, Up, Down

DAMAGE X100
Up, Down, Up, Down, Left, Right, Left, Right

XBOX®

BATTLEFIELD 2: MODERN COMBAT

ALL WEAPONS
During gameplay, hold Black + White and press Right, Right, Down, Up, Left, Left.

BLAZING ANGELS: SQUADRONS OF WWII

ALL MISSIONS, MEDALS, & PLANES
At the Main menu, hold Left Trigger + Right Trigger and press X, White, Black, Y, Y, Black, White, X.

GOD MODE
Pause the game, hold Left Trigger and press X, Y, Y, X. Release Left Trigger, hold Right Trigger and press Y, X, X, Y. Re-enter the code to disable it.

DAMAGE INCREASED
Pause the game, hold Left Trigger and press White, White, Black. Release Left Trigger, hold Right Trigger and press Black, Black, White. Re-enter the code to disable it.

CAPCOM CLASSICS COLLECTION

ALL LOCKS OPENED
At the Title screen, press Left Trigger, Right Trigger, Up on Right Thumbstick, Down on Right Thumbstick, Left Trigger, Right Trigger, Up on Left Thumbstick, Down on Left Thumbstick, Left Trigger, Right Trigger, Up, Down.

CARS

UNLOCK EVERYTHING
Select Cheat Codes from the Options menu and enter IF900HP.

ALL CHARACTERS
Select Cheat Codes from the Options menu and enter YAYCARS.

ALL CHARACTER SKINS
Select Cheat Codes from the Options menu and enter R4MONE.

ALL MINI-GAMES AND COURSES
Select Cheat Codes from the Options menu and enter MATTL66.

MATER'S COUNTDOWN CLEAN-UP MINI-GAME & MATER'S SPEEDY CIRCUIT
Select Cheat Codes from the Options menu and enter TRGTEXC.

FAST START
Select Cheat Codes from the Options menu and enter IMSPEED.

INFINITE BOOST
Select Cheat Codes from the Options menu and enter VROOOOM.

ART
Select Cheat Codes from the Options menu and enter CONC3PT.

VIDEOS
Select Cheat Codes from the Options menu and enter WATCHIT.

THE CHRONICLES OF NARNIA: THE LION, THE WITCH AND THE WARDROBE

ENABLE CHEATS
At the Title screen, press A and hold Left Trigger + Right Trigger and press Down, Down, Right, Up. The text should turn green when entered correctly. When this occurs, you can enter the following codes.

LEVEL SELECT
At the wardrobe, hold Left Trigger and press Up, Up, Right, Right, Up, Right, Down.

ALL BONUS LEVELS
At the Bonus Drawer, hold Left Trigger and press Down, Down, Right, Right, Down, Right, Up.

LEVEL SKIP
During gameplay, hold Left Trigger and press Down, Left, Down, Left, Down, Right, Down, Right, Up.

INVINCIBILITY
During gameplay, hold Left Trigger and press Down, Up, Down, Right, Right.

RESTORE HEALTH
During gameplay, hold Left Trigger and press Down, Left, Left, Right.

10,000 COINS
During gameplay, hold Left Trigger and press Down, Left, Right, Down, Down.

ALL ABILITIES
During gameplay, hold Left Trigger and press Down, Left, Right, Left, Up.

FILL COMBO METER
During gameplay, hold Left Trigger and press Up, Up, Right, Up.

COLD WAR

INVULNERABILITY
Pause the game and press X, White, Y, Black, Left.

WIN CURRENT LEVEL
Pause the game and press X, White, Y, Black, X.

ALL ITEMS, GADGETS, & TECH POINTS
Pause the game and press X, White, Y, Black, Y.

COMMANDOS STRIKE FORCE

MISSION SELECT
Enter TRUCO as a profile name.

UNLIMITED AMMO
Pause the game, hold Left Trigger + Right Trigger and press A, Y, A, B, X, Y.

CONSTANTINE

BIG DEMON HEADS
Press Back to get to the Journal and press Black, Left, Right, Left, Left, Right, Left, Black.

BIG WEAPON MODE
Press Back to get to the Journal and press Left, X, X, X, Y, Y, Y.

INFINITE AMMO
Press Back to get to the Journal and press Left, Right, Left, X, Y, X, X, Y, Y, X, Y, X, X, Y, Y.

INFINITE SPELL SOUL ENERGY
Press Back to get to the Journal and press Left, Right, Right, Left, Left, Right, Right, Left, Y, Y.

RAPID FIRE SHOTGUN
Press Back to get to the Journal and press White, Left, Black, Left, Y, X, Y, X.

SHOOT LARGE FIREBALLS
Press Back to get to the Journal and press Y, Y, Y, Left, Right, Right, Left, Left, Right.

EXPLOSIVE HOLY BOMBS
Press Back to get to the Journal and press Right, Left, X, Y, X, Y, Left, Right.

DANCE DANCE REVOLUTION ULTRAMIX 3

ALL SONGS
Select Credits from the Options menu and play the Credits mini-game, then press the opposite of what the game indicates. (For example, press Up when it says Down and so on. Or, if it says Left + Right, press Up + Down.) You'll hear applause when the code is entered correctly.

THE DA VINCI CODE

GOD MODE
Select Codes from the Options menu and enter VITRUVIAN MAN.

EXTRA HEALTH
Select Codes from the Options menu and enter SACRED FEMININE.

MISSION SELECT
Select Codes from the Options menu and enter CLOS LUCE 1519.

1-HIT FIST KILL
Select Codes from the Options menu and enter PHILLIPS EXETER.

XBOX

ONE-HIT WEAPON KILL
Select Codes from the Options menu and enter ROYAL HOLLOWAY.

ALL VISUAL DATABASE
Select Codes from the Options menu and enter APOCRYPHA.

ALL VISUAL DATABASE & CONCEPT ART
Select Codes from the Options menu and enter ET IN ARCADIA EGO.

DEF JAM: FIGHT FOR NY

Select Cheats from the Extras menu and enter the following:

100 REWARD POINTS
Enter NEWJACK, THESOURCE, CROOKLYN, DUCKETS, or GETSTUFF. You can only enter each code once.

UNLOCK SONG: "AFTERHOURS" BY NYNE
Enter LOYALTY.

UNLOCK SONG: "ANYTHING GOES" BY C-N-N
Enter MILITAIN.

UNLOCK SONG: "BUST" BY OUTKAST
Enter BIGBOI.

UNLOCK SONG: "BLINDSIDE" BY BAXTER
Enter CHOPPER.

UNLOCK SONG: "COMP" BY COMP
Enter CHOCOCITY.

UNLOCK SONG: "DRAGON HOUSE" BY CHIANG
Enter AKIRA.

UNLOCK SONG: "GET IT NOW" BY BLESS
Enter PLATINUMB.

UNLOCK SONG: "KOTO" BY CHIANG
Enter GHOSTSHELL.

UNLOCK SONG: "LIL' BRO" BY RIC-A-CHE
Enter GONBETRUBL.

UNLOCK SONG: "MAN UP" BY STICKY FINGAZ
Enter KIRKJONES.

UNLOCK SONG: "MOVE!" BY PUBLIC ENEMY
Enter RESPECT.

UNLOCK SONG: "O. G. ORIGINAL GANGSTER" BY ICE T
Enter POWER.

UNLOCK SONG: "POPPA LARGE" BY ULTRAMAGNETIC MC'S
Enter ULTRAMAG.

UNLOCK SONG: "SIEZE THE DAY" BY BLESS
Enter SIEZE.

UNLOCK SONG: "TAKE A LOOK AT MY LIFE" BY FAT JOE
Enter CARTAGENA.

UNLOCK SONG: "WALK WITH ME" BY JOE BUDDEN
Enter PUMP.

DESTROY ALL HUMANS! 2

SALAD DAYS WITH POX & CRYPTO MOVIE
Pause the game and select Archives. Hold Left Thumbstick and press A, X, Y, B, X, B, Y, A, A.

DRAGON BALL Z: SAGAS

ALL UPGRADES
Pause the game, select Controller and press Up, Left, Down, Right, Back, Start, Y, X, A, B.

INVINCIBILITY
Pause the game, select Controller and press Down, A, Up, Y, Back, Start, Right, X, Left, B.

DRIV3R

At the Main menu, enter the following cheats. Then select Cheats from the Options menu to toggle them on and off.

ALL MISSIONS
Enter X, X, Y, Y, R, R, L.

ALL WEAPONS
Enter L, L, X, Y, Y, R, R.

UNLIMITED AMMO
Enter R, R, L, L, X, Y, Y.

INVINCIBILITY (TAKE A RIDE)
Enter X, Y, L, R, L, R, R.

IMMUNITY
Enter X, Y, R, R, L, L, Y.

ALL VEHICLES
Enter X, X, Y, Y, L, R, L.

EA SPORTS ARENA FOOTBALL

BIG BALL
While at the line of scrimmage, press Left Trigger + Y, Up, Up.

SMALL BALL
While at the line of scrimmage, press Left Trigger + Y, Down, Down.

NORMAL SIZE BALL
While at the line of scrimmage, press Left Trigger + Y, Up, Down.

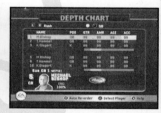

MAX STATS IN QUICK PLAY
Load a profile with the name IronMen. This will maximize all players' stats in Quick Play.

ERAGON

FURY MODE
Pause the game, hold Left Trigger + Right Trigger and press X, X, B, B.

FAR CRY: INSTINCTS—EVOLUTION

ALL MAPS
Enter GiveMeTheMaps at the Cheats menu.

FERAL ATTACKS (EARLY LEVELS)
Enter FeralAttack at the Cheats menu.

RESTORE HEALTH
Enter ImJackCarver at the Cheats menu.

INFINITE AMMO
Enter UnleashHell at the Cheats menu.

INFINITE ADRENALINE
Enter BloodLust at the cheats menu.

FLATOUT 2

ALL CARS AND 1,000,000 CREDITS
Select Enter Code from Extras and enter GIEVEPIX.

1,000,000 CREDITS
Select Enter Code from the Extras and enter GIVECASH.

PIMPSTER CAR
Select Enter Code from Extras and enter RUTTO.

FLATMOBILE CAR
Select Enter Code from Extras and enter WOTKINS.

MOB CAR
Select Enter Code from the Extras and enter BIGTRUCK.

SCHOOL BUS
Select Enter Code from Extras and enter GIEVCARPLZ.

ROCKET CAR
Select Enter Code from Extras and enter KALJAKOPPA.

TRUCK
Select Enter Code from the Extras and enter ELPUEBLO.

FULL SPECTRUM WARRIOR: TEN HAMMERS

ALL LEVELS
Enter FULLSPECTRUMPWNAGE at the Cheat menu.

THE GODFATHER

$5,000
Pause the game and press X, Y, X, X, Y, Left Thumbstick.

FULL AMMO
Pause the game and press Y, Left, Y, Right, X, Right Thumbstick.

FULL HEALTH
Pause the game and press Left, X, Right, Y, Right, Left Thumbstick.

UNLOCK ENTIRE FILM ARCHIVE
After loading a game and before joining the family, press Y, X, Y, X, X, Left Thumbstick. Select Film Archive to view films.

GRAND THEFT AUTO 3

BETTER VEHICLE HANDLING

Press Right Trigger, Left Trigger, Black, Left Trigger, Left, Right Trigger, Right Trigger, Y while *outside* your vehicle. This code makes all vehicles handle better. When entered correctly, press the Left Thumbstick to cause the vehicle to hop.

VEHICLE HEALTH

Press Black, Black, Left Trigger, Right Trigger, Left, Down, Right, Up, Left, Down, Right, Up while *inside* a vehicle. The car will remain damaged, but it will stop smoking and retain its perfect "health" status.

EXPLODE ALL VEHICLES

Press White, Black, Left Trigger, Right Trigger, White, Black, Y, X, B, Y, White, Left Trigger.

RHINO

Press B (x6), Right Trigger, White, Left Trigger, Y, B, Y.

INVISIBLE CAR CHASSIS

Press Left Trigger, Left Trigger, X, Black, Y, Left Trigger, Y.

FLYING VEHICLES

Press Right, Black, B, Right Trigger, White, Down, Left Trigger, Right Trigger.

FOGGY

Press Left Trigger, White, Right Trigger, Black, Black, Right Trigger, White, A.

CLOUDY

Press Left Trigger, White, Right Trigger, Black, Black, Right Trigger, White, X.

RAIN

Press Left Trigger, White, Right Trigger, Black, Black, Right Trigger, White, B.

NORMAL WEATHER

Press Left Trigger, White, Right Trigger, Black, Black, Right Trigger, White, Y.

PEDESTRIANS RIOT

Press Down, Up, Left, Up, A, Right Trigger, Black, White, Left Trigger. Please note that this code is irreversible, so do NOT enter the code and save your game.

PEDESTRIANS OUT TO GET YOU

Press Down, Up, Left, Up, A, Right Trigger, Black, Left Trigger, White. Please note that this code is irreversible, so do NOT enter the code and save your game.

PEDESTRIANS PACKING HEAT

Press Black, Right Trigger, Y, A, White, Left Trigger, Up, Down. Please note that this code is irreversible, so do NOT enter the code and save your game.

WANTED LEVEL INCREASE

Press Black, Black, Left Trigger, Black, Left, Right, Left, Right, Left to increase your Wanted Level by two each time the code is entered.

WANTED LEVEL DECREASE

Press Black, Black, Left Trigger, Black, Up, Down, Up, Down, Up, Down to decrease your Wanted Level.

WEAPON CHEAT

Press Black, Black, Left Trigger, Black, Left, Down, Right, Up, Left, Down, Right, Up. Continue to enter the code until the maximum ammo capacity of 9999 is reached for each weapon. When a weapon reaches its maximum ammo capacity, its ammunition supply becomes infinite.

CHANGE CHARACTER MODEL

Press Right, Down, Left, Up, Left Trigger, White, Up, Left, Down, Right. Please note that this code is irreversible, so do NOT enter the code and save your game.

HEALTH CHEAT

Press Black, Black, Left Trigger, Right Trigger, Left, Down, Right, Up, Left, Down, Right, Up.

ARMOR CHEAT

Press Black, Black, Left Trigger, White, Left, Down, Right, Up, Left, Down, Right, Up.

MONEY CHEAT ($250,000)

Press Black, Black, Left Trigger, Left Trigger, Left, Down, Right, Up, Left, Down, Right, Up.

INCREASED GORE FACTOR

Press X, Left Trigger, B, Down, Left Trigger, Right Trigger, Y, Right, Left Trigger, A to make victims lose body parts.

SLOW MOTION

Press Y, Up, Right, Down, X, Right Trigger, Black. Enter this cheat three times for even more slowdown.

FASTER GAMEPLAY

Press Y, Up, Right, Down, X, Left Trigger, White. Enter this cheat three times for even faster gameplay.

INCREASE TIME
Press B (x3), X (x5), Left Trigger, Y, B, Y. Enter this cheat a second time to return to "normal" time.

GRAND THEFT AUTO: VICE CITY
Enter the following cheats during gameplay. Note that some of these codes may affect your gameplay, so don't save your game unless you want the code to stay in effect.

HEALTH CHEAT
Press Right Trigger, Black, Left Trigger, B, Left, Down, Right, Up, Left, Down, Right, Up.

ARMOR CHEAT
Press Right Trigger, Black, Left Trigger, A, Left, Down, Right, Up, Left, Down, Right, Up.

LOW GRAVITY
Press Right, Black, B, Right Trigger, White, Down, Left Trigger, Right Trigger.

BETTER DRIVING
Press Y, Right Trigger, Right Trigger, Left, Right Trigger, Left Trigger, Black, Left Trigger. Press the Left Thumbstick to jump.

SUICIDE
Press Right, White, Down, Right Trigger, Left, Left, Right Trigger, Left Trigger, White, Left Trigger.

WANTED LEVEL UP 2 STARS
Press Right Trigger, Right Trigger, B, Black, Left, Right, Left, Right, Left, Right.

WANTED LEVEL DOWN 2 STARS
Press Right Trigger, Right Trigger, B, Black, Up, Down, Up, Down, Up, Down.

SLOW MOTION
Press Y, Up, Right, Down, X, Black, Right Trigger.

SPEED UP TIME
Press B, B, Left Trigger, X, Left Trigger, X, X, X, Left Trigger, Y, B, Y.

BLACK CARS
Press B, White, Up, Right Trigger, Left, A, Right Trigger, Left Trigger, Left, B.

PINK CARS
Press B, Left Trigger, Down, White, Left, A, Right Trigger, Left Trigger, Right, B.

CHANGE WHEELS
Press Right Trigger, A, Y, Right, Black, X, Up, Down, X.

CAR SPEED X2
Press Right Trigger, Black, Left Trigger, L, Left, Down, Right, Up, Left, Down, Right, Up.

CARS FLOAT
Press Right, Black, B, Right Trigger, White, X, Right Trigger, Black.

ALL CARS EXPLODE
Press Black, White, Right Trigger, Left Trigger, White, Black, X, Y, B, Y, White, Left Trigger.

ROBOCOPS
Press B, Left Trigger, Down, White, Left, A, Right Trigger, Left Trigger, Right, A.

CARS DON'T STOP
Press Black, B, Right Trigger, White, Left, Right Trigger, Left Trigger, Black, White.

PEDESTRIANS RIOT
Press Down, Left, Up, Left, A, Black, Right Trigger, White, Left Trigger.

PEDESTRIANS ATTACK
Press Down, Up (x3), A, Black, Right Trigger, White, White.

ARMED PEDESTRIANS
Press Black, Right Trigger, A, Y, A, Y, Up, Down.

WOMEN WITH GUNS
Press Right, Left Trigger, B, White, Left, A, Right Trigger, Left Trigger, Left Trigger, A.

WOMEN FOLLOW YOU
Press B, A, Left Trigger, Left Trigger, Black, A, A, B, Y.

MEDIA LEVEL METER
Press Black, B, Up, Left Trigger, Right, Right Trigger, Right, Up, X, Y.

The following codes provide one weapon for each weapon class:

WEAPONS SET 1
Press Black, Black, Right Trigger, Black, Left Trigger, Black, Left, Down, Right, Up, Left Down, Right, Up.

WEAPONS SET 2
Press Right Trigger, Black, Left Trigger, Black, Left, Down, Right, Up, Left, Down, Down, Left.

WEAPONS SET 3
Press Right Trigger, Black, Left Trigger, Black, Left, Down, Right, Up, Left, Down, Down, Down.

CLEAR WEATHER
Press Black, A, Left Trigger, Left Trigger, White, White, White, Down.

SUNNY
Press Black, A, Left Trigger, Left Trigger, White (x3), Y.

OVERCAST
Press Black, A, Left Trigger, Left Trigger, White (x3), X.

RAIN
Press Black, A, Left Trigger, Left Trigger, White (x3), B.

FOG
Press Black, A, Left Trigger, Left Trigger, White (x3), A.

RED LEATHER
Press Right, Right, Left, Up, Left Trigger, White, Left, Up, Down, Right.

CANDY SUXXX
Press B, Black, Down, Right Trigger, Left, Right, Right Trigger, Left Trigger, A, White.

HILARY KING
Press Right Trigger, B, Black, Left Trigger, Right, Right Trigger, Left Trigger, A, Black.

KEN ROSENBERG
Press Right, Left Trigger, Up, White, Left Trigger, Right, Right Trigger, Left Trigger, A, R.

LANCE VANCE
Press B, White, Left, A, Right Trigger, Left Trigger, A, Left Trigger.

LOVE FIST 1
Press Down, Left Trigger, Down, White, Left, A, Right Trigger, Left Trigger, A, A.

LOVE FIST 2
Press Right Trigger, White, Black, Left Trigger, Right, Black, Left, A, X, Left Trigger.

MERCEDES
Press Black, Left Trigger, Up, Left Trigger, Right, Right Trigger, Right, Up, B, Y.

PHIL CASSADY
Press Right, Right Trigger, Up, Black, Left Trigger, Right, Right Trigger, Left Trigger, Right, B.

RICARDO DIAZ
Press Left Trigger, White, Right Trigger, Black, Down, Left Trigger, Black, White.

SONNY FORELLI
Press B, Left Trigger, B, White, Left, A, Right Trigger, Left Trigger, A, A.

BLOODRING BANGER
Press Up, Right, Right, Left Trigger, Right, Up, X, White.

BLOODRING BANGER
Press Down, Right Trigger, B, White, White, A, Right Trigger, Left Trigger, Left, Left.

CADDY
Press B, Left Trigger, Up, Right Trigger, White, A, Right Trigger, Left Trigger, B, A.

HOTRING RACER 1
Press Black, Left Trigger, B, Right, Left Trigger, Right Trigger, Right, Up, B, Black.

HOTRING RACER 2
Press Right Trigger, B, Black, Right, Left Trigger, White, A, A, X, Right Trigger.

LOVE FIST LIMO
Press Black, Up, White, Left, Left, Right Trigger, Left Trigger, B, Right.

RHINO TANK
Press B, B, Left Trigger, B (x3), Left Trigger, White, Right Trigger, Y, B, Y.

ROMERO'S HEARSE
Press Down, Black, Down, Right Trigger, White, Left, Right Trigger, Left Trigger, Left, Right.

SABRE TURBO
Press Right, White, Down, White, White, A, Right Trigger, Left Trigger, B, Left.

TRASHMASTER
Press B, Right Trigger, B, Right Trigger, Left, Left, Right Trigger, Left Trigger, B, Right.

GRAND THEFT AUTO: SAN ANDREAS
During gameplay, enter the following cheats:

FULL HEALTH, FULL ARMOR, & $250,000
Press Right Trigger, Black, Left Trigger, A, Left , Down, Right, Up, Left, Down, Right, Up.

INFINITE HEALTH
Press Down, A, Right, Left, Right, Right Trigger, Right, Down, Up, Y.

INFINITE AMMO
Press Left Trigger, Right Trigger, X, Right Trigger, Left, Black, Right Trigger, Left, X, Down, Left Trigger, Left Trigger.

INFINITE LUNG CAPACITY
Press Down, Left, Left Trigger, Down, Down, Black, Down, White, Down.

MAX RESPECT
Press Left Trigger, Right Trigger, Y, Down, Black, A, Left Trigger, Up, White, White, Left Trigger, Left Trigger.

MAX SEX APPEAL
Press B, Y, Y, Up, B, Right Trigger, White, Up, Y, Left Trigger, Left Trigger, Left Trigger

MAX VEHICLE STATS
Press X, White, A, Right Trigger, White, White, Left, Right Trigger, Right, Left Trigger, Left Trigger, Left Trigger.

0 FAT AND 0 MUSCLE
Press Y, Up, Up, Left, Right, X, B, Right.

MAXIMUM MUSCLES
Press Y, Up, Up, Left, Right, X, B, Left.

MAXIMUM FAT
Press Y, Up, Up, Left, Right, X, B, Down.

BIG JUMPS
Press Up, Up, Y, Y, Up, Up, Left, Right, X, Black, Black.

BIG BUNNY HOPS ON BMX
Press Y, X, B, B, X, B, B, Left Trigger, White, White, Right Trigger, Black

SUICIDE
Press Right, White, Down, Right Trigger, Left, Left, Right Trigger, Left Trigger, White, Left Trigger.

MIDNIGHT
Press X, Left Trigger, Right Trigger, Right, A, Up, Left Trigger, Left, Left.

FASTER GAMEPLAY
Press Y, Up, Right, Down, White, Left Trigger, X.

SLOWER GAMEPLAY
Press Y, Up, Right, Down, X, Black, Right Trigger.

FASTER TIME
Press B, B, Left Trigger, X, Left Trigger, X, X, X, Left Trigger, Y, B, Y.

JUNK CARS
Press White, Right, Left Trigger, Up, A, Left Trigger, White, Black, Right Trigger, Left Trigger, Left Trigger, Left Trigger.

FARM VEHICLES
Press Left Trigger, Left Trigger, Right Trigger, Right Trigger White, Left Trigger, Black, Down, Left, Up.

BLACK CARS
Press B, White, Up, Right Trigger, Left, A, Right Trigger, Left Trigger, Left, B.

PINK CARS
Press B, Left Trigger, Down, White, Left, A, Right Trigger, Left Trigger, Right, B.

FAST CARS
Press Up, Left Trigger, Right Trigger, Up, Right, Up, A, White, A, Left Trigger.

NITROUS FOR ALL CARS
Press Left, Y, Right Trigger, Left Trigger, Up, X, Y, Down, B, White, Left Trigger, Left Trigger.

NITROUS FOR TAXIS & HOP
Press Up, A, Y, A, Y, A, X, Black, Right.

INVISIBLE VEHICLES
Press Y, Left Trigger, Y, Black, X, Left Trigger, Left Trigger.

INVINCIBLE VEHICLE
Press Left Trigger, White, White, Up, Down, Down, Up, Right Trigger, Black, Black.

DRIVE-BY WHILE DRIVING
Press Up, Up, X, White, Right, A, Right Trigger, Down, Black, B.

GREEN STOPLIGHTS
Press Right, Right Trigger, Up, White, White, Left, Right Trigger, Left Trigger, Right Trigger, Right Trigger.

AGGRESSIVE DRIVERS
Press Right, Black, Up, Up, Black, B, X, Black, Left Trigger, Right, Down, Left Trigger.

AGGRESSIVE TRAFFIC
Press Black, B, Right Trigger, White, Left, Right Trigger, Left Trigger, Black, White.

LESS TRAFFIC
Press A, Down, Up, Black, Down, Y, Left Trigger, Y, Left.

FASTER CARS
Press Right, Right Trigger, Up, White, White, Left, Right Trigger, Left Trigger, Right Trigger, Right Trigger.

BETTER HANDLING CARS
Press Y, Right Trigger, Right Trigger, Left, Right Trigger, Left Trigger, Black, Left Trigger.

FLOATING CARS
Press Right, Black, B, Right Trigger, White, X, Right Trigger, Black.

FLYING CARS
Press X, Down, White, Up, Left Trigger, B, Up, A, Left.

EXPLODING CARS
Press Black, White, Right Trigger, Left Trigger, White, Black, X, Y, B, Y, White, Left Trigger.

FLYING BOATS
Press Black, B, Up, Left Trigger, Right, Right Trigger, Right, Up, X, Y.

PEDESTRIANS ATTACK
Press Down, Up, Up, Up, A, Black, Right Trigger, White, White.

PEDESTRIANS ATTACK WITH GUNS
Press A, Left Trigger, Up, X, Down, A, White, Y, Down, Right Trigger, Left Trigger, Left Trigger.

PEDESTRIANS ATTACK EACH OTHER
Press Down, Left, Up, Left, A, Black, Right Trigger, White, Left Trigger.

PEDESTRIANS CARRY WEAPONS
Press Black, Right Trigger, A, Y, A, Y, Up, Down.

ELVIS IS EVERYWHERE
Press Left Trigger, B, Y, Left Trigger, Left Trigger, X, White, Up, Down, Left.

ATTRACT LADIES OF THE NIGHT
Press X, Right, X, X, White, A, Y, A, Y.

LADIES OF THE NIGHT PAY YOU
Press Right, White, White, Down, White, Up, Up, White, Black.

MULTIPLE UNLOCKABLES
When this code is entered, CJ turns into a Clown, civilians appear in fast food apparel and as clowns, there are BF Injections, HotDogs and so on. Press Y, Y, Left Trigger, X, X, B, X, Down, B.

PEOPLE IN SWIMSUITS
Press Up, Up, Down, Down, X, B, Left Trigger, Right Trigger, Y, Down.

GANGS
Press White, Up, Right Trigger, Right Trigger, Left, Right Trigger, Right Trigger, Black, Right, Down.

DECREASE WANTED LEVEL
Press Right Trigger, Right Trigger, B, Black, Up, Down, Up, Down, Up, Down.

INCREASE WANTED LEVEL
Press Right Trigger, Right Trigger, B, Black, Right, Left, Right, Left, Right, Left.

CLEAR WEATHER
Press Black, A, Left Trigger, Left Trigger, White, White, White, X.

NIGHT
Press Black, A, Left Trigger, Left Trigger, White, White, White, Y.

SUNNY WEATHER
Press Black, A, Left Trigger, Left Trigger, White, White, White, Down.

ORANGE SKY
Press Left, Left, White, Right Trigger, Right, X, X, Left Trigger, White, A.

FOGGY WEATHER
Press Black, A, Left Trigger, Left Trigger, White, White, White, A.

CLOUDY WEATHER
Press White, Down, Down, Left, X, Left, Black, X, A, Right Trigger, Left Trigger, Left Trigger.

OVERCAST
Press Black, A, Left Trigger, Left Trigger, White, White, White, X.

SAND STORM
Press Up, Down, Left Trigger, Left Trigger, White, White, Left Trigger, White, Right Trigger, Black.

RAINY WEATHER
Press Black, A, Left Trigger, Left Trigger, White, White, White, B.

HITMAN RANK
Press Down, X, A, Left, Right Trigger, Black, Left, Down, Down, Left Trigger, Left Trigger, Left Trigger.

WEAPONS SET 1
Press Right Trigger, Black, Left Trigger, Black, Left, Down, Right, Up, Left, Down, Right, Up.

WEAPONS SET 2
Press Right Trigger, Black, Left Trigger, Black, Left, Down, Right, Up, Left, Down, Down, Left.

WEAPONS SET 3
Press Right Trigger, Black, Left Trigger, Black, Left, Down, Right, Up, Left , Down, Down, Down.

PARACHUTE
Press Left, Right, Left Trigger, White, Right Trigger, Black, Black, Up, Down, Right, Left Trigger.

JETPACK
Press Left, Right, Left Trigger, White, Right Trigger, Black, Up, Down, Left, Right.

BLOODRING BANGER
Press Down, Right Trigger, B, White, White, A, Right Trigger, Left Trigger, Left, Left.

CADDY
Press B, Left Trigger, Up, Right Trigger, White, A, Right Trigger, Left Trigger, B, A.

DOZER
Press Black, Left Trigger, Left Trigger, Right, Right, Up, Up, A, Left Trigger, Left.

HOTRING RACER 1
Press Right Trigger, B, Black, Right, Left Trigger, White, A, A, X, Right Trigger.

HOTRING RACER 2
Press Black, Left Trigger, B, Right, Left Trigger, Right Trigger, Right, Up, B, Black.

HUNTER
Press B, A, Left Trigger, B, B, Left Trigger, B, Right Trigger, Black, White, Left Trigger, Left Trigger.

HYDRA
Press Y, Y, X, B, A, Left Trigger, Left Trigger, Down, Up.

MONSTER
Press Right, Up, Right Trigger, Right Trigger, Right Trigger, Down, Y, Y, A, B, Left Trigger, Left Trigger.

QUADBIKE
Press Left, Left, Down, Down, Up, Up, X, B, Y, Right Trigger, Black.

RANCHER
Press Up, Right, Right, Left Trigger, Right, Up, X, White.

RHINO
Press B, B, Left Trigger, B, B, B, Left Trigger, White, Right Trigger, Y, B, Y.

ROMERO
Press Down, Black, Down, Right Trigger, White, Left, Right Trigger, Left Trigger, Left, Right.

STRETCH
Press Black, Up, White, Left, Left, Right Trigger, Left Trigger, B, Right.

STUNTPLANE
Press B, Up, Left Trigger, White, Down, Right Trigger, Left Trigger, Left Trigger, Left, Left, A, Y.

TANKER
Press Right Trigger, Up, Left, Right, Black, Up, Right, X, Right, White, Left Trigger, Left Trigger.

TRASHMASTER
Press B, Right Trigger, B, Right Trigger, Left, Left, Right Trigger, Left Trigger, B, Right.

VORTEX
Press Y, Y, X, B, A, Left Trigger, White, Down, Down.

THE INCREDIBLE HULK: ULTIMATE DESTRUCTION

You must first collect a specific comic in the game to activate each code. After collecting the appropriate comic, you can enter the following. If you don't have the comic and enter the code, you get the following message: "That code cannot be activated…yet". You can access the cheats on the Code Input screen.

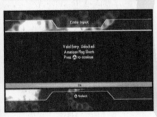

UNLOCKED: CABS GALORE
Select Code Input from the Extras menu and enter CABBIES.

UNLOCKED: GORILLA INVASION
Select Code Input from the Extras menu and enter KINGKNG.

UNLOCKED: MASS TRANSIT
Select Code Input from the Extras menu and enter TRANSIT.

UNLOCKED: 5000 SMASH POINTS
Select Code Input from the Extras menu and enter SMASH5.

UNLOCKED: 10000 SMASH POINTS
Select Code Input from the Extras menu and enter SMASH10.

UNLOCKED: 15000 SMASH POINTS
Select Code Input from the Extras menu and enter SMASH15.

UNLOCKED: AMERICAN FLAG SHORTS
Select Code Input from the Extras menu and enter AMERICA.

UNLOCKED: CANADIAN FLAG SHORTS
Select Code Input from the Extras menu and enter OCANADA.

UNLOCKED: FRENCH FLAG SHORTS
Select Code Input from the Extras menu and enter Drapeau.

UNLOCKED: GERMAN FLAG SHORTS
Select Code Input from the Extras menu and enter DEUTSCH.

UNLOCKED: ITALIAN FLAG SHORTS
Select Code Input from the Extras menu and enter MUTANDA.

UNLOCKED: JAPANESE FLAG SHORTS
Select Code Input from the Extras menu and enter FURAGGU.

UNLOCKED: SPANISH FLAG SHORTS
Select Code Input from the Extras menu and enter BANDERA.

UNLOCKED: UK FLAG SHORTS
Select Code Input from the Extras menu and enter FSHNCHP.

UNLOCKED: COW MISSILES
Select Code Input from the Extras menu and enter CHZGUN.

UNLOCKED: DOUBLE HULK'S DAMAGE
Select Code Input from the Extras menu and enter DESTROY.

UNLOCKED: DOUBLE POWER COLLECTABLES
Select Code Input from the Extras menu and enter BRINGIT.

UNLOCKED: BLACK AND WHITE
Select Code Input from the Extras menu and enter RETRO.

UNLOCKED: SEPIA
Select Code Input from the Extras menu and enter HISTORY.

UNLOCKED: ABOMINATION
Select Code Input from the Extras menu and enter VILLAIN.

UNLOCKED: GRAY HULK
Select Code Input from the Extras menu and enter CLASSIC.

UNLOCKED: JOE FIXIT SKIN
Select Code Input from the Extras menu and enter SUITFIT.

UNLOCKED: WILD TRAFFIC
Select Code Input from the Extras menu and enter FROGGIE.

UNLOCKED: LOW GRAVITY
Select Code Input from the Extras menu and enter PILLOWS.

JAMES BOND 007: EVERYTHING OR NOTHING

CHEATS

To access the following codes, you must first earn the given number of Platinum. Upon doing so, pause the game and enter the corresponding code.

EFFECT	PLATINUM	CODE
Golden Gun	1	B, Y, A, B, Y
Improved Traction	3	B, A, A, X, Y
Improved Battery	5	B, X, X, A, B
Double Ammunition	7	B, B, A, B, Y
Double Damage	9	B, Y, Y, X, B
Full Ammunition	11	B, B, Y, X, X
Cloak	13	B, Y, A, Y, X
Full Battery	15	B, Y, Y, A, B
All Weapons	17	B, Y, A, A, B
Unlimited Battery	19	B, X, B, X, Y
Unlimited Ammo	23	B, A, X, A, Y
Slow Motion Driving	25	B, Y, A, Y, A
Platinum Gun	27	B, X, X, B, A

LEGO STAR WARS II: THE ORIGINAL TRILOGY

BEACH TROOPER
At Mos Eisley Canteena, select Enter Code and enter UCK868. You still need to select Characters and purchase this character for 20,000 studs.

BEN KENOBI (GHOST)
At Mos Eisley Canteena, select Enter Code and enter BEN917. You still need to select Characters and purchase this character for 1,100,000 studs.

BESPIN GUARD
At Mos Eisley Canteena, select Enter Code and enter VHY832. You still need to select Characters and purchase this character for 15,000 studs.

BIB FORTUNA
At Mos Eisley Canteena, select Enter Code and enter WTY721. You still need to select Characters and purchase this character for 16,000 studs.

BOBA FETT

At Mos Eisley Canteena, select Enter Code and enter HLP221. You still need to select Characters and purchase this character for 175,000 studs.

DEATH STAR TROOPER

At Mos Eisley Canteena, select Enter Code and enter BNC332. You still need to select Characters and purchase this character for 19,000 studs.

EWOK

At Mos Eisley Canteena, select Enter Code and enter TTT289. You still need to select Characters and purchase this character for 34,000 studs.

GAMORREAN GUARD

At Mos Eisley Canteena, select Enter Code and enter YZF999. You still need to select Characters and purchase this character for 40,000 studs.

GONK DROID

At Mos Eisley Canteena, select Enter Code and enter NFX582. You still need to select Characters and purchase this character for 1,550 studs.

GRAND MOFF TARKIN

At Mos Eisley Canteena, select Enter Code and enter SMG219. You still need to select Characters and purchase this character for 38,000 studs.

GREEDO

At Mos Eisley Canteena, select Enter Code and enter NAH118. You still need to select Characters and purchase this character for 60,000 studs.

HAN SOLO (HOOD)

At Mos Eisley Canteena, select Enter Code and enter YWM840. You still need to select Characters and purchase this character for 20,000 studs.

IG-88

At Mos Eisley Canteena, select Enter Code and enter NXL973. You still need to select Characters and purchase this character for 30,000 studs.

IMPERIAL GUARD

At Mos Eisley Canteena, select Enter Code and enter MMM111. You still need to select Characters and purchase this character for 45,000 studs.

IMPERIAL OFFICER

At Mos Eisley Canteena, select Enter Code and enter BBV889. You still need to select Characters and purchase this character for 28,000 studs.

IMPERIAL SHUTTLE PILOT

At Mos Eisley Canteena, select Enter Code and enter VAP664. You still need to select Characters and purchase this character for 29,000 studs.

IMPERIAL SPY

At Mos Eisley Canteena, select Enter Code and enter CVT125. You still need to select Characters and purchase this character for 13,500 studs.

JAWA

At Mos Eisley Canteena, select Enter Code and enter JAW499. You still need to select Characters and purchase this character for 24,000 studs.

LOBOT

At Mos Eisley Canteena, select Enter Code and enter UUB319. You still need to select Characters and purchase this character for 11,000 studs.

PALACE GUARD

At Mos Eisley Canteena, select Enter Code and enter SGE549. You still need to select Characters and purchase this character for 14,000 studs.

REBEL PILOT

At Mos Eisley Canteena, select Enter Code and enter CYG336. You still need to select Characters and purchase this character for 15,000 studs.

REBEL TROOPER (HOTH)

At Mos Eisley Canteena, select Enter Code and enter EKU849. You still need to select Characters and purchase this character for 16,000 studs.

SANDTROOPER

At Mos Eisley Canteena, select Enter Code and enter YDV451. You still need to select Characters and purchase this character for 14,000 studs.

SKIFF GUARD

At Mos Eisley Canteena, select Enter Code and enter GBU888. You still need to select Characters and purchase this character for 12,000 studs.

SNOWTROOPER

At Mos Eisley Canteena, select Enter Code and enter NYU989. You still need to select Characters and purchase this character for 16,000 studs.

STROMTROOPER

At Mos Eisley Canteena, select Enter Code and enter PTR345. You still need to select Characters and purchase this character for 10,000 studs.

THE EMPEROR

At Mos Eisley Canteena, select Enter Code and enter HHY382. You still need to select Characters and purchase this character for 275,000 studs.

TIE FIGHTER

At Mos Eisley Canteena, select Enter Code and enter HDY739. You still need to select Characters and purchase this character for 60,000 studs.

TIE FIGHTER PILOT

At Mos Eisley Canteena, select Enter Code and enter NNZ316. You still need to select Characters and purchase this character for 21,000 studs.

TIE INTERCEPTOR

At Mos Eisley Canteena, select Enter Code and enter QYA828. You still need to select Characters and purchase this character for 40,000 studs.

TUSKEN RAIDER

At Mos Eisley Canteena, select Enter Code and enter PEJ821. You still need to select Characters and purchase this character for 23,000 studs.

UGNAUGHT

At Mos Eisley Canteena, select Enter Code and enter UGN694. You still need to select Characters and purchase this character for 36,000 studs.

MADDEN NFL 07

MADDEN CARDS

Select Madden Cards from My Madden. Then select Madden Codes and enter the following:

CARD	PASSWORD
#199 Gold Lame Duck Cheat	5LAWO0
#200 Gold Mistake Free Cheat	XL7SP1
#210 Gold QB on Target Cheat	WROA0R
#220 Super Bowl XLI Gold	RLA9R7
#221 Super Bowl XLII Gold	WRLUF8
#222 Super Bowl XLIII Gold	NIEV4A
#223 Super Bowl XLIV Gold	M5AB7L
#224 Aloha Stadium Gold	YI8P8U
#225 1958 Colts Gold	B57QLU
#226 1966 Packers Gold	1PL1FL
#227 1968 Jets Gold	MIE6WO
#228 1970 Browns Gold	CL2TOE
#229 1972 Dolphins Gold	NOEB7U
#230 1974 Steelers Gold	YO0FLA
#231 1976 Raiders Gold	MOA11I
#232 1977 Broncos Gold	C8UM7U
#233 1978 Dolphins Gold	VIU0O7
#234 1980 Raiders Gold	NLAPH3
#235 1981 Chargers Gold	COAGI4
#236 1982 Redskins Gold	WL8BRI
#237 1983 Raiders Gold	H0EW71

XBOX

CARD	PASSWORD
#238 1984 Dolphins Gold	M1AM1E
#239 1985 Bears Gold	QOETO8
#240 1986 Giants Gold	ZI8S2L
#241 1988 49ers Gold	SP2A8H
#242 1990 Eagles Gold	2L4TRO
#243 1991 Lions Gold	J1ETRI
#244 1992 Cowboys Gold	W9UVI9
#245 1993 Bills Gold	DLA3I7
#246 1994 49ers Gold	DR7EST
#247 1996 Packers Gold	F8LUST
#248 1998 Broncos Gold	FIES95
#249 1999 Rams Gold	S9OUSW
#250 Bears Pump Up the Crowd	B1OUPH
#251 Bengals Cheerleader	DRL2SW
#252 Bills Cheerleader	1PLUYO
#253 Broncos Cheerleader	3ROUJO
#254 Browns Pump Up the Crowd	T1UTOA
#255 Buccaneers Cheerleader	S9EWRI
#256 Cardinals Cheerleader	57IEPI
#257 Chargers Cheerleader	F7UHL8
#258 Chiefs Cheerleader	PRI5SL
#259 Colts Cheerleader	1R5AMI
#260 Cowboys Cheerleader	Z2ACHL
#261 Dolphins Cheerleader	C5AHLE
#262 Eagles Cheerleader	PO7DRO
#263 Falcons Cheerleader	37USPO
#264 49ers Cheerleader	KL0CRL
#265 Giants Pump Up the Crowd	C4USPI
#266 Jaguars Cheerleader	MIEH7E
#267 Jets Pump Up the Crowd	C0LUXI
#268 Lions Pump Up the Crowd	3LABLU
#269 Packers Pump Up the Crowd	4HO7VO
#270 Panthers Cheerleader	F2IASP
#282 All AFC Team Gold	PRO9PH
#283 All NFC Team Gold	RLATH7

MAJOR LEAGUE BASEBALL 2K7

MICKEY MANTLE ON THE FREE AGENTS LIST
Select Enter Cheat Code from the My 2K7 menu and enter themick.

ALL CHEATS
Select Enter Cheat Code from the My 2K7 menu and enter Black Sox.

ALL EXTRAS
Select Enter Cheat Code from the My 2K7 menu and enter Game On.

UNLOCK EVERYTHING
Select Enter Cheat Code from the My 2K7 menu and enter Derek Jeter. This does not unlock the Topps cheats.

MIGHTY MICK CHEAT
Select Enter Cheat Code from the My 2K7 menu and enter mightymick.

TRIPLE CROWN CHEAT
Select Enter Cheat Code from the My 2K7 menu and enter triplecrown.

PINCH HIT MICK CHEAT
Select Enter Cheat Code from the My 2K7 menu and enter phmantle.

BIG BLAST CHEAT
Select Enter Cheat Code from the My 2K7 menu Rand enter m4murder.

MANHUNT

CHEAT CODES
The following codes cannot be used until they are unlocked. To unlock them, you must earn a five-star rating (which is only possible on Hardcore mode) in each pair of two consecutive scenes. After unlocking the codes, enter them at the Title screen.

EFFECT	CODE
Runner	White, White, L, White, Left, Right, Left, Right (Scenes 01 and 02)
Silence	R, L, White, L, Right, Left (x3) (Scenes 03 and 04)
Regenerate	White, Right, B, White, Black, Down, B, Left (Scenes 05 and 06)
Helium Hunters	R, R, Y, B, X, Black, L, Down (Scenes 07 and 08)
Fully Equipped	R, White, L, Black, Down, Up, Left, Up (Scenes 09 and 10)
Super Punch	L, Y (x3), B (x3), R (Scenes 11 and 12)
Rabbit Skin	Left, R, R, Y, R, R, X, L (Scenes 13 and 14)
Monkey Skin	X, X, White, Down, Y, X, B, Down (Scenes 15 and 16)
Invisibility	X (x3), Down, X, Down, B, Up (Scenes 17 and 18)
Piggsy Skin	Up, Down, Left, Left, R, White, L, L (Scenes 19 and 20)

GOD MODE
After defeating the game on Fetish mode, press Down, Down, B, Up, X, Y, X, White, Up, Up, L, Y.

MARC ECKO'S GETTING UP: CONTENTS UNDER PRESSURE

ALL LEVELS
Select Codes from the Options menu and enter IPULATOR.

INFINITE HEALTH
Select Codes from the Options menu and enter MARCUSECKOS.

MAX HEALTH
Select Codes from the Options menu and enter BABYLONTRUST.

INFINITE SKILLS
Select Codes from the Options menu and enter FLIPTHESCRIPT.

MAX SKILLS
Select Codes from the Options menu and enter VANCEDALLISTER.

ALL COMBAT UPGRADES
Select Codes from the Options menu and enter DOGTAGS.

ALL CHARACTERS IN VERSUS MODE
Select Codes from the Options menu and enter STATEYOURNAME.

ALL VERSUS ARENAS
Select Codes from the Options menu and enter WORKBITCH.

ALL ART
Select Codes from the Options menu and enter SIRULLY.

ALL BLACK BOOK
Select Codes from the Options menu and enter SHARDSOFGLASS.

ALL IPOD
Select Codes from the Options menu and enter GRANDMACELIA.

ALL LEGENDS
Select Codes from the Options menu and enter NINESIX.

ALL MOVIES
Select Codes from the Options menu and enter DEXTERCROWLEY.

NARC

ALL DRUGS
During a game, press R, L, R, L, R, L, Left Thumbstick.

ALL WEAPONS
During a game, press R, L, R, L, R, L, Right Thumbstick.

INVINCIBILITY
During a game, press R, L, R, L, R, L, A.

XBOX®

SHOW HIDDEN STASHES

During a game, press R, L, R, L, R, L, Left.

UNLIMITED AMMO FOR CURRENT WEAPON

During a game, press R, L, R, L, R, L, Down.

THE REFINERY

During a game, press R, L, R, L, R, L, X.

NASCAR 07

$10,000,000

In Fight to the Top mode, enter your name as GiveMe More.

10,000,000 FANS

In Fight to the Top mode, enter your name as AllBow ToMe.

PRESTIGE LEVEL 10 WITH 2,000,000 POINTS

In Fight to the Top mode, enter your name as Outta MyWay.

100% TEAM PRESTIGE

In Fight to the Top mode, enter your name as MoMoney BlingBling.

ALL CHASE PLATES

In Fight to the Top mode, enter your name as ItsAll ForMe.

OLD SPICE TRACKS AND CARS

In Fight to the Top mode, enter your name as KeepCool SmellGreat.

WALMART TRACK AND CARS

In Fight to the Top mode, enter your name as Walmart EveryDay.

NBA 2K7

MAX DURABILITY

Select Codes from the Features menu and enter ironman.

UNLIMITED STAMINA

Select Codes from the Features menu and enter norest.

+10 DEFENSIVE AWARENESS

Select Codes from the Features menu and enter getstops.

+10 OFFENSIVE AWARENESS

Select Codes from the Features menu and enter inthezone.

TOPPS 2K SPORTS ALL-STARS

Select Codes from the Features menu and enter topps2ksports.

ABA BALL

Select Codes from the Features menu and enter payrespect.

NBA LIVE 07

ADIDAS ARTILLERY II BLACK & THE RBK ANSWER 9 VIDEO

Select NBA Codes from My NBA Live and enter 99B6356HAN.

ADIDAS ARTILLERY II

Select NBA Codes and enter NTGNFUE87H.

ADIDAS BTB LOW AND THE MESSAGE FROM ALLEN IVERSON VIDEO

Select NBA Codes and enter 7FB3KS9JQ0.

ADIDAS C-BILLUPS

Select NBA Codes and enter BV6877HB9N.

ADIDAS C-BILLUPS BLACK
Select NBA Codes and enter
85NVLDMWS5.

ADIDAS CAMPUS LT
Select NBA Codes and enter
CLT2983NC8.

ADIDAS CRAZY 8
Select NBA Codes and enter
CC98KKL814.

ADIDAS EQUIPMENT BBALL
Select NBA Codes and enter
22OIUJKMDR.

ADIDAS GARNETT BOUNCE
Select NBA Codes and enter
HYIOUHCAAN.

ADIDAS GARNETT BOUNCE BLACK
Select NBA Codes and enter
KDZ2MQL17W.

ADIDAS GIL-ZERO
Select NBA Codes and enter
23DN1PPOG4.

ADIDAS GIL-ZERO BLACK
Select NBA Codes and enter
QQQ3JCUYQ7.

ADIDAS GIL-ZERO MID
Select NBA Codes and enter
1GSJC8JWRL.

ADIDAS GIL-ZERO MID BLACK
Select NBA Codes and enter
369V6RVU3G.

ADIDAS STEALTH
Select NBA Codes and enter
FE454DFJCC.

ADIDAS T-MAC 6
Select NBA Codes and enter
MCJK843NNC.

ADIDAS T-MAC 6 WHITE
Select NBA Codes and enter
84GF7EJG8V.

AIR JORDAN V
Select NBA Codes and enter
PNBBX1EVT5.

AIR JORDAN V
Select NBA Codes and enter
VIR13PC451.

AIR JORDAN V
Select NBA Codes and enter
IB7G8NN91Z.

JORDAN MELO M3
Select NBA Codes and enter
JUL38TC485.

**CHARLOTTE BOBCATS 2006-07
ALTERNATE JERSEY**
Select NBA Codes and enter
WEDX671H7S.

UTAH JAZZ 2006-07 ALTERNATE JERSEY
Select NBA Codes and enter
VCBI89FK83.

**NEW JERSEY NETS 2006-07 ALTERNATE
JERSEY**
Select NBA Codes and enter
D4SAA98U5H.

**WASHINGTON WIZARDS 2006-07
ALTERNATE JERSEY**
Select NBA Codes and enter
QV93NLKXQC.

**EASTERN ALL-STARS 2006-07 ROAD
JERSEY**
Select NBA Codes and enter
WOCNW4KL7L.

**EASTERN ALL-STARS 2006-07 HOME
JERSEY**
Select NBA Codes and enter
5654ND43N6.

**WESTERN ALL-STARS 2006-07 ROAD
JERSEY**
Select NBA Codes and enter
XX93BVL20U.

**WESTERN ALL-STARS 2006-07 HOME
JERSEY**
Select NBA Codes and enter
993NSKL199.

NCAA FOOTBALL 07

PENNANT CODES
Select Pennant Collection from My NCAA, then press Select to enter the
following codes.

CODE NAME	ENTER		CODE NAME	ENTER
#16 Baylor	Sic Em		#207 Extra Credit	Touchdown
#16 Nike Speed TD	Light Speed		#208 Helium	In The Zone
#63 Illinois	Oskee Wow		#209 Hurricane	Turnover
#160 Texas Tech	Fight		#210 Instant Freeplay	Impact
#200 First and Fifteen	Thanks		#211 Jumbalaya	Heisman
#201 Blink	For		#212 Molasses	Game Time
#202 Boing	Registering		#213 Nike Free	Break Free
#204 Butter Fingers	With EA		#214 Nike Magnigrip	Hand Picked
#205 Crossed the Line	Tiburon		#215 Nike Pro	No Sweat
#206 Cuffed	EA Sports		#219 QB Dud	Elite 11
			#221 Steel Toe	Gridiron

XBOX

CODE NAME	ENTER		CODE NAME	ENTER
#222 Stiffed	NCAA		#293 All-Oklahoma	Boomer
#223 Super Dive	Upset		#294 All-Oklahoma State	Go Pokes
#224 Take Your Time	Football		#295 All-Oregon	Quack Attack
#225 Thread & Needle	06		#296 All-Penn State	We Are
#226 Tough As Nails	Offense		#297 All-Pittsburgh	Lets Go Pitt
#227 Trip	Defense		#298 All-Purdue	Boiler Up
#228 What a Hit	Blitz		#299 All-Syracuse	Orange Crush
#229 Kicker Hex	Sideline		#300 All-Tennessee	Big Orange
#273 2004 All-Americans	Fumble		#301 All-Texas	Hook Em
#274 All-Alabama	Roll Tide		#302 All-Texas A&M	Gig Em
#276 All-Arkansas	Woopigsooie		#303 All-UCLA	MIGHTY
#277 All-Auburn	War Eagle		#304 All-USC	Fight On
#278 All-Clemson	Death Valley		#305 All-Virginia	Wahoos
#279 All-Colorado	Glory		#306 All-Virginia Tech	Tech Triumph
#280 All-Florida	Great To Be		#307 All-Washington	Bow Down
#281 All-FSU	Uprising		#308 All-Wisconsin	U Rah Rah
#282 All-Georgia	Hunker Down		#311 Ark Mascot	Bear Down
#283 All-Iowa	On Iowa		#329 GT Mascot	RamblinWreck
#284 All-Kansas State	Victory		#333 ISU Mascot	Red And Gold
#285 All-LSU	Geaux Tigers		#335 KU Mascot	Rock Chalk
#286 All-Miami	Raising Cane		#341 Minn Mascot	Rah Rah Rah
#287 All-Michigan	Go Blue		#344 Mizzou Mascot	Mizzou Rah
#288 All-Mississippi State	Hail State		#346 MSU Mascot	Go Green
#289 All-Nebraska	Go Big Red		#349 NCSU Mascot	Go Pack
#290 All-North Carolina	Rah Rah		#352 NU Mascot	Go Cats
#291 All-Notre Dame	Golden Domer		#360 S Car Mascot	Go Carolina
#292 All-Ohio State	Killer Nuts		#371 UK Mascot	On On UK
			#382 Wake Forest	Go Deacs Go
			#385 WSU Mascot	All Hail
			#386 WVU Mascot	Hail WV

NEED FOR SPEED UNDERGROUND 2

ALL CIRCUIT TRACKS
At the Main menu, press Down, Right Trigger, Right Trigger, Right Trigger, Black, Black, Black, X.

BEST BUY VINYL
At the Main menu, press Up, Down, Up, Down, Down, Up, Right, Left.

BURGER KING VINYL
At the Main menu, press Up, Up, Up, Up, Down, Up, Up, Left.

H2 CAPONE
At the Main menu, press Up, Left, Up, Up, Down, Left, Down, Left.

NISSIAN SKYLINE
At the Main menu, press Down, Down, Left Trigger, White, Left Trigger, White, Left Trigger, Down.

LEVEL 1 PERFORMANCE PARTS
At the Main menu, press Left Trigger, Right Trigger, Left Trigger, Right Trigger, Left, Left, Right, Up.

LEVEL 2 PERFORMANCE PARTS
At the Main menu, press Right Trigger, Right Trigger, Left Trigger, Right Trigger, Left, Right, Up, Down.

LEVEL 1 VISUAL PARTS
At the Main menu, press Right Trigger, Right Trigger, Up, Down, Left Trigger, Left Trigger, Up, Down.

LEVEL 2 VISUAL PARTS
At the Main menu, press Left Trigger, Right Trigger, Up, Down, Left Trigger, Up, Up, Down.

NFL HEAD COACH

CLOWN
Name your coach Red Nose.

JOHN MADDEN
Name your coach John Madden.

SANTA CLAUS
Name your coach Merry Christmas.

SUPER BOWL ALWAYS AT HOMETOWN
Name your coach Hometown Hero.

ORIGINAL BLUE NINJA COSTUME
Highlight New Game and press Left
Trigger + Right Trigger, then press
the A button.

OUTRUN 2

Select OutRun Challenge and go to the Gallery screen. Choose Enter Code
and input the following.

ALL CARS
Enter DREAMING.

ALL MISSION STAGES
Enter THEJOURNEY.

BONUS TRACKS
Enter TIMELESS.

REVERSE TRACKS
Enter DESREVER.

ALL MUSIC
Enter RADIOSEGA.

ORIGINAL OUTRUN
Enter NINETEEN86.

ALL CARDS
Enter BIRTHDAY.

OVER THE HEDGE

COMPLETE LEVELS
Pause the game, hold Left Trigger
+ Right Trigger and press Y, B, Y,
B, B, X.

ALL MINIGAMES
Pause the game, hold Left Trigger
+ Right Trigger and press Y, B, Y,
Y, X, X.

ALL MOVES
Pause the game, hold Left Trigger
+ Right Trigger and press Y, B, Y,
X, X, B.

EXTRA DAMAGE
Pause the game, hold Left Trigger
+ Right Trigger and press Y, B, Y,
B, Y, X.

MORE HP FROM FOOD
Pause the game, hold Left Trigger
+ Right Trigger and press Y, B, Y,
B, X, Y.

ALWAYS POWER PROJECTILE
Pause the game, hold Left Trigger
+ Right Trigger and press Y, B, Y,
B, X, B.

BONUS COMIC 14
Pause the game, hold Left Trigger
+ Right Trigger and press Y, B, X,
X, B, Y.

BONUS COMIC 15
Pause the game, hold Left Trigger
+ Right Trigger and press Y, Y, X,
B, X, B.

PAINKILLER: HELL WARS

GOD MODE
During a game, hold White + L and press B.

TOGGLE DEMON MODE
During a game, hold White + L and press X.

ALL AMMO
Select Cheat Codes from the Settings menu and press Down, Up, Down, Y

GOD MODE
Select Cheat Codes from the Settings menu and press Up, Left Trigger, X, Left Trigger.

ALL SINGLE-PLAYER LEVELS
Select Cheat Codes from the Settings menu and press Y, Down, Right Trigger, Down.

LOCATION STATUS
Select Cheat Codes from the Settings menu and press X, Right, Left Trigger, Left.

BEST BUY MULTIPLAYER LEVEL
Select Cheat Codes from the Settings menu and press Left Trigger, Black, White, Right Trigger.

EB MULTIPLAYER LEVEL
Select Cheat Codes from the Settings menu and press White, Y, X, Black.

GAMESTOP MULTIPLAYER LEVEL
Select Cheat Codes from the Settings menu and press Left, Left Trigger, X, Left.

TOYS 'R' US MULTIPLAYER LEVEL
Select Cheat Codes from the Settings menu and press Left, Up, White, Black.

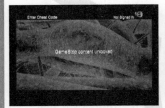 

PRINCE OF PERSIA: THE TWO THRONES

BABY TOY HAMMER WEAPON
Pause the game and press Left, Left, Right, Right, Y, X, X, Y, Up, Down.

CHAINSAW WEAPON
Pause the game and press Up, Up, Down, Down, Left, Right, Left, Right, Y, X, Y, X.

SWORDFISH WEAPON
Pause the game and press Up, Down, Up, Down, Left, Right, Y, X, Y, X.

TELEPHONE OF SORROW WEAPON
Pause the game and press Right, Left, Right, Left, Down, Down, Up, Up, Y, X, Y, Y, X, X.

PSYCHONAUTS

ALL POWERS
During a game, hold Left Trigger + Right Trigger and press B, B, Y, White, Left Thumbstick, Y.

9999 LIVES
During a game, hold Left Trigger + Right Trigger and press Left Thumbstick, White, White, B, A, Right Thumbstick.

9999 AMMO (BLAST, CONFUSION)
During a game, hold Left Trigger + Right Trigger and press Right Thumbstick, A, Left Thumbstick, Left Thumbstick, Y, B.

GLOBAL ITEMS (NO PSI-BALL COLORIZER, NO DREAM FLUFFS)
During a game, hold Left Trigger + Right Trigger and press Right Thumbstick, B, White, White, Left Thumbstick, Y.

ALL POWERS UPGRADED (MAX RANK)
During a game, hold Left Trigger + Right Trigger and press Left Thumbstick, Right Thumbstick, Left Thumbstick, White, B, White.

9999 ARROWHEADS
During a game, hold Left Trigger + Right Trigger and press A, Right Thumbstick, Right Thumbstick, White, Y, X.

INVINCIBILITY
During a game, hold Left Trigger + Right Trigger and press B, White, B, B, Y, Black.

WEIRD TEXT
During a game, hold Left Trigger + Right Trigger and press White, A, click Left Thumbstick, White, White, B.

RESERVOIR DOGS

ALL LEVELS
Select Cheats from the Extras menu and enter Black, White, Black, White, Left Trigger, Right Trigger, Start.

ADRENALINE RUSH-INFINITE ADRENALINE
Select Cheats from the Extras menu and enter A, Left Trigger, Y, A, Left Trigger, A, Start.

BATTERING RAM-INSTANT CRASH
Select Cheats from the Extras menu and enter Black, Black, A, A, Y, White, Start.

BULLETPROOF-INFINITE HEALTH
Select Cheats from the Extras menu and enter Left Trigger, Right Trigger, Y, Y, Right Trigger, Y, Start.

FULLY LOADED-INFINITE AMMO
Select Cheats from the Extras menu and enter White, Black, Y, Black, A, White, Start.

MAGIC BULLET-ONE SHOT KILLS
Select Cheats from the Extras menu and enter Right Trigger, Black, Y, A, Right Trigger, A, Start.

TIME OUT-INFINITE TIMER
Select Cheats from the Extras menu and enter Right Trigger, Right Trigger, White, Y, A, Black, Start.

ART GALLERY
Select Cheats from the Extras menu and enter Y, A, Black, White, Y, A, Start.

MOVIE GALLERY
Select Cheats from the Extras menu and enter Left Trigger, Left Trigger, Y, A, Left Trigger, Right Trigger, Start.

ROBOTS

BIG HEAD FOR RODNEY
Pause the game and press Up, Down, Down, Up, Right, Right, Left, Right.

UNLIMITED HEALTH
Pause the game and press Up, Right, Down, Up, Left, Down, Right, Left.

UNLIMITED SCRAP
Pause the game and press Down, Down, Left, Up, Up, Right, Up, Down.

After entering the following cheats, highlight the cheat and press A to "DO IT."

MAX AMMO
Pause the game, select Cheats and enter AMMO.

REFILL HEALTH
Pause the game, select Cheats and enter MEDIK.

FILL BALLS METER
Pause the game, select Cheats and enter FPATCH.

KILL TONY
Pause the game, select Cheats and enter KILTONY.

DECREASE COP HEAT
Pause the game, select Cheats and enter FLYSTRT.

INCREASE COP HEAT
Pause the game, select Cheats and enter DONUT.

DECREASE GANG HEAT
Pause the game, select Cheats and enter NOBALLS.

INCREASE GANG HEAT
Pause the game, select Cheats and enter GOBALLS.

REPAIR TONY'S VEHICLE
Pause the game, select Cheats and enter TBURGLR.

SPAWN ARIEL MK III
Pause the game, select Cheats and enter OLDFAST.

SPAWN BACINARI
Pause the game, select Cheats and enter 666999.

SPAWN BODOG STAMPEDE
Pause the game, select Cheats and enter BUMMER.

SPAWN BULLDOZER
Pause the game, select Cheats and enter DOZER.

SPAWN ODIN VH88
Pause the game, select Cheats and enter DUMPER.

BLACK SUIT TONY
Pause the game, select Cheats and enter BLACK.

BLUE PINSTRIPE SUIT TONY WITH SHADES
Pause the game, select Cheats and enter BLUESH.

GRAY SUIT TONY
Pause the game, select Cheats and enter GRAY.

GRAY SUIT TONY WITH SHADES
Pause the game, select Cheats and enter GRAYSH.

HAWAIIAN SHIRT TONY
Pause the game, select Cheats and enter HAWAII.

HAWAIIAN SHIRT TONY WITH SHADES
Pause the game, select Cheats and enter HAWAIIG.

SANDY SHIRT TONY
Pause the game, select Cheats and enter SANDY.

SANDY SHIRT TONY WITH SHADES
Pause the game, select Cheats and enter SANDYSH.

WHITE SUIT TONY
Pause the game, select Cheats and enter WHITE.

WHITE SUIT TONY WITH SHADES
Pause the game, select Cheats and enter WHITESH.

CHANGE TIME OF DAY
Pause the game, select Cheats and enter MARTHA.

TOGGLE LIGHTNING
Pause the game, select Cheats and enter SHAZAAM.

TOGGLE RAIN
Pause the game, select Cheats and enter RAINY.

BREAL "THE WORLD IS YOURS" MUSIC TRACK
Pause the game, select Cheats and enter TUNEME.

SKIP CURRENT WEEK IN CAMPAIGN MODE

At the US Map, press Start for the Options. Then select Cheat Menu and press X, Y, X, B, A.

WIN CIVIL WAR IN CAMPAIGN MODE

At the US Map, press Start for the Options. Then select Cheat Menu and press X, B, A, B, Y.

$100,000

At the US Map, press Start for the Options. Then select Cheat Menu and press X, X, A, A, Y.

ARCADIA PLAINS

At the US Map, press Start for the Options. Then select Cheat Menu and press B, X, X, X, A.

ARIZONA TERRITORY

At the US Map, press Start for the Options. Then select Cheat Menu and press B, X, X, A, X.

CAROLINAS

At the US Map, press Start for the Options. Then select Cheat Menu and press B, X, Y, X, A.

CENTRAL CASCADES

At the US Map, press Start for the Options. Then select Cheat Menu and press B, X, X, X, Y.

CENTRAL HEARTLAND

At the US Map, press Start for the Options. Then select Cheat Menu and press B, X, X, B, Y.

CUMBERLANDS

At the US Map, press Start for the Options. Then select Cheat Menu and press B, X, Y, X, Y.

DAKOTAS

At the US Map, press Start for the Options. Then select Cheat Menu and press B, X, X, B, X.

EASTERN SHENANDOAH

At the US Map, press Start for the Options. Then select Cheat Menu and press B, X, Y, Y, B.

FLORIDA

At the US Map, press Start for the Options. Then select Cheat Menu and press B, X, Y, X, B.

GREAT BASIN

At the US Map, press Start for the Options. Then select Cheat Menu and press B, X, X, Y, A.

GREAT LAKES

At the US Map, press Start for the Options. Then select Cheat Menu and press B, X, X, B, A.

GREAT PLAINS

At the US Map, press Start for the Options. Then select Cheat Menu and press B, X, X, B, B.

MISSISSIPPI DELTA

At the US Map, press Start for the Options. Then select Cheat Menu and press B, X, Y, X, X.

NEW MEXICO

At the US Map, press Start for the Options. Then select Cheat Menu and press B, X, X, Y, B.

NEW YORK

At the US Map, press Start for the Options. Then select Cheat Menu and press B, X, Y, Y, Y.

NORTHERN CALIFORNIA

At the US Map, press Start for the Options. Then select Cheat Menu and press B, X, X, Y, X.

NORTHERN CASCADES

At the US Map, press Start for the Options. Then select Cheat Menu and press B, X, X, X, B.

NORTHERN NEW ENGLAND

At the US Map, press Start for the Options. Then select Cheat Menu and press B, X, Y, Y, A.

NORTHERN TEXAS

At the US Map, press Start for the Options. Then select Cheat Menu and press B, X, X, A, A.

OHIO VALLEY

At the US Map, press Start for the Options. Then select Cheat Menu and press B, X, Y, Y, X.

OKLAHOMA GRASSLANDS

At the US Map, press Start for the Options. Then select Cheat Menu and press B, X, A, X, Y.

SOUTHEASTERN CASCADES

At the US Map, press Start for the Options. Then select Cheat Menu and press B, X, X, X, X.

SOUTHERN CALIFORNIA

At the US Map, press Start for the Options. Then select Cheat Menu and press B, X, X, Y, Y.

SOUTHERN TEXAS

At the US Map, press Start for the Options. Then select Cheat Menu and press B, X, X, A, B.

SID MEIER'S PIRATES!

FOOD NEVER DWINDLES
Name your character Sweet Tooth.

INVINCIBLE SHIP
Name your character Bloody Bones Baz.

JEFF BRIGGS AS ABBOTT
Name your character Firaxis.

SNAPPY DRESSER
Name your character Bonus Frag.

BEST SHIP AND FULL CREW
Name your character D.Gackey.

FLEET IS TWICE AS FAST
Name your character Sprinkler.

HIGHEST MORALE
Name your character B.Caudizzle.

DUELING INVINCIBILITY
Name your character Dragon Ma.

SID MEIER AS MYSTERIOUS STRANGER
Name your character Max Remington.

SONIC HEROES

METAL CHARACTERS IN 2-PLAYER
After selecting a level in 2-Player mode, hold A + Y.

SPY VS SPY

ALL CLASSIC MAPS
Enter RETROSPY at the password screen.

ALL STORY MODE LEVELS
Enter ANTONIO at the password screen.

ALL LEVELS FOR SINGLE-PLAYER MODERN MODE
Enter PROHIAS at the password screen.

ALL MULTIPLAYER MAPS
Enter MADMAG at the password screen.

ALL OUTFITS
Enter DISGUISE at the password screen.

ALL WEAPONS
Enter WRKBENCH at the password screen.

INVULNERABILITY
Enter ARMOR at the password screen.

SUPER DAMAGE
Enter BIGGUNZ at the password screen.

PERMANENT FAIRY IN MODERN MODE
Enter FAIRY at the password screen.

NO DROPPED ITEMS WHEN KILLED
Enter NODROP at the password screen.

INVISIBLE HUD
Enter BLINK at the password screen.

ALL MOVIES
Enter SPYFLIX at the password screen.

CONCEPT ART
Enter SPYPICS at the password screen.

SSX ON TOUR

NEW THREADS
Select Cheats from the Extras menu and enter FLYTHREADS.

THE WORLD IS YOURS
Select Cheats from the Extras menu and enter BACKSTAGEPASS.

SHOW TIME (ALL MOVIES)
Select Cheats from the Extras menu and enter THEBIGPICTURE.

BLING BLING (INFINITE CASH)
Select Cheats from the Extras menu and enter LOOTSNOOT.

FULL BOOST, FULL TIME
Select Cheats from the Extras menu and enter ZOOMJUICE.

MONSTERS ARE LOOSE (MONSTER TRICKS)
Select Cheats from the Extras menu and enter JACKALOPESTYLE.

SNOWBALL FIGHT
Select Cheats from the Extras menu and enter LETSPARTY.

FEEL THE POWER (STAT BOOST)
Select Cheats from the Extras menu and enter POWERPLAY.

CHARACTERS ARE LOOSE
Select Cheats from the Extras menu and enter ROADIEROUNDUp.

UNLOCK CONRAD
Select Cheats from the Extras menu and enter BIGPARTYTIME.

UNLOCK MITCH KOOBSKI
Select Cheats from the Extras menu and enter MOREFUNTHANONE.

UNLOCK NIGEL
Select Cheats from the Extras menu and enter THREEISACROWD.

UNLOCK SKI PATROL
Select Cheats from the Extras menu and enter FOURSOME.

STAR WARS KNIGHTS OF THE OLD REPUBLIC II THE SITH LORDS

CHANGE VOICES
Add a controller to the controller port 4 and press Black or White to raise and lower character voices.

STOLEN

LEVEL SKIP
At the Title screen, press Right Trigger, Left Trigger, Start + Down.

99 OF ALL ITEMS
During gameplay, go to Equipment and press Right Trigger, Left Trigger, Right.

XBOX®

SUPERMAN RETURNS: THE VIDEOGAME

INFINITE STAMINA
Pause the game, select Options and press Up, Up, Down, Down, Left, Right, Left, Right, Y, X.

INFINITE CITY HEALTH
Pause the game, select Options and press Y, Right, Y, Right, Up, Left, Right, Y.

ALL MOVES
Pause the game, select Options and press Left, Y, Right, X, Down, Y, Up, Down, X, Y, X.

ALL COSTUMES, TROPHIES AND THEATER ITEMS
Pause the game, select Options and press Left, Up, Right, Down, Y, X, Y, Up, Right, X.

TAK: THE GREAT JUJU CHALLENGE

BONUS SOUND EFFECTS
In Juju's Potions, select Universal Card and enter the following numbers for Bugs, Crystals and Fruits: 20, 17, 5.

BONUS SOUND EFFECTS 2
In Juju's Potions, select Universal Card and enter the following numbers for Bugs, Crystals and Fruits: 50, 84, 92.

BONUS MUSIC TRACK 1
In Juju's Potions, select Universal Card and enter the following numbers for Bugs, Crystals and Fruits: 67, 8, 20.

BONUS MUSIC TRACK 2
In Juju's Potions, select Universal Card and enter the following numbers for Bugs, Crystals and Fruits: 6, 18, 3.

MAGIC PARTICLES
In Juju's Potions, select Universal Card and enter the following numbers for Bugs, Crystals and Fruits: 24, 40, 11.

MORE MAGIC PARTICLES
In Juju's Potions, select Universal Card and enter the following numbers for Bugs, Crystals and Fruits: 48, 57, 57.

VIEW JUJU CONCEPT ART
In Juju's Potions, select Universal Card and enter the following numbers for Bugs, Crystals and Fruits: Art 33, 22, 28.

VIEW VEHICLE ART
In Juju's Potions, select Universal Card and enter the following numbers for Bugs, Crystals and Fruits: 11, 55, 44.

VIEW WORLD ART
In Juju's Potions, select Universal Card and enter the following numbers for Bugs, Crystals and Fruits: 83, 49, 34.

THRILLVILLE

$50,000
During a game, press X, B, Y, X, B, Y, A. Repeat this code as much as desired.

ALL PARKS
During a game, press X, B, Y, X, B, Y, X.

ALL RIDES
During a game, press X, B, Y, X, B, Y, Y. Some rides still need to be researched.

COMPLETE MISSIONS
During a game, press X, B, Y, X, B, Y, B. Then, at the Missions menu, highlight a mission and press X to complete that mission. Some missions have Bronze, Silver, and Gold objectives. For these missions the first press of X earns the Bronze, the second earns the Silver, and the third earns the Gold.

TIGER WOODS PGA TOUR 07

NIKE ITEMS

Select the Password option and enter JUSTDOIT.

TOMB RAIDER: LEGEND

You must unlock the following codes in the game before using them.

BULLETPROOF

During gameplay, hold Left Trigger and press A, Right Trigger, Y, Right Trigger, X, Black.

DRAIN ENEMY HEALTH

During gameplay, hold Left Trigger and press X, B, A, Black, Right Trigger, Y.

INFINITE ASSAULT RIFLE AMMO

During gameplay, hold Black and press A, B, A, Left Trigger, X, Y.

INFINITE GRENADE LAUNCHER AMMO

During gameplay, hold Black and press Left Trigger, Y, Right Trigger, B, Left Trigger, X.

INFINITE SHOTGUN AMMO

During gameplay, hold Black and press Right Trigger, B, X, Left Trigger, X, A.

INFINITE SMG AMMO

During gameplay, hold Black and press B, Y, Left Trigger, Right Trigger, A, B.

EXCALIBUR

During gameplay, hold Black and press Y, A, B, Right Trigger, Y, Left Trigger.

SOUL REAVER

During gameplay, hold Black and press A, Right Trigger, B, Right Trigger, Left Trigger, X.

NO TEXTURE MODE

During gameplay, hold Left Trigger and press Black, A, B, A, Y, Right Trigger.

TONY HAWK'S AMERICAN WASTELAND

ALWAYS SPECIAL

Select Cheat Codes from the Options menu and enter uronfire. Pause the game and select Cheats from the Game Options to enable the cheat.

PERFECT RAIL

Select Cheat Codes from the Options menu and enter grindxpert. Pause the game and select Cheats from the Game Options to enable the cheat.

PERFECT SKITCH

Select Cheat Codes from the Options menu and enter h!tchar!de. Pause the game and select Cheats from the Game Options to enable the cheat.

PERFECT MANUAL

Select Cheat Codes from the Options menu and enter 2wheels!. Pause the game and select Cheats from the Game Options to enable the cheat.

MOON GRAVITY

Select Cheat Codes from the Options menu and enter 2them00n. Pause the game and select Cheats from the Game Options to enable the cheat.

MAT HOFFMAN

Select Cheat Codes from the Options screen and enter the_condor.

JASON ELLIS

Select Cheat Codes from the Options menu and enter sirius-dj.

TOTAL OVERDOSE: A GUNSLINGER'S TALE IN MEXICO

CHEAT MODE
Hold Left Trigger + Right Trigger + White + Black + Left Thumbstick + Right Thumbstick for a few seconds. Now enter any of the following cheats.

RESTORE HEALTH
Press A, X, B, Y.

ALL LOCO MOVES
Press B, B, White, Black.

MAXIMUM REWINDING
Press Right Trigger, Black, White, A.

ALL WEAPONS
Press Y, Left Trigger, Black, X.

TY THE TASMANIAN TIGER 3: NIGHT OF THE QUINKAN

100,000 OPALS
During a game, press Start, Start, Y, Start, Start, Y, B, A, B, A.

ALL RINGS
During a game, press Start, Start, Y, Start, Start, Y, B, X, B, X.

ULTIMATE SPIDER-MAN

ALL CHARACTERS
Pause the game and select Controller Setup from the Options menu. Press Right, Down, Right, Down, Left, Up, Left, Right.

ALL COVERS
Pause the game and select Controller Setup from the Options menu. Press Left, Left, Right, Left, Up, Left, Left, Down.

ALL CONCEPT ART
Pause the game and select Controller Setup from the Options menu. Press Down, Down, Down, Up, Down, Up, Left, Left.

ALL LANDMARKS
Pause the game and select Controller Setup from the Options menu. Press Up, Right, Down, Left, Down, Up, Right, Left.

THE WARRIORS

100% COMPLETE
During a game, press Right Trigger, Back, X, Down, Left Trigger, Right.

99 CREDITS IN ARMIES OF THE NIGHT
During the Armies of the Night mini-game, press Up, Up, Down, Down, Left, Right.

$200, FLASH, & SPRAY PAINT
During gameplay, press Black, Left Thumbstick, Right Trigger, A, Down, R.

INFINITE HEALTH
During gameplay, press Up, Y, White, Back, A, Left Trigger, Down, X, Left, A, Right Trigger, Back.

INFINITE RAGE
During gameplay, press X, B, Y, Back, A, Left.

INFINITE SPRINT
During gameplay, press Down, X, Left, A, R, Back.

COMPLETE MISSION
During gameplay, press Down, X, A, Back, Back, Left.

BAT
During gameplay, press X, Left Thumbstick, Down, Down, Right Trigger, Right Trigger.

UNBREAKABLE BAT
During gameplay, press White, White, B, Up, B, Back.

BRASS KNUCKLES
During gameplay, press B, B, B, R, Back, Y.

KNIFE
During gameplay, press Down, Down, Back, Up, Up, White.

MACHETE
During gameplay, press Right Trigger, A, Black, Black, Back, Left Thumbstick.

PIPE
During gameplay, press Left Thumbstick, B, Back, Up, Right Trigger, Right.

STEEL-TOE BOOTS
During gameplay, press Click Right Thumbstick, Click Left Thumbstick, Black, White, Left Trigger, Right Trigger.

BUM ADVICE UPGRADE
During gameplay, press B, B, Down, Click Left Thumbstick, Left Trigger, B.

COMBAT STAMINA UPGRADE
During gameplay, press A, Right Trigger, Down, X, Up, A.

FLASH CAPACITY UPGRADE
During gameplay, press Left Trigger, A, Click Left Thumbstick, Right Trigger, Right Trigger, B.

FLASH UPGRADE
During gameplay, press Down, Left, Up, Up, X, Right.

SPRINT STAMINA UPGRADE
During gameplay, press Left Trigger, Back, Back, Back, Back, Y.

CUFF DROPS
During gameplay, press Up, A, Up, Back, White, Right Trigger.

CUFF KEY DROPS
During gameplay, press Left, A, A, Click Left Thumbstick, Right Trigger, Down.

UNCUFF SELF
During gameplay, press Y, Y, Y, Back, Y, Black.

LOSE THE POLICE
During gameplay, press Up, Back, A, Y, Y, B.

HOBO ALLIANCE
During gameplay, press Black, Black, Right Trigger, Black, Right Trigger, Up.

WEAPONS DEALER
During gameplay, press Right, Black, B, A, Back, X.

X-MEN: THE OFFICIAL GAME

DANGER ROOM ICEMAN
At the Cerebro Files menu, press Right, Right, Left, Left, Down, Up, Down, Up, Start.

DANGER ROOM NIGHTCRAWLER
At the Cerebro Files menu, press Up, Up, Down, Down, Left, Right, Left, Right, Start.

DANGER ROOM WOLVERINE
At the Cerebro Files menu, press Down, Down, Up, Up, Right, Left, Right, Left, Start.

YU-GI-OH! THE DAWN OF DESTINY

COSMO QUEEN CARD IN DECK
Enter your name as KONAMI.

TRI-HORN DRAGON CARD IN DECK
Enter your name as HEARTOFCARDS.

ZERA THE MANT CARD IN DECK
Enter your name as XBOX.

XBOX®

GAMECUBE™

GAMES

ANIMAL CROSSING

TOM NOOK PASSWORDS

Talk to Tom Nook and select the Other Things option. Then, select Say Code and enter the following passwords. You will be able to enter only three at a time.

PASSWORD	ITEM
CbDahLBdaDh98d 9ub8ExzZKwu7Zl	Balloon Fight NES Game
1n5%N%8JUjE5fj lEcGr4%ync5eUp	Baseball NES Game
Crm%h4BNRyu98d 9uu8exzZKwu7Zl	Clu Clu Land NES Game
bA5PC%8JUjE5fj ljcGr4%ync5EUp	DK Jr. Math NES Game
2n5@N%8JUjE5fj ljcGr4%ync5EUp	Donkey Kong NES Game
3%Q4fhMTRByAY3 05yYAK9zNHxLd7	Excitebike NES Game
Crm%h4BNRbu98d 9un8exzZKwo7Zl	Golf NES Game
bA5PC%8JUjE5fj 1EcGr4%ync5eup	Wario's Woods NES Game
Wn2&SAVAcgIC7N POudE2Tk8JHyUH	10,000 Bells from Project Hyrule
WB2&pARAcnOwnU jMCK%hTk8JHyrT	30,000 Bells from Project Hyrule
#SbaUIRmw#gwkY BK66q#LGscTY%2	? Block
IboOBCeHz3YblC B5igPvQYsfMZMd	Block Flooring
1mWYg6lfB@&q75 8XzSNKpfWj76ts	Brick Block
4UT6T6L89ZnOW3 dw&%jtL3qjLZBf	Cannon
4UT6T948GZnOW3 dw#%jtLEqj5ZBf	Fire Flower
4UT6T6L89ZnOW3 dwU%jtL3qjLZBf	Flagpole
1mWYg6lfB@&q7z 8XzSNwpfij76ts	Green Pipe
BCQ4iZFK%i5xqo SnyrjcrwAeDMkQ	Luigi Trophy
Ql6DLEnhm23CqH zrUHk3cXd#HOr9	Mushroom Mural
4UF6T948GZ3ZW3 dw#%jtLEqj5ZBf	Starman
1LhOwvrDA23fmt dsgnvzbClBAsyd	Station Model 1

LETTER TO VILLAGER PASSWORDS

For the following codes, send the password to one of the animals living in your town. Only include the password in the body of the letter. Be sure to include a line break between the two lines of code.

PASSWORD	ITEM
rSbaUlRmwUgwkA 1K6tq#LMscTY%2	Coin
rSbaUlAmwUgwkY 1K6tq#LGscTY%2	Koopa Shell
ECzihy%rtHbHuk o3XlP3lslEql#K	Mario Trophy
#SbaUlRmw#gwkY Bh66qeLMscTY%2	Super Mushroom

BATMAN BEGINS

GALLERY OF FEAR
Finish the game on any difficulty mode.

ALL MOVIES AND INTERVIEWS
Finish the game on any difficulty mode.

ALTERNATE COSTUMES
Finish the game on any difficulty mode.

PROTOTYPE BATMOBILE
Finish the game on any difficulty mode.

BRATZ: FOREVER DIAMONDZ

1000 BLINGZ
While in the Bratz Office, use the Cheat computer to enter SIZZLN.

2000 BLINGZ
While in the Bratz Office, use the Cheat computer to enter FLAUNT.

PET TREATS
While in the Bratz Office, use the Cheat computer to enter TREATZ.

GIFT SET A
While in the Bratz Office, use the Cheat computer to enter STYLIN.

GIFT SET B
While in the Bratz Office, use the Cheat computer to enter SKATIN.

GIFT SET C
While in the Bratz Office, use the Cheat computer to enter JEWELZ.

GIFT SET E
While in the Bratz Office, use the Cheat computer to enter DIMNDZ.

CARS

UNLOCK EVERYTHING
Select Cheat Codes from the Options screen and enter IF900HP.

ALL CHARACTERS
Select Cheat Codes from the Options screen and enter YAYCARS.

ALL CHARACTER SKINS
Select Cheat Codes from the Options screen and enter R4MONE.

ALL MINI-GAMES AND COURSES
Select Cheat Codes from the Options screen and enter MATTL66.

MATER'S COUNTDOWN CLEAN-UP MINI-GAME AND MATER'S SPEEDY CIRCUIT
Select Cheat Codes from the Options menu and enter TRGTEXC.

FAST START
Select Cheat Codes from the Options menu and enter IMSPEED.

INFINITE BOOST
Select Cheat Codes from the Options menu and enter VROOOOM.

ART
Select Cheat Codes from the Options menu and enter CONC3PT.

VIDEOS
Select Cheat Codes from the Options menu and enter WATCHIT.

OVERLOAD

GAMECUBE™

THE CHRONICLES OF NARNIA: THE LION, THE WITCH AND THE WARDROBE

ENABLE CHEATS
At the Title screen, press A then hold L + R and press Down, Down, Right, Up. When entered correctly, the text turns green. Now you can enter the following:

LEVEL SELECT
At the wardrobe, hold L and press Up, Up, Right, Right, Up, Right, Down.

ALL BONUS LEVELS
At the Bonus Drawer, hold L and press Down, Down, Right, Right, Down, Right, Up.

LEVEL SKIP
During gameplay, hold L and press Down, Left, Down, Left, Down, Right, Down, Right, Up.

INVINCIBILITY
During gameplay, hold L and press Down, Up, Down, Right, Right.

RESTORE HEALTH
During gameplay, hold L and press Down, Left, Left, Right.

10,000 COINS
During gameplay, hold L and press Down, Left, Right, Down, Down.

ALL ABILITIES
During gameplay, hold L and press Down, Left, Right, Left, Up.

FILL COMBO METER
During gameplay, hold L and press Up, Up, Right, Up.

CURIOUS GEORGE

CURIOUS GEORGE GOES APE
Pause the game, hold Z and press B, B, A, Y, B.

UNLIMITED BANANAS
Pause the game, hold Z and press A, X, X, Y, A.

ROLLERSKATES & FEZ HAT
Pause the game, hold Z and press X, A, A, A, B.

UPSIDE DOWN GRAVITY MODE
Pause the game, hold Z and press Y, Y, B, A, A.

ICE AGE 2: THE MELTDOWN

ALL BONUSES
Pause the game and press Down, Left, Up, Down, Down, Left, Right, Right.

LEVEL SELECT
Pause the game and press Up, Right, Right, Left, Right, Right, Down, Down.

UNLIMITED PEBBLES
Pause the game and press Down, Down, Left, Up, Up, Right, Up, Down.

INFINITE ENERGY
Pause the game and press Down, Left, Right, Down, Down, Right, Left, Down.

INFINITE HEALTH
Pause the game and press Up, Right, Down, Up, Left, Down, Right, Left.

THE INCREDIBLE HULK: ULTIMATE DESTRUCTION

You must collect a specific comic in the game to activate each code. After collecting the appropriate comic, you can enter the following codes. If you don't have the comic and enter the code, you receive a message "That code cannot be activated… yet". Enter the cheats at the Code Input screen.

UNLOCKED: CABS GALORE
Select Code Input from the Extras menu and enter CABBIES.

UNLOCKED: GORILLA INVASION
Select Code Input from the Extras menu and enter kingkng.

UNLOCKED: MASS TRANSIT
Select Code Input from the Extras menu and enter TRANSIT.

UNLOCKED: 5000 SMASH POINTS
Select Code Input from the Extras menu and enter SMASH5.

UNLOCKED: 10000 SMASH POINTS
Select Code Input from the Extras menu and enter SMASH10.

UNLOCKED: 15000 SMASH POINTS
Select Code Input from the Extras menu and enter SMASH15.

UNLOCKED: AMERICAN FLAG SHORTS
Select Code Input from the Extras menu and enter AMERICA.

UNLOCKED: CANADIAN FLAG SHORTS
Select Code Input from the Extras menu and enter OCANADA.

UNLOCKED: FRENCH FLAG SHORTS
Select Code Input from the Extras menu and enter Drapeau.

UNLOCKED: GERMAN FLAG SHORTS
Select Code Input from the Extras menu and enter DEUTSCH.

UNLOCKED: ITALIAN FLAG SHORTS
Select Code Input from the Extras menu and enter MUTANDA.

UNLOCKED: JAPANESE FLAG SHORTS
Select Code Input from the Extras menu and enter FURAGGU.

UNLOCKED: SPANISH FLAG SHORTS
Select Code Input from the Extras menu and enter BANDERA.

UNLOCKED: UK FLAG SHORTS
Select Code Input from the Extras menu and enter FSHNCHP.

UNLOCKED: COW MISSILES
Select Code Input from the Extras menu and enter CHZGUN.

UNLOCKED: DOUBLE HULK'S DAMAGE
Select Code Input from the Extras menu and enter DESTROY.

UNLOCKED: DOUBLE POWER COLLECTABLES
Select Code Input from the Extras menu and enter BRINGIT.

UNLOCKED: BLACK AND WHITE
Select Code Input from the Extras menu and enter RETRO.

UNLOCKED: SEPIA
Select Code Input from the Extras menu and enter HISTORY.

UNLOCKED: ABOMINATION
Select Code Input from the Extras menu and enter VILLAIN.

UNLOCKED: GRAY HULK
Select Code Input from the Extras menu and enter CLASSIC.

UNLOCKED: JOE FIXIT SKIN
Select Code Input from the Extras menu and enter SUITFIT.

UNLOCKED: WILD TRAFFIC
Select Code Input from the Extras menu and enter FROGGIE.

UNLOCKED: LOW GRAVITY
Select Code Input from the Extras menu and enter PILLOWS.

LEGO STAR WARS II: THE ORIGINAL TRILOGY

BEACH TROOPER
At Mos Eisley Canteena, select Enter Code and enter UCK868. You must then select Characters and purchase this character for 20,000 studs.

BEN KENOBI (GHOST)
At Mos Eisley Canteena, select Enter Code and enter BEN917. You must then select Characters and purchase this character for 1,100,000 studs.

BESPIN GUARD
At Mos Eisley Canteena, select Enter Code and enter VHY832. You must then select Characters and purchase this character for 15,000 studs.

BIB FORTUNA
At Mos Eisley Canteena, select Enter Code and enter WTY721. You must then select Characters and purchase this character for 16,000 studs.

BOBA FETT
At Mos Eisley Canteena, select Enter Code and enter HLP221. You must then select Characters and purchase this character for 175,000 studs.

DEATH STAR TROOPER
At Mos Eisley Canteena, select Enter Code and enter BNC332. You must then select Characters and purchase this character for 19,000 studs.

EWOK
At Mos Eisley Canteena, select Enter Code and enter TTT289. You must then select Characters and purchase this character for 34,000 studs.

GAMORREAN GUARD

At Mos Eisley Canteena, select Enter Code and enter YZF999. You must then select Characters and purchase this character for 40,000 studs.

Gamorrean Guard! Cheat Unlocked!

GONK DROID

At Mos Eisley Canteena, select Enter Code and enter NFX582. You must then select Characters and purchase this character for 1,550 studs.

GRAND MOFF TARKIN

At Mos Eisley Canteena, select Enter Code and enter SMG219. You must then select Characters and purchase this character for 38,000 studs.

GREEDO

At Mos Eisley Canteena, select Enter Code and enter NAH118. You must then select Characters and purchase this character for 60,000 studs.

HAN SOLO (HOOD)

At Mos Eisley Canteena, select Enter Code and enter YWM840. You must then select Characters and purchase this character for 20,000 studs.

IG-88

At Mos Eisley Canteena, select Enter Code and enter NXL973. You must then select Characters and purchase this character for 30,000 studs.

IMPERIAL GUARD

At Mos Eisley Canteena, select Enter Code and enter MMM111. You must then select Characters and purchase this character for 45,000 studs.

IMPERIAL OFFICER

At Mos Eisley Canteena, select Enter Code and enter BBV889. You must then select Characters and purchase this character for 28,000 studs.

IMPERIAL SHUTTLE PILOT

At Mos Eisley Canteena, select Enter Code and enter VAP664. You must then select Characters and purchase this character for 29,000 studs.

IMPERIAL SPY

At Mos Eisley Canteena, select Enter Code and enter CVT125. You must then select Characters and purchase this character for 13,500 studs.

JAWA

At Mos Eisley Canteena, select Enter Code and enter JAW499. You must then select Characters and purchase this character for 24,000 studs.

LOBOT

At Mos Eisley Canteena, select Enter Code and enter UUB319. You must then select Characters and purchase this character for 11,000 studs.

PALACE GUARD

At Mos Eisley Canteena, select Enter Code and enter SGE549. You must then select Characters and purchase this character for 14,000 studs.

REBEL PILOT

At Mos Eisley Canteena, select Enter Code and enter CYG336. You must then select Characters and purchase this character for 15,000 studs.

REBEL TROOPER (HOTH)

At Mos Eisley Canteena, select Enter Code and enter EKU849. You must then select Characters and purchase this character for 16,000 studs.

SANDTROOPER

At Mos Eisley Canteena, select Enter Code and enter YDV451. You must then select Characters and purchase this character for 14,000 studs.

SKIFF GUARD

At Mos Eisley Canteena, select Enter Code and enter GBU888. You must then select Characters and purchase this character for 12,000 studs.

SNOWTROOPER

At Mos Eisley Canteena, select Enter Code and enter NYU989. You must then select Characters and purchase this character for 16,000 studs.

STORMTROOPER

At Mos Eisley Canteena, select Enter Code and enter PTR345. You must then select Characters and purchase this character for 10,000 studs.

THE EMPEROR

At Mos Eisley Canteena, select Enter Code and enter HHY382. You must then select Characters and purchase this character for 275,000 studs.

TIE FIGHTER

At Mos Eisley Canteena, select Enter Code and enter HDY739. You must then select Characters and purchase this item for 60,000 studs.

TIE FIGHTER PILOT

At Mos Eisley Canteena, select Enter Code and enter NNZ316. You must then select Characters and purchase this character for 21,000 studs.

TIE INTERCEPTOR

At Mos Eisley Canteena, select Enter Code and enter QYA828. You must then select Characters and purchase this item for 40,000 studs.

TUSKEN RAIDER

At Mos Eisley Canteena, select Enter Code and enter PEJ821. You must then select Characters and purchase this character for 23,000 studs.

UGNAUGHT

At Mos Eisley Canteena, select Enter Code and enter UGN694. You must then select Characters and purchase this character for 36,000 studs.

MADDEN NFL 07

MADDEN CARDS

Select Madden Cards from My Madden. Then select Madden Codes and enter the following:

CARD	PASSWORD
#199 Gold Lame Duck Cheat	5LAWO0
#200 Gold Mistake Free Cheat	XL7SP1
#210 Gold QB on Target Cheat	WROA0R
#220 Super Bowl XLI Gold	RLA9R7
#221 Super Bowl XLII Gold	WRLUF8
#222 Super Bowl XLIII Gold	NIEV4A
#223 Super Bowl XLIV Gold	M5AB7L
#224 Aloha Stadium Gold	YI8P8U
#225 1958 Colts Gold	B57QLU
#226 1966 Packers Gold	1PL1FL
#227 1968 Jets Gold	MIE6WO
#228 1970 Browns Gold	CL2TOE
#229 1972 Dolphins Gold	NOEB7U
#230 1974 Steelers Gold	YO0FLA
#231 1976 Raiders Gold	MOA11I
#232 1977 Broncos Gold	C8UM7U
#233 1978 Dolphins Gold	VIU0O7
#234 1980 Raiders Gold	NLAPH3
#235 1981 Chargers Gold	COAGI4
#236 1982 Redskins Gold	WL8BRI
#237 1983 Raiders Gold	H0EW71
#238 1984 Dolphins Gold	M1AM1E
#239 1985 Bears Gold	QOETO8
#240 1986 Giants Gold	ZI8S2L
#241 1988 49ers Gold	SP2A8H
#242 1990 Eagles Gold	2L4TRO
#243 1991 Lions Gold	J1ETRI
#244 1992 Cowboys Gold	W9UVI9
#245 1993 Bills Gold	DLA3I7
#246 1994 49ers Gold	DR7EST
#247 1996 Packers Gold	F8LUST
#248 1998 Broncos Gold	FIES95
#249 1999 Rams Gold	S9OUSW
#250 Bears Pump Up the Crowd	B1OUPH
#251 Bengals Cheerleader	DRL2SW

OVERLORD

GAMECUBE™

CARD	PASSWORD
#252 Bills Cheerleader	1PLUYO
#253 Broncos Cheerleader	3ROUJO
#254 Browns Pump Up the Crowd	T1UTOA
#255 Buccaneers Cheerleader	S9EWRI
#256 Cardinals Cheerleader	57IEPI
#257 Chargers Cheerleader	F7UHL8
#258 Chiefs Cheerleader	PRI5SL
#259 Colts Cheerleader	1R5AMI
#260 Cowboys Cheerleader	Z2ACHL
#261 Dolphins Cheerleader	C5AHLE
#262 Eagles Cheerleader	PO7DRO
#263 Falcons Cheerleader	37USPO
#264 49ers Cheerleader	KL0CRL
#265 Giants Pump Up the Crowd	C4USPI
#266 Jaguars Cheerleader	MIEH7E
#267 Jets Pump Up the Crowd	C0LUXI
#268 Lions Pump Up the Crowd	3LABLU
#269 Packers Pump Up the Crowd	4HO7VO
#270 Panthers Cheerleader	F2IASP
#282 All AFC Team Gold	PRO9PH
#283 All NFC Team Gold	RLATH7

MARIO GOLF: TOADSTOOL TOUR

At the Title screen, press Start + Z to access the Password screen. Enter the following to open the bonus tournaments.

TARGET BULLSEYE TOURNAMENT
Enter CEUFPXJ1.

HOLLYWOOD VIDEO TOURNAMENT
Enter BJGQBULZ.

CAMP HYRULE TOURNAMENT
Enter 0EKW5G7U.

BOWSER BADLANDS TOURNAMENT
Enter 9L3L9KHR.

BOWSER JR.'S JUMBO TOURNAMENT
Enter 2GPL67PN.

MARIO OPEN TOURNAMENT
Enter GGAA241H.

PEACH'S INVITATIONAL TOURNAMENT
Enter ELBUT3PX.

MARIO POWER TENNIS

EVENT MODE
At the Title screen, press Z + Start.

MARIO SUPERSTAR BASEBALL

STAR DASH MINI GAME
Complete Star difficulty on all mini-games.

BABY LUIGI
Complete Challenge Mode with Yoshi.

DIXIE KONG
Complete Challenge Mode with Donkey Kong.

HAMMER BRO
Complete Challenge Mode with Bowser.

MONTY MOLE
Complete Challenge Mode with Mario.

PETEY PIRANHA
Complete Challenge Mode with Wario.

TOADETTE
Complete Challenge Mode with Peach.

KOOPA CASTLE STADIUM
Complete Challenge Mode.

TITLE SCREEN

At the Title screen, press the following for a variety of options.

Press R to make the Pikmin form the word NINTENDO.
Press L to go back to PIKMIN 2.
Press X to get a beetle.
Use the C-Stick to move the beetle around.
Press L to dispose of the Beetle.
Press Y to get a Chappie.
Use the C-Stick to move the Chappie around.
Press Z to eat the Pikmin.
Press L to dispose of the Chappie.

PRINCE OF PERSIA: THE TWO THRONES

BABY TOY HAMMER WEAPON

Pause the game and press Left, Left, Right, Right, A, Y, Y, A, Up, Down.

CHAINSAW WEAPON

Pause the game and press Up, Up, Down, Down, Left, Right, Left, Right, A, Y, A, Y.

SWORDFISH WEAPON

Pause the game and press Up, Down, Up, Down, Left, Right, Left, Right, A, Y, A, Y.

TELEPHONE OF SORROW WEAPON

Pause the game and press Right, Left, Right, Left, Down, Down, Up, Up, A, Y, A, A, Y, Y.

THE SIMS 2: PETS

CHEAT GNOME

During a game, press L, L, R, A, A, Up.

ADVANCE 6 HOURS

After activating the Cheat Gnome, press Up, Left, Down, Right, R during a game. Select the Gnome to access the cheat.

GIVE SIM SIMOLEONS

After activating the Cheat Gnome, enter the Advance 6 Hours cheat. Access the Gnome and exit. Enter the cheat again. Now, Give Sim Simoleons should be available from the Gnome.

CAT AND DOG CODES

When creating a family, press X to Enter Unlock Code. Enter the following for new fur patterns.

FUR PATTERN/CAT OR DOG	UNLOCK CODE
Bandit Mask Cats	EEGJ2YRQZZAIZ9QHA64
Bandit Mask Dogs	EEGJ2YRQZQARQ9QHA64
Black Dot Cats	EEGJ2YRZQQ1IQ9QHA64
Black Dot Dogs	EEGJ2YRQZZ1IQ9QHA64
Black Smiley Cats	EEGJ2YRQQZ1RQ9QHA64
Black Smiley Dogs	EEGJ2YRZQQARQ9QHA64
Blue Bones Cats	EEGJ2YRQZZARQ9QHA64
Blue Bones Dogs	EEGJ2YRZZZ11Z9QHA64
Blue Camouflage Cats	EEGJ2YRZZQ1IQ9QHA64
Blue Camouflage Dogs	EEGJ2YRZZZ1RQ9QHA64
Blue Cats	EEGJ2YRQZZAIQ9QHA64
Blue Dogs	EEGJ2YRQQQ1IZ9QHA64
Blue Star Cats	EEGJ2YRQQZ1IZ9QHA64
Blue Star Dogs	EEGJ2YRQZQ1IQ9QHA64
Deep Red Cats	EEGJ2YRQQQAIQ9QHA64
Deep Red Dogs	EEGJ2YRQZQ1RQ9QHA64
Goofy Cats	EEGJ2YRQZQ1IZ9QHA64
Goofy Dogs	EEGJ2YRZZZARQ9QHA64
Green Cats	EEGJ2YRZQQAIZ9QHA64
Green Dogs	EEGJ2YRQZQAIQ9QHA64
Green Flower Cats	EEGJ2YRZQZAIQ9QHA64

FUR PATTERN/CAT OR DOG	UNLOCK CODE
Green Flower Dogs	EEGJ2YRQZZ1RQ9QHA64
Light Green Cats	EEGJ2YRZZQ1RQ9QHA64
Light Green Dogs	EEGJ2YRZZQQ1RQ9QHA64
Navy Hearts Cats	EEGJ2YRZQZ1IQ9QHA64
Navy Hearts Dogs	EEGJ2YRQQZ1IQ9QHA64
Neon Green Cats	EEGJ2YRZZQAIQ9QHA64
Neon Green Dogs	EEGJ2YRQQQAIQ9QHA64
Neon Yellow Cats	EEGJ2YRZZQARQ9QHA64
Neon Yellow Dogs	EEGJ2YRQQQAIZ9QHA64
Orange Diagonal Cats	EEGJ2YRQQZAIQ9QHA64
Orange Diagonal Dogs	EEGJ2YRZQZ1IZ9QHA64
Panda Cats	EEGJ2YRQZQAIZ9QHA64
Pink Cats	EEGJ2YRQZZ1IZ9QHA64
Pink Dogs	EEGJ2YRZQZ1RQ9QHA64
Pink Vertical Strip Cats	EEGJ2YRQQQARQ9QHA64
Pink Vertical Strip Dogs	EEGJ2YRZZZAIQ9QHA64
Purple Cats	EEGJ2YRQQZARQ9QHA64
Purple Dogs	EEGJ2YRQQZAIZ9QHA64
Star Cats	EEGJ2YRZQZARQ9QHA64
Star Dogs	EEGJ2YRZQZAIZ9QHA64
White Paws Cats	EEGJ2YRQQQ1RQ9QHA64
White Paws Dogs	EEGJ2YRZQQ1IZ9QHA64
White Zebra Stripe Cats	EEGJ2YRZZQ1IZ9QHA64
White Zebra Stripe Dogs	EEGJ2YRZZZ1IQ9QHA64
Zebra Stripes Dogs	EEGJ2YRZZQAIZ9QHA64

SSX ON TOUR

NEW THREADS
Select Cheats from the Extras menu and enter FLYTHREADS.

THE WORLD IS YOURS
Select Cheats from the Extras menu and enter BACKSTAGEPASS.

SHOW TIME (ALL MOVIES)
Select Cheats from the Extras menu and enter THEBIGPICTURE.

BLING BLING (INFINITE CASH)
Select Cheats from the Extras menu and enter LOOTSNOOT.

FULL BOOST, FULL TIME
Select Cheats from the Extras menu and enter ZOOMJUICE.

MONSTERS ARE LOOSE (MONSTER TRICKS)
Select Cheats from the Extras menu and enter JACKALOPESTYLE.

SNOWBALL FIGHT
Select Cheats from the Extras menu and enter LETSPARTY.

FEEL THE POWER (STAT BOOST)
Select Cheats from the Extras menu and enter POWERPLAY.

CHARACTERS ARE LOOSE
Select Cheats from the Extras menu and enter ROADIEROUNDUP.

UNLOCK CONRAD
Select Cheats from the Extras menu and enter BIGPARTYTIME.

UNLOCK MITCH KOOBSKI
Select Cheats from the Extras menu and enter MOREFUNTHANONE.

UNLOCK NIGEL
Select Cheats from the Extras menu and enter THREEISACROWD.

UNLOCK SKI PATROL
Select Cheats from the Extras menu and enter FOURSOME.

LEVEL SELECT (COOPERATIVE MODE)
Enter SWGRCQPL, then enter UCHEATED.

ALL SINGLE-PLAYER MISSIONS
Enter HYWSC!WS, then enter NONGAMER.

ALL SINGLE-PLAYER MISSIONS & BONUS MISSIONS
Enter EEQQ?YPL, then enter CHE!ATER.

BEGGAR'S CANYON RACE (COOPERATIVE MODE)
Enter FRLL!CSF, then enter FARMBOY?.

ASTEROID FIELD MISSION (COOPERATIVE MODE)
Enter RWALPIGC, then enter NOWAYOUT.

DEATH STAR ESCAPE MISSION (COOPERATIVE MODE)
Enter YFCEDFRH, then enter DSAGAIN?.

ENDURANCE MISSION (COOPERATIVE MODE)
Enter WPX?FGC!, then enter EXCERSIZ.

ALL SHIPS (VERSUS MODE)
Enter W!WSTPQB, then enter FREEPLAY.

MILLENNIUM FALCON
Enter QZCRPTG!, then enter HANSRIDE.

NABOO STARFIGHTER
Enter RTWCVBSH, then enter BFNAGAIN.

SLAVE I
Enter TGBCWLPN, then enter ZZBOUNTY.

TIE BOMBER
Enter JASDJWFA, then enter !DABOMB!.

TIE HUNTER
Enter FRRVBMJK, then enter LOOKOUT!.

TIE FIGHTER (COOPERATIVE MODE)
Enter MCKEMAKD, then enter ONESHOT!.

TIE ADVANCE IN COOPERATIVE
Enter VDX?WK!H, then enter ANOKSHIP.

RUDY'S CAR
Enter AXCBPRHK, then enter WHATTHE?.

CREDITS
Enter LOOKMOM!. This option is available in the Special Features menu.

STAR WARS ARCADE GAME
Enter RTJPFC!G, then enter TIMEWARP.

EMPIRE STRIKES BACK ARCADE GAME
Enter !H!F?HXS, then enter KOOLSTUF.

DOCUMENTARY
Enter THEDUDES.

ART GALLERY
Enter !KOOLART.

MUSIC HALL
Enter HARKHARK.

BLACK & WHITE
Enter NOCOLOR?.

TAK: THE GREAT JUJU CHALLENGE

BONUS SOUND EFFECTS
In Juju's Potions, select Universal Card and enter the following numbers for Bugs, Crystals and Fruit: 20, 17, 5.

BONUS SOUND EFFECTS 2
In Juju's Potions, select Universal Card and enter the following numbers for Bugs, Crystals and Fruit: 50, 84, 92.

BONUS MUSIC TRACK 1
In Juju's Potions, select Universal Card and enter the following numbers for Bugs, Crystals and Fruit: 67, 8, 20.

BONUS MUSIC TRACK 2
In Juju's Potions, select Universal Card and enter the following numbers for Bugs, Crystals and Fruit: 6, 18, 3.

MAGIC PARTICLES
In Juju's Potions, select Universal Card and enter the following numbers for Bugs, Crystals and Fruit: 24, 40, 11.

MORE MAGIC PARTICLES
In Juju's Potions, select Universal Card and enter the following numbers for Bugs, Crystals and Fruit: 48, 57, 57.

VIEW JUJU CONCEPT ART
In Juju's Potions, select Universal Card and enter the following numbers for Bugs, Crystals and Fruit: Art 33, 22, 28.

VIEW VEHICLE ART

In Juju's Potions, select Universal Card and enter the following numbers for Bugs, Crystals and Fruit: 11, 55, 44.

VIEW WORLD ART

In Juju's Potions, select Universal Card and enter the following numbers for Bugs, Crystals and Fruit: 83, 49, 34.

ULTIMATE SPIDER-MAN

ALL CHARACTERS

Pause the game and select Controller Setup from the Options menu. Press Right, Down, Right, Down, Left, Up, Left, Right.

ALL COVERS

Pause the game and select Controller Setup from the Options menu. Press Left, Left, Right, Left, Up, Left, Left, Down.

ALL CONCEPT ART

Pause the game and select Controller Setup from the Options menu. Press Down, Down, Down, Up, Down, Up, Left, Left.

ALL LANDMARKS

Pause the game and select Controller Setup from the Options menu. Press Up, Right, Down, Left, Down, Up, Right, Left.

X-MEN: THE OFFICIAL GAME

DANGER ROOM ICEMAN

At the Cerebro Files menu, press Right, Right, Left, Left, Down, Up, Down, Up, Start.

DANGER ROOM NIGHTCRAWLER

At the Cerebro Files menu, press Up, Up, Down, Down, Left, Right, Left, Right, Start.

DANGER ROOM WOLVERINE

At the Cerebro Files menu, press Down, Down, Up, Up, Right, Left, Right, Left, Start.

GAMES

ADVANCE WARS: DAYS OF RUIN

UNLOCK COS

Complete the following missions to unlock the corresponding CO.

COMPLETE MISSION	CO UNLOCKED
12	Tasha
13	Gage
14	Forthsythe
20	Waylon
21	Greyfield
24	Penny
25	Tabitha
26	Caulder

ADVANCE WARS: DUAL STRIKE

ADVANCE WARS MAP

Select Map from the Design Room menu and immediately press and hold L + R. This reveals a map that spells out Advance Wars.

ADVANCE WARPAPER

Insert Advance Wars into the GBA slot of your Nintendo DS. Start Advance Wars: Dual Strike. Select Battle maps and purchase Advance Warpaper. Select Display from the Design Room and choose Classic 1.

HACHI'S LAND

Insert Advance Wars into the GBA slot of your Nintendo DS. Start Advance Wars: Dual Strike. Select Battle Maps and purchase Hachi's Land for 1.

NELL'S LAND

Insert Advance Wars into the GBA slot of your Nintendo DS. Start Advance Wars: Dual Strike. Select Battle Maps and purchase Nell's Land for 1.

ADVANCE WARPAPER 2

Insert Advance Wars 2: Black Hole Rising into the GBA slot of your Nintendo DS. Start Advance Wars: Dual Strike. Select Battle maps and purchase Advance Warpaper 2. Select Display from the Design Room and choose Classic 2.

LASH'S LAND

Insert Advance Wars 2: Black Hole Rising into the GBA slot of your Nintendo DS. Start Advance Wars: Dual Strike. Select Battle Maps and purchase Lash's Land for 1.

STRUM'S LAND

Insert Advance Wars 2: Black Hole Rising into the GBA slot of your Nintendo DS. Start Advance Wars: Dual Strike. Select Battle Maps and purchase Strum's Land for 1.

ANIMANIACS: LIGHTS, CAMERA, ACTION!

SKIP LEVEL

Pause the game and press L, L, R, R, Down, Down.

DISABLE TIME

Pause the game and press L, R, Left, Left, Up, Up.

KINGSIZE PICK-UPS

Pause the game and press Right, Right, Right, Left, Left, Left, R, L.

PASSWORDS

LEVEL	PASSWORD
1	Wakko, Wakko, Wakko, Wakko, Wakko
2	Dot, Yakko, Brain, Wakko, Pinky
3	Yakko, Dot, Wakko, Wakko, Brain
4	Pinky, Yakko, Yakko, Dot, Brain
5	Pinky, Pinky, Yakko, Wakko, Wakko
6	Brain, Dot, Brain, Pinky, Yakko
7	Brain, Pinky, Wakko, Pinky, Brain
8	Brain Pinky, Pinky, Wakko, Wakko
9	Dot, Dot, Yakko, Pinky, Wakko

LEVEL	PASSWORD
10	Brain, Dot, Brain, Yakko, Wakko
11	Akko, Yakko, Pinky, Dot, Dot
12	Pinky, Pinky, Brain, Dot, Wakko
13	Yakko, Wakko, Pinky, Wakko, Brain
14	Pinky, Wakko, Brain, Wakko, Yakko
15	Dot, Pinky, Wakko, Wakko, Yakko

BEN 10: PROTECTOR OF EARTH

GWEN 10 SKINS
At the level select, press Left, Right, Left, Right, L, R, Select.

GALACTIC ENFORCER SKINS
At the level select, press A, B, X, Y, L, R, Select.

ULTRA BEN SKINS
At the level select, press Up, Right, Down, Left, A, B, Select.

BRAIN AGE: TRAIN YOUR BRAIN IN MINUTES A DAY

BRAIN AGE CHECK SELECTION MENU
At the Daily Training Menu, hold Select while choosing Brain Age Check.

TOP 3 LISTS
At the Daily Training Menu, hold Select while choosing Graph.

BRAIN VOYAGE

ALL GOLD MEDALS
At the World Map, press A, B, Up, L, L, Y.

INFINITE COINS
At the World Tour Mode, press L, Up, X, Up, R, Y.

BUBBLE BOBBLE REVOLUTION

BONUS LEVELS IN CLASSIC MODE
At the Classic Mode title screen, press L, R, L, R, L, R, Right, Select. Touch the door at Level 20.

POWER UP! MODE IN CLASSIC VERSION
At the Classic Mode title screen, press Select, R, L, Left, Right, R, Select, Right.

SUPER BUBBLE BOBBLE IN CLASSIC VERSION
You must first defeat the boss with two players. Then at the Classic Mode title screen, press Left, R, Left, Select, Left, L, Left, Select.

BUST-A-MOVE DS

DARK WORLD
Complete the game then press A Left Right A at the Title screen.

SOUND TEST
At the Main menu, press Select, A, B, Left, Right, A, Select, Right.

CARS

SECRET MUSIC TRACK FOR RAMONE'S STYLE
At the Title screen, press Up, Down, Up, Down, A, B, X, Y.

EVERYTHING EXCEPT HIDDEN MUSIC
At the Title screen, press Up, Up, Down, Down, Left, Right, Left, Right, B, A, B.

CARTOON NETWORK RACING

The following codes will disable the ability to save:

UNLOCK EVERYTHING
Select Nickname from the Options and enter GIMMIE.

ENABLES ALL HAZARDS AND PICKUPS IN TIME TRIAL
Select Nickname from the Options and enter AAARGH.

ROCKETS TURN NON-INVULNERABLE OPPONENTS INTO STONE
Select Nickname from the Options and enter STONEME.

UNLIMITED DUMB ROCKETS
Select Nickname from the Options and enter ROCKETMAN.

UNLIMITED SUPERPOWER ENERGY
Select Nickname from the Options and enter SPINACH.

TOP-DOWN VIEW
Select Nickname from the Options and enter IMACOPTER.

CASTLEVANIA: DAWN OF SORROW

POTION
Complete Boss Rush Mode.

RPG
Complete Boss Rush Mode in less than 5 minutes.

DEATH'S ROBE
Complete Boss Rush Mode in less than 6 minutes.

TERROR BEAR
Complete Boss Rush Mode in less than 7 minutes.

NUNCHAKUS
Complete Boss Rush Mode in less than 8 minutes.

CASTLEVANIA: PORTRAIT OF RUIN

JAPANESE VOICEOVERS
At the Main menu, hold L and press A.

THE CHRONICLES OF NARNIA: THE LION, THE WITCH AND THE WARDROBE

RESTORE HEALTH
At the Main menu, press Left, Right, Up, Down, A (x4).

INVINCIBILITY
At the Main menu, press A, Y, X, B, Up, Up, Down, Down.

ARMOR
At the Main menu, press A, X, Y, B, Up, Up, Up, Down.

EXTRA MONEY
At the Main menu, press Up, X, Up, X, Down, B, Down, B.

ALL BLESSINGS
At the Main menu, press Left, Up, A, B, Right, Down, X, Y.

MAXIMUM ATTRIBUTES
At the Main menu, press Left, B, Up, Y, Down, X, Right, A.

MAX SKILLS
At the Main menu, press A, Left, Right, B, Down, Up, X, X.

STRONGER ATTACKS
At the Main menu, press A, Up, B, Down, X, X, Y, Y.

CODE LYOKO

CODELYOKO.COM SECRET FILES
Enter the following as Secret Codes on the My Secret Album page of www.codelyoko.com:

SECRET FILE	CODE
Dark Enemies Wallpaper	9L8Q
Desert Sketch	6G7T
Fight Video	4M9P
FMV Ending	5R5K
Forest Sketch	8C3X
Ice Sketch	2F6U
Mountain Sketch	7E5V
Overbike	3Q4L

SECRET FILE	CODE
Overboard	8P3M
Overwing	8N2N
Scorpion Video	9H8S
Scorpion Wallpaper	3D4W
Sector 5 Sketch	5J9R
Ulrich	9A9Z
Yumi	4B2Y

CONTRA 4

SUPER C

10 LIVES
At the title screen, press Right, Left, Down, Up, B, Y.

SOUND TEST
As the logo fades in to the title screen, hold Y + B and press Start.

CONTRA

30 LIVES
At the title screen, press Up, Up, Down, Down, Left, Right Left, Right, Y, B.

UPGRADE WEAPONS
Pause the game and press Up, Up, Down, Down, Left, Right Left, Right, B, A, Start. This code can be used once per life. If you enter it a second time, you will die.

DISGAEA DS

ETNA MODE
At the Main menu, highlight New Game and press X, Y, B, X, Y, B, A.

DRAGLADE

CHARACTERS

CHARACTER	TO UNLOCK
Asuka	Defeat Daichi's story
Gyamon	Defeat Guy's story
Koki	Defeat Hibito's story
Shura	Defeat Kairu's story

HIDDEN QUEST: SHADOW OF DARKNESS
Defeat Story Mode with all of the main characters. This unlocks this hidden quest in Synethesia.

ZEKE
Complete all of the quests including Shadow of Darkness to unlock Zeke in wireless battle.

DRAGON QUEST HEROES: ROCKET SLIME

KNIGHTRO TANK IN MULTIPLAYER
While inside the church, press Y, L, L, Y, R, R, Y, Up, Down, Select.

THE NEMESIS TANK IN MULTIPLAYER
While inside the church, press Y, R, R, up, L, L, Y, Down, Down, Down, Y, Select.

NINTENDO DS™

DRAGON QUEST MONSTERS: JOKER

CAPTAIN CROW
As you travel between the islands on the sea scooters, you are occasionally attacked by pirates. Find out which route the pirates are located on the bulletin board in any scoutpost den. When you face them between Infant Isle and Celeste Isle, Captain Crow makes an appearance. Defeat him and he forces himself into your team.

SOLITAIRE'S CHALLENGE
After completing the main game, load your game back up for a new endeavor. The hero is in Solitaire's office where she proposes a new non-stop challenge known as Solitaire's Challenge.

METAL KING SLIME
Acquire 100 different skills for your library and talk to the woman in Solitaire's office.

METAL KAISER SLIME
Acquire 150 different skills for your library and talk to the woman in Solitaire's office.

LEOPOLD
Acquire all of the skills for your library and talk to the woman in Solitaire's office.

LIQUID METAL SLIME
Collect 100 monsters in your library and talk to the man in Solitaire's office.

GRANDPA SLIME
Collect 200 monsters in your library and talk to the man in Solitaire's office.

EMPYREA
Collect all of the monsters in your library and talk to the man in Solitaire's office.

TRODE AND ROBBIN' HOOD
Complete both the skills and monster libraries and talk to both the man and woman in Solitaire's office.

DRAWN TO LIFE

HEAL ALL DAMAGE
During a game, press Start, hold L and press Y, X, Y, X, Y, X, A.

INVINCIBLITY
During a game, press Start, hold L and press A, X, B, B, Y.

ALIEN TEMPLATES
During a game, press Start, hold L and press X, Y, B, A, A.

ANIMAL TEMPLATES
During a game, press Start, hold L and press B, B, A, A, X.

ROBOT TEMPLATES
During a game, press Start, hold L and press Y, X, Y, X, A.

SPORTS TEMPLATES
During a game, press Start, hold L and press Y, A, B, A, X.

DRAWN TO LIFE: SPONGEBOB SQUAREPANTS EDITION

9,999,999 REWARD COINS
Select Cheat Entry and enter Down, Down, B, B, Down, Left, Up, Right, A.

FINAL FANTASY FABLES: CHOCOBO TALES

OMEGA – WAVE CANNON CARD
Select Send from the Main Menu and then choose Download Pop-Up Card. Press L, L, Up, B, B, Left.

GODZILLA UNLEASHED: DOUBLE SMASH

ANGUIRUS
Defeat Hedorah Terrorizes San Francisco.

DESTOROYAH
Defeat Monster Island, The Final Battle.

FIRE RODAN
Defeat Biollante Attacks Paris.

KING GHIDORAH
Defeat Mecha King Ghidorah Ravages Bangkok.

UNLOCK ALL
Select Cheat Codes from the Options and enter 233558.

INVULNERABILITY
Select Cheat Codes from the Options and enter 161650.

DRIFT MASTER
Select Cheat Codes from the Options and enter 789520.

PERFECT GRIP
Select Cheat Codes from the Options and enter 831782.

HIGH ROLLER
Select Cheat Codes from the Options and enter 401134.

GHOST CAR
Select Cheat Codes from the Options and enter 657346.

TOY CARS
Select Cheat Codes from the Options and enter 592014.

MM MODE
Select Cheat Codes from the Options and enter 800813.

IZUNA: LEGEND OF THE UNEMPLOYED NINJA

PATH OF TRAILS BONUS DUNGEON
After completing the game, touch the crystal from the beginning.

JACKASS THE GAME

CHANGE MUSIC
Press A + Y + Up.

JAKE HUNTER: DETECTIVE CHRONICLES

PASSWORDS
Select Password from the Main menu and enter the following:

UNLOCKABLE	PASSWORD
1 Password Info	AAAA
2 Visuals	LEET
3 Visuals	GONG
4 Visuals	CARS
5 Movies	ROSE
6 Jukebox	BIKE
7 Hints	HINT

JAM SESSIONS

BONUS SONGS
At the Free Play menu, press Up, Up, Down, Down, Left, Right, Left, Right.
This unlocks I'm Gonna Miss Her by Brad Paisley, Needles and Pins by Tom
Petty, and Wild Thing by Jimi Hendrix.

JUICED 2: HOT IMPORT NIGHTS

$5000
At the Cheat menu, enter HSAC.

ALL RACES
At the Cheat menu, enter EDOM.

ALL CARS
At the Cheat menu, enter SRAC.

ALL TRACKS
At the Cheat menu, enter KART.

KIRBY: CANVAS CURSE

JUMP GAME
Defeat the game with all five characters, then select the game file to get
Jump Game next to the Options on the Main menu.

LEGO BATMAN

You should hear a confirmation sound after the following codes are entered.

ALL CHARACTERS
At the Main menu, press X, Up, B, Down, Y, Left, Start, Right, R, R, L, R, R, Down, Down, Up, Y, Y, Start, Select.

ALL EPISODES AND FREE PLAY MODE
At the Main menu, press Right, Up, R, L, X, Y, Right, Left, B, L, R, L, Down, Down, Up, Y, Y, X, X, B, B, Up, Up, L, R, Start, Select.

ALL EXTRAS
At the Main menu, press Up, Down, L, R, L, R, L, Left, Right, X, X, Y, Y, B, B, L, Up, Down, L, R, L, R, Up, Up, Down, Start, Select.

1 MILLION STUDS
At the Main menu, press X, Y, B, B, Y, X, L, L, R, R, Up, Down, Left, Right, Start, Select.

3 MILLION STUDS
At the Main menu, press Up, Up, B, Down, Down, X, Left, Left, Y, L, R, L, R, B, Y, X, Start, Select.

LEGO INDIANA JONES: THE ORIGINAL ADVENTURES

You should hear a confirmation sound after the following codes are entered.

ALL CHARACTERS
At the Title screen, press X, Up, B, Down, Y, Left, Start, Right, R, R, L, R, R, Down, Down, Up, Y, Y, Y, Start, Select.

ALL EPISODES AND FREE PLAY MODE
Right, Up, R, L, X, Y, Right, Left, B, L, R, L, Down, Down, Up, Y, Y, X, X, B, B, Up, Up, L, R, Start, Select.

ALL EXTRAS
Up, Down, L, R, L, R, L, Left, Right, X, X, Y, Y, B, B, L, Up, Down, L, R, L, R, Up, Up, Down, Start, Select.

1,000,000 STUDS
At the Title screen, press X, Y, B, B, Y, X, L, L, R, R, Up, Down, Left, Right, Start, Select.

3,000,000 STUDS
At the Title screen, press Up, Up, B, Down, Down, X, Left, Left, Y, L, R, L, R, B, Y, X, Start, Select.

LEGO STAR WARS: THE COMPLETE SAGA

3,000,000 STUDS
At the main menu, press Start, Start, Down, Down, Left, Left, Up, Up, Select. This cheat can only be used once.

DEBUG MENUS
At the main menu, press Up, Left, Down, Right, Up, Left, Down, Right, Up, Left, Down, Right, R, L, Start, Select.

BONUS TOUCH GAME 1
At the main menu, press Up, Up, Down, L, L, R, R.

LEGO STAR WARS II: THE ORIGINAL TRILOGY

10 STUDS
At the Mos Eisley cantina, enter 4PR28U.

OBI WAN GHOST
At the Mos Eisley cantina, enter BEN917.

LOCK'S QUEST

REPLACE CLOCKWORKS WITH KINGDOM FORCE
After completing the game, hold R and select your profile.

ENDING STORY
After completing the game, hold L and select your profile.

LUNAR KNIGHTS

SOUND DATA (BOKTAI)
With Boktai in the GBA slot, purchase this from the General Store in Acuna.

SOUND DATA (BOKTAI 2)
With Boktai 2 in the GBA slot, purchase this from the General Store in Acuna.

MARIO PARTY DS

BOSS BASH
Complete Story Mode.

EXPERT CPU DIFFICULTY LEVEL
Complete Story Mode.

MUSIC AND VOICE ROOM
Complete Story Mode.

SCORE SCUFFLE
Complete Story Mode.

TRIANGLE TWISTER PUZZLE MODE
Complete Story Mode.

MEGAMAN BATTLE NETWORK 5: DOUBLE TEAM

NUMBERMAN CODES
When the Numberman machine is available in Higsby's Shop, enter the following codes.

CODE	ENTER
Area Steal *	99428938
Dark Recovery *	91182599
DoroTsunamiBall *	78234329
Leaders Raid L	01285874
Lord of Chaos X	39285712
MagmaSeed *	29387483
NumberBall *	64836563
P. Battle Pack 1	22323856
P. Battle Pack 2	66426428
P.Attack+3	76820385
P.Chip+50	48582829
P.HP+100	28475692
P.HP+50	53891756
Super Kitakaze *	29486933
Sword *	12495783
TP Chip	85375720
Tsunami Hole *	19283746
Unlocker	15733751

NUMBERMAN NAVI CUSTOMIZER PROGRAM
Enter the following codes in the Numberman Lotto Number.

CODE	ENTER
Attack Max Yellow	63231870
Beat Blue	79877132
BodyPack Green	30112002
BustPack Blue	80246758
Charge Max White	87412146
HP+200 Pink	90630807
HP+300 Pink	48785625
HP+300 White	13926561
HP+400 Pink	03419893
HP+400 Yellow	45654128

CODE	ENTER
HP+500 Pink	50906652
HP+500 White	72846472
Mega Folder 2 Green	97513648
Rush Yellow	09609807
SoulT+1 Yellow	28256341
Speed Max Pink	36695497
Spin Blue	12541883
Spin Green	78987728
Spin Red	30356451
Tango Green	54288793

METROID PRIME PINBALL

PHAZON MINES
Complete Omega Pirate in Multi Mission Mode.

PHENDRANA DRIFTS
Complete Thardus in Multi Mission Mode.

MY WORD COACH

WORD POPPERS MINIGAME
After reaching 200 word successes, at the options menu, press A, B, X, Y, A, B.

N+

ATARI BONUS LEVELS
Select Unlockables from the Main menu, hold L + R and press A, B, A, B, A, A, B.

NARUTO: PATH OF THE NINJA

After defeating the game, talk to Knohamaru on the roof of the Ninja Academy. He allows you go get certain cheats by tapping four successive spots on the touch screen in order. There are 12 different spots on the screen, we have numbered them from left to right, top to bottom as follows:

1	2	3	4
5	6	7	8
9	10	11	12

Now enter the following by touching the four spots in the order given.

UNLOCK	CODE
4th Hokage's Sword	4, 7, 11, 5
Fuji Fan	8, 11, 2, 5
Jiraiya	11, 3, 1, 6
Rajin's Sword	7, 6, 5, 11
Rasengan	9, 2, 12, 7

NARUTO: PATH OF THE NINJA 2

CHARACTER PASSWORDS
Talk to Konohamaru at the school to enter the following passwords. You must first complete the game for the passwords to work.

CHARACTER	PASSWORD
Gaara	DKFIABJL
Gai	IKAGDEFL
Iruka	JGDLKAIB
Itachi Uchiha	GBEIDALF
Jiraiya	EBJDAGFL
Kankuro	ALJKBEDG
Kyuubi Naruto	GJHLBFDE
Orochimaru	AHFBLEJG

CHARACTER	PASSWORD
Temari	HFICLKBG
The Third Hokage	CGHAJBEL

MISSION PASSWORDS

Talk to Konohamaru at the school to enter the following passwords. You must first complete the game for the passwords to work.

MISSION	PASSWORD
An Extreme Battle!	HLBAKGCD
The Legendary Haze Ninja!	FGEHIDAL
The Legendary Sannin!	BCEGKFHL

NEED FOR SPEED CARBON: OWN THE CITY

INFINITE NITROUS
At the Main menu, press Up, Up, Down, Left, A, B, B, A.

NEW SUPER MARIO BROS.

PLAY AS LUIGI IN SINGLE-PLAYER MODE
At the Select a File screen, press and hold L + R while selecting a saved game.

SECRET CHALLENGE MODE
While on the map, pause the game and press L, R, L, R, X, X, Y, Y.

THE NEW YORK TIMES CROSSWORDS

BLACK & WHITE
At the Main menu, press Up, Up, Down, Down, B, B, Y, Y.

NICKTOONS: ATTACK OF THE TOYBOTS

DANNY PHANTOM 2
Select Unlock Code from the Options and enter Tak, Jimmy, Zim, El Tigre.

SPONGEBOB 2
Select Unlock Code from the Options and enter Patrick, Jenny, Timmy, Tak.

PIRATES OF THE CARIBBEAN: DEAD MAN'S CHEST

10 GOLD
During a game, press Right, X, X, Right, Left.

INVINCIBILITY
During a game, press Up, Down, Left, Right (x5), Left, Right, Up, Down, Left, Right, Up (x5), Left.

UNLIMITED POWER
During a game, press Up, Up, Down, Down, Left, Right, Left, Right, L, R.

RESTORE HEALTH
During a game, press Y, Y, Select, Left, Right, Left, Right, Left.

RESTORE SAVVY
During a game, press X, X, Select, Up, Down, Up, Down, Up.

GHOST FORM MODE
During a game, press Y, X, Y, X, Y, X.

SEASICKNESS MODE
During a game, press X, X, Y, X, X, Y.

SILLY WEAPONS
During a game, press Y, Y, X, Y (x3).

AXE
During a game, press Left, L, L, Down, Down, Left, Up, Up, Down, Down.

BLUNDERBUSS
During a game, press Down, L, L, Down (x3).

CHICKEN
During a game, press Right, L, L, Up, Down, Down.

EXECUTIONER AXE
During a game, press Right, L, L, Up, Down, Up, Right, Right, Left (x2).

PIG
During a game, press Right, R, R, Down, Up, Up.

PISTOL
During a game, press Down, L, L, Down, Down, Right.

RIFLE
During a game, press Left, L, L, Up (x3).

FAST MUSIC
During a game, press Y, Select, Y (x4).

SLOW MUSIC
During a game, press Y, Select, X (x4).

DISABLE CHEATS
During a game, press X (x6).

POKEMON MYSTERY DUNGEON: EXPLORERS OF DARKNESS/ TIME

Select Wonder Mail before starting your game, and then enter the following passwords to add a mission to your Job List. These are listed by the reward you receive for completing the mission.

Each password can only be used once. There are many possible passwords, here we list some examples. These passwords work on Explorers of Darkness and Explorers of Time.

ACCESSORY

ACCESSORY	PASSWORD
Gold Ribbon	5+KPKXT9RYP754&M2-58&&1-
Golden Mask	@QYPSJ@-N-J%TH6=4-SK32CR
Joy Ribbon	597C6#873795@Q6=F+TSQ68J
Mobile Scarf	R2MQ0X0&&-RN+64#4S0R+&-1
Miracle Chest	FX199P@CW@-XK54Q%4628XT#
No-Stick Cap	1@484PJ7NJW@XCHC2&-+H=@P
Pecha Scarf	8%2R-T&T1F-KR5#08P#&T=@=
Persim Band	TCX#TJQ0%#46Q6MJYMH2S#C9
Power Band	FHSM5950-2QNFTH9S-JM3Q9F
Racket Band	-F773&1XM0FRJT7Y@PJ%9C40
Special Band	752PY8M-Q1NHY@QX92836MHT
Stamina Band	F9RM4Y6W1&2T7@%SWF=R0NK&
X-Ray Specs	C#7H-#P2J9QPHCFPM5F674H=
Wonder Chest	0@R#3-+&7SC2K3@4NQ0-JQX9
Zinc Band	@WWHK8X18@C+C8KTN51H#213

ITEM

ITEM	PASSWORD
Beauty Scarf	@+CWF98#5CPYR13RJ#3YWKS5
Calcium	Y=59NRNS-#M2%C25725NJMQQ
Coronet Rock	S%9@47NTYP#Y105SR#%QH9MX
Dawn Stone	N54=MK=FSH1FCR8=R@HN14#Y
Deepseascale	WT192-H2=K@-WTJ3=JJ64C16
Deepseatooth	WQCM0-H=QH&-W+JP7FKT4CP+
Dusk Stone	X0=-JQ&X1X4KRY=8Y=23M=FH
Electrilizer	4SJYCFNX0-N@JN%NQ#+7-Q7#
Frozen Rock	YT&8WY&+278+2QJT@53TM3M8
Heal Seed	TWTN%RFRK+39-P#M2X+CXQS#
Joy Seed	PQS39&-7WC+R&QJQM2Y@@1KN
Leaf Stone	NP96N4K0HW3CJX8#FNK%=F&+
Link Box	&%8FXT9C76F4Q4SP5F8X3RW%
Lost Loot	J%0+F18XW5%P-9@&17+F8P9M
Lunar Ribbon	%-94RKFY%505XXMMC=FYK45N
Magmarizer	=TK+0KH72MNJNRW5P@RS&Y6=
Max Elixir	4Q9F-K6X66YW5TJY6MXK+RX7
Metal Coat	NP3SMTH-T&TMQFY@N1Q&SFNK
Mossy Rock	@JH#ST1&S14W3T2XJ8=7KR+7
Mystery Part	PXJ634F44Q3FQW&KYRX538+=
Oval Stone	@&FYQ977C#@0YN-77TM&=X&+Q
Razor Claw	6JK2T26&MPC7&%-HWRXK2&-W
Reviver Seed	W+P0MYKJFNN3&Q%&-J12J2QH
Secret Slab	K=&4Q=@908N7=X&XHQ+Q1-CS
Shiny Stone	69-HHQX%K@#%7+5SMSPSQP#2
Sun Ribbon	7C8W308RYJ2XM@&QTYSJ%3=9
Thunderstone	+4QQK3PY84Y39P&=KN3=@XYR

| Vile Seed | 8#8%4496C#=JKRX9M&RKQW4% |
| Zinc | X=S#N&RNYSP9R2S01HT4MP8& |

309

TM

TM	PASSWORD
Attract	Y@=JC48#K4SQ0NS9#S7@32%3
Blizzard	Y#ST42FMC4H+NM@M=T999#PR
Brick Break	@MF=%8400Y8X#T8FCTQC5XTS
Brine	9C04WP5XXN@=4NPFR08SS&03
Calm Mind	SH&YH&96C%&JK9Y0H99%3WM9
Dig	SQ96Y08RXJJXMJJ7=SSQK3K3
Embargo	1PQ7K%JX#4=HFHXPPK%7K04H
Energy Ball	5016-@1X8@&5H46#51M&+-XC
Fire Blast	W0T+NF98J13+F&NN=XNR&J-7
Flamethrower	JQ78%-CK%1PTP-77M740=F98
Flash	FS272Y61F1@MNN8FCSSTJ6TP
Gyro Ball	C#S@Y4%9YFQ+SQ6WRK36@1N0
Iron Tail	8+R006Y-&X57XX#&N-PT@R&6
Overheat	F=X5&K=FYJ3FC-N-@QXK34QJ
Payback	K3%0=W61FQCMN-FPHP=J5&W3
Poison Jab	S==YMX%92R54TSK6=F8%-%MN
Protect	Q#6762JK@967H#CMX#RQ3&M3

TM	PASSWORD
Psych Up	6=49WKH72&-JN%14SKNF&40N
Recycle	M@56C+=@H%K13WF4Q%RJ2JP9
Reflect	F=YTCK297HC02MT+MF13SQ4W
Rest	KR=WT#JC#@+HFS5K0JJM-0-2
Roar	C&0FWPTCRMKT&7NQ@N0&RQS+
Rock Slide	CN%+TMSHM0&3#&5YC4M1#C@2
Skill Swap	-H4TNNKY&1-P%4HSJY&XHW%Q
Sleep Talk	1M5972RY8X6NCC3CPPRS0K8J
Swords Dance	=633=JSY147RT=&0R9PJJ1FM
Thunder	WKY&7==@HR2%32YX6755JQ85
Vacuum-Cut	7PS2#26WN7HNX83M23J6F@C5
X-Scissor	S6P&198+-5QYR&22FJMKW1XF

PRINCESS NATASHA

ALL GADGETS
Select Codes from the Extras menu and enter OLEGSGIZMO.

EXTRA LEVELS
Select Codes from the Extras menu and enter SMASHROBOT.

INFINITE LIVES
Select Codes from the Extras menu and enter CRUSHLUBEK.

RACE DRIVER: CREATE & RACE

ALL CHALLENGES
Select Cheat Codes from Extras and enter 942785.

ALL CHAMPIONSHIPS
Select Cheat Codes from Extras and enter 761492.

ALL REWARDS
Select Cheat Codes from Extras and enter 112337.

FREE DRIVE
Select Cheat Codes from Extras and enter 171923.

NO DAMAGE
Select Cheat Codes from Extras and enter 505303.

EASY STEERING
Select Cheat Codes from Extras and enter 611334.

MINIATURE CARS
Select Cheat Codes from Extras and enter 374288.

MM VIEW
Select Cheat Codes from Extras and enter 467348.

NINTENDO DS™

RIDGE RACER DS

00-AGENT CAR
Finish more than 10 races in Multiplayer.

CADDY CAR
Finish more than 10 races in Multiplayer.

GALAGA '88 CAR
Finish more than 10 races in Multiplayer.

MARIO RACING CAR
Finish more than 10 races in Multiplayer.

POOKA CAR
Finish more than 10 races in Multiplayer.

RED SHIRT RAGE CAR
Finish more than 10 races in Multiplayer.

SHY GUY CAR
Finish more than 10 races in Multiplayer.

GALAGA PAC JAM SONG
Unlock the Pooka car.

MUSHROOM KINGDOM II SONG
Unlock the DK Team Racing car.

SHREK SUPERSLAM

ALTERNATE OUTFIT FOR SHREK
Start the game with the GBA version of Shrek SuperSlam in the GBA slot.

SIMCITY CREATOR

99999999 MONEY
Enter MONEYBAGS as a password.

AMERICAN PROSPERITY AGE MAP
Enter NEWWORLD as a password.

ASIA AGE MAP
Enter SAMURAI as a password.

ASIA AGE BONUS MAP
Enter FEUDAL as a password.

DAWN OF CIVILIZATION MAP
Enter ANCIENT as a password.

GLOBAL WARMING MAP
Enter MODERN as a password.

GLOBAL WARMING BONUS MAP
Enter BEYOND as a password.

RENAISSANCE BONUS MAP
Enter HEREANDNOW as a password.

SIMCITY DS

LANDMARK BUILDINGS
Select Landmark Collection from the Museum menu. Choose Password and enter the following:

BUILDING	PASSWORD
Anglican Cathedral (UK)	kipling
Arc de Triomphe (France)	gaugin
Atomic Dome (Japan)	kawabata
Big Ben (UK)	orwell
Bowser Castle (Nintendo)	hanafuda
Brandenburg Gate (Germany)	gropius
Coit Tower	kerouac
Conciergerie (France)	rodin
Daibutsu (Japan)	mishima
Edo Castle (Japan)	shonagon
Eiffel Tower (France)	camus
Gateway Arch (USA)	twain
Grand Central Station (USA)	f.scott
Great Pyramids (Egypt)	mahfouz
Hagia Sofia (Turkey)	ataturk

BUILDING	PASSWORD
Helsinki Cathedral (Finland)	kivi
Himeji Castle (Japan)	hokusai
Holstentor (Germany)	durer
Independence Hall (USA)	mlkingjr
Jefferson Memorial (USA)	thompson
Kokkai (Japan)	soseki
LA Landmark (USA)	hemingway
Lincoln Memorial (USA)	melville
Liver Building (UK)	dickens
Melbourne Cricket Ground (Australia)	damemelba
Metropolitan Cath. (UK)	austen
Moai (Chile)	allende
Mt. Fuji (Japan)	hiroshige
National Museum (Taiwan)	yuanlee
Neuschwanstein Castle (Germany)	beethoven
Notre Dame (France)	hugo
Palace of Fine Arts (USA)	bunche
Palacio Real (Spain)	cervantes
Paris Opera (France)	daumier
Parthenon (Greece)	callas
Pharos of Alexandria (Egypt)	zewail
Building	Password
Rama IX Royal Park (Thailand)	phu
Reichstag (Germany)	goethe
Sagrada Familia (Spain)	dali
Shuri Castle (Japan)	basho
Smithsonian Castle (USA)	pauling
Sphinx (Egypt)	haykal
St Paul's Cathedral (UK)	defoe
St. Basil's Cathedral (Russia)	tolstoy
St. Stephen's Cathedral (Austria)	mozart
Statue of Liberty (USA)	pollack
Stockholm Palace (Sweden)	bergman
Taj Mahal (India)	tagore
Tower of London (UK)	maugham
Trafalgar Square (UK)	joyce
United Nations (UN)	amnesty
United States Capitol (USA)	poe
Washington Monument	capote
Westminster Abbey (UK)	greene
White House (USA)	Steinbeck

THE SIMS 2

MONGOO MONKEY FOR THE CASINO
Start the game with Sims 2 in the GBA slot of your Nintendo DS.

SOUL BUBBLES

REVEAL ALL CALABASH LOCATIONS
Pause the game and press A, L, L, R, A, Down, A, R.

ALL LEVELS
At the World Select, press L, Up, X, Up, R, Y.

ALL GALLERY ITEMS
At the Gallery, press B, Up, B, B, L, Y.

SPECTROBES

CARD INPUT SYSTEM
When the Upsilon Cube is unearthed and shown to Aldous, the Card Input System feature becomes available. This will allow you to input data from Spectrobe Cards. These give you new Spectrobes and Custom Parts.

OVERLOAD

If you get your hands on a Spectrobe Card and the system is unlocked, investigate the card input system in the spaceship's lower deck. Follow the instructions on the upper screen to match the four corner points of the card to the corners of the touch screen. Touch the screen through the seven holes in the card in the order indicated on the card. If the code you input is correct, you receive Spectrobes, custom Parts, minerals or Cubes.

You can input the same card a maximum of four times. This means that you can only obtain four of the same Spectrobes from a single card. Some cards are only able to be inputted once. And some cards cannot be input until you have reached a certain point in the game.

Here we give you the codes without needing the actual cards. There are 16 different spots that are used for these codes. These spots are labeled on the following image as A through P.

The following table gives you a seven character code which refers to the spots you touch in order. The first four characters have you touching the four corners in order. The final three are spots among the 12 in the middle. To get Cyclone Geo, Hammer Geo, Ice Geo, Plasma Geo, or Thunder Geo; you must first beat the game.

EFFECT	CODE
Aobasat Apex	BACD HEP
Cyclone Geo	CDAB LGM
Danaphant Tuska	ABDC ELI
Danilob	DABC GLO
Emerald Mineral	BACD FKN
Grilden Biblad	ABDC FIH
Grildragos Drafly	CDAB MHK
Gristar	BACD EJN
Effect	Code
Hammer Geo	ABDC ELH
Harumitey Lazos	DABC ILM
Ice Geo	CDAB HEK
Inataflare Auger	ABDC IGH
Inkalade	ABDC GLP
Iota Cube	ABDC OHE
Komainu	CDAB HMJ
Kugaster Sonara	DABC LOE
Mossax Jetspa (Custom Color 1)	BACD JML
Naglub	ABDC EJM
Plasma Geo	BACD KLE
Rho Cube	BACD PNI
Ruby Mineral	CDAB FKO
Samukabu	ABDC OIL
Samurite Voltar	BACD LHM
Sapphire Mineral	ABDC FJO
Segulos Propos	CDAB KIH
Seguslice	CDAB GKP
Shakor Bristle	DABC MLK
Sigma Cube	CDAB PML
Tau Cube	DABC LIF
Thunder Geo	DABC MEL
Vilagrisp (Custom Part)	DABC EIN
Vilakroma	BACD NLM
Vilakroma (Custom Color 1)	CDAB LJI
Vilakroma (Custom Color 2)	DABC EGP
Windora	ABDC MGP
Windora (Custom Color 1)	DABC EHG
Windora (Custom Color 2)	CDAB JPM
Windora Ortex	BACD IPG
Windora Ortex (Custom Color 1)	ABDC MPH
Windora Ortex (Custom Color 2)	DABC MGH
Windora Sordina	CDAB PEO

OVERLOAD

EFFECT	CODE
Windora Sordina (Custom Color 1)	BACD MOH
Windora Sordina (Custom Color 2)	ABDC LEN
Wing Geo (must beat game	DABC MNP

STAR WARS: THE FORCE UNLEASHED

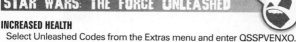

INCREASED HEALTH
Select Unleashed Codes from the Extras menu and enter QSSPVENXO.

MAX OUT FORCE POWERS
Select Unleashed Codes from the Extras menu and enter CPLOOLKBF.

UNLIMITED FORCE ENERGY
Select Unleashed Codes from the Extras menu and enter TVENCVMJZ.

MORE POWERFUL LIGHTSABER
Select Unleashed Codes from the Extras menu and enter lightsaber.

UBER LIGHTSABER
Select Unleashed Codes from the Extras menu and enter MOMIROXIW.

ROM KOTA
Select Unleashed Codes from the Extras menu and enter mandalore.

CEREMONIAL JEDI ROBES
Select Unleashed Codes from the Extras menu and enter CURSEZRUX.

DAD'S ROBES
Select Unleashed Codes from the Extras menu and enter wookiee.

DARTH VADER'S COSTUME
Select Unleashed Codes from the Extras menu and enter HRMXRKVEN.

KENTO'S ROBE
Select Unleashed Codes from the Extras menu and enter KBVMSEVNM.

KOTA'S OUTFIT
Select Unleashed Codes from the Extras menu and enter EEDOPVENG.

SITH ROBE
Select Unleashed Codes from the Extras menu and enter ZWSFVENXA.

SITH ROBES
Select Unleashed Codes from the Extras menu and enter holocron.

SITH STALKER ARMOR
Select Unleashed Codes from the Extras menu and enter CPLZKMZTD.

SUPER PRINCESS PEACH

MINI-GAME
At the Title screen, hold R and press Start.

TAMAGOTCHI CONNECTION: CORNER SHOP 3

DOUBLE LAYERED CAKE
Select Enter Code from the Special menu and enter R6194BJD6F.

TOM CLANCY'S SPLINTER CELL CHAOS THEORY

UNLIMITED AMMO/GADGETS
Defeat the game.

CHARACTER SKINS
Defeat the game.

TONY HAWK'S DOWNHILL JAM

ALWAYS SNOWSKATE
Select Buy Stuff from the Skateshop. Choose Enter Code and enter SNOWSK8T.

ABOMINABLE SNOWMAN OUTFIT
Select Buy Stuff from the Skateshop. Choose Enter Code and enter BIGSNOWMAN.

MIRRORED MAPS
Select Buy Stuff from the Skateshop. Choose Enter Code and enter MIRRORBALL.

ZOMBIE SKATER OUTFIT
Select Buy Stuff from the Skateshop. Choose Enter Code and enter ZOMBIEALIVE.

OVERLOAD

NINTENDO DS™

TRAUMA CENTER: UNDER THE KNIFE

X1: KYRIAKI MISSION
Defeat the game. Find the X Missions under Challenge Mode.

X2: DEFTERA MISSION
Defeat X1: Kyriaki Mission. Find the X Missions under Challenge Mode.

X3: TRITI MISSION
Defeat X2: Deftera Mission. Find the X Missions under Challenge Mode.

X4: TETARTI MISSION
Defeat X3: Triti Mission. Find the X Missions under Challenge Mode.

X5: PEMPTI MISSION
Defeat X4: Tetarti Mission. Find the X Missions under Challenge Mode.

X6: PARAKEVI MISSION
Defeat X5: Pempti Mission. Find the X Missions under Challenge Mode.

X7: SAVATO MISSION
Defeat X6: Parakevi Mission. Find the X Missions under Challenge Mode.

ULTIMATE MORTAL KOMBAT

VS CODES
At the VS screen, each player must use LP, BLK, and LK to enter the following codes:

EFFECT	PLAYER 1	PLAYER 2
You are now entering the realm	642	468
Blocking Disabled	020	020
Dark Kombat	448	844
Infinite Run	466	466
Play in Kahn's Kave	004	700
Play in the Kombat Temple	600	N/A
Play in the Soul Chamber	123	901
Play on Jade's Deset	330	033
Play on Kahn's Tower	880	220
Play on Noob Saibot Dorfen	050	050
Play on Rooftops	343	343
Play on Scislac Busorez	933	933
Play on Subway	880	088
Play on the Belltower	091	190
Play on the Bridge	077	022
Play on the Graveyard	666	333
Play on the Pit 3	820	028
Play on the Street	079	035
Play on the Waterfront	002	003
Play Scorpions Lair	666	444
Player 1 Half Power	033	N/A
Player 1 Quarter Power	707	N/A
Player 2 Half Power	N/A	033
Player 2 Quarter Power	N/A	707
Power Bars Disabled	987	123
Random Kombat	444	444
Revision 1.2	999	999
Sans Power	044	440
Silent Kombat	300	300
Throwing Disabled	100	100
Throwing Encouraged	010	010
Winner of round fights Motaro	969	141
Winner of round fights Noob Saibot	769	342
Winner of round fights Shao Kahn	033	564
Winner of round fights Smoke	205	205

UNLOCK ERMAC, MILEENA, CLASSIC SUB-ZERO

At the Ultimate Kombat Kode screen input the following codes:
(Note: To easily access the Ultimate Kombat Kode screen just get defeated and dont continue)

CLASSIC SUB-ZERO

At the Ultimate Kombat Kode screen, enter 81835. You can reach this screen by losing and not continuing.

ERMAC

At the Ultimate Kombat Kode screen, enter 12344. You can reach this screen by losing and not continuing.

MILEENA

At the Ultimate Kombat Kode screen, enter 22264. You can reach this screen by losing and not continuing.

HUMAN SMOKE

Select ROBO Smoke. Hold Block + Run + High Punch + High Kick + Back before the fight begins.

WORLD CHAMPIONSHIP POKER

UNLOCK CASINOS

At the Title screen, press Y, X, Y, B, L, R. Then press the following direction:

DIRECTION	CASINO
Left	Amazon
Right	Nebula
Down	Renaissance

YU-GI-OH! NIGHTMARE TROUBADOUR

CREDITS

Unlock the Password Machine by defeating the Expert Cup. Enter the Duel Shop and select the Slot Machine, then enter 00000375.

SOUND TEST

Unlock the Password Machine by defeating the Expert Cup. Enter the Duel Shop and select the Slot Machine, then enter 57300000.

YU-GI-OH! WORLD CHAMPIONSHIP 2007

CARD PASSWORDS

Select Password from the Shop and enter one of the Card Passwords. You must already have that card or have it in a pack list for the password to work.

Refer to the Card List for YU-GI-OH! GX TAG FORCE for PSP. All cards may not be available in World Championship 2007.

YU-GI-OH! WORLD CHAMPIONSHIP 2008

CARD PASSWORDS

Enter the following in the password machine to receive the corresponding card. You need to have the card already to use the password.

CARD	PASSWORD
7	67048711
7 Colored Fish	23771716
7 Completed	86198326
A Feint Plan	68170903
A Hero Emerges	21597117
Abyss Soldier	18318842
Acid Rain	21323861
Acid Trap Hole	41356845
Adhesive Explosive	53828196
Agido	16135253
Airknight Parshath	18036057

NINTENDO DS™

OVERLOAD

CARD	PASSWORD
Aitsu	48202661
Alkana Knight Joker	06150044
Alligator's Sword	64428736
Alligator's Sword Dragon	03366982
Alpha the Magnet Warrior	99785935
Altar for Tribute	21070956
Amazon Archer	91869203
Amazoness Archers	67987611
Amazoness Blowpiper	73574678
Amazoness Chain Master	29654737
Amazoness Fighter	55821894
Amazoness Paladin	47480070
Amazoness Spellcaster	81325903
Amazoness Swords Woman	94004268
Amazoness Tiger	10979723
Amphibian Beast	67371383
Amplifier	00303660
Anti-Spell	53112492
Aqua Madoor	85639257
Aqua Spirit	40916023
Archfiend of Gilfer	50287060
Armed Changer	90374791
Armed Ninja	09076207
Armored Glass	21070956
Armored Zombie	20277860
Array of Revealing Light	69296555
Arsenal Bug	42364374
Arsenal Robber	55348096
Assault on GHQ	62633180
Asura Priest	02134346
Attack and Receive	63689843
Autonomous Action Unit	71453557
Axe of Despair	40619825
Axe Raider	48305365
B. Skull Dragon	11901678
Baby Dragon	88819587
Back to Square One	47453433
Backfire	82705573
Bad Reaction to Simochi	40633297
Bait Doll	07165085
Ballista of Rampart Smashing	00242146
Banisher of the Light	61528025
Banner of Courage	10012614
Bark of The Dark Ruler	41925941
Baron of the Fiend Sword	86325596
Barrel Behind the Door	78783370
Barrel Dragon	81480460
Battery Charger	61181383
Batteryman AA	63142001
Batteryman C	19733961
Batteryman D	55401221
Battle Ox	05053103
Battle Warrior	55550921
Beast Fangs	46009906
Beast Soul Swap	35149085
Beastking of the Swamps	99426834
Beautiful Headhuntress	16899564
Beckoning Light	16255442
Berfomet	77207191
Berserk Gorilla	39168895
Beta the Magnet Warrior	39256679
Bickuribox	25655502
Big Bang Shot	61127349

CARD	PASSWORD
Big Eye	16768387
Big Shield Gardna	65240384
Birdface	45547649
Black Illusion Ritual	41426869
Black Luster Ritual	55761792
Black Luster Soldier	72989439
Black Magic Ritual	76792184
Black Pendant	65169794
Bladefly	28470714
Blast Held by a Tribute	89041555
Blast Magician	21051146
Blast Sphere	26302522
Blast with Chain	98239899
Blasting the Ruins	21466326
Blessings of the Nile	30653173
Blowback Dragon	25551951
Blue Medicine	20871001
Blue-Eyes Toon Dragon	53183600
Blue-Eyes Ultimate Dragon	23995346
Blue-Eyes White Dragon	80906030
Blue-Eyes White Dragon	80906030
Book of Taiyou	38699854
Bottomless Trap Hole	29401950
Bowganian	52090844
Bracchio-Raidus	16507828
Brain Control	87910978
Breaker the Magical Warrior	71413901
Breath of Light	20101223
Bright Castle	82878489
Burning Land	24294108
Burning Spear	18937875
Burst Return	27191436
Burst Stream of Destruction	17655904
Buster Rancher	84740193
Cannon Soldier	11384280
Cannonball Spear Shellfish	95614612
Card Destruction	72892473
Card of Sanctity	04266498
Card Shuffle	12183332
Castle of Dark Illusions	00062121
Castle Walls	44209392
Catapult Turtle	95727991
Ceasefire	36468556
Celtic Guardian	91152256
Cemetery Bomb	51394546
Centrifugal Field	01801154
Cestus of Dagla	28106077
Chain Destruction	01248895
Chain Disappearance	57139487
Chain Energy	79323590
Chaos Command Magician	72630549
Chaos End	61044390
Chaos Greed	97439308
Chimera the Flying Mythical Beast	04796100
Chiron the Mage	16956455
Chorus of Sanctuary	81380218
Chthonian Alliance	46910446
Chthonian Blast	18271561
Chthonian Polymer	72287557
Clay Charge	22479888
Cocoon of Evolution	40240595
Coffin Seller	65830223
Cold Wave	60682203

CARD	PASSWORD
Command Knight	10375182
Conscription	31000575
Continuous Destruction Punch	68057622
Contract with Exodia	33244944
Contract with the Dark Master	96420087
Convulsion of Nature	62966332
Copycat	26376390
Cosmo Queen	38999506
Covering Fire	74458486
Crass Clown	93889755
Crawling Dragon #2	38289717
Crimson Sunbird	46696593
Crush Card Virus	57728570
Curse of Anubis	66742250
Curse of Darkness	84970821
Curse of Dragon	28279543
Curse of the Masked Beast	94377247
Cursed Seal of the Forbidden Spell	58851034
Cyber Raider	39978267
Cyber Shield	63224564
Cyber-Tech Alligator	48766543
D.D. Borderline	60912752
D.D. Designator	33423043
D.D. Assailant	70074904
D.D. Dynamite	08628798
D.D. Trap Hole	05606466
D.D. Warrior	37043180
D.D. Warrior Lady	07572887
D. Tribe	02833249
Dark Artist	72520073
Dark Deal	65824822
Dark Dust Spirit	89111398
Dark Elf	21417692
Dark Energy	04614116
Dark Factory of Mass Production	90928333
Dark Jeroid	90980792
Dark Magic Attack	02314238
Dark Magic Curtain	99789342
Dark Magician	46986414
Dark Magician Girl	38033121
Dark Magician of Chaos	40737112
Dark Master - Zorc	97642679
Dark Mimic LV1	74713516
Dark Mimic LV3	01102515
Dark Mirror Force	20522190
Dark Necrofear	31829185
Dark Paladin	98502113
Dark Rabbit	99261403
Dark Room of Nightmare	85562745
Dark Sage	92377303
Dark Snake Syndrome	47233801
Dark Spirit of the Silent	93599951
Dark World Lightning	93554166
Darkness Approaches	80168720
Dark-Piercing Light	45895206
Deck Devastation Virus	35027493
Decoy Dragon	02732323
Dedication through Light and Darkness	69542930
De-Fusion	95286165
Delta Attacker	39719977
Despair from the Dark	71200730
De-Spell	19159413
Destiny Board	94212438

CARD	PASSWORD
Destruction Ring	21219755
Dian Keto the Cure Master	84257639
Dice Re-Roll	83241722
Different Dimension Capsule	11961740
Different Dimension Dragon	50939127
Different Dimension Gate	56460688
Diffusion Wave-Motion	87880531
Dimension Fusion	23557835
Dimension Wall	67095270
Dimensional Prison	70342110
Dimensionhole	22959079
Disappear	24623598
Disarmament	20727787
Divine Sword - Phoenix Blade	31423101
Divine Wrath	49010598
DNA Surgery	74701381
Doomcaliber Knight	78700060
Double Coston	44436472
Double Snare	03682106
Double Spell	24096228
Dragged Down into the Grave	16435235
Dragon Capture Jar	50045299
Dragon Seeker	28563545
Dragon Treasure	01435851
Dragonic Attack	32437102
Dragon's Mirror	71490127
Draining Shield	43250041
Dramatic Rescue	80193355
Dream Clown	13215230
Drill Bug	88733579
Driving Snow	00473469
Drop Off	55773067
Dunames Dark Witch	12493482
Dust Barrier	31476755
Dust Tornado	60082867
Earth Chant	59820352
Earthbound Spirit's Invitation	65743242
Earthquake	82828051
Eatgaboon	42578427
Ectoplasmer	97342942
Ekibyo Drakmord	69954399
Electro-Whip	37820550
Elegant Egotist	90219263
Elemental Hero Avian	21844576
Elemental Hero Burstinatrix	58932615
Elemental Hero Clayman	84327329
Elemental Hero Flame Wingman	35809262
Elemental Hero Rampart Blaster	47737087
Elemental Hero Sparkman	20721928
Elemental Hero Thunder Giant	61204971
Embodiment of Apophis	28649820
Emergency Provisions	53046408
Enchanted Arrow	93260132
Enchanting Fitting Room	30531525
Enemy Controller	98045062
Energy Drain	56916805
Enervating Mist	26022485
Enraged Battle Ox	76909279
Eradicating Aerosol	94716515
Eternal Drought	56606928
Eternal Rest	95051344
Exarion Universe	63749102
Exchange	05556668

NINTENDO DS™

CARD	PASSWORD
Exhausting Spell	95451366
Exodia Necross	12600382
Exodia the Forbidden One	33396948
Fairy Box	21598948
Fairy King Truesdale	45425051
Fairy Meteor Crush	97687912
Fairy's Hand Mirror	17653779
Fake Trap	03027001
Feather Shot	19394153
Feather Wind	71060915
Fengsheng Mirror	37406863
Feral Imp	41392891
Fiend Comedian	81172176
Fiend Skull Dragon	66235877
Fiend's Hand Mirror	58607704
Fiend's Sanctuary	24874630
Final Countdown	95308449
Final Destiny	18591904
Firewing Pegasus	27054370
Fissure	66788016
Flame Cerebrus	60862676
Flame Manipulator	34460851
Flame Swordsman	40502030
Flying Kamakiri #1	84834865
Foolish Burial	81439173
Forced Ceasefire	97806240
Forest	87430998
Fortress Whale	62337487
Fortress Whale's Oath	77454922
Frozen Soul	57069605
Fulfillment of the Contract	48206762
Full Salvo	70865988
Fusilier Dragon, the Duel-Mode Beast	51632798
Fusion Gate	24094653
Fusion Sage	26902560
Fusion Sword Murasame Blade	37684215
Gaia Power	56594520
Gaia the Dragon Champion	66889139
Gaia the Fierce Knight	06368038
Gamma the Magnet Warrior	11549357
Garoozis	14977074
Garuda the Wind Spirit	12800777
Gazelle the King of Mythical Beasts	05818798
Gear Golem the Moving Fortress	30190809
Gearfried the Iron Knight	00423705
Gearfried the Swordmaster	57046845
Gemini Elf	69140098
Generation Shift	34460239
Germ Infection	24668830
Getsu Fuhma	21887179
Giant Flea	41762634
Giant Germ	95178994
Giant Rat	97017120
Giant Red Seasnake	58831685
Giant Soldier of Stone	13039848
Giant Trunade	42703248
Gigantes	47606319
Gilasaurus	45894482
Gilford the Legend	69933858
Gilford the Lightning	36354007
Gil Garth	38445524
Goblin Attack Force	78658564
Goblin Fan	04149689

CARD	PASSWORD
Goblin King	18590133
Goblin Thief	45311864
Goblin's Secret Remedy	11868825
Goddess of Whim	67959180
Goddess with the Third Eye	53493204
Gokibore	15367030
Gorgon's Eye	52648457
Graceful Dice	74137509
Gradius' Option	14291024
Granadora	13944422
Grand Tiki Elder	13676474
Gravedigger Ghoul	82542267
Gravekeeper's Assailant	25262697
Gravekeeper's Cannonholder	99877698
Gravekeeper's Chief	62473983
Gravekeeper's Commandant	17393207
Gravekeeper's Curse	50712728
Gravekeeper's Guard	37101832
Gravekeeper's Servant	16762927
Gravekeeper's Spear Soldier	63695531
Gravekeeper's Spy	24317029
Gravekeeper's Vassal	99690140
Gravekeeper's Watcher	26084285
Gravity Axe - Grarl	32022366
Gravity Bind	85742772
Great Moth	14141448
Greed	89405199
Green Baboon, Defender of the Forest	46668237
Greenkappa	61831093
Ground Collapse	90502999
Gust	73079365
Gust Fan	55321970
Gyaku-Gire Panda	09817927
Hammer Shot	26412047
Hand Collapse	74519184
Hannibal Necromancer	05640330
Harpie Lady	76812113
Harpie Lady 1	91932350
Harpie Lady 2	27927359
Harpie Lady 3	54415063
Harpie Lady Sisters	12206212
Harpies' Hunting Ground	75782277
Harpie's Pet Dragon	52040216
Headless Knight	5434080
Heart of Clear Water	64801562
Heart of the Underdog	35762283
Heavy Mech Support Platform	23265594
Heavy Slump	52417194
Heavy Storm	19613556
Helpoemer	76052811
Hercules Beetle	52584282
Hero Kid	32679370
Hero Signal	22020907
Hidden Book of Spell	21840375
Hieroglyph Lithograph	10248192
Hinotama	46130346
Hiro's Shadow Scout	81863068
Hitotsu-Me Giant	76184692
Horn Imp	69669405
Horn of Light	38552107
Horn of the Unicorn	64047146
Hoshiningen	67629977
House of Adhesive Tape	15083728

CARD	PASSWORD
Human-Wave Tactics	30353551
Illusionist Faceless Mage	28546905
Impenetrable Formation	96631852
Inferno	74823665
Inferno Fire Blast	52684508
Infinite Cards	94163677
Infinite Dismissal	54109233
Injection Fairy Lily	79575620
Insect Armor with Laser Cannon	03492538
Insect Barrier	23615409
Insect Imitation	96965364
Insect Queen	91512835
Inspection	16227556
Interdimensional Matter Transporter	36261276
Invigoration	98374133
Jack's Knight	90876561
Jade Insect Whistle	95214051
Jam Breeding Machine	21770260
Jam Defender	21558682
Jar of Greed	83968380
Jigen Bakudan	90020065
Jinzo	77585513
Jinzo #7	77585513
Jowgen the Spiritualist	41855169
Jowls of Dark Demise	05257687
Judge Man	30113682
Judgment of the Pharaoh	55948544
Just Desserts	24068492
Kabazauls	51934376
Kabazauls	51934376
Kanan the Swordsmistress	12829151
Killer Needle	88979991
Kinetic Soldier	79853073
King of the Skull Servants	36021814
King of the Swamp	79109599
King Tiger Wanghu	83986578
King's Knight	64788463
Koitsu	69456283
Krokodilus	76512652
Kryuel	82642348
Kunai with Chain	37390589
Kuriboh	40640057
Kycoo the Ghost Destroyer	88240808
Labyrinth of Nightmare	66526672
Labyrinth Tank	99551425
Larvae Moth	87756343
Laser Cannon Armor	77007920
Last Day of the Witch	90330453
Launcher Spider	87322377
Lava Battleguard	20394040
Lava Golem	00102380
Left Arm of the Forbidden One	07902349
Left Leg of the Forbidden One	44519536
Legacy of Yata-Garasu	30461781
Legendary Sword	61854111
Level Conversion Lab	84397023
Level Limit - Area A	54976796
Level Limit - Area B	03136426
Level Modulation	61850482
Level Up!	25290459
Light of Judgment	44595286
Lighten the Load	37231841
Lightforce Sword	49587034

CARD	PASSWORD
Lightning Vortex	69162969
Little Chimera	68658728
Luminous Soldier	57482479
Luminous Spark	81777047
Luster Dragon	11091375
Machine Duplication	63995093
Machine King	46700124
Mad Sword Beast	79870141
Mage Power	83746708
Magic Cylinder	62279055
Magic Drain	59344077
Magic Formula	67227834
Magic Jammer	77414722
Magical Arm Shield	96008713
Magical Dimension	28553439
Magical Explosion	32723153
Magical Hats	81210420
Magical Stone Excavation	98494543
Magical Thorn	53119267
Magician of Black Chaos	30208479
Magician of Faith	31560081
Magician's Circle	00050755
Magician's Unite	36045450
Magician's Valkyria	80304126
Maha Vailo	93013676
Maharaghi	40695128
Maiden of the Aqua	17214465
Major Riot	09074847
Malevolent Catastrophe	01224927
Malevolent Nuzzler	99597615
Malfunction	06137091
Malice Dispersion	13626450
Man-Eater Bug	54652250
Man-Eating Treasure Chest	13723605
Manga Ryu-Ran	38369349
Marauding Captain	02460565
Marie the Fallen One	57579381
Marshmallon	31305911
Marshmallon Glasses	66865880
Mask of Brutality	82432018
Mask of Darkness	28933734
Mask of Dispel	20765952
Mask of Restrict	29549364
Mask of the Accursed	56948373
Mask of Weakness	57882509
Masked Sorcerer	10189126
Mass Driver	34906152
Master Kyonshee	24530661
Mataza the Zapper	22609617
Mausoleum of the Emperor	80921533
Mechanicalchaser	07359741
Mega Ton Magical Cannon	32062913
Megamorph	22046459
Melchid the Four-Faced Beast	86569121
Meltiel, Sage of the Sky	49905576
Mesmeric Control	48642904
Messenger of Peace	44656491
Metal Detector	75646520
Metal Reflect Slime	26905245
Metalmorph	68540058
Metalzoa	50705071
Meteor Black Dragon	90660762
Meteor Dragon	64271667

CARD	PASSWORD
Michizure	37580756
Micro Ray	18190572
Millennium Shield	32012841
Milus Radiant	07489323
Mind Control	37520316
Mind Crush	15800838
Miracle Dig	63434080
Miracle Kids	55985014
Miracle Restoring	68334074
Mirror Force	44095762
Mispolymerization	58392024
Mist body	47529357
Moisture Creature	75285069
Mokey Mokey	27288416
Mokey Mokey King	13803864
Mokey Mokey Smackdown	01965724
Molten Destruction	19384334
Monster Gate	43040603
Monster Recovery	93108433
Monster Reincarnation	74848038
Mooyan Curry	58074572
Morphing Jar	33508719
Morphing Jar #2	79106360
Mother Grizzly	57839750
Mountain	50913601
Muka Muka	46657337
Multiplication of Ants	22493811
Multiply	40703222
Mushroom Man	14181608
My Body as a Shield	69279219
Mysterious Puppeteer	54098121
Mystic Box	25774450
Mystic Horseman	68516705
Mystic Probe	49251811
Mystic Swordsman LV2	47507260
Mystic Swordsman LV4	74591968
Mystic Swordsman LV6	60482781
Mystic Tomato	83011277
Mystical Elf	15025844
Mystical Moon	36607978
Mystical Refpanel	35563539
Mystical Sheep #1	30451366
Mystical Space Typhoon	05318639
Narrow Pass	40172183
Necrovalley	47355498
Needle Wall	38299233
Needle Worm	81843628
Negate Attack	14315573
Neo the Magic Swordsman	50930991
Newdoria	04335645
Next to be Lost	07076131
Nightmare Wheel	54704216
Nimble Momonga	22567609
Nitro Unit	23842445
Non Aggression Area	76848240
Non-Fusion Area	27581098
Non-Spellcasting Area	20065549
Numinous Healer	02130625
Nuvia the Wicked	12953226
Obnoxious Celtic Guard	52077741
Ojama Black	79335209
Ojama Delta Hurricane!!	08251996
Ojama Green	12482652

CARD	PASSWORD
Ojama King	90140980
Ojama Trio	29843091
Ojama Yellow	42941100
Ojamagic	24643836
Ojamuscle	98259197
Ominous Fortunetelling	56995655
Ookazi	19523799
Opti-Camouflage Armor	44762290
Order to Charge	78986941
Order to Smash	39019325
Otohime	39751093
Overpowering Eye	60577362
Panther Warrior	42035044
Paralyzing Potion	50152549
Parasite Paracide	27911549
Parrot Dragon	62762898
Patrician of Darkness	19153634
Pendulum Machine	24433920
Penguin Knight	36039163
Penguin Soldier	93920745
Perfectly Ultimate Great Moth	48579379
Petit Moth	58192742
Pharaoh's Treasure	63571750
Pigeonholing Books of Spell	96677818
Pikeru's Second Sight	58015506
Pinch Hopper	26185991
Pitch-Black Power Stone	34029630
Poison Fangs	76539047
Poison of the Old Man	08842266
Polymerization	35550694
Pot of Avarice	67169062
Premature Burial	70828912
Prepare to Strike Back	04483989
Prevent Rat	00549481
Princess of Tsurugi	51371017
Prohibition	43711255
Protector of the Sanctuary	24221739
Pumpking the King of Ghosts	29155212
Queen's Knight	25652259
Rabid Horseman	94905343
Radiant Jeral	84177693
Radiant Mirror Force	21481146
Raigeki Break	04178474
Rapid-Fire Magician	06337436
Ray of Hope	82529174
Ready for Intercepting	31785398
Really Eternal Rest	28121403
Reaper of the Cards	33066139
Reckless Greed	37576645
Recycle	96316857
Red Archery Girl	65570596
Red Medicine	38199696
Red-Eyes B. Chick	36262024
Red-Eyes Black Dragon	74677422
Red-Eyes Black Metal Dragon	64335804
Reflect Bounder	02851070
Reinforcement of the Army	32807846
Reinforcements	17814387
Release Restraint	75417459
Relieve Monster	37507488
Relinquished	64631466
Remove Trap	51482758
Respect Play	08951260

NINTENDO DS™

CARD	PASSWORD
Restructer Revolution	99518961
Reversal Quiz	05990062
Reverse Trap	77622396
Revival Jam	31709826
Right Arm of the Forbidden One	70903634
Right Leg of the Forbidden One	08124921
Rigorous Reaver	39180960
Ring of Magnetism	20436034
Riryoku Field	70344351
Rising Energy	78211862
Rite of Spirit	30450531
Ritual Weapon	54351224
Robbin' Goblin	88279736
Robbin' Zombie	83258273
Robotic Knight	44203504
Rock Bombardment	20781762
Rocket Warrior	30860696
Rod of Silence - Kay'est	95515060
Rogue Doll	91939608
Roll Out!	91597389
Royal Command	33950246
Royal Decree	51452091
Royal Magical Library	70791313
Royal Oppression	93016201
Royal Surrender	56058888
Royal Tribute	72405967
Rude Kaiser	26378150
Rush Recklessly	70046172
Ryu Kokki	57281778
Ryu-Kishin	15303296
Ryu-Ran	02964201
Sage's Stone	13604200
Saggi the Dark Clown	66602787
Sakuretsu Armor	56120475
Salamandra	32268901
Salvage	96947648
Sangan	26202165
Sasuke Samurai #3	77379481
Sasuke Samurai #4	64538655
Satellite Cannon	50400231
Second Coin Toss	36562627
Sengenjin	76232340
Serial Spell	49398568
Serpentine Princess	71829750
Seven Tools of the Bandit	03819470
Shadow Ghoul	30778711
Shadow of Eyes	58621589
Share the Pain	56830749
Shield & Sword	52097679
Shield Crush	30683373
Shift	59560625
Shifting Shadows	59237154
Shinato, King of a Higher Plane	86327225
Shinato's Ark	60365591
Shining Abyss	87303357
Shining Angel	95956346
Shooting Star Bow - Ceal	95638658
Shrink	55713623
Silver Bow and Arrow	01557499
Simultaneous Loss	92219931
Skilled Dark Magician	73752131
Skilled White Magician	46363422
Skull Dice	00126218

CARD	PASSWORD
Skull Servant	32274490
Skull-Mark Ladybug	64306248
Skyscraper	63035430
Slate Warrior	78636495
Slot Machine	03797883
Smashing Ground	97169186
Smoke Grenade of the Thief	63789924
Snake Fang	00596051
Sogen	86318356
Solar Ray	44472639
Solemn Judgment	41420027
Solemn Wishes	35346968
Sorcerer of the Doomed	49218300
Soul Absorption	68073522
Soul Demolition	76297408
Soul Exchange	68005187
Soul of Purity and Light	77527210
Soul of the Pure	47852924
Soul Release	05758500
Soul Resurrection	92924317
Soul Reversal	78864369
Soul Taker	81510157
Spark Blaster	97362768
Spatial Collapse	20644748
Special Hurricane	42598242
Spell Absorption	51481927
Spell Reproduction	29228529
Spell Vanishing	29735721
Spellbinding Circle	18807108
Spell-stopping Statute	10069180
Spiral Spear Strike	49328340
Spirit Message "A"	94772232
Spirit Message "I"	31893528
Spirit Message "L"	30170981
Spirit Message "N"	67287533
Spirit of Flames	13522325
Spirit of the Pharaoh	25343280
Spirit's Invitation	92394653
Spiritual Earth Art - Kurogane	70156997
Spiritual Energy Settle Machine	99173029
Spiritual Fire Art - Kurenai	42945701
Spiritual Water Art - Aoi	06540606
Spiritual Wind Art - Miyabi	79333300
Spiritualism	15866454
St. Joan	21175632
Staunch Defender	92854392
Steel Ogre Grotto #2	90908427
Steel Scorpion	13599884
Stim-Pack	83225447
Stone Statue of the Aztecs	31812496
Stop Defense	63102017
Stray Lambs	60764581
Stumbling	34646691
Swamp Battleguard	40453765
Swift Gaia the Fierce Knight	16589042
Sword of Deep-Seated	98495314
Sword of the Soul-Eater	05371656
Swords of Concealing Light	12923641
Swords of Revealing Light	72302403
Swordsman of Landstar	03573512
System Down	07672244
Tailor of the Fickle	43641473
Terraforming	73628505

CARD	PASSWORD
The A. Forces	00403847
The Agent of Force - Mars	91123920
The Agent of Judgement - Saturn	91345518
The Big March of Animals	01689516
The Bistro Butcher	71107816
The Cheerful Coffin	41142615
The Creator	61505339
The Creator Incarnate	97093037
The Dark Door	30606547
The Earl of Demise	66989694
The Fiend Megacyber	66362965
The First Sarcophagus	31076103
The Flute of Summoning Kuriboh	20065322
The Forgiving Maiden	84080938
The Gross Ghost of Fled Dreams	68049471
The Illusory Gentleman	83764996
The Inexperienced Spy	81820689
The Last Warrior from Another Planet	86099788
The Law of the Normal	66926224
The League of Uniform Nomenclature	55008284
The Little Swordsman of Aile	25109950
The Masked Beast	49064413
The Portrait's Secret	32541773
The Regulation of Tribe	00296499
The Reliable Guardian	16430187
The Rock Spirit	76305638
The Sanctuary in the Sky	56433456
The Second Sarcophagus	04081094
The Secret of the Bandit	99351431
The Shallow Grave	43434803
The Snake Hair	29491031
The Spell Absorbing Life	99517131
The Statue of Easter Island	10261698
The Third Sarcophagus	78697395
The Unhappy Girl	27618634
The Unhappy Maiden	51275027
The Warrior Returning Alive	95281259
The Wicked Worm Beast	06285791
Thestalos the Firestorm Monarch	26205777
Thousand Dragon	41462083
Thousand Energy	05703682
Thousand Knives	63391643
Thousand-Eyes Idol	27125110
Threatening Roar	36361633
Three-Headed Geedo	78423643
Thunder Crash	69196160
Thunder Dragon	31786629
Thunder Nyan Nyan	70797118
Time Machine	80987696
Time Wizard	06285791
Token Feastevil	83675475
Toon Alligator	59383041
Toon Cannon Soldier	79875176
Toon Dark Magician Girl	90960358
Toon Defense	43509019
Toon Gemini Elf	42386471
Toon Goblin Attack Force	15270885
Toon Masked Sorcerer	16392422
Toon Mermaid	65458948
Toon Summoned Skull	91842653
Toon Table of Contents	89997728
Toon World	15259703
Tornado	61068510

CARD	PASSWORD
Tornado Wall	18605135
Torpedo Fish	90337190
Tower of Babel	94256039
Tragedy	35686187
Transcendent Wings	25573054
Trap Hole	04206964
Trap Jammer	19252988
Trap Master	46461247
Tremendous Fire	46918794
Triage	30888983
Triangle Ecstasy Spark	12181376
Triangle Power	32298781
Tribute Doll	02903036
Tribute to the Doomed	79759861
Tri-Horned Dragon	39111158
Twin Swords of Flashing Light - Tryce	21900719
Twin-Headed Behemoth	43586926
Twin-Headed Thunder Dragon	54752875
Two-Headed King Rex	94119974
Two-Pronged Attack	83887306
Tyhone	72842870
Type Zero Magic Crusher	35346968
UFO Turtle	60806437
Ultimate Offering	80604091
Ultra Evolution Pill	22431243
Umiiruka	82999629
Union Attack	60399954
United We Stand	56747793
Unity	14731897
Upstart Goblin	70368879
Uraby	01784619
Valkyrion the Magna Warrior	75347539
Versago the Destroyer	50259460
Vile Germs	39774685
Vorse Raider	14898066
Waboku	12607053
Wall of Illusion	13945283
Wall of Revealing Light	17078030
Wall Shadow	63162310
Warrior Elimination	90873992
Warrior Lady of the Wasteland	05438492
Wasteland	98239899
Weapon Change	10035717
Weather Report	72053645
Weed Out	28604635
White Magical Hat	15150365
White-Horned Dragon	73891874
Wicked-Breaking Flamberge - Baou	68427465
Widespread Ruin	77754944
Wild Nature's Release	61166988
Winged Dragon, Guardian of the Fortress #1	87796900
Winged Kuriboh	57116033
Winged Kuriboh LV10	98585345
Witch's Apprentice	80741828
Wolf	49417509
Wolf Axwielder	56369281
Woodland Sprite	06979239
World Suppression	12253117
Xing Zhen Hu	76515293
Yamata Dragon	76862289
Yami	59197169
Yellow Luster Shield	04542651

CARD	PASSWORD
Yu-Jo Friendship	81332143
Zaborg the Thunder Monarch	51945556
Zero Gravity	83133491
Zoa	24311372
Zolga	16268841
Zombie Warrior	31339260

GAMES

300: MARCH TO GLORY

25,000 KLEOS

Pause the game and press Down, Left, Down, Left, Up, Left.

ATV OFFROAD FURY: BLAZIN' TRAILS

UNLOCK EVERYTHING EXCEPT THE FURY BIKE

Select Player Profile from the Options menu. Choose Enter Cheat and enter All Access.

1500 CREDITS

Select Player Profile from the Options menu. Choose Enter Cheat and enter $moneybags$.

ALL RIDER GEAR

Select Player Profile from the Options menu. Choose Enter Cheat and enter Duds.

TIRES

Select Player Profile from the Options menu. Choose Enter Cheat and enter Dubs.

MUSIC VIDEOS

Select Player Profile from the Options menu. Choose Enter Cheat and enter Billboards.

BEN 10: ALIEN FORCE THE GAME

LEVEL LORD

Enter Gwen, Kevin, Big Chill, Gwen as a code.

INVINCIBILITY

Enter Kevin, Big Chill, Swampfire, Kevin as a code.

ALL COMBOS

Enter Swampfire, Gwen, Kevin, Ben as a code.

INFINITE ALIENS

Enter Ben, Swampfire, Gwen, Big Chill as a code.

BEN 10: PROTECTOR OF EARTH

INVINCIBILITY

Select a game from the Continue option. Go to the Map Selection screen, press Start and choose Extras. Select Enter Secret Code and enter XLR8, Heatblast, Wildvine, Fourarms.

ALL COMBOS

Select a game from the Continue option. Go to the Map Selection screen, press Start and choose Extras. Select Enter Secret Code and enter Cannonblot, Heatblast, Fourarms, Heatblast.

ALL LOCATIONS
Select a game from the Continue option. Go to the Map Selection screen, press Start and choose Extras. Select Enter Secret Code and enter Heatblast, XLR8, XLR8, Cannonblot.

DNA FORCE SKINS
Select a game from the Continue option. Go to the Map Selection screen, press Start and choose Extras. Select Enter Secret Code and enter Wildvine, Fourarms, Heatblast, Cannonbolt.

DARK HEROES SKINS
Select a game from the Continue option. Go to the Map Selection screen, press Start and choose Extras. Select Enter Secret Code and enter Cannonbolt, Cannonbolt, Fourarms, Heatblast.

ALL ALIEN FORMS
Select a game from the Continue option. Go to the Map Selection screen, press Start and choose Extras. Select Enter Secret Code and enter Wildvine, Fourarms, Heatblast, Wildvine.

MASTER CONTROL
Select a game from the Continue option. Go to the Map Selection screen, press Start and choose Extras. Select Enter Secret Code and enter Cannonbolt, Heatblast, Wildvine, Fourarms.

BLITZ: OVERTIME

The following codes only work for Quick Play mode.

BALL TRAILS ALWAYS ON
Select Extras from the menu and enter ONFIRE.

BEACH BALL
Select Extras from the menu and enter BOUNCY.

DOUBLE UNLEASH ICONS
Select Extras from the menu and enter PIPPED.

STAMINA DISABLED
Select Extras from the menu and enter NOTTIRED.

SUPER CLASH MODE
Select Extras from the menu and enter CLASHY.

SUPER UNLEASH CLASH MODE
Select Extras from the menu and enter BIGDOGS.

INSTANT WIN IN CAMPAIGN MODE
Select Extras from the menu and enter CHAMPS. In Campaign mode, highlight a team and press ●, ●, ▲ to win against that team.

TWO PLAYER CO-OP MODE
Select Extras from the menu and enter CHUWAY.

BROTHERS IN ARMS D-DAY

LEVEL SELECT
Enter JUNESIX as your profile name.

BURNOUT LEGENDS

COP RACER
Earn a Gold in all Pursuit events.

FIRE TRUCK
Earn a Gold in all Crash Events.

GANGSTER BOSS
Earn Gold in all Race events.

CAPCOM CLASSICS COLLECTION REMIXED

UNLOCK EVERYTHING
At the title screen, press Left on D-pad, Right on D-pad, Left on Analog stick, Right on Analog stick, ●, ●, Up on D-pad, Down on D-pad.

CAPCOM PUZZLE WORLD

SUPER BUSTER BROS.

LEVEL SELECT IN TOUR MODE

At the Main menu, highlight Tour Mode, hold Down and press ✪.

SUPER PUZZLE FIGHTER

PLAY AS AKUMA

At the character select, highlight Hsien-Ko and press Down.

PLAY AS DAN

At the character select, highlight Donovan and press Down.

PLAY AS DEVILOT

At the character select, highlight Morrigan and press Down.

PLAY AS ANITA

At the character select, hold L + R and choose Donovan.

PLAY AS HSIEN-KO'S TALISMAN

At the character select, hold L + R and choose Hsien-Ko.

PLAY AS MORRIGAN AS A BAT

At the character select, hold L + R and choose Morrigan.

CARS

BONUS SPEEDWAY (REVERSED) IN CUSTOM RACE

At the Main menu, hold L and press ✪, ▣, ▲, ✪, ▲, ▣.

ALL CARS, PAINTJOBS, TRACKS, MOVIE CLIPS AND MODES

At the Main menu, hold L and press ▲, ▣, ✪, ▣, ▲, ✪, ▣, ▲, ▣, ✪.

UNLIMITED NITROUS

At the Main menu, hold L and ✪, ▣, ▣, ▣, ▣, ▲, ▣, ✪.

CASTLEVANIA: THE DRACULA X CHRONICLES

SYMPHONY OF THE NIGHT

After clearing the game as Alucard, select New Game and enter the following as your name:

PLAY AS ALUCARD, WITH 99 LUCK AND THE LAPIS LAZULI

X-X!V''Q

PLAY AS ALUCARD, WITH THE AXE LORD ARMOR

AXEARMOR

PLAY AS MARIA RENARD

MARIA

PLAY AS RICHTER BELMONT

RICHTER

CRASH TAG TEAM RACING

FASTER VEHICLES

At the Main menu, hold L + R and press ▣, ▣, ▲, ▲.

1-HIT KO

At the Main menu, hold L + R and press ✪, ▣, ▣, ✪.

DISABLE HUD

At the Main menu, hold L + R and press ✪, ▣, ▲, ▣.

CHICKEN HEADS

At the Main menu, hold L + R and press ✪, ▣, ▣, ▣.

JAPANESE CRASH

At the Main menu, hold L + R and press ▣, ▣, ▣, ▣.

DRIVE A BLOCK VEHICLE

At the Main menu, hold L + R and press ▣, ▣, ▲, ▣.

NEW GAME+

After completing the game, you'll be prompted to make a new save. Loading a game from this new save will begin a New Game+, starting the game over while allowing Zack to retain almost everything he's earned.

The following items transfer to a New Game+:

- Level, Experience, SP, Gil, Playtime, Non-Key Items, Materia, and DMW Completion Rate

The following items do not transfer:

- Key Items, Materia/Accessory Slot Expansion, Ability to SP Convert, DMW Images, Mission Progress, Mail, and Unlocked Shops

DARKSTALKERS CHRONICLE: THE CHAOS TOWER

EX OPTIONS

At the Main menu, hold L and select Options.

MARIONETTE IN ARCADE MODE

At the Character Select screen, highlight ? and press START (x7), then press P or K.

OBORO BISHAMON IN ALL MODES

At the Character Select screen, highlight Bishamon, hold START, and press P or K.

REVENGER'S ROOST

SHADOW IN ARCADE MODE

At the Character Select screen, highlight ? and press START (x5), then press P or K.

DAXTER

THE MATRIX DREAM SEQUENCE

Collect 1 Precursor Orb.

BRAVEHEART DREAM SEQUENCE

Collect 100 Precursor Orbs.

THE LORD OF THE RINGS DREAM SEQUENCE

Collect 200 Precursor Orbs.

INDIANA JONES DREAM SEQUENCE

Collect 300 Precursor Orbs.

THE MATRIX DREAM SEQUENCE 2

Collect 400 Precursor Orbs.

THE LORD OF THE RINGS DREAM SEQUENCE 2

Collect 500 Precursor Orbs.

E3 2005 TRAILER

Collect 600 Precursor Orbs, then pause the game and select Extras from the Secrets menu.

CONCEPT ART

Collect 700 Precursor Orbs, then pause the game and select Extras from the Secrets menu.

INTRO ANIMATIC

Collect 800 Precursor Orbs, then pause the game and select Extras from the Secrets menu.

GAME UNDER CONSTRUCTION

Collect 900 Precursor Orbs, then pause the game and select Extras from the Secrets menu.

BEHIND THE SCENES

Collect 1000 Precursor Orbs, then pause the game and select Extras from the Secrets menu.

PANTS

Earn Gold on The Lord of the Rings Dream Sequence 2, then pause the game and select Cheats from the Secrets menu.

HAT

Earn Gold on the Indiana Jones Dream Sequence, then pause the game and select Cheats from the Secrets menu.

WEBSITE CLUE A
Earn Gold on The Matrix Dream Sequence, then pause the game and select Cheats from the Secrets menu.

WEBSITE CLUE B
Earn Gold on the Braveheart Dream Sequence, then pause the game and select Cheats from the Secrets menu.

WEBSITE CLUE C
Earn Gold on The Lord of the Rings Dream Sequence, then pause the game and select Cheats from the Secrets menu.

WEBSITE CLUE D
Earn Gold on The Matrix Dream Sequence 2, then pause the game and select Cheats from the Secrets menu.

DEATH JR.

CAN'T TOUCH THIS (INVINCIBILITY)
Pause the game, hold L + R and press Up, Up, Down, Down, Left, Left, Right, Right, ●, ▲.

INCREASED HEALTH
Pause the game, hold L + R and press Up, Up, Down, Down, ✕, ●, ▲, ■, ●, ✕, ✕.

WEAPONS UPGRADED (GIVES ALL WEAPONS)
Pause the game, hold L + R and press Up, Up, Down, Down, Left, Right, Left, Right, ✕, ●.

AMMO REFILLED
Pause the game, hold L + R and press ▲, ▲, ✕, ✕, ■, ●, ■, ●, Down, Right.

UNLIMITED AMMO
Pause the game, hold L + R and press ▲, ▲, ✕, ✕, ■, ●, ■, ●, Right, Down.

MY HEAD FEELS FUNNY (BIG HEAD)
Pause the game, hold L + R and press ▲, ●, ✕, ■, ▲, Up, Right, Down, Left, Up. Re-enter the code for normal head size.

GIANT BLADE (BIG SCYTHE)
Pause the game, hold L + R and press ▲, ■, ✕, ●, ▲, Up, Left, Down, Right, Up.

FREE SEEP
Pause the game, hold L + R and press Left, Left, Right, Right, Left, Right, Left, Right, ✕, ✕.

A LITTLE MORE HELP (ASSIST EXTENDER)
Pause the game, hold L + R and press Up, Up, Down, Down, ▲, ▲, ✕, ✕, ▲, ▲.

FREE WIDGET
Pause the game, hold L + R and press Right, Up, Down, Up, ▲, Up, Left, ●, ▲, Right.

ALL LEVELS & FREE ALL CHARACTERS

Pause the game, hold L + R and press Up (x4), Down (x4), ✗, ✗. Enter a stage and exit back to the museum for the code to take effect.

I'D BUY THAT FOR A DOLLAR (FILL PANDORA ASSIST METER)

Pause the game, hold L + R and press Up, Up, Down, Down, Up, Right, Down, Left, ✗, ✗.

THIS WAS JED'S IDEA (ATTACKS HAVE DIFFERENT NAMES)

Pause the game, hold L + R and press Up, Up, Down, Left, ▲, ▲, ●, ✗, ◉, ●.

WEAPON NAMES = NORMAL (WEAPONS HAVE DIFFERENT NAMES)

Pause the game, hold L + R and press Down, Down, Up, Up, Left, Right, Left, Right, ●, ▲.

EYEDOOR SOLIDITY QUESTIONABLE (NO LONGER REQUIRE SOULS)

Pause the game, hold L + R and press Up, Left, Down, Right, Left, ▲, ●, ✗, ◉, ◉.

BUDDY DECALS (BULLET HOLES BECOME PICTURES)

Pause the game, hold L + R and press Up, Right, Down, Left, Up, ▲, ◉, ✗, ●, ▲.

STAGE WARP

Pause the game, hold L + R and enter the following codes to warp to that stage.

STAGE	CODE
Advanced Training	Down, K, Down, K, Down, K, Down, K, Down, I
The Basement	Down, K, Down, K, Down, K, Down, K, Up, J
Basic Training	Up, J, Up, K, Down, K, Down, K, Down, K
Big Trouble in Little Downtown	Up, J, Down, K, Down, K, Down, K, Down, K
Bottom of the Bell Curve	Down, K, Down, K, Down, K, Down, K, Down, J
The Burger Tram	Down, K, Down, K, Down, K, Up, K, Down, K
Burn It Down	Down, K, Up, J, Down, K, Down, K, Down, K
The Corner Store	Down, K, Up, K, Down, K, Down, K, Down, K
Final Battle	Down, K, Down, K, Down, K, Down, J, Up, K
Growth Spurt	Down, K, Down, K, Down, K, Down, K, Up, K
Happy Trails Insanitarium	Down, K, Down, J, Up, K, Down, K, Down, K
Higher Learning	Down, K, Down, K, Down, K, Down, J, Down, K
How a Cow Becomes a Steak	Down, K, Down, K, Down, J, Down, K, Down, K
Inner Madness	Down, K, Down, K, Up, J, Down, K, Down, K
Into the Box	Down, K, Down, K, Down, K, Up, J, Down, K
Moving on Up	Down, J, Up, K, Down, K, Down, K, Down, K
The Museum	Up, K, Down, K, Down, K, Down, K, Down, K
My House	Down, K, Down, J, Down, K, Down, K, Down, K
Seep's Hood	Down, J, Down, K, Down, K, Down, K, Down, K
Shock Treatment	Down, K, Down, K, Down, J, Up, K, Down, K
Udder Madness	Down, K, Down, K, Up, K, Down, K, Down, K

DISGAEA: AFTERNOON OF DARKNESS

ETNA MODE

At the Main menu, highlight New Game and press ▲, ●, ◉, ▲, ●, ◉, ✗.

DRAGON BALL Z: SHIN BUDOKAI

MINI-GAME

At the Main menu, press L and then press R to begin the mini-game.

DUNGEON SIEGE: THRONE OF AGONY

ITEM CODES

Talk to Feydwer and Klaars in Seahaven and enter the following codes. Enter the Master Code and one of the item codes.

ITEM	CODE
Master Code	MPJNKBHAKANLPGHD
Bloodstained Warboots	MHFMCJIFNDHOKLPM

ITEM	CODE
Bolt Flingers	OBMIDNBJNPFKADCL
Enkindled Cleaver	MJPOBGFNLKELLLLP
Malignant Force	JDGJHKPOLNMCGHNC
Polychromatic Shiv	PJJEPCFHEIHAJEEE
Teasha's Ire	GDIMBNLEIGNNLOEG
Traveler's Handbook	PIJNPEGFJJPFALNO

ELITE MODE
Defeat the game to unlock this mode.

EA REPLAY

B.O.B.

PASSWORDS

LEVEL	PASSWORD
Anciena 1	672451
Anciena 2	272578
Anciena 3	652074
Anciena 4	265648
Anciena 5	462893
Anciena 6	583172
Goth 2	171058
Goth 3	950745
Goth 4	472149
Ultraworld 1	743690
Ultraworld 2	103928
Ultraworld 3	144895
Ultraworld 4	775092
Ultraworld 5	481376

DESERT STRIKE

10 LIVES
At the Desert Strike menu, press ● to bring up the Password screen. Enter BQQQAEZ.

JUNGLE STRIKE

PASSWORDS
Press ● at the Jungle Strike menu to bring up the Password screen. Enter the following:

LEVEL	PASSWORD
Mountains	7LSPFBVWTWP
Night Strike	X4MFB4MHPH4
Puloso City	V6HGY39XVXL
Return Home	N4MK9N6MHM7
River Raid	TGB76MGCZCC
Training Ground	9NHDXMGCZCG
Washington D.C	BXYTNMGCYDB

WING COMMANDER

INVINCIBILITY AND STAGE SELECT
At the Wing Commander menu, press ⊗, ◉⊗, ◉, ⊗, ◉, L, ◉, R, ◉, Start.

ROAD RASH 2

WILD THING MOTORCYCLE
At the title screen, hold Up + ● + ◉ and press Start.

FAMILY GUY

ALL STAGES
At the Main menu, press Up, Left, Up, Left, Down, Right, Start.

MUSIC TEST MODE

Enter the main character's name as PolkaPolka at the name entry screen.

FLATOUT: HEAD ON

1 MILLION CREDITS

Select Enter Code from the Extras menu and enter GIVECASH.

ALL CARS AND 1 MILLION CREDITS

Select Enter Code from the Extras menu and enter GIEVEPIX.

BIG RIG

Select Enter Code from the Extras menu and enter ELPUEBLO.

BIG RIG TRUCK

Select Enter Code from the Extras menu and enter RAIDERS.

FLATMOBILE CAR

Select Enter Code from the Extras menu and enter WOTKINS.

MOB CAR

Select Enter Code from the Extras menu and enter BIGTRUCK.

PIMPSTER CAR

Select Enter Code from the Extras menu and enter RUTTO.

ROCKET CAR

Select Enter Code from the Extras menu and enter KALJAKOPPA.

SCHOOL BUS

Select Enter Code from the Extras menu and enter GIEVCARPLZ.

FULL AUTO 2: BATTLELINES

ALL CARS

Select Cheats from the Options and press Up, Up, Up, Up, Left, Down, Up, Right, Down, Down, Down, Down.

ALL EVENTS

Select Cheats from the Options and press Start, Left, Select, Right, Right, ▲, ✕, ●, Start, R, Down, Select.

THE GODFATHER: MOB WARS

Each of the following codes will work once every five minutes.

$1000

Pause the game and press ●, ●, ●, ●, ●, L.

FULL AMMO

Pause the game and press ●, Left, ●, Right ●, R.

FULL HEALTH

Pause the game and press Left, ●, Right, ●, Right, L.

GRADIUS COLLECTION

AALL WEAPONS & POWER-UPS

Pause the game and press Up, Up, Down, Down, Left, Right, Left, Right, L, R. This code can be used once per level.

$250,000
During a game, press L, R, ▲, L, R, ●, L, R.

FULL HEALTH
During a game, press L, R, ✕, L, R, ●, L, R.

FULL ARMOR
During a game, press L, R, ●, L, R, ✕, L, R.

WEAPON SET 1
During a game, press Up, ●, ●, Down, L, ●, ●, R.

WEAPON SET 2
During a game, press Up, ●, ●, Down, Left, ●, ●, R.

WEAPON SET 3
During a game, press Up, ✕, ✕, Down, L, ✕, ✕, R.

CHROME PLATED CARS
During a game, press ▲, R, L, Down, Down, R, R, ▲.

BLACK CARS
During a game, press ●, ●, R, ▲, ▲, L, ●, ●.

WHITE CARS
During a game, press ✕, ✕, R, ●, ●, L, ▲, ▲.

CARS DRIVE ON WATER
During a game, press ●, ✕, Down, ●, ✕, Up, L, L.

PERFECT TRACTION
During a game, press L, Up, L, R, ▲, ●, Down, ✕.

CHANGE BICYCLE TIRE SIZE
During a game, press ●, Right, ✕, Up, R, ✕, L, ●.

AGGRESSIVE DRIVERS
During a game, press ●, ●, R, ✕, ✕, L, ●, ●.

ALL GREEN LIGHTS
During a game, press ▲, ▲, R, ●, ●, L, ✕, ✕.

DESTROY ALL CARS
During a game, press L, L, Left, L, L, R, ✕, ●.

RAISE MEDIA ATTENTION
During a game, press L, Up, R, R, ▲, ●, Down, ✕.

RAISE WANTED LEVEL
During a game, press L, R, ●, L, R, ▲, L, R.

NEVER WANTED
During a game, press L, L, ▲, R, R, ✕, ●, ●.

CHANGE OUTFIT
During a game, press L, L, L, L, L, Right, ●, ▲.

BOBBLE HEAD WORLD
During a game, press Down, Down, Down, ●, ●, ✕, L, R.

PEOPLE ATTACK YOU
During a game, press L, L, R, L, L, R, Up, ▲.

PEOPLE FOLLOW YOU
During a game, press Down, Down, Down, ▲, ▲, ●, L, R.

PEOPLE HAVE WEAPONS
During a game, press R, R, L, R, R, L, R, ●.

PEOPLE RIOT
During a game, press L, L, R, L, L, R, L, ●.

SPAWN RHINO
During a game, press L, L, L, L, L, R, ▲, ●.

SPAWN TRASHMASTER
During a game, press ▲, ●, Down, ▲, ●, Up, L, L.

FASTER CLOCK
During a game, press L, L, L, L, L, R, ●, ✕.

FASTER GAMEPLAY
During a game, press R, R, L, R, R, L, Down, ✕.

SLOWER GAMEPLAY
During a game, press R, ▲, ✕, R, ●, ●, L, R.

ALL CHARACTERS, CARS, & ENTIRE CITY (MULTIPLAYER)
During a game, press Up (x3), ▲, ▲, ●, L, R.

43 CHARACTERS & 7 GANGS (MULTIPLAYER)
During a game, press Up (x3), ✕, ✕, ●, R, L.

28 CHARACTERS & 4 GANGS (MULTIPLAYER)
During a game, press Up (x3), ●, ●, ✕, L, R.

14 CHARACTERS & 2 GANGS (MULTIPLAYER)
During a game, press Up (x3), ●, ●, ▲, R, L.

CLEAR WEATHER
During a game, press Up, Down, ●, Up, Down, ●, L, R.

FOGGY WEATHER
During a game, press Up, Down, ▲, Up, Down, ✕, L, R.

OVERCAST WEATHER
During a game, press Up, Down, ✕, Up, Down, ▲, L, R.

RAINY WEATHER
During a game, press Up, Down, ●, Up, Down, ●, L, R.

OVERLOAD

SUNNY WEATHER
During a game, press L, L, ⊙, R, R, ⊙, ▲, ✖

UPSIDE DOWN
During a game, press Down, Down, Down, ✖, ✖, ⊙, R, L.

UPSIDE UP
During a game, press ✖, ✖, ✖, Down, Down, Right, L, R.

RIGHT SIDE UP
During a game, press ▲, ▲, ▲, Up, Up, Right, L, R.

COMMIT SUICIDE
During a game, press L, Down, Left, R, ✖, ⊙, Up, ▲.

GAME CREDITS
During a game, press L, R, L, R, Up, Down, L, R.

GRAND THEFT AUTO: VICE CITY STORIES

Enter the following cheats during a game.

$250000
Press Up, Down, L, R, ✖, ✖, L, R.

ARMOR
Press Up, Down, L, R, ⊙, ⊙, L, R.

HEALTH
Press Up, Down, L, R, ⊙, ⊙, L, R.

NEVER WANTED
Press Up, R, ▲, ▲, Down, L, ⊙, ⊙.

LOWER WANTED LEVEL
Press Up, R, ▲, ▲, Down, L, ✖, ✖.

RAISE WANTED LEVEL
Press Up, R, ⊙, ⊙, Down, L, ⊙, ⊙.

WEAPON SET 1
Press L, R, ✖, Up, Down, ⊙, L, R.

WEAPON SET 2
Press L, R, ⊙, Up, Down, ▲, L, R.

WEAPON SET 3
Press L, R, ▲, Up, Down, ⊙, L, R.

SPAWN RHINO
Press Up, L, Down, R, L, L, R, R.

SPAWN TRASHMASTER
Press Down, Up, R, ▲, L, ▲, L, ▲.

BLACK CARS
Press L, R, L, R, L, ⊙, Up, ✖.

CHROME CARS
Press R, Up, L, Down, ▲, ▲, L, R.

CARS AVOID YOU
Press Up, Up, R, L, ▲, ⊙, ⊙, ⊙.

DESTROY ALL CARS
Press L, R, R, L, R, ⊙, Down, R.

GUYS FOLLOW YOU
Press R, L, Down, L, ⊙, Up, L, ⊙.

PERFECT TRACTION
Press Down, Left, Up, L, R, ▲, ⊙, ✖.
Press Down to jump into a car.

PEDESTRIAN GETS INTO YOUR VEHICLE
Press Down, Up, R, L, L, ⊙, Up, L.

PEDESTRIANS ATTACK YOU
Press Down, ▲, Up, ✖, L, R, L, R.

PEDESTRIANS HAVE WEAPONS
Press Up, L, Down, R, L, ⊙, R, ▲.

PEDESTRIANS RIOT
Press R, L, L, Down, L, ⊙, Down, L.

SUICIDE
Press R, R, ⊙, ⊙, L, R, Down, ✖.

UPSIDE DOWN 1
Press ⊙, ⊙, ⊙, L, L, R, L, R.

UPSIDE DOWN 2
Press L, L, L, R, R, L, R, L.

FASTER CLOCK
Press R, L, L, Down, Up, ✖, Down, L.

FASTER GAMEPLAY
Press L, L, R, R, Up, ▲, Down, ✖.

SLOWER GAMEPLAY
Press L, L, ⊙, ⊙, Down, Up, ▲, ✖.

CLEAR WEATHER
Press L, Down, R, L, R, Up, L, ✖.

FOGGY WEATHER
Press L, Down, ▲, ✖, R, Up, L, L.

OVERCAST WEATHER
Press L, Down, L, R, R, Up, L, ⊙.

RAINY WEATHER
Press L, Down, L, R, R, Up, Left, ▲.

SUNNY WEATHER
Press L, Down, R, L, R, Up, L, ⊙.

GUN SHOWDOWN

ALL CHAPTERS IN QUICK PLAY
Enter hunter as a profile name.

PLAY AS JENNY
Enter allies as a profile name.

UNLOCKS ALL WEAPONS IN STORY MODE
Enter nedwhite as a profile name. This does not unlock the final weapon.

FASTER GUN FIRING
Enter quivira as a profile name.

INCREASE AMMUNTION CAPACITY
Enter campbell as a profile name.

INFINITE AMMUNITION IN STORY MODE
Enter barton as a profile name.

NEW MULTIPLAYER MAP
Enter badlands as a profile name.

HOT BRAIN

119.99 TEMPERATURE IN ALL 5 CATEGORIES
Select New Game and enter Cheat.

HOT SHOTS GOLF 2

UNLOCK EVERYTHING
Enter 2gsh as your name.

IRON MAN

ARMOR SUITS
Iron Man's different armor suits are unlocked by completing certain missions.

COMPLETE MISSION	SUIT UNLOCKED
1, Escape	Mark I
2, First Flight	Mark II
3, Fight Back	Mark III
5, Maggia Compound	Gold Tin Can
8, Frozen Ship	Classic
11, Island Meltdown	Stealth
13, Showdown	Titanium Man

PSP MINIGAMES
Minigames can be unlocked by completing the following missions. Access the minigames through the Bonus menu.

COMPLETE MISSION	PSP MINIGAME UNLOCKED
1, Escape	Tin Can Challenge 1 + 2
2, First Flight	DEATH RACE: STARK INDUSTRY
3, Fight Back	BOSS FIGHT: DREADNOUGHT
4, Weapons Transport	DEATH RACE: AFGHAN DESERT BOSS FIGHT: WHIPLASH
5, Maggia Compound	DEATH RACE: MAGGIA MANSION
6, Flying Fortress	SPEED KILL: FLYING FORTRESS SURVIVAL: FLYING FORTRESS
7, Nuclear Winter	DEATH RACE: ARTIC CIRCLE
8, Frozen Ship	SPEED KILL: FROZEN SHIP SURVIVAL: FROZEN SHIP
9, Home Front	BOSS FIGHT: TITANIUM MAN
10, Save Pepper	DEATH RACE: DAM BASSIN
11, Island Meltdown	SPEED KILL: GREEK ISLANDS SURVIVAL: GREEK ISLANDS
12, Battlesuit Factory	SPEED KILL: TINMEN FACTORY SURVIVAL: TINMEN FACTORY
13, Showdown	BOSS FIGHT: IRON MONGER

CONCEPT ART
As you progress through the game and destroy the Weapon Crates, bonuses are unlocked. You can find all of these in the Bonus menu once unlocked.

CONCEPT ART UNLOCKED	NUMBER OF WEAPON CRATES FOUND
Environments Set 1	6
Environments Set 2	12
Iron Man	18
Environments Set 3	24
Enemies	30
Environments Set 4	36
Villains	42
Vehicles	48
Covers	50

LAST MAN STANDING CHALLENGE AND AN ASCARI KZ1

Select Cheats and Challenges from the DNA Lab menu and enter KNOX. Defeat the challenge to earn the Ascari KZ1.

SPECIAL CHALLENGE AND AN AUDI TT 1.8 QUATTRO

Select Cheats and Challenges from the DNA Lab menu and enter YTHZ. Defeat the challenge to earn the Audi TT 1.8 Quattro.

SPECIAL CHALLENGE AND A BMW Z4

Select Cheats and Challenges from the DNA Lab menu and enter GVDL. Defeat the challenge to earn the BMW Z4.

SPECIAL CHALLENGE AND A HOLDEN MONARO

Select Cheats and Challenges from the DNA Lab menu and enter RBSG. Defeat the challenge to earn the Holden Monaro.

SPECIAL CHALLENGE AND A HYUNDAI COUPE 2.7 V6

Select Cheats and Challenges from the DNA Lab menu and enter BSLU. Defeat the challenge to earn the Hyundai Coupe 2.7 V6.

SPECIAL CHALLENGE AND AN INFINITY G35

Select Cheats and Challenges from the DNA Lab menu and enter MRHC. Defeat the challenge to earn the Infinity G35.

SPECIAL CHALLENGE AND AN INFINITY RED G35

Select Cheats and Challenges from the DNA Lab menu and enter MNCH. Defeat the challenge to earn the Infinity G35.

SPECIAL CHALLENGE AND A KOENIGSEGG CCX

Select Cheats and Challenges from the DNA Lab menu and enter KDTR. Defeat the challenge to earn the Koenigsegg CCX.

SPECIAL CHALLENGE AND A MITSUBISHI PROTOTYPE X

Select Cheats and Challenges from the DNA Lab menu and enter DOPX. Defeat the challenge to earn the Mitsubishi Prototype X.

SPECIAL CHALLENGE AND A NISSAN 350Z

Select Cheats and Challenges from the DNA Lab menu and enter PRGN. Defeat the challenge to earn the Nissan 350Z.

SPECIAL CHALLENGE AND A NISSAN SKYLINE R34 GT-R

Select Cheats and Challenges from the DNA Lab menu and enter JWRS. Defeat the challenge to earn the Nissan Skyline R34 GT-R.

SPECIAL CHALLENGE AND A SALEEN S7

Select Cheats and Challenges from the DNA Lab menu and enter WIKF. Defeat the challenge to earn the Saleen S7.

SPECIAL CHALLENGE AND A SEAT LEON CUPRA R

Select Cheats and Challenges from the DNA Lab menu and enter FAMQ. Defeat the challenge to earn the Seat Leon Cupra R.

JUSTICE LEAGUE HEROES

UNLOCK EVERYTHING

Pause the game, hold L + R and press Down, Left, Up, Right.

INVINCIBLE

Pause the game, hold L + R and press Left, Down, Right, Up, Left, Down, Right, Up.

UNLIMITED ENERGY

Pause the game, hold L + R and press Down, Down, Right, Right, Up, Up, Left, Left.

MAX ABILITIES

Pause the game, hold L + R and press Right, Down, Right, Down.

20 FREE SHIELDS

Pause the game, hold L + R and press Up, Up, Down, Down.

25 BOOSTS

Pause the game, hold L + R and press Left, Right, Left, Right.

LEGO BATMAN

BATCAVE CODES

Using the computer in the Batcave, select Enter Code and enter the following:

CHARACTERS

CHARACTER	CODE
Alfred	ZAQ637
Batgirl	JKR331
Bruce Wayne	BDJ327
Catwoman (Classic)	M1AAWW
Clown Goon	HJK327
Commissioner Gordon	DDP967
Fishmonger	HGY748
Freeze Girl	XVK541
Joker Goon	UTF782
Joker Henchman	YUN924
Mad Hatter	JCA283
Man-Bat	NYU942
Military Policeman	MKL382
Nightwing	MVY759
Penguin Goon	NKA238
Penguin Henchman	BJH782
Penguin Minion	KJP748
Poison Ivy Goon	GTB899
Police Marksman	HKG984
Police Officer	JRY983
Riddler Goon	CRY928
Riddler Henchman	XEU824
S.W.A.T.	HTF114
Sailor	NAV592
Scientist	JFL786
Security Guard	PLB946
The Joker (Tropical)	CCB199
Yeti	NJL412
Zoo Sweeper	DWR243

VEHICLES

VEHICLE	CODE
Bat-Tank	KNTT4B
Bruce Wayne's Private Jet	LEA664
Catwoman's Motorcycle	HPL826
Garbage Truck	DUS483
Goon Helicopter	GCH328
Harbor Helicopter	CHP735
Harley Quinn's Hammer Truck	RDT637
Mad Hatter's Glider	HS000W
Mad Hatter's Steamboat	M4DM4N
Mr. Freeze's Iceberg	ICYICE
The Joker's Van	JUK657
Mr. Freeze's Kart	BCT229
Penguin Goon Submarine	BTN248
Police Bike	LJP234
Police Boat	PLC999
Police Car	KJL832
Police Helicopter	CWR732
Police Van	MAC788
Police Watercraft	VJD328
Riddler's Jet	HAHAHA
Robin's Submarine	TTF453
Two-Face's Armored Truck	EFE933

CHEAT	CODE
Always Score Multiply	9LRGNB
Fast Batarangs	JRBDCB
Fast Walk	ZOLM6N
Flame Batarang	D8NYWH
Freeze Batarang	XPN4NG
Extra Hearts	ML3KHP
Fast Build	EVG26J
Immune to Freeze	JXUDY6
Invincibility	WYD5CP
Minikit Detector	ZXGH9J
More Batarang Targets	XWP645
Piece Detector	KHJ554
Power Brick Detector	MMN786
Regenerate Hearts	HJH7HJ
Score x2	N4NR3E
Score x4	CX9MAT
Score x6	MLVNF2
Score x8	WCCDB9
Score x10	18HW07

LEGO INDIANA JONES: THE ORIGINAL ADVENTURES

CHARACTERS

Approach the blackboard in the Classroom and enter the following codes.

CHARACTER	CODE
Bandit	12N68W
Bandit Swordsman	1MK4RT
Barranca	04EM94
Bazooka Trooper (Crusade)	MK83R7
Bazooka Trooper (Raiders)	S93Y5R
Belloq	CHN3YU
Belloq (Jungle)	TDR197
Belloq (Robes)	VEO29L
British Commander	B73EUA
British Officer	VJ5TI9
British Soldier	DJ5I2W
Captain Katanga	VJ3TT3
Chatter Lal	ENW936
Chatter Lal (Thuggee)	CNH4RY
Chen	3NK48T
Colonel Dietrich	2K9RKS
Colonel Vogel	8EAL4H
Dancing Girl	C7EJ21
Donovan	3NFTU8
Elsa (Desert)	JSNRT9
Elsa (Officer)	VMJ5US
Enemy Boxer	8246RB
Enemy Butler	VJ48W3
Enemy Guard	VJ7R51
Enemy Guard (Mountains)	YR47WM
Enemy Officer	572E61
Enemy Officer (Desert)	2MK45O
Enemy Pilot	B84ELP
Enemy Radio Operator	1MF94R
Enemy Soldier (Desert)	4NSU7Q
Fedora	V75YSP
First Mate	0GIN24

CHARACTER	CODE
Grail Knight	NE6THI
Hovitos Tribesman	H0V1SS
Indiana Jones (Desert Disguise)	4J8S4M
Indiana Jones (Officer)	VJ85OS
Jungle Guide	24PF34
Kao Kan	WMO46L
Kazim	NRH23J
Kazim (Desert)	3M29TJ
Lao Che	2NK479
Maharajah	NFK5N2
Major Toht	13NS01
Masked Bandit	N48SF0
Mola Ram	FJUR31
Monkey Man	3RF6YJ
Pankot Assassin	2NKT72
Pankot Guard	VN28RH
Sherpa Brawler	VJ37WJ
Sherpa Gunner	ND762W
Slave Child	0E3ENW
Thuggee	VM683E
Thuggee Acolyte	T2R3F9
Thuggee Slave Driver	VBS7GW
Village Dignitary	KD48TN
Village Elder	4682E1
Willie (Dinner Suit)	VK93R7
Willie (Pajamas)	MEN4IP
Wu Han	3NSLT8

EXTRAS

Approach the blackboard in the Classroom and enter the following codes. Some cheats need to be enabled by selecting Extras from the pause menu.

CHEAT	CODE
Artifact Detector	VIKED7
Beep Beep	VNF59Q
Character Treasure	VIES2R
Disarm Enemies	VKRNS9
Disguises	4ID1N6
Fast Build	V83SLO
Fast Dig	378RS6
Fast Fix	FJ59WS
Fertilizer	B1GW1F
Ice Rink	33GM7J
Parcel Detector	VUT673
Poo Treasure	WWQ1SA
Regenerate Hearts	MDLP69
Secret Characters	3X44AA
Silhouettes	3HE85H
Super Scream	VN3R7S
Super Slap	0P1TA5
Treasure Magnet	H86LA2
Treasure x10	VI3PS8
Treasure x2	VM4TS9
Treasure x4	VLWEN3
Treasure x6	V84RYS
Treasure x8	A72E1M

BEACH TROOPER

At Mos Eisley Canteena, select Enter Code and enter UCK868. You still need to select Characters and purchase this character for 20,000 studs.

BEN KENOBI (GHOST)

At Mos Eisley Canteena, select Enter Code and enter BEN917. You still need to select Characters and purchase this character for 1,100,000 studs.

BESPIN GUARD

At Mos Eisley Canteena, select Enter Code and enter VHY832. You still need to select Characters and purchase this character for 15,000 studs.

BIB FORTUNA

At Mos Eisley Canteena, select Enter Code and enter WTY721. You still need to select Characters and purchase this character for 16,000 studs.

BOBA FETT

At Mos Eisley Canteena, select Enter Code and enter HLP221. You still need to select Characters and purchase this character for 175,000 studs.

DEATH STAR TROOPER

At Mos Eisley Canteena, select Enter Code and enter BNC332. You still need to select Characters and purchase this character for 19,000 studs.

EWOK

At Mos Eisley Canteena, select Enter Code and enter TTT289. You still need to select Characters and purchase this character for 34,000 studs.

GAMORREAN GUARD

At Mos Eisley Canteena, select Enter Code and enter YZF999. You still need to select Characters and purchase this character for 40,000 studs.

GONK DROID

At Mos Eisley Canteena, select Enter Code and enter NFX582. You still need to select Characters and purchase this character for 1,550 studs.

GRAND MOFF TARKIN

At Mos Eisley Canteena, select Enter Code and enter SMG219. You still need to select Characters and purchase this character for 38,000 studs.

GREEDO

At Mos Eisley Canteena, select Enter Code and enter NAH118. You still need to select Characters and purchase this character for 60,000 studs.

HAN SOLO (HOOD)

At Mos Eisley Canteena, select Enter Code and enter YWM840. You still need to select Characters and purchase this character for 20,000 studs.

IG-88

At Mos Eisley Canteena, select Enter Code and enter NXL973. You still need to select Characters and purchase this character for 30,000 studs.

IMPERIAL GUARD
At Mos Eisley Canteena, select Enter Code and enter MMM111. You still need to select Characters and purchase this character for 45,000 studs.

IMPERIAL OFFICER
At Mos Eisley Canteena, select Enter Code and enter BBV889. You still need to select Characters and purchase this character for 28,000 studs.

IMPERIAL SHUTTLE PILOT
At Mos Eisley Canteena, select Enter Code and enter VAP664. You still need to select Characters and purchase this character for 29,000 studs.

IMPERIAL SPY
At Mos Eisley Canteena, select Enter Code and enter CVT125. You still need to select Characters and purchase this character for 13,500 studs.

JAWA
At Mos Eisley Canteena, select Enter Code and enter JAW499. You still need to select Characters and purchase this character for 24,000 studs.

LOBOT
At Mos Eisley Canteena, select Enter Code and enter UUB319. You still need to select Characters and purchase this character for 11,000 studs.

PALACE GUARD
At Mos Eisley Canteena, select Enter Code and enter SGE549. You still need to select Characters and purchase this character for 14,000 studs.

REBEL PILOT
At Mos Eisley Canteena, select Enter Code and enter CYG336. You still need to select Characters and purchase this character for 15,000 studs.

REBEL TROOPER (HOTH)
At Mos Eisley Canteena, select Enter Code and enter EKU849. You still need to select Characters and purchase this character for 16,000 studs.

SANDTROOPER
At Mos Eisley Canteena, select Enter Code and enter YDV451. You still need to select Characters and purchase this character for 14,000 studs.

SKIFF GUARD
At Mos Eisley Canteena, select Enter Code and enter GBU888. You still need to select Characters and purchase this character for 12,000 studs.

SNOWTROOPER
At Mos Eisley Canteena, select Enter Code and enter NYU989. You still need to select Characters and purchase this character for 16,000 studs.

STORMTROOPER
At Mos Eisley Canteena, select Enter Code and enter PTR345. You still need to select Characters and purchase this character for 10,000 studs.

THE EMPEROR
At Mos Eisley Canteena, select Enter Code and enter HHY382. You still need to select Characters and purchase this character for 275,000 studs.

TIE FIGHTER
At Mos Eisley Canteena, select Enter Code and enter HDY739. You still need to select Characters and purchase this item for 60,000 studs.

TIE FIGHTER PILOT
At Mos Eisley Canteena, select Enter Code and enter NNZ316. You still need to select Characters and purchase this character for 21,000 studs.

TIE INTERCEPTOR
At Mos Eisley Canteena, select Enter Code and enter QYA828. You still need to select Characters and purchase this item for 40,000 studs.

TUSKEN RAIDER
At Mos Eisley Canteena, select Enter Code and enter PEJ821. You still need to select Characters and purchase this character for 23,000 studs.

UGNAUGHT
At Mos Eisley Canteena, select Enter Code and enter UGN694. You still need to select Characters and purchase this character for 36,000 studs.

MICKEY MANTLE ON THE FREE AGENTS LIST
Select Enter Cheat Code from the My 2K7 menu and enter themick.

MICKEY PINCH HITS
Select Enter Cheat Code from the My 2K7 menu and enter phmantle.

UNLOCK EVERYTHING
Select Enter Cheat Code from the My 2K7 menu and enter Derek Jeter. This does not unlock the Topps cheats.

ALL CHEATS
Select Enter Cheat Code from the My 2K7 menu and enter Black Sox.

ALL EXTRAS
Select Enter Cheat Code from the My 2K7 menu and enter Game On.

MIGHTY MICK CHEAT
Select Enter Cheat Code from the My 2K7 menu and enter mightymick.

TRIPLE CROWN CHEAT
Select Enter Cheat Code from the My 2K7 menu and enter triplecrown.

BIG BLAST CHEAT
Select Enter Cheat Code from the My 2K7 menu and enter m4murder.

MANHUNT 2

EXTRA LEVEL AS LEO
Defeat the game.

RELIVE SCENE
Defeat the game. This allows you to replay any level.

MARVEL TRADING CARD GAME

COMPLETE CARD LIBRARY
At the Deck menu, select new deck and name it BLVRTRSK.

ALL PUZZLES
At the Deck menu, select new deck and name it WHOWANTSPIE.

MARVEL ULTIMATE ALLIANCE

UNLOCK ALL SKINS
At the Team menu, press Up, Down, Left, Right, Left, Right, Start.

UNLOCK ALL HERO POWERS
At the Team menu, press Left, Right, Up, Down, Up, Down, Start.

ALL HEROES TO LEVEL 99
At the Team menu, press Up, Left, Up, Left, Down, Right, Down, Right, Start.

UNLOCK ALL HEROES
At the Team menu, press Up, Up, Down, Down, Left, Left, Left, Start Unlock Daredevil
At the Team Menu, press Left, Left, Right, Right, Up, Down, Up, Down, Start.

UNLOCK SILVER SURFER
At the Team menu, press Down, Left, Left, Up, Right, Up, Down, Left, Start.

GOD MODE
During gameplay, press Up, Down, Up, Down, Up, Left, Down, Right, Start.

TOUCH OF DEATH
During gameplay, press Left, Right, Down, Down, Right, Left, Start.

SUPER SPEED
During gameplay, press Up, Left, Up, Right, Down, Right, Start.

FILL MOMENTUM
During gameplay, press Left, Right, Right, Left, Up, Down, Down, Up, Start.

UNLOCK ALL COMICS
At the Review menu, press Left, Right, Right, Left, Up, Up, Right, Start.

UNLOCK ALL CONCEPT ART
At the Review menu, press Down, Down, Down, Right, Right, Left, Down, Start.

UNLOCK ALL CINEMATICS
At the Review menu, press Up, Left, Left, Up, Right, Right, Up, Start.

UNLOCK ALL LOAD SCREENS
At the Review menu, press Up, Down, Right, Left, Up, Up Down, Start.

UNLOCK ALL COURSES
At the Comic Missions menu, press Up, Right, Left, Down, Up, Right, Left, Down, Start.

MEDIEVIL: RESURRECTION

INVINCIBILITY & ALL WEAPONS
Pause the game, hold R and press Down, Up, ●, ▲, ▲, ●, Down, Up, ●, ▲. Pause the game to access the Cheat menu.

CHEAT MENU
Pause the game, hold R and press Down, Up, ●, ▲, ▲, ●, Down, Up, ●+▲. This gives you invincibility and all weapons.

ALL ARTIFACTS AND KEYS
Pause the game and press L + R, ✪, ✪, ●, ●, ▲, ✪.

METAL GEAR ACID 2

CARD NO. 046—STRAND
Enter nojiri as a password.

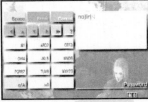

CARD NO. 099—GIJIN-SAN
Enter shinta as a password.

CARD NO. 119—REACTION BLOCK
Enter konami as a password.

CARD NO. 161—VIPER
Enter viper as a password.

CARD NO. 166—MIKA SLAYTON
Enter mika as a password.

CARD NO. 170—KAREN HOJO
Enter karen as a password.

CARD NO. 172—JEHUTY
Enter jehuty as a password.

CARD NO. 187—XM8
Enter xmeight as a password.

CARD NO. 188—MR. SIGINT
Enter sigint as a password.

CARD NO. 197—SEA HARRIER
Enter shrr as a password.

CARD NO. 203—DECOY OCTOPUS
Enter dcy as a password.

CARD NO. 212—ROGER MCCOY
Enter mccy as a password.

CARD NO. 281—REIKO HINOMOTO
Enter hnmt as a password.

CARD NO. 285—AYUMI KINOSHITA
Enter aym as a password.

CARD NO. 286—MEGURU ISHII
Enter mgr as a password.

CARD NO. 287—NATSUME SANO
Enter ntm as a password.

CARD NO. 288—MGS4
Enter nextgen as a password.

CARD NO. 289—EMMA'S PARROT
Enter ginormousj as a password.

CARD NO. 290—BANANA SKIN
Enter ronaldsiu as a password.

CARD NO. 292—POSSESSED ARM
Enter thespaniard as a password.

CARD NO. 293—SOLID EYE
Enter tobidacid as a password.

CARD NO. 294—SOLID SNAKE (MGS4)
Enter snake as a password.

CARD NO. 295—OTACON (MGS4)
Enter otacon as a password.

CARD NO. 296—GEKKO
Enter gekko as a password.

CARD NO. 297—METAL GEAR MK. II (MGS4)
Enter mk2 as a password.

CARD NO. 298—NO SMOKING
Enter smoking as a password.

METAL GEAR SOLID: PORTABLE OPS

CUNNINGHAM
Enter JUNKER as a password.

ELISA
Enter THE-L as a password.

EVA
Enter E.APPLE as a password.

GA KO
Enter !TRAUMER as a password.

GENE
Enter ERBE as a password.

NULL
Enter Hunter-n as a password.

OCELOT
Enter R.R.R. as a password.

PARAMEDIC
Enter PM-EMS as a password.

PYTHON
Enter LQ.N2 as a password.

RAIKOV
Enter IVN =RV as a password.

SIGINT
Enter DARPA-1 as a password.

SOKOLOV
Enter SATURNV as a password.

TELIKO
Enter T.F-ACID as a password.

URSULA
Enter PK +ESP as a password.

VENUS
Enter MGA2VE as a password.

ZERO
Enter 1+2-3 as a password.

METAL GEAR SOLID: PORTABLE OPS PLUS

SOLDIER PASSWORDS
Enter the following as a password.

SOLDIER	PASSWORD
Alabama	BB6K768KM9
Alaska	XL5SW5NH9S
Arizona	ZHEFPVV947
Arkansas	VNRE7JNQ8WE
Black Genome	WYNGG3JBP3YS
Blue Genome	9GNPHGFFLH
California	6MSJQYWNCJ8
Colorado	W6TAH498DJ
Connecticut	2N2AB3JV2WA

SOLDIER	PASSWORD
Delaware	AJRL6E7TT9
Female Scientist 1	3W8WVRGB2LNN
Female Scientist 2	FUC72C463KZ
Female Scientist 3	UCAWYTMXB5V
Female Soldier 1	UZZQYRPXM86
Female Soldier 2	QRQQ7GWKHJ
Female Soldier 3	MVNDAZAP8DWE
Florida	A44STZ3BHY5
Fox Soldier 1	FMXT79TPV4U8
Fox Soldier 2	HGMK3WCYURM
Fox Soldier 3	6ZY5NYW4TGK
Georgia	VD5H53JJCRH
Green Genome	TGQ6F5TUHD
GRU Soldier	9V8S7DVYFTR
Gurlukovich's Soldier	6VWM6A22FSS8
Hawaii	TW7ZMZHCBL
Hideochan Soldier	RU8XRCLPUUT
High Official	ADPS2SE5UC8
High Rank Officer 1	DVB2UDTQ5Z
High Rank Officer 2	84ZEC4X5PJ6
High Ranking Officer 3	DTAZ3QRQQDU
High-Tech Soldier	M4MSJ6R87XPP
Idaho	XAFGETZGXHGA
Illinois	QYUVCNDFUPZJ
Indiana	L68JVXVBL8RN
Iowa	B8MW36ZU56S
Kansas	TYPEVDEE24YT
Kentucky	LCD7WGS5X5
KGB Soldier	MNBVYRZP4QH
Louisiana	EHR5VVMHUSG
Maine	T5GYHQABGAC3
Maintenance Crew Member 1	T8EBSRK6F38
Maintenance Crew Member 2	YHQU74J6LLQ
Maintenance Crew Member 3	MFAJMUXZHHKJ
Male Scientist 1	ZFKHJKDEA2
Male Scientist 2	QQ4N3TPCL8PF
Male Scientist 3	CXFCXF4FP9R6
Maryland	L2W9G5N76MH7
Massachusetts	ZLU2S3ULDEVF
Michigan	HGDRBUB5P3SA
Minnesota	EEBBM888ZRA
Mississippi	TBF7H9G6TJH7
Missouri	WJND6M9N738
Montana	9FYUFV29B2Y
Nebraska	MCNB5S5K47H
Nevada	Z9D4UGG8T4U6
New Hampshire	7NQYDQ9Y4KMP
New Jersey	LGHTBU9ZTGR
New Mexico	RGJCMHNLSX
New York	6PV39FKG6X
Normal Soldier Long Sleeve	QK3CMV373Y
Normal Soldier Long Sleeve Magazine Vest	D8RV32E9774
Normal Soldier Short Sleeve	N524ZHU9N4Z
Normal Soldier Short Sleeve Magazine Vest	6WXZA7PTT9Z
North Carolina	JGVT2XV47UZ
North Dakota	T5LSAVMPWZCY
Ocelot Female A	9FS7QYSHZ56N
Ocelot Female B	F94XDZSQSGJ8
Ocelot Female C	CRF8PZGXR28
Ocelot Unit	GE6MU3DXL3X
Ohio	AUWGAXWCA3D

SOLDIER	PASSWORD
Oklahoma	ZQT75NUJH8A3
Oregon	HKSD3PJ5E5
Pennsylvania	PL8GVVUM4HD
Pink Genome	7WRG3N2MRY2
Red Genome	9CM4SY23C7X8
Rhode Island	MMYC99T3QG
Seal	X56YCKZP2V
South Carolina	ZR4465MD8LK
South Dakota	RY3NUDDPMU3
Tengu Soldier	PHHB4TY4J2D
Tennessee	TD2732GCX43U
Texas	QM84UPP6F3
Tsuhan soldier	A9KK7WYWVCV
USSR Female Soldier A	2VXUZQVH9R
USSR Female Soldier B	HPMRFSBXDJ3Y
USSR Female Soldier C	QXQVW9R3PZ
USSR Female Soldier D	GMC3M3LTPVW7
USSR Female Soldier E	5MXVX6UFPMZ5
USSR Female Soldier F	76AWS7WDAV
Utah	V7VRAYZ78GW
Vermont	L7T66LFZ63C8
Virginia	DRTCS77F5N
Washington	G3S4N42WWKTV
Washington DC	Y5YCFYHVZZW
West Virginia	72M8XR99B6
White Genome	QJ4ZTQSLUT8
Wisconsin	K9BUN2BGLMT3
Wyoming	C3THQ749RA
Yellow Genome	CE5HHYGTSSB

MLB 07: THE SHOW

SILVER ERA AND GOLD ERA TEAMS
At the Main menu, press Left, Up, Right, Down, Down, Left, Up, Down.

MAX BREAK PITCHES
Pause the game and press Right, Up, Right, Down, Up, Left, Left, Down.

MAX SPEED PITCHES
Pause the game and press Up, Left, Down, Up, Left, Right, Left, Down.

MLB 08: THE SHOW

CLASSIC FREE AGENTS AT THE PLAYER MOVEMENT MENU
At the Main menu, press Left, Right, Up, Left, Right, Up, Right, Down.

SILVER ERA AND GOLDEN ERA TEAMS
At the Main menu, press Right, Up, Right, Down, Down, Left, Up, Down.

BIG BALL
Pause the game and press Right, Down, Up, Left, Right, Left, Down, Up.

BIG HEAD MODE
Pause the game and press Right, Left, Down, Up, Left, Up, Down, Left.

SMALL HEAD MODE
Pause the game and press Left, Right, Down, Up, Right, Left, Down, Left.

MTX MOTOTRAX

ALL TRACKS
Enter BA7H as a password.

ALL BONUSES
Enter 2468GOA7 as a password.

SUPER SPEED
Enter JIH345 as a password.

MAXIMUM AIR
Enter BFB0020 as a password.

BUTTERFINGER GEAR
Enter B77393 as a password.

LEFT FIELD GEAR
Enter 12345 as a password.

SOBE GEAR
Enter 50BE as a password.

MVP BASEBALL

ALL REWARDS
Select My MVP and create a player with the name Dan Carter.

MX VS. ATV UNLEASHED: ON THE EDGE

UNLOCK EVERYTHING
Select Cheat Codes from the Options screen and enter TOOLAZY.

1,000,000 POINTS
Select Cheat Codes from the Options screen and enter BROKEASAJOKE.

PRO PHYSICS
Select Cheat Codes from the Options screen and enter IAMTOOGOOD.

ALL GEAR
Select Cheat Codes from the Options screen and enter WARDROBE.

ALL BIKES
Select Cheat Codes from the Options screen and enter BRAPP.

50CC BIKE CLASS
Select Cheat Codes from the Options screen and enter MINIMOTO.

500CC BIKE CLASS
Select Cheat Codes from the Options screen and enter BIGBORE.

ALL ATVS
Select Cheat Codes from the Options screen and enter COUCHES.

ALL MACHINES
Select Cheat Codes from the Options screen and enter LEADFOOT.

ALL FREESTYLE TRACKS
Select Cheat Codes from the Options screen and enter HUCKIT.

ALL NATIONAL TRACKS
Select Cheat Codes from the Options screen and enter GOOUTSIDE.

ALL OPEN CLASS TRACKS
Select Cheat Codes from the Options screen and enter NOTMOTO.

ALL SUPERCROSS TRACKS
Select Cheat Codes from the Options screen and enter GOINSIDE.

ALL TRACKS
Select Cheat Codes from the Options screen and enter PITPASS.

N+

25 EXTRA LEVELS
At the Main menu, hold L + R and press ✖, ◉, ✖, ◉, ✖, ✖, ◉.

NASCAR

ALL CHASE PLATES
Go to Fight to the Top mode. Next, edit the driver's first and last name so that it says ItsAll ForMe. Note that the code is case-sensitive.

$10,000,000
In Fight to the Top mode, enter your driver's name as GiveMe More.

10,000,000 FANS
In Fight to the Top mode, enter your driver's name as AllBow ToMe.

ALL CHASE PLATES
In Fight to the Top mode, enter your driver's name as ItsAll ForMe.

OLD SPICE TRACKS AND CARS
In Fight to the Top mode, enter your driver's name as KeepCool SmellGreat.

NBA BALLERS: REBOUND

VERSUS SCREEN CHEATS
You must enter the following codes at the Vs screen. The ◉ button corresponds to the first number in the code, the ▲ is the second number, and the ◉ button corresponds to the last number. Press the D-pad in any direction to enter the code. The name of the code will appear when entered correctly. Some of the codes will give you the wrong code name when entered.

EFFECT	CODE
Big Head	1 3 4
Pygmy	4 2 5
Alternate Gear	1 2 3
Show Shot Percentage	0 1 2
Expanded Move Set	5 1 2
Super Push	3 1 5
Super Block Ability	1 2 4

EFFECT	CODE
Great Handles	3 3 2
Unlimited Juice	7 6 3
Super Steals	2 1 5
Perfect Free Throws	3 2 7
Better Free Throws	3 1 7
Speedy Players	2 1 3
Alley-Oop Ability	7 2 5
Back-In Ability	1 2 2
Hotspot Ability	6 2 7
Pass 2 Friend Ability	5 3 6
Put Back Ability	3 1 3
Stunt Ability	3 7 4
2x Juice Replenish	4 3 1
Legal Goal Tending	7 5 6
Play As Afro Man	5 1 7
Play As Agent	5 5 7
Play As Business-A	5 3 7
Play As Business-B	5 2 7
Play As Coach	5 6 7
Play As Secretary	5 4 7
Super Back-Ins	2 3 5
Half House	3 6 7
Random Moves	3 0 0
Tournament Mode	0 1 1

PHRASE-OLOGY CODES

Select Phrase-ology from the Inside Stuff option and enter the following to unlock that bonus.

BONUS	PHRASE
All Players and Cinemas	NBA BALLERS TRUE PLAYA
Special Shoe #2	COLD STREAK
Special Shoe #3	LOST YA SHOES

CRIBS

Select Phrase-ology from the Inside Stuff option and enter the following to unlock player cribs.

CRIB	PHRASE
Allen Iverson's Recording Studio	THE ANSWER
Karl Malone's Devonshire Estate	ICE HOUSE
Kobe Bryant's Italian Estate	EURO CRIB
Ben Gordon's Yacht	NICE YACHT
Yao Ming's Childhood Grade School	PREP SCHOOL

NEED FOR SPEED CARBON: OWN THE CITY

UNLOCK EVERYTHING

At the Start menu, press X, X, Right, Left, ●, Up, Down.

JET CAR

At the Start menu, press Up, Down, Left, R1, L1, ●, ▲.

LAMBORGINI MERCIALAGO

At the Start menu, press X, X, Up, Down, Left, Right, ●, ●.

TRANSFORMERS CAR

At the Start menu, press X, X, X, ●, ▲, ▲, Up, Down.

START GAME WITH 5 CHOCOLATE TREATS
Enter treat4u as your Petpet's name. You can then rename your character.
The chocolate treats are shaped according to the character you chose.

PAC-MAN WORLD 3

ALL LEVELS AND MAZES
At the Main menu, press Left, Right, Left, Right, ●, Up.

PINBALL HALL OF FAME

CUSTOM BALLS OPTION
Enter CKF as a code.

TILT OPTION
Enter BZZ as a code.

PAYOUT MODE
Enter WGR as a code.

ACES HIGH IN FREEPLAY
Enter UNO as a code.

CENTRAL PARK IN FREEPLAY
Enter NYC as a code.

LOVE MACHINE IN FREEPLAY
Enter HOT as a code.

PLAYBOY TABLE IN FREEPLAY
Enter HEF as a code.

STRIKES 'N SPARES IN FREEPLAY
Enter PBA as a code.

TEE'D OFF IN FREEPLAY
Enter PGA as a code.

XOLTEN IN FREEPLAY
Enter BIG as a code.

POCKET POOL

ALL PICTURES AND VIDEOS
At the Title screen, press L, R, L, L, R, R, L (x3), R (x3), L (x4), R (x4).

SEGA GENESIS COLLECTION

Before using the following cheats, select the ABC Control option. This sets
the controller to the following: ● is A, ✖ is B, ● is C.

ALTERED BEAST

OPTIONS MENU
At the Title screen, hold B and press Start.

LEVEL SELECT
After enabling the Options menu, select a level from the menu. At the Title
screen, hold A and press Start.

BEAST SELECT
At the Title screen, hold A + B + C + Down/Left and then press Start

SOUND TEST
At the Title screen, hold A + C + Up/Right and press Start.

COMIX ZONE

INVINCIBILITY
At the Jukebox screen, press C on the following sounds:
3, 12, 17, 2, 2, 10, 2, 7, 7, 11

LEVEL SELECT
At the Jukebox screen, press C on the following sounds:
14, 15, 18, 5, 13, 1, 3, 18, 15, 6
Press C on the desired level.

ECCO THE DOLPHIN

INVINCIBILITY
When the level name appears, hold A + Start until the level begins.

DEBUG MENU
Pause the game with Ecco facing the screen and press Right, B, C, B, C, Down, C, Up.

INFINITE AIR
Enter LIFEFISH as a password.

PASSWORDS

LEVEL	PASSWORD
The Undercaves	WEFIDNMP
The Vents	BQDPXJDS
The Lagoon	JNSBRIKY
Ridge Water	NTSBZTKB
Open Ocean	YWGTTJNI
Ice Zone	HZIFZBMF
Hard Water	LRFJRQLI
Cold Water	UYNFRQLC
Island Zone	LYTIOQLZ
Deep Water	MNOPOQLR
The Marble	RJNTOQLZ
The Library	RTGXQQLE
Deep City	DDXPQQLJ
City of Forever	MSDBRQLA
Jurassic Beach	IYCBUNLB
Pteranodon Pond	DMXEUNLI
Origin Beach	EGRIUNLB
Trilobite Circle	IELMUNLB
Dark Water	RKEQUNLN
City of Forever 2	HPQIGPLA
The Tube	JUMFKMLB
The Machine	GXUBKMLF
The Last Fight	TSONLMLU

FLICKY

ROUND SELECT
Begin a new game. Before the first round appears, hold A + C + Up + Start. Press Up or Down to select a Round.

GAIN GROUND

LEVEL SELECT
At the Options screen, press A, C, B, C.

GOLDEN AXE

LEVEL SELECT
Select Arcade Mode. At the character select, hold Down/Left + B and press Start. Press Up or Down to select a level.

RISTAR

Select Passwords from the Options menu and enter the following:

LEVEL SELECT
ILOVEU

BOSS RUSH MODE
MUSEUM

TIME ATTACK MODE
DOFEEL

TOUGHER DIFFICULTY
SUPER

ONCHI MUSIC
MAGURO. Activate this from the Sound Test.

CLEARS PASSWORD
XXXXXX

SONIC THE HEDGEHOG

LEVEL SELECT

At the title screen, press Up, Down, Left, Right. Hold A and press Start.

SONIC THE HEDGEHOG 2

LEVEL SELECT

Select Sound Test from the options. Press C on the following sounds in order: 19, 65, 09, 17. At the title screen, hold A and press Start.

VECTORMAN

DEBUG MODE

At the options screen, press A, B, B, A, Down, A, B, B, A.

REFILL LIFE

Pause the game and press A, B, Right, A, C, A , Down, A, B, Right, A.

VECTORMAN 2

LEVEL SELECT

Pause the game and press Up, Right, A, B, A, Down, Left, A, Down.

EXTRA LIFE

Pause the game and press Right, Up, B, A, Down, Up, B, Down, Up, B. Repeat for more lives.

FULL ENERGY

Pause the game and press B, A, B, A, Left, Up, Up.

NEW WEAPON

Pause the game and press C, A, Left, Left, Down, A, Down. Repeat for more weapons.

SHREK THE THIRD

10,000 BONUS COINS

Press Up, Up, Down, Up, Right, Left at the Gift Shop.

SILENT HILL: ORIGINS

CODEBREAKER SUIT

During a game, press Up, Up, Down, Down, Left, Right, Left, Right, ✕, ◎. You must first finish the game to get this suit.

THE SIMPSONS GAME

UNLIMITED POWER FOR ALL CHARACTERS

At the Extras menu, press ▲, Left, Right, ▲, ◉, L.

ALL MOVIES

At the Extras menu, press ◉, Left, ◉, Right, ▲, R.

ALL CLICHÉS

At the Extras menu, press Left, ◉, Right, ▲, Right, L.

THE SIMS 2

PERK CHEAT

At the Buy Perks screen, hold L + R + ◉. Buy the Cheat Perk to get some money, skills, and more.

THE SIMS 2: CASTAWAY

CHEAT GNOME

During a game, press L, R, Up, ✕, R. You can now use this Gnome to get the following during Live mode:

ALL PLANS

During a game, press ✕, R, ✕, R, ✕.

ALL CRAFT AND RESOURCES

During a game, press ◉, ▲, R, Down, Down, Up.

MAX FOOD AND RESOURCES

During a game, press ◉(x4), L.

PSP®

THE SIMS 2: PETS

CHEAT GNOME
During a game, press L, L, R, ✖, ✖, Up. Now you can enter the following cheats:

ADVANCE TIME 6 HOURS
During a game, press Up, L, Down, R, R.

GIVE SIM PET POINTS
During a game, press ▲, ●, ✖, ●, L, R.

$10,000
During a game, press ▲, Up, Left, Down, R.

SPIDER-MAN: FRIEND OR FOE

NEW GREEN GOBLIN AS A SIDEKICK
While standing in the Helicarrier between levels, press Left, Down, Right, Right, Down, Left.

SANDMAN AS A SIDEKICK
While standing in the Helicarrier between levels, press Right, Right, Right, Up, Down, Left.

VENOM AS A SIDEKICK
While standing in the Helicarrier between levels, press Left, Left, Right, Up, Down, Down.

5000 TECH TOKENS
While standing in the Helicarrier between levels, press Up, Up, Down, Down, Left, Right.

NEW GOBLIN
At the stage complete screen, hold L + R and press ●, Down, ✖, Right, ●, Up, ▲, Left.

STAR WARS: THE FORCE UNLEASHED

CHEATS
Once you have accessed the Rogue Shadow, select Enter Code from the Extras menu. Now you can enter the following:

CHEAT	CODE
Invincibility	CORTOSIS
Unlimited Force	VERGENCE
1,000,000 Force Points	SPEEDER
All Force Powers	TYRANUS
Max Force Power Level	KATARN
Max Combo Level	COUNTDOOKU
Amplified Lightsaber Damage	LIGHTSABER

COSTUMES
Once you have accessed the Rogue Shadow, select Enter Code from the Extras menu. Now you can enter the following:

COSTUME	CODE
All Costumes	GRANDMOFF
501st Legion	LEGION
Aayla Secura	AAYLA
Admiral Ackbar	ITSATWAP
Anakin Skywalker	CHOSENONE
Asajj Ventress	ACOLYTE
Ceremonial Jedi Robes	DANTOOINE
Chop'aa Notimo	NOTIMO
Classic stormtrooper	TK421
Count Dooku	SERENNO
Darth Desolous	PAUAN
Darth Maul	ZABRAK
Darth Phobos	HIDDENFEAR
Darth Vader	SITHLORD
Drexl Roosh	DREXLROOSH

OVERLOAD

COSTUME	CODE
Emperor Palpatine	PALPATINE
General Rahm Kota	MANDALORE
Han Solo	NERFHERDER
Heavy trooper	SHOCKTROOP
Juno Eclipse	ECLIPSE
Kento's Robe	WOOKIEE
Kleef	KLEEF
Lando Calrissian	SCOUNDREL
Luke Skywalker	T16WOMPRAT
Luke Skywalker (Yavin)	YELLOWJCKT
Mace Windu	JEDIMASTER
Mara Jade	MARAJADE
Maris Brook	MARISBROOD
Navy commando	STORMTROOP
Obi Wan Kenobi	BENKENOBI
Proxy	HOLOGRAM
Qui Gon Jinn	MAVERICK
Shaak Ti	TOGRUTA
Shadow trooper	INTHEDARK
Sith Robes	HOLOCRON
Sith Stalker Armor	KORRIBAN
Twi'lek	SECURA

STAR WARS: LETHAL ALLIANCE

ALL LEVELS
Select Create Profile from the Profiles menu and enter HANS0L0.

ALL LEVELS AND REFILL HEALTH WHEN DEPLETED
Select Create Profile from the Profiles menu and enter JD1MSTR.

REFILL HEALTH WHEN DEPLETED
Select Create Profile from the Profiles menu and enter B0BAF3T.

SUPER MONKEY BALL ADVENTURE

ALL CARDS
At the mode select, press ⬤, ▲, ◉, ⬤, ▲, ◉, ⬤, ▲, ◉, ⬤, ▲, ◉.

THRILLVILLE: OFF THE RAILS

$50,000
During a game, press ⬤, ◉, ▲, ⬤, ◉, ▲, ✖. Repeat this code as much as desired.

ALL PARKS
During a game, press ⬤, ◉, ▲, ⬤, ◉, ▲, ⬤.

ALL RIDES
During a game, press ⬤, ◉, ▲, ⬤ ◉, ▲, ▲. Some rides still need to be researched.

COMPLETE MISSIONS
During a game, press ⬤, ◉, ▲, ⬤, ◉, ▲, ◉. Then, at the Missions menu, highlight a mission and press ⬤ to complete that mission. Some missions have Bronze, Silver, and Gold objectives. For these missions the first press of ⬤ earns the Bronze, the second earns the Silver, and the third earns the Gold.

TOMB RAIDER: LEGEND

You must unlock the following cheats before you can use them.

BULLETPROOF
During a game, hold L and press ✖, R, ▲, R, ⬤, R.

DRAW ENEMY HEALTH
During a game, hold L and press ⬤, ◉, ✖, R, R, ▲.

INFINITE ASSUALT RIFLE AMMO
During a game, hold L and press ✖, ◉, ✖, R, ⬤, ▲.

INFINITE GRENADE LAUNCHER
During a game, hold L and press R, ▲, R, ◉, R, ⬤.

INFINITE SHOTGUN AMMO
During a game, hold L and press R, ●, ■, R, ●, ✕.

INFINITE SMG AMMO
During a game, hold L and press ●, ▲, R, R, ✕, ●.

1-SHOT KILL
During a game, hold L and press ▲, ✕, ▲, ■, R, ●.

TEXTURELESS MODE
Hold L and press R, ✕, ●, ✕, ▲, R.

WIELD EXCALIBUR
During a game, hold L and press ▲, ✕, ●, R, ▲, R.

TWISTED METAL: HEAD-ON

Note that the following codes will not work for Multiplayer or Online modes.

HEALTH RECHARGED
Hold L + R and press ▲, ✕, ■, ●.

INFINITE AMMO
Hold L + R and press ▲, ▲, Down, Down, Left.

INVULNERABLE
Hold L + R and press Right, Left, Down, Up.

INFINITE WEAPONS
Hold L + R and press ▲, ▲, Down, Down.

KILLER WEAPONS
Hold L + R and press ✕, ✕, Up, Up.

MEGA GUNS
Hold L + R and press ✕, ▲, ✕, ▲

WALL-E

KILL ALL
Select Cheats and then Secret Codes. Enter BOTOFWAR.

UNDETECTED BY ENEMIES
Select Cheats and then Secret Codes. Enter STEALTHARMOR.

LASERS CHANGE COLORS
Select Cheats and then Secret Codes. Enter RAINBOWLAZER.

CUBES ARE EXPLOSIVE
Select Cheats and then Secret Codes. Enter EXPLOSIVEWORLD.

LIGHTEN DARK AREAS
Select Cheats and then Secret Codes. Enter GLOWINTHEDARK.

GOGGLES
Select Cheats and then Secret Codes. Enter BOTOFMYSTERY.

GOLD TRACKS
Select Cheats and then Secret Codes. Enter GOLDENTRACKS.

THE WARRIORS

100% COMPLETION IN STORY MODE
During a game, press L, Select, ■, Down, L, Right.

COMPLETE CURRENT MISSION
During a game, press Down, ■, ✕, Select, R, Left.

UNLIMITED HEALTH
During a game, press Up, ▲, R, Select, ✕, L.

UPGRADES STAMINA
During a game, press ✕, L, Down, ■, Up, ✕.

UNLIMITED RAGE
During a game, press ■, ●, ▲, Select, ✕, Left.

BRASS KNUCKLES
During a game, press ●, ●, ●, L, Select, ▲.

HAND CUFFS
During a game, press ✕, Up, Select, L, L.

HAND CUFF KEYS
During a game, press Left, ✕, ✕, R, L, Down.

KNIFE
During a game, press Down, Down, Select, Up, Up, L.

MACHETE
During a game, press L, ✕, R(x2), Select, R.

UNBREAKABLE BAT
During a game, press L, L, ●, Up, ●, Select.

ALL DEALERS
During a game, press right, R, ●, ✕, Select, ■.

UPGRADE FLASH CAPACITY
During a game, press L, ✖, R, L, L, ●.

99 CREDITS IN ARMIES OF THE NIGHT
During a game of Armie of the Night, press Up, Up, Down, Down, Left, Right.

WRC: FIA WORLD RALLY CHAMPIONSHIP

UNLOCK EVERYTHING
Create a new profile with the name PADLOCK.

EXTRA AVATARS
Create a new profile with the name UGLYMUGS.

GHOST CAR
Create a new profile with the name SPOOKY.

SUPERCHARGER
Create a new profile with the name MAXPOWER.

TIME TRIAL GHOST CARS
Create a new profile with the name AITRIAL.

BIRD CAMERA
Create a new profile with the name dovecam.

REVERSES CONTROLS
Create a new profile with the name REVERSE.

X-MEN LEGENDS II: RISE OF APOCALYPSE

ALL CHARACTERS
At the Team Management screen, press Right, Left, Left, Right, Up, Up, Up, Start.

LEVEL 99 CHARACTERS
At the Team Management screen, press Up, Down, Up, Down, Left, Up, Left, Right, Start.

ALL SKILLS
At the Team Management screen, press Left, Right, Left, Right, Down, Up, Start.

SUPER SPEED
Pause the game and press Up, Up, Up, Down, Up, Down, Start.

UNLIMITED XTREME POWER
Pause the game and press Left, Down, Right, Down, Up, Up, Down, Up Start.

100,000 TECHBITS
At Forge or Beast's equipment screen, press Up, Up, Up, Down, Right, Right, Start.

ALL CINEMATICS
At the Review menu, press Left, Right, Right, Left, Down, Down, Left, Start.

ALL COMIC BOOKS
At the Review menu, press Right, Left, Left, Right, Up, Up, Right, Start.

PSP

BOOSTER PACK

At the card shop, press Up, Up, Down, Down, Left, Right, Left, Right, ✗, ◉.

RENTAL CARD PASSWORDS

Enter the following in the Password Machine to obtain for rental:

CARD	PASSWORD	CARD	PASSWORD
30,000-Year White Turtle	11714098	Ancient Gear Cannon	80045583
4-Starred Ladybug of Doom	83994646	Ancient Gear Castle	92001300
7	67048711	Ancient Gear Drill	67829249
7 Colored Fish	23771716	Ancient Gear Golem	83104731
7 Completed	86198326	Ancient Gear Soldier	56094445
A Cat of Ill Omen	24140059	Ancient Lamp	54912977
A Deal with Dark Ruler	06850209	Ancient Lizard Warrior	43230671
A Feather of the Phoenix	49140998	Andro Sphinx	15013468
A Feint Plan	68170903	Anteatereatingant	13250922
A Hero Emerges	21597117	Anti-Aircraft Flower	65064143
A Legendary Ocean	00295517	Anti-Spell	53112492
A Man with Wdjat	51351302	Apprentice Magician	09156135
A Rival Appears!	05728014	Appropriate	48539234
A Wingbeat of Giant Dragon	28596933	Aqua Madoor	85639257
A-Team: Trap Disposal Unit	13026402	Aqua Spirit	40916023
Abare Ushioni	89718302	Arcane Archer of the Forest	55001420
Absolute End	27744077	Archfiend of Gilfer	50287060
Absorbing Kid From the Sky	49771608	Archfiend Soldier	49881766
Abyss Soldier	18318842	Archlord Zerato	18378582
Abyssal Designator	89801755	Armaill	53153481
Acid Rain	21323861	Armed Changer	90374791
Acid Trap Hole	41356845	Armed Dragon LV 3	00980973
Acrobat Monkey	47372349	Armed Dragon LV 5	46384672
Adhesion Trap Hole	62325062	Armed Dragon LV 7	73879377
Adhesive Explosive	53828396	Armed Dragon LV 10	59464593
After the Struggle	25345186	Armed Ninja	09076207
Agido	16135253	Armed Samurai - Ben Kei	84430950
Airknight Parshath	18036057	Armor Axe	07180418
Aitsu	48202661	Armor Break	79649195
Alkana Knight Joker	06150044	Armored Lizard	15480588
Alpha the Magnet Warrior	99785935	Armored Starfish	17535588
Altar for Tribute	21070956	Armored Zombie	20277860
Amazon Archer	91869203	Array of Revealing Light	69296555
Amazoness Archers	67987611	Arsenal Bug	42364374
Amazoness Blowpiper	73574678	Arsenal Robber	55348096
Amazoness Chain Master	29654737	Arsenal Summoner	85489096
Amazoness Paladin	47480070	Assault on GHQ	62633180
Amazoness Swords Woman	94004268	Astral Barrier	37053871
Amazoness Tiger	10979723	Asura Priest	02134346
Ambulance Rescueroid	98927491	Aswan Apparition	88236094
Ambulanceroid	36378213	Atomic Firefly	87340664
Ameba	95174353	Attack and Receive	63689843
Amphibian Beast	67371383	Attack Reflector Unit	91989718
Amphibious Bugroth MK-3	64342551	Aussa the Earth Charmer	37970940
Amplifier	00303660	Autonomous Action Unit	71453557
An Owl of Luck	23927567	Avatar of the Pot	99284890
Ancient Elf	93221206	Axe Dragonute	84914462
Ancient Gear	31557782	Axe of Despair	40619825
Ancient Gear Beast	10509340	B. Skull Dragon	11901678
		B.E.S. Covered Core	15317640
		B.E.S. Crystal Core	22790789
		B.E.S. Tetran	44954628
		Baby Dragon	88819587
		Back to Square One	47453433

CARD	PASSWORD
Backfire	82705573
Backup Soldier	36280194
Bad Reaction to Simochi	40633297
Bait Doll	07165085
Ballista of Rampart Smashing	00242146
Banisher of the Light	61528025
Bark of Dark Ruler	41925941
Barrel Dragon	81480460
Basic Insect	89091579
Battery Charger	61181383
Batteryman AA	63142001
Batteryman C	19733961
Batteryman D	55401221
Battle Footballer	48094997
Battle Ox	05053103
Battle-Scarred	94463200
Bazoo The Soul-Eater	40133511
Beast Soul Swap	35149085
Beaver Warrior	32452818
Beckoning Light	16255442
Beelze Frog	49522489
Begone, Knave	20374520
Behemoth the King of All Animals	22996376
Beiige, Vanguard of Dark World	33731070
Berserk Dragon	85605684
Berserk Gorilla	39168895
Beta the Magnet Warrior	39256679
Bickuribox	25655502
Big Bang Shot	61127349
Big Burn	95472621
Big Core	14148099
Big Eye	16768387
Big Koala	42129512
Big Shield Gardna	65240384
Big Wave Small Wave	51562916
Big-Tusked Mammoth	59380081
Bio-Mage	58696829
Birdface	45547649
Black Illusion Ritual	41426869
Black Luster Soldier - Envoy of the Beginning	72989439
Black Pendant	65169794
Black Tyranno	38670435
Blackland Fire Dragon	87564352
Blade Knight	39507162
Blade Rabbit	58268433
Blade Skater	97023549
Bladefly	28470714
Blast Held By a Tribute	89041555
Blast Magician	21051146
Blast with Chain	98239899
Blasting the Ruins	21466326
Blazing Inpachi	05464695
Blind Destruction	32015116
Blindly Loyal Goblin	35215622
Block Attack	25880422
Blockman	48115277
Blowback Dragon	25551951
Blue-Eyes Shining Dragon	53347303
Blue-Eyes Toon Dragon	53183600

CARD	PASSWORD
Blue-Eyes Ultimate Dragon	23995346
Blue-Eyes White Dragon	89631139
Blue-Winged Crown	41396436
Bokoichi the Freightening Car	08715625
Bombardment Beetle	57409948
Bonding - H2O	45898858
Boneheimer	98456117
Book of Life	02204140
Book of Moon	14087893
Book of Taiyou	38699854
Boss Rush	66947414
Bottom Dweller	81386177
Bottomless Shifting Sand	76532077
Bottomless Trap Hole	29401950
Bountiful Artemis	32296881
Bowganian	52090844
Bracchio-Raidus	16507828
Brain Control	87910978
Brain Jacker	40267580
Branch	30548775
Breaker the Magical Warrior	71413901
Broww, Huntsman of Dark World	79126789
Brron, Mad King of Dark World	06214884
Bubble Blaster	53586134
Bubble Illusion	80075749
Bubble Shuffle	61968753
Bubonic Vermin	06104968
Burning Algae	41859700
Burning Beast	59364406
Burning Land	24294108
Burst Breath	80163754
Burst Return	27191436
Burst Stream of Destruction	17655904
Buster Blader	78193831
Buster Rancher	84740193
Butterfly Dagger - Elma	69243953
Byser Shock	17597059
Call of The Haunted	97077563
Call of the Mummy	04861205
Cannon Soldier	11384280
Cannonball Spear Shellfish	95614612
Card of Safe Return	57953380
Card Shuffle	12183332
Castle of Dark Illusions	00062121
Cat's Ear Tribe	95841282
Catapult Turtle	95727991
Cathedral of Nobles	29762407
Catnipped Kitty	96501677
Cave Dragon	93220472
Ceasefire	36468556
Celtic Guardian	91152256
Cemetery Bomb	51394546
Centrifugal	01801154
Ceremonial Bell	20228463
Cetus of Dagala	28106077
Chain Burst	48276469

CARD	PASSWORD
Chain Destruction	01248895
Chain Disappearance	57139487
Chain Energy	79323590
Chain Thrasher	88190453
Chainsaw Insect	77252217
Change of Heart	04031928
Chaos Command Magician	72630549
Chaos Emperor Dragon-Envoy of the End	82301904
Chaos End	61044390
Chaos Greed	97439308
Chaos Necromancer	01434352
Chaos Sorcerer	09596126
Chaosrider Gutaph	47829960
Charcoal Inpachi	13179332
Charm of Shabti	50412166
Charubin the Fire Knight	37421579
Chiron the Mage	16956455
Chopman the Desperate Outlaw	40884383
Chorus of Sanctuary	81380218
Chthonian Alliance	46910446
Chthonian Blast	18271561
Chthonian Polymer	72287557
Chu-Ske the Mouse Fighter	08508055
Clay Charge	22479888
Cliff the Trap Remover	06967870
Cobra Jar	86801871
Cobraman Sakuzy	75109441
Cold Wave	60682203
Collected Power	07565547
Combination Attack	08964854
Command Knight	10375182
Commander Covington	22666164
Commencement Dance	43417563
Compulsory Evacuation Device	94192409
Confiscation	17375316
Conscription	31000575
Continuous Destruction Punch	68057622
Contract With Exodia	33244944
Contract With the Abyss	69035382
Contract with the Dark Master	96420087
Convulsion of Nature	62966332
Cost Down	23265313
Covering Fire	74458486
Crab Turtle	91782219
Crass Clown	93889755
Creature Swap	31036355
Creeping Doom Manta	52571838
Crimson Ninja	14618326
Criosphinx	18654201
Cross Counter	37083210
Crush D. Gandra	64681432
Cure Mermaid	85802526
Curse of Aging	41398771
Curse of Anubis	66742250
Curse of Darkness	84970821
Curse of Dragon	28279543

CARD	PASSWORD
Curse of the Masked Beast	94377247
Curse of Vampire	34294855
Cyberdark Dragon	40418351
Cyberdark Horn	41230939
Cyberdark Keel	03019642
D - Sheild	62868900
D - Time	99075257
D. D. Assailant	70074904
D. D. Borderline	60912752
D. D. Trainer	86498013
D. D. Warrior Lady	07572887
D.D. Crazy Beast	48148828
D.D. Dynamite	08628798
D.D. Trap Hole	05606466
D.D.M. - Different Dimension Master	82112775
Dancing Fairy	90925163
Dangerous Machine TYPE-6	76895648
Dark Artist	72520073
Dark Bat	67049542
Dark Blade	11321183
Dark Blade the Dragon Knight	86805855
Dark Driceratops	65287621
Dark Dust Spirit	89111398
Dark Elf	21417692
Dark Energy	04614116
Dark Factory of Mass Production	90928333
Dark Flare Knight	13722870
Dark Hole	53129443
Dark Magic Attack	02314238
Dark Magic Ritual	76792184
Dark Magician	46986414
Dark Magician Girl	38033121
Dark Magician of Chaos	40737112
Dark Magician's Tome of Black Magic	67227834
Dark Master - Zorc	97642679
Dark Mirror Force	20522190
Dark Paladin	98502113
Dark Paladin	98502113
Dark Room of Nightmare	85562745
Dark Sage	92377303
Dark Snake Syndrome	47233801
Dark-Piercing Light	45895206
Darkfire Dragon	17881964
Darkfire Soldier #1	05388481
Darkfire Soldier #2	78861134
Darkworld Thorns	43500484
De-Spell	19159413
Deal of Phantom	69122763
Decayed Commander	10209545
Dedication Through Light And Darkness	69542930
Deepsea Shark	28593363
Dekoichi the Battlechanted Locomotive	87621407
Delinquent Duo	44763025
Demotion	72575145
Des Counterblow	39131963
Des Croaking	44883830

CARD	PASSWORD
Des Dendle	12965761
Des Feral Imp	81985784
Des Frog	84451804
Des Kangaroo	78613627
Des Koala	69579761
Des Lacooda	02326738
Des Wombat	09637706
Desert Sunlight	93747864
Destertapir	13409151
Destiny Board	94212438
Destiny Hero - Captain Tenacious	77608643
Destiny Hero - Diamond Dude	13093792
Destiny Hero - Doom Lord	41613948
Destiny Hero - Dreadmaster	40591390
Destiny Signal	35464895
Destroyer Golem	73481154
Destruction Ring	21219755
Dian Keto the Cure Master	84257639
Dice Jar	03549275
Dimension Distortion	95194279
Dimensional Warrior	37043180
Dimenional Fissure	816747482
Disappear	24623598
Disarmament	20727787
Disc Fighter	19612721
Dissolverock	40826495
Divine Dragon Ragnarok	62113340
Divine Wrath	49010598
DNA Surgery	74701381
DNA Transplant	56769674
Doitsu	57062206
Dokurorider	99721536
Dokuroyaiba	30325729
Don Turtle	03493978
Don Zaloog	76922029
Doriado	84916669
Doriado's Blessing	23965037
Dragon Seeker	28563545
Dragon Treasure	01435851
Dragon Zombie	66672569
Dragon's Mirror	71490127
Dragon's Rage	54178050
Dragoness the Wicked Knight	70681994
Draining Shield	43250041
Dream Clown	13215230
Drillago	99050989
Drillroid	71218746
Dunames Dark Witch	12493482
Dust Tornado	60082867
Earth Chant	59820352
Earthbound Spirit	67105242
Earthquake	82828051
Eatgaboon	42578427
Ebon Magician Curran	46128076
Electro-Whip	37820550
Elegant Egotist	90219263
Element Dragon	30314994
Elemental Burst	61411502
Elemental Hero Avian	21844576

CARD	PASSWORD
Elemental Hero Bladedge	59793705
Elemental Hero Bubbleman	79979666
Elemental Hero Burstinatrix	58932615
Elemental Hero Clayman	84327329
Elemental Hero Electrum/Erekshieler	29343734
Elemental Hero Flame Wingman	35809262
Elemental Hero Mariner	14225239
Elemental Hero Necroid Shaman	81003500
Elemental Hero Neos	89943723
Elemental Hero Phoenix Enforcer	41436536
Elemental Hero Shining Flare Wingman	25366484
Elemental Hero Shining Phoenix Enforcer	88820235
Elemental Hero Sparkman	20721928
Elemental Hero Thunder Giant	61204971
Elemental Mistress Doriado	99414158
Elemental Recharge	36586443
Elf's Light	39897277
Emblem of Dragon Destroyer	06390406
Embodiment of Apophis	28649820
Emergency Provisions	53046408
Emes the Infinity	43580269
Empress Judge	15237615
Empress Mantis	58818411
Enchanted Javelin	96355986
Enchanting Mermaid	75376965
Enraged Battle Ox	76909279
Enraged Muka Muka	91862578
Eradicating Aerosol	94716515
Eternal Draught	56606928
Eternal Rest	95051344
Exhausting Spell	95451366
Exile of the Wicked	26725158
Exiled Force	74131780
Exodia Necross	12600382
Exodia the Forbidden One	33396948
Fairy Box	21598948
Fairy Dragon	20315854
Fairy King Truesdale	45425051
Fairy Meteor Crush	97687912
Faith Bird	75582395
Fatal Abacus	77910045
Fenrir	00218704
Feral Imp	41392891
Fiber Jar	78706415
Fiend Comedian	81172176
Fiend Scorpion	26566878
Fiend's Hand	52800428
Fiend's Mirror	31890399
Final Countdown	95308449
Final Destiny	18591904
Final Flame	73134081
Final Ritual of the Ancients	60369732

CARD	PASSWORD
Fire Darts	43061293
Fire Eye	88435542
Fire Kraken	46534755
Fire Princess	64752646
Fire Reaper	53581214
Fire Sorcerer	27132350
Firegrass	53293545
Firewing Pegasus	27054370
Fireyarou	71407486
Fissure	66788016
Five God Dragon (Five-Headed Dragon)	99267150
Flame Cerebrus	60862676
Flame Champion	42599677
Flame Dancer	12883044
Flame Ghost	58528964
Flame Manipulator	34460851
Flame Swordsman	45231177
Flame Viper	02830619
Flash Assailant	96890582
Flower Wolf	95952802
Flying Fish	31987274
Flying Kamakiri #1	84834865
Flying Kamakiri #2	03134241
Follow Wind	98252586
Foolish Burial	81439173
Forest	87430998
Fortress Whale	62337487
Fortress Whale's Oath	77454922
Frenzied Panda	98818516
Frozen Soul	57069605
Fruits of Kozaky's Studies	49998907
Fuh-Rin-Ka-Zan	01781310
Fuhma Shuriken	09373534
Fulfillment of the Contract	48206762
Fushi No Tori	38538445
Fusion Gate	33550694
Fusion Recovery	18511384
Fusion Sage	26902560
Fusion Weapon	27967615
Fusionist	01641883
Gadget Soldier	86281779
Gagagigo	49003308
Gaia Power	56594520
Gaia the Dragon Champion	66889139
Gaia the Fierce Knight	06368038
Gale Dogra	16229315
Gale Lizard	77491079
Gamble	37313786
Gamma the Magnet Warrior	11549357
Garma Sword	90844184
Garma Sword Oath	78577570
Garoozis	14977074
Garuda the Wind Spirit	12800777
Gatling Dragon	87751584
Gazelle the King of Mythical Beasts	05818798
Gear Golem the Moving Fortress	30190809
Gearfried the Iron Knight	00423705

CARD	PASSWORD
Gearfried the Swordmaster	57046845
Gemini Elf	69140098
Getsu Fuhma	21887179
Giant Axe Mummy	78266168
Giant Germ	95178994
Giant Kozaky	58185394
Giant Orc	73698349
Giant Rat	97017120
Giant Red Seasnake	58831685
Giant Soldier of Stone	13039848
Giant Trunade	42703248
Gift of the Mystical Elf	98299011
Giga Gagagigo	43793530
Giga-Tech Wolf	08471389
Gigantes	47606319
Gigobyte	53776525
Gil Garth	38445524
Gilasaurus	45894482
Giltia the D. Knight	51828629
Girochin Kuwagata	84620194
Goblin Attack Force	78658564
Goblin Calligrapher	12057781
Goblin Elite Attack Force	85306040
Goblin Thief	45311864
Goblin's Secret Remedy	11868825
Gogiga Gagagigo	39674352
Golem Sentry	82323207
Good Goblin Housekeeping	09744376
Gora Turtle	80233946
Graceful Charity	79571449
Graceful Dice	74137509
Gradius	10992251
Gradius' Option	14291024
Granadora	13944422
Grand Tiki Elder	13676474
Granmarg the Rock Monarch	60229110
Gravedigger Ghoul	82542267
Gravekeeper's Cannonholder	99877698
Gravekeeper's Curse	50712728
Gravekeeper's Guard	37101832
Gravekeeper's Servant	16762927
Gravekeeper's Spear Soldier	63695531
Gravekeeper's Spy	24317029
Gravekeeper's Vassal	99690140
Graverobber's Retribution	33737664
Gravity Bind	85742772
Gray Wing	29618570
Great Angus	11813953
Great Long Nose	02356994
Great Mammoth of Goldfine	54622031
Green Gadget	41172955
Gren Maju Da Eiza	36584821
Ground Attacker Bugroth	58314394
Ground Collapse	90502999
Gruesome Goo	65623423
Gryphon Wing	55608151

CARD	PASSWORD
Gryphon's Feather Duster	34370473
Guardian Angel Joan	68007326
Guardian of the Labyrinth	89272878
Guardian of the Sea	85448931
Guardian Sphinx	40659562
Guardian Statue	75209824
Gust Fan	55321970
Gyaku-Gire Panda	09817927
Gyroid	18325492
Hade-Hane	28357177
Hamburger Recipe	80811661
Hammer Shot	26412047
Hamon	32491822
Hand of Nephthys	98446407
Hane-Hane	07089711
Hannibal Necromancer	05640330
Hard Armor	20060230
Harpie Girl	34100324
Harpie Lady 1	91932350
Harpie Lady 2	27927359
Harpie Lady 3	54415063
Harpie Lady Sisters	12206212
Harpie's Brother	30532390
Harpies' Hunting Ground	75782277
Hayabusa Knight	21015833
Headless Knight	05434080
Heart of Clear Water	64801562
Heart of the Underdog	35762283
Heavy Mech Support Platform	23265594
Heavy Storm	19613556
Helios - the Primordial Sun	54493213
Helios Duo Megistus	80887952
Helios Tris Megiste	17286057
Helping Robo for Combat	47025270
Hero Barrier	44676200
HERO Flash!	00191749
Hero Heart	67951831
Hero Kid	32679370
Hero Ring	26647858
Hero Signal	22020907
Hidden Book of Spell	21840375
Hidden Soldier	02047519
Hieracosphinx	82260502
Hieroglyph Lithograph	10248192
High Tide Gyojin	54579801
Hiita the Fire Charmer	00759393
Hino-Kagu-Tsuchi	75745607
Hinotama Soul	96851799
Hiro's Shadow Scout	81863068
Hitotsu-Me Giant	76184692
Holy Knight Ishzark	57902462
Homunculus the Alchemic Being	40410110
Horn of Heaven	98069388
Horn of Light	38552107
Horn of the Unicorn	64047146
Horus The Black Flame Dragon LV 4	75830094
Horus The Black Flame Dragon LV 6	11224103

CARD	PASSWORD
Horus The Black Flame Dragon LV 8	48229808
Hoshiningen	67629977
House of Adhesive Tape	15083728
Howling Insect	93107608
Huge Revolution	65396880
Human-Wave Tactics	30353551
Humanoid Slime	46821314
Humanoid Worm Drake	05600127
Hungry Burger	30243636
Hydrogeddon	22587018
Hyena	22873908
Hyozanryu	62397231
Hyper Hammerhead	02671330
Hysteric Fairy	21297224
Icarus Attack	53567095
Illusionist Faceless Mage	28546905
Impenetrable Formation	96631852
Imperial Order	61740673
Inaba White Rabbit	77084837
Incandescent Ordeal	33031674
Indomitable Fighter Lei Lei	84173492
Infernal Flame Emperor	19847532
Infernal Queen Archfiend	08581705
Inferno	74823665
Inferno Fire Blast	52684508
Inferno Hammer	17185260
Inferno Reckless Summon	12247206
Inferno Tempest	14391920
Infinite Cards	94163677
Infinite Dismissal	54109233
Injection Fairy Lily	79575620
Inpachi	97923414
Insect Armor with Laser Cannon	03492538
Insect Barrier	23615409
Insect Imitation	96965364
Insect Knight	35052053
Insect Princess	37957847
Insect Queen	91512835
Insect Soldiers of the Sky	07019529
Inspection	16227556
Interdimensional Matter Transporter	36261276
Invader From Another Dimension	28450915
Invader of Darkness	56647086
Invader of the Throne	03056267
Invasion of Flames	26082229
Invigoration	98374133
Iron Blacksmith Kotetsu	73431236
Island Turtle	04042268
Jack's Knight	90876561
Jade Insect Whistle	95214051
Jam Breeding Machine	21770260
Jam Defender	21558682
Jar of Greed	83968380
Jar Robber	33784505
Javelin Beetle	26932788
Javelin Beetle Pact	41182875
Jellyfish	14851496

CARD	PASSWORD
Jerry Beans Man	23635815
Jetroid	43697559
Jinzo	77585513
Jinzo #7	32809211
Jirai Gumo	94773007
Jowgen the Spiritualist	41855169
Jowls of Dark Demise	05257687
Judge Man	30113682
Judgment of Anubis	55256016
Just Desserts	24068492
KA-2 Des Scissors	52768103
Kabazauls	51934376
Kagemusha of the Blue Flame	15401633
Kaibaman	34627841
Kaiser Dragon	94566432
Kaiser Glider	52824910
Kaiser Sea Horse	17444133
Kaminari Attack	09653271
Kaminote Blow	97570038
Kamionwizard	41544074
Kangaroo Champ	95789089
Karate Man	23289281
Karbonala Warrior	54541900
Karma Cut	71587526
Kelbek	54878498
Keldo	80441106
Killer Needle	88979991
Kinetic Soldier	79853073
King Dragun	13756293
King Fog	84686841
King of the Skull Servants	36021814
King of the Swamp	79109599
King of Yamimakai	69455834
King Tiger Wanghu	83986578
King's Knight	64788463
Kiryu	84814897
Kiseitai	04266839
Kishido Spirit	60519422
Knight's Title	87210505
Koitsu	69456283
Kojikocy	01184620
Kotodama	19406822
Kozaky	99171160
Kozaky's Self-Destruct Button	21908319
Kryuel	82642348
Kumootoko	56283725
Kurama	85705804
Kuriboh	40640057
Kuwagata Alpha	60802233
Kwagar Hercules	95144193
Kycoo The Ghost Destroyer	88240808
La Jinn The Mystical Genie of The Lamp	97590747
Labyrinth of Nightmare	66526672
Labyrinth Tank	99551425
Lady Assailant of Flames	90147755
Lady Ninja Yae	82005435
Lady of Faith	17358176
Larvas	94675535
Laser Cannon Armor	77007920

CARD	PASSWORD
Last Day of Witch	90330453
Last Turn	28566710
Launcher Spider	87322377
Lava Battleguard	20394040
Lava Golem	00102380
Layard the Liberator	67468948
Left Arm of the Forbidden One	07902349
Left Leg of the Forbidden One	44519536
Legendary Black Belt	96438440
Legendary Flame Lord	60258960
Legendary Jujitsu Master	25773409
Legendary Sword	61854111
Leghul	12472242
Lekunga	62543393
Lesser Dragon	55444629
Lesser Fiend	16475472
Level Conversion Lab	84397023
Level Limit - Area A	54976796
Level Limit - Area B	03136426
Level Modulation	61850482
Level Up	25290459
Levia-Dragon	37721209
Levia-Dragon - Daedalus	37721209
Light of Intervention	62867251
Light of Judgment	44595286
Lighten the Load	37231841
Lightforce Sword	49587034
Lightning Blade	55226821
Lightning Conger	27671321
Lightning Vortex	69162969
Limiter Removal	23171610
Liquid Beast	93108297
Little Chimera	68658728
Little-Winguard	90790253
Lizard Soldier	20831168
Lord of the Lamp	99510761
Lost Guardian	45871897
Luminous Soldier	57282479
Luminous Spark	81777047
Luster Dragon	11091375
Luster Dragon #2	17658803
M-Warrior #1	56342351
M-Warrior #2	92731455
Machine Conversion Factory	25769732
Machine Duplication	63995093
Machine King	46700124
Machine King Prototype	89222931
Machiners Defender	96384007
Machiners Force	58054262
Machiners Sniper	23782705
Machiners Soldier	60999392
Mad Dog of Darkness	79182538
Mad Lobster	97240270
Mad Sword Beast	79870141
Mage Power	83746708
Magic Drain	59344077
Magic Jammer	77414722
Magical Cylinder	62279055
Magical Dimension	28553439
Magical Explosion	32723153

CARD	PASSWORD
Magical Hats	81210420
Magical Labyrinth	64389297
Magical Marionette	08034697
Magical Merchant	32362575
Magical Plant Mandragola	07802006
Magical Scientist	34206604
Magical Thorn	53119267
Magician of Black Chaos	30208479
Magician of Faith	31560081
Magician's Circle	00050755
Magician's Unite	36045450
Magician's Valkyria	80304126
Magnet Circle	94940436
Maha Vailo	93013676
Maharaghi	40695128
Maiden of the Aqua	17214465
Maji-Gire Panda	60102563
Maju Garzett	08794435
Makiu	27827272
Makyura the Destructor	21593977
Malevolent Nuzzler	99597615
Malfunction	06137095
Malice Ascendant	14255590
Malice Dispersion	13626450
Mammoth Graveyard	40374923
Man Eater	93553943
Man-Eater Bug	54652250
Man-Eating Black Shark	80727036
Man-Eating Treasure Chest	13723605
Man-Thro' Tro	43714890
Manga Ryu-Ran	38369349
Manju of the Ten Thousand Hands	95492061
Manticore of Darkness	77121851
Marauding Captain	02460565
Marie the Fallen One	57579381
Marine Beast	29929832
Marshmallon	31305911
Marshmallon Glasses	66865880
Maryokutai	71466592
Masaki the Legendary Swordsman	44287299
Mask of Brutality	82432018
Mask of Darkness	28933734
Mask of Restrict	29549364
Mask of Weakness	57882509
Masked Dragon	39191307
Masked of the Accursed	56948373
Masked Sorcerer	10189126
Mass Driver	34906152
Master Kyonshee	24530661
Master Monk	49814180
Master of Dragon Knight	62873545
Master of Oz	27134689
Mataza the Zapper	22609617
Mavelus	59036972
Maximum Six	30707994
Mazera DeVille	06133894
Mech Mole Zombie	63545455
Mecha-Dog Marron	94667532
Mechanical Hound	22512237
Mechanical Snail	34442949

CARD	PASSWORD
Mechanical Spider	45688586
Mechanicalchaser	07359741
Meda Bat	76211194
Medusa Worm	02694423
Mefist the Infernal General	46820049
Mega Thunderball	21817254
Mega Ton Magical Cannon	32062913
Megamorph	22046459
Megarock Dragon	71544954
Melchid the Four-Face Beast	86569121
Memory Crusher	48700891
Mermaid Knight	24435369
Messenger of Peace	44656491
Metal Armored Bug	65957473
Metal Dragon	09293977
Metallizing Parasite	07369217
Metalmorph	68540058
Metalzoa	50705071
Metamorphosis	46411259
Meteor B. Dragon	90660762
Meteor Dragon	64271667
Meteor of Destruction	33767325
Meteorain	64274292
Michizure	37580756
Micro-Ray	18190572
Mid Shield Gardna	75487237
Mighty Guard	62327910
Mikazukinoyaiba	38277918
Millennium Golem	47986555
Millennium Scorpion	82482194
Millennium Shield	32012841
Milus Radiant	07489323
Minar	32539892
Mind Control	37520316
Mind Haxorz	75392615
Mind on Air	66690411
Mind Wipe	52718046
Mine Golem	76321376
Minefield Eruption	85519211
Minor Goblin Official	01918087
Miracle Dig	06343408
Miracle Fusion	45906428
Miracle Kid	55985014
Miracle Restoring	68334074
Mirage Dragon	15960641
Mirage Knight	49217579
Mirage of Nightmare	41482598
Mirror Force	44095762
Mirror Wall	22359980
Misfortune	01036974
Mispolymerization	58392024
Mistobody	47529357
Moai Interceptor Cannons	45159319
Mobius the Frost Monarch	04929256
Moisture Creature	75285069
Mokey Mokey	27288416
Mokey Mokey King	13803864
Mokey Mokey Smackdown	01965724

CARD	PASSWORD
Molten Behemoth	17192817
Molten Destruction	19384334
Molten Zombie	04732017
Monk Fighter	03810071
Monster Egg	36121917
Monster Eye	84133008
Monster Gate	43040603
Monster Reborn	83764718
Monster Recovery	93108433
Monster Reincarnation	74848038
Mooyan Curry	58074572
Morale Boost	93671934
Morphing Jar	33508719
Morphing Jar #2	79106360
Mother Grizzly	57839750
Mountain	50913601
Mr. Volcano	31477025
Mudora	82108372
Muka Muka	46657337
Multiplication of Ants	22493811
Multiply	40703222
Musician King	56907389
Mustering of the Dark Scorpions	68191243
Mysterious Puppeteer	54098121
Mystic Horseman	68516705
Mystic Lamp	98049915
Mystic Plasma Zone	18161786
Mystic Swordsman LV 2	47507260
Mystic Swordsman LV 4	74591968
Mystic Swordsman LV 6	60482781
Mystic Tomato	83011277
Mystic Wok	80161395
Mystical Beast Serket	89194033
Mystical Elf	15025844
Mystical Knight of Jackal	98745000
Mystical Moon	36607978
Mystical Sand	32751480
Mystical Sheep #	30451366
Mystical Shine Ball	39552864
Mystical Space Typhoon	05318639
Mystik Wok	80161395
Mythical Beast Cerberus	55424270
Nanobreaker	70948327
Necklace of Command	48576971
Necrovalley	47355498
Needle Ball	94230224
Needle Burrower	98162242
Needle Ceiling	38411870
Needle Wall	38299233
Needle Worm	81843628
Negate Attack	14315573
Nemuriko	90963488
Neo Aqua Madoor	49563947
Neo Bug	16587243
Neo the Magic Swordsman	50930991
Neo-Space	40215635
Neo-Spacian Aqua Dolphin	17955766
Newdoria	04335645
Next to be Lost	07076131
Night Assailant	16226786
Nightmare Horse	59290628

CARD	PASSWORD
Nightmare Penguin	81306586
Nightmare Wheel	54704216
Nightmare's Steelcage	58775978
Nimble Momonga	22567609
Nin-Ken Dog	11987744
Ninja Grandmaster Sasuke	04041838
Ninjitsu Art of Decoy	89628781
Ninjitsu Art of Transformation	70861343
Nitro Unit	23842445
Niwatori	07805359
Nobleman of Crossout	71044499
Nobleman of Extermination	17449108
Nobleman-Eater Bug	65878864
Non Aggression Area	76848240
Non-Fusion Area	27581098
Non-Spellcasting Area	20065549
Novox's Prayer	43694075
Nubian Guard	51616747
Numinous Healer	02130625
Nutrient Z	29389368
Nuvia the Wicked	12953226
O - Oversoul	63703130
Obnoxious Celtic Guardian	52077741
Ocubeam	86088138
Offerings to the Doomed	19230407
Ojama Black	79335209
Ojama Delta Hurricane	08251996
Ojama Green	12482652
Ojama King	90140980
Ojama Trio	29843091
Ojama Yellow	42941100
Ojamagic	24643836
Ojamuscle	98259197
Old Vindictive Magician	45141844
Ominous Fortunetelling	56995655
Oni Tank T-3	66927994
Opti-Camaflauge Armor	44762290
Opticlops	14531242
Option Hunter	33248692
Orca Mega-Fortress of Darkness	63120904
Ordeal of a Traveler	39537362
Order to Charge	78986941
Order to Smash	39019325
Otohime	39751093
Outstanding Dog Marron	11548522
Overdrive	02311603
Oxygeddon	58071123
Painful Choice	74191942
Paladin of White Dragon	73398797
Pale Beast	21263083
Pandemonium	94585852
Pandemonium Watchbear	75375465
Parasite Paracide	27911549
Parasitic Ticky	87978805
Patrician of Darkness	19153634
Patroid	71930383
Penguin Knight	36039163
Penumbral Soldier Lady	64751286

CARD	PASSWORD
People Running About	12143771
Perfect Machine King	18891691
Performance of Sword	04849037
Petit Angel	38142739
Petit Dragon	75356564
Petit Moth	58192742
Phantasmal Martyrs	93224848
Pharaoh's Servant	52550973
Pharonic Protector	89959682
Phoenix Wing Wind Blast	63356631
Photon Generator Unit	66607691
Pikeru's Circle of Enchantment	74270067
Pikeru's Second Sight	58015506
Pinch Hopper	26185991
Pineapple Blast	90669991
Piranha Army	50823978
Pitch-Black Power Stone	34029630
Pitch-Black Warwolf	88975532
Pitch-Dark Dragon	47415292
Poison Draw Frog	56840658
Poison Fangs	76539047
Poison Mummy	43716289
Poison of the Old Man	08842266
Polymerization	24094653
Possessed Dark Soul	52860176
Pot of Avarice	67169062
Pot of Generosity	70278545
Pot of Greed	55144522
Power Bond	37630732
Power Capsule	54289683
Precious Card from Beyond	68304813
Premature Burial	70828912
Prepare to Strike Back	04483989
Prevent Rat	00549481
Prickle Fairy	91559748
Primal Seed	23701465
Princess Curran	02316186
Princess of Tsurugi	51371017
Princess Pikeru	75917088
Protective Soul Ailin	11678191
Protector of the Sanctuary	24221739
Protector of the Throne	10071456
Proto-Cyber Dragon	26439287
Pumpking the King of Ghosts	29155212
Punished Eagle	74703140
Pyramid of Light	53569894
Pyramid Turtle	77044671
Queen's Knight	25652259
Rabid Horseman	94905343
Rafflesia Seduction	31440542
Raging Flame Sprite	90810762
Raigeki	12580477
Raigeki Break	04178474
Rain Of Mercy	66719324
Rainbow Flower	21347810
Rancer Dragonute	11125718
Rapid-Fire Magician	06337436
Rare Metalmorph	12503902
Raregold Armor	07625614

CARD	PASSWORD
Raviel, Lord of Phantasms	69890967
Ray & Temperature	85309439
Ray of Hope	82529174
Re-Fusion	74694807
Ready For Intercepting	31785398
Really Eternal Rest	28121403
Reaper of the Cards	33066139
Reaper of the Nightmare	85684223
Reasoning	58577036
Reborn Zombie	23421244
Reckless Greed	37576645
Recycle	96316857
Red Archery Girl	65570596
Red Gadget	86445415
Red Medicine	38199696
Red Moon Baby	56387350
Red-Eyes B. Chick	36262024
Red-Eyes B. Dragon	74677422
Red-Eyes Black Metal Dragon	64335804
Red-Eyes Darkness Dragon	96561011
Reflect Bounder	02851070
Regenerating Mummy	70821187
Reinforcement of the Army	32807846
Release Restraint	75417459
Relinquished	64631466
Reload	22589918
Remove Trap	51482758
Rescue Cat	14878871
Rescueroid	24311595
Reshef the Dark Being	62420419
Respect Play	08951260
Return from the Different Dimension	27174286
Return of the Doomed	19827717
Reversal of Graves	17484499
Reversal Quiz	05990062
Revival Jam	31709826
Right Arm of the Forbidden One	70903634
Right Leg of the Forbidden One	08124921
Ring of Destruction	83555666
Ring of Magnetism	20436034
Riryoku Field	70344351
Rising Air Current	45778932
Rising Energy	78211862
Rite of Spirit	30450531
Ritual Weapon	54351224
Robbin' Goblin	88279736
Robbin' Zombie	83258273
Robolady	92421852
Robotic Knight	44203504
Roboyarou	38916461
Rock Bombardment	20781762
Rock Ogre Grotto	68846917
Rocket Jumper	53890795
Rocket Warrior	30860696
Rod of the Mind's Eye	94793422
Roll Out	91597389
Root Water	39004808
Rope of Life	93382620

CARD	PASSWORD
Rope of Spirit	37383714
Roulette Barrel	46303688
Royal Command	33950246
Royal Decree	51452091
Royal Keeper	16509093
Royal Knight	68280530
Royal Magical Library	70791313
Royal Surrender	56058888
Royal Tribute	72405967
Ruin, Queen of Oblivion	46427957
Rush Recklessly	70046172
Ryu Kokki	57281778
Ryu Senshi	49868263
Ryu-Kishin Clown	42647539
Ryu-Kishin Powered	24611934
Saber Beetle	49645921
Sacred Crane	30914564
Sacred Phoenix of Nephthys	61441708
Saggi the Dark Clown	66602787
Sakuretsu Armor	56120475
Salamandra	32268901
Salvage	96947648
Samsara	44182827
Sand Gambler	50593156
Sand Moth	73648243
Sangan	26202165
Sanwitch	53539634
Sasuke Samurai	16222645
Sasuke Samurai 2#	11760174
Sasuke Samurai 3#	77379481
Sasuke Samurai 4#	64538655
Satellite Cannon	50400231
Scapegoat	73915051
Scarr, Scout of Dark World	05498296
Science Soldier	67532912
Scroll of Bewitchment	10352095
Scyscraper	63035430
Sea Serpent Warrior of Darkness	42071342
Sealmaster Meisei	02468169
Second Coin Toss	36562627
Second Goblin	19086954
Secret Barrel	27053506
Self-Destruct Button	57585212
Senri Eye	60391791
Serial Spell	49398568
Serpent Night Dragon	66516792
Serpentine Princess	71829750
Servant of Catobolism	02792265
Seven Tools of the Bandit	03819470
Shadow Ghoul	30778711
Shadow Of Eyes	58621589
Shadow Tamer	37620434
Shadowknight Archfiend	09603356
Shadowslayer	20939559
Share the Pain	56830749
Shield & Sword	52097679
Shield Crash	30683373
Shien's Spy	07672244
Shift	59560625
Shifting Shadows	59237154

CARD	PASSWORD
Shinato's Ark	60365591
Shinato, King of a Higher Plane	86327225
Shining Abyss	87303357
Shining Angel	95956346
Shooting Star Bow - Ceal	95638658
Silent Insect	40867519
Silent Magician Lv 4	73665146
Silent Magician Lv 8	72443568
Silent Swordsman LV 3	01995985
Silent Swordsman LV 5	74388798
Silent Swordsman LV 7	37267041
Sillva, Warlord of Dark World	32619583
Silpheed	73001017
Silver Fang	90357090
Simultaneous Loss	92219931
Sinister Serpent	08131171
Sixth Sense	03280747
Skill Drain	82732705
Skilled Dark Magician	73752131
Skilled White Magician	46363422
Skull Archfiend of Lightning	61370518
Skull Descovery Knight	78700060
Skull Dog Marron	86652646
Skull Invitation	98139712
Skull Lair	06733059
Skull Mariner	05265750
Skull Red Bird	10202894
Skull Servant	32274490
Skull Zoma	79852326
Skull-Mark Ladybug	64306248
Skyscraper	63035430
Slate Warrior	78636495
Smashing Ground	97169186
Smoke Grenade of the Thief	63789924
Snatch Steal	45986603
Sogen	86318356
Soitsu	60246171
Solar Flare Dragon	45985838
Solar Ray	44472639
Solemn Judgment	41420027
Solemn Wishes	35346968
Solomon's Lawbook	23471572
Sonic Duck	84696266
Sonic Jammer	84550200
Sorcerer of Dark Magic	88619463
Soul Absorption	68073522
Soul Exchange	68005187
Soul of Purity and Light	77527210
Soul Release	05758500
Soul Resurrection	92924317
Soul Reversal	78864369
Soul Tiger	15734813
Soul-Absorbing Bone Tower	63012333
Souleater	31242786
Souls Of The Forgotten	04920010
Space Mambo	36119641
Spark Blaster	97362768
Sparks	76103675

CARD	PASSWORD
Spatial Collapse	20644748
Spear Cretin	58551308
Spear Dragon	31553716
Spell Canceller	84636823
Spell Economics	04259068
Spell Purification	01669772
Spell Reproduction	29228529
Spell Shield Type-8	38275183
Spell Vanishing	29735721
Spell-Stopping Statute	10069180
Spellbinding Circle	18807108
Spherous Lady	52121290
Sphinx Teleia	51402177
Spiral Spear Strike	49328340
Spirit Barrier	53239672
Spirit Caller	48659020
Spirit Message "A"	94772232
Spirit Message "I"	31893528
Spirit Message "L"	30170981
Spirit Message "N"	67287533
Spirit of Flames	13522325
Spirit of the Breeze	53530069
Spirit of the Harp	80770678
Spirit of the Pharaoh	25343280
Spirit Reaper	23205979
Spirit Ryu	67957315
Spiritual Earth Art - Kurogane	70156997
Spiritual Energy Settle Machine	99173029
Spiritual Fire Art - Kurenai	42945701
Spiritual Water Art - Aoi	06540606
Spiritual Wind Art - Miyabi	79333300
Spiritualism	15866454
St. Joan	21175632
Stamping Destruction	81385346
Star Boy	08201910
Statue of the Wicked	65810489
Staunch Defender	92854392
Stealth Bird	03510565
Steam Gyroid	05368615
Steamroid	44729197
Steel Ogre Grotto #1	29172562
Steel Ogre Grotto #2	90908427
Stim-Pack	83225447
Stop Defense	63102017
Storming Wynn	29013526
Stray Lambs	60764581
Strike Ninja	41006930
Stronghold	13955608
Stumbling	34646691
Success Probability 0%	06859683
Summon Priest	00423585
Summoned Skull	70781052
Summoner of Illusions	14644902
Super Conductor Ttranno	85520851
Super Rejuvenation	27770341
Super Robolady	75923050
Super Roboyarou	01412158
Supply	44072894
Susa Soldier	40473581

CARD	PASSWORD
Swarm of Locusts	41872150
Swarm of Scarabs	15383415
Swift Gaia the Fierce Knight	16589042
Sword Hunter	51345461
Sword of Deep-Seated	98495314
Sword of Dragon's Soul	61405855
Sword of the Soul Eater	05371656
Swords of Concealing Light	12923641
Swords of Revealing Light	72302403
Swordsman of Landstar	03573512
Symbol of Heritage	45305419
System Down	18895832
T.A.D.P.O.L.E	10456559
Tactical Espionage Expert	89698120
Tailor of the Fickle	43641473
Taunt	90740329
Tenkabito Shien	41589166
Terra the Terrible	63308047
Terraforming	73628505
Terrorking Archfiend	35975813
Terrorking Salmon	78060096
Teva	16469012
The Agent of Creation - Venus	64734921
The Agent of Force - Mars	91123920
The Agent of Judgment - Saturn	91345518
The Agent of Wisdom - Mercury	38730226
The All-Seeing White Tiger	32269855
The Big March of Animals	01689516
The Bistro Butcher	71107816
The Cheerful Coffin	41142615
The Creator	61505339
The Creator Incarnate	97093037
The Dark - Hex Sealed Fusion	52101615
The Dark Door	30606547
The Dragon Dwelling in the Cave	93346024
The Dragon's Bead	92408984
The Earl of Demise	66989694
The Earth - Hex Sealed Fusion	88696724
The Emperor's Holiday	68400115
The End of Anubis	65403020
The Eye Of Truth	34694160
The Fiend Megacyber	66362965
The Flute of Summoning Dragon	43973174
The Flute of Summoning Kuriboh	20065322
The Forceful Sentry	42829885
The Forces of Darkness	29826127
The Forgiving Maiden	84080938
The Furious Sea King	18710707
The Graveyard in the Fourth Dimension	88089103
The Gross Ghost of Fled Dreams	68049471

CARD	PASSWORD
The Hunter With 7 Weapons	01525329
The Illusionary Gentleman	83764996
The Immortal of Thunder	84926738
The Kick Man	90407382
The Last Warrior From Another Planet	86099788
The Law of the Normal	66926224
The League of Uniform Nomenclature	55008284
The Legendary Fisherman	03643300
The Light - Hex Sealed Fusion	15717011
The Little Swordsman of Aile	25109950
The Masked Beast	49064413
The Portrait's Secret	32541773
The Regulation of Tribe	00296499
The Reliable Guardian	16430187
The Rock Spirit	76305638
The Sanctuary in the Sky	56433456
The Second Sarcophagus	04081094
The Secret of the Bandit	99351431
The Shallow Grave	43434803
The Spell Absorbing Life	99517131
The Thing in the Crater	78243409
The Third Sarcophagus	78697395
The Trojan Horse	38479725
The Unhappy Girl	27618634
The Unhappy Maiden	51275027
The Warrior returning alive	95281259
Theban Nightmare	51838385
Theinen the Great Sphinx	87997872
Thestalos the Firestorm Monarch	26205777
Thousand Dragon	41462083
Thousand Energy	05703682
Thousand Needles	33977496
Thousand-Eyes Idol	27125110
Thousand-Eyes Restrict	63519819
Threatening Roar	36361633
Three-Headed Geedo	78423643
Throwstone Unit	76075810
Thunder Crash	69196160
Thunder Dragon	31786629
Thunder Nyan Nyan	70797118
Thunder of Ruler	91781589
Time Seal	35316708
Time Wizard	71625222
Timeater	44913552
Timidity	40350910
Token Festevil	83675475
Token Thanksgiving	57182235
Tongyo	69572024
Toon Cannon Soldier	79875176
Toon Dark Magician Girl	90960358
Toon Defense	43509019
Toon Gemini Elf	42386471
Toon Goblin Attack Force	15270885

CARD	PASSWORD
Toon Masked Sorcerer	16392422
Toon Mermaid	65458948
Toon Summoned Skull	91842653
Toon Table of Contents	89997728
Toon World	15259703
Tornado Bird	71283180
Tornado Wall	18605135
Torpedo Fish	90337190
Torrential Tribute	53582587
Total Defense Shogun	75372290
Tower of Babel	94256039
Tradgedy	35686187
Transcendent Wings	25573054
Trap Dustshoot	64697231
Trap Hole	04206964
Trap Jammer	19252988
Treeborn Frog	12538374
Tremendous Fire	46918794
Tri-Horned Dragon	39111158
Triage	30888983
Trial of Nightmare	77827521
Trial of the Princesses	72709014
Triangle Ecstasy Spar	12181376T
Triangle Power	32298781
Tribe-Infecting Virus	33184167
Tribute Doll	02903036
Tribute to The Doomed	79759861
Tripwire Beast	45042329
Troop Dragon	55013285
Tsukuyomi	34853266
Turtle Oath	76806714
Turtle Tiger	37313348
Twin Swords of Flashing Light	21900719
Twin-Headed Behemoth	43586926
Twin-Headed Fire Dragon	78984772
Twin-Headed Thunder Dragon	54752875
Twin-Headed Wolf	88132637
Twinheaded Beast	82035781
Two Thousand Needles	83228073
Two-Man Cell Battle	25578802
Two-Mouth Darkruler	57305373
Two-Pronged Attack	83887306
Tyhone	72842870
Type Zero Magic Crusher	21237481
Tyranno Infinity	83235263
Tyrant Dragon	94568601
UFOroid	07602840
UFOroid Fighter	32752319
Ultimate Insect LV 1	49441499
Ultimate Insect LV 3	34088136
Ultimate Insect LV 5	34830502
Ultimate Insect LV 7	19877898
Ultimate Obedient Fiend	32240937
Ultimate Tyranno	15894048
Ultra Evolution Pill	22431243
Umi	22702055
Umiiruka	82999629
Union Attack	60399954
United Resistance	85936485
United We Stand	56747793

CARD	PASSWORD
Unity	14731897
Unshaven Angler	92084010
Upstart Goblin	70368879
Uraby	01784619
Uria, Lord of Sealing Flames	06007213
V-Tiger Jet	51638941
Valkyrion the Magna Warrior	75347539
Vampire Genesis	22056710
Vampire Lord	53839837
Vampire Orchis	46571052
Vengeful Bog Spirit	95220856
Victory D	44910027
Vilepawn Archfiend	73219648
VW-Tiger Catapult	58859575
VWXYZ-Dragon Catapult Cannon	84243274
W-Wing Catapult	96300057
Waboku	12607053
Wall of Revealing Light	17078030
Wandering Mummy	42994702
Warrior Dai Grepher	75953262
Warrior of Zera	66073051
Wasteland	23424603
Water Dragon	85066822
Water Omotics	02483611
Wave Motion Cannon	38992735
Weed Out	28604635
Whiptail Crow	91996584
Whirlwind Prodigy	15090429
White Dragon Ritual	09786492
White Horn Dragon	73891874
White Magical Hat	15150365
White Magician Pikeru	81383947
White Ninja	01571945
Wicked-Breaking Flameberge-Baou	68427465
Wild Nature's Release	61166988
Winged Dragon, Guardian of the Fortress #1	87796900

CARD	PASSWORD
Winged Kuriboh	57116033
Winged Kuriboh LV1	98585345
Winged Minion	89258225
Winged Sage Falcos	87523462
Wingweaver	31447217
Witch Doctor of Chaos	75946257
Witch of the Black Forest	78010363
Witch's Apprentice	80741828
Witty Phantom	36304921
Wolf Axwielder	56369281
Woodborg Inpachi	35322812
Woodland Sprite	06979239
Worm Drake	73216412
Wroughtweiler	06480253
Wynn the Wind Charmer	37744402
X-Head Cannon	62651957
Xing Zhen Hu	76515293
XY-Dragon Cannon	02111707
XYZ-Dragon Cannon	91998119
XZ-Tank Cannon	99724761
Y-Dragon Head	65622692
Yamata Dragon	76862289
Yami	59197169
Yata-Garasu	03078576
Yellow Gadget	13839120
Yellow Luster Shield	04542651
Yomi Ship	51534754
YZ-Tank Dragon	25119460
Z-Metal Tank	64500000
Zaborg the Thunder Monarch	51945556
Zero Gravity	83133491
Zoa	24311372
Zolga	16268841
Zombie Tiger	47693640
Zombyra the Dark	88472456
Zure, Knight of Dark World	07459013

YU-GI-OH! GX TAG FORCE 2

MIDDDAY CONSTELLATION BOOSTER PACK
When buying booster packs, press Up, Up, Down, Down, Left, Right, Left, Right, ✕, ◉.

CARD PASSWORDS

CARD	PASSWORD
4-Starred Ladybug of Doom	83994646
7 Colored Fish	23771716
A Cat of Ill Omen	24140059
A Deal With Dark Ruler	06850209
A Feather of the Phoenix	49140998
A Feint Plan	68170903
A Hero Emerges	21597117
A Legendary Ocean	00295517
A Man With Wdjat	51351302
A Rival Appears!	05728014
A Wingbeat of Giant Dragon	28596933

CARD	PASSWORD
A-Team: Trap Disposal Unit	13026402
Abare Ushioni	89718302
Absolute End	27744077
Absorbing Kid From the Sky	49771608
Abyss Soldier	18318842
Abyssal Designator	89801755
Acid Trap Hole	41356845
Acrobat Monkey	47372349
Adhesion Trap Hole	62325062
Adhesive Explosive	53828396
After the Struggle	25345186

CARD	PASSWORD
Agido	16135253
Airknight Parshath	18036057
Aitsu	48202661
Alkana Knight Joker	06150044
Alpha the Magnet Warrior	99785935
Altar for Tribute	21070956
Amazon Archer	91869203
Amazoness Archers	67987611
Amazoness Blowpiper	73574678
Amazoness Chain Master	29654737
Amazoness Paladin	47480070
Amazoness Swords Woman	94004268
Amazoness Tiger	10979723
Ambulance Rescueroid	98927491
Ambulanceroid	36378213
Ameba	95174353
Amphibian Beast	67371383
Amphibious Bugroth MK-3	64342551
Amplifier	00303660
An Owl of Luck	23927567
Ancient Elf	93221206
Ancient Gear	31557782
Ancient Gear Beast	10509340
Ancient Gear Cannon	80045583
Ancient Gear Castle	92001300
Ancient Gear Drill	67829249
Ancient Gear Golem	83104731
Ancient Gear Soldier	56094445
Ancient Lamp	54912977
Ancient Lizard Warrior	43230671
Andro Sphinx	15013468
Anteatereatingant	13250922
Anti-Aircraft Flower	65064143
Anti-Spell	53112492
Apprentice Magician	09156135
Appropriate	48539234
Aqua Madoor	85639257
Aqua Spirit	40916023
Arcane Archer of the Forest	55001420
Archfiend of Gilfer	50287060
Archfiend Soldier	49881766
Archlord Zerato	18378582
Armaill	53153481
Armed Changer	90374791
Armed Dragon LV 3	00980973
Armed Dragon LV 5	46384672
Armed Dragon LV 7	73879377
Armed Dragon LV10	59464593
Armed Ninja	09076207
Armed Samurai - Ben Kei	84430950
Armor Axe	07180418
Armor Break	79649195
Armored Lizard	15480588
Armored Starfish	17535588
Armored Zombie	20277860
Array of Revealing Light	69296555
Arsenal Bug	42364374
Arsenal Robber	55348096

CARD	PASSWORD
Arsenal Summoner	85489096
Assault on GHQ	62633180
Astral Barrier	37053871
Asura Priest	02134346
Aswan Apparition	88236094
Atomic Firefly	87340664
Attack and Receive	63689843
Attack Reflector Unit	91989718
Aussa the Earth Charmer	37970940
Autonomous Action Unit	71453557
Avatar of the Pot	99284890
Axe Dragonute	84914462
Axe of Despair	40619825
B. Skull Dragon	11901678
B.E.S. Covered Core	15317640
B.E.S. Crystal Core	22790789
B.E.S. Tetran	44954628
Baby Dragon	88819587
Back to Square One	47453433
Backfire	82705573
Backup Soldier	36280194
Bad Reaction to Simochi	40633297
Bait Doll	07165085
Ballista of Rampart Smashing	00242146
Banisher of the Light	61528025
Bark of Dark Ruler	41925941
Barrel Dragon	81480460
Basic Insect	89091579
Battery Charger	61181383
Batteryman AA	63142001
Batteryman C	19733961
Batteryman D	55401221
Battle Footballer	48094997
Battle Ox	05053103
Battle-Scarred	94463200
Bazoo The Soul-Eater	40133511
Beast Soul Swap	35149085
Beaver Warrior	32452818
Beckoning Light	16255442
Beelze Frog	49522489
Begone, Knave	20374520
Behemoth the King of All Animals	22996376
Beiige, Vanguard of Dark World	33731070
Berserk Dragon	85605684
Berserk Gorilla	39168895
Beta the Magnet Warrior	39256679
Bickuribox	25655502
Big Bang Shot	61127349
Big Burn	95472621
Big Core	14148099
Big Koala	42129512
Big Shield Gardna	65240384
Big Wave Small Wave	51562916
Big-Tusked Mammoth	59380081
Bio-Mage	58696829
Birdface	45547649
Black Illusion Ritual	41426869
Black Luster Soldier - Envoy of the Beginning	72989439

CARD	PASSWORD
Black Pendant	65169794
Black Tyranno	38670435
Blackland Fire Dragon	87564352
Blade Knight	39507162
Blade Rabbit	58268433
Blade Skater	97023549
Bladefly	28470714
Blast Held By a Tribute	89041555
Blast Magician	21051146
Blast with Chain	98239899
Blasting the Ruins	21466326
Blazing Inpachi	05464695
Blind Destruction	32015116
Blindly Loyal Goblin	35215622
Block Attack	25880422
Blockman	48115277
Blowback Dragon	25551951
Blue-Eyes Shining Dragon	53347303
Blue-Eyes Toon Dragon	53183600
Blue-Eyes Ultimate Dragon	23995346
Blue-Eyes White Dragon	89631139
Blue-Winged Crown	41396436
Bokoichi the Freightening Car	08715625
Bombardment Beetle	57409948
Bonding - H2O	45898858
Boneheimer	98456117
Book of Life	02204140
Book of Moon	14087893
Book of Taiyou	38699854
Boss Rush	66947414
Bottom Dweller	81386177
Bottomless Shifting Sand	76532077
Bottomless Trap Hole	29401950
Bountiful Artemis	32296881
Bowganian	52090844
Bracchio-Raidus	16507828
Brain Control	87910978
Brain Jacker	40267580
Branch!	30548775
Breaker the Magical Warrior	71413901
Broww, Huntsman of Dark World	79126789
Brron, Mad King of Dark World	06214884
Bubble Blaster	53586134
Bubble Illusion	80075749
Bubble Shuffle	61968753
Bubonic Vermin	06104968
Burning Algae	41859700
Burning Beast	59364406
Burning Land	24294108
Burst Breath	80163754
Burst Return	27191436
Burst Stream of Destruction	17655904
Buster Blader	78193831
Buster Rancher	84740193
Butterfly Dagger - Elma	69243953
Byser Shock	17597059

CARD	PASSWORD
Call of The Haunted	97077563
Call of the Mummy	04861205
Cannon Soldier	11384280
Cannonball Spear Shellfish	95614612
Card of Safe Return	57953380
Card Shuffle	12183332
Castle of Dark Illusions	00062121
Cat's Ear Tribe	95841282
Catapult Turtle	95727991
Cathedral of Nobles	29762407
Catnipped Kitty	96501677
Cave Dragon	93220472
Ceasefire	36468556
Celtic Guardian	91152256
Cemetery Bomb	51394546
Centrifugal	01801154
Ceremonial Bell	20228463
Cetus of Dagala	28106077
Chain Burst	48276469
Chain Destruction	01248895
Chain Disappearance	57139487
Chain Energy	79323590
Chain Thrasher	88190453
Chainsaw Insect	77252217
Change of Heart	04031928
Chaos Command Magician	72630549
Chaos Emperor Dragon - Envoy of the End	82301904
Chaos End	61044390
Chaos Greed	97439308
Chaos Necromancer	01434352
Chaos Sorcerer	09596126
Chaosrider Gutaph	47829960
Charcoal Inpachi	13179332
Charm of Shabti	50412166
Charubin the Fire Knight	37421579
Chiron the Mage	16956455
Chopman the Desperate Outlaw	40884383
Chorus of Sanctuary	81380218
Chthonian Alliance	46910446
Chthonian Blast	18271561
Chthonian Polymer	72287557
Chu-Ske the Mouse Fighter	08508055
Clay Charge	22479888
Cliff the Trap Remover	06967870
Cobra Jar	86801871
Cobraman Sakuzy	75109441
Cold Wave	60682203
Collected Power	07565547
Combination Attack	08964854
Command Knight	10375182
Commander Covington	22666164
Commencement Dance	43417563
Compulsory Evacuation Device	94192409
Confiscation	17375316
Conscription	31000575
Continuous Destruction Punch	68057622
Contract With Exodia	33244944

CARD	PASSWORD
Contract With the Abyss	69035382
Contract with the Dark Master	96420087
Convulsion of Nature	62966332
Cost Down	23265313
Covering Fire	74458486
Crab Turtle	91782219
Crass Clown	93889755
Creature Swap	31036355
Creeping Doom Manta	52571838
Crimson Ninja	14618326
Criosphinx	18654201
Cross Counter	37083210
Crush D. Gandra	64681432
Cure Mermaid	85802526
Curse of Aging	41398771
Curse of Anubis	66742250
Curse of Darkness	84970821
Curse of Dragon	28279543
Curse of the Masked Beast	94377247
Curse of Vampire	34294855
Cyber Dragon	70095154
Cyber End Dragon	01546123
Cyber Twin Dragon	74157028
Cyber-Dark Edge	77625948
Cyber-Stein	69015963
Cyberdark Dragon	40418351
Cyberdark Horn	41230939
Cyberdark Keel	03019642
D - Shield	62868900
D - Time	99075257
D. D. Assailant	70074904
D. D. Borderline	60912752
D. D. Crazy Beast	48148828
D. D. Dynamite	08628798
D. D. M. - Different Dimension Master	82112775
D. D. Trainer	86498013
D. D. Trap Hole	05606466
D. D. Warrior Lady	07572887
Dancing Fairy	90925163
Dangerous Machine TYPE-6	76895648
Dark Artist	72520073
Dark Bat	67049542
Dark Blade	11321183
Dark Blade the Dragon Knight	86805855
Dark Driceratops	65287621
Dark Dust Spirit	89111398
Dark Elf	21417692
Dark Energy	04614116
Dark Factory of Mass Production	90928333
Dark Flare Knight	13722870
Dark Hole	53129443
Dark Magic Attack	02314238
Dark Magic Ritual	76792184
Dark Magician	46986414
Dark Magician Girl	38033121
Dark Magician of Chaos	40737112
Dark Magician's Tome of Black Magic	67227834

CARD	PASSWORD
Dark Master - Zorc	97642679
Dark Mirror Force	20522190
Dark Paladin	98502113
Dark Room of Nightmare	85562745
Dark Sage	92377303
Dark Snake Syndrome	47233801
Dark-Piercing Light	45895206
Darkfire Dragon	17881964
Darkfire Soldier #1	05388481
Darkfire Soldier #2	78861134
Darkworld Thorns	43500484
De-Spell	19159413
Deal of Phantom	69122763
Decayed Commander	10209545
Dedication Through Light And Darkness	69542930
Deepsea Shark	28593363
Dekoichi the Battlechanted Locomotive	87621407
Delinquent Duo	44763025
Demotion	72575145
Des Counterblow	39131963
Des Croaking	44883830
Des Dendle	12965761
Des Feral Imp	81985784
Des Frog	84451804
Des Kangaroo	78613627
Des Koala	69579761
Des Lacooda	02326738
Des Wombat	09637706
Desert Sunlight	93747864
Destertapir	13409151
Destiny Board	94212438
Destiny Hero - Captain Tenacious	77608643
Destiny Hero - Diamond Dude	13093792
Destiny Hero - Doom Lord	41613948
Destiny Hero - Dreadmaster	40591390
Destiny Signal	35464895
Destroyer Golem	73481154
Destruction Ring	21219755
Dian Keto the Cure Master	84257639
Dice Jar	03549275
Dimension Distortion	95194279
Dimensional Warrior	37043180
Disappear	24623598
Disarmament	20727787
Disc Fighter	19612721
Dissolverock	40826495
Divine Dragon Ragnarok	62113340
Divine Wrath	49010598
DNA Surgery	74701381
DNA Transplant	56769674
Doitsu	57062206
Dokurorider	99721536
Dokuroyaiba	30325729
Don Turtle	03493978
Don Zaloog	76922029
Doriado	84916669

CARD	PASSWORD
Doriado's Blessing	23965037
Dragon Seeker	28563545
Dragon Treasure	01435851
Dragon Zombie	66672569
Dragon's Mirror	71490127
Dragon's Rage	54178050
Dragoness the Wicked Knight	70681994
Draining Shield	43250041
Dream Clown	13215230
Drillago	99050989
Drillroid	71218746
Dunames Dark Witch	12493482
Dust Tornado	60082867
Earth Chant	59820352
Earthbound Spirit	67105242
Earthquake	82828051
Eatgaboon	42578427
Ebon Magician Curran	46128076
Electro-Whip	37820550
Elegant Egotist	90219263
Element Dragon	30314994
Elemental Burst	61411502
Elemental Hero Avian	21844576
Elemental Hero Bladedge	59793705
Elemental Hero Bubbleman	79979666
Elemental Hero Burstinatrix	58932615
Elemental Hero Clayman	84327329
Elemental Hero Electrum/Erekshieler	29343734
Elemental Hero Flame Wingman	35809262
Elemental Hero Mariner	14225239
Elemental Hero Necroid Shaman	81003500
Elemental Hero Neos	89943723
Elemental Hero Phoenix Enforcer	41436536
Elemental Hero Shining Flare Wingman	25366484
Elemental Hero Shining Phoenix Enforcer	88820235
Elemental Hero Sparkman	20721928
Elemental Hero Thunder Giant	61204971
Elemental Mistress Doriado	99414158
Elemental Recharge	36586443
Elf's Light	39897277
Emblem of Dragon Destroyer	06390406
Embodiment of Apophis	28649820
Emergency Provisions	53046408
Emes the Infinity	43580269
Empress Judge	15237615
Empress Mantis	58818411
Enchanted Javelin	96355986
Enchanting Mermaid	75376965
Enemy Controller	98045062
Enraged Battle Ox	76909279
Enraged Muka Muka	91862578
Eradicating Aerosol	94716515

CARD	PASSWORD
Eternal Draught	56606928
Eternal Rest	95051344
Exhausting Spell	95451366
Exile of the Wicked	26725158
Exiled Force	74131780
Exodia Necross	12600382
Exodia the Forbidden One	33396948
Fairy Box	21598948
Fairy Dragon	20315854
Fairy King Truesdale	45425051
Fairy Meteor Crush	97687912
Faith Bird	75582395
Fatal Abacus	77910045
Fenrir	00218704
Feral Imp	41392891
Fiber Jar	78706415
Fiend Comedian	81172176
Fiend Scorpion	26566878
Fiend's Hand	52800428
Fiend's Mirror	31890399
Final Countdown	95308449
Final Destiny	18591904
Final Flame	73134081
Final Ritual of the Ancients	60369732
Fire Darts	43061293
Fire Eye	88435542
Fire Kraken	46534755
Fire Princess	64752646
Fire Reaper	53581214
Fire Sorcerer	27132350
Firegrass	53293545
Firewing Pegasus	27054370
Fireyarou	71407486
Fissure	66788016
Five God Dragon (Five Headed Dragon)	99267150
Flame Cerebrus	60862676
Flame Champion	42599677
Flame Dancer	12883044
Flame Ghost	58528964
Flame Manipulator	34460851
Flame Swordsman	45231177
Flame Viper	02830619
Flash Assailant	96890582
Flower Wolf	95952802
Flying Fish	31987274
Flying Kamakiri #1	84834865
Flying Kamakiri #2	03134241
Follow Wind	98252586
Foolish Burial	81439173
Forest	87430998
Fortress Whale	62337487
Fortress Whale's Oath	77454922
Frenzied Panda	98818516
Frozen Soul	57069605
Fruits of Kozaky's Studies	49998907
Fuh-Rin-Ka-Zan	01781310
Fuhma Shuriken	09373534
Fulfillment of the Contract	48206762
Fushi No Tori	38538445

CARD	PASSWORD
Fusion Gate	33550694
Fusion Recovery	18511384
Fusion Sage	26902560
Fusion Weapon	27967615
Fusionist	01641883
Gadget Soldier	86281779
Gagagigo	49003308
Gaia Power	56594520
Gaia the Dragon Champion	66889139
Gaia the Fierce Knight	06368038
Gale Dogra	16229315
Gale Lizard	77491079
Gamble	37313786
Gamma the Magnet Warrior	11549357
Garma Sword	90844184
Garma Sword Oath	78577570
Garoozis	14977074
Garuda the Wind Spirit	12800777
Gatling Dragon	87751584
Gazelle the King of Mythical Beasts	05818798
Gear Golem the Moving Fortress	30190809
Gearfried the Iron Knight	00423705
Gearfried the Swordmaster	57046845
Gemini Elf	69140098
Getsu Fuhma	21887179
Giant Axe Mummy	78266168
Giant Germ	95178994
Giant Kozaky	58185394
Giant Orc	73698349
Giant Rat	97017120
Giant Red Seasnake	58831685
Giant Soldier of Stone	13039848
Giant Trunade	42703248
Gift of the Mystical Elf	98299011
Giga Gagagigo	43793530
Giga-Tech Wolf	08471389
Gigantes	47606319
Gigobyte	53776525
Gil Garth	38445524
Gilasaurus	45894482
Giltia the D. Knight	51828629
Girochin Kuwagata	84620194
Goblin Attack Force	78658564
Goblin Calligrapher	12057781
Goblin Elite Attack Force	85306040
Goblin Thief	45311864
Goblin's Secret Remedy	11868825
Gogiga Gagagigo	39674352
Golem Sentry	82323207
Good Goblin Housekeeping	09744376
Gora Turtle	80233946
Graceful Charity	79571449
Graceful Dice	74137509
Gradius	10992251
Gradius' Option	14291024
Granadora	13944422
Grand Tiki Elder	13676474

CARD	PASSWORD
Granmarg the Rock Monarch	60229110
Gravedigger Ghoul	82542267
Gravekeeper's Cannonholder	99877698
Gravekeeper's Curse	50712728
Gravekeeper's Guard	37101832
Gravekeeper's Servant	16762927
Gravekeeper's Spear Soldier	63695531
Gravekeeper's Spy	24317029
Gravekeeper's Vassal	99690140
Graverobber's Retribution	33737664
Gravity Bind	85742772
Gray Wing	29618570
Great Angus	11813953
Great Long Nose	02356994
Great Mammoth of Goldfine	54622031
Green Gadget	41172955
Gren Maju Da Eiza	36584821
Ground Attacker Bugroth	58314394
Ground Collapse	90502999
Gruesome Goo	65623423
Gryphon Wing	55608151
Gryphon's Feather Duster	34370473
Guardian Angel Joan	68007326
Guardian of the Labyrinth	89272878
Guardian of the Sea	85448931
Guardian Sphinx	40659562
Guardian Statue	75209824
Gust Fan	55321970
Gyaku-Gire Panda	09817927
Gyroid	18325492
Hade-Hane	28357177
Hamburger Recipe	80811661
Hammer Shot	26412047
Hamon	32491822
Hand of Nephthys	98446407
Hane-Hane	07089711
Hannibal Necromancer	05640330
Hard Armor	20060230
Harpie Girl	34100324
Harpie Lady 1	91932350
Harpie Lady 2	27927359
Harpie Lady 3	54415063
Harpie Lady Sisters	12206212
Harpie's Brother	30532390
Harpies' Hunting Ground	75782277
Hayabusa Knight	21015833
Headless Knight	05434080
Heart of Clear Water	64801562
Heart of the Underdog	35762283
Heavy Mech Support Platform	23265594
Heavy Storm	19613556
Helios - The Primordial Sun	54493213
Helios Duo Megistus	80887952
Helios Tris Megiste	17286057

CARD	PASSWORD
Helping Robo for Combat	47025270
Hero Barrier	44676200
HERO Flash!!	00191749
Hero Heart	67951831
Hero Kid	32679370
Hero Ring	26647858
Hero Signal	22020907
Hidden Book of Spell	21840375
Hidden Soldier	02047519
Hieracosphinx	82260502
Hieroglyph Lithograph	10248192
High Tide Gyojin	54579801
Hiita the Fire Charmer	00759393
Hino-Kagu-Tsuchi	75745607
Hinotama Soul	96851799
Hiro's Shadow Scout	81863068
Hitotsu-Me Giant	76184692
Holy Knight Ishzark	57902462
Homunculus the Alchemic Being	40410110
Horn of Heaven	98069388
Horn of Light	38552107
Horn of the Unicorn	64047146
Horus The Black Flame Dragon LV4	75830094
Horus The Black Flame Dragon LV6	11224103
Horus The Black Flame Dragon LV8	48229808
Hoshiningen	67629977
House of Adhesive Tape	15083728
Howling Insect	93107608
Huge Revolution	65396880
Human-Wave Tactics	30353551
Humanoid Slime	46821314
Humanoid Worm Drake	05600127
Hungry Burger	30243636
Hydrogeddon	22587018
Hyena	22873798
Hyozanryu	62397231
Hyper Hammerhead	02671330
Hysteric Fairy	21297224
Icarus Attack	53567095
Illusionist Faceless Mage	28546905
Impenetrable Formation	96631852
Imperial Order	61740673
Inaba White Rabbit	77084837
Incandescent Ordeal	33031674
Indomitable Fighter Lei Lei	84173492
Infernal Flame Emperor	19847532
Infernal Queen Archfiend	08581705
Inferno	74823665
Inferno Fire Blast	52684508
Inferno Hammer	17185260
Inferno Reckless Summon	12247206
Inferno Tempest	14391920
Infinite Cards	94163677
Infinite Dismissal	54109233
Injection Fairy Lily	79575620
Inpachi	97923414

CARD	PASSWORD
Insect Armor with Laser Cannon	03492538
Insect Barrier	23615409
Insect Imitation	96965364
Insect Knight	35052053
Insect Princess	37957847
Insect Queen	91512835
Insect Soldiers of the Sky	07019529
Inspection	16227556
Interdimensional Matter Transporter	36261276
Invader From Another Dimension	28450915
Invader of Darkness	56647086
Invader of the Throne	03056267
Invasion of Flames	26082229
Invigoration	98374133
Iron Blacksmith Kotetsu	73431236
Island Turtle	04042268
Jack's Knight	90876561
Jade Insect Whistle	95214051
Jam Breeding Machine	21770260
Jam Defender	21558682
Jar of Greed	83968380
Jar Robber	33784505
Javelin Beetle	26932788
Javelin Beetle Pact	41182875
Jellyfish	14851496
Jerry Beans Man	23635815
Jetroid	43697559
Jinzo	77585513
Jinzo #7	32809211
Jirai Gumo	94773007
Jowgen the Spiritualist	41855169
Jowls of Dark Demise	05257687
Judge Man	30113682
Judgment of Anubis	55256016
Just Desserts	24068492
KA-2 Des Scissors	52768103
Kabazauls	51934376
Kagemusha of the Blue Flame	15401633
Kaibaman	34627841
Kaiser Dragon	94566432
Kaiser Glider	52824910
Kaiser Sea Horse	17444133
Kaminari Attack	09653271
Kaminote Blow	97570038
Kamionwizard	41544074
Kangaroo Champ	95789089
Karate Man	23289281
Karbonala Warrior	54541900
Karma Cut	71587526
Kelbek	54878498
Keldo	80441106
Killer Needle	88979991
Kinetic Soldier	79853073
King Dragun	13756293
King Fog	84686841
King of the Skull Servants	36021814
King of the Swamp	79109599
King of Yamimakai	69455834

CARD	PASSWORD
King Tiger Wanghu	83986578
King's Knight	64788463
Kiryu	84814897
Kiseitai	04266839
Kishido Spirit	60519422
Knight's Title	87210505
Koitsu	69456283
Kojikocy	01184620
Kotodama	19406822
Kozaky	99171160
Kozaky's Self-Destruct Button	21908319
Kryuel	82642348
Kumootoko	56283725
Kurama	85705804
Kuriboh	40640057
Kuwagata Alpha	60802233
Kwagar Hercules	95144193
Kycoo The Ghost Destroyer	88240808
La Jinn The Mystical Genie of The Lamp	97590747
Labyrinth of Nightmare	66526672
Labyrinth Tank	99551425
Lady Assailant of Flames	90147755
Lady Ninja Yae	82005435
Lady of Faith	17358176
Larvas	94675535
Laser Cannon Armor	77007920
Last Day of Witch	90330453
Last Turn	28566710
Launcher Spider	87322377
Lava Battleguard	20394040
Lava Golem	00102380
Layard the Liberator	67468948
Left Arm of the Forbidden One	07902349
Left Leg of the Forbidden One	44519536
Legendary Black Belt	96438440
Legendary Flame Lord	60258960
Legendary Jujitsu Master	25773409
Legendary Sword	61854111
Leghul	12472242
Lekunga	62543393
Lesser Dragon	55444629
Lesser Fiend	16475472
Level Conversion Lab	84397023
Level Limit - Area A	54976796
Level Limit - Area B	03136426
Level Modulation	61850482
Level Up!	25290459
Levia-Dragon	37721209
Light of Intervention	62867251
Light of Judgment	44595286
Lighten the Load	37231841
Lightforce Sword	49587034
Lightning Blade	55226821
Lightning Conger	27671321
Lightning Vortex	69162969
Limiter Removal	23171610
Liquid Beast	93108297
Little Chimera	68658728

CARD	PASSWORD
Little-Winguard	90790253
Lizard Soldier	20831168
Lord of D.	17985575
Lord of the Lamp	99510761
Lost Guardian	45871897
Luminous Soldier	57282479
Luminous Spark	81777047
Luster Dragon	11091375
Luster Dragon #2	17658803
M-Warrior #1	56342351
M-Warrior #2	92731455
Machine Conversion Factory	25769732
Machine Duplication	63995093
Machine King	46700124
Machine King Prototype	89222931
Machiners Defender	96384007
Machiners Force	58054262
Machiners Sniper	23782705
Machiners Soldier	60999392
Mad Dog of Darkness	79182538
Mad Lobster	97240270
Mad Sword Beast	79870141
Mage Power	83746708
Magic Drain	59344077
Magic Jammer	77414722
Magical Cylinder	62279055
Magical Dimension	28553439
Magical Explosion	32723153
Magical Hats	81210420
Magical Labyrinth	64389297
Magical Marionette	08034697
Magical Merchant	32362575
Magical Plant Mandragola	07802006
Magical Scientist	34206604
Magical Thorn	53119267
Magician of Black Chaos	30208479
Magician of Faith	31560081
Magician's Circle	00050755
Magician's Unite	36045450
Magician's Valkyrie	80304126
Magnet Circle	94940436
Maha Vailo	93013676
Maharaghi	40695128
Maiden of the Aqua	17214465
Maji-Gire Panda	60102563
Maju Garzett	08794435
Makiu	27827272
Makyura the Destructor	21593977
Malevolent Nuzzler	99597615
Malfunction	06137095
Malice Ascendant	14255590
Malice Dispersion	13626450
Mammoth Graveyard	40374923
Man Eater	93553943
Man-Eater Bug	54652250
Man-Eating Black Shark	80727036
Man-Eating Treasure Chest	13723605
Man-Thro' Tro'	43714890
Manga Ryu-Ran	38369349
Manju of the Ten Thousand Hands	95492061

CARD	PASSWORD
Manticore of Darkness	77121851
Marauding Captain	02460565
Marie the Fallen One	57579381
Marine Beast	29929832
Marshmallon	31305911
Marshmallon Glasses	66865880
Maryokutai	71466592
Masaki the Legendary Swordsman	44287299
Mask of Brutality	82432018
Mask of Darkness	28933734
Mask of Restrict	29549364
Mask of Weakness	57882509
Masked Dragon	39191307
Masked of the Accursed	56948373
Masked Sorcerer	10189126
Mass Driver	34906152
Master Kyonshee	24530661
Master Monk	49814180
Master of Dragon Knight	62873545
Master of Oz	27134689
Mataza the Zapper	22609617
Mavelus	59036972
Maximum Six	30707994
Mazera DeVille	06133894
Mech Mole Zombie	63545455
Mecha-Dog Marron	94667532
Mechanical Hound	22512237
Mechanical Snail	34442949
Mechanical Spider	45688586
Mechanicalchaser	07359741
Meda Bat	76211194
Medusa Worm	02694423
Mefist the Infernal General	46820049
Mega Thunderball	21817254
Mega Ton Magical Cannon	32062913
Megamorph	22046459
Megarock Dragon	71544954
Melchid the Four-Face Beast	86569121
Memory Crusher	48700891
Mermaid Knight	24435369
Messenger of Peace	44656491
Metal Armored Bug	65957473
Metal Dragon	09293977
Metallizing Parasite	07369217
Metalmorph	68540058
Metalzoa	50705071
Metamorphosis	46411259
Meteor B. Dragon	90660762
Meteor Dragon	64271667
Meteor of Destruction	33767325
Meteorain	64274292
Michizure	37580756
Micro-Ray	18190572
Mid Shield Gardna	75487237
Mighty Guard	62327910
Mikazukinoyaiba	38277918
Millennium Golem	47986555
Millennium Scorpion	82482194
Millennium Shield	32012841
Milus Radiant	07489323

CARD	PASSWORD
Minar	32539892
Mind Control	37520316
Mind Haxorz	75392615
Mind on Air	66690411
Mind Wipe	52718046
Mine Golem	76321376
Minefield Eruption	85519211
Minor Goblin Official	01918087
Miracle Dig	06343408
Miracle Fusion	45906428
Miracle Kid	55985014
Miracle Restoring	68334074
Mirage Dragon	15960641
Mirage Knight	49217579
Mirage of Nightmare	41482598
Mirror Force	44095762
Mirror Wall	22359980
Misfortune	01036974
Mispolymerization	58392024
Mistobody	47529357
Moai Interceptor Cannons	45159319
Mobius the Frost Monarch	04929256
Moisture Creature	75285069
Mokey Mokey	27288416
Mokey Mokey King	13803864
Mokey Mokey Smackdown	01965724
Molten Behemoth	17192817
Molten Destruction	19384334
Molten Zombie	04732017
Monk Fighter	03810071
Monster Egg	36121917
Monster Eye	84133008
Monster Gate	43040603
Monster Reborn	83764718
Monster Recovery	93108433
Monster Reincarnation	74848038
Mooyan Curry	58074572
Morale Boost	93671934
Morphing Jar	33508719
Morphing Jar #2	79106360
Mother Grizzly	57839750
Mountain	50913601
Mr. Volcano	31477025
Mudora	82108372
Muka Muka	46657337
Multiplication of Ants	22493811
Multiply	40703222
Musician King	56907389
Mustering of the Dark Scorpions	68191243
Mysterious Puppeteer	54098121
Mystic Horseman	68516705
Mystic Lamp	98049915
Mystic Plasma Zone	18161786
Mystic Swordsman LV 2	47507260
Mystic Swordsman LV 4	74591968
Mystic Swordsman LV 6	60482781
Mystic Tomato	83011277
Mystic Wok	80161395
Mystical Beast Serket	89194033
Mystical Elf	15025844

CARD	PASSWORD
Mystical Knight of Jackal	98745000
Mystical Moon	36607978
Mystical Sand	32751480
Mystical Sheep #2	30451366
Mystical Shine Ball	39552864
Mystical Space Typhoon	05318639
Mystik Wok	80161395
Mythical Beast Cerberus	55424270
Nanobreaker	70948327
Necklace of Command	48576971
Necrovalley	47355498
Needle Ball	94230224
Needle Burrower	98162242
Needle Ceiling	38411870
Needle Wall	38299233
Needle Worm	81843628
Negate Attack	14315573
Nemuriko	90963488
Neo Aqua Madoor	49563947
Neo Bug	16587243
Neo the Magic Swordsman	50930991
Neo-Space	40215635
Neo-Spacian Aqua Dolphin	17955766
Newdoria	04335645
Next to be Lost	07076131
Night Assailant	16226786
Nightmare Horse	59290628
Nightmare Penguin	81306586
Nightmare Wheel	54704216
Nightmare's Steelcage	58775978
Nimble Momonga	22567609
Nin-Ken Dog	11987744
Ninja Grandmaster Sasuke	04041838
Ninjitsu Art of Decoy	89628781
Ninjitsu Art of Transformation	70861343
Nitro Unit	23842445
Niwatori	07805359
Nobleman of Crossout	71044499
Nobleman of Extermination	17449108
Nobleman-Eater Bug	65878864
Non Aggression Area	76848240
Non-Fusion Area	27581098
Non-Spellcasting Area	20065549
Novox's Prayer	43694075
Nubian Guard	51616747
Numinous Healer	02130625
Nutrient Z	29389368
Nuvia the Wicked	12953226
O - Oversoul	63703130
Obnoxious Celtic Guardian	52077741
Ocubeam	86088138
Offerings to the Doomed	19230407
Ojama Black	79335209
Ojama Delta Hurricane	08251996
Ojama Green	12482652
Ojama King	90140980
Ojama Trio	29843091

CARD	PASSWORD
Ojama Yellow	42941100
Ojamagic	24643836
Ojamuscle	98259197
Old Vindictive Magician	45141844
Ominous Fortunetelling	56995655
Oni Tank T-34	66927994
Opti-Camaflauge Armor	44762290
Opticlops	14531242
Option Hunter	33248692
Orca Mega-Fortress of Darkness	63120904
Ordeal of a Traveler	39537362
Order to Charge	78986941
Order to Smash	39019325
Otohime	39751093
Outstanding Dog Marron	11548522
Overdrive	02311603
Oxygeddon	58071123
Painful Choice	74191942
Paladin of White Dragon	73398797
Pale Beast	21263083
Pandemonium	94585852
Pandemonium Watchbear	75375465
Parasite Paracide	27911549
Parasitic Ticky	87978805
Patrician of Darkness	19153634
Patroid	71930383
Penguin Knight	36039163
Penumbral Soldier Lady	64751286
People Running About	12143771
Perfect Machine King	18891691
Performance of Sword	04849037
Petit Angel	38142739
Petit Dragon	75356564
Petit Moth	58192742
Phantasmal Martyrs	93224848
Phantom Beast Cross-Wing	71181155
Phantom Beast Thunder-Pegasus	34961968
Phantom Beast Wild-Horn	07576264
Pharaoh's Servant	52550973
Pharonic Protector	89959682
Phoenix Wing Wind Blast	63356631
Photon Generator Unit	66607691
Pikeru's Circle of Enchantment	74270067
Pikeru's Second Sight	58015506
Pinch Hopper	26185991
Pineapple Blast	90669991
Piranha Army	50823978
Pitch-Black Power Stone	34029630
Pitch-Black Warwolf	88975532
Pitch-Dark Dragon	47415292
Poison Draw Frog	56840658
Poison Fangs	76539047
Poison Mummy	43716289
Poison of the Old Man	08842266
Polymerization	24094653
Possessed Dark Soul	52860176

CARD	PASSWORD
Pot of Avarice	67169062
Pot of Generosity	70278545
Pot of Greed	55144522
Power Bond	37630732
Power Capsule	54289683
Precious Card from Beyond	68304813
Premature Burial	70828912
Prepare to Strike Back	04483989
Prevent Rat	00549481
Prickle Fairy	91559748
Primal Seed	23701465
Princess Curran	02316186
Princess of Tsurugi	51371017
Princess Pikeru	75917088
Protective Soul Ailin	11678191
Protector of the Sanctuary	24221739
Protector of the Throne	10071456
Proto-Cyber Dragon	26439287
Pumpking the King of Ghosts	29155212
Punished Eagle	74703140
Pyramid of Light	53569894
Pyramid Turtle	77044671
Queen's Knight	25652259
Rabid Horseman	94905343
Rafflesia Seduction	31440542
Raging Flame Sprite	90810762
Raigeki	12580477
Raigeki Break	04178474
Rain Of Mercy	66719324
Rainbow Flower	21347810
Rallis the Star Bird	41382147
Rancer Dragonute	11125718
Rapid-Fire Magician	06337436
Rare Metalmorph	12503902
Raregold Armor	07625614
Raviel, Lord of Phantasms	69890967
Ray & Temperature	85309439
Ray of Hope	82529174
Re-Fusion	74694807
Ready For Intercepting	31785398
Really Eternal Rest	28121403
Reaper of the Cards	33066139
Reaper of the Nightmare	85684223
Reasoning	58577036
Reborn Zombie	23421244
Reckless Greed	37576645
Recycle	96316857
Red Archery Girl	65570596
Red Gadget	86445415
Red Medicine	38199696
Red Moon Baby	56387350
Red-Eyes B. Chick	36262024
Red-Eyes B. Dragon	74677422
Red-Eyes Black Metal Dragon	64335804
Red-Eyes Darkness Dragon	96561011
Reflect Bounder	02851070
Regenerating Mummy	70821187

CARD	PASSWORD
Reinforcement of the Army	32807846
Release Restraint	75417459
Relinquished	64631466
Reload	22589918
Remove Trap	51482758
Rescue Cat	14878871
Rescueroid	24311595
Reshef the Dark Being	62420419
Respect Play	08951260
Return from the Different Dimension	27174286
Return of the Doomed	19827717
Reversal of Graves	17484499
Reversal Quiz	05990062
Revival Jam	31709826
Right Arm of the Forbidden One	70903634
Right Leg of the Forbidden One	08124921
Ring of Defense	58641905
Ring of Destruction	83555666
Ring of Magnetism	20436034
Riryoku Field	70344351
Rising Air Current	45778932
Rising Energy	78211862
Rite of Spirit	30450531
Ritual Weapon	54351224
Robbin' Goblin	88279736
Robbin' Zombie	83258273
Robolady	92421852
Robotic Knight	44203504
Roboyarou	38916461
Rock Bombardment	20781762
Rock Ogre Grotto	68846917
Rocket Jumper	53890795
Rocket Warrior	30860696
Rod of the Mind's Eye	94793422
Roll Out!	91597389
Root Water	39004808
Rope of Life	93382620
Rope of Spirit	37383714
Roulette Barrel	46303688
Royal Command	33950246
Royal Decree	51452091
Royal Keeper	16509093
Royal Knight	68280530
Royal Magical Library	70791313
Royal Surrender	56058888
Royal Tribute	72405967
Ruin, Queen of Oblivion	46427957
Rush Recklessly	70046172
Ryu Kokki	57281778
Ryu Senshi	49868263
Ryu-Kishin Clown	42647539
Ryu-Kishin Powered	24611934
Saber Beetle	49645921
Sacred Crane	30914564
Sacred Phoenix of Nephthys	61441708
Saggi the Dark Clown	66602787
Sakuretsu Armor	56120475
Salamandra	32268901
Salvage	96947648

CARD	PASSWORD
Samsara	44182827
Sand Gambler	50593156
Sand Moth	73648243
Sangan	26202165
Sanwitch	53539634
Sasuke Samurai	16222645
Sasuke Samurai #2	11760174
Sasuke Samurai #3	77379481
Sasuke Samurai #4	64538655
Satellite Cannon	50400231
Scapegoat	73915051
Scarr, Scout of Dark World	05498296
Science Soldier	67532912
Scroll of Bewitchment	10352095
Scyscraper	63035430
Sea Serpent Warrior of Darkness	42071342
Sealmaster Meisei	02468169
Second Coin Toss	36562627
Second Goblin	19086954
Secret Barrel	27053506
Self-Destruct Button	57585212
Senri Eye	60391791
Serial Spell	49398568
Serpent Night Dragon	66516792
Serpentine Princess	71829750
Servant of Catabolism	02792265
Seven Tools of the Bandit	03819470
Shadow Ghoul	30778711
Shadow Of Eyes	58621589
Shadow Tamer	37620434
Shadowknight Archfiend	09603356
Shadowslayer	20939559
Share the Pain	56830749
Shield & Sword	52097679
Shield Crash	30683373
Shien's Spy	07672244
Shift	59560625
Shifting Shadows	59237154
Shinato's Ark	60365591
Shinato, King of a Higher Plane	86327225
Shining Abyss	87303357
Shining Angel	95956346
Shooting Star Bow - Ceal	95638658
Silent Insect	40867519
Silent Magician Lv4	73665146
Silent Magician Lv8	72443568
Silent Swordsman LV3	01995985
Silent Swordsman LV5	74388798
Silent Swordsman LV7	37267041
Sillva, Warlord of Dark World	32619583
Silpheed	73001017
Silver Fang	90357090
Simorgh, Bird of Divinity	14989021
Simultaneous Loss	92219931
Sinister Serpent	08131171
Sixth Sense	03280747
Skill Drain	82732705

CARD	PASSWORD
Skilled Dark Magician	73752131
Skilled White Magician	46363422
Skull Archfiend of Lightning	61370518
Skull Descovery Knight	78700060
Skull Dog Marron	86652646
Skull Invitation	98139712
Skull Lair	06733059
Skull Mariner	05265750
Skull Red Bird	10202894
Skull Servant	32274490
Skull Zoma	79852326
Skull-Mark Ladybug	64306248
Skyscraper	63035430
Slate Warrior	78636495
Smashing Ground	97169186
Smoke Grenade of the Thief	63789924
Snatch Steal	45986603
Sogen	86318356
Soitsu	60246171
Solar Flare Dragon	45985838
Solar Ray	44472639
Solemn Judgment	41420027
Solemn Wishes	35346968
Solomon's Lawbook	23471572
Sonic Duck	84696266
Sonic Jammer	84550200
Sorcerer of Dark Magic	88619463
Soul Absorption	68073522
Soul Exchange	68005187
Soul of Purity and Light	77527210
Soul Release	05758500
Soul Resurrection	92924317
Soul Reversal	78864369
Soul Tiger	15734813
Soul-Absorbing Bone Tower	63012333
Souleater	31242786
Souls Of The Forgotten	04920010
Space Mambo	36119641
Spark Blaster	97362768
Sparks	76103675
Spatial Collapse	20644748
Spear Cretin	58551308
Spear Dragon	31553716
Spell Canceller	84636823
Spell Economics	04259068
Spell Purification	01669772
Spell Reproduction	29228529
Spell Shield Type-8	38275183
Spell Vanishing	29735721
Spell-Stopping Statute	10069180
Spellbinding Circle	18807108
Spherous Lady	52121290
Sphinx Teleia	51402177
Spiral Spear Strike	49328340
Spirit Barrier	53239672
Spirit Caller	48659020
Spirit Message A	94772232
Spirit Message I	31893528
Spirit Message L	30170981
Spirit Message N	67287533

CARD	PASSWORD
Spirit of Flames	13522325
Spirit of the Breeze	53530069
Spirit of the Harp	80770678
Spirit of the Pharaoh	25343280
Spirit Reaper	23205979
Spirit Ryu	67957315
Spiritual Earth Art - Kurogane	70156997
Spiritual Energy Settle Machine	99173029
Spiritual Fire Art - Kurenai	42945701
Spiritual Water Art - Aoi	06540606
Spiritual Wind Art - Miyabi	79333300
Spiritualism	15866454
St. Joan	21175632
Stamping Destruction	81385346
Star Boy	08201910
Statue of the Wicked	65810489
Staunch Defender	92854392
Stealth Bird	03510565
Steam Gyroid	05368615
Steamroid	44729197
Steel Ogre Grotto #1	29172562
Steel Ogre Grotto #2	90908427
Stim-Pack	83225447
Stop Defense	63102017
Storming Wynn	29013526
Stray Lambs	60764581
Strike Ninja	41006930
Stronghold	13955608
Stumbling	34646691
Success Probability 0%	06859683
Summon Priest	00423585
Summoned Skull	70781052
Summoner of Illusions	14644902
Super Conductor Tyranno	85520851
Super Rejuvenation	27770341
Super Robolady	75923050
Super Roboyarou	01412158
Supply	44072894
Susa Soldier	40473581
Swarm of Locusts	41872150
Swarm of Scarabs	15383415
Swift Gaia the Fierce Knight	16589042
Sword Hunter	51345461
Sword of Deep-Seated	98495314
Sword of Dragon's Soul	61405855
Sword of the Soul Eater	05371656
Swords of Concealing Light	12923641
Swords of Revealing Light	72302403
Swordsman of Landstar	03573512
Symbol of Heritage	45305419
System Down	18895832
T.A.D.P.O.L.E.	10456559
Tactical Espionage Expert	89698120
Tailor of the Fickle	43641473
Taunt	90740329
Tenkabito Shien	41589166

CARD	PASSWORD
Terra the Terrible	63308047
Terraforming	73628505
Terrorking Archfiend	35975813
Terrorking Salmon	78060096
Teva	16469012
The Agent of Creation - Venus	64734921
The Agent of Force - Mars	91123920
The Agent of Judgment - Saturn	91345518
The Agent of Wisdom - Mercury	38730226
The All-Seeing White Tiger	32269855
The Big March of Animals	01689516
The Bistro Butcher	71107816
The Cheerful Coffin	41142615
The Creator	61505339
The Creator Incarnate	97093037
The Dark - Hex Sealed Fusion	52101615
The Dark Door	30606547
The Dragon Dwelling in the Cave	93346024
The Dragon's Bead	92408984
The Earl of Demise	66989694
The Earth - Hex Sealed Fusion	88696724
The Emperor's Holiday	68400115
The End of Anubis	65403020
The Eye Of Truth	34694160
The Fiend Megacyber	66362965
The Flute of Summoning Dragon	43973174
The Flute of Summoning Kuriboh	20065322
The Forceful Sentry	42829885
The Forces of Darkness	29826127
The Forgiving Maiden	84080938
The Furious Sea King	18710707
The Graveyard in the Fourth Dimension	88089103
The Gross Ghost of Fled Dreams	68049471
The Hunter With 7 Weapons	01525329
The Illusionary Gentleman	83764996
The Immortal of Thunder	84926738
The Kick Man	90407382
The Last Warrior From Another Planet	86099788
The Law of the Normal	66926224
The League of Uniform Nomenclature	55008284
The Legendary Fisherman	03643300
The Light - Hex Sealed Fusion	15717011
The Little Swordsman of Aile	25109950
The Masked Beast	49064413
The Portrait's Secret	32541773
The Regulation of Tribe	00296499

CARD	PASSWORD
The Reliable Guardian	16430187
The Rock Spirit	76305638
The Sanctuary in the Sky	56433456
The Second Sarcophagus	04081094
The Secret of the Bandit	99351431
The Shallow Grave	43434803
The Spell Absorbing Life	99517131
The Thing in the Crater	78243409
The Third Sarcophagus	78697395
The Trojan Horse	38479725
The Unhappy Girl	27618634
The Unhappy Maiden	51275027
The Warrior Returning Alive	95281259
Theban Nightmare	51838385
Theinen the Great Sphinx	87997872
Thestalos the Firestorm Monarch	26205777
Thousand Dragon	41462083
Thousand Energy	05703682
Thousand Needles	33977496
Thousand-Eyes Idol	27125110
Thousand-Eyes Restrict	63519819
Threatening Roar	36361633
Three-Headed Geedo	78423643
Throwstone Unit	76075810
Thunder Crash	69196160
Thunder Dragon	31786629
Thunder Nyan Nyan	70797118
Thunder of Ruler	91781589
Time Seal	35316708
Time Wizard	71625222
Timeater	44913552
Timidity	40350910
Token Festevil	83675475
Token Thanksgiving	57182235
Tongyo	69572024
Toon Cannon Soldier	79875176
Toon Dark Magician Girl	90960358
Toon Defense	43509019
Toon Gemini Elf	42386471
Toon Goblin Attack Force	15270885
Toon Masked Sorcerer	16392422
Toon Mermaid	65458948
Toon Summoned Skull	91842653
Toon Table of Contents	89997728
Toon World	15259703
Tornado Bird	71283180
Tornado Wall	18605135
Torpedo Fish	90337190
Torrential Tribute	53582587
Total Defense Shogun	75372290
Tower of Babel	94256039
Tradgedy	35686187
Transcendent Wings	25573054
Trap Dustshoot	64697231
Trap Hole	04206964
Trap Jammer	19252988
Treeborn Frog	12538374
Tremendous Fire	46918794

CARD	PASSWORD
Tri-Horned Dragon	39111158
Triage	30888983
Trial of Nightmare	77827521
Trial of the Princesses	72709014
Triangle Ecstasy Spark	12181376
Triangle Power	32298781
Tribe-Infecting Virus	33184167
Tribute Doll	02903036
Tribute to The Doomed	79759861
Tripwire Beast	45042329
Troop Dragon	55013285
Tsukuyomi	34853266
Turtle Oath	76806714
Turtle Tiger	37313348
Twin Swords of Flashing Light	21900719
Twin-Headed Beast	82035781
Twin-Headed Behemoth	43586926
Twin-Headed Fire Dragon	78984772
Twin-Headed Thunder Dragon	54752875
Twin-Headed Wolf	88132637
Two Thousand Needles	83228073
Two-Man Cell Battle	25578802
Two-Mouth Darkruler	57305373
Two-Pronged Attack	83887306
Tyhone	72842870
Type Zero Magic Crusher	21237481
Tyranno Infinity	83235263
Tyrant Dragon	94568601
UFOroid	07602840
UFOroid Fighter	32752319
Ultimate Insect LV1	49441499
Ultimate Insect LV3	34088136
Ultimate Insect LV5	34830502
Ultimate Insect LV7	19877898
Ultimate Obedient Fiend	32240937
Ultimate Tyranno	15894048
Ultra Evolution Pill	22431243
Umi	22702055
Umiiruka	82999629
Union Attack	60399954
United Resistance	85936485
United We Stand	56747793
Unity	14731897
Unshaven Angler	92084010
Upstart Goblin	70368879
Uraby	01784619
Uria, Lord of Sealing Flames	06007213
V-Tiger Jet	51638941
Valkyrion the Magna Warrior	75347539
Vampire Genesis	22056710
Vampire Lord	53839837
Vampire Orchis	46571052
Vengeful Bog Spirit	95220856
Victory D	44910027
Vilepawn Archfiend	73219648
VW-Tiger Catapult	58859575
VWXYZ-Dragon Catapult Cannon	84243274

CARD	PASSWORD
W-Wing Catapult	96300057
Waboku	12607053
Wall of Revealing Light	17078030
Wandering Mummy	42994702
Warrior Dai Grepher	75953262
Warrior of Zera	66073051
Wasteland	23424603
Water Dragon	85066822
Water Omotics	02483611
Wave Motion Cannon	38992735
Weed Out	28604635
Whiptail Crow	91996584
Whirlwind Prodigy	15090429
White Dragon Ritual	09786492
White Horn Dragon	73891874
White Magical Hat	15150365
White Magician Pikeru	81383947
White Ninja	01571945
Wicked-Breaking Flameberge-Baou	68427465
Wild Nature's Release	61166988
Winged Dragon, Guardian of the Fortress #1	87796900
Winged Kuriboh	57116033
Winged Kuriboh LV10	98585345
Winged Minion	89258225
Winged Sage Falcos	87523462
Wingweaver	31447217
Witch Doctor of Chaos	75946257
Witch of the Black Forest	78010363
Witch's Apprentice	80741828

CARD	PASSWORD
Witty Phantom	36304921
Wolf Axwielder	56369281
Woodborg Inpachi	35322812
Woodland Sprite	06979239
Worm Drake	73216412
Wroughtweiler	06480253
Wynn the Wind Charmer	37744402
X-Head Cannon	62651957
Xing Zhen Hu	76515293
XY-Dragon Cannon	02111707
XYZ-Dragon Cannon	91998119
XZ-Tank Cannon	99724761
Y-Dragon Head	65622692
Yamata Dragon	76862289
Yami	59197169
Yata-Garasu	03078576
Yellow Gadget	13839120
Yellow Luster Shield	04542651
Yomi Ship	51534754
YZ-Tank Dragon	25119460
Z-Metal Tank	64500000
Zaborg the Thunder Monarch	51945556
Zero Gravity	83133491
Zoa	24311372
Zolga	16268841
Zombie Tiger	47693640
Zombyra the Dark	88472456
Zure, Knight of Dark World	07459013

GAME BOY® ADVANCE

GAMES

ACE COMBAT ADVANCE

COMPLETE GAME WITH ALL PLANES & LEVELS OPEN
Select Enter Code and enter QF9B9F59.

BANJO PILOT

GRUNTY
Defeat Grunty in the Broomstick battle race. Then you can purchase Grunty from Cheato.

HUMBA WUMBA
Defeat Humba Wumba in the Jiggu battle race. Then you can purchase Humba Wumba from Cheato.

JOLLY

Defeat Jolly in the Pumpkin battle race. Then you can purchase Jolly from Cheato.

KLUNGO

Defeat Klungo in the Skull battle race. Then you can purchase Klungo from Cheato.

BARBIE AS THE PRINCESS AND THE PAUPER

PASSWORDS

LEVEL	PASSWORD
1-2	Preminger, Wolfie, Erika, Serafina
1-3	Wolfie, Preminger, Serafina, Preminger
1-4	Preminger, Wolfie, Serfania, Wolfie
Boss 1	Serafina, Woflia. Erika, Preminger
2-1	Princess Anneliese, Preminger, Wolfie, Erika
2-2	Preminger, Princess Anneliese, Wolfie, Erika
2-3	Preminger, Serafina, Preminger, Erika
2-4	Serafina, Erika, Preminger, Wolfie
Boss 2	Preminger, Erika, Serafina, Wolfie
3-1	Wolfie, Preminger, Wolfie, Erika
3-2	Serafina, Preminger, Erika, Serafina
3-3	Erika, Wolfie, Serafina, Princess Anneliese
3-4	Erika, Serafina, Erika, Preminger
Boss 3	Preminger, Serafina, Princess Anneliese, Serafina
4-1	Wolfie, Serafina, Preminger, Serafina
4-2	Preminger, Serafina, Princess Anneliese, Preminger
4-3	Wolfie, Serafina, Erika, Serafina
Boss 4	Erika, Serafina, Princess Anneliese, Wolfie
Final Boss	Erika, Princess Anneliese, Princess Anneliese, Man
Arcade Level	Princess Anneliese, Serafina, Erika, Wolfie

BIONICLE: TALES OF THE TOHUNGA

EVERYTHING BUT THE MINI-GAMES
Enter B9RBRN as a name.

GALI MINI-GAME
Enter 9MA268 as a name.

KOPAKA MINI-GAME
Enter V33673 as a name.

LEWA MINI-GAME
Enter 3LT154 as a name.

ONUA MINI-GAME
Enter 8MR472 as a name.

POHATU MINI-GAME
Enter 5MG834 as a name.

TAHU MINI-GAME
Enter 4CR487 as a name.

CAR BATTLER JOE

BIG BANG

At the Main menu, select Battle League. When the game asks "Use which machine," choose password and enter HAMA!333.

BLUE GALPE EV

At the Main menu, select Battle League. When the game asks "Use which machine," choose password and enter SHISYO!!.

CASEY'S WHLS

At the Main menu, select Battle League. When the game asks "Use which machine," choose password and enter !KOKICHI.

 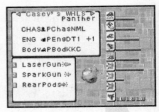

CAVALIER

At the Main menu, select Battle League. When the game asks "Use which machine," choose password and enter CUREWAND.

COPA ZONE23

At the Main menu, select Battle League. When the game asks "Use which machine," choose password and enter CDMACAPA.

EMP FORCE X

At the Main menu, select Battle League. When the game asks "Use which machine," choose password and enter EMPIRE!!.

ISSUE X

At the Main menu, select Battle League. When the game asks "Use which machine," choose password and enter 8998981!.

JOE JIM ZERO

At the Main menu, select Battle League. When the game asks "Use which machine," choose password and enter Todoroki.

 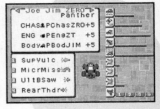

LONG VALLEY

At the Main menu, select Battle League. When the game asks "Use which machine," choose password and enter NAGOYADB.

MATSU K MK4

At the Main menu, select Battle League. When the game asks "Use which machine," choose password and enter MR!HURRY.

MAX-K

At the Main menu, select Battle League. When the game asks "Use which machine," choose password and enter GANKOMAX.

MEGA M

At the Main menu, select Battle League. When the game asks "Use which machine," choose password and enter M!M!M!M!.

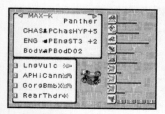

MILLENNIUM90

At the Main menu, select Battle League. When the game asks "Use which machine," choose password and enter 90!60!92.

MRIN'S DREAM

At the Main menu, select Battle League. When the game asks "Use which machine," choose password and enter MARRON!!.

MSSL DOLLY

At the Main menu, select Battle League. When the game asks "Use which machine," choose password and enter KINNIKU!.

PISTON GH

At the Main menu, select Battle League. When the game asks "Use which machine," choose password and enter GO!HOME!.

SOLID WIND

At the Main menu, select Battle League. When the game asks "Use which machine," choose password and enter RED!GUNS.

TAKAH'S LSR

At the Main menu, select Battle League. When the game asks "Use which machine," choose password and enter TK000056.

WNN SPECIAL

At the Main menu, select Battle League. When the game asks "Use which machine," choose password and enter BOM!BOM!.

CARS

ALL LEVELS & 90 BOLTS

At the Title screen, press Up, Up, Down, Down, Left, Right, Left, Right, B, A.

ALL CARS

At the Title screen, press Right, Down, Right, B.

ALL CAR COLORS

At the Title screen, press Up, Up, Left, Right, Right, Left, Down, Down.

RADIATOR CAP SECRET CIRCUIT

At the Title screen, press Left, Left, Right, Right, B, B, A.

ALL SCREENSHOTS AT THE DRIVE-IN

At the Title screen, press Left, Down, Right, A.

CASTLEVANIA: ARIA OF SORROW

NO ITEMS

Start a new game with the name NOUSE to use no items in the game.

NO SOULS

Start a new game with the name NOSOUL to use no souls in the game.

CLASSIC NES SERIES: PAC-MAN

PAC-ATTACK PUZZLE MODE

STAGE	PASSWORD
1	STR
2	HNM
3	KST
4	TRT
5	MYX
6	KHL
7	RTS
8	SKB
9	HNT
10	SRY
11	YSK
12	RCF
13	HSM
14	PWW
15	MTN
16	TKY
17	RGH

CT SPECIAL FORCES 3: NAVY OPS

LEVEL PASSWORDS

LEVEL #	ENTER
Level 1-2	5073
Level 2-1	1427
Level 2-2	2438
Level 2-3	7961
Level 2-4	8721
Level 3-1	5986
Level 3-2	2157
Level 3-3	4796
Level 3-4	3496
Level 3-5	1592
Level 3-6	4168
Level 3-7	1364
Level 4-1	7596
Level 4-2	9108
Level 4-3	6124
Level 4-4	7234
Level 4-5	6820
Level 5-1	2394
Level 5-2	4256
Level 5-3	0842

DAREDEVIL: THE MAN WITHOUT FEAR

UNLOCK EVERYTHING
Enter the password 41TK1S6ZNGV.

DK: KING OF SWING

ATTACK BATTLE 3
At the Title screen, press Up + L + A + B to access a password screen. Enter 65942922.

CLIMBING RACE 5
At the Title screen, press Up + L + A + B to access a password screen. Enter 55860327.

OBSTACLE RACE 4
At the Title screen, press Up + L + A + B to access a password screen. Enter 35805225.

UNLOCK TIME ATTACK
Complete the game as DK.

UNLOCK DIDDY MODE
Collect 24 medals as DK.

UNLOCK BUBBLES
Complete Diddy Mode with 24 Medals.

UNLOCK KREMLING
Collect 6 gold medals in Jungle Jam.

UNLOCK KING K. ROOL
Collect 12 gold medals in Jungle Jam.

DONKEY KONG COUNTRY 2: DIDDY KONG'S QUEST

ALL LEVELS
Select Cheats from the Options menu and enter freedom.

START WITH 15 LIVES
Select Cheats from the Options menu and enter helpme.

START WITH 55 LIVES
Select Cheats from the Options menu and enter weakling.

START WITH 10 BANANA COINS
Select Cheats from the Options menu and enter richman.

START WITH 50 BANANA COINS
Select Cheats from the Options menu and enter wellrich.

NO DK OR HALFWAY BARRELS
Select Cheats from the Options menu and enter rockard.

MUSIC PLAYER
Select Cheats from the Options menu and enter onetime.

CREDITS
Select Cheats from the Options menu and enter kredits.

E.T.: THE EXTRA-TERRESTRIAL

PASSWORDS

LEVEL	PASSWORD
2	Up, Up, A, Down, Down, B, R, L
3	Left, Up, Right, Down, L, A, R, B
4	A, Left, B, Right, L, Up, R, Down
5	L, R, R, L, A, Up, B, Left
6	L, Left, R, Right, A, A, B, A
7	B, R, B, L, A, Up, B, Up
8	Up, Up, A, Down, Down, Left, A, B
9	Right, B, B, Left, Up, R, R, L
10	Left, Left, A, L, Right, Right, B, R

GAMEBOY® ADVANCE

FINAL FANTASY I & II: DAWN OF SOULS

FF I TILE GAME
During a game of Final Fantasy I and after you get the ship, hold A and press B about 55 times.

FF II CONCENTRATION GAME
After obtaining the Snowcraft, hold B and press A about 20 times.

FLUSHED AWAY

LEVEL SELECT
Enter 60861775 at the password screen.

GRADIUS GALAXIES

SLOWER
Pause the game and press Left, Right, Up, Down, Left, Left, Right, Start.

ALL WEAPONS
Pause the game and press Up, Up, Down, Down, L, R, L, R, B, A.

SELF-DESTRUCT
Pause the game and press Up, Up, Down, Down, Left, Right, Left, Right, B, A, Start.

GRAND THEFT AUTO

CHEAT MODE/COORDINATES
During a game, press A + B + Start.

ALL WEAPONS
After entering the Cheat Mode code, press Left, Right, Up, Down, A, A.

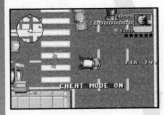

RESTORE ARMOR
After entering the Cheat Mode code, press Left, Right, Up, Down, A, L.

15,000 DOLLARS
After entering the Cheat Mode code, press Left, Right, Up, Down, L, L.

RESTORE HEALTH
After entering the Cheat Mode code, press Left, Right, Up, Down, B, B.

LOWER WANTED LEVEL
After entering the Cheat Mode code, press Left, Right, Up, Down, A, R.

RAISE WANTED LEVEL
After entering the Cheat Mode code, press Left, Right, Up, Down, R, A.

TOGGLE BETWEEN 0 STARS AND 6 STARS
After entering the Cheat Mode code, press Left, Right, Up, Down, R, R.

TOGGLE GANG HOSTILITY
After entering the Cheat Mode code, press Left, Right, Up, Down, B, R.

THE INCREDIBLE HULK

STAGE SKIP
Pause the game and press Down, Right, Down, Right, Left, Left, Left, Up.

TUTORIAL
Enter XL9ZMD as a password.

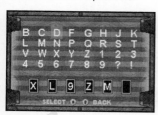

GIANT ROBOT FACTORY 1
Enter G!G1DK as a password.

GIANT ROBOT FACTORY 2
Enter DXY6FK as a password.

GIANT ROBOT FACTORY 3
Enter BBT7FK as a password.

BLIZZARD BACKDOOR 1
Enter ZPGVFK as a password.

BLIZZARD BACKDOOR 2
Enter B94GFK as a password.

BLIZZARD BACKDOOR 3
Enter J2B?FK as a password.

STAGE CORRUPTORATOR 1
Enter QF1XFK as a password.

STAGE CORRUPTORATOR 2
Enter SW3!FK as a password.

STAGE CORRUPTORATOR 3
Enter QQ?7DK as a password.

UNDERMINER
Enter 24NCGK as a password.

JAZZ JACKRABBIT

500 CREDITS
Pause the game and press Right,
Left, Right, Left, L, R, Up, Up, R, R,
L, L.

1000 CREDITS
Pause the game and press Up,
Down, Up, Down, Left, Right, L, R,
L, R, R, L.

5000 CREDITS
Pause the game and press Up, Right,
Down, Left, L, L, Right, Left, R, R, L, L.

KONG: KING OF ATLANTIS

LEVEL PASSWORDS
Enter the following passwords to unlock certain levels in the game.

LEVEL	PASSWORD
Level 1-2	FJLJBDG
Level 1-3	GGJJJBF
Level 1-4	BFBGLJG
Level 2-1	LDBMLMD
Level 2-2	GMLLDDD
Level 2-3	LDFMLJD
Level 2-4	DGDDGML
Level 3-1	GMMMDFB
Level 3-2	MPFDMLB
Level 3-3	FMJBFFP
Level 3-4	LFGPMGB
Level 4-1	GPPMBGB
Level 4-2	DLBGDPP
Level 4-3	LGFPPJB

GAMEBOY® ADVANCE

OVERLORD

LEGO STAR WARS II: THE ORIGINAL TRILOGY

ALDERAAN
At Mos Eisley Cantina, enter 27000 as a code.

BUBBLE BLASTER
At Mos Eisley Cantina, enter 80873 as a code.

CARBONITE CHAMBER
At Mos Eisley Cantina, enter 08433 as a code.

DANCING GIRL
At Mos Eisley Cantina, enter 70546 as a code.

DEATH STAR
At Mos Eisley Cantina, enter 52577 as a code.

DEATH STAR 2
At Mos Eisley Cantina, enter 52583 as a code.

DEATH STAR HANGER
At Mos Eisley Cantina, enter 80500 as a code.

DEATH STAR SUBSECTOR 1
At Mos Eisley Cantina, enter 51999 as a code.

EMPEROR'S LAIR
At Mos Eisley Cantina, enter 20876 as a code.

EWOK VILLAGE
At Mos Eisley Cantina, enter 31299 as a code.

JEDI SPIRIT
At Mos Eisley Cantina, enter 75046 as a code.

MILLENIUM FALCON
At Mos Eisley Cantina, enter 89910 as a code.

MOS EISELY
At Mos Eisley Cantina, enter 82434 as a code.

MOS EISLEY CANTINA
At Mos Eisley Cantina, enter 13197 as a code.

OBI WAN'S HOUSE
At Mos Eisley Cantina, enter 40214 as a code.

SENSOR BALCONY
At Mos Eisley Cantina, enter 61806 as a code.

SITH MODE
At Mos Eisley Cantina, enter 11340 as a code.

THE DARK CAVE
At Mos Eisley Cantina, enter 50250 as a code.

TRASH COMPACTOR
At Mos Eisley Cantina, enter 11911 as a code.

WAMPA CAVE
At Mos Eisley Cantina, enter 42352 as a code.

YODA'S HUT
At Mos Eisley Cantina, enter 06881 as a code.

MADAGASCAR: OPERATION PENGUIN

CHRISTMAS
During gameplay, press Select, Up, L, Left, R, Right, L, Down, R.

MONSTER FORCE

RESTART LEVEL
Pause the game, hold L + R and press A.

FINISH LEVEL
During a game, hold L + R + A and press Up.

PLAY AS MINA OR DREW
At the Character Select screen, hold L + R + B and press Right.

NANCY DREW: HAUNTED MANSION

LEVEL PASSWORDS

LEVEL	PASSWORD
2	Ox, Horse, Tiger, Sheep
3	Rooster, Pig, Rabbit, Dragon
4	Rat, Dog, Monkey, Snake
5	Sheep, Tiger, Horse, Ox
6	Dragon, Rabbit, Pig, Rooster
7	Snake, Monkey, Dog, Rat

NICKTOONS UNITE!

LEVEL 2: FENTON LAB
Select Continue and enter JAZMINE.

LEVEL 3: VLAD'S CHATEAU
Select Continue and enter PAULINA.

LEVEL 4: BIKINI BOTTOM
Select Continue and enter SKULKER.

LEVEL 5: CHUM BUCKET
Select Continue and enter PATRICK.

LEVEL 6: PLANKTON
Select Continue and enter MERMAID.

LEVEL 7: TIMMY'S HOME
Select Continue and enter SCALLOP.

LEVEL 8: DIMMSDALE DUMP
Select Continue and enter BABYSIT.

LEVEL 9: CROCKER'S LOCKER ROOM
Select Continue and enter GODDARD.

LEVEL 10: JIMMY'S LAB
Select Continue and enter ESTEVEZ.

LEVEL 11: SUBTERRANEAN CAVES
Select Continue and enter LIBERTY.

LEVEL 12: PROF CALAMITOUS' LAB
Select Continue and enter SKYLARK.

THE PINBALL OF THE DEAD

BOSS MODE
Enter D0NTN33DM0N3Y as a password.

PRINCESS NATASHA: STUDENT SECRET AGENT

ALL GADGETS
Select Codes from the Extras menu and enter OLEGSGIZMO.

EXTRA LEVELS
Select Codes from the Extras menu and enter SMASHROBOT.

INFINITE LIVES
Select Codes from the Extras menu and enter CRUSHLUBEK.

R-TYPE III: THE THIRD LIGHTNING

PASSWORDS

LEVEL	PASSWORD
2	5bdgb
3	5hhlq
4	5mglt
5	5rflx
6	5wdl0

RACING GEARS ADVANCE

You can enter up to three codes at a time. Note that entering a wrong code resets the codes.

AAA
After selecting the Circuit, hold R and press A, L, B, Right, Right, Up, A. This code eliminates damage.

ARMAGEDDON
After selecting the Circuit, hold R and press B, B, L, Right, Left, Down. This unlocks unlimited ammo.

OVERLOAD

GAMEBOY® ADVANCE

BLINDSPOT

After selecting the Circuit, hold R and press Right, A, B, B, Left. With this code activated, all opponents become invisible.

CASHCROP

After selecting the Circuit, hold R and press Right, L, Up, A, Left, B. This makes dollar signs worth more.

ENDURANCE

After selecting the Circuit, hold R and press Left, B, A, Right, L, L, Down. This makes the race five laps long.

EQUALIZER

After selecting the Circuit, hold R and press Up, Up, B, Down, A.

HAMBURGER

After selecting the Circuit, hold R and press A, A, L, Left, Right, Up. This code unlocks weapons from the start of the race.

SPRINT

After selecting the Circuit, hold R and press Down, Up, B, Left, Right, A. This makes the race one lap long.

TAXMAN

After selecting the Circuit, hold R and press L, A, B, L, Down, Down. This makes dollar signs worth less.

WUSSY

After selecting the Circuit, hold R and press B, A, B, B, L. This code eliminates weapons.

RATATOUILLE

INVINCIBILITY
Enter X4V!3RJ as a password.

ALL CHAPTERS
Enter H3L!X3! as a password. Press L or R at chapter select screen.

ALL MINI GAMES
Enter JV4ND1Z as a password.

ALL BONUS PICTURES
Enter 3R1CQRR as a password.

RIVER CITY RANSOM EX

Select the status menu and change your name to one of the following.

MAX STATS
DAMAX

$999999.99
PLAYA

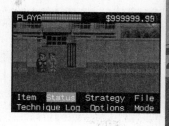

CUSTOM CHAR
XTRA0

CUSTOM SELF
XTRA1

CUSTOM MOVE
XTRA2

CLEAR SAVE
ERAZE

TECHNIQUES 1
FUZZY. This group includes Mach Punch, Dragon Kick, Acro Circus, Grand Slam, Javelin Man, Slick Trick, Nitro Port, Twin Kick, Deadly Shot, Top Spin, Helicopter, Torpedo.

TECHNIQUES 2
WUZZY. This group includes Slap Happy, Pulper, Headbutt, Kickstand, Big Bang, Wheel Throw, Glide Chop, Head Bomb, Chain Chump, Jet Kick, Shuriken, Flip Throw.

TECHNIQUES 3
WAZZA. This group includes Boomerang, Charge It, Bat Fang, Flying Kick, Speed Drop, Bomb Blow, Killer Kick, Bike Kick, Slam Punk, Dragon Knee, God Fist, Hyperguard.

TECHNIQUES 4
BEAR*. This group includes PhoenixWing, Inlines, Springlines, Rocketeers, Air Merc's Narcishoes, Magic Pants, Pandora Box, Skaterz, Custom Fit.

ROCK 'EM SOCK 'EM ROBOTS

TITLE FIGHT PASSWORDS
Select Passwords from the Select Game Mode screen and enter one of the following.

TITLE FIGHT	PASSWORD
Black Bruiser	LSTL2B
Blue Bomber	B5T32J
Brown Bully	J[]T7KH
Green Grappler	NMTZKQ
Orange Oppressor	2XT9KN
Pink Pummeller	6QT1KK
Purple Pyro	02TX2T
Silver Stretcher	GZTV2K
Yellow Yahoo	W8T52Q
End	3CTNKS

OVERLOAD

GAMEBOY® ADVANCE

SERIOUS SAM ADVANCE

EASY PASSWORDS

LEVEL	PASSWORD
Amon Thule, Subterranean Palace of the Pharaohs	HEXMODE
Baths of Diocletian	NEED
Caesar's Palace	WAFTY
Gladiator Training School	COINAGE
Praetorian Fort	NORTHERN
Pyramid Entrance Maze	BADDUN
Slave Compound	BOBBINS
Slave Quarters	TOAST
The Forum of Mars	GAMES
The Temple of Herkat Lower	MNIP
Tomb Of Ramses	MEGAMUNT

NORMAL PASSWORDS

LEVEL	PASSWORD
Amon Thule, Subterranean Palace of the Pharaohs	OPEE
Baths OF Diocletian	OWL
Caesar's Palace	MOOPAY
Gladiator Training School	FRYUP
Praetorian Fort	FILLY
Pyramid Entrance Maze	BETTERER
Slave Compound	PILCH
Slave Quarters	BEVIL
The Forum Of Mars	DUCKAROO
The Temple of Herkat Lower	KIPPAGE
Tomb of Ramses	HORSE

HARD PASSWORDS

LEVEL	PASSWORD
Amon Thule, Subterranean Palace of the Pharaohs	WOLF
Baths OF Diocletian	LIMO
Caesar's Palace	MOCKNEY
Gladiator Training School	MADEUP
Praetorian Fort	MIRROR
Pyramid Entrance Maze	CHIPPER
Slave Compound	FORREST
Slave Quarters	BEAK
The Forum Of Mars	FOZZER
The Temple of Herkat Lower	TITHES
Tomb of Ramses	EYE

SPONGEBOB SQUAREPANTS: REVENGE OF THE FLYING DUTCHMAN

DEBUG MODE
Enter the password D3BVG-M0D3.

100 GEMS

At the Mode menu, press L + R, then enter V1S10NS.

 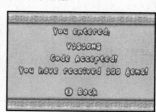

ORANGE GAME

At the Mode menu, press L + R, then enter SP4RX.

PURPLE GAME

At the Mode menu, press L + R, then enter P0RT4L.

ORANGE SPYRO

At the Mode menu, press L + R, then enter SPYR0.

SHEEP MODE

At the Mode menu, press L + R, then enter SH33P.

SHEEP FLAME MODE

At the Mode menu, press L + R, then enter B41S0KV.

CRASH PARTY USA MINI-GAME

Start up your Game Boy Advance and hold L + R.

SPYRO: SEASON OF FLAME

BLUE SPYRO

At the Title screen, press Up, Up, Up, Up, Down, Left, Right, Down, B.

ALL PORTALS

At the Title screen, press Up, Left, Up, Right, Up, Down, Up, Down, B.

ALL WORLDS IN ATLAS

At the Title screen, press Left, Right, Up, Up, Right, Left, Right, Up, B.

ATLAS WARPING

At the Title screen, press Down, Up, Left, Left, Up, Left, Left, Right, B.

INFINITE LIVES

At the Title screen, press Left, Right, Left, Right (x3), Up, Down, B.

INFINITE SHIELD FOR AGENT 9

At the Title screen, press Left, Down, Up, Right, Left, Up, Up, Left, B.

INFINITE AMMO

At the Title screen, press Right, Left, Up, Down, Right, Down, Up, Right, B.

NEVER DROWN

At the Title screen, press Down, Up, Right, Left, Right, Up, Right, Left, B.

ALL BREATH TYPES

At the Title screen, press Right, Down, Up, Right, Left, Up, Right, Down, B.

SUPER CHARGE

At the Title screen, press Left, Left, Down, Up, Up, Right, Left, Left, B.

DRAGON DRAUGHTS MINI-GAME

At the Title screen, press Right, Up, Down, Down, Down, Right, Up, Down, B.

OVERLORD

STREET FIGHTER ALPHA 3

ALL FIGHTERS
At the Title screen, press Left, Right, Down, Right, L, L, A, L, L, B, R, A, Up.

ALL MODES
At the Title screen, press A, Up, A, L, R, Right, L, Right, A, Down, Right.
Then press L, Right, A, R, Up, L, Right, B, A, Up, Right, Down, Right.

PLAY AS SUPER BISON
At the Character Select screen, hold Start and select Bison.

PLAY AS SHIN AKUMA
At the Character Select screen, hold Start and select Akuma.

ALTERNATE COSTUMES
At the Character Select screen, press L or R.

FINAL BATTLE
At the Speed Select screen, hold A + B.

THAT'S SO RAVEN 2: SUPERNATURAL STYLE

COSTUME MODE
At the Title screen, press Left, Right, Up, Down, B, B, B, Up, Down.

UNLIMITED ENERGY MODE
At the Title screen, press B, B, L, R, Up, Down, Up, Left, Right.

TREASURE PLANET

PASSWORDS

LEVEL	PASSWORD
1	MUSHROOM
2	TRUMPET
3	CLOUDY
4	RABBIT
5	SUNSHINE
6	SPIDER
7	APRON
8	RAINBOW
9	GOOSE
10	ENGLAND
11	MOUNTAIN
12	CAPTAIN
13	SNOWMAN
14	WITCHES
15	MONKEY
16	PRINCESS
17	WINDOW
18	COCONUT
19	FOOTBALL
20	CONCRETE
21	ELEPHANT
22	PHANTOM
23	DRAGON

TRON 2.0: KILLER APP

ALL MINI-GAMES
At the Title screen, press Left, Left, Left, Left, Up, Right, Down, Down,
Select.

UNFABULOUS

PASSWORDS

Select Continue and enter the following:

PASSWORD	EFFECT
End of Game	Zach, Brandywine, Addie, Addie
Credits	Geena, Ben, Addie, Ben
Mini Game	Ben, Zach, Ben, Addie

WORLD CHAMPIONSHIP POKER

10 MILLION DOLLAR

Enter the following as a password: 7 Hearts, King Spades, 2 Hearts, Queen Clubs, 9 Hearts, Jack Hearts.

YOSHI TOPSY-TURVY

CHALLENGE MODE & CHALLENGE 1

Defeat Bowser for the second time in Story Mode.

CHALLENGES 2, 3, 4

Complete the Egg Gallery in Story Mode.

FINAL CHALLENGE

Earn all Golds in Story Mode.

YU-GI-OH! ULTIMATE MASTERS: WORLD CHAMPIONSHIP TOURNAMENT 2006

CARD PASSWORDS

Enter the 8-digit codes at the Password screen to unlock that card for purchase. Refer to the Card List for YU-GI-OH! GX TAG FORCE for PSP. All cards may not be available in World Championship Tournament 2006.

DK/BradyGames, a division of Penguin Group (USA) Inc.
800 East 96th Street, 3rd Floor
Indianapolis, IN 46240

PlayStation® 2, PlayStation® 3, and PSP™ are registered trademarks or trademarks of
Sony Computer Entertainment, Inc. Xbox® and Xbox 360™ are registered trademarks or
trademarks of Microsoft Corporation. Game Boy® Advance, GameCube™, Nintendo DS™,
and Nintendo Wii™ are registered trademarks of trademarks of Nintendo of America, Inc.
All rights reserved. All other trademarks and trade names are properties of their respective
owners.

Please be advised that the ESRB ratings icons, "EC", "E", "E10+", "T", "M", "AO", and "RP"
are trademarks owned by the Entertainment Software Association, and may only be used
with their permission and authority. For information regarding whether a product has been
rated by the ESRB, please visit www.esrb.org. For permission to use the ratings icons,
please contact the ESA at esrblicenseinfo@theesa.com.

ISBN: 978-0-7440-1083-1

Printing Code: The rightmost double-digit number is the year of the book's printing; the
rightmost single-digit number is the number of the book's printing. For example, 08-1
shows that the first printing of the book occurred in 2008.

11 10 09 08   4 3 2 1

Manufactured in the United States of America.

Limits of Liability and Disclaimer of Warranty: THE AUTHOR AND PUBLISHER MAKE
NO WARRANTY OF ANY KIND, EXPRESSED OR IMPLIED, WITH REGARD TO THESE
PROGRAMS OR THE DOCUMENTATION CONTAINED IN THIS BOOK. THE AUTHOR
AND PUBLISHER SPECIFICALLY DISCLAIM ANY WARRANTIES OF MERCHANTABILITY
OR FITNESS FOR A PARTICULAR PURPOSE. THE AUTHOR AND PUBLISHER SHALL
NOT BE LIABLE IN ANY EVENT FOR INCIDENTAL OR CONSEQUENTIAL DAMAGES IN
CONNECTION WITH, OR ARISING OUT OF, THE FURNISHING, PERFORMANCE, OR USE
OF THESE PROGRAMS.

BRADYGAMES STAFF

Publisher
David Waybright

Editor-In-Chief
H. Leigh Davis

Licensing Director
Mike Degler

Marketing Director
Debby Neubauer

CREDITS

Senior Development Editor
David Bartley

Screenshot Editor
Michael Owen

Book Designers
Keith Lowe, Brent Gann

Production Designer
Wil Cruz